TOTAL QUALITY
CONTRIBUTIONS TO THEORY AND APPLICATION

Edited By

Professor Mohamed Zairi

European Centre for
Best Practice Management

PUBLISHING HOUSE

Total Quality Management
Contributions to Theory and Application

1st Edition 2009

ISBN 978-1-906993-00-9

9 781906 993009 >

Published by:
European Centre for Best Practice Management
1, Carriage Fold
Cullingworth
Keighley. West Yorkshire
BD13 5DW
UK
Tel: +44-1535-275030
www.ECBPM.com

Cover Design
UpStart Design & Media
25 Aireville Crescent
Bradford
BD9 4EU
UK

CONTENTS

INTRODUCTION

To determine whether quality management has made an effective contribution to theory building, one has to go back to some of the fundamentals, and refer to some of the key references where eminent authors and researchers constantly have attempted to argue the merits and demerits of TQM contribution and the evaluation of its soundness as a concept, philosophy and a new management discipline. As we have stated in a paper published in the TQM journal, (B.G.Dale et al, 2001) we argued that:

> "Theory is important to researchers as it provides the guidance and framework to analyze problems, helping them to focus on key issues when undertaking a piece of research. It also helps to explain relationships between variables and provides the basis for answering questions and understanding issues which arise in research".

In a special issue of The Academy of Management Review on TQM the editor, Dr Klimoski (1994) has argued that although TQM has been around for quite some time it has however, been given little attention by research teams in top universities. On closer analysis, however, it appears that there is a consensus from different researchers on TQM in terms of its soundness, its value and its contribution to management theory. On the whole, most researchers conclude that TQM is a sound concept and it has enabled organizations to address some of the competitive issues. It was also found to have an impact on raising performance and improving work flow in organizations. Similarly there is a consensus on TQM informing other management theories about succinct issues and also TQM itself being influenced by existing management theories.

Reed & Lemak (1996) present a very clear description of TQM. They state that:

> "TQM is not a quick fix or a golden egg solution".

TQM is a business level strategy with components of process and content that both demand attention. Further, Spencer (1994) states that TQM is conceptualized, not as a new paradigm, but as a comprehensive management practice that captures signals from established models of organization and amplifies them by providing a methodology for use. The real issue it appears, as Spencer (1994) states is that TQM origins lie mainly outside the academic world, it has therefore little connection to management theory and these connections are yet to be made explicit.

Whilst the arguments about the merits of TQM as a pioneering concept that has emerged and been significant in most of the 20th century may continue, it is useful however, to go back to basics and revisit certain aspects of theory building, theory testing, theory management. First of all in relation to understanding Total Quality Management as a concept, it seems that in most cases academicians particularly look at TQM in very simplistic terms. They argue that the issue of causality has to be transparently established and If it is to be given any due credibility it has therefore got to demonstrate through empirical testing that it can impact on organizational performance and that its workability is therefore no longer an issue. Furthermore, contributions to theory building should also be accepted as a spectrum of strategies, some are to look at causality of a concept, some are to look at the credibility and the soundness of the concept itself, some have to look at the relevance of certain concepts and some have to look at the value rendered through a newly developed and introduced concept.

The compilation introduced in this text addresses some of the difficulties associated with proving the soundness of Total Quality Management, demonstrating tangible contribution and value it renders to improvement that takes place in organizations and support it the latter gives in raising performance standards and sustaining competitive advantage. Since Total Quality Management feeds from existing management theories, on the whole it is very difficult to look at the concept from the point of view of originality rather than the sound logical approach that needs to be adopted. Rather, there is more merit in looking at synergy, interconnectedness and the integration and the workings of various management theories presented together and enhanced by new thinking and new ideas. TQM feeds from theories of management linked to strategy, financial management, human resource management, to operations management, customer focus and marketing, and to other disciplines particularly in most recent years in the areas of information technology, information management and the development of socio technical work environments. This complexity therefore makes the issue of investigating causality and contributions much more difficult because there are hundreds of variables that are working together all the time to create the synergy and to support the performance of organizations and the implementation of new ideas and thinking, for the purpose of raising competitive standards.

In general, it has to be accepted that Total Quality Management is a set of integrated management concepts, a bundle of theories and innovations and an amalgamation of management thinking and tools and techniques that work in harmony for the purpose of supporting organizational excellence and their drive for achieving sustainable performance. To answer the question therefore, "What has been the main contribution of Total Quality Management to the development of theory", this compilation attempts to present some facts to describe some of the initiatives and to argue and discuss some of the key findings, and to present some of the new ideas, new models, new tools and techniques that have evolved from investigating the workings of Total Quality Management in hundreds of organizations and in various parts of the world.

The compilation presents ideas and thoughts of TQM investigation going back to the mid-nineties, some of the ideas are related to scrutinizing the implementation of aspects of Total Quality Management in different organizational contexts and also in different cultures. The understanding, therefore of the drivers of TQM Implementation and the factors that inhibit the workings of TQM and particularly understanding the subtle differences between cultures is to be considered as a major contribution to bringing enlightenment in so far as introducing new innovations is concerned, but also in supporting the practicality of the existing management theories and blended theories, enriched by the addition of Total Quality Management thinking.

There is also important work that has been done to isolate key factors of success that enable the implementation of TQM and which really provide the fundamentals of the TQM thinking and its implementation. The compilation of several studies which, through empirical means have attempted to verify the soundness of certain factors that have been collected from the existing literature and incorporated through observations and scrutinizing the experience of many organizations that have been successful in the introduction of TQM.

One useful link that the compilation does also present is the one between TQM and performance measurement, TQM and business excellence. This is important since TQM, although very often presented as a concept that deals with long term issues, nonetheless by relaying its workings to various aspects of performance measurement and performance enhancement and the drive for excellence, this adds credibility to the concept and particularly supports the implementation effort in organizations where skeptical leaders and executives who may question the soundness and who probably may not have sufficient patience to focus on long term issues.

It is hoped that this compilation can help clarify further some of the blurred thinking that still exists in some of the management schools of thought and particularly this will help convince the cynics who still regard Total Quality Management as a fad, as a lightweight concept and as a topic that has had very little impact on theory development.

The compilation demonstrates that the case is made for Total Quality Management to be easily implementable in any cultural context. Various empirical studies have consistently come to the same conclusion, that it is the focus on a list of critical factors of the success that generate success in implementation rather than focusing on unique and peculiar, cultural aspect that will dictate the outcomes of TQM implementation effort. These critical factors have been verified in different cultural contexts and they are therefore now produced as a generic list of items that senior management must adhere to when contemplating the introduction of quality initiatives. Another contribution to TQM thinking is the ability of the concept to create a seamless, integrated value chain that focuses on customers and creates customer orientation.

Lastly, in terms of causality, Total Quality Management through various empirical studies, has demonstrated that it impacts positively on enhancing competitive performance of those organizations that have embraced the concepts fully, and can assist in the delivery of sustainable performance and the creation of competitive advantage.

In summary, Total Quality Management, it can be argued, has made a significant contribution to the development theory enhancement and to demonstrating how various management theories can be blended together and be put to work in harmony for the benefit of organization excellence. The credibility of TQM philosophy is not an issue any longer and cannot be questioned at all since it has been demonstrated in various countries in the world, that competitive advantages can be created and sustained by complying through the adoption of TQM thinking. The best examples to quote are: Japan has dominated the world's economy for over a period of 50 years; the USA has regained its competitive position by encouraging the adoption of Total Quality Management thinking, not just in the private sector but also in government services and the public sector as a whole. The proliferation of journals and publications focusing on TQM thinking, the research that addresses challenges and opportunities that Total Quality Management offers, and the thousands of courses at graduate and post graduate levels offered at universities throughout the world, the establishment of quality associations and professional bodies that encourage the development of the quality professionals at all levels, the regular events and conferences of an international nature, bring together scholars and practitioners together to exchange views share new thinking and debate some aspects of TQM implementation is a testimony of how well the concept is regarded, how credible it is in terms of its value and impact generated and how supportive it is to the development of a new thinking also in the development of individual professionals.

Editor: **Professor Mohamed Zairi**
Director of the European Centre for TQM
Juran Chair in TQM

References:

Dale B.G., Wu P.Y., Zairi M., Williams A.R.T.,(2001), "Total quality management and theory: An exploratory study of contribution", Total Quality Management, Volume 12, No. 4, 2001, pp. 439-449

Klimoski R.,(1994) : Guest editorial: a total quality special issue, Accademy of Management Review 19, pp.390-391

Reed R., Lemak D.J., (1996) "Beyond Process: TQM Content and Firm Performance," Academy of Management Review, 1996, Vol. 21, No. 1, pp. 173-202

Spencer Barbara A. (1994): Mississippi State University : Academy of Management Review 1994. Vol. 19. No. 3. 446-471

Acknowledgement

'No book is ever written alone and no research endeavour is ever carried out in solitude'. First and foremost, my biggest appreciation has to go to my research teams past and present and in particular, the individuals who are closely involved in these compilations and whose research projects I have enjoyed leading and closely supervising.

My sincere thanks also go to my support teams, past and present who make our work possible everyday of the week, all months of the year and who have helped sustain our focus and our determination to continue pioneering.

Lastly, my thanks and appreciation go to my wife Alweena and my children Adel, Bilal and Nadir for their unconditional love and unwavering support.

Dedication

"But when I searched, I found no work so meritorious
as the discovery and development of the arts and inventions
that tend to civilise the life of man."

- Francis Bacon

This book is dedicated to all the men and women whose mission in life is to pioneer, validate and enlighten others with knowledge and the discovery of facts and the truth. It is also dedicated to all those who can help by developing solutions to problems and finding answers to enquiries. Dr. Joseph Juran has once said: 'My job of contributing to the welfare of my fellow man is the great unfinished business'.

It is therefore hoped that the content of this book will help move forward the human thinking capacity, will assist in the development of the enquiry mind and will support the future quests for knowledge and advancement of theory and practice in the field of Total Quality Management and related topics.

Our biggest thrill would be to see that the content of this book is used, the knowledge presented consumed and the various ideas applied. It may of coruse be wishful thinking but we remain hopeful that the efforts made in putting this text together are not futile and that there will be some useful use for the various concepts presented.
As Rita C. Richey (October, 1999) wrote:

Ideas often take a substantial amount of time to be appreciated, and even for those few that attract attention quickly, there is an assumption that one needs the perspective of hindsight to determine their lasting value. Consequently, an intellectual inheritance is usually determined by the survivors rather than by the donor, and the labels that describe the merit of one's ideas are affixed by subsequent generations.

The Theory behind TQM

Section -1

66 *…every successful quality revolution has included the participation of upper management. We know of no exceptions.* *99*

- Joseph Juran

Total Quality Management (TQM) A Contemporary Perspective

By
Ian Librud,

Professor Mohamed Zairi, and

Dr. Yasar Jarrar

1. A historical perspective of TQM

In any attempt to discuss the historical perspective of TQM it may be prudent to first examine its definitions, a task which has proven to be a difficult one since so many pundits have submitted their own definitions which are based on their personal beliefs and/or particular experiences. Many organisations which have introduced a TQM approach to managing their businesses, have likewise experienced difficulty in finding a universally accepted definition of what it actually means, although this scenario seem to be changing in more recent times.

For some people TQM means statistical process control (SPC) or quality management systems, whilst to others it means teamwork and involvement of the workforce. However, despite the divergence of views on what constitutes TQM, there are number of common dimensions in the various definitions which include, top management support, customer and supplier relationships, also employee involvement. The baseline issues that capture.

TQM are thus shown in the diagram below as per Figure 1.

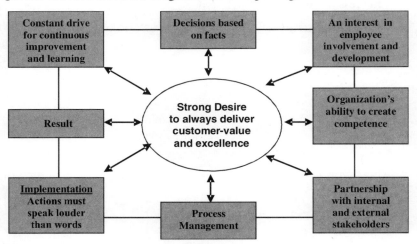

Figure 1 **Baseline issues that capture TQM**

The baseline issues referred to in the above-diagram, attempt to capture the different dimensions that shape TQM which are:

- A strong desire to always deliver customer-value and excellence
- A constant drive for continuous improvement and learning
- A management process
- Decisions based on facts
- An interest in employee involvement and development
- Partnership with internal and external stakeholders
- Organisation's ability to create competence
- Result-focused

"TQM is one of the subjects which tends to raise many questions about meaning and eventually about enhancing competitiveness through supporting financial results" – (Zairi 1996). The definition of TQM that takes an organisation-wide approach and is meant to include a wide range of critical factors covering leadership elements such as quality decisions and customer/market focus, hard elements like systems, tools and techniques and soft elements such as continuous improvement philosophy and team-work was suggested earlier by Zairi et al in 1994 and is quoted hereunder:

"A positive attempt by the organisations concerned to improve structural, infrastructural, attitudinal, behavioral and methodological ways of delivering to the end customer, with emphasis on: consistency, improvements in quality, competitive enhancements, all with the aim of satisfying or delighting the end customer".

According to Zairi (1996), this proposed definition is meant to highlight that TQM is not a separate initiative supporting 'Business as usual' but rather it is business itself and represents a comprehensive modern philosophy of management. Boaden (1997) noted that many of the quality gurus did not actually use the term TQM, although their work has subsequently been recognised as being relevant and sometimes quoted as referring to TQM. The

term 'quality management' is often used without the documentation of the 'total' element and Boaden (1997) goes on to suggest that however TQM is defined, there is no doubt that in some way it developed from, and has its roots in, the work of the major gurus of quality management like Deming, Juran and Crosby and others working at the same time. It is speculated that it may have been affected by the many translations of the original works from Japanese in the 1960s. Many of the recognised quality gurus did not actually use the term TQM, although their work has subsequently been recognised as being relevant and sometimes quoted as TQM. Dale et al (1994) described this as part of the TQM evolution.

Dale et al (1998) later suggests that perhaps, the main reason for the origin of the term TQM could be a substitution in the previously used term of total quality control (TQC), the word "control" by "management" with the reasoning that quality is not just a matter of control, it has to be managed. The Japanese developed its approach to TQM from the end of the second world war and by the end of the 1970s and the beginning of the 1980s, Japanese pressure along with the success of American writers like Crosby, Deming, Feigenbaum and Juran created a general concern about the focus on quality management in the USA, and this spread to the rest of the world. The publication of the Malcolm Baldrige National Quality Award (MBNQA) in the USA and similar awards in other Countries gave official recognition to the importance of TQM.

2. Stages of Evolution of TQM

In recent years Total Quality Management has started to play a more significant role in influencing and shaping the competitive strategy of many businesses and organisations.

The TQM philosophy is however not new and it is only comparatively recently in the latter part of the twentieth century, that an identifiable quality assurance movement emerged, with professional bodies devoted to developing a specialist literature and a technology of the subject, but as many writers have pointed out, the roots lie deeply buried in history (Dale and Plunkett 1990).

Quality in the past was the exclusive domain of manufacturing and operations departments but now it embraces the diverse functions of purchasing, finance, marketing research, human resource management also research and development and demands the attention of chief executive officers. Most modern approaches to quality have emerged gradually and are a product of a series of discoveries that were organised in the USA into four distinct quality eras (Garvin 1988) namely:-

- Inspection
- Statistical Quality Control
- Quality Assurance and
- Strategic Quality Management.

The first world war stimulated mass production and formal inspection became necessary as volumes increased and the process required large pools of skilled labour which was costly and time consuming. These and other pressures gave rise to what was called the American system of manufacturing which used special-purpose machinery to produce interchangeable parts by following a pre-established sequence of operations.

The 1930s marked the turning point for the quality movement as a result of the work of W A Shewhart (1931) who was the first to recognise that variability was a fact of industrial life and could be understood using the principles of probability and statistics.

Statistical Quality Control (SQC) methods were successfully applied in the USA and the UK during the second world war to find solutions to the procurement of large quantities of arms and ammunitions from multiple suppliers at acceptable levels of quality.

The Japanese also made great strides in quality control as a result of post-war American style SQC courses that were conducted in Japan by Deming in the first instance and later by Juran. A detailed historical study of quality assurance in Japan reveals that their approach was to try out all the western-style quality control techniques, retain only those that worked well for them, after which they made their own contributions through ingenuity and inventiveness. The Taguchi methods and most notably the contribution of the Japanese guru

Ishikawa (Japan's foremost authority on quality) with his cause-and-effect diagrams are worthy of note. Above all however, the implementation of a national quality policy with a top-down managerial approach has enabled Japan to achieve world dominance through peaceful economic means.

The quest for quality in organisations has taken different forms varying with an evolving paradigm and conceptualisation (Hermel 1997). When one examines the evolution of the quality movement, the progressive appearance of the following four principal trends become quite visible:

- The first approaches to quality were much more quantitative after which there was an increasing importance of qualitative factors among the performance criteria of organisations.

- The original function of inspection became a dynamic and preventive function thus moving from a reactive to a proactive vision of quality.

- The notion of quality spread into different new areas and instead of just focusing on the final product, this new approach concentrated mainly on the quality of daily tasks, and on the quality of processes.

- A global perspective of the organisation emerged as a result of the increasingly important integration of different functional aspects of quality. Economic, social and other organisational aspects were now added to the commercial dimension of organisations.

3. Development and Concepts

As a concept, quality has been with us for a millennia and only recently has it emerged as a formal management function (Garvin 1988). Although still evolving, originally it was reactive and inspection-oriented but in the world today quality-related activities have broadened and are now seen as essential for strategic success.

The concept of quality in the early phase was related to products and the degree of conformance to specified standards was the main consideration. The traditional product development process which occurred in many industries however, was best described as a sequential process commonly known as "throwing it over the wall" (Tompkins 1989) as shown in Figure 2.

8

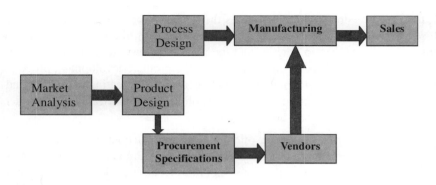

Figure 2 Traditional Product Development (Source: Tompkins 1989)

The process as outlined in Figure 1.2 above is not only sequential, but also walled into separate product development functions. In essence, marketing threw the product goals over the wall to the product designers who altered these goals and designed a product to meet the corrected market analysis, if they believed that said goals were unrealistic and did not reflect a clear understanding of available technology. Product design then threw the design over the wall to both the process designers and purchasing.

When the process designers discovered parts that could not be manufactured and other design flaws, they had no choice but to correct the product design and this led to scheduling problems. Without adequate time to check their work, the process sheets was then thrown over the wall to manufacturing. Similarly, when the interaction between purchasing and the vendors indicated that the product design was flawed, procurement had to work with the vendors to redesign the product and this placed pressure on manufacturing who had to hurry into production, after which the first set of products are thrown over the wall to sales.

Upon reviewing this traditional product development process, it can soon be realised that even though in theory, market analysis may have recorded the wants and needs of customers, the customer is not really a part of the process.

Little or no feedback occurred across the walls, no one was accountable for the results of the process and the length of time from the market analysis to the point of sale was so lengthy that the market analysis was often no longer valid. This was so because at each stage of the product development process, the entire product development process was restarted, creating expensive and time-consuming duplication. It is therefore obvious that this traditional product development process just did not work.

In the early phase of the quality evolution the meaning of control was understood as inspection, detection or test of the final products. Gradually, Joseph Juran's term "fitness for use" became more important as he included the managerial dimensions of planning, organising and controlling, and focused on the responsibility of management to achieve quality, as well as the need for setting goals. Quality was defined by Juran (1974) as fitness for use, in terms of design, conformance, availability, safety and field-use. Later on quality meant "meeting requirements" of the customers. His proposed managerial processes for implementing a quality program has come to be known as the Juran quality trilogy as listed below:

- Quality planning
- Quality control
- Quality improvement

One of the strongest proponents of quality management was W. Edwards Deming who was a member of the select few credited with contributing to the rapid revitalisation of the Japanese economy after World War II (Deming, 1986; Walton, 1986; Yoshida, 1989).

The Deming management method, is currently embraced by many firms in the United States and around the world (Hodgson, 1987). Deming who is credited with the original concept of quality that is used in management circles today, defines it as "satisfying the customer" by not merely meeting expectations but exceeding them.

"Meeting requirements" was thus changed to "satisfying the customer" then to "delight the customer" and in this changing process the objects of the quality concept have also changed from products of tangible character to an all-inclusive approach to the customer of both tangibles and intangibles. This movement from tangible to intangible factors is quite evident in the quality management area, where in the beginning quality activities were primarily concerned with the manufacturing sector, but in parallel with a more profound understanding of the concept of quality, quality management activities have spread to the service sector and other sectors. In the service sector the main issues that pertain to quality activities are intangible in nature, for example the attitudes and mindsets of people.

In an article by Anderson et al (1994), a theory of quality management was proposed and articulated in order to describe and explain the effects of adopting the Deming management method which is a set of 14 points developed by Deming using anectdotes and examples containing morals for everyone in the organisation in order to convey the meaning of these points. The proposed theory was based on the conceptual synthesis of Deming's writings, available literature on the Deming management method, observations and practice, and, more specifically, on the results of a Delphi study on the Deming management method. The analysis presented by Anderson et al arrived at the conclusion, that the theoretical essence of the Deming management method concerns the creation of an organisational system that fosters cooperation and learning for facilitating the implementation of process management practices, which in turn leads to continuous improvement of processes, products and services, and to employee fulfillment, both of which are critical to customer satisfaction and ultimately to the survival of the organisation.

What is implied in this theoretical proposition, is the crucial role that has to be played by the leadership of the organisation so as to ensure the success of quality management, because it is the responsibility of top management to create and communicate a vision within the organisation which gravitates toward continuous improvement, also to provide formal and informal support that will enable the creating and sustaining of an organisational system that is receptive to the processing of management practices.

The Delphi method is a technique developed at the RAND Corporation in the early 1950s, intended for systematically soliciting, organising, and structuring judgments and opinions on a particularly complex subject matter from a panel of experts until a consensus on the topic is reached (Helmer and Rescher, 1959), or until it becomes evident that further convergence is not possible. This method was used by Anderson et al (1994) to aid in the preliminary identification and definition of concepts suggested in Deming's 14 points and the members of the Delphi panel were asked to identify what they thought were the underlying concepts for each of these points and to define or operationalise each of their concepts. These members identified and defined 37 concepts, which they believed were suggested by the 14 points and after three iterations members of the panel consistently agreed to the meaning of the 37 concepts. The results of this abstraction effort are seven more abstract concepts that serve as the "Whats" or building blocks of their proposed theory of quality management. These seven concepts and their nominal definitions are shown hereunder:

- **Visionary Leadership** - relates to the role of top management in defining a long-range vision of an organisation's development, communicating this vision, implementing a plan of action, and inspiring and motivating the entire organisation toward the fulfillment of this vision

- **Internal and External Cooperation** - in this context, is synonymous with collaboration among different individuals, groups, or organisations, where all entities are engaging in noncompetitive, mutually beneficial, win-win activities.

- **Learning** - is the ability and willingness of the organisation to engage in learning or knowledge-seeking activities at the individual, group, and organisational levels which is critical to the implementation of process management practices.

- **Process Management** - in the context of the proposed theory, connotes a set of practices that combine methodological approaches with human resource management, and these are implemented in order to manage and improve processes that produce products and services.

- **Continuous Improvement** - this concept defines the purpose of the Deming management method and consistently means "better and better quality, less and less variation" which results from process management practices that bring forth incremental improvements and innovations in processes, products, and services.

- **Employee Fulfilment** - is a multidimensional concept defined as the degree to which employees of an organisation believe that the organisation continually satisfies their needs, and this arises fundamentally from employees' being able to derive pride of workmanship, satisfaction, and commitment from the work they do.

- **Customer Satisfaction** – is based on a customer's perception of the quality of products and services. Satisfaction levels have been theorised in the literature as a result of subtractive disconfirmation, subjective disconfirmation, expectation and perceived performance of a particular attribute, or set of attributes, of a product or service (Tse and Wilton, 1988).

Armand Feigenbaum regards quality as a way of managing a business organisation, with quality improvement being achieved by the participation of the whole workforce, who need a good understanding of what management is trying to do (Boaden, 1997).

Feigenbaum does not propose 14 points but his approach is summarised in following three criteria to which management must commit themselves:

- Strengthening the quality improvement process itself

- Making sure that quality improvement becomes a habit, and

- Managing quality and cost as complimentary objectives

Philip Crosby also has 14 points for quality management and has achieved significant commercial success through the promotion of his ideas, based around the notion that poor quality costs money (Crosby, 1979). He lists the four absolutes of quality mentioned below:

13

- Quality is defined as conformance to requirements, not as goodness

- The system for achieving quality is prevention, not appraisal

- The performance standard is zero defects

- The measurement of quality is the price of non-conformance

It can thus be summarised, that Deming can be best remembered for statistical process control, Juran for project management, Feigenbaum for systems management and Crosby for company-wide management (Dale et al., 1994). The different approaches of Deming, Crosby and Juran, are discussed by Ross (1994) who pinpoints some common themes in their work as:

- Inspection is never the answer to quality improvement, nor is it policing

- Involvement of and leadership by top management, are essential to the necessary culture of commitment to quality.

- A program for quality requires organisation-wide efforts and long-term commitment, accompanied by the necessary investment in training

- Quality is first and schedules are secondary

4. The 1970s, 1980s, 1990s and Current Era

The focus of quality gradually moved from product control to process improvement, from inspection to prevention. The view of quality as an added cost gradually changed to a recognition that it brings cost reduction and improved productivity. Two major changes of the postwar period were a better understanding of the role of management in quality improvement and the understanding that quality applied everywhere, not just to the production line. Juran must be given credit for initiating the first of these changes whilst Deming, who earlier promoted statistical quality control, added his voice to Juran's call for management involvement (Burrill, Ledolter, 1999). Juran expressed the view that it was important for top management to be quality-minded because in the absence of sincere manifestation of interest at the top, little will happen below.

One can glean from a glance at the world of quality today, that other major quality gurus have built various parts of a richly detailed quality model, on the original foundation of Shewhart. In some instances these parts seem to interlock, at times there is an element of overlap and in other cases the quality gurus approach similar concepts from extremely different vantage points. Figure 3 attempts to illustrate the changes that have taken place in the quality movement since the 1970s to the current era, and in the process it highlights some of the critical success factors in the respective era.

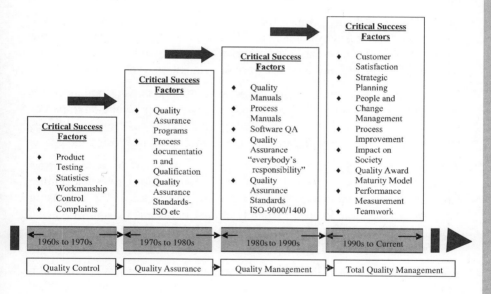

Figure 3 Evolution from Quality Control to Total Quality Management

The second major change in the direction of the quality effort emerged during the 1960s when the focus shifted from the factory floor to the entire production process. This view was expounded by Feigenbaum (1961) who proposed extending the quality effort to all functional areas. This Feigenbaum dubbed as total quality control (TQC) which was attempt to integrate the quality development, quality maintenance and quality improvement efforts within all areas of the organisation, in order to enable the most economical levels of production and service which allows for complete customer satisfaction. This concept broadened the horizon of the quality movement to the entire production process at that time which included marketing, engineering, purchasing and manufacturing.

The 1970s were difficult times for the United States and by extension the western world. Dogged by political problems, a faltering economy and a severe recession which followed the huge oil price hikes early in the decade after the rise of OPEC, quality thus received very little attention as an issue of the day.

In the interim, Japan's erosion of the American markets went unnoticed for years and it was not until the US car industry, which represent a large part of its GNP, came under siege and captured much attention, as the United States which had won the war with Japan was in serious danger of losing the peace.

The dawn of the 1980s brought the promise of salvation to dispel the worries of the late 1970s as the United States discovered quality circles and Phillip Crosby (Burrill, Ledolter, 1999). In light of the recession and increasing Japanese competition, interest in quality circles, but it was Crosby who had a more dramatic impact on the United States as he expounded the absolutes of quality in his book 'Quality is Free'.

A major quality event of the 1980s was the establishment in 1987 of Malcolm Baldrige National Quality Award. Suffice to add nevertheless, by the 1990s a small number of American organisations had raised their quality to world-class levels and those successful Baldrige Award winners displayed characteristics that can be described as a total quality management (TQM) approach to quality.

The large and growing importance of world trade is a phenomenon of this current era. To deal confidently with any supplier, a customer needs to be assured that quality products will be supplied and such assurance becomes even more salient in this era of trade liberalisation or globalisation. The growing acceptance of ISO 9000, an internationally acknowledged quality management standard, is the main quality story of the 1990s. The ISO 9000 series, which will be also discussed later, are generic standards for quality management and quality assurance that apply to all types of companies (large and small) in all sectors of the economy.

5.   A Classification of Issues per Era

Each quality era built on the previous one, and during the first three eras quality was viewed as a problem to be solved with the focus being on the internal operations of the organisation. In the 1980s however, quality was seen for the first time as a competitive opportunity or a strategic weapon that could be used against competitors. Thus, in the fourth quality era the focus was on the customer and organisations became more proactive in anticipating and responding to both customer and market needs (Kaye, Anderson 1999).

A similar view was earlier advanced by Zairi and Leonard (1994) who suggested that quality by definition referred to certain standards and the ways and means by which those standards were achieved, maintained and improved upon, until gradually quality became to be more associated with what the customer wanted and thus definitions began to appear with this point of view in mind. Zairi and Leonard (1994) cited two examples to wit :– quality is driven by the market place, by the competition and especially by the customer also, quality is a key attribute that customers use to evaluate products or services.

The continued commitment and involvement of top management is crucial to ensuring the full integration of quality into business strategy and plans, also its adequate deployment throughout the organisation. Kaye and Anderson (1999) also submit the view that the strategic quality management approach however, is still inadequate to meet today's rapidly changing business environment, that is characterised by uncertainty and unpredictability.

In order to meet these challenges, Kaye and Dyason (1995) identified a fifth quality era – competitive continuous improvement. Here, it is suggested that the primary concern is with the organisation being flexible, responsive and capable of adapting quickly to changes needed in strategy as a result of feedback from customers and from benchmarking against competitors. The implementation of a sound strategy of continuous improvement is therefore essential, if an organisation is to achieve flexibility, responsiveness and the ability to adapt quickly to changes within the environment in which it operates.

Self-assessment is an approach that is used to underpin continuous improvement by measuring the current performance of an organisation against a model which represents a position of "excellence". Two of the most frequently used self-assessment models are the Malcolm Baldrige Quality Award (MBNQA), and the European Business Excellence Model.

COMMENT

TQM:
What is Wrong
with the Terminology?

Mohamed Zairi

First Published in

The TQM Magazine,
Vol. 6 No. 4, 1994, pp. 6-8
MCB University Press, 0954-478X

It is quite surprising to realize that even in the mid-1990s there is still a lot of confusion about the meaning of total quality management (TQM) and the way it is perceived by many senior managers in both industry and commerce. There seems to be a lot of wrestling with questions such as "Is TQM a programme?", "Is it a concept?", "Is it a management philosophy?", "Is it something else in disguise?" Rather than leap into a defensive mode and attempt to answer the above questions, let us first of all try to understand the context under which the above questions tend to get asked:

(1) Most business organizations start the implementation of TQM programmes with lots of vigour, enthusiasm and perhaps even excitement. The more they move forward with their attempts to change the culture of business through TQM, the more they realize that it is a hard and very painful process. The requirements from business organizations tend very often to be of a short-term nature; TQM as a philosophy delivers long-term benefits. Most managers who are more concerned by the delivery of short-term business results will, if and when their business stalls, come up with statements such as:

TQM has given all it has got; as an *initiative* it is completely drained now. We need something else to rejuvenate the business and give it a new lease of life.

(2) Less enthusiastic senior managers than those referred to in the previous section will take every opportunity to apportion blame, look for scapegoats and when perhaps their organizations run into difficulties will announce that TQM has failed and does not really work. They would not of course qualify the meaning of the term "failure". Very often, however, failure associated with TQM implementation is not really the *failure of TQM to deliver results* but rather *the failure of managers to introduce TQM effectively.*

(3) The third school of thought is the cynical one which includes those who constantly refer to TQM as "a fad, label of the month, rain- dance", among others. These people are always very anxious to see the TQM terminology disappear and will take every opportunity to diminish its value and discredit its workings. What these people have failed to realize, however, is the fact

that TQM as a philosophy is not being *imposed* on people but that customers are demanding it in various ways:

- quality of products/service;
- speed and reliability of delivery;
- price;
- innovation and differentiation;
- professionalism.

The customer (industrial) or consumer (domestic) ought to be the focal point for the way business organizations are being managed. TQM is all around us, it is being demanded even in the context of public sector and non-profit making organizations; it is a global and universal philosophy of management and is here to stay.

(4) Rather than talk about "terminology destruction" it may be a more positive approach to discuss the "process construction". This is perhaps the point at which I would like to introduce a "gentle" definition of TQM:

TQM is essentially a whole array of techniques, management principles, technologies and methodologies which are put together to work for the benefit of the end customer. TQM seeks to develop organizations by creating better planning, better external focus, better design and prioritization. It is also aimed at strengthening weak processes and protecting strong areas which give the organizations concerned an edge over their competitors (through continuous improvement and benchmarking). TQM helps organizations build strong *capability* enabling them respond to current and future market pressures. It ensures that the voice of the customer (level of demand) is always matched by the voice the process (level of delivery ability). TQM values people and people productivity through innovation, creativity, problem solving and a commitment continuously to improve quality and optimize value-creation for the benefit of the end customer. TQM is a corporate-wide process and has to involve all levels of employees. In addition, TQM is about the continuous process of introducing best practice to ensure sustainability and positive competitiveness.

In a sense, it is about the management of change; it is therefore *limitless* and *timeless* in its approach.

(5) It is perhaps time to accept that there is nothing wrong with the terminology and that TQM as a philosophy is fine, provided that we understand its workings and its benefits (which are long-term). It is also perhaps time for all the cynics to admit to themselves that the problem is not really TQM as a philosophy but rather one of *attitudes and behaviour.* TQM will not stand a chance to succeed with half-hearted commitment, moving goalposts, being obsessed with short-term results, doing things because there is a clear and tangible benefit rather than because they are the right things to do from the customer perspective and treating employees with much suspicion and with "rigid and hard control".

(6) The wider perspective–shareholder dilemma: It is also time to tackle this paradox. Business organizations have to deliver quality products and services to customers for them to survive and prosper; their holding and parent company has a duty to its customers (shareholders) who expect good returns on their investment. In the former case, TQM has to be regarded as a *must.* In the latter case TQM has no direct relevance or meaning. It is therefore incumbent on all those who have faith and belief in TQM as a modern management philosophy to keep spreading the message and change attitudes and behaviours for achieving positive outcomes. This is a long-term process, and there are already positive signs in the way corporate reporting is being used by leading organizations to convey the TQM message.

(7) *Education and training:* With regard to confusion in terminologies, there are many people who still fail to distinguish between education and training. In the context of TQM, it is very important to report that most initiatives undertaken by business organizations were those geared towards *training* rather than *education per se.* Training addresses the skills and knowledge base to deal with a specific task, project or current job. Education is the development of people regardless of the job(s) they are doing. It is futuristic and based on the belief that well-educated people can contribute more effectively because they raise their creative potential. In addition, better

educated people are more flexible and more adaptable to change.

Many organizations will find it easier to accept, for instance, investing a great deal of money on preventive maintenance programmes because they strongly believe that productivity is important and production processes have to be serviced on a regular basis. What about maintenance of humans? Productivity in the 1990s is measured in people's terms; the modern approach is to work *smart* rather than work *hard*.

There is a large mismatch between industry and commerce

Educational establishments need also to rise to the challenge. There is a large mismatch between what industry and commerce are demanding and what universities and colleges are offering. This can easily be measured by the number of courses on TQM and related areas. There is a very urgent need to develop syllabuses which reflect the current and future needs of industry and commerce in terms of knowledge and skill provision.

Finally, let us examine the situation in Japan. Japan is, after all, the place where the concept of TQM was born, referred to as company-wide quality control (CWQC). In Japan, the philosophy of TQM is well embedded in all aspects of business life and even in the public sector. It is a truly powerful management philosophy and nobody challenges its workings or credibility. All education and training is based on a broad knowledge basis where quality is strongly featured in almost all syllabuses. In addition, the whole Japanese society understands the workings of TQM and the priorities are: "Customer first, employee second, shareholder last". This really means that without customers, there can be no jobs and no dividends but, on the other hand, the Japanese believe that people are the most important asset that delivers to the customer and ultimately delivers dividends to the shareholder.

The challenge for all of us is to make TQM work effectively

In conclusion therefore one has to say that there is nothing wrong with the terminology TQM. It is more important to understand how it works as a philosophy, appreciate it for its long-term nature and be inspired by the Japanese who after all have made it work, who are considered to be supreme competitors in every sense and who do not find problems with the terminology. The challenge for all of us is perhaps to make TQM work effectively in any sector, to ensure that organizations optimize its benefits, to develop it as a philosophy of modern management so that it can address future challenges, to disseminate widely ideas, definitions, examples of TQM and its workings and to integrate it in our education systems.

We have to share the vision of all the gurus of quality who devoted their entire life defending its workings and trying to convince sceptics about its wide benefits. In particular, one name stands out when one considers the long list of gurus' names; it is Professor Ishikawa, perhaps the guru who introduced TQM to our lives, since he introduced CWQC in Japan in the early 1960s. A few years before his death, in 1985, he wrote the following:

> As I look back on my life with QC, the following becomes my hope and prayer: "That QC and QC circle activities be spread everywhere in the world, that quality all over the world be improved, that cost be lowered, that productivity be increased, that raw materials and energy be saved, that people all over the world be happy, and that the world prosper and be peaceful".

Mohamed Zairi is Unilever Lecturer in TQM, Bradford University Management Centre, Bradford, UK.

A review of total quality Management in practice: Understanding the Fundamentals through Examples of best Practice Applications - Part I

T. Thiagarajan and M. Zairi

First Published in

The TQM Magazine
Volume 9 : Number 6 1997 pp. 270-286
© MCB University Press : ISSN 0954-478X

The authors

T. Thiagarajan is Senior Quality Manager, Palm Oil Research Institute (PORIM), Malaysia.

M. Zairi is SABIC Chair in Best Practice Management, Bradford University, Bradford, UK.

Abstract

Represents a comprehensive review of the literature by discussing critical factors of TQM in key areas often stressed in implementation case studies, and supported by quality gurus and writers. Such factors are considered as being conducive to the success of TQM implementation. Discusses these factors from the point of view of how and why. There appears to be little agreement on the what, so an understanding of the "processes" involved in implementation allows for the appropriate framing and objective classification of key factors for TQM implementation. Part I discusses quality factors related to: leadership; internal stakeholders' management; policy and strategy. In all, 98 examples of best practice are referred to, to illustrate how the various critical fields of TQM have successfully been put in place.

Introduction

The principle of self-assessment using various models such as the Malcolm Baldrige National Quality Award (MBNQA), the European Quality Award (EQA) and the Deming Prize is becoming globally pervasive. Indeed such models are found to be the best means for assessing organizational excellence and the criteria used are found to reflect the most important components of effectiveness and competitiveness. By linking means and drives such as leadership to results (ends) one could relate capability and competence to achievements.

This review of the literature was therefore an attempt to map total quality management using similar sets of criteria to those of the European Quality Award Model (see Appendix 1 for an example of the EQA and MBNQA). More importantly, this is the first attempt at reviewing the literature from the point of view of what, how and why.

Leadership

Everything starts with a committed and passionate leader of the business organization. A leader who is really committed to making fundamental changes. Without that very little else is possible (Steven Stanton in Watts, 1996).

The critical role of top management and their leadership in quality management is emphasized over and over again in the literature covering implementation case studies and the writings of quality gurus. Top management commitment to the quality process and their leadership in fostering an environment where quality is a way of life sets the foundation for the implementation of TQM in an organization.

Deming [1] calls for managers to institute leadership to usher the transformation process. Feigenbaum[2] views senior executives' commitment as the means for promoting organizational commitment[3,4]. Kano[3] talks about senior executives' commitment as a (more) important factor of TQM, and their doubt as the greatest enemy. Crosby [5] places management commitment on top of the essentials of TQM implementation. Juran[6] attributes the quality excellence of the Japanese companies to senior managers' commitment to quality.

In explaining why most of the quality initiatives failed in the West in the 1970s and 1980s, Juran[6] focuses on senior managers' lack of personal involvement in managing quality; leaving such responsibility to middle managers and confining it to the quality department. The quote by Theodor Krantz, the president of Velcro USA, put this reality into perspective:

A year earlier we had made a toothless attempt to modernise Velcro's quality programme. The effort had been delegated to the quality assurance manager, and it ended stillborn[7].

Quality is too important to be delegated; it must be the responsibility of top management[1,5]. Bertram[8] echoes the gurus' caution by stressing that TQM is not just another management policy decision to be implemented by others. He states that a lack of requisite management commitment is the main reason for 80 per cent of TQM failures[9] . Easton[10] also pinpoints deficient leadership as the reason why TQM programmes of some of the American companies achieve only moderate results.

Given the importance of leadership, it is not surprising to find that, in all quality awards, leadership issues are not only placed at the top of the list of criteria but also are emphasized in the other criteria as necessary to make a quality implementation successful [11,12].

The importance of top management commitment and involvement is also highlighted in the findings of several studies in the USA and Europe. In a study carried out using Malcolm Baldrige National Quality Award (MBNQA) winners as respondents, Ramirez and Loney[13] reported that management commitment was rated as the most critical step in quality-improvement-process activity. In fact, management-related activities such as the need for a clear vision statement, and focusing the business processes on customer satisfaction, were listed among the top ten critical steps for a successful quality-improvement process. The overall conclusion of the study was that success or failure of a quality process hinges in a significant way on what happens regarding management commitment and other related top management activities. Similar conclusions were obtained by Zairi and Youssef[14] when Ramirez and Loney's [13] study was repeated in the UK and six other countries in the Middle and Far East.

Based on a study, Porter and Parker[15] showed that the presence of certain management behaviours was the single most critical success factor. Johnston and Daniel [16] described that senior management on both sides of the Atlantic, visited during a study tour, assumed active responsibility for the success of the TQM process in their companies. A similar conclusion was reported by Bertsch and Williams[17] from a study of 20 large international companies based in the USA, Europe and the Far East.

Based on his experience as an MBNQA examiner, Easton[10], in capturing the state of leadership of top management in the Baldrige applicants, states that senior management are committed to quality. Senior managers are actively involved in promoting the importance of quality and customer satisfaction and they devote a substantial part of their time to quality-related issues. Their involvement includes activities such as meeting with employees, meeting customers, giving formal and informal recognition, receiving training and training others. Senior management also develop and communicate key company quality values which place emphasis on the importance of the customer, process orientation, continuous improvement, teamwork, management-by-fact, mutual respect and dignity, and value of individual employees and their contributions. They ensure that the entire workforce understands its role in satisfying the customer. To support and promote the quality process of the organization, senior management develop and put in place elements of quality management structure. These include a senior management TQM council or division and departmental councils.

Discussions of implementation case studies in the literature are also unanimous in reinforcing this reality. The examples range from large to small companies, service to manufacturing, multinationals to family business, and government to non-profit agencies[18-21]. At ICL Product Distribution UK, the chief executive and senior executives spearheaded the company-wide quality drive, while at Ciba-Geigy Italy, the total quality initiative was led by the group chief executive, with the active support and involvement of senior executives [22].

First and foremost in the quality evolution process, senior management must start by understanding what TQM really means [23]. They must be convinced of its benefits to the organization, and acknowledge the fundamental change it will bring in the running of the organization. It is critical that they build the requisite commitment before getting the rest of the staff involved. There must be consensus among themselves regarding what the organization needs to achieve its quality goal.

At the Aluminum Company of America (Alcoa), it was the chief executive officer who initiated the quality initiative. The directors and senior managers then laboured over six months to identify the challenges and opportunities, and then to design and begin the total quality process there. During this period, the top management team, including the CEO, spent many hours in quality education and training, and visiting and benchmarking companies that had acquired reputations as leaders in quality management. All these helped form a consensus among top management about why they were interested in quality and what needed to be done to achieve the goals[24].

At Ciba-Geigy Italy, the management team spent two years "owning" and shaping the quality initiatives themselves before consultants were involved [22]. At Rockware Glass Ltd, UK, a series of workshops for senior executives was held at the outset resulting in an unanimous recognition of the importance of quality management for the organization's survival [25]. The first stage of implementing TQM at Ilford Ltd was the acceptance by top management that they had to change fundamentally the way they operated. "Acceptance of this was difficult but vital to achieving real change" [26].

One of the precepts of TQM is employees' greater involvement and commitment to the process and its goal. It is through the actions and behaviour of the management that employees identify with the goals of the company and extend their commitment towards its success[2-4,20]. Ramirez and Loney's[13] study also highlighted the fact that it is not sufficient for management just to be committed, but they must also be obvious[5,27]. Bertsch and Williams' [17] study also found that senior executives see being visible in their commitment to quality sends strong signals about what is expected and desired from the staff. It is through their demonstrated actions and behaviour that management can harness the involvement of employees, and thence their commitment to the quality goals of the company will be assured [28].

Johnston and Daniel [16] in relating Fuji Xerox experiences, stress that if top management command employees to improve but are not themselves constantly seeking ways to improve systems, continuous improvement initiatives will fail. In describing the experiences of TQM implementation at Johnston Matthey plc, UK, George[19] emphasizes that senior management demonstrating involvement in the quality process is just as critical as commitment. There were initial hiccups in the implementation process when staff felt that senior executives were not committed [19].

The CEO of Alcoa stressed the need for his directors and senior managers to be visible in terms of their commitment in the eyes of the staff involved [24]. The findings of a survey carried out among employees at two Hewlett-Packard factories in the UK showed that the degree of buy-in amongst the respondents was favourable amongst those who saw their management staff using the TQM techniques themselves to improve processes [29].

Some of the ways CEOs and senior executives of best companies make this commitment evident is by leading quality initiatives and investing the requisite time and effort. A study found that most of the CEOs of the 62 major US-based companies spend at least 10 per cent of their time in quality improvement efforts [20]. At Southern Pacific Lines, leadership meant role modelling. This involved leaders being out on the "track and yards" with the employees to demonstrate and speak about the quality-driven approach to doing business[30]. The CEO of Motorola spent a significant amount of time explaining the corporate vision to enable every employee to translate it into personal work goals [21]. The president and his senior executives at Shorts Brothers were the first to be trained in the theory, practice and tools of quality improvement [31] . The managing director of Rock-ware Glass Ltd, UK, meets every employee in a series of TQM-related sessions at various locations and times convenient to the workers [25] . A high-powered steering committee to manage the TQM process at Paul Revere Insurance Group is a visible sign of top-level commitment to the process [32]. The vice-president at Philips Electronics personally leads a company-wide task force on quality improvement of software development, while at Ericsson Sweden, a top executive took ownership of analysing and improving the order-make-market system[17].

According to Juran[6], there are seven steps that a responsible CEO must take
to achieve quality in any organization:

(1) Set up and serve on the company's quality council.

(2) Establish corporate quality goals and make them a part of the business
plan.

(3) Make provision for training the entire company hierarchy in managing for
quality.

(4) Establish the means to measure quality results against quality goals.

(5) Review results against goals on a regular basis.

(6) Give recognition for superior quality performance.

(7) Revise the reward system to respond to the changes demanded by world
class quality.

Oakland [4] lists the five requirements for effective leadership:

(1) Clear beliefs and objectives in the form of a mission statement.

(2) Clear and effective strategies and supporting plans.

(3) The critical success factors and critical process.

(4) The appropriate management structure.

(5) Employee participation through empowerment, and the EPDCA (evaluate,
plan, do, check, amend) helix.

Internal stakeholders' management

Employee involvement

While top management involvement and leadership are essential for TQM
success, they are not sufficient on their own[33]. TQM succeeds only with
employees' involvement in the TQM process and their commitment to its
goals[3,5,32,34]. In 1979, when the founder president of Matsushita Japan
spoke of how Japanese products swept aside Western products in the world
market, he attributed it to the involvement of everyone in the company in the
quest for quality[32]. This fact was also captured in a study which found that

organizations with a high level of employee involvement stand a greater change of success[35].

Crosby [36] talks about the need for every individual in the organization to understand his or her role in making quality happen. In fact, the need to maximize the involvement of all employees is one of the basic principles of change implementation in an organization. It involves the employees having a common understanding of quality and the importance of their involvement to maintain the quality momentum.

According to the chief executive of Federal Express, the foundation for the success of the quality improvement process at this company is the involvement of every employee in that process[27]. He calls it the "human side of quality". LeaRonal (UK) believes that "fora quality improvement programme to be successful, the commitment to total quality must encompass a whole workforce who must be encouraged to participate actively in the search for continuous improvement[37]. The success of the quality improvement process at Mitel Telecom Ltd UK is attributed to the total involvement of the workforce [38]. In implementing the quality process, Shorts Brothers views greater involvement of its workforce as important evidence that the company is progressing in the right direction[31].

The critical importance of employees' involvement in the quality process of an organization is based on the belief that the best process innovation ideas come from the people actually doing the job [33]. The quality reputation of Japanese companies is mainly credited to their great success in this area.

A total quality environment demands that people participate in continuous improvement activities in an unhindered manner, that pushing decision making to the lowest practical level is the way. In TQM terminology, this is called empowerment. Deming[1] and Juran[39] also stress the importance of empowerment or giving employees the authority and autonomy to do their job when they talk about "pride of workmanship", "self-improvement", "self-control" and "self-inspection" respectively. AtTioxide Group Limited, empowerment to enable its employees to participate in continuous improvement activities was seen as a key element in the development of its total quality strategy [31].

Zink[40] emphasizes that employee empowerment is an important area of assessment of major quality awards around the world. Empowered employees go by many labels: self-managing teams, self-directing teams, autonomous groups. Zink[40] even includes participation in employee suggestion schemes.

Promoting employee involvement by operating employee suggestion schemes is common in the majority of the 158 US companies in the Fortune 1000 surveyed (Conference Board in Olian and Rynes[20]). While such schemes are also common in non-TQ organizations, enthusiasm is often stifled due to poor follow-up from management. TQ organizations, however, generally design schemes that are responsive and user-friendly. Employees who wish to make a suggestion at Thomas Interior Systems simply fill out a half-page pre-printed form and drop it in a designated suggestion box[16]. Response to the suggestions is ensured within 72 hours. At Thomas, ideas are submitted at an average monthly rate of 40, with an implementation at 80 per cent.

At Milliken, which received 262,000 ideas in 1989, suggestions are acknowledged within 24 hours and acted on within 72 hours, while at Globe Metallurgical, ideas discussed at the weekly quality circle meeting are implemented the same day where possible[41]. However, at Eastman Chemical Company, the suggestion system was eliminated because it was found to impede teamwork[42].

Greater employee involvement in quality efforts can only come about when the employees know that the organization cares for them[27]. Baldrige winners treat their employees as partners rather than hired hands [41]. The chief executive of Wainwright Industries, the 1994 winner of the Baldrige Award, sums up this point well when he said:

> An internal customer (employee) will treat the external customer the way he or she is treated by the company[43].

This message is echoed by Townsend and Gebhardt[27]:

> Without the co-operation of the latter group (employees), the loyalty of the former (external customers) is always in jeopardy.

Middle management role

The act of maximizing employee involvement in the quality process requires middle managers within the organization to make major adjustments. They must give up some authority as power and control are pushed to lower levels in the organization. In addition, managing according to the philosophy of TQM requires new attitudes and skills from middle managers[44]. The transition towards TQM can be an uncertain and troubling process for middle managers[27,45].

Only when middle managers are convinced that the transition process that may cost them in status, power and recognition leads to a better world, can the implementation of TQM be smooth [16]. If they do not see it, they may react with suspicion, uncertainty and resistance[25,44-46]. Crosby[36] says:

> It is hard to get people interested in improvement of any kind if they perceive it is a threat to their authority or life style.

Unless there is a middle management buy-in, they soon become barriers to rather than champions of the new system. According to Manz and Sims[45]:

On the road to a total quality culture, the biggest obstacle to success is the middle management brick wall.

This fact was also reflected in a survey of 161 organizations. It was established that one of the elements that differentiated the successful TQ organizations from the less than successful ones was middle management support. A survey concluded that without middle managers' committed support for the quality process, the process will be derailed.

Another survey, reported in *Quality Progress[47]*, which examined 536 organizations using TQM, returned similar findings. The study, which aimed to identify specific practices that have contributed to or detracted from TQM success, revealed that middle management are the main roadblocks to successful TQM. The study recommends that senior management should work hard to understand and involve middle managers in TQM efforts such as involvement in designing and promoting TQM, creating different but meaningful roles for them in supporting widespread quality improvement initiatives, and providing training and development not only in TQM concepts and practices, but also in new leadership skills.

In this sense, getting middle managers to buy-in and be involved in a positive manner is viewed as key to the success of TQM[20,36,48-50]. Ishikawa[48] says that middle management can contribute greatly to quality improvement but conventional organizational arrangements do not encourage their contributions. He calls for senior management to provide greater attention to encourage new roles for middle managers.

At Norand Corporation, management discovered that without middle management's committed support, the total quality process can fail. Middle management training and acceptance were made a priority. Training was created for middle managers to show them how to manage empowered employees and to become facilitators of quality improvement initiatives and coaches of employee development [46].

At Charrette Corporation, it was recognized at the outset that the new role of middle managers, especially in the transition stage, would be critical to achieving a successful implementation[45]. At Nissan UK, the supervisors have a wide range of responsibilities where people management skills feature prominently. For example, supervisors are involved in staff selection, developing and training their staff and motivating and maintaining morale. They are also the channel for all communications to manufacturing staff.

Training and education

Introducing new systems such as TQM when people do not have the fundamental skills to work in the new system is a prescription for disaster[51]. There should be no doubt that for TQM to succeed, the entire workforce must acquire new knowledge, skills and abilities. Training and education based on total quality must be planned and provided if this is to be realized. Oakland [4] stresses that training strategy should be addressed early alongside other strategies within the quality policy. He goes on to say that training is the single most important factor in improving quality once the necessary commitment has been assured.

The importance of training and education is also echoed by other quality gurus. Ishikawa[48] says "Quality begins and ends with training" (also Imai, in Clemmer[52]). Crosby[36], Juran[53] and Feigenbaum[2] also emphasized the need for organization-wide education and quality awareness programmes.

Top management of best organizations, recognizing the link between education and successful TQM, also focus their implementation process around it. This point is well summed up by Durrant[25] in discussing TQM initiatives at Rockware Glass Ltd, UK:

There would be more training for all in one year than the previous ten years.

At Shorts Brothers, training is a number one priority [35]. Some 400 training sessions were conducted, catering for the president, the management committee and the shopfloor workers.

Rank Xerox has had a comprehensive training programme for all its employees since the beginning of its TQ initiatives. It considers training to be an essential element in developing the TQ process throughout the company [54]. AT&T Istel UK and Mitel Telecom Ltd UK have also ensured that all employees are provided with formal and rigorous education at the outset of the TQM process[38,55]. Both organizations believed that education provides a firm foundation for a common language and for understanding the organization's quality aspirations.

Best companies do not just confine education and training to their shopfloor employees and managers. Top executives are actively involved in the learning process themselves. Wallace Company's five top leaders each underwent more than 200 hours of intensive training in the methods and philosophy of continuous improvement. The managing director of Grundos spends an average of 30 days a year sitting in seminars with all levels of managers [22].

According to Garvin[56], organizations failing to grasp the basic truth that TQM requires a commitment to learning is the reason why failed programmes far outnumber successes and success rates remain distressingly low. This statement may come as a surprise as many organizations embarking on total quality initiatives allocate a considerable amount of resources in providing the employees' with training in new skills and knowledge. Garvin[56] is not just referring to the mechanism of providing skills and knowledge but is including the accompanying - and perhaps more critical - process of applying what was learnt in the workplaces. Potential for involvement will not exist just by creating systems and processes for the provision of training. Skills and knowledge acquired must be applied and integrated into the fabric of daily operations. He says that some of the less than successful initiatives, although effective at creating or acquiring new knowledge, may have been less successful in applying the knowledge to the workplace.

It is critical for training and education programmes to be linked explicitly to implementation if they are to have maximum effectiveness. Management should not assume that the new knowledge from such programmes will be applied when trainees return to their workplaces. Management should have in place a system to ensure employees follow through what they have learnt when they return to their jobs after training. For example, the management at GTE have put in place a system whereby employees know that they will be evaluated on the implementation of the new knowledge acquired during training. Organizations such as Honda, Corning and General Electric are other examples where new knowledge had been effectively translated into new ways of behaving. These companies actively manage the training process to ensure that it occurs by design rather than by chance.

Best organizations also direct training towards supporting other quality initiatives within the organization. For example, Baxter Healthcare Corporation believes that the objectives of its Baxter Quality Award can only be realized if applicants receive training relating to the award - the process, criteria, and the scoring system - and the examiners are familiar with the objectives of the award and how to conduct assessment[57]. At Mercury Marine, the absence of relevant training resulted in setbacks to its quality circle initiative[58]. Problemsolving teams set up as part of the quality process at Hilti (Great Britain) Ltd encountered problems during the early stages when project teams were set up without the requisite skills [59].

Proper timing and spacing of training programmes to ensure what is learnt is applied right away and not lost is also crucial. Maximizing the impact of training by the correct timing of training programmes was highlighted in a recent study of 536 TQM organizations in the USA[60]. Hence, conducting organization-wide training in TQM before the need or desire for TQM is created could have a negative impact in the TQM implementation process. Employees unable to apply their knowledge forget the details by the time they encounter a real need, and thence lose enthusiasm in the quality initiative.

As training and education prepare employees for greater involvement in the organization's quality process, providing them with the right type of training is crucial. Generally, leading organizations ensure their education and training programmes include both the basics of quality and TQM and the set of skills for continuous quality improvement.

The literature gives a good degree of indication of the type of new skills bestorganizations provide for their workforce to nurture a quality ethic[16,30,32,57,61-63]. A study in the USA reported that training in continuous improvement skills, interpersonal skills and leadership skills is common amongst 536 TQM organizations [60]. Another study of 20 companies that were high scorers in 1988/89 MBNQA assessment rounds found that initial training typically encompasses TQM awareness and leadership, followed by sessions in problemsolving and continuous skills [20].

It is also evident from the studies that organizations are emphasizing both interactive and technical skills. According to a survey, good communication skills is one of the two employee characteristics most valued by quality-driven organizations[64]. British Airways' training for its crew is a 50-50 split between the technical and the behavioural. The latter type of training includes treating customers as individuals and taking ownership of their problems. At Charrette Corporation, training for supervisors and managers to develop the necessary facilitator skills and behaviours was essential to overcome the initial uncertainty and suspicion amongst middle managers[45]. Only with a considerable amount of suitable training and education can this be achieved.

Organizations such as Fuji Xerox commence training for all employees immediately on hiring. They believe that putting everyone through the same

TQM training provides the employees across the organization with a common language of quality and a shared way of thinking. TQM concepts are generally understood and used, making communication much easier [16].

TQM is a leadership issue at all levels. Middle managers become leaders of empowered employees, facilitators of the new management system, and coaches of new methods. Only with a considerable degree of training and education can this changed role be assumed[27]. Organizations are investing a significant amount of resources in preparing their managers to be different types of leaders. Based on a survey among UK managers[44], it was concluded that the effective training of managers may be an important factor in the success of TQM implementation.

At Nissan UK where supervisors are empowered to recruit their own staff and people management skills feature prominently in their functions, the company puts a great deal of emphasis on training and developing supervisors as leaders. In addition to standard training elements, professional programmes conducted cover personal effectiveness and impart knowledge required by a supervisor in one function which is different from that needed by his or her peer in another function[65].

AMP of Canada Ltd has implemented a training programme whereby managers participate in learning a different way of managing. This ongoing programme, which takes 300 hours during the first year, deals with the soft side of managing and draws extensively on the disciplines of psychology, sociology and philosophy. Milliken managers take a seven-week Leadership Orientation Programme, which is topped up by at least 40 more hours in a year [16].

It is important that education and training materials used should be readily associated with the company, its "culture" and implementation strategy:

A week of training in a vacuum ... doesn't make TQM happen [60].

Kano[3] stresses the importance of adapting training programmes to the company's work-place. At British Steel, top management spent considerable time defining the challenges to be faced by the organization and clarifying their vision and values before embarking on training. In designing their training courses, they matched the methodologies and content to the specific culture and values of their organization[16]. At Rank Xerox, a task force was set up to develop a training curriculum to support the implementation plan.

On the same note, Oakland[4] cautioned that training for quality is too important to be totally left to the so-called external quality professionals [37]. Bought-in training courses may not be compatible with the philosophies and culture of the company. In fact, some TQ organizations perceive the generic nature of off-the-rack education and training materials as a barrier to steady progress in the quality drive[62]. GPT Ltd is one such organization. It produced its own education package comprising a work book, manual and videos.

In many TQ organizations that conduct internal training, cascading of training is common [66]. This basically involves a number of managers and supervisors who, after undergoing training and education themselves, are selected to be trained as course instructors for internal training. These trainers then develop their own training package best suited to their team's needs. In some organizations, the process starts at the top [17]. The CEO, who is trained first, trains managers who report to him or her, and who in turn teach their immediate staff and so forth.

By accepting responsibility for and conducting training courses themselves, managers are seen as visible supporters and get buy-in from their "students". Training will have more impact as a result as employees, seeing that management is committed, will also be more willing to get involved. In the process, managers also develop self-discipline and expertise in promoting TQM within the organization [67].

GPT Ltd UK call such training "family group training" [62]. The majority of its training workshops were designed and run by line managers. The cascading approach was used at Ilford Ltd to great effect [26]. A top management committee delivered the training, starting with themselves and followed by the next level. This level then trained their reporting managers. At Southern Pacific Lines, internal staff deliver most of the formal quality training for the company's 23,000 employees[30]. Rank Xerox Limited, whose firstline managers also worked with their staff during training, sees the line management ownership of the training process as critical to effective continuing implementation[68].

In some TQ organizations, however, training is led by employees who are recognized by the management as having particular inter-personal skills. This is done without reducing or compromising the role of the work group leader in any way. At LeaRonal (UK), training achieved a high degree of success using dedicated in-house trainers [23].

Before they develop tailor-made training packages, some organizations start by using training materials put together by external consultants, gradually reducing their involvement. BP Chemicals UK started by using the Crosby programme [69]. While they retained Crosby's key principles and philosophy, the training materials were now their own. After getting training help externally in the initial years, Paul Revere Insurance Group has now taken responsibility for its own training[32]. At Shorts Brothers, the training was initially consultantled[31]. In the later stages, the employees took ownership of all courses. The three organizations view the ownership of the training process as an important factor in their quality initiatives.

In almost all the 20 best companies surveyed in the USA, Europe and the Far East, Bertsch and Williams[17] found that quality training is frequently conducted by line managers with consultants used sparingly and for specific short-term assignments. The use of cascade systems is common.

In TQ organizations, most employees receive a substantial amount of annual training. Employees of Baldrige applicants receive 40 to 80 hours of training per year [10]. At Grundos, an average of 4 per cent of employees' working time is devoted to training[22]. In terms of training expenditures, top American organizations, Baldrige applicants included, commit 2-5 per cent of total corporate payroll.

In the USA, several top companies, in recognizing the importance of training and education, have come together to form a co-operative venture to identify training's best practices and generate comparative data to set a standard for their individual efforts. The American Society for Training and Development's Benchmarking Forum is represented by 37 companies, and includes many

Baldrige winners. One of their motives is a desire to learn how to adopt or adapt training practices that clearly provide a competitive advantage [70].

Rewards and recognition

Drawing a conclusion based on best practices of quality leaders in the USA, Europe and Japan, Johnston and Daniel[16] cited rewards and recognition as one of the enablers which maximizes employees' potential and involvement and, in doing so, become one of the main contributors to the company's journey to quality. A study which focused on 86 major corporations found that best practice units within these organizations used rewards as incentives to advance their TQM process[35]. According to Easton[10], the practice of providing an employee recognition scheme for quality is widespread amongst Baldrige applicants.

Crosby [36] considers recognition as one of the most important steps of the quality improvement process. Many other authors also talk about recognition and rewards as being part and parcel of a well-defined quality process[10,16,22,27,33,54,69,71].Inbest organizations, rewards and recognition are linked to sustaining the appropriate behaviour[17,72].

Titman and Callum[71], in discussing the experience of Exxon Chemicals Ltd UK, see reward and recognition as an essential element of the TQ process and a prerequisite to achieving and maintaining a corporate culture which embraces the TQ process. Rank Xerox Ltd identified recognition as one of the major areas of change to be leveraged within its quality initiative strategy[23]. At IBM UK Ltd's Havant site, it is generally recognized that the company's recognition programme had played a major part in the overall success of the site's quality initiative[73]. The emphasis on recognition of its employees' contributions and achievements is a special feature of the TQ initiative at Hartford Insurance Group [54]. When the enthusiasm of its employees of the TQ work faded after two years, top management at Ciba-Geigy Italy rekindled their enthusiasm by rethinking the reward system to include quality objectives [22].

At Exxon Chemical Ltd UK, both reward and recognition systems are in place. The reward mechanism comprises an across-the-board salary increment and individual merit awards. Those whose behaviour is in line with company business needs are made known to management and encouraged. Individuals who succeed in establishing the desired behaviour and results are provided with higher benefits.

As the individual reward mechanism gives little external recognition, the company provides a channel for more public recognition through the Reward of Teams. The annual presentation of the President's Awards are for outstanding and exemplary achievement in certain well-defined areas, including TQ. Here there are no direct financial rewards. However, winners are accorded worldwide publicity through company news bulletins.

Rewards do not have to be monetary[33]. Employees are motivated by different things and organizations need to ascertain in each case what these are. Paul Revere Insurance Group designed its recognition awards for successful ideas from quality teams along the lines of Olympic medals, i.e. bronze, silver and gold lapel pin medals. Employees attach value to and proudly wear them[32]. Employees at Florida Power & Light Company wanted as recognition the full implementation of their improvement suggestions [16].

It is also important that employees perceive that the achievement of the goals tied to rewards and recognition is within their power. A system in which employees cannot have direct impact on the achievement of the goal will cause frustration and a lack of identification with the goal[16]. On a similar note, Titman and Callum[71] stress the importance of clear communication as a tool to support the reward mechanism, i.e. employees need to know what is expected of them, what it is that they are trying to achieve and why they are trying to achieve it. Rewards and recognition schemes must continually evolve to meet the organization's changing needs.

Teamwork

According to Koichi Tsukamoto, President, Wascoal Corporation, Japan: "One step by 100 persons is better than 100 steps by one person" (quoted in [52]).

Teamwork is a critical element if TQM is to succeed[32,36,45,67,74-76]]. Teamwork promotes a bottom-up thrust for quality improvement [77] and

44

delivers synergistic enhancement of quality efforts [32].

Successful organizations are run with teams for solving problems, for improving quality, for introducing new processes and products[78]. Compared to employees who work individually, effective teams tend to have higher morale and productivity, and take pride in the job and the company. A 1991 Conference Board study [16] found the formation of teams working together for continuous improvement to be the single most commonly-employed TQM implementation tactic amongst 158 companies. In Japan, teams are a fundamental component of the management system [79]. Perlman and Zacharias[80] say that in many organizations, one of the greatest barriers to TQM is the territorialism that has evolved over many years.

At Southern Pacific Lines, there is a strong emphasis on teamwork. It was in fact made clear at the onset that the quality process would survive only if the employees could form themselves into teams. There are now over 890 teams, of which 25 per cent are cross functional [30].

The importance of active participation by every employee and a team approach were recognized as vital at an early stage of implementation at Tioxide Group Ltd[31]. At IBM UK Ltd's Havant site, the success of its quality "programme" is due to each and every one of its employees working as a team [7 3]. Teamwork is one of the guiding principles of total quality at Bama Pie in the USA[18]. At STC Cables Products UK, the team approach is seen to create an environment where employee involvement is maximized, morale improved and job satisfaction increased[81]. At Rank Xerox, people from all levels come together to share ideas and best practices in an effort to innovate and continuously improve business processes.

Team working and the breaking down of functional barriers were given great emphasis in Ilford Ltd's quality initiatives[26]. This helped to underpin a total company approach rather than allow initiatives to become too functionalized. At the heart of Eastman Chemical Company's quality is the interlocking team structure [82]. This structure starts with a team composed of Eastman's president and the vice-presidents who report to him. Each vice-president then forms a team with his or her reports. This continues all the way down the organization until, essentially, all 17,750 employees are involved in teams. With this structure, teamwork is improved and information flows both up and down the organization.

Employees who involve themselves in quality group activities are also better convinced of the benefits of the quality process. The findings for a survey carried out among employees at two Hewlett-Packard factories in the UK showed that the degree of buy-in amongst the survey respondents was favourable with those who were part of a quality team [28].

In pursuit of teamwork, some organizations set up formal team systems. Such systems can play a major role in promoting employee involvement - one of the cornerstones of TQM. Florida Power & Light Company which maintains a team process improvement system saw a significant involvement of its employees in the quality process as a result [16].

There are typically two types of formal team system. One of these is the natural, or functional, team which usually focuses on the regular daily work processes, and involves a voluntary problem-solving group made up of workers in the same work area. The quality circle is an example of a voluntary work area team. Organizations attempting to foster a teamwork ethic may find this type of team allows discrete pilot development [83]. Given its existence across a wide range of industries, including the public sector since the 1970s, the opportunities for learning from the experiences of others are also plentiful.

Although functional teams help towards the improvement of teamwork within local work areas, working within functional boundaries keeps individuals and groups isolated and reinforces preconceptions[84,85]. This may create resistance to integration within organizations and thus hamper the creation of a total quality culture.

Best organizations such as Xerox Canada and General Electric are blurring functional boundaries to integrate all players across the organization to work together as a team towards greater accomplishments in the organization's quality journey [84]. Organizations are linking together traditional functions by forming a second type of team system -cross functional teams. Price and Chen[86], believe that a properly managed cross-functional team system can assist in

46

scaling down organizational boundaries to satisfy the customer [4]. According to National West-minster Bank plc UK, cross-functional teams are important in the design of quality delivery service [87].

Getting employees together in groups does not guarantee a successful outcome [62]. Members need to work effectively as a team. Organizations keen to promote integration through teams create an enabling system which promotes teamwork and eliminates barriers to successful performance. Florida Power & Light Company employees are trained on how to work in teams, and have officially been given the responsibility and authority to form natural teams as they see fit[16].

The role of employee unions

There is a lot of debate on the role of employee unions within the concept of employee involvement. For the unions, past experiences of management "productivity" initiatives to turn around the organizations had often resulted in job losses and redundancies. Productivity and efficiency are thus not positive words for them to support new initiatives in whatever form.

Some hold the view that if an organization is substantially unionized, management must take the initiative to encourage union involvement. It is recognized that because most unions exert tremendous influence at the grassroots level - where quality must become an uncontentious way of life - some form of workable partnership is needed for TQM to succeed. Glover[49] also stresses the importance of keeping the union informed and involved in what the organization is doing with the TQM transformation process.

At the outset of the implementation of the quality process, the management at Shorts Brothers was very aware that one of the potential barriers to progress was trade union resistance. However, by involving the trade union at the early stages and in discussing the objectives of the initiatives, resistance was avoided [31].

Southern Pacific Lines also involved the unions in its quality initiative from the very beginning with much success. Union officers were briefed on the poor economic and performance status of the company and asked to discuss the plan with their locals and participate in the TQ process. In fact, the union leaders know about the strategy before middle and lower managers[30]. At Rover Cars, its total quality improvement initiative yielded significant gains in performance with the support and co-operation of the unions [88].

While the above organizations would agree wholeheartedly on the importance of union involvement in the TQ initiative, Ciba-Geigy Italy is one organization that felt unions should be kept at arms' length in the corporate TQM projects [22]. They believe that this will enable the management to establish a stronger direct line of control and communication to the shopfloor, which is vital to effective TQ process. Its TQM initiative was started without union involvement. In fact, when the union asked to be included, the company refused.

Policy and strategy

It is clearly evident that successfully implementing TQM in any organization requires the alignment of every member's efforts with the aim of the organization[20]. Deming[1] through his first point, "strive for consistency of purpose", stresses the need to link quality efforts within an organization to a larger sense of corporate purpose. Crosby [5] sees quality policy as a standard for practice that sets priorities by influencing the entire organization on what to do and what not to do.

Management of best organizations are using the process of policy development and deployment to make sure that employees understand the objectives of the company, and how they will contribute to meeting the objectives[20]. A critical factor for success in the management of quality would appear to be attention to policy development and goal setting and planning, and the effective deployment of goals.

Quality gurus and writers of TQM are also unanimous in stressing the importance of a strategic planning process based on total quality[1,4,5,33,37,53,89]. The process determines customer and other stakeholders' requirements, competitors' position and process capability, and then deploys them within the organization, where they are translated into specific activities.

Easton[10] revealed that Baldrige applicants usually develop some sort of written quality plan, which may be separate from or part of the overall strategic or business plans. Coulson-Thomas [90], in summarizing the findings of three 1991 TQM-related surveys with top management, reported that clear vision and strategy, along with top management commitment, were ranked as the most important requirements for successful management of change. A case study of six companies concluded that those without a formalized quality policy are unlikely to have an effective quality-related decision-making process, and tend to adopt an inspection-oriented approach to the management of quality [91]. When Rank Xerox Limited made the commitment in 1984 to adopt quality principles and practices into its business processes, the first step was to articulate a simple and direct quality policy, and communicate it to all employees [92]. For Grundos, quality policy is central to their efforts to win a sustainable competitive edge [22]. In this sense, quality policy provides the context and launching platform for the implementation of TQM. Typically the quality strategy, goals, vision/mission and values are contained within the larger quality policy.

The CEO of Procter & Gamble stresses that strategic planning is management leadership's job[42] . Policy development is an integral part of management's commitment to quality[53]. Having a clear, specific quality policy as part of the management commitment step is also defined in Crosby's 14 steps[5]. He explains that the quality policymust be given the same emphasis as the financial policy and is the responsibility of top executives. Mitel Telecom Ltd UK views the publishing of its quality policy as the first evidence of its commitment to quality improvement[38]. Carman[30], in relating the experience of Southern Pacific Lines in implementing continuous quality improvement, emphasized that a strong and clear leadership statement of mission and strategy is essential. This statement must make clear that quality is the strategy.

Although most organizations have sophisticated planning processes, the many strategies fail to deliver because "what is planned and what is implemented are not the same" [93].

This contention is supported by Easton[10]: The [strategic quality] plans generally stop at setting goals and objectives and developing budgets. They do not realistically address implementation issues or deployment of the plan throughout the organization. Even in companies with a fairly well-developed planning process, failure to realistically consider implementation issues is common and is a key reason the planning process is ineffective.

This is not surprising as policy deployment and implementation are generally acknowledged as difficult processes [94]. A study of strategy development and implementation found that 73 per cent of managers believed that implementation is more difficult than development [89]. Zairi[93] views the problem as being due to strategies often under-going frequent changes and causing misalignment and disruption in performance. Failure to address this fundamental link was attributed to ICL Product Distribution[22] and GPT Ltd UK [62] who had little success with their quality initiatives in the early years.

However, best organizations such as Procter & Gamble, NEC Japan, Komatsu, Unilever Personal Products, Hewlett-Packard, Rank Xerox, and Florida Power & Light attain much success in developing, communicating and reviewing strategic plans at levels within their organizations by using a structured strategic planning process. This is sometimes termed quality policy deployment[16,23,42,89] and is defined by Rank Xerox as:

A key process [through] which Rank Xerox can articulate and communicate the Vision, Mission, Goals and Vital Few Programmes to all employees. It provides answers to the two questions. What do we need to do? and How are we going to do it?[89].

At NEC Japan, the quality policy deployment process (called *hoshin kanri)* starts with the chief executive first setting the long-term policy in line with the aims and philosophy of the corporation [2 3]. This is done after full discussion with his senior managers and when consensus is achieved. Out of this, a few strategic factors *(kanri)* that will give the corporation an edge in the marketplace are created. The long-term plan is then divided down into medium- and short-term objectives. This is handed down the line and debated with the three levels involved, thus overlapping discussions. This will go up and down and across the lines until the plan has a shape and everyone understands and agrees to it. The strategic aims generally stay intact - the debate is mostly about how to achieve them and the acceptance of responsibilities. At Rank Xerox, the process is also deployed in a top-down fashion, with active participation at all levels [89]. In order to gain organization-wide commitment, a "catchball" technique is used. The technique is similar to NEC Japan's, whereby through negotiation at all levels, across levels and across departments using hard data and facts "thrown" at each other, goals are accepted and everyone is committed to delivering them. At Thomas Cork SML, the board directors and senior management had a joint meeting to reach consensus on the two sets of company policy and objectives drawn up by each group[30].

The next step of policy deployment is taking the defined corporate focus and converting it into action with targets within every department and at every level of the organization. Smith[23] sees this step as "a key way of locking the quality process into the management process; making linkages from a five- or ten-year vision into daily actions". Johnston and Daniel[16] explain how corporate objectives are translated into meaningful ones and cascaded down the levels at Suntory Brewery in Japan:

The policy deployment process forces the organization to develop plans for action ... after the plant manager announces his policy, section managers set targets. Supervisors then set targets for each group and individual operators define their role, targets and plans of action.

At Rank Xerox, with the company's objective defined, each director identifies a list of actions to meet his objective. These are then cascaded down the organization, with each level agreeing their own list of actions. At the end of the cascade, all its 28,000 employees have personal objectives[23].

An important element of QPD is the regular monitoring of progress and performance checks to ensure that goals are still achievable [16] . At NEC Japan, the *kanri* element ensures that progress to goals is monitored[23]. Annual presidential audits are conducted to track if the plan is on schedule, and regular checks on progress at all levels are made before the president's audit. Changes are made whenever necessary. At the Soap Sector of Procter & Gamble, management reviews are conducted for the purposes of ensuring the quality of results, assessing strengths and weaknesses, and ensuring that there is goal congruence and total alignment within the company [89].

Johnston and Daniel [16] reported that Deming Award-winning organizations also continuously standardize or modify processes based on the results of the review. The actual results, and the processes used to achieve them, become input for the planning phase the following year.

While the subject of strategic quality planning in organizations is not widely discussed in the literature, unlike many other topics of TQM, what is reported generally tends to give a good degree of indication of how best organizations achieve success, namely, they ensure that it:

- is a corporate-wide process;

- focuses on the vital few;

- builds contributions from all levels into the planning;

- approaches deployment through consensus;

- is accessible to everyone and open to challenge;

- ensures everyone understands and is committed to it;

- keeps it a live document by regular review and adjustment.

References

1   Deming, W.E., *Out of the Crisis,* MIT Centre for Advanced Engineering Study, Cambridge, MA, 1986.

2   Feigenbaum, A.V., *Total Quality Control,* McGraw-Hill, London, 1961.

3   Kano, N., "A perspective on quality activities in American firms", *California Management Review,* Vol. 35 No. 3, 1993, pp. 12-31.

4   Oakland, J.S., *Total Quality Management,* Butterworth-Heinemann, Oxford, 1993.

5 Crosby, P., *Quality Is Free: The Art of Making Quality Certain,* Penguin Books, New York, NY, 1979.

6   Juran, J.M., "Made in USA: a renaissance in quality", *Harvard Business Review,* Vol. 71 No. 4, 1993, pp. 42-50.

7 Krantz, K.T.," How Velcro got hooked on quality", *Harvard Business Review,* Vol. 67 No. 5,1989, pp. 34-40.

8 Bertram, D., "Getting started in total quality management", *Total Quality Management,* Vol. 2 No. 3,1991, pp. 279-82.

9 Atkinson, R., "Motivating people for success", *The TQM Magazine,* Vol. 4 No. 4,1992, p. 2513.

10 Easton, G.S., "The 1993 state of US total quality management: a Baldrige examiner's perspective", *California Management Review,* Vol. 35 No. 3,1993, pp. 32-54.

11 NIST, *Malcolm Baldrige National Quality Award: 1994 Award Criteria,* National Institute of Standards and Technology, US Department of Commerce, Gaithersburg, MD, 1994.

12 EFQM, *Total Quality Management: The European Model for Self-appraisal,* ISBN 90-5236-035-9, European Foundation for Quality Management, 1992.

13 Ramirez, C. and Loney, T., "Baldrige Award winners identify the essential activities of a successful quality process", *Quality Digest,* January 1993, pp. 38-40.

14 Zairi, M.andYoussef, M.A., "Benchmarkingcritical factors for TQM: PartI: Theory and foundation", *Benchmarking for Quality Management & Technology,* Vol. 2 No. 1,1995, pp. 5-20.

15 Porter, L.J. and Parker, A.J., "Total quality management - the critical success factors", *Total Quality Management, Vol. 4 No.* 1,1993, pp. 13-22.

16 Johnston, C.G. and Daniel, M.J., *Customer Satisfaction through Quality. An International Perspective,* The Conference Board of Canada, Ottawa, Ontario, Canada, 1991.

17 Bertsch, B. and Williams, R.," How multinational CEOs make change programme stick", *Long Range Planning,* Vol. 27 No. 5,1994, pp. 3-11.

18 Powers, V., "The sweet smell of success", *Continuous\ Journey,* October/ November 1994, pp. 18-24.

19 George, D., "The routine involvement of senior managers in the quality improvement process", in Oakland, J.S. (Ed.), *Proceedings of the 3rd International Conference on Total Quality Management,* Warwick, IFS Ltd, Bedford, 1990.

20 Olian, J.D. and Rynes, S.L., "Making total quality work: aligning organizational processes, performance measures, and stakeholders", *Human Resource Management,* Vol. 30 No. 3,1991, pp. 303-33.

21 Wiggenhorn, W., "Motorola U: when training becomes an education", *Harvard Business Review,* Vol. 68 No. 4,1990, pp. 71-83.

22 Binney, G., *Making Quality Work: Lessons from Europe's Leading Companies,* The Economist Intelligence Unit, London, 1992.

23 Smith, S., *The Quality Revolution,* Management Books 2000 Ltd, Didcot, 1994.

24 Kolesar, P.J., "Vision, values, milestones: Paul O'Neill starts total quality at Alcoa", *California Management Review,* Vol. 35 No. 3,1993, pp. 133-65.

25 Durrant, P.W., "TQM and the cultural changes required", in Oakland, J.S. (Ed.), *Proceedings of the 3rd International Conference on Total Quality Management,* Warwick, IFS Ltd, Bedford 1990.

26 Hunt, W. and Hillman, G.P., "Achieving the real culture change necessary for TQM", in Oakland, J.S. (Ed.), *Proceedings of the 3rd International Conference on Total Quality Management,* Warwick, IFS Ltd, Bedford, 1990.

27 Townsend, P.L. and Gebhardt, J.E., *Quality in Action,* John Wiley & Sons, New York, NY, 1992.

28 Barker, R.L., "Basic improvement tools and total quality management", in Oakland, J.S. (Ed.), *Total Quality Management: Proceedings of the 4th International Conference,* Warwick, 3-5, IFS Ltd, Bedford, 1991.

29 Browning, S.A. and Shaw, W.N., "Employees' views of TQM at two Hewlett-Packard manufacturing plants", in Oakland, J.S. (Ed.), *Proceedings of the*

3rd International Conference on Total Quality Management, Warwick, IFS Ltd, Bedford, 1990.

30 Carman, J.M., "Continuous quality improvement as a survival strategy: the Southern Pacific experience", *California Management Review,* Vol. 35 No. 3,1993, pp. 118-32.

31 Oakland, J.S. and Porter, L., *Cases in Total Quality Management,* Butterworth-Heinemann, Oxford, 1994.

32 Bank, J., *The Essence of Total Quality Management,* Prentice-Hall, London, 1992.

33 Haksever, C., "Total quality management in the small business environment", *Business Horizons,* March- April 1996, pp. 33-40.

34 Reeves, C.A. and Bednar, D.A., "What prevents TQM implementation in health care organizations?", *Quality Progress,* April 1993, pp. 41-4.

35 *Quality Progress,"* Companies that link quality to reward program report success", *Quality Progress,* Vol. 27 No. 4,1994, pp. 15,18.

36 Crosby, P., *Let's Talk Quality: 96 Questions that You Always Wanted to Ask Phil Crosby,* McGraw-Hill, New York, NY, 1989.

37 Smith, P.K. and Tee, M.R., "Total quality-the issues and realities for a leading supplier of advanced surface treatment technology", in Oakland, J.S. (Ed.), *Proceedings of the 3rd International Conference on Total Quality Management,* Warwick, IFS Ltd, Bedford, UK, 1990.

38 Boyer, S.M., "Total quality management and new product development", *Total Quality Management,* Vol. 2 No. 3,1991, pp. 283-90.

39 Juran, J.M., *Juran on Quality by Design,* Free Press, New York, NY, 1991.

40 Zink, K.J., "Total quality management and people management" in Kanji, G.K. (Ed.), *Total Quality Management: Processing of the First World Congress,* Chapman & Hall, London, 1995.

41 Nadkarni, R.A., "A not-so-secret recipe for successful TQM", *Quality Progress,* Vol. 28 No. 11,1995, pp. 91-6.

42 Bemowski, K., "Carrying on the P&G tradition", *Quality Progress,* Vol. 25 No. 5,1992, pp. 21-5.

43 Bemowski, K.," 1994 Baldrige Award recipients share their expertise", *Quality Progress,* 1994, Vol. 28 No. 2, pp. 35-40.

44 Wilkinson, A., Redman, T. and Snape, E., "Quality management and the manager", *Employee Relations,* Vol. 16 No. 1,1994, pp. 62-70.

45 Manz, C.C. and Sims, H.P., *Business without Bosses,* John Wiley, New York, NY, 1993.

46 Wacker, K.A.,"Uncommon common sense", *Quality Progress,* Vol. 26 No. 7,1993, pp. 97-100.

47 Quality Progress, "Middle managers can inhibit TQM", *Quality Progress,* Vol. 26 No. 7,1993, pp. 16, 18.

48 Ishikawa, K., *What Is Total Quality Control? The Japanese Way,* Prentice-Hall, Englewood Cliffs, NJ, 1985.

49 Glover, J., "Achieving the organizational change necessary for successful TQM", *International Journal of Quality & Reliability Management,* Vol. 10 No. 6, 1993, pp. 47-64.

50 McDermott, L., "Jump-starting managers on quality", *Training & Development,* Vol. 47 No. 9,1993, pp. 37- 40.

51 Dumas, R., "Organizational quality: how to avoid common pitfalls", *Quality Progress,* Vol. 22 No. 5, 1989, pp. 41-4.

52 Clemmer, J., *Firing on All Cylinders,* Judy Piatkus Publishers, London, 1990.

53 Juran, J.M., *Quality Control Handbook,* McGraw-Hill, London, 1974.

54 Cullen, J. and Hollingum, J., *Implementing Total Quality, IFS* Ltd, Bedford, 1987.

55 Hutt, G., "Quality-theproperwayof managing", in Oakland, J.S. (Ed.), *Proceedings of the 3rd International Conference on Total Quality*

Management, Warwick, IFS Ltd, Bedford, UK, 1990.

56 Garvin, D.A., "Building a learning organization", *Harvard Business Review,* Vol. 71 No. 4,1993, pp. 78- 91.

57 Sanford, R.L., "Baxter Healthcare uses its own quality award to help achieve excellence", *National Productivity Review,* Winter 1992, pp. 37-43.

58 Ingle, S., "How to avoid quality circle failure in your company", *Training and Development Journal,Vol.* 36 No. 6,1982, pp. 54-9.

59 Findlay, I., Wilshaw, G. and Dale, B.G., "Total quality management in sales and marketing organizations: introduction and development", in Oakland, J.S. (Ed.), *Proceedings of the 3rd International Conference on Total Quality Management,* Warwick, IFS Ltd, Bedford, UK, 1990.

60 DDI, *TQM: Forging ahead or Falling behind-A Study of Quality Practices,* Development Dimensions International Inc., Bridgeville, PA, 1994.

61 Oakland, J.S. and Beardmore, D.," Best practice customer service", *Total Quality Management,* Vol. 6 No. 2,1995, pp. 135-48.

62 Cashbourne, B.R., "Organizingfortotalquality management", in Oakland, J.S. (Ed.), *Proceedings of the 4th International Conference on Total Quality Management,* Warwick, Bedford, UK, IFS Ltd, 1991.

63 Westbrook, R. and Barwise, P., "Total quality management in leading fast-moving consumer goods companies", *Total Quality Management,* Vol. 6 No. 4,1995, pp. 365-82.

64 *Quality Progress,* "Workforce study identifies most valued employee characteristics", *Quality Progress,* Vol. 28 No. 9,1995, p. 14.

65 Vallely, I., "Why supervisors can with Nissan", *Works Management,* October 1993, pp. 18-21.

66 Bendell, T., Boulter, L. and Kelly, J., *Benchmarking for Competitive Advantage,* Pitman Publishing, London, 1993.

67 Kanji, G.K. and Asher, M., *Total Quality Management Process - A Systematic Approach. Advances in Total Quality Management Series,* Carfax

Publishing, Abingdon, 1993.

68 Wright, J.," Rank Xerox approach to implementation", in Oakland, J.S. (Ed.), *Proceedings of the 1st International Conference on Total Quality Management,* Warwick, IFS Ltd, Bedford, 1988.

69 Stark, J.A.L., "Experience of TQM at BP Chemicals", in Oakland, J.S. (Ed.), *Proceedings of the 3rd International Conference on Total Quality Management,* War- wick, IFS Ltd, Bedford, 1990.

70 Kimmerling, G., "Gathering best practices", *Training & Development,* Vol. 47 No. 9,1993, pp. 29-36.

71 Titman, C.R. and Callum, W.S., "Recognition and reward", in Oakland, J.S. (Ed.), *Total Quality Management: Proceedings of the 4th International Conference on Total Quality Management,* Warwick, IFS Ltd, Bedford, 1991.

72 Williams, A., Dodson, P. and Walters, M., *Changing Culture,* 2nd ed., Institute of Personnel Management, London, 1993.

73 Kyte, R., "Departmental purpose analysis/quality policy deployment", in Oakland, J.S. (Ed.), *Total Quality Management: Proceedings of the 4th International Conference on Total Quality Management,* Warwick, IFS Ltd, Bedford, UK, 1991.

74 Creech, B., *The Five Pillars of TQM,* Penguin Group, New York, NY, 1994.

75 Clemmer, J., "The coming team crisis: five stumbling blocks or stepping stones to success", *CMA Magazine,* Vol. 67 No. 4,1993, p. 30.

76 Aune, A., "A recipe for success", *TQM Magazine,* February 1991, pp. 33-7.

77 Heath, P.M., "The path to quality achievement through teamwork plus commitment", *International Journal of Quality & Reliability Management,* Vol. 1 No. 2,1989, pp. 51-9.

78 Hoevemeyer, V.A.," How effective is your team?", *Training & Development,* Vol. 47 No. 9,1993, pp. 67- 71.61

79 Garvin, D., "Quality on line", *Harvard Business Review,* Vol. 61 No. 5,1983, pp. 65-75.

80 Perlman, S.L. and Zacharias, M., "Can the quality movement succeed in healthcare?", *Journal for Quality and Participation,* January/February 1991, pp. 54-8.

81 Davies, B. and Wilson, D., "TQM - organizing for success", in Oakland, J.S. (Ed.), *Proceedings of the 3rd International Conference on Total Quality Management,* Warwick, IFS Ltd, Bedford, 1990.

82 Bemowski, K., "A pat on the back is worth a thousand words", *Quality Progress,* Vol. 27 No. 3,1994, pp. 51-4.

83 Lawler III, E.E. and Mohrman, S.E., "Quality circle after the fad", *Harvard Business Review,* Vol. 63 No. 1, 1985, pp. 65-71.

84 Hirschhorn, L. and Gilmore, T., "The new boundaries of the boundaryless company", *Harvard Business Review,* Vol. 70 No. 3,1992, pp. 104-15.

85 Kordupleski, R.E., Rust, R.T. and Zahorik, A.J., "Why improving quality doesn't improve quality (or whatev- er happened to marketing)?", *California Management Review,* Vol. 35 No. 3,1993, pp. 82-95.

86 Price, M. and Chen, E.E., "Total quality management in a small, high-technology company", *California Management Review,* Vol. 35 No. 3,1993, pp. 96-117.

87 Goodstadt, P., "Exceeding customer satisfaction", in Oakland, J.S. (Ed.), *Proceedings of the 3rd International Conference on Total Quality Management,* Warwick, IFS Ltd, Bedford, 1990.

88 Rose, E., Woolley, "Shifting sands? Trade unions and productivity at Rover Cars", *Industrial Relations Journal,* Vol. 23 No. 4,1992, pp. 257-67.

89 Zairi, M., *Measuring Performance for Business Results,* Chapman & Hall, London, 1994.

90 Coulson-Thomas, C.J., "Quality: where do we go from here?", *International Journal of Quality & Reliability Management,* Vol. 9 No. 1,1992, pp. 38-55.

91 Dale, B.G. and Duncalf, A.J., "Quality-related decision making: a study of six British companies", *International Journal of Operations & Production Management,* Vol. 5 No. 1,1988, pp. 15-25.

92 Coleman, R., "People and training-the progressive evolution of a training strategy in support of the implementation of total quality management", in Oakland, J.S. (Ed.), *Proceedings of the 4th International Conference on Total Quality Management,* IFS Ltd, Bedford, 1991.

93 Zairi, M., "Strategic planning through quality policy deployment: a benchmarking approach" in Kanji, G.K. (Ed.), *Total Quality Management: Proceedings of the First World Congress,* Chapman & Hall, London, 1995.

94 Groocock, J.M., *The Chain of Quality,* John Wiley, Chichester, 1986.

Appendix: Names of companies referred to in this review

Aluminum Company of America (Alcoa)

AMP of Canada Ltd

AT&T

Baxter Healthcare Group

Bekaeit in Belgium

BMA plc

BP Chemicals UK

British Airways

British Construction Machinery

Manufacturer British Steel Carnaud Metalbox plc Caterpillar Tractor Company Catton and Company (UK) Ltd Charrette Corporation Ciba-Geigy Italy Club Med

Co-operative Bank plc Corning

Digital Equipment DuPont

Eastman Chemical Company Electrolux

Elida Gibbs Ltd in Belgium Ericsson Sweden

in this review

Esso Research Centre UK

Exxon Chemicals Ltd UK

Federal Express

Florida Power & Light

Ford

Fuji Xerox

General Electric

Global Contribution Circle

Globe Metallurgical

GPT Ltd

Grundos of Denmark

GTE Directories

Hartford Insurance Group

Heinz

Hewlett-Packard UK

Hilti (GB) Ltd

Honda

IBM UK Ltd

ICL Product Distribution UK

Ilford Ltd

Istel UK

ITT Hancock Industries

Jaguar Cars

Johnston Maltkey plc UK

Komatsu

L L Beau Inc.

LeaRonal (UK)

Matsushita Japan

Mercury Marine

Milliken Industrial

Mitel

Mitel Telecom UK Ltd

Motorola

National Westminster Bank plc

NEC Japan

Nestlé

Nissan UK

Norand Corporation

Oklahoma City Works

Panasonic

Pascal Corporation Japan

Paul Revere Insurance Group

Philips Electronics

Philips Signetics

Post Office Counters Ltd

Procter & Gamble

Prudential Assurance Company

Rank Xerox

Rockware Glass Ltd, UK

Rover Cars

Royal Mail

Saturn Corporation

Shell Chemicals UK

Shorts Brothers

Solectron Corporation

Southern Pacific Lines

STC Cables Products Ltd

Suntory Brewery Japan

Telecom Ltd UK

Thomas Cork SML

Thomas Interior Systems

Thomas Interior Systems (USA)

Tioxide Group Ltd

Toyota

Unilever Personal Products

Unipart

Velcro USA

Wainwright Industries

Wallace Co.

Yutaka Gigen

3M

Aluminum Company of America (Alcoa)

AMP of Canada Ltd

AT&T

Baxter Healthcare Group

Bekaeit in Belgium

BMA plc

BP Chemicals UK

British Airways

British Construction Machinery Manufacturer

British Steel

Carnaud Metalbox plc

Caterpillar Tractor Company

Catton and Company (UK) Ltd

Charrette Corporation

Ciba-Geigy Italy

Club Med

Co-operative Bank plc

Corning

Digital Equipment

DuPont

Eastman Chemical Company

Electrolux

Elida Gibbs Ltd in Belgium

Ericsson Sweden

Esso Research Centre UK
Exxon Chemicals Ltd UK
Federal Express
Florida Power & Light
Ford
Fuji Xerox
General Electric
Global Contribution Circle
Globe Metallurgical
GPT Ltd
Grundos of Denmark
GTE Directories
Hartford Insurance Group
Heinz Hewlett-Packard UK
Hilti (GB) Ltd
Honda
IBM UK Ltd
ICL Product Distribution UK
Ilford Ltd
Istel UK
ITT Hancock Industries
Jaguar Cars
Johnston Maltkey plc UK
Komatsu
L L Beau Inc.

LeaRonal (UK)
Matsushita Japan
Mercury Marine
Milliken Industrial
Mitel
Mitel Telecom UK Ltd
Motorola
National Westminster Bank plc
NEC Japan
Nestlé
Nissan UK
Norand Corporation
Oklahoma City Works
Panasonic
Pascal Corporation Japan
Paul Revere Insurance Group
Philips Electronics
Philips Signetics
Post Office Counters Ltd
Procter & Gamble
Prudential Assurance Company
Rank Xerox

Rockware Glass Ltd, UK

Rover Cars

Royal Mail

Saturn Corporation

Shell Chemicals UK

Shorts Brothers

Solectron Corporation

Southern Pacific Lines

STC Cables Products Ltd

Suntory Brewery Japan

Telecom Ltd UK

Thomas Cork SML

Thomas Interior Systems

Thomas Interior Systems (USA)

Tioxide Group Ltd

Toyota

Unilever Personal Products

Unipart

Velcro USA

Wainwright Industries

Wallace Co.

Yutaka Gigen

Commentary

The first part of an important and thoughtful review of where we are and where we are going, co-authored by one of the best thinkers in the world in this subject, Mohamed Zairi.

A review of total quality management in practice: understanding the fundamentals through examples of best practice applications - Part II

T Thiagarajan and M. Zairi

First Published in

The TQM Magazine
Volume 9 · Number 5 · 1997 · pp. 344–356
© MCB University Press · ISSN 0954-478X

The authors

T. Thiagarajan is Senior Quality Manager at Palm Oil Research Institute (PORIM), Malaysia.

M. Zairi is SABIC Chair in Best Practice Management at Bradford University, UK.

Abstract

Part II of a three-part series, presents a comprehensive review of the literature by discussing critical factors of TQM in key areas often stressed in implementation case studies, and supported by quality gurus and writers. Such factors are considered as being conducive to the success of TQM implementation. Discusses these factors from the point of view of how and why. There appears to be little agreement on the what, so an understanding of the "processes" involved in implementation allows for the appropriate framing and objective classification of key factors for TQM implementation. Discusses those quality factors related to resource management and systems and process management.

Introduction

The principle of self-assessment using various models such as the Malcolm Baldrige National Quality Award (MBNQA), the European Quality Award (EQA) and the Deming Prize is becoming globally pervasive. Indeed such models are found to be the best means for assessing organizational excellence and the criteria used are found to reflect the most important components of effectiveness and competitiveness. By linking means and drives such as leadership to results (ends) it is possible to relate capability and competence to achievements.

This review of the literature is therefore an attempt to map total quality management using similar sets of criteria to those of the European Quality Award model. More importantly, this is the first attempt at reviewing the literature from the point of view of what, how and why.

Resources management

Communicating for quality

The need for continuous quality improvement must be conveyed effectively and regularly if TQM is to take root and be sustained (Oakland, 1993; Smith, 1994). Kanji and Asher (1993) are most forthright about the need for effective communication for the development of awareness of, and commitment to, quality in an organization's environment:

> Communication is part of the cement that holds together the bricks of the total quality process supporting the principle of people-based management.

Best organizations also recognize that communication could make the difference between success and failure. They see effective communication as a means of maintaining enthusiasm for quality initiatives within the organization. At IBM UK Ltd Havant, communication, along with management direction, was identified as most important if the quality process was to succeed (Kyte, 1991). At ICL Product Distribution UK, various modes of communication were used in an effort to motivate staff and increase understanding of the role that everyone could play in improving quality (Binney, 1992). At Ciba-Geigy Italy, a comprehensive communication campaign was launched to support the TQ initiative. A special feature of the TQ initiatives at Hartford Insurance Group is the emphasis on communications up and down the hierarchy and between departments (Cullen and Hollingum, 1987).

Effective communication is vital in aligning the workforce towards corporate expectations. Leaders of Grundos of Denmark believe that effective communication brings out the best in people:

> The key is to keep people as informed as possible. People want to do things right. It's up to management to give them the chance to do so. (Binney, 1992)

Unclear and inconsistent communication results in employees, front-line and middle managers focusing on priorities which have little or no relevance to the organizational focus (Williams, *etaJ.,* 1993). Smith (1994), in citing the experience of Elida Gibbs in Belgium, also warns that poor communication can lead to loss in momentum in the quality drive.

Typically, best organizations tend to use a wide range of techniques to communicate. At Ciba-Geigy Italy, management briefings are held regularly in an effort to develop commitment to quality, supported by posters, brochures and noticeboards, all emphasizing the need for quality improvement. The company even used its suggestion scheme to improve communication and inter-depart-mental understanding by requiring that suggestions had to be outside the person's own area of work. IBM UK Ltd in Havant even set up a communication department to keep everyone informed of quality activities (Kyte, 1991). In ICL Product Distribution UK, posters and slogans were used in an effort to motivate staff and increase understanding of the role that everyone could play in improving quality. Measurement charts dealing with customer service levels, process improvement and personal and departmental performance were widely maintained and displayed (Binney, 1992).

Many TQ organizations have realized that over and above the usual array of newsletters, memos and bulletins, personal communication needs to be emphasized, (Bertsch and Williams, 1994). Smith (1994) says that there is no real substitute for direct contact.

A survey of 158 US companies in *Fortune* 1000 concluded that not only do they empha-size top-down communication, but also they increase bottom-up and lateral communications (Olian and Rynes, 1991). The need to develop channels to receive feedback from workers is also stressed by many writers. Employees need ways to present ideas, vent their feelings, and voice their opinions.

Open, two-way communication also helps foster good relationships between management and employees, which is vital if quality is to be an integral part of "business as usual". British Airways has a programme whereby, in a public form, the CEO answers questions that have been previously submitted by the staff (Binney, 1992). Bertsch and Williams (1994) also reported that top managers in 20 best companies in the USA, Europe and the Far East make a point of personally interacting with staff at various levels. Regular luncheon meetings where CEOs discuss quality matters with a cross-section of the staff are common in Philips Signetics and Bekaert in Belgium. The CEO of Philips Electronics conducts question-and-answer sessions about the company's TQM process with all his employees in 18 European countries via TV-satellite connection. Crosby (1989) also talks about TQ organizations having communication systems that utilize in-house TV circuits and satellite transmission to ensure that the communication linkage is maintained.

Nissan UK, on the other hand, does not rely on corporate videos, in-house news bulletins or noticeboards for communication with its staff. Its supervisors are the channel for all communication to manufacturing staff. At the start of every shift, each has a five minute meeting with his team (Ashton, 1992).

Lateral communication or communication across the organization is vital if the customer is to be continuously satisfied. Digital has a worldwide system called "notes" which literally allows any one of 100,000 Digital employees to talk to anyone else and obtain information on any subject (Smith, 1994).

The literature also highlights the fact that clear and effective communication is also vital to support other quality initiatives such as performance-related reward mechanisms and training (Titman and Callum, 1991). In the former case, for example, the appraiser needs to communicate to the employee what is expected of him or her, and why is it important. Having in place a feedback mechanism from training course attendees is useful to monitor and improve the quality of subsequent events.

Communication is vital in the empowerment process. If employees are to share the decision making in the company, they must know and understand company objectives and values, and have access to the information relevant to their area of responsibility. British Steel communicates to its employees the results of all customer surveys, highlighting both positive and negative comments. It has monthly newsletters, and even mails relevant information to employees' houses (Johnston and Daniel, 1991). British Airways has a programme whereby, in a public forum, the CEO answers questions that have been previously submitted by the staff (Johnston and Daniel, 1991).

Managing suppliers

No total quality process is complete if it does not address the issues related to the process of managing suppliers (Elshennawy etah, 1991). This notion stems from the quality management philosophy of "prevention rather than detection". TQ organizations aim for "design and purchase" quality, rather than "inspecting" quality to produce services and products that meet customer requirements.

Quality gurus such as Crosby (1989), Deming (1986), Ishikawa (1985) and Peters (1989), preach about the need for suppliers to be viewed as an integral part of the organization's operation. Crosby (1989) says that the relationship between supplier and buyer is one of the most important parts of the quality improvement process. He estimates that 50 per cent of an organization's quality non-conformances are due to defective in-coming materials (Smock, 1982).

TQ organizations tend to manage and control their supply chain better (Hirschhorn and Gilmore, 1992) by pursuing approaches such as supplier base reduction, limited sourcing arrangement, and closer integration and strategic alliance with suppliers (DeRose, 1987). According to the Japanese Ministry of International Trade and Industry, the Japanese manufacturing industry owes its competitive advantage and strength to its supplier relationship structure (Dyer and Ouchi, 1993). Japanese automakers have elaborate supplier-relationship programmes. Toyota and Nissan have large supplier-assistance management consulting groups with specialized expertise that work full-time - "free of charge" - with suppliers. They help suppliers to improve their production techniques and achieve total quality in products and service. Both Toyota and Nissan have at least one consultant for every four to six suppliers (Dyer and Ouchi, 1993). At Jaguar Cars, where appropriate, representatives of its suppliers are brought in as team members of task forces set up to deal with specific quality problems (Cullen and Hollingum, 1987).

According to Easton (1993), many Baldrige applicants have set up extensive quality programmes with their suppliers. These include supplier quality systems audits, supplier rating and qualification systems, training, joint design teams, joint quality improvement teams, and supplier (and supplier employee) recognition schemes. In this way, they ensure that the quality movement spreads gradually throughout their entire supplier chain (Crosby, 1989). They offer partnership and extend as much assistance as possible to suppliers to help them manage quality effectively. Florida Power & Light Company provides a two-week training course for its suppliers on how to implement a total quality management initiative in their own company, while Wallace Company has provided over 100 of its suppliers with training on TQM (Johnston and Daniel, 1991).

Deming (1986) strongly advocates supplier base reduction. His fourth principle states: End the practice of awarding business on price tag alone. Instead, minimise total cost by working with a single supplier.

According to Dyer and Ouchi (1993), reducing the total number of direct suppliers can increase quality while lowering costs. Suppliers developing competence in the customer's requirements, less or no inspection owing to confidence in supply quality and quicker and better responsiveness from the suppliers are some of the reasons for this (Kyte, 1991). Shorts Brothers is continually attempting to reduce the supply base and to build long-term lasting relationships with a number of preferred suppliers (Oakland and Porter, 1994). It encourages suppliers to embrace total quality by extending support through training services and an invitation to participate in joint improvement teams.

As a vital preventive measure against non-conformance of incoming materials,

TQ organizations also undertake supplier evaluation (Newman, 1988). As a key criterion, they select suppliers based on their capability and commitment to product and service quality. Evaluation may be performed by analysing the supplier's history or audits such as on-site assessments or interview. One of the key factors in ICL Product Distribution UK's success in getting its supplies right is its supplier evaluation programme (Binney, 1992). Rover and Ford in the UK also have similar programmes (Gilroy, 1994).

Systems and process management

Accredited quality management system

En route to a TQ culture, registration with a quality management system such as BS 5750/ISO 9000 is seen by many organizations as a starting point and an important element of the implementation process (Hirschhorn and Gilmore, 1992; Oakland and Porter, 1994; Porter and Parker, 1993). At Carnaud Metalbox plc, the BS 5750/ISO 9000 registration process provided the foundation on which a quality culture was built and helped the company to move on in developing the total quality process (Oakland and Porter, 1994). At Tioxide Group Ltd, the registration programme pushed quality to a much higher profile in the company as everyone was actively involved in the process. The company also saw itself in a better position to meet the specific requirements of customers and improve its strategic relationships (Oakland and Porter, 1994). In discussing the implementation of the quality management process at Esso Research Centre, UK, Price and Gaskill (1990) assert that the use of the discipline of a recognized industry accreditation for a quality management system such as the ISO 9000 helps in the integration of the quality process into the site culture. The systematic approach, as stipulated under the various elements such as calibration and maintenance of laboratory equipment, staff training, and sample management, assists in minimizing errors and increases the incidents of "right first time".

Companies such as Nissan Motor UK, Federal Express and Club Med view operating standards as an important requirement in the quality stakes. However, they do not see the need to have a recognized industry accreditation (Binney, 1992).

Organizing for quality

The success of the quality improvement process depends on effective and systematic implementation (Crosby, 1989). Given the corporate-wide nature of TQM, a suitable infrastructure to support quality initiatives is required (Johnston and Daniel, 1991). Oakland and Porter (1994) in fact, highlighted that one of the responsibilities of senior management at the outset of introducing TQM is the need to set up a defined quality organization structure in order to create a framework which will enable quality improvement to develop and flourish (Bendell *etal,* 1993; Davies and Wilson, 1990; Easton, 1993). In fact, they see the structure as a key element in ensuring the success of TQM.

Some authors such as Oakland and Porter (1994) propose a three-tier quality structure, made up of a quality council, process quality committees (or site steering committees) and quality improvement teams to devise and implement TQM within an organization. The quality council, comprising a top management team and headed by the CEO, reviews the strategic direction on TQM, decides resources, monitors, facilitates, and handles impediments to progress (Bendell *et ah,* 1993) . Glover (1993) views a quality council as usually beneficial in planning and designing the TQM system. He goes on to say that it is important that the council is high-powered if this is to be realized.

The process quality committees support the council by overseeing and managing quality at process or site levels, depending on the size of the organization. Oakland and Porter (1994) recommend that every senior manager should be a member of at least one committee, and believes that this provides the top-down support for full employee participation, through either a quality improvement team or quality circle programme. The committees control the quality improvement teams and assist by selecting projects, appointing team members and monitoring progress. The team members, themselves cross-functional, are brought together to tackle and solve specific problems on a project basis.

A case example of a threetier structure is a quality structure introduced at a major British construction machinery manufacturer (Goulden and Rawlins,

1995). The structure is made up of a plant quality council, steering groups and cross-functional/multilevel project teams. Overall strategy and management of the quality programme is provided by the council. The steering groups sponsor and support individual teams, ensuring the required resources are made available.

Members of the teams come from areas closely associated with the project.

The quality structure at Shorts Brothers is another example (Oakland and Porter, 1994). To direct a quality management implementation process, a total quality organizational structure was formed at the outset of the implementation process. This consisted of a quality council chaired by the CEO, two divisional councils chaired by their respective vice-presidents, and 18 functional quality teams chaired by senior managers. A total quality secretariat was also established to co-ordinate the quality initiatives and to take a leading role in assisting the quality council to develop a total quality strategy.

The quality structure at STC Cables Products UK is aimed at total employee involvement in the quality improvement process (Davies and Wilson, 1990). The company designed a five-element quality structure to harness their full potential at every level of the organization (see Table I).

It is evident from the literature that support structures for quality management vary widely (Black, 1993). Smith (1994) suggests that the differences reflect the cultures of the organizations. The structures are also seen to be live, evolving as the TQM matures. This may suggest that there is more concern with promoting ownership of the quality process than there is with the structure required.

Promoting ownership of the quality process through structures becomes even more beneficial within organizations with geographically dispersed operating units. At Southern Pacific Lines, several regional steering committees reporting directly to the central quality council were set up (Carman, 1993).

Support structures for quality management are typically changed or dismantled when goals and objectives for setting up have been achieved. For example, BP Chemicals, UK modified and changed its quality structures as its quality system evolved and moved from the planning and education phase to the implementation phase (Stark, 1990). At Thomas Cork SML, the high-powered quality council set up at the outset to oversee the introduction of total quality was disbanded and its functions taken over by the management committee, once the quality initiatives got off the ground (Oakland and Porter, 1994).

Townsend and Gebhardt (1992) recommend the need to have a full-time post to facilitate and manage the day-to-day running of the quality process, especially if the organization is large (Smith, 1994). An individual such as this can provide a vital support function to the corporate quality council. At STC Cables Products UK, the facilitator (quality improvement process manager) has a major role in the ongoing success of the QIP. He is responsible for establishing the quality teams and putting together the training programme at the initial launch. According to Davies and Wilson (1990), the individual selected must be an efficient organizer, a motivator, enthusiastic and sufficiently senior. At Tioxide

Table I Five-element quality structure

Quality improvement team	Comprising general manager, senior managers and a facilitator
	Ensures visibility of management commitment
	Determines quality policy
	Establishes direction
	Provides support
Quality improvement groups (QIGs)	Operate at all levels on a departmental basis
	Supervisors as leaders
	Address quality issues within work area

Corrective action teams (CATs)	Brought together to address specific problems allocated
	Disbanded when permanent solution found
	Leader is appointed
	Leader selects members
Quality improvement process manager	Senior manager
	Facilitates day-to-day operations of QIGs and CATs
	Co-ordinates quality activities
Individuals	The employee is expected to strive for excellence and be totally involved in the quality process

Group Ltd, a group quality manager reporting directly to the executive director responsible for quality was appointed to facilitate the implementation process (Oakland and Porter, 1994).

The vital role of the facilitator is also high-lighted by a study at two Hewlett-Packard factories in the UK (Barker, 1991). The finding showed that the degree of buy-in among the survey respondents was better in the factory which had a full-time TQM facilitator who actively coached and supported quality teams and activities.

Managing by processes

Although most, if not all, organization activities are considered as processes which cross traditional functional boundaries (Kanji, 1995), many organizations maintain and operate along vertical functional structures, stifling the people within the organization and thus preventing them from understanding how their work affects the overall process of providing customer satisfaction. The functional approach therefore allows barriers to customer satisfaction to evolve

(Oakland and Beardmore, 1995). It allows critical control points between departments to be vulnerable to organizational "noise" (Edson and Shannahan, 1991) such as "turf protection" and poor communication.

If employee involvement is key to the attainment of customer satisfaction, managing by process is key to engaging an organization's employees to take responsibility for what they are doing in relation to satisfying the customers (Oakland and Beardmore, 1995); (Juran, 1993). In many best organizations such as Rank Xerox (Coleman, 1991), IBM (Snowden, 1991), ICL and Shell Chemicals UK (Sinclair, 1994), there is a growing recognition of the need to move away from the traditional functionally-based approach to managing through a set of clearly-defined, customer-driven processes. McAdam (1996), in relating the experiences of Shorts Brothers, says that the process-based approach or managing by process improves customer focus and avoids the limitations of managing by vertical functions.

If the aim of implementing TQM in an organization is to achieve customer satisfaction, then a first step is managing the internal customer-supplier relationship to support the management of processes. Within each organization there exists an intricate structure of both internal customer (one individual/ process/department dependent on another) and internal supplier (one individual/ process/ department supplying another). Any weak link or break at any point in the internal customer-supplier chain may find its way to the interface between the organization and the external customer (Oakland, 1993). Deming (1986) and Kanji (1995) also talk about understanding the notion of internal customer-supplier as absolutely critical to a quality transformation. In this sense, the concept of an internal and external customer-supplier relationship forms the core of total quality (Kanji and Asher, 1993; Oakland, 1993).

Best organizations ensure that everyone within the organization understands that they are dependent on one another, know where their work goes, and continuously ensures that the necessary quality at each interface meets overall customer expectations (Bendell et al., 1993; Crosby, 1989). To orient the perspective of its employees to the "next internal customer", the management at Catton and Company (UK) Ltd requested every-one to ask: Who are my immediate customers? What are their requirements? Do I have the necessary capabilities to meet their requirements? Who are my immediate suppliers? What are my true requirements? Do I communicate my requirements? (NIST, 1994). At the outset of the TQ programme at Thomas Cork SML, an exercise called Needs and Expectations was carried out which involved everyone asking similar questions (Oakland and Porter, 1994). At Shorts Brothers, everyone understood the concept of the internal customer-supplier and that satisfying the internal customer must be realized in order for the company to succeed in its quality quest (Oakland and Porter, 1994).

In his study, Sinclair (1994) found that the identifying and mapping of processes is one of the activities pursued by TQM organizations to support the management of processes (Hardaker and Ward, 1987; McAdam, 1996).

Benchmarking

Benchmarking is an integral part of a total quality process (Bank, 1992; Beadle and Searstone, 1995; Bendell *etal,* 1993; Kleiner, 1994; Mitchell, 1995). But what is benchmarking? Rank Xerox, which developed benchmarking as part of its quality process, provides the most practical definition:

> A continuous, systematic, process of evaluating companies recognised as industry leaders, to determine business and work processes that represent best practices, establish rational performance goals (Zairi, 1994).

The primary objective of benchmarking is performance improvement. Identifying opportunities for performance improvement by comparing one organization's performance with that of another is a reflex of TQM (Bank, 1992). Zairi (1994) draws the link between TQM and benchmarking:

> TQM is the wheel of improvement. ... doing an internal, value-adding activity for the end customer. Benchmarking ... is the external activity for identifying opportunities and ensuring that the wheel of improvement is turning in the right direction and is making the necessary effort towards the end destination, i.e. achieving high standards of competitiveness.

Many best organizations are using benchmarking as a tool for obtaining the information to be used in the continuous improvement process, and to gain competitive edge (Booth, 1995; McNair and Leibfried, 1992). They are attracted to it because it stimulates and challenges the improvement process (Smith, 1994).

At Post Office Counters Limited (POCL), benchmarking is a quality improvement tool (Mitchell, 1995). It used benchmarking inputs to set realistic targets to benefit the customer. At Southern Pacific Lines, benchmarking is viewed as essential for an increased rate of improvement (Carman, 1993). Saturn Corporation built and successfully launched a brand - Saturn - in a saturated market using the benchmarking approach (Bemowski, 1995). Motorola benchmarks itself against 125 companies, while Wainwright Industries has benchmarked 16 past MBNQA winners (Nadkarni, 1995).

Unipart, a UK car components manufacturer, has an information sharing scheme -Global Contribution Circle - with Yutaka Gigen, a counterpart in Japan. Bank (1992) reported that organizations such as Royal Mail, 3M, Heinz, British Airways and Federal express also employ benchmarking as a vital component of their total quality initiatives.

All Baldrige winners used various types of benchmarking to learn best practices (Nadkarni, 1995). There are essentially four types of benchmarking (Zairi, 1994):

(1) Competitive benchmarking: comparisons with primary competitors.

(2) Functional benchmarking: comparisons with similar functions or processes within the same broad industry leaders as partners.

(3) Generic benchmarking: comparison with similar functions or processes regardless of type of industry.

(4) Internal benchmarking.

The fourth type, internal benchmarking, involves comparison within the set-up of the corporation, for example, between sister organizations or branch offices. It is generally ignored in many definitions and played down as unimportant by some writers. However, Rank Xerox used internal benchmarking with much success, transmitting best practices experiences between its 20 different operating companies across Europe (Smith, 1994).

Typically, the process of benchmarking involves the acquisition both of outputs (the actual benchmark) and information on how those outputs are achieved.

Zairi (1994) labels this as process-driven benchmarking. Focusing on just outputs - cost-driven benchmarking - while often resulting in cost reduction, may commit people to unrealistic targets to the detriment of the quality process (Zairi, 1994).

Pulat (1994), in describing AT&T Oklahoma City Works benchmarking experience, offers benchmarking as a continuous process using the plan-do-check-act (PDCA) cycle. The plan phase defines processes to be benchmarked. The do phase involves collecting data on own processes and those of others that are similar. The check phase requires performing gap analysis (numbers and practices). The act phase involves implementing projects to close negative gaps and maintain positive ones.

Haksever (1996), in reference to results of the International Quality Study by Ernst & Young and American Quality Foundation, cautions against the application of bench-marking before a comprehensive quality process is in place. However, Southern Pacific Lines disputed the findings and conducted benchmarking early in their implementation process to set targets for improvement (Carman, 1993).

> The target for any particular performance indicator has no credibility unless it is based on what the competition is doing.

Rank Xerox, the concept creator, claims to have worked and benchmarked with competitors. Milliken benchmarked Xerox's approach to benchmarking.

Benchmarking is a qualifying criterion for organizations aiming for the European Quality Award, and the US Malcolm Baldrige National Quality Award (MBNQA). In the MBNQA, applicants are required to demonstrate competitive analysis and benchmarking activities for 510 of the total 1,000 points.

Self-assessment

Self-assessment is an effective technique to measure the culture of quality within an organization (Zairi, 1994). In this sense, management can use self-assessment as the means to assess whether its implementation efforts are deployed in the right way. Such was the case at Prudential Life Administration, part of Prudential Assurance Company Limited (Porter and Tanner, 1995).

The ability to assess an organization's progress against an accepted set of criteria would be most valuable (Oakland, 1993; Porter and Tanner, 1995). The Malcolm Baldrige National Quality Award (MBNQA) and the European Quality Award (EQA) assessment models are available to organizations for self-assessment (Conti, 1991). For example, it has been suggested that thousands of TQM organizations use the MBNQA criteria annually (Sunday and Liberty, 1992). In this sense, these provide a more widely-accepted technique to measure progress towards TQM than those suggested by authors such as Saraph *etal.* (1989), Black (1993), Cupello (1994).

At 3M, a self-assessment using the MBNQA criteria is performed annually at all business units (Bertsch and Williams, 1994). Prudential Life Administration used the MBNQA criteria during the first year, before moving on to use the EQ's (Porter and Tanner, 1995). Tioxide Group Ltd used the EQA criteria (Oakland and Porter, 1994). Many organizations adapt these well known criteria to suit their needs and objectives.

In recent years, researchers have attempted to develop a scientifically-based diagnostic framework for TQM (Black, 1993; Saraph *et al,* 1989).

There are three commonly-used methodologies for self-assessment, namely, discussion group methods, survey methods and award type processes using written reports (Finn and Porter, 1994). The award type self-assessment is deemed to be the most objective. Prudential Life Administration used a hybrid approach of discussion and award type (Porter and Tanner, 1995).

In common with other quality initiatives, providing the necessary training is vital to make self-assessment work. A study of self-assessment practices in 117 leading European organizations found training to be one of the initiatives used to support self-assessment (van der Wiele, 1996). Tioxide Group Ltd has over the years produced a team of professional auditors (Oakland and Porter, 1994). Nearly 400 employees have been trained to undertake quality audits through the group.

Cost of quality

Quality costing is one quality tool that has been used to help justify the adoption of quality improvement efforts to top management (Israeli and Fisher, 1991; Plunkett and Dale, 1990). Dale and Plunkett (1991) consider quality costing as useful first steps along the TQM journey. Crosby (1979) calls the measurement of quality costs one of the absolutes of quality management.

Thomas Interior Systems (USA), which modelled its 14-step quality process on that of Milliken & Co, winner of the 1989 Baldrige Award, considers the cost of quality as an important stage in its quality process (Johnson, 1993). To ensure its people are comfortable with the improvement process, the company introduced the cost of quality in the first year to everyone. It is believed that putting this exercise at the beginning helped employees to believe in the quality process. Hilti (Great Britain) Ltd also conducted a cost of quality analysis as an integral part of the TQM process to show the staff in the early stages the tangible benefits of introducing total quality (Findlay *etal.* 1990).

At Shorts Brothers, management were quick to realize at the outset of the TQM implementation that the total quality process would only survive if it could provide tangible benefits to the company. It involved the work-force in the cost of quality projects relevant to the business objectives (Oakland and Porter, 1994). The success in savings convinced the staff of the benefits of total quality.

In order to get the efforts in tracking of the cost of quality started, several organizations confine tracking to costs where measurable improvements can be obtained in the short to medium term. LeaRonal (UK) concentrated initially on costs such as scrap and rework, quality assurance, compensation claims, staff turnover, and poor inventory management. National Westminster Bank plc discovered early in its quality journey that straight rework offered the largest opportunity for improving quality cost (Goodstadt, 1990). Thomas Interior Systems (USA) introduced the quality cost concept without getting too specific or to try to account for every penny of cost by looking at errors in specifications, lack of training, cost of not doing things right the first time, missed opportunities and loss of repeat business (Johnson, 1993).

The prevention-appraisal-failure (PAF) model, developed by Feigenbaum is the most widely-applied scheme for categorizing quality costs (Plunkett and

Dale, 1990; Porter and Rayner, 1992). It is also adopted as the quality cost standard for the American Society for Quality Control (Black, 1993). Feigenbaum (1961) breaks down the quality costs into three categories:

(1) Cost of prevention: the costs of any action taken to investigate, prevent or reduce the risk of non-conformity or defects.

(2) Cost of appraisal: the costs of evaluating the achievement of quality requirements.

(3) Failure costs: the costs of non-conformity, both internal and external.

Both Rank Xerox and LeaRonal (UK) added two additional elements to the model:

(1) Cost of exceeding requirements: the costs incurred to provide information or services which are unnecessary or unimportant or for which no agreed requirement has been established.

(2) Cost of lost opportunities: the lost profits resulting from purchases of competitors' products and services or from cancellation of products or services which did not meet customer requirements.

As the cost of introducing its TQM process is included as part of the prevention element, LeaRonal accepts the fact that the prevention costs could increase, pass through a maximum and possibly decline over a total four-year period. The other five elements would be expected to decline progressively from year 1, until after some three to four years, the sum total of all elements would be less than half of the initial year 1 cost.

Quality control techniques

Juran (1974) states that quality control techniques are important tools, not only for low-defect production but also for quality improvement. Shewhart defines quality control as the use of statistical procedures to provide guides to produce good parts and to disclose the cause of variations (Modaress and Aussari, 1989). Other quality gurus such as Deming and Taguchi strongly support a comprehensive quality control system to aid the management of quality. Deming says the key to achieving high quality conformance and to overcoming process-related problems is the use of statistical quality control

A review of total quality management in practice: understanding the
fundamentals through examples of best practice
applications - part III

(SQC) techniques (Modaress and Aussari, 1989). The techniques deal with
the collection, analysis and interpretation of data related to the causes of
variations in quality characteristics.

According to Juran, there are over 50 SQC techniques (Quiros, 1994). However,
the fundamental ones, originally assembled by Ishikawa (1985) as the seven
QC tools, are process flow charting, check sheets or tally charts, histograms,
Pareto analysis, cause and effect diagrams, scatter diagrams and control charts.

SQC for defect prevention is one of the cornerstones of the quality strategy at
Electrolux (Cullen and Hollingum, 1987). The use of SQC techniques was
also seen as one of the key elements in the development of Tioxide Group
Ltd's total quality strategy, while at CarnaudMetalbox plc, the SQC initiative
was seen as an important vehicle for wider participation in teamwork and gave
the total quality process a new boost (Oakland and Porter, 1994). ITT Hancock
Industries considers SQC an important tool in controlling key process
parameters and monitoring quality improvements (Cullen and Hollingum,
1987). Each level of its workforce is trained in the techniques of SQC.

Measuring customer wants and satisfaction

Quality should be customer driven, (Takeuchi and Quelch, 1983). In the
Baldrige Award criteria, a key concept is that quality should be "based on the
customer" (NIST, 1994). Nearly a third of the award score is related to the
customer. Among best companies, there is a passionate and generally held
commitment to serve customers to the best of their abilities (Easton, 1993;
Peters, 1989). A major conclusion of Peters and Waterman (1982) was that
best organizations align their corporate strategies to their customers'
requirements.

Satisfying customers' requirements better than the competition can is widely
recognized today as a key to success in the marketplace (Peters, 1989).

Central to the success of Baldrige winners was their constant focus on satisfying
customers and measuring their satisfaction (Nakarni, 1995). Measuring
customer satisfaction is a cornerstone of TQM (Zairi, 1994). Best organizations
use a variety of techniques such as customer surveys, focus groups and advisory

panels, service visit teams, and close-up interviews to measure customer satisfaction (Berry, 1991; Clemmer, 1990; Taylor, 1995).

Customer survey is the method most commonly used to track customer satisfaction (Bergendahl and Wachmeister, 1993; Oakland and Beardmore, 1995). At Hilti (Great Britain) Ltd, surveys were carried out to assess customers' perception of Hilti quality (Findlay *etal,* 1990). Caterpillar Tractor Company conducts two customer satisfaction surveys following each purchase, one after 300 hours of product use and the second after 500 hours of use (Takeuchi and Quelch, 1983). Baldrige winner Solectron Corporation calls on each of its 120 customers to enquire about satisfaction with their products and service, while another winner, Wain-wright Industries collects weekly and monthly feedback information from customers to determine quality trends and customer satisfaction (Nadkarni, 1995).

While customer satisfaction surveys potentially offer the most efficient and objective means of assessing satisfaction, Deming (1986) calls for frequent direct interaction with customers to determine the level of satisfaction of a continual basis. L L Bean Inc., a mail order company, maintains direct contacts with its customers to track customer and non-customer perceptions of the quality of its own and its competitors' products and services (Takeuchi and Quelch, 1983). At Shorts Brothers, customer representatives are regularly consulted on the level of customer satisfaction (Oakland and Porter, 1994). Xerox holds a visitor quality day for customers every six week (Nadkarni, 1995).

Without understanding customers, there can be no true customer satisfaction (Crosby, 1989; Kordupleski *etal.,* 1993). Peters (1989) even equates survival to customer responsiveness.

Best organizations listen to their customers in order to serve their requirements effectively (Nadkarni, 1995). National Westminster Bank plc, UK considers understanding and staying close to its customers' requirements and expectations as the cornerstone of its quality service programme (Goodstadt, 1990). Through surveys, NatWest can identify critical service elements as required by the customers. The CEO of GTE Directories, the 1994 Baldrige winner, attributes its success to the "religion" of listening and responding to the customer (Bemowski, 1995).

In his study, Garvin (1993) found that the Japanese quality leaders had a clear understanding of consumers' wants by collecting expensive customer data. Like measuring customer satisfaction, a variety of methods are used to collect information on customer requirements (Berry, 1991; Clemmer, 1990). At Shorts Brothers, customer representatives are invited to contribute to multidisciplinary design teams (Oakland and Porter, 1994).

Determining customers' needs is the start; translating these needs in the organization and satisfying them is a major challenge. In recent years, many best organizations have adopted the technique of quality function deployment (QFD) to "bring the voice of the customer into everything they do" (Zairi, 1994). It is a system for translating consumer requirements into appropriate organizational requirements at each stage, from research and product development to engineering and manufacturing to marketing. Best organizations such as Ford, Rank Xerox, Hewlett-Packard and Digital Equipment have started adopting QFD as a method of designing and optimizing the process of developing new products based on the wants of the customers (Zairi, 1994).

The process of QFD involves systematic conversion of non-measurable customer requirements - "what" - into technical specifications/design requirements - "how" (Zairi, 1994). At the centre of the QFD process is the "house of quality". The house of quality is the essential tool used to chart customer requirements and the translation of those requirements into tangible goods and services. The resulting matrix depicts customer requirements, technical specifications/design requirements, target values, and competitive ratings on products/services.

Some best organizations, recognizing the need to look beyond customers' immediate needs, are also investigating the requirements of customers' customers (Vandermerwe, 1993). IBM, DuPont, AT&T and Panasonic have stopped creating products with just the buyer in mind and have started considering the end user as well.

References

Ashton, C. (1992), "Employing habitual success", *The TQM Magazine,* Vol. 4 No. 4, pp. 225-58.

Bank, J. (1992), *The Essence of Total Quality Management,* Prentice Hall, London.

Barker, R.L. (1991), "Basic improvement tools and total quality management", in Oakland, J.S. (Ed.), *Total Qualify Management: Proceedings of the 4th International* Conference, Warwick, IFS Ltd, Bedford.

Beadle, I. and Searstone, K. (1995), "An investigation into the use of benchmarking within quality programme", in Kanji, G.K. (Ed.), *Total Qualify Management, Proceedings of the First World Congress,* Chapman-Hall, London.

Bemowski, K. (1995), "To boldly go where so many have gone before", *Quality Progress,* Vol. 28 No. 2, pp. 29-33.

Bendell, T., Boulter, L. and Kelly, J. (1993), *Benchmarking for Competitive Advantage,* Pitman Publishing, London.

Bergendahl, S. and Wachmeister, A. (1993), "Creating an index", *Managing Service Quality,* May, pp. 19-22.

Berry, T.H. (1991), *Managing the Total Quality Transformation,* McGraw-Hill, New York, NY.

Bertsch, B. and Williams, R. (1994), "How multinational CEOs make change programme stick", *Long Range Planning,* Vol 27 No. 5, pp. 3-11.

Binney, G. (1992), *Making Quality Work: Lessons from Europe's Leading Companies,* The Economist Intelligence Unit, London.

Black, S.A. (1993), "Measuring the critical factors of total quality management", University of Bradford, Unpublished PhD thesis.

Booth, D. (1995)," Benchmarking - the essential phase of preparation", in Kanji, G.K. (Ed.), *Total Quality Management, Proceedings of the First World Congress,* Chapman & Hall, London.

A review of total quality management in practice: understanding the
fundamentals through examples of best practice
applications - part III

Carman, J.M. (1993), "Continuousquality improvementas a survival strategy: the Southern Pacific experience", *California Management Review,* Vol. 35 No. 3, pp. 118-32.

Clemmer, J. (1990), *Firing on all Cylinders,* Judy Piatkus, London.

Coleman, R. (1991), "People and training the progressive evolution of a training strategy in support of the implementation of Total Quality Management", in Oakland, J.S. (Ed.), *Proceedings of the 4th International Conference on Total Quality Management,* IFS Ltd, Bedford.

Conti, T. (1991), "Company quality assessment", *The TQM Magazine,* June/July, pp. 14-27.

Crosby, P. (1979), *Quality is Free: the Art of Making Quality Certain,* Penguin Books, New York, NY.

Crosby, P. (1989), *Let's Talk Quality: 96 Questions that you always wanted to ask Phil* Crosby, McGraw-Hill, New York, NY.

Cullen, J. and Hollingum, J. (1987), *Implementing Total Quality,* IFS Ltd, Bedford.

Cupello, J.M. (1994), "A new paradigm for measuring TQM progress", *Quality Progress,* May, pp.79-82.

Dale, B.G. and Plunkett, J.J. (1991), *Quality Costing,* Chapman and Hall, London.

Davies, B. and Wilson, D. (1990), "TQM -organizing for success", in Oakland, J.S. (Ed.), *Proceedings of the 3rd International Conference on Total Quality Management,* Warwick, IFS Ltd, Bedford.

Deming, W.E. (1986), *Outofthe Crisis,* Cambridge University Press, Cambridge.

DeRose, L.J. (1987), "Changing procurement practices", *Purchasing World,* Vol. 31 No. 3, pp. 32,88.

Dyer, J.H. and Ouchi, W.G. (1993), "Japanesestyle partnerships - giving company a competitive edge", *Sloan Management Review,* Vol. 35 No. 1, pp. 51-63.

Easton, G.S. (1993), "The 1993 state of US total quality management: a Baldrige examiner's perspective", *California Management Review,* Vol. 35 No. 3, pp. 32-54.

Edson, J. and Shannahan, R. (1991),"Managing quality across barriers", *Quality Progress,* February, pp. 45-7.

Elshennawy,A.K.,Maytubby, V.J. andAly, N.A. (1991), "Concepts and attributes of total quality management", *Total Quality Management,* Vol. 2 No. 1, pp. 75-98.

Feigenbaum, A.V. (1961), *Total Quality Control,* McGraw-Hill, London.

Findlay, I., Wilshaw, G. and Dale, B.G. (1990), "Total quality management in sales and marketing organization: introduction and development", in Oakland, J.S. (Ed.), *Proceedings of the 3rd International Conference on Total Quality* Management, Warwick, IFS Ltd, Bedford.

Finn, M. and Porter, L.J. (1994), "TQM self-assessment in the UK", *TQM Magazine,* Vol. 6 No. 4, pp. 56-61.

Garvin, David A. (1993), "Building a learning organization", *Harvard Business Review,* Vol. 71 No. 4, pp. 78-91.

Gilroy, A.J. (1994), "Automotive purchasing management's comparative approaches to supplier interface and development", University of Bradford, unpublished MBA dissertation.

Glover, J. (1993), "Achieving the organizational change necessary for successful TQM", *International Journal of Quality & Reliability Management,* Vol. 10 No. 6, pp. 47-64.

Goodstadt, P. (1990), "Exceeding customer satisfaction", in Oakland, J.S. (Ed.), *Proceedings of the 3rd International Conference on Total Quality Management,* Warwick, IFS Ltd., Bedford.

Goulden, C. and Rawlins, L. (1995), "A hybrid model for process quality costing", *International Journal of Quality & Reliability Management,* Vol. 12 No. 8, pp. 32-47.

A review of total quality management in practice: understanding the
fundamentals through examples of best practice
applications - part III

Haksever, C. (1996), "Total quality management in the small business environment", *Business Horizons,* March-April, pp. 33-40.

Hardaker, M. and Ward, B.K. (1987), "How to make a team work", *Harvard Business Review,* Vol. 65 No. 6, pp. 112-20.

Hirschhorn, L. and Gilmore, T. (1992), "The new boundaries of the boundaryless company", *Harvard Business Review,* Vol. 70 No. 3, pp. 104-15.

Ishikawa, K. (1985), *What is Total Quality Control? The Japanese Way,* Prentice-Hall, Englewood Cliffs, NJ.

Israeli, A. and Fisher, B. (1991), "Cutting quality costs", *Quality Progress,* January, pp. 46-8.

Johnson, R.S. (1993), "TQM: leadership for the quality transformation", *Quality Progress,* Vol. 26 No. 1-5.

Johnston, C.G. and Daniel, M.J. (1991), *Customer Satisfaction Through Quality. An International Perspective,* The Conference Board of Canada, Ottawa, Ontario.

Juran, J. M. (1974), *Quality Control Handbook,* McGraw-Hill, London.

Juran, J.M. (1993), "Made in the USA: a renaissance in quality", *Harvard Business Review, Vol.* 71 No. 4, pp. 34-40.

Kanji, G.K. (1995), "Quality and statistical concepts", in Kanji, G.K. (Ed.), *Total Quality Management: Proceedings of the First World Congress,* Chapman & Hill, London.

Kanji, G.K. and Asher, M. (1993), "Total quality management process - a systematic approach", *Advances in Total Quality Management Series,* Carfax Publishing Co., Abingdon.

Kleiner, B.M. (1994), "Benchmarking for continuous performance improvement", *Total Quality Environmental Management,* Spring, pp. 283-95.

Kordupleski, R.E., Rust, R.T. and Zahorik, A.J. (1993), "Why improving quality doesn't improve quality (or whatever happened to marketing?)", *California Management Review,* Vol. 35 No. 3, pp. 82-95.

Kyte, R. (1991), "Departmental purpose analysis/quality policy deployment", in Oakland, J.S., (Ed.), *Proceedings of the 4th International Conference on Total Quality Management, Warwick,* IFS Ltd, Bedford.

McAdam, R. (1996), "An integrated business improvement methodology to refocus business improvement efforts", *Business Process Re-engineering & Management Journal,* Vol. 2 No. 1, pp. 63-71.

McNair, C.J. and Leibfried, L. (1992), *Benchmarking: A Tool for Continuous Improvement,* Harper Business, New York, NY.

Mitchell, CM. (1995), "Preparing for benchmarking: an effective benchmarking strategy", in Kanji, G.K.(Ed.), *Total Quality Management: Proceedings of the First World Congress,* Chapman-Hall, London.

Modaress, B. and Aussari, M. (1989), "Quality control techniques in US firms: a survey", *Production and Inventory Management Journal,* 2nd quarter.

Nadkarni, R.A. (1995), "A not-so-secret recipe for successful TQM", *Quality Progress,* Vol. 28 No. 11, pp. 91-6.

Newman, R.G. (1988), "Primary source qualification", *Journal of Purchasing & Material Management,* Summer, pp. 10-17.

NIST (1994), *Malcolm Baldrige National Quality Award: 1994 Award Criteria,* National Institute of Standards and Technology, US Department of Commerce, Gaithersburg, MD.

Oakland, J.S. (1993), *Total Quality Management,* Butter-worth-Heinemann, Oxford.

Oakland, J.S. and Beardmore, D. (1995)," Best practice customer service", *Total Quality Management,* Vol. 6 No. 2, pp. 135-48.

Oakland, J.S. and Porter, L. (1994), *Cases in Total Quality Management,* Butterworth Heinemann, Oxford.

A review of total quality management in practice: understanding the
fundamentals through examples of best practice
applications - part III

Olian, J.D. and Rynes, S.L. (1991), "Making total quality work: Aligning
organizational processes, performance measures, and stakeholders", *Human
Resource Management,* Vol. 30 No. 3, pp.303-33.

Peters, T. (1989), *Thriving on Chaos,* Pan Books Ltd, London.

Peters, T. and Waterman, R. (1982), *In Search of Excellence,* Harper and Row,
New York, NY.

Plunkett, J.J.and Dale, B.G. (1990), "Quality costing", in Dale, B.G. *etal.* (Eds),
Managing Quality, Philip Allan, Hemel Hempstead.

Porter, L.I. and Tanner, S.I. (1995), "Business improvement through self-
assessment - a case study from financial services", in Kanji, G.K. (Ed.),
Total Quality Management. Proceedings of the First World Congress,
Chapman & Hall, London.

Porter, L.J. and Parker, A.J. (1993), "Total quality management - the critical
success factors", *Total Quality Management,* Vol. 4 No. 1, pp. 13-22.

Porter, L.J. and Rayner, P. (1992), "Quality costing for total quality
management", *International Journal for Production Economics,* Vol.27 No.
1, pp. 69-81.

Price, R.C. and Gaskill, G.P. (1990), Total quality management in research
philosophy and practice", in Oakland, J.S. (Ed.), *Proceedings of the 3rd
International Conference on Total Quality Management, Warwick,* IFS Ltd,
Bedford.

Pulat, B.M. (1994), "Total quality management: a frame-work for application
in manufacturing", *The TQM Magazine,* Vol.6 No.4, pp. 44-9.

Quiros, G.M. (1994), "Integrated performance measurement", unpublished
MBA dissertation, University of Bradford.

Saraph, J.V., Benson, P.G. and Schroeder, R.G. (1989), "An instrument for
measuring the critical factors of quality management", *Decision Sciences,*
Vol. 20 No.4, pp. 810-29.

Sinclair, D.A.C. (1994), "Total quality-based performance measurement: an empirical study of best practice", unpublished PhD thesis, University of Bradford.

Smith, S. (1994), *The Quality Revolution,* Management Books 2000 Ltd, Didcot.

Smock, D. (1982)," How to stem the tide of shoddy materials", *Purchasing,* May, pp. 51-7

Snowden, D. (1991), "Business process management and TQM", in Oakland, J.S. (Ed.), Proceedings of the 4th International Conference on Total Quality Manage-ment, Warwick, IFS Ltd, Bedford.

Stark, J.A.L. (1990), "Experience of TQM at BP chemicals", in Oakland, J.S. (Ed.), Proceedings of the 3rd Interna-tional Conference on Total Quality Management. Warwick, IFS Ltd, Bedford.

Sunday, J.L. and Liberty, L. (1992), "Benchmarking the Baldrige Award", Quality Progress,Vol. 25 No. 9, pp. 75-7.

Takeuchi, H. and Quelch, J.A. (1983), "Quality is more than making a good product", Harvard Business Review, Vol. 61 No. 4.

Taylor, W.A. (1995), "Total quality management and the need for organizational self-assessment: some empirical evidence", Total Quality Management, Vol. 6 No. 1, pp. 3-12.

Titman,C.R. and Callum,W.S. (1991), "Recognition and reward", in Oakland, J.S. (Ed.), Total Quality Management: Proceedings of the 4th International Conference on Total Quality Management, Warwick, 3-5 June, IFS Ltd, Bedford.

Townsend, P.L. and Gebhardt, J.E. (1992), Quality in Action, John Wiley & Sons Ltd, New York, NY.

Vandermerwe, S. (1993), "Jumping into the customer's activity cycle. A new role for customer services in the 1990s", The Columbia Journal of World Business, Vol. 28 No. 2, pp. 46-65.

van der Wiele, A. and company (1996), "Self-assessment: a study of progress in Europe's leading organiza-tions in quality management practices", Internation-al Journal of Quality & Reliability Management, Vol. 13 No. 1, pp. 84-104.

A review of total quality management in practice: understanding the
fundamentals through examples of best practice
applications - part III

Williams, A., Dodson, P. and Walters, M. (1993), Changing Culture2nd ed,
    Institute of Personnel Management, London.

Zairi, M. (1994), Measuring Performance for Business Results,Chapman &
    Hall, London.

Commentary

*More in-depth reviews from the head of Bradford University's European Centre
    for TQM*

A review of total quality management in practice: understanding the fundamentals through examples of best practice applications - part III

T. Thiagarajan and M. Zairi

First Published in

The TQM Magazine
Volume 9 : Number 6 1997 pp. 414-417
© MCB University Press : ISSN 0954-478X

The authors

T. Thiagarajan is a Senior Quality Manager, based at Palm Oil Research Institute (PORIM), Malaysia. M. Zairi is SABIC Chair in Best Practice Management at the University of Bradford, UK.

Abstract

Part III of a three-part series which represents a compre-hensive review of the literature by discussing critical factors of TQM in key areas often stressed in implementa-tion case studies, and supported by quality gurus and writers. Such factors are considered as being conducive to the success of TQM implementation. Covers issues related to the implementation aspects such as the role of culture, reasons for TQ programme failures, gestation period, etc. Presents a co-ordinated approach to the literature which aims to link in all key elements.

Introduction

The principle of self-assessment using various models such as the Malcolm Baldrige Nation-al Quality Award (MBNQA), the European Quality Award (EQA) and the Deming Prize is becoming globally pervasive. Indeed, such models are found to be the best means for assessing organizational excellence and the criteria used are found to reflect the most important components of effectiveness and competitiveness. By linking means and drives such as leadership to results (ends) one could relate capability and competence to achieve-ments.

This review of the literature was therefore an attempt to map total quality management (TQM) using similar sets of criteria to those of the EQA model. More importantly, this is the first attempt at reviewing the literature from the point of view of what, how and why.

Issues in implementation

In an effort to understand the essentials of effective TQM implementation, the overview in the previous sections revolved primarily around the key components of TQM. However, to appreciate the complexity of TQM implementation (Glover, 1993), it is imperative that an understudying of other issues in the context of this research is developed.

TQM and national culture

Many assumptions are made about the cultur-al influences on TQM implementation. Juran (1993), for example, says that there is no need to redesign a country's culture to instil the disciplines of quality improvements. He stresses that what is needed to make TQM work is the adherence to its principles, prac-tices and techniques. Kano (1993), on the other hand, says that one needs to take cultur-al background into account when implement-ing TQM. However, he stresses that culture is not a barrier to the implementation of TQM.

A Bradford-based benchmarking study of 22 critical factors of TQM across several countries of widely differing cultures found that not all the critical factors are relevant in a generic sense (Zairi, 1994). Fundamental factors such as top management commit-ment, the need for a clear mission statement and focus on the customer were, however, emphasized as absolutely essential to the success of TQM across borders.

TQM failures

The success of implementing TQM in an organization is ultimately judged by its cus-tomers, Zairi (1994). A TQM initiative is therefore considered a failure if it fails to optimize operations to continuously add value for customer satisfaction.

Given that implementing a TQM system is one of the most complex tasks which an orga-nization might ever encounter (Glover, 1993; Kanji and Asher, 1993), it is not surprising to note that there are as many TQM failures as there are success stories (Gilbert, 1992). For obvious reasons, reports of failures in the open literature are few and far between. Several writers, however, have discussed general patterns in TQM failures (Glover, 1993).

"...Given that implementing a TQM system is one of the most important tasks which an organization might ever encounter it is not surprising to note that.. .there are as many TQM failures as there are success stories.

Common reasons for TQM setbacks and failures are highlighted below:

- The absence of, or inadequate attention to, several of the key quality factors discussed in the earlier sections (Longenecker and Scazerro, 1993). This appears as the most cited element in predicting the failure of a TQM implementation.

- Failure to devise an implementation strate-gy that fits an organization's unique cir- cumstances (Hart and Schlesinger, 1991). Rather a generic "off-the-shelf" model or a copy of a system that was successful in another organization was used.

- TQM implemented as an "add-on pro-gramme" to "business as usual" (Alloway, 1994). TQM is seen as a motivational programme, wholesale training of employees or simply the use of tools and techniques.

- High expectations of quick results from TQM initiatives (Merron, 1994).

Gestation period

It is generally acknowledged that the longer organizations work at TQM, the more suc-cessful they will be. Two-to-three years into implementation have been quoted in the literature as the period after which the tangi-ble benefits of TQM are more likely to be evident (Mann, 1992). A study reported in *Quality Progress* (1994) showed that those organizations that have been actively imple-menting TQM for more than two years are more likely to have "very successful" initiatives as opposed to those that have had programmes for less than two years.

Another American study, which examined 536 TQM organizations, concluded that those that had implemented TQM for more than three years had significantly better successes than those using TQM for two years or less, in three TQM outcomes, namely customer satisfaction and retention, operational results, and organizational climate (DDI, 1994).

Hard and soft quality factors

Reflecting on the model of TQM proposed by Oakland (1993), the review of the literature suggests that the key components that impact on TQM implementation are a synergetic blend of "hard" and "soft" quality factors. Systems and tools and techniques such as those that impact on internal efficiency (e.g. quality management systems, cost of quality and statistical process control (SPC)) and external effectiveness (e.g. benchmarking and customer satisfaction surveys) are examples of hard quality factors. Soft quality factors are intangible and difficult-to-measure issues and are primarily related to leadership and employee involvement.

While Black (1993) contends that it is difficult to classify factors along soft-hard criteria, Wilkinson *etal.* (1991) highlight that it has a practical reality by referring to experi-ences at the Co-operative Bank plc and Black & Decker UK. At the Esso Research Centre UK, quality process is also seen in terms of "hard" and "soft" (Price and Chen, 1993).

The "soft" quality factors may best be seen as issues discussed under leadership, internal stakeholders management and policy. They are issues that impact on maximizing organization-wide support and involvement in attaining the quality goals of an organization. They may be seen as "internal marketing" issues (Wilkinson and Witcher, 1992). They include:

- senior executives commitment and involve- ment, actively demonstrated;
- comprehensive policy development and effective deployment of goals;
- entire workforce commitment to quality goals of the organization;
- supervisors, unit heads and divisional managers assume active new roles;
- empowerment;
- effective communication;
- internal customer supplier concept;
- teamwork;
- system for recognition and appreciation of quality efforts; and
- training and education.

It is evident from the list that "soft" factors are long-term issues, something that cannot be switched on and off, and therefore, must be emphasized and addressed accord-ingly in an organization's TQM implementa-tion plan.

'... the effective manipulation of the "soft" factors must be supported by the "hard" factors...'

There is a good chance that the TQM process will end up in failure if there is insufficient attention to "soft" factors (Wilkinson and Witcher, 1992). It would be expected that "soft" factors would all rate highly in terms of criticality and emphasis in the TQM imple-mentation process.

While the effective manipulation of the "soft" factors is essential to the attainment of the quality goals of the organization, they must be supported by the "hard" factors to manage, track and improve the journey towards achieving the goals. They include:

- Benchmarking.
- Performance measurement.

- Management by fact.
- Managing by processes.
- Self-assessment.
- Quality control tools and techniques.
- Cost of quality process.
- Documented quality management system.
- Supplier management.
- Customer management.

Some writers describe the above factors as tactics rather than strategies (Pegels, 1993) and those that extend the power of TQM in an organization (Black, 1993). In Ramirez and Loney's (1993) study, the majority of Baldrige winners perceive these types of factors as important not essential to the suc-cess of TQM.

Conclusion

This review has demonstrated that there is a vast array of literature on TQM and its key components. Previous literature reviews tended, however, to be presented in anecdotal and impressionistic ways.

This effort is, however, more systematic and has tried to present the body of the litera-ture in a co-ordinated supportive approach by linking in all the key elements. By covering theory, concepts and applications this makes a real contribution to understanding:

- What is the importance of individual elements? (Why?) and how are they imple- mented in practice?
- What benefits have been derived from using these elements?

A further attempt through this review, was to discuss wider issues of implementation, such as cultural differences, the need for a gestation period, failures and the reason why, and the need to consider TQM from the point of view of "hard" and "soft" issues.

References

Alloway, J.A. (1994), "The card drop shop", *Quality Progress,* Vol. 27 No. 7, pp. 99-104.

Black, S.A. (1993)," Measuring the critical factors of total quality management", unpublished PhD thesis, University of Bradford, Bradford.

DDI (1994), *TQM: Forging Ahead or Falling Behind-A Study of Quality Practices,* Development Dimensions International Inc, Bridgeville, PA.

Gilbert, J.D. (1992), "TQM flops: a chance to learn from the mistakes of others", *National Productivity Review,* Autumn, pp. 491-99.

Glover, J. (1993), "Achieving the organisational change necessary for successful TQM", *International Journal of Quality & Reliability Management,* Vol. 10 No. 6, pp. 47-64.

Hart, C. and Schlesinger, L. (1991), "Total quality manage-ment and the human resource professional: applying the Baldrige framework to human resources", *Human Resource Management,* Vol. 30 No. 3, pp. 433-54.

Juran, J.M. (1993), "Made in USA: a renaissance in quality", *Harvard Business Review,* Vol. 71 No. 4, pp. 42-50.

Kanji, G.K. and Asher, M. (1993), *Total Quality Manage-ment Process - A Systematic Approach. Advances in Total Quality Management Series,* Carfax Publishing Co., Abingdon.

Kano, N. (1993), "A perspective on quality activities in American firms", *California Management Review,* Vol. 35 No. 3, pp. 12-31.

Longenecker, CO. and Scazzero, J.A. (1993), "Total quality management from theory to practice: a case study", *International Journal of Quality & Reliability Man-agement,* Vol. 10 No. 5, pp. 24-31.

Mann, R.S. (1992), "The development of a framework to assist in the implementation of TQM", unpublished PhD thesis, University of Liverpool, Liverpool.

Merron, K.A. (1994), "Creating TQM organisations", *Quality Progress,* Vol. 27 No. 1, pp. 51-4.

Oakland, IS. (1993), *Total Quality Management,* Butter-worth-Heinemann, Oxford.

Pegels, C.C. (1993), "Total quality management defined in terms of reported practice", *International Journal of Quality & Reliability Management,* Vol. 11 No. 5, pp. 6-18.

Price, M. and Chen, E.E. (1993), "Total quality management in a small, high-technology company", *California Management Review,* Vol. 35 No. 3, pp. 96-117.

Ramirez, C. and Loney, T. (1993), "Baldrige award winners identify the essential activities of a success-ful quality process", *Quality Digest,* January, pp. 38-40.

Willkinson, A. andWitcher, B. (1992), "Conference review: quality concerns for management", *International Journal of Quality & Reliability Management,* Vol. 9 No. 2, pp. 64-8.

Wilkinson, A.; Allen, P. and Snape, E. (1991), "TQM and the management of labour", *Employee Relations,* Vol. 13 No. 1, pp. 24-31.

Zairi, M. (1994), *Measuring Performance for Business Results,* Chapman & Hall, London.

Commentary

If you haven't tried it yet - take half an hour only and make some notes on your business against one of the assessment frameworks.

> " My job of
> contributing to the
> welfare of my fellow
> man is the great
> unfinished business. "

- Joseph Juran

Benchmarking critical factors for TQM Part I: theory and foundations

Mohamed Zairi
TQM Centre, Bradford University, Bradford, UK and

Mohamed A. Youssef
School of Business, Ithaca College, Ithaca, USA

First Published in

Benchmarking for Quality Management &
Technology, Vol. 2 No. 1, 1995, pp. 5-20.
© MCB University Press, 1351-3036

Introduction

Total quality management (TQM) is one of the subjects which tends to raise many questions about meaning, benefits and eventually about enhancing competitiveness through supporting financial results. Although it is widely agreed that TQM has to be defined in customer terms, organizations tend to take various routes, adopt different approaches and exhibit varying degrees and levels of commitment.

In this part of the article we lay the foundations for the empirical part which will follow. First, we define TQM from two perspectives and show that any TQM definition should go beyond the internal boundaries of an organization. Second, with a view to the existing TQM literature as related to the subject of this article. Third, we analyse the critical factors for TQM success. Finally, we discuss some of the self-assessment frameworks of quality programmes. This will pave the way for the second part of the article.

TQM defined

There are many definitions for the TQM philosophy. Zairi *et al.*[1] define TQM as:

> A positive attempt by the organizations concerned to improve structural, infrastructural, attitudinal, behavioral and methodological ways of delivering to the end customer, with emphasis on: consistency, improvements in quality, competitive enhancements, all with the aim of satisfying or delighting the end customer.

The above definition is meant to include a wide range of critical factors which cover the following three areas:

(1) Leadership elements:

- mission/vision statement;
- quality policy;
- direction;
- goals;

- communication processes;
- measurement;
- quality decisions;
- strategic planning and deployment;
- customer/market focus.

(2) Hard elements:

- tools and techniques;
- measurement;
- systems;
- procedures;
- specifications;
- standards.

(3) Soft elements:

- problem-solving approach;
- teamwork;
- innovation/creativity;
- continuous improvement philosophy;
- empowerment;
- incentives;
- process-based approach.

This definition emphasizes that TQM is not a separate initiative supporting "business as usual", but rather it is the business itself and represents a comprehensive modern philosophy of management.

Youssef[2], on the other hand, defines TQM as:

An overall philosophy whose objective is to meet or exceed the needs of the internal and the external customer by creating an organizational culture in which everyone at every stage of creating the product as well as every level of management is committed to quality and clearly understands its strategic importance.

The essence of Youssef's definition is pictorially depicted in Figure 1.

The above two definitions share many common elements. First, they consider the customer as the centre of attention and the driving force in the TQM philosophy. Second, they consider management commitment as an essential element for TQM success. Finally, they promote cultural and organizational changes as necessary conditions for TQM success. Unfortunately there is simple evidence which indicates that senior managers at large are still confused about the real potential of TQM and in some cases still very suspicious of its potential and the benefits which might accrue from its introduction.

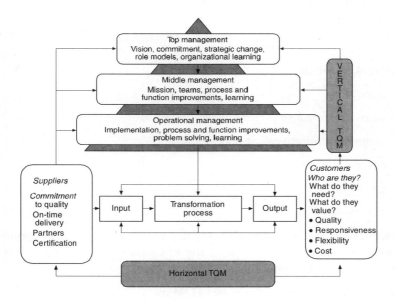

Figure 1. Horizontal and vertical TQM

108

Relevant literature

TQM is not a quick-fix scheme[2]. Many firms in different industries have encountered difficulties in implementing TQM. They fail to realize the TQM benefits for one simple reason: lack of support by top management. Lakhe and Mohanty[3] surveyed the TQM literature and identified some of the problems encountered in the process of implementing TQM. Table I summarizes their findings.

A survey which looked at the level of understanding of TQM from fund analysts and fund investment managers[4] led to the conclusion that TQM is only recognized and endorsed by a small minority of chairmen of public limited companies (plcs). Furthermore, the survey established that, as far as the City of London is concerned, the concept of TQM is alien and there is little or no interest in the subject at all.

It appears that the chairmen of plcs are constantly under pressure and that messages they convey to fund analysts and investment managers must be carefully thought out since there are clear implications of their decisions on the stock exchange ratings of their companies' shares. Senior managers and chairmen of plcs, therefore, only incorporate in the company reports information which is not detrimental to them and the company.

This is clearly at the expense of showing leadership and a high level of commitment by, for example, incorporating up-to-date information which relates to the performance of various processes, their plans for internal improvements, their commitment to raising customer services and maximizing benefits through driving down waste and costs in order to remain competitive.

Three main conclusions emerged from this survey. First, the level of awareness of TQM and its impact is limited, particularly in service-type organizations. Second, there is little or no knowledge of TQM and its potential

Application area	Author(s)	Problems encountered
Health care	Matherly and Laster[20] Materna and Rothe[21] Gopalkrishnan and McIntyre[22] Fried[23] Muller[24] Morrison[25] Zentmyer[26]	(1) Lack of commitment at senior level (2) Limited resources (3) Fear of change (4) Heavy workload (5) Difficulty in establishing measures and quality indicators that truly reflect the objectives of organization
Education and research organization structure	Price and Gaskill[27] Bemowski[28] Axland[29]	(1) Improper communication between business and education systems (2) Many layers of existing (3) Autonomous status of faculty (4) Tenure system (5) Conflicting practices
Federal agencies	Burstein and Sedlak[30] Carr and Littman[31]	(1) Lack of accountability structure (2) Uneven support from top management (3) Measurement system not widely understood (4) Scarcity of needed investment
Environment	Colling Jr[32] Stratton[33] Bemowski[34] Kelly[35]	(1) Resistance to change (2) Lack of commitment at all levels (3) Inadequate education and training (4) Measurement difficulties
Bank	Goodstadt[36] Ballantyne[37]	(1) Difficulty in defining standards (2) Problem in framing reward structure (3) Resistance to change
Manufacturing quality	Jeans[38] Hansen and Hilman Browning and Shaw[40] Dale[41] Boyer[42] Davis and Wilson[43] Stark[44] Smith and Tee[45]	(1) Lack of involvement in total [39] activity at all levels of management (2) Poor internal communication (3) Fragmented structured approach to the management (4) Fear and insecurity (5) Resistance to change (6) Measurement problems (7) Cost and investment

benefits in the business institutions, which are more concerned about shortterm business returns. Consequently, these institutions indicated that they are not really interested in TQM. Finally, fund analysis and fund investment institutions do not put pressure on their "supplier", i.e. business organizations in manufacturing and the service sectors, to subscribe to the TQM philosophy.

The City's "customers" (pensioners, savers, shareholders, etc.) are thereby denied extra benefits because their suppliers are not interested in TQM and do not demand it consistently in performance from their own suppliers.

A worldwide survey reported in [1], which targeted 3,000 managers, showed that more than 90 per cent of the respondents believed that customer issues will be the most critical to business success in the coming years. Most, however, reported that their organizations had a long way to go before achieving customer satisfaction. The survey did reveal that customer satisfaction is more often based on gut feelings than data collection and organized intelligence systems. Furthermore, the survey revealed that most companies do not assess competitor performance in a systematic way. It is not a process but a part-time activity.

These two studies indicate that TQM implementation is still failing in many organizations and its potential as a modern business philosophy is still underestimated. In addition to the lack of appreciation of TQM benefits, there is another school of thought which tries to negate the usefulness of TQM altogether and many attempts are being made to discredit its potential by a continuous effort of referring to failures, obstacles and difficulties in implementation. This school of thought, for example, still advocates the use of the financial management approach which has created in the West particularly a business culture based on short-termism and the exaggerated emphasis on financial results to the detriment of performance improvement and sustainability through the building of capability, innovation and distinct competitive advantages.

Schaffer[5] and Schaffer and Thompson[6] argue that TQM (referred to as the activity-centred approach) does not lead to benefits and is a waste of resources and time. It has been described as the "rain dance", "a fundamentally flawed logic that confuses ends with means, processes with outcomes". Financial management (referred to as a results-driven approach) is the quickest and most effective way of obtaining results. Shaffer and Thompson[6] argue that:

> Any payoffs from the infusion of activities will be meager at best. And there is in fact an alternative: results-driven improvement processes that focus on achieving specific, measurable operations improvements within a few months. This means increased yields, reduced delivery time, increased inventory turns, improved customer satisfaction and reduced product development time. With results-driven improvements, a company introduces only those innovations in management methods and business processes that can help achieve specific goals.

Understanding the workings of TQM and its critical factors becomes therefore an essential task to assist in:

- guiding organizations in understanding what is required, the size of the challenge, the level of resources and commitment needed for achievingsuccessful implementation of TQM;

- persuading sceptics by indicating that critical factors of TQM are conducive to positive business results if adhered to;

- beginning to support organizations in integrating TQM into their business, through the development of a management approach entirely dependent on TQM principles.

The critical factors of TQM

One of the problems of critical factors of TQM is how to define them and what should be the measure of their impact before they become critical. When one scans through the literature, numerous factors tend to be stressed as facilitators for successful TQM implementation. Table II gives some examples.

Table II. Facilitators for successful TQM implementation

	Element	Author
Leadership and commitment	(1) Active senior management involvement	Juran[7]
	(2) Top management consciousness and overall embracement of responsibility for TQM implementation	Kano[11]
	(3) Top management motivation to be part of TQM and a warning that the greatest enemy of TQM is top management doubt	Kano[11]
	(4) Co-ordinated approach at a corporate-wide level through active leadership Barker[12]	
	(5) Commitment of top management through devoting a substantial amount of time for TQM issues	Easton[13]
Employee involvement	(1) Success of departmental purpose analysis (DPA) at IBM UK Ltd was due to employee ownership of the process	Kyte[14]
	(2) Employees' total involvement in innovation and determining the best alternative for NPD in terms of cost, safety, quality and productivity	Vallely[15]
	(3) Union involvement can lead to successful TQM implementation	Carman[16]
Education and training	(1) "Quality begins with education"	Ishikawa[17]
	(2) "Continuous improvement requires a commitment to learning"	Garvin[18]

(3) TQ projects can only succeed
through training all teams and team
leaders in teamwork, leadership skills
and problem-solving techniques   Casbourne[19]

(4) Employees of applicants for Malcolm
Baldrige National Quality Award receive
between 40-80 hours of training per year
with expenditures around 3.5 per cent
of the payroll   Easton[13]

Juran[7], for instance, recommends seven critical areas which senior managers need to take into consideration, in order to demonstrate their commitment and also ensure that TQM implementation will succeed in their organizations:

(1) It is incumbent on senior management to set up and serve on the company's quality council.

(2) Senior management need to establish corporate quality goals and make them an integral part of the business plan.

(3) Senior management need to make provision for training all the employees for effective management of quality.

(4) Senior management need to establish the means for measuring quality results against quality goals.

(5) Senior management need to review results against quality goals on a regular basis.

(6) Senior management need to provide recognition for superior quality performance.

(7) Senior management have an obligation to revisit reward systems and to ensure that they are completely compatible with changes demanded by world-class quality.

These are only three areas which are very often stressed in case studies and seem to be conducive to successful TQM implementation programmes. There are, however, many other factors both at the strategic and operational levels which are considered to be vital for the positive introduction of TQM. Generally speaking, there has not been a lot of work carried out on critical factors of TQM. This is perhaps due to the fact that TQM still remains poorly understood by senior managers and its potential for enhancing competitiveness is not well appreciated.

Defining TQM critical factors

The first real attempt which was made at grouping a list of critical factors for TQM was a study conducted in the USA by Saraph et al.[8], which led to the proposal of a list of 78 factors. This was followed by a research project conducted in the UK[9], which replicated the study undertaken in the USA. Responses were obtained from 101 quality managers and, out of all the critical factors, the ten highest and lowest scoring items are exhibited in Table III.

In addition to the important factors which one would expect, such as senior management leadership and commitment, it is surprising to see that there is heavy emphasis on inspection, review and checking. The results also indicated that employee participation and involvement were not considered to be critical and that data utilization for improving quality is not so important. This seems to be contrary to the workings of the TQM philosophy and the teachings of all the gurus who clearly emphasize the importance of teamwork, employee participation and involvement and the use of data and reliance on facts rather than subjective opinions.

Item	Mean
The highest mean scoring items	
Quality departments' access to divisions' top management	3.7
Extent to which sales and marketing people consider quality a saleable attribute	3.6
Amount of final inspection, review or checking	3.6
Importance of inspection, review or checking of work	3.5
Autonomy of the quality department	3.4
Commitment of the divisional top management to employee training	3.4
Extent to which divisional top management supports the long-term quality improvement process	3.4
Clarity of product/service specifications and procedures	3.3
Degree to which divisional top management considers quality improvement as a way to increase profits	3.3
Amount of in-process inspection/review/checking	3.3
The ten lowest mean scoring items	
Extent to which quality data are used as tools to manage quality	2.2
Degree of participation in quality decisions by hourly/non-supervisory employees	2.2
Extent to which inspection, review or checking of work is automated	2.1
Extent to which quality data, control charts, etc. are displayed at employee workstations	2.1
Extent to which quality data are used to evaluate supervisor and managerial performance	2.1
Training in basic statistical techniques in the division as a whole	2.0
Impact of trade unions on quality improvement	2.0
Use of statistical control charts for process control	2.0
Availability of cost of quality data in the division	1.9
Training in advanced statistical techniques in the division as a whole	1.5

Table III. Mean score for the 20 TQM factors

The study by Black in 1993[9] was an attempt at developing a model for measuring the critical factors of TQM. Using the MBNQA criteria, a questionnaire with 39 critical factors was produced and through the use of a ratio scaling method respondents were asked to assign a ratio score of importance to each of the 39 criteria. The list of the 39 items was factor analysed and ten factors were identified as the most critical. These are represented in Table IV. These factors appear to be compatible with successful TQM implementation programmes. They represent strategic elements, people involvement, emphasis on communication, a focus on the customer, an awareness of the external market, the need to develop supplier partnerships, measurement and the long-term emphasis on developing a culture for quality improvement.

Self-assessment frameworks for determining critical factors of TQM
Self-assessment helps organizations in many ways, including, for example, the following areas[10]:

- providing the opportunity to take a broader view on how TQM is impacting on various business operations;

Table IV. Critical factors for TQM

Critical factors of total quality management

1. People and customer management Education, training, involvement schemes, role definition, service standards and recognition in line with quality and performance plans

2. Supplier partnerships Quality audits, reviews, improvement action and long-term relations

3. Communication of improvement information Quality costs information, assessment of training needs, benchmarking of processes, promotion of quality

4. Customer satisfaction orientation Policies, warranties, customer satisfaction determination and comparison, benchmarking of products

5. External interface management Public responsibilities, future customer requirements, integration of requirements and operations constraints

6. Strategic quality management Use of process control, active quality leadership, employee wellbeing considerations, executive commitment, long-term planning, prioritization of improvements

7. Teamwork structures for process improvement Organizational structures, identification of key processes and requirements

8. Operational quality planning Short-term plans and goals relating to quality

9. Improvement measurement systems Assessment and improvement of processes/products, management of data and datagathering cycle

10. Corporate quality culture
Long-term goals related to quality, company-wide culture

   • measuring performance of processes, enablers and their relationship with results;

   • measuring in financial and non-financial areas;

   • measuring internally and externally, including the community and the environment;

   • encouraging objective assessment through third-party involvement;

   • providing the opportunity to benchmark and compare like with like;

   • measuring for improvement rather than for hard control;

   • creating the desire to do better and perhaps even win awards.

In the next few paragraphs we are going to examine these self assessment frameworks and show the role they play in determining the TQM critical factors.

The Deming Prize. The Deming Prize is the oldest self-assessment framework, developed in Japan in 1951. Since its origination, 53 prizes have been awarded for individuals' achievements; 126 prizes to companies; and 13 prizes to divisions among 12 corporations.

The following ten criteria are used for assessing Deming Prize applications:

(1) company policy and planning;

(2) organization and its management;

(3) quality circle education and dissemination;

(4) collection, transmission and utilization of information on quality;

(5) analysis;

(6) standardization;

(7) control (*kanri*);

(8) quality assurance (QA);

(9) effects;

(10) future plans.

Table V illustrates a complete list of critical factors distributed among the ten key areas described above.

The Malcolm Baldrige National Quality Award (MBNQA). The MBNQA was established by US Congress back in 1987 to raise awareness about quality and its importance for American business organizations. Based on the 1994 award examination criteria, there are 28 critical factors covering seven key areas. These are represented in Table VI.

The European Quality Award (EQA). The EQA was developed and introduced by the European Foundation for Quality Management (EFQM) in 1991. The EFQM itself was created in 1988 by leading business organizations to alert European business organizations to the need to incorporate quality management in all operations and also to raise the level of knowledge and awareness of the benefits of TQM.

The EQA criteria are split, 50 per cent representing enablers and 50 per cent representing results. The criteria are represented in nine broad categories. These are:

(1) leadership;

(2) customer satisfaction;

(3) people satisfaction;

(4) impact on society;

(5) policy and strategy;

(6) people management;

(7) resources;

(8) processes;

(9) business results.

The Australian Quality Award. The Australian Quality Award (AQA) was introduced in 1988 for similar reasons to those linked to MBNQA and EQA,

Table V. Checklist for the Deming Prize criteria

(1) Policy and objectives

- Policy with regard to management, quality and quality control
- Methods in determining policy and objectives
- Appropriateness and consistency of the contents of objectives
- Utilization of statistical methods
- Deployment, dissemination and permeation of objectives
- Checking objectives and their implementation
- Relationships with long-range and short-range plans

(2) Organization and its operations

- A clear-cut line of responsibilities
- Appropriateness of delegation of power

- Co-operation between divisions
- Activities of committees
- Utilization of the staff
- Utilization of quality circle activities
- Quality control audit

(3) Education and its extension

- Education plan and actual accomplishment
- Consciousness about quality and control, understanding of quality control
- Education concerning statistical concepts and methods, and degree of permeation
- Ability to understand the effects
- Education for subcontractors and outside organizations
- Quality circle activities
- Suggestion system and its implementation

(4) Assembling and dissemination of information and its utilization

- Assembling outside information
- Disseminating information between divisions
- Speed in disseminating information (use of computers)
- (Statistical) analysis of information and its utilization

(5) Analysis

- Selection of important problems and themes
- Appropriateness of the analytical method
- Utilization of statistical methods
- Tying in with own engineering technology

121

- Quality analysis, process analysis
- Utilization of results of analysis
- Positiveness of suggestions for improvement

6) Standardization

- System of standardization
- Methods of establishing, revising and withdrawing standards
- Actual records in establishing, revising and withdrawing standards
- Contents of standards
- Utilization of statistical methods
- Accumulation of technology
- Utilization of standards

7) Control (*kanri*)

- Control systems for quality and in related areas such as cost, delivery and quantity
- Control points and control items
- Utilization of statistical methods such as the control chart and general acceptance of the statistical way of thinking
- Contributions of quality circle activities
- Actual conditions of control activities
- Actual conditions of control state

8) Quality assurance (QA)

- Procedures for new product development– quality deployment (breakdown of quality function) and its analysis, reliability and design review, etc.
- Safety and product liability prevention

122

- Process design, control and improvement (*kaizen*)
- Process capabilities
- Measurement and inspection
- Control of facilities/equipment, sub- contracting, purchasing, services, etc.
- Quality assurance system and its audit
- Utilization of statistical methods
- Evaluation and audit of quality
- Practical conditions of quality assurance

9) Effects

- Measuring effects
- Visible effects, such as quality, service- ability, date of delivery, cost, profit, safety, environment, etc.
- Invisible effects
- Compatibility between prediction of effects and actual records

10) Future plans

- Understanding of the status quo, and concreteness
- Policies adopted to solve shortcomings
- Plans of promotion of TQC for the future
- Relations with the company's long-range plans

Table VI. Malcolm Baldrige National Quality Award criteria

(1) Leadership

- Senior executive leadership
- Management for quality

- Public responsibility and corporate citizenship

(2) Information and analysis

- Scope and management of quality and performance data and information
- Competitive comparisons and benchmarking
- Analysis and uses of company-level data

(3) Strategic quality planning

- Strategic quality and company performance planning process
- Quality and performance plans

(4) Human resource development and management

- Human resource planning and management
- Employee involvement
- Employee education and training
- Employee performance and recognition
- Employee wellbeing and satisfaction

(5) Management of process quality

- Design and introduction of quality products and services
- Process management: product and service production and delivery process
- Process management: business and support service processes
- Supplier quality
- Quality assessment

(6) Quality and operation results

- Product and service quality results

- Company operational results
- Business and support service results
- Supplier quality results

(7) Customer focus and satisfaction

- Customer expectations: current and future
- Customer relationship management
- Commitment to customers
- Customer satisfaction determination
- Customer satisfaction results
- Customer satisfaction comparison

Source: National Institute for Standards and Technology

mainly to recognize the efforts of outstanding organizations, to encourage other companies to follow suit and to raise the level of education and awareness on the importance of quality in raising competitive standards and its impact on the community. The AQA criteria include leadership, policy and planning, information and analysis, people, customer focus, and quality of process, product and service.

The NASA Quality and Excellence Award. This is also referred to as the George M. Low Trophy and is specifically targeted at the aerospace industry. George Low was a distinguished scientist and educator in the 1950s and this award is a recognition of his efforts. The NASA award is to encourage high quality from contractors, subcontractors and suppliers to NASA and to reward innovation and excellence. The NASA Quality Award criteria are represented in Table VII.

International quality rating system (IQRS). Det Norske Veritas (DNV) is a key member of the European Foundation for Quality Management (EFQM) and is a consultancy offering services in 130 countries. The critical areas which DNV considers to be important include quality management, safety

125

management and environmental management. DNV has over the past few years developed support tools for the management and control of the international safety rating system (ISRS, 1978), the international quality rating system (IQRS, 1992) and the international environment rating system (IERS, 1992).

Table VII. NASA Award criteria

Evaluation criteria elements	Total points
Performance achievements	600
(1) Customer satisfaction	
•Contract performance	120
•Schedule	50
• Cost	50
(2) Quality	
• QA (hardware/software/service)	120
• Vendor quality assurance and involvement	50
• External communication	40
• Problem prevention and resolution	40
(3) Productivity	
• Software utilization	40
• Process improvement and equipment modernization	30
• Resources conservation	30
• Effective use of human resources	30
Process achievements	400
(1) Commitment and communication	
• Top management/commitment/involvement	100

• Goals, planning and measurement	80
• Internal communciation	40
(2) Human resource activities	
• Training	50
• Workforce involvement	50
• Awards and recognition	40
• Health and safety	40
Total points	1,000

The IQRS system is structured in 18 key elements including 176 sub-elements and 800 questions. The 18 critical factors are:

(1) leadership and administration;

(2) communication;

(3) quality system documentation;

(4) human resources;

(5) support functions;

(6) marketing and sales;

(7) development and design;

(8) purchasing and subcontracting;

(9) production process control;

(10) distribution and warehousing;

(11) after-sales service;

(12) quality inspection and testing;

(13) quality results;

(14) document control and quality records;

(15) non-conformities and corrective actions;

(16) continuous improvements;

(17) quality audits;

(18) customer satisfaction.

Conclusion

It is apparent from this review that all the models covered have many similarities between them. In fact, most of them seem to be based on the Deming Prize model, which is the oldest and perhaps the most credible. Winners of the Deming Prize have demonstrated that great strides can be achieved with TQM and competitiveness can be sustained and maintained by adhering to the practices covered comprehensively in the Deming Prize criteria.

The second part of this article (Vol. 2 No. 2) will empirically examine the critical success factors for TQM.

References

1. Zairi, M., Letza, S.R. and Oakland, J.S., *TQM: Its Impact on BottomLine Results*, Technical Communications (Publishing) Ltd, Letchworth, 1994.

2. Youssef, M.A., "The impact of TQM on firms' responsiveness: an empirical study", in progress for the *Total Quality Management Journal,* 1995.

3. Lakhe, R.R. and Mohanty, R.P., "Understanding TQM", *Production Planning and Control*, Vol. 5 No. 5, 1994, pp. 426-41.

4. Howard, D., "A limited understanding", *Total Quality Management*, April 1991, pp. 91-4.

5. Schaffer, R.H., "Demand better results – and get them", *Harvard Business Review*, March- April 1991, pp. 14-29.

6. Schaffer, R.H. and Thomson, H.A., "Successful change programs begin with results", *Harvard Business Review*, January-February 1992, pp. 80-89.

7. Juran, J.M., "Made in USA: a renaissance in quality", *Harvard Business Review*, Vol. 71 No. 4, 1993, pp. 42-50.

8. Saraph, J.V., Benson, P.G. and Schroeder, R.G., "An instrument for measuring critical factors of quality management", *Decision Sciences*, Vol. 20 No. 4, 1989, pp. 457-78.

9. Black, S.A., "Measuring the critical factors of total quality management", PhD thesis, University of Bradford Management Centre, Bradford, 1993.

10. Zairi, M., *Measuring Performance for Business Results*, Chapman & Hall, London, 1994.

11. Kano, N., "A perspective on quality activities in American firms", *California Management Review*, Vol. 35 No. 3, 1993, pp. 12 31.

12. Barker, R.L., "Basic improvement tools and total quality management", *Proceedings of the 4th International Conference on Total Quality Management*, IFS Ltd, Kempston, Bedford, 1991.

13. Easton, G.S., "The 1991 state of US total quality management: a Baldrige examiner's perspective", *California Management Review*, Vol. 35 No. 3, 1993, pp. 32-54.

14. Kyte, R., "Departmental purpose analysis/quality policy deployment", *Proceedings of the 4th International Conference on Total Quality Management*, IFS Ltd, Kempston, Bedford, 1991.

15. Vallely, I., "Why supervisors can with Nissan", *Works Management*, October 1993, pp. 18- 21.

16. Carman, J.M., "Continuous quality improvement as a survival strategy: the southern Pacific experience", *California Management Review*, Vol. 35 No. 3, 1993, pp. 118-32.

17. Ishikawa, K., *What Is Total Quality Control? The Japanese Way*, Prentice-Hall, Inc., Englewood Cliffs, NJ, 1985.

18. Garvin, D.A., "Building a learning organization", *Harvard Business Review*, Vol. 71 No. 4, 1993, pp. 78-91.

19. Casbourne, B.R., "Organizing for total quality management", *Proceedings of the 4th International Conference on Total Quality Management*, IFS Ltd, Kempston, Bedford, 1991.

20. Maherly, L.L. and Laster, H.A., "Implementing TQM in a hospital", *Quality Progress*, Vol. 25, 1992, pp. 81-3.

21. Materna, S. and Rothe, K., "A Canadian hospital implements continuous quality improvement", *Quality Progress*, Vol. 25, 1992, pp. 89-91.

22. Gopalkrishnan, K.N. and McIntyre, B.E., "Hurdles to quality health care", *Quality Progress*, Vol. 25, 1992, pp. 93-5.

23. Fried, R.A., "A crisis in health care", *Quality Progress*, Vol. 25, 1992, pp. 67-9.

24. Muller, R.A., "Implementing TQM in health care requires adaptation and innovation", *Quality Progress*, Vol. 25, 1992, pp. 57-9.

25. Morrison, P.E. and Heineke, J., "Why do health care practitioners resist quality management?", *Quality Progress*, Vol. 25, 1992, pp. 51-5.

26. Zentmyer, R.K., "The journey from bureaucracy to TQM", *Quality Progress*, Vol. 24, 1991, pp. 61-6.

27. Price, R.C., and Gaskill, G.P., "TQM in research and practice", *Proceedings of the 3rd International Conference on Total Quality Management*, London, 1990, pp. 77-87.

28. Bemowski, K., "Sorting facts from fiction", *Quality Progress*, Vol. 24, 1991, pp. 21-5.

29. Axland, S., "Looking for quality education", *Quality Progress*, Vol. 24, 1991, pp. 61-5.

30. Burstein, C. and Sedlak, K., "The federal quality and productivity improvement efforts", *Quality Progress*, Vol. 21, 1988, pp. 35-40.

31. Carr, D. and Littman, I., "Quality in Federal Government", *Quality Progress*, Vol. 23, 1990, pp. 49-52.

32. Collins, F.C. Jr, "New era at the Environmental Protection Agency", *Quality Progress*, Vol. 21, 1988, pp. 43-4.

33. Stratton, B., "Going beyond pollution control", *Quality Progress*, Vol. 24, 1991, pp. 18-20.

34. Bemowski, K., "Restoring the pillars of higher education", *Quality Progress*, Vol. 24, 1991, pp. 37-42.

35. Kelly, T., "GEMI: the superhero of environmental management", *Quality Progress*, Vol. 24, 1991, pp. 26-8.

36. Goodstadt, P., "Exceeding customer expectations", *Proceedings of the 3rd International Conference on Total Quality Management*, London, 1990, pp. 115-22.

37. Ballantyne, D., "Managing the diagnostic review process in service quality management", *Proceedings of the 3rd International Conference on Total Quality Management*, London, 1990, pp. 19-26.

38. Jeans, C., "What is TQM (and what is not)", *Proceedings of the 3rd International Conference on Total Quality Management*, London, 1990, pp. 3-7.

39. Hansen, W. and Hilman, G.P., "Achieving the real culture change necessary for TQM", *Proceedings of the 3rd International Conference on Total Quality Management*, London, 1990, pp. 27-36.

40. Browning, S. and Shaw, W.N., "Employees' view of TQM at two Hewlett Packard manufacturing plants", *Proceedings of the 3rd International Conference on Total Quality Management*, London, 1990, pp. 43-56.

41. Findlay, I., Wilshaw, G. and Dale, B.G., *Proceedings of the 3rd International Conference on Total Quality Management*, London, 1990, pp. 59-70.

42. Boyer, S.M., "TQM and new product development", *Proceedings of the 3rd International Conference on Total Quality Management*, London, 1990, pp. 97-104.

43. Davis, B. and Wilson, D., "TQM – organizing for success", *Proceedings of the 3rd International Conference on Total Quality Management*, London, 1990, pp. 105-12.

44. Stark, J.A., "Experience of TQM at BP Chemicals", *Proceedings of the 3rd International Conference on Total Quality Management*, London, 1990, pp. 123-31.

45. Smith, P.K. and Tee, M.R., "Total quality: the issues and realities for a leading supplier of advanced surface treatment technology", *Proceedings of the 3rd International Conference on Total Quality Management*, London, 1990, pp. 59-67.

Further reading

Morgan, J. and Everett, T., "Introducing quality management in the NHS", *International Journal for Healthcare Quality Assurance*, Vol. 3 No. 5, 1990, pp. 23-5.

Ramirez, C. and Loney, T., "Baldrige Award winners identify the essential activities of a successful quality process", *Quality Digest*, January 1993, pp. 38-40.

Roth, J.E., *Total Quality Management: Text Cases and Reading,* St Lucie Press, Delray Beach, FL, 1993.

Sloan, M.D., "A prescription for the healthcare industry", *Quality Progress*, 1991, pp. 75-9.

Zairi, M. and Matthew, A., "TQM in primary care: an evaluation", a research report submitted to the management executive of the NHS, Bradford University, August 1993.

Zairi, M. and Simintiras, A.C., "The sales link in the supplier-customer chain", *Productivity*, Vol. 32, 1991, pp. 427-34.

Benchmarking Critical Factors for TQM

Part II – empirical results from different regions in the world

Mohamed A. Youssef
Norfolk State University, Virginia, USA, and

Mohamed Zairi
TQM Centre, Bradford University, UK

First Published in

Benchmarking for Quality Management & Technology,
Vol. 2 No. 2, 1995, pp. 3-19.
© MCB University Press, 1351-3036

Introduction

In the first part of this article (*BQMT*, Vol. 2 No. 1), we reviewed the TQM literature on the critical factors for TQM success. Specifically, two studies were examined in detail. The first was by Saraph *et al.*[1] and the second was by Black[2]. In addition, we examined a number of self assessment frameworks for determining these factors. The self assessment frameworks include: the Deming prize, The Malcolm Baldrige National Quality Award (MBNQA), the European Quality Award (EQA), the Australian Quality Award (AQA), The NASA Quality and Excellence Award (Q&E), and International Quality Rating Systems (IQRS). This part of the article deals with the empirical analysis of the TQM critical factors in different regions of the world. We compare and contrast the findings from these studies.

Benchmarking critical factors of TQM

This project was an attempt to verify the applicability of a list of 22 critical factors based on the MBNQA criteria and the teachings of three TQM gurus to organizations operating on a global basis. Three important issues were considered before the survey was undertaken:

(1) If total quality management as a "soft technology", modern philosophy of management is transferable, one would see that organizations would subscribe to the same critical factors regardless of where they are operating and regardless of market conditions, location, etc.

(2) If TQM is to be considered as a generic philosophy of management, one would see that its applicability will cut across various sectors of industry, service, commerce and public sector. This presented an opportunity, therefore, to check the relevance of the 22 factors in the context of health care in the UK.

(3) There are many assumptions made about the cultural influences on TQM implementation. By spreading the survey on an international basis, this assumption could be verified and if cultural influences would be having an impact, then this could easily be assessed.

The original study

This project was carried out by Ramirez and Loney[3] to identify activities which are critical for the success of TQM implementation. A questionnaire based on 22 critical factors short listed from the teachings of quality gurus such as Deming, Crosby and Juran was devised. The list was then finalized by comparing it with activities which award winning organizations tend to undertake. Ninety-two organizations were targeted, including national quality award winning organizations in the USA and various quality experts. The winning organizations included:

- winners of the MBNQA Award;
- the presidential and Prototype Quality Award;
- NASA Q&E George M. Low Award.

The response rate to the questionnaire was 68 per cent, including 37 quality award winners and 26 consultant firms.

The results illustrated in Figure 1 demonstrate that:

- For TQM to be introduced successfully there has to be top management commitment and this is to be demonstrated through active involvement, setting clear goals and a vision for the organization and integrating TQM into the strategic quality planning process.

- The primary purpose for introducing TQM is to achieve complete customer satisfaction. This will in turn impact on business organizations' level of competitiveness and prosperity.

- TQM introduction is heavily reliant on employee involvement and participation and TQ-based performance is dependent on people productivity. As such, investment in people through education and training is fundamental to the success of TQM implementation.

- TQM is long term, and can only succeed if there is a serious attempt at changing methods, ways of working, ideas, technologies etc. In a sense it requires a fundamentally new culture.

- The Ramirez and Loney[3] project does also indicate that TQM is certainly not just about using simple tools such as statistical process control (SPC), quality costing and a zero defect attitude.

It is surprising, however, that factors such as measurement and vendor partnerships were not considered as very critical. They were both ranked in the middle tier. Measurement, however, is the catalyst for improvement and also is the essential ingredient for goal setting, monitoring and review. Vendor partnerships on the other hand are essential for establishing high competitive standards, based on low cost, high quality, speed of responsiveness, innovation, among others.

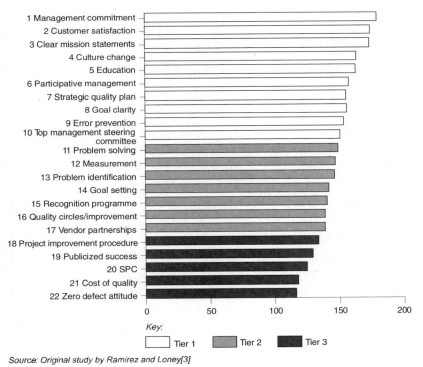

Source: Original study by Ramirez and Loney[3]

Figure 1. Benchmarking critical factors of TQM, USA

The survey highlighted other factors which the respondents did not considerto be covered sufficiently enough in the list of 22, including for example:

- process management;
- union participation;
- benchmarking;
- match quality plan to business plan;
- CEO and senior executives must believe;
- commitment of resources;
- emphasis on team – not individual;
- full-time quality consultant and professionals;
- strong communication plan.

In relation to reasons for introducing TQM in the first place, the following were given by the respondents:

- competition, loss of market share;
- survival;
- desire to improve, be a leader in our field, be a world-class company;
- negative publicity, customer dissatisfaction, crisis in operation;
- ordered or required to implement a quality process by management;
- practice what we preach, "walk the talk";
- need to reduce costs, maximize productivity.

Out of all the critical factors, respondents were asked to highlight those ones which were particularly difficult to implement and where they have encountered difficulties most. The following factors were particularly mentioned by some of the respondents:

- getting management commitment and support;
- getting buy-in related;

- vision, goal or strategy related;
- culture change related;
- finding time to devote to quality issues;
- training all employees;
- focus on quality instead of numbers;
- patience – it takes a long time.

Figure 2 illustrates a chart of the 22 critical factors being compared with the mean score obtained from repeating the survey in other countries and in different sectors. This was an attempt to see whether the US sample are over-emphasizing or under-emphasizing some of the factors. As Figure 2 indicates, there is an over-emphasis on all the 22 factors and the order of criticality is in line with the three-tier classification carried out by Ramirez and Loney[3].

The NHS/UK study

The Ramirez and Loney[3] study provided an opportunity to check whether the list of critical factors is applicable to the UK situation and in particular if TQM is a genetic and transferable philosophy to check whether the same critical factors do apply to other sectors such as health care.

There are radical changes taking place in health care in the UK, and TQM is widely considered as an opportunity for bringing about the necessary changes and restructuring for modern management. The arguments for TQM in health care are numerous[4]. Sloan[5] for instance mentions the following arguments:

- modern medical miracles were unchallenged;
- the escalating costs in health care;
- societal demand and the growth of consumerism;
- growth of TQM in the industrial and commercial sector and its application to the health service.

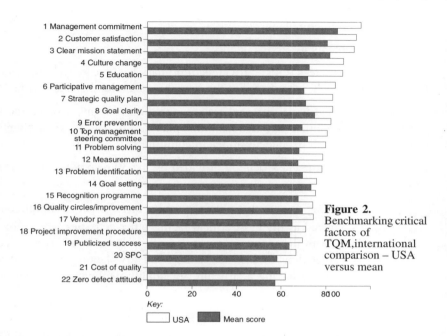

Figure 2.
Benchmarking critical factors of TQM, international comparison – USA versus mean

There is also strong evidence that TQM in health care does work, and various benefits could be derived from its introduction. Morgan and Everett[6] report the following benefits:

- managers' competence, confidence and interest in service improved;
- staff interest and commitment improved;
- staff collaboration improved;
- efficiency savings;
- improved interdisciplinary working;
- establishment of practice standards;
- clearer information;
- improved consistency of standards;

- reduction in complaints;
- improvements in service quality.

Thirty general practices (GPs), providers of primary health care were targeted for the survey and all were based in the Yorkshire and Humberside regions.

The GPs concerned have different sizes (according to number of partners involved), and are either autonomous in the purchase of care for their clients (fund holders) or still dependent of health authorities.

Figure 3 illustrates the classification provided by the 30 responding GPs and reveals that:

- It is interesting to note that although senior management commitment was recognized as the most critical factor, other activities which are associated with the senior management role were not perceived to be so critical, including, for instance, strategic quality planning, goal setting, goal clarity and having a structure for quality deployment through a steering committee.

- In health care, vendor partnership is considered to be critical. This is understandable, as GPs are heavily dependent on local hospitals providing secondary care, and very often refer patients to consultants for closer examinations.

- Because the nature of work processes in health care is people intensive, quality is considered to have more impact through local involvement and working in discrete areas. This is why quality circles and a focus on improvement though projects were considered high on the list.

- It is surprising to see that education is not considered to be very critical. Once again, this is perhaps because people are trained on clinical grounds and they perceive their knowledge to be adequate for the provision of quality service to patients.

- One area which is surprisingly high on the list is that of publicized successes. This seems to suggest that health care providers do good work which is not often made visible and that they should highlight successes more often.

Figure 4 compares the ratings given by the health-care respondents against the mean score. Most factors are under-emphasized. The areas which are overemphasized because of their perceived importance include:

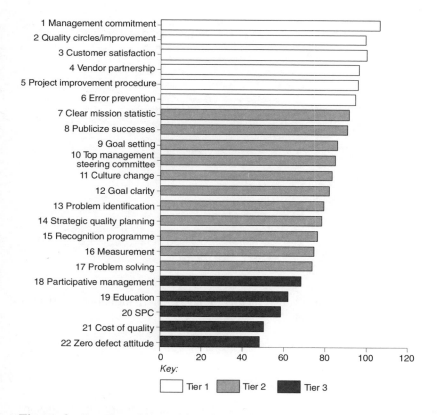

Figure 3. Benchmarking critical factors of TQM, UK health-care sector

141

- quality circles/improvement programmes;

- vendor partnerships;

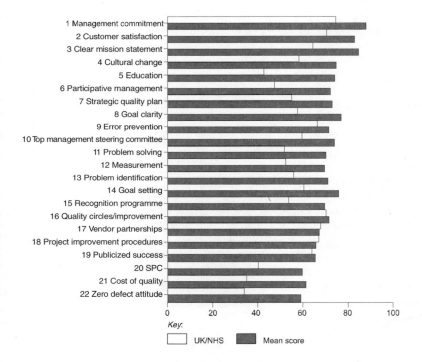

Figure 4. Benchmarking critical factors of TQM, international comparison – UK/NHS versus mean score

- project improvement processes;

- publicized successes.

Middle East study

The quality revolution is spreading all over the world. There are various reasons which could be attributed to the phenomenon. The nature of competitiveness has changed from regional to a global one. Third World countries offer a good base for foreign capital investment because of low costs, availability of labour, good access to neighbouring markets, etc. There is also a growing desire by developing countries to become more competitive, to exploit natural resources at their disposal and to modernize.

In the Middle East, for instance, many organizations are embracing TQM principles. ISO 9000 registration is growing all the time and there is wider appreciation that embarking on TQM programmes could lead to substantial benefits.

A sample of 30 senior/middle managers representing five Middle Eastern countries and coming from different industry sectors were targeted for this study. Details of the responses are included in Tables AI-AIV in the Appendix.

Figure 5 illustrates the rankings of the 22 critical factors.

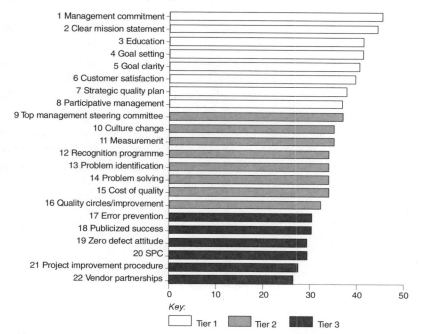

Figure 5. Benchmarking critical factors of TQM, Saudi Arabia, Kuwait, Bahrain, Qatar, UAE

143

Figure 5 reveals that:

- Most factors considered very critical pertain to senior management role, commitment and support. This is an indication that management from the top in the Middle East is a problem, and particularly in relation to TQM implementation. One can assume many things in relation to this; is there lack of leadership for instance? Do senior managers not really appreciate the potential of TQM?

- Education is considered very high on the list, perhaps because most industrial projects in the Middle East are new and there is still a lot of potential for growth – therefore there is a need for learning though transfer of technology, practices and methods from developed economies. Education is also considered high perhaps for raising top management awareness and appreciation of the importance of TQM and to achieve their commitment and involvement.

- One factor which was considered quite low on the list is vendor partnerships. This does perhaps suggest that the nature of industrial projects is such that partnership with suppliers is not considered to be of paramount importance. Most industries are in the commodities sectors, most rely on the exploitation of natural resources such as oil and natural gas.

Figure 6 indicates the ratings of the 22 factors by the Middle East sample and compared against the mean score. In addition to the factors of senior management role and commitment which are over-emphasized, the following factors are more emphasized than the mean:

- measurement;

- recognition programme;

- SPC;

- cost of quality;

- zero defect attitude.

The cost of quality for instance is an area which is extremely important to many organizations in the Middle East, since they are under a lot of pressure to remain attractive for foreign capital investment projects and joint venture programmes.

Malaysia and Singapore study

These two countries consider TQM to be very important for similar reasons given for the previous sample. Malaysia in particular is a country which is enjoying strong economic growth; together with Singapore, both are countries attractive to foreign capital investment because of low cost, high level of skills and political stability. Altogether, 120 managers representing both countries and serving in different industry sectors, were targeted for this study. The details of responses are provided in the Appendix.

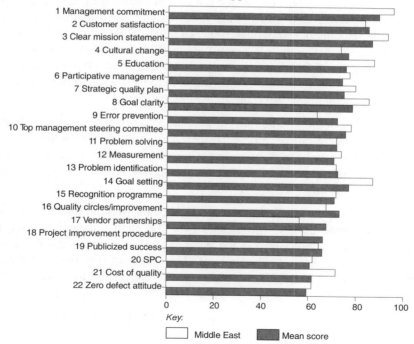

Figure 6. Benchmarking critical factors of TQM, international comparison – Middle East versus mean

145

Figure 7 illustrates the ratings of the 22 critical factors provided by the respondents which indicate that:

- It is apparent that there is little difference between most critical factors. Senior management role and commitment are considered to be most critical alongside customer satisfaction.

- There is, however, emphasis on culture change. This suggests that there is an urgent need to completely modify attitudes and methods of work to ensure total compatibility with modern business requirements.

- The middle tier includes the bulk of critical factors all considered to be equally important. It is perhaps surprising to see that a factor such as strategic quality planning which is a very important senior management task is ranked very low. This tends to suggest that there is poor understanding of senior management's role in TQM implementation, or even perhaps that there is a confusion on the role of TQM. Is it perhaps thought that TQM implementation is a separate programme from the running of the business? Why is the need to have a senior management steering committee also considered low on the list?

- Similarly to the Middle East sample, the area of vendor partnerships is not considered to be very important. This could be attributed to reasons suggested above or even perhaps the fact that there is lack of appreciation on how managing suppliers could impact on quality and business results.

Figure 8 illustrates the 22 critical factors ranked by the Malaysia and Singapore sample and compared with the mean score. The chart indicates that most factors are at least emphasized in the same degree as the mean and in many instances over-emphasis is also present. This suggests that the 22 factors found to be critical in the US situation are also considered to be critical in Malaysia and Singapore.

The factors which are apparently more emphasized than others include:

- clear mission statement;

- education;

- participative management;

- goal clarity;

- top management steering committee;

- problem solving;

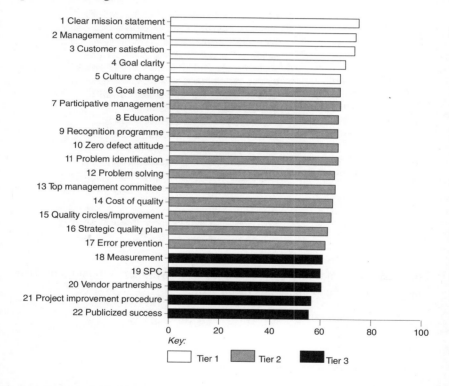

Figure 7. Benchmarking critical factors of TQM, Malaysia and Singapore

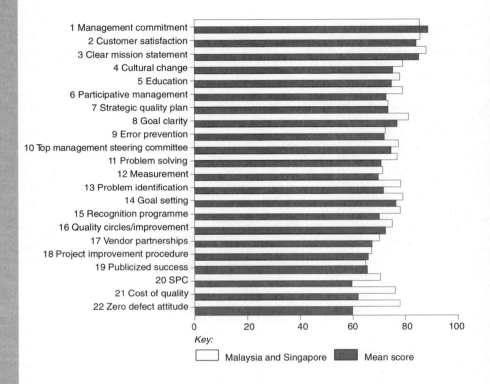

Figure 8. Benchmarking critical factors of TQM, international comparison – Malaysia and Singapore versus mean score

- problem identification;

- goal setting;

- recognition programmes;

- quality circles/improvement programmes;

- SPC;

148

- cost of quality;

- zero defect attitude.

Similarly to the Middle East sample, there is an over-emphasis on cost of quality and zero defect attitude. This again highlights the importance of cost and making the countries very attractive for foreign capital investment and joint venture programmes.

Conclusions

This survey is a useful attempt to provide better understanding of critical factors of TQM. The list of 22 factors generated by Ramirez and Loney[3] proved to be a very useful vehicle for checking applicability, order of criticality and relevance of TQM in a much wider context.

By benchmarking the 22 factors across countries and industry sectors, the following points were noted:

Figure 9. Benchmarking critical factors of TQM, international comparison

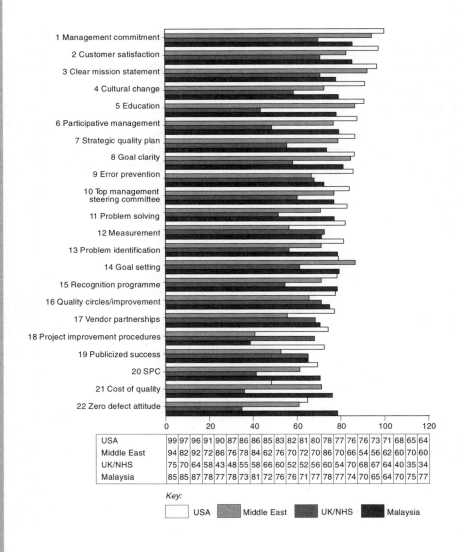

	USA	Middle East	UK/NHS	Malaysia
1 Management commitment	99	94	75	85
2 Customer satisfaction	97	82	70	85
3 Clear mission statement	96	92	64	87
4 Cultural change	91	72	58	78
5 Education	90	86	43	77
6 Participative management	87	76	48	78
7 Strategic quality plan	86	78	55	73
8 Goal clarity	86	84	58	81
9 Error prevention	85	62	66	72
10 Top management steering committee	83	76	60	76
11 Problem solving	82	70	52	76
12 Measurement	81	72	52	71
13 Problem identification	80	70	56	77
14 Goal setting	78	86	60	78
15 Recognition programme	77	70	54	77
16 Quality circles/improvement	76	66	70	74
17 Vendor partnerships	76	54	68	70
18 Project improvement procedures	73	56	67	65
19 Publicized success	71	62	64	64
20 SPC	68	60	40	70
21 Cost of quality	65	70	35	75
22 Zero defect attitude	64	60	34	77

Key:

☐ USA ▨ Middle East ▨ UK/NHS ■ Malaysia

- cost of quality;

- zero defect attitude.

Similarly to the Middle East sample, there is an over-emphasis on cost of quality and zero defect attitude. This again highlights the importance of cost and making the countries very attractive for foreign capital investment and joint venture programmes.

Conclusions

This survey is a useful attempt to provide better understanding of critical factors of TQM. The list of 22 factors generated by Ramirez and Loney[3] proved to be a very useful vehicle for checking applicability, order of criticality and relevance of TQM in a much wider context.

By benchmarking the 22 factors across countries and industry sectors, the following points were noted:

Figure 9. Benchmarking critical factors of TQM, international comparison

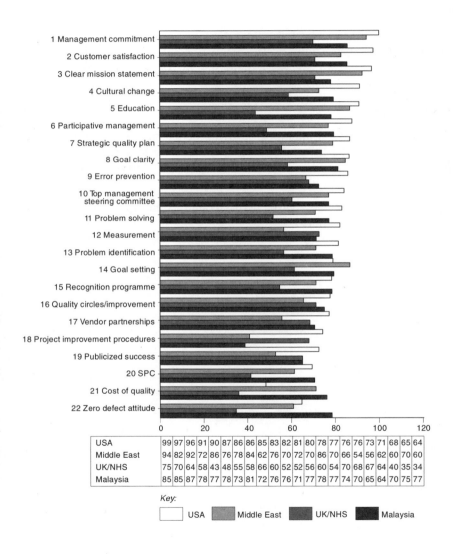

	USA	Middle East	UK/NHS	Malaysia
USA	99 97 96 91 90 87 86 86 85 83 82 81 80 78 77 76 76 73 71 68 65 64			
Middle East	94 82 92 72 86 76 78 84 62 76 70 72 70 86 70 66 54 56 62 60 70 60			
UK/NHS	75 70 64 58 43 48 55 58 66 60 52 52 56 60 54 70 68 67 64 40 35 34			
Malaysia	85 85 87 78 77 78 73 81 72 76 76 71 77 78 77 74 70 65 64 70 75 77			

Key:

☐ USA   ▨ Middle East   ▨ UK/NHS   ■ Malaysia

150

- Not all of the 22 critical factors are relevant in a generic sense to any organization (Figure 9).

- Some factors are emphasized with the same degree of criticality, including for instance top management commitment, having a clear mission statement and a clear commitment towards customer satisfaction.

- There is a need for goal clarity and having a quality strategic planning process and a senior management structure for driving quality forward and deploying quality goals throughout the organization.

- Successful TQM implementation can only come from radically challenging and changing the culture of the organization.

Figure 10. Benchmarking critical factors of TQM, mean average score

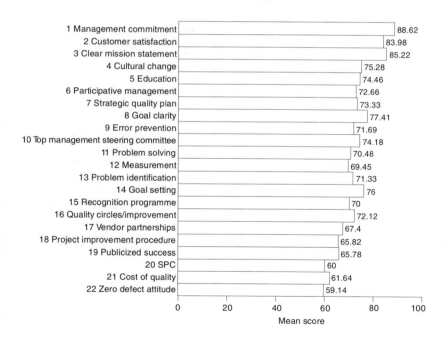

- Quality management is a long-term process which relies on relative achievements though continuous improvement. Problem solving, problem identification, teamwork and quality circles are all important aspects for driving the improvement wheel forward.

- Emphasis on continuous learning through education and training. TQM relies on people creativity, innovation and ability to add value for the benefit of the end customer.

- TQM implementation is certainly not about just doing the bare minimum through using simple tools and techniques of quality such as SPC, being obsessed with zero defects as a tangible goal and wanting just to drive down costs. These are important elements but not the core elements (Figure 10).

References

1. Saraph, J.V., Benson, P.G. and Schroeder, R.G., "An instrument for measuring critical factors of quality management", *Decision Sciences*, Vol. 20 No. 4, 1989, pp. 457-78.

2. Black, S.A., "Measuring the critical factors of total quality management", PhD thesis, University of Bradford Management Centre, Bradford, 1993.

3. Ramirez, C. and Loney, T., "Baldrige Award Winners identify the essential activities of a successful quality process", *Quality Digest*, January 1993, pp. 38-40.

4. Zairi, M. and Matthew, A., "TQM in primary care: an evaluation", research report submitted to the Management Executive of the NHS, Bradford University, August 1993.

5. Sloan, M.D., "A prescription for the healthcare industry", *Quality Progress*, 1991, pp. 75-9.

6. Morgan, J. and Everett, T., "Introducing quality management in the NHS", *International Journal for Healthcare Quality Assurance*, Vol. 3 No. 5, 1990, pp. 23-5.

Appendix

Tier	Score (out of 90)
Tier 1	
1 Clear mission statement	79
2 Management commitment	77
3 Customer satisfaction	77
4 Goal clarity	73
5 Culture change	71
Tier 2	
6 Goal setting	71
7 Participative management	71
8 Education	70
9 Recognition programme	70
10 Zero defects attitude	70
11 Problem identification	70
12 Problem solving	69
13 Top management steering committee	69
14 Cost of quality	68
15 Quality circles/improvement teams	67
16 Strategic quality planning	66
17 Error prevention	65
Tier 3	
18 Measurement	64
19 Statistical process control	63
20 Vendor partnership	63
21 Project improvement process	59
22 Publicized successes	58
$n = 30$	

Tier	Score (out of 51)
Tier 1	
1 Management commitment	48
2 Clear mission statement	47

Table AI. Ranking of quality activities: Malaysia

3 Education	44
4 Goal setting	44
5 Goal clarity	43
6 Customer satisfaction	42
7 Strategic quality planning	40
8 Participative management	39

Tier	Score (out of 51)
Tier 2	
9 Top management steering committee	39
10 Culture change	37
11 Measurement	37
12 Recognition programme	36
13 Problem identification	36
14 Problem solving	36
15 Cost of quality	36
16 Quality circles/improvement teams	34
Tier 3	
17 Error prevention	32
18 Publicized successes	32
19 Zero defects attitude	31
20 Statistical process control	31
21 Project improvement process	29
22 Vendor partnership	28

$n = 17$

Notes: The items listed in Tier 1 were those that the majority of the respondents rated as critical and absolutely essential to a successful quality management process

Tier 2 consists of items that the majority of the respondents rated as important. However they do not consider these items as essential nor critical

Table AII. Ranking of quality activities: Middle East

Tier 3 items were rated by most respondents as non-critical. Less than a third of them indicated that these items were essential to the success of a quality management process

Table AII.

Tier	Score (out of 150)	Percentage
Tier 1		
1 Management commitment	113	75.33
2 Quality circles/improvement teams	106	70.67
3 Customer satisfaction	106	70.67
4 Vendor partnership	102	68.00
5 Project improvement process	101	67.33
6 Error prevention	100	66.67
Tier 2		
7 Clear mission statement	97	64.67
8 Publicized successes	96	64.00
9 Goal setting	91	60.67
10 Top management steering committee	90	60.00
11 Culture change	88	58.67
12 Goal clarity	87	58.00
13 Problem identification	84	56.00
14 Strategic quality planning	83	55.33
15 Recognition programme	81	54.00
16 Measurement	79	52.67
17 Problem solving	78	52.00
Tier 3		
18 Participative management	72	48.00
19 Education	65	43.33
20 Statistical process control	61	40.67
21 Cost of quality	53	35.33
22 Zero defects attitude	51	34.00
$n = 30$		

Table AIII. Health-care list

Tier	Score (out of 189)	Percentage
Tier 1		
1 Management commitment	188	99.47
2 Customer satisfaction	184	97.35
3 Clear mission statement	182	96.30
4 Culture change	172	91.01
5 Education	171	90.48
6 Participative management	165	87.30
7 Strategic quality planning	163	86.24
8 Goal clarity	163	86.24
9 Error prevention	161	85.19
10 Top management steering committee	158	83.60
Tier 2		
11 Problem solving	156	82.54
12 Measurement	154	81.48
13 Problem identification	153	80.95
14 Goal setting	148	78.31
15 Recognition programme	147	77.78
16 Quality circles/improvement teams	145	76.72
17 Vendor partnership	145	76.72
Tier 3		
18 Project improvement process	139	73.54
19 Publicized successes	136	71.96
20 Statistical process control	130	68.78
21 Cost of quality	123	65.08
22 Zero defects attitude	121	64.02

Source: [3]

Table AIV. Ramirez and Loney

An empirical analysis of critical factors of TQM

A proposed tool for self-assessment and benchmarking purposes

T. Thiagarajan
Palm Oil Research Institute, Malaysia, and

M. Zairi
University of Bradford, Bradford, UK

First Published in

Benchmarking for Quality Management & Technology,
Vol. 5 No. 4, 1998, pp. 291-303,
© MCB University Press, 1351-3036

Introduction

Traditionally, the study of ideal or desired management practices in work organisations has tended to be normative; that is, it relied on the knowledge and judgement of the respondents for the development of "what ought to be". Studies in quality management (see Benson *et al.*, 1991; Black, 1993) employed a normative approach in "identifying the critical factors of TQM". The normative approach has been criticised on the grounds that in such an approach it is necessary to make certain basic assumptions regarding perfect knowledge and judgement in the respondents (Cooke and Slack, 1984).

In studies of critical quality factors for effective total quality management (TQM) implementation, a descriptive approach rather than a normative one was considered more appropriate. A descriptive approach in the context of this study involves best organisations agreeing to a set of quality factors critical to a successful TQM implementation in their organisations. The emphasis is on "what is"; that is, what best organisations do or did in practice. The questionnaire must thus be designed to enable respondents to indicate the quality factors that he or she perceives to be critical to a successful implementation of TQM in his or her organisation.

For the purpose of the study discussed in this paper, a slight adaptation was carried out on the approach devised by Ramirez and Loney (1993). Respondents were asked to rate each of the quality factors (labelled as quality-related factors in the questionnaire) as to their level of importance to a successful implementation of quality management processes in their organisations, using the following criteria:

- *Critical.* Factors that you feel are critical and absolutely essential. The process stands a good chance of ending in failure if these factors are not part of the quality management process.

- *Important.* Factors that you feel are important but not absolutely essential. The process will survive if these are not addressed, but the organisation may experience some unnecessary delays to its quality management process until these factors are eventually addressed.

- *Minor importance.* Factors that you feel are of minor importance. These factors will not seriously affect the success or failure of the quality management process.

Analysis and interpretation of the responses to the questionnaire would then allow objective judgement to be used in identifying consensus on the level of perceived importance of the quality factors, a requisite to developing a hierarchical critical quality factor structure.

Very early in the questionnaire design stage, a pretest was done to test the workability of the rating to be used, using the questionnaire developed by Ramirez and Loney (1993). Nunnally (1978) advises that any pretest must be carried out on a similar group, in this case Malaysian managers. As in the case of the US respondents, Malaysian managers had no difficulties in rating the critical factors using the ratings. Respondents were also asked if the rating created any difficulties. All respondents replied that they faced no problems in completing the questionnaires.

Choice of variables
The set of variables used in the questionnaire is the product of an in-depth review of the literature and a robust reiterative process of verification and validation. The set of variables, termed as quality factors in this study, used in the questionnaire are illustrated in the Appendix.

Survey management

Administration of the survey questionnaire The administration of the questionnaire represents a departure from several of the earlier studies. Only one form was sent per organisation, instead of the multi-forms approach used by earlier researchers (see Black, 1993; Saraph *et al.*, 1989). Like the study initiated by Ramirez and Loney (1993), the unit of analysis for this investigation is the organisation: that is, the subject matter is the respondents' organisations, measured by the perceptions of the respondents. A single form approach was deemed to be appropriate.

While the single form approach allows working with only a smaller pool of respondents, it eliminates the potential for bias and skew in the results from the multi-forms approach due to an uneven number of returns across the organisation. It also allows an accurate and precise demographics to variables analysis to be carried out. The multi-forms approach exposes some confusion in terms of the unit of analysis in some of the studies.

Response rate
As the sample size is small, it was decided at the outset to set a high response rate of at least 90 percent. This rate was chosen so that the rate of returns is large enough to establish a representative and credible set of data.

The questionnaire, with a covering letter addressed to the TQM director/manager and explaining the objectives of the survey, were mailed or hand-delivered to each of the 86 organisations in the sample. This was followed by telephone enquiries to all respondents after a fortnight.

A total of 81 usable questionnaires were returned, representing a 94.2 percent response rate. This rate compares very favourably with similar studies involving Sinclair (1994) and Ramirez and Loney (1993).

Figure 1 shows the breakdown of the organisations. It can be seen that, allowing for the constraints imposed by the small population of TQ organisations in Malaysia, the 81 organisations form a fairly heterogeneous mixture.

Data analysis

The results of this investigation suggest that there are 22 critical quality factors identified, which form a constellation of mutually supportive and interdependent "processes" that together increase the chance of a successful TQM implementation.

Table I shows the critical quality factor structure comprising the 22 critical quality factors, sorted in descending order of criticality and stratified into three tiers representing stages of priorities emphasis.

The critical quality factor structure suggests that TQM must begin with senior management commitment. All the nine core critical quality factors are either top management-related or share some connection which requires top management support.

Most, if not all, of tier I critical quality factors are acknowledged in the TQM literature as prerequisites or fundamental elements that must be addressed early in the implementation, namely, commitment and involvement from the top, communication of statement of mission, maximising employees' support and involvement, internal customer-supplier attitude, and effective communication. This validates the interpretation of tier I critical quality factors as factors that impact on the success of the TQM implementation the most.

It comes as no surprise that all the Malaysian-based organisations surveyed returned q1 (senior executives assume active responsibility for evaluation and improvement of management system, and leading quality drive) as critical and absolutely essential to the success of TQM implementation. The finding, in tandem with the information in the literature review, places senior management's own commitment to the quality and involvement in leading the quality drive at the pinnacle of key quality intervention. All quality gurus and every author of TQM are unanimous on the importance of top management commitment and involvement. Management leadership and commitment is also an important category in all major quality awards.

The uniqueness of q1 as the only critical quality factor that is unanimously returned as absolutely essential supports the conclusions from the literature review that, while there is disagreement concerning the appropriate emphasis on many quality interventions, there is unanimity in opinions among TQM authorities and practitioners that success in TQM implementation is ultimately rooted in senior management taking active responsibility for quality (Hackman and Wageman, 1995).

The development of a clear mission statement and the consistent communication of objectives defining values expectations and focus (q3) is seen as one of the first steps of Malaysian top management commitment. Quality and Tier I

- Senior executives assume active responsibility for evaluation and improvement of management system, and leading quality drive

- Clear, consistent communication of mission statement and objectives defining quality values, expectations and focus

- The entire workforce understands, and is committed to, vision, values, and quality goals of the organisation

161

Figure 1. Breakdown of respondents' organisations

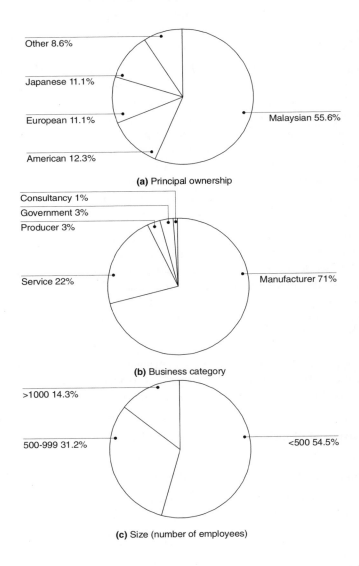

(a) Principal ownership

(b) Business category

(c) Size (number of employees)

- Visibility of senior executive commitment to quality and customer satisfaction
- Training for employees in problem identification and solving skills, quality improvement skills and other technical skills
- The entire organisation understands that each individual and each process has internal customers and suppliers
- Supervisors, unit heads and divisional managers assume active roles as facilitators of continuous improvement, coaches of new method, mentors and leaders of empowered employees
- Systems for recognition and appreciation of quality efforts and success of individuals and teams
- Effective top-down, bottom-up and lateral communication

Tier II

- Problem-solving and continuous improvement processes, based on facts and systemic analysis
- Comprehensive policy development and effective deployment of goals
- A team approach (such as quality circles, cross-functional teams) in problem solving and continuous improvement
- Comprehensive identification of customers and customer needs and alignment of processes to satisfy the needs
- The use of customer surveys and feedback process, and tracking of other key measures to assess customer satisfaction
- Training for employees to improve interactive skills (such as communication skills, effective meeting skills, empowerment and leadership skills)

Tier III

- Elements of quality deployment structure in place to manage the organisation's quality journey
- Employee suggestion scheme in place, with target time scales for management response

- The use of self-assessment tools and other mechanisms to track and improve performance gaps in the implementation and effectiveness of systems, processes and practices
- Competitive benchmarking made against primary competitors
- Cost of quality process to track rework, waste, rejects, and for continuous improvement
- Informal benchmarking and other forms of information acquisition and sharing with organisation in different sectors and industries to identify best practices for improvement and opportunities
- Informal benchmarking and other forms of information acquisition and sharing with organisations in different sectors and industries to identify best practices for improvement and opportunities
- Systemic review and analysis of key process measures that have a direct or indirect impact on value-addition to customer satisfaction

commitment to customer satisfaction is also seen to play an important part in the top management daily priorities (q2). Such commitment of the top management, actively demonstrated, is the means for promoting organisational commitment, such as identification by the workforce with the vision, values and goals of the organisation (q9) and middle management assuming their new roles (q12).

Education and training is often reported as an important element in the development of a suitable continuous improvement culture. Malaysian organisations view employee training in problem solving and continuous improvement (q16) as the main emphasis here. However, top management must sell the need to create such a culture to engage the commitment of the employees. Effective top-down and bottom-up communication (q6) is perceived as a critical enabler here. A system for recognition and appreciation of quality efforts and success of individual and teams (q14), as a core concept of TQM, appears to be set-up by the top management to reinforce the message.

The critical quality factor list also shares most of the values covered by key principles espoused by the Baldrige award and EQA criteria, namely:

- Top management take responsibility for creating the enabling environment for quality to take roots and to be sustained. Their role includes policy development and goal setting and planning process, promoting quality awareness, providing role models through demonstrated commitment and involvement, and setting up elements of a quality management structure.

- Aligning employee active involvement to corporate expectations by uniting them behind the vision, values and quality goals of the organisations.

- Maximising employee involvement through teamwork, understanding and meeting their needs, setting up the means to tap improvement ideas, recognition for quality efforts and training and education.

- Creation of continuous improvement ethics. Use of quality improvement tools and techniques.

- Emphasis on management by fact.

- Importance of external customer focus. The concept of internal customeris understood.

- Having a system for measuring key indicators that impact the way the organisation adds value to customers.

- Benchmarking and self-assessment are carried out.

Toward an index of comparative criticality: a measure of criticality

A critical quality factor has been defined as a quality factor that is critical and absolutely essential to the success of TQM implementation. This definition is qualified to mean that the implementation process stands a good chance of ending in failure if this critical quality factor is not part of TQM. It is also implied that the more critical a quality factor is, the higher the chances of failure if it is not part of TQM. A comparative quantitative measure of how critical a critical quality factor is, therefore, is useful. Such measure of criticality has several applications for the purpose of research in the field of TQM.

Ramirez and Loney (1993) ordered the quality factors in terms of importance using of factor score computed by assigning arbitrary weights to ordinal scales. This approach could, however, be challenged.

From the analysis of the returned questionnaires it has been established that:

- a quality factor with critical as the modal category be defined as a critical quality factor;

- the extent of consensus in opinions amongst respondents in categorising a quality factor as critical be equated to show how critical a critical quality factor is;

- variation ratio as a measure of how descriptive the modal category is of the data (Weisberg, 1992) be equated to the extent of consensus in opinions;

- variation ratio, thus, be equated to show how critical a critical quality factor is.

By its definition, variation ratio is corrected for the unequal valid responses (N). Thus, ratio values can be compared across response distributions with differing numbers of valid responses within a single survey sample. It also permits crosssample comparisons between survey samples of differing sizes with an identical number of categories. Variation ratio is, therefore, appropriate as a surrogate measure of comparative criticality.

A variation ratio of zero for a critical quality factor is obtained when every single organisation perceives a quality factor to be absolutely essential to the success of TQM implementation. Thus, a zero value represents the extreme end or pinnacle of criticality. Any value greater than zero means relatively fewer organisations returning the quality factor as critical. At the other extreme end of criticality, the maximal value is obtained when just a third of the organisations return the quality factor as critical.

The maximum value is never an integer and depends on the number of categories (K) (Weisberg, 1992). This feature is awkward and does not allow easy interpretation when the measure is used as a stand-alone indicator of criticality. It would be more useful were the measures normed to go from 0 to 1. Introducing an index of comparative criticality for critical quality factors with end values of 0 for most critical and 1 for least critical is thus in order. (From here on the index will be referred to as comparative criticality index or simply CC Index.)

Dividing the variation ratio by the maximal value norms the CC Index so that the value of 1 always represents the least critical. The criticality index for each critical quality factor is therefore best calculated from a modified variation ratio equation:

CC Index $= (1 - f^{critical}/N)/(K - 1/K)$ where critical is the maximal value. Table II is the CC Index of the 22 critical quality factors distilled in this investigation. To enable ease of interpretation when used as a stand-alone, the CC Index is superimposed with tiers.

Index

value	Quality factor
Tier I critical quality factors	
0.000	Senior executives assume active responsibility for evaluation and improvement of management systems, and leading quality drive
0.132	Clear, consistent communication of mission statement and objectives defining quality values, expectations and focus
0.166	The entire workforce understands, and is committed to, vision, values, and quality goals of the organisation
0.171	Visibility of senior executive commitments to quality and customer satisfaction
0.205	Training for employees in problem identification and solving skills, quality improvement skills and other technical skills
0.240	The entire organisation understands that each individual and each process has internal customers and suppliers
0.304	Supervisors, unit heads and divisional managers assume active roles as facilitators of continuous improvement, coaches of new methods, mentors and leaders of empowered employees
0.370	System for recognition and appreciation of quality efforts and success of individuals and teams

167

| 0.388 | Effective top-down and bottom-up communication |

Tier II critical quality factors

0.408	Problem-solving and continuous improvement processes, based on facts and systemic analysis
0.493	Comprehensive policy development and effective deployment of goals
0.519	A team approach (such as quality circles, cross-functional teams) in problem solving and continuous improvement
0.519	Comprehensive identification of customers and customer needs and alignment of processes to satisfy the needs
0.519	The use of customer surveys and feedback process, and tracking of other key measures to assess customer satisfaction
0.544	Training for employees to improve interactive skills (such as communication skills, effective meeting skills, empowerment and leadership skills)

Tier III critical quality factors

0.759	Elements of quality management structure in place to manage the organisation's quality journey
0.759	Employee suggestion scheme in place, with target time scales for management response
0.759	The use of self-assessment tools and other mechanisms to track and improve performance gaps in the implementation and effectiveness of systems, processes and practices
0.769	Competitive benchmarking made against primary competitors
0.769	Cost of quality process to track rework, waste, rejects, and for continuous improvement
0.787	Informal benchmarking and other forms of information acquisition and sharing with organisations in different sectors and industries to identify best practices for improvement and opportunities

0.826   Systemic review and analysis of key process measures that have a direct or indirect impact on value-addition to customer satisfaction

A self-assessment tool using TQ quality factors

A self-assessment tool can be useful in two ways. First, to assess TQM implementation within an organisation during the early years. The 22 critical quality factors provide a more realistic checklist for assessment of implementation progress during the early years of implantation than those suggested in national quality awards. It is generally recognised that selfassessment using the criteria of quality awards such as MBNQA and EQA are appropriate for organisations that are usually advanced in the use of TQM (see Boaden and Dale, 1994; van der Wiele *et al.*, 1996).

Second, the self-assessment tool can be used to assess TQM understanding among the workforce. Such an assessment is of importance in an appraisal of training requirements, especially during the early years.

In designing an instrument, consideration has to be given to subject-matter for the assessment – the unit of analysis (Nachmias and Nachmias, 1981). For TQM implementation assessment, the organisation is the unit of analysis. The instrument is designed to measure an individual's perception of the level of implementation of each quality factor, and therefore the development of the overall programme as a whole within the organisation. To assess TQM understanding, an individual is the unit of analysis. The instrument is designed to measure an individual's perception of the relative importance of the quality factors.

The selection of measurement scales to solicit such responses must be taken into consideration for both respondents and those who administer the tool. Features like ease of completion and scoring are important to the former, while ease in interpretation (and mathematical manipulation) are important to the latter.

The survey questionnaire used in this study could be used with minor modification as a tool for assessing the implementation of the critical quality factors. A significant modification to the questionnaire will be the exclusion of non-critical quality factors.

The use of a Likert-type scale with a rating of, say, 1 to 5 or even 1 to 10 to express the extent of implantation can be limiting and pose difficulties in interpretation. The alternative of a continuous scale, where respondents ark a line, say from very high to very low, is impractical, as measuring and coding each response could be time consuming (Black, 1993).

A practical and tested alternative for performance assessment is to adapt the approaches of scoring used for quality awards such as Baldrige and EFQA. It will be easier to mask for respondents to rate the degree of implementation as a score out of a maximum point. The maximum score represents the organisation performing to the full extent of the quality factors. It is convenient to work with a single maximum point for all quality factors. Working with integers such as 10, 100 or 1,000 as maximum points is practical and convenient when it comes to interpretation and mathematical conversion. A maximum of 100 is ideal as it is neither limiting nor awkwardly large to score and sum.

Figure 2. Criticality matrix

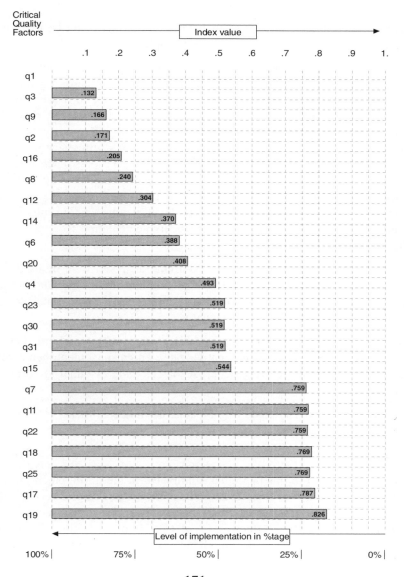

Using self-assessment tool for benchmarking

A useful analysis to perform is benchmarking using the CC Index. The information gathered from the benchmarking analysis could be used as the basis to prioritise areas for improvement (implementation) action.

Benchmarking analysis involves the comparison of the degree of implementation of critical quality factors against the CC Index as the standard. A gap analysis is performed on a matrix chart called criticality matrix shown in Figure 2. Critical quality factors in order of criticality are listed on the left y-axis from top to bottom. Benchmark "scores" for each critical quality factor are incorporated on the matrix using horizontal lines with varying lengths representing values of the CC Index. Implementation scores of the respective critical quality factors represented as lines are plotted from right to left on the criticality lines. Implementation score plots that fall short of the benchmark line range are negative gaps (that is, the level of implantation falls short of standard). Positive gaps are ones where the implementation score plots fall on the line range.

The information gathered from benchmarking analysis could be used as the basis to prioritise areas for improvement (implementation) action. Negative gaps indicate actions required. Prioritisation of actions is performed along the criticality scale from the top downwards.

Positive gaps are of little concern, unless in instances where there are significantly large numbers of negative gaps. The management then needs to realign quality strategies and tactics, resources and personnel to correct the imbalances.

Benchmarking analysis could also be done across departments of past trends using similar approach.

Summary

The work covered in this paper has culminated in the development of a tool which can be used, both as a self-assessment means and also for benchmarking purposes. The analysis has revealed that there are 22 critical factors which impinge on the degree of effectiveness of TQM implementation. The findings from this study are significant enough in the sense that there is total consensus with previous findings and also establishes the fact that the "context" of implementation may not be very relevant and that there are no specific cultural issues to be observed.

References

Benson, P.G., Saraph, J.V. and Schroeder, R.G. (1991), "The effects of organisational context on quality management: an empirical investigation", *Management Science*, Vol. 37 No. 9, pp.1107-24.

Black, S.A. (1993a), "Measuring the critical factors of total quality management", unpublished PhD thesis, University of Bradford.

Boaden, R.J. and Dale, B.G. (1994), "A generic framework for managing quality improvement: theory and practice", *Quality Management Journal*, July, pp. 11-29.

Cooke, S. and Slack, N. (1984), *Making Management Decision*, Prentice-Hall International, London.

Hackman, J.R. and Wageman (1995), "Total quality management: empirical, conceptual, and practical issues", *Administrative Science Quarterly*, Vol. 40 No. 2, pp. 309-42.

Nachmias, C. and Nachmias, D. (1981), *Research Methods in the Social Sciences*, Edward Arnold, London.

Nunnally, J.C. (1978), *Psychometric Theory*, McGraw-Hill, New York, NY.

Raimirez, C. and Loney, T. (1993), "Baldrige Award winners identify the essential activities of a successful quality process", *Quality Digest*, January, pp.38-40

Saraph, J.V., Benson, P.G. and Schroeder, R.G. (1989), "An instrument for measuring the critical factors of quality management", *Decision Sciences*, Vol. 20 No. 4, pp. 810-29.

Sinclair, D.A.C. (1994), "Total quality-based performance measurement: an empirical study of best practice", unpublished PhD thesis, University of Bradford.

Van der Wiele, A. *et al.* (1996), "Self-assessment: a study of progress in Europe's leading organisations in quality management practices", *International Journal of Quality & Reliability Management*, Vol. 13 No. 1, pp. 84-104.

Weisberg, H.F. (1992), *Central Tendency and Variability*, Sage University Paper Series on Quantitative Applications in the Social Series No. 07-083, Sage, Newbury Park, CA.

Appendix. Mail questionnaire survey response

1 – critical	2 – important	3 – minor importance		Responses	
Quality factor			1	2	3
q1. Senior executives assume active responsibility for evaluation and improvement of management system, and leading quality drive			81	0	0
q2. Visibility of senior executive commitment to quality and customer satisfaction			70	9	0
q3. Clear, consistent communication of mission statement and objectives defining quality values, expectations and focus			73	7	0
q4. Comprehensive policy development and effective deployment of goals			53	24	2
q5. Top management push decision making to the lowest practical level			30	37	12
q6. Effective top-down and bottom-up communication			60	21	0
q7. Elements of quality management structure in place to manage the organisation's quality journey			40	35	6
q8. The entire organisation understands that each individual and each process has internal customers and suppliers			68	13	0
q9. The entire workforce understands, and is committed to the vision, values and quality goals of the organisation			72	9	0
q10. The use of employee surveys and tracking of other key measures to assess employee support of, and involvement in, the quality initiatives			22	48	10
q11. Employees suggestion scheme in place, with target time scales for management response			40	26	15

q12. Supervisors, unit heads and divisional managers assume active roles as facilitators of continuous improvement, coaches of new methods, mentors and leaders of empowered employees   63 16 0

q13. Employees' union support of the organisation's quality initiatives   25 33 21

q14. System for recognition and appreciation of quality efforts and success of individuals and teams   61 20 0

q15. Training for employees to improve interactive skills (such as communication skills, effective meeting skills, empowerment and leadership skills)   51 27 2

q16. Training for employees in problem identification and solving skills, quality improvement skills and other technical skills   69 11 0

q17. Informal benchmarking and other forms of information acquisition and sharing with organisations in different sectors and industries to identify best practices for improvements and opportunities   38 28 14

q18. Competitive benchmarking made against primary competitors   39 28 13

q19. Systematic review and analysis of key process measures that have a direct or indirect impact on value-addition to customer satisfaction   35 31 12

q20. Problem-solving and continuous improvement processes, based on facts and systematic analysis   59 19 3

q21. Application of total quality approach to the management of support services and business processes   29 38 13

q22. The use of self-assessment tools and other mechanisms to track and improve performance gaps in the implementation and effectiveness of systems, processes and practices   39 31 9

q23. A team approach (such as quality circles, cross-functional teams) in problem solving and continuous improvement   53 26 2

q24. The use of SPC (statistical process control) to control variability and improve processes   22 29 27

q25. Cost of quality process to track rework, waste, rejects, and for continuous improvement   39 29 12

q26. Zero defects as the quality performance standard   27 29 24

q27. A formal documented quality management system in place   27 30 23

q28. Reliance on reasonably few dependable suppliers who are   29   38 13
      evaluated and selected based on their capability and commitment to
      product and service quality, and value for money

q29. Long-term relationship and working partnership with key suppliers   32   35 13

q30. Comprehensive identification of customers and customer needs   53   25   3
      and alignment of processes to satisfy the needs

q31. The use of customer surveys and feedback process, and tracking   53   24   4
      of other key measures to assess customer satisfaction

Critical Factors of TQM: An international Comparative Benchmarking Analysis

Dr Al-Nofal A.
Associate of the European Centre for TQM

Professor Zairi M.
Director of ECTQM
m.zairi@bradford.ac.uk

Dr Ahmed A. M.
Lecturer in TQM, University of Bradford, UK

ABSTRACT

Total Quality Management (TQM) as a management philosophy is attaining greater and wider acceptance, but it does still continue to provide various challenges in so far as understanding the impact of various critical factors are concerned. This paper examines critical factors of TQM Implementation in a specific geographical context (Kuwait) and compares the outcomes with other settings in order to establish the degree of consensus and generisis that might exist between various cultural settings. Survey questionnaires were used to investigate the various Critical Quality Factors (CQFs). Semi-structured interviews were conducted to discover how these CQFs are understood. Leadership and related behaviours such as top management commitment, maximising employee commitment; involvement and empowerment, managing by customer-driven systems and processes, and continuous improvement, are most essential and fundamental to effective and successful implementation of TQM. These are some of the key CQFs that have emerged to be of significance. This paper compares the key findings in the Kuwaiti context with similar studies in Malaysia, Palestine and Saudi Arabia. These comparative studies have produced inspiring results and suggest that the quality culture has big impacts on successful TQM implementation.

Keywords:

Total Quality Management (TQM), empirical research, TQM implementation framework, best practice, Critical Quality Factors (CQFs), quality culture

1.0 INTRODUCTION

Critical factors are factors that determine the progress of an orientation. In TQM, factors that influence success or failure in TQM implementation have received much research interest (Baidoun, 2000; Salegna and Fazel, 2000). These factors are sometimes referred to as soft and hard factors.

The 'soft' and 'hard' quality factors reflect the TQM model proposed by Oakland (2000) and Thiagarajan and Zairi (1997). However, making the differentiation between 'soft' and 'hard' quality factors is difficult and unnecessary; and an issue, such as leadership, can contain both 'soft' and 'hard' aspects. It is argued that the 'soft' quality factors may best be seen as issues discussed under leadership, internal stakeholders management and policy. They are issues that impact on maximising organisation-wide support and involvement in attaining the quality goals of an organisation. They include:

Senior executives' commitment and involvement, actively demonstrated; comprehensive policy development and effective deployment of goals; entire workforce commitment to quality goals of the organisation; supervisors, unit heads and divisional managers assume active new roles; empowerment; effective communication; internal customer-supplier concept; teamwork; system for recognition and appreciation of quality efforts; and Training and education (Thiagarajan and Zairi, 1997).

'Soft' factors are regarded as long-term issues, something that cannot be switched on and off, and therefore must be emphasised and addressed accordingly in an organisation's TQM implementation plan. It is also argued that the TQM process will end up in failure if there is insufficient attention to 'soft' factors. It would be expected that 'soft' factors would all rate highly in terms of criticality and emphasis in the TQM implementation process. While the effective manipulation of the 'soft' factors is essential to the attainment of the quality goals of the organisation, they must be supported by the 'hard' factors to manage, track and improve the journey towards achieving the goals. They include: benchmarking, performance measurement; management by fact, managing by processes, self-assessment, quality control tools and techniques, cost of quality process, documented quality management system, supplier management, and customer management. However, the differentiation between hard and soft factors is not without its problems. Under what criteria can we say that leadership is a 'soft' factor, while customer management is 'hard'? This kind of dichotomy further confuses our focus on the diversity and multi-dimensional nature of TQM (Cravens et al., 2000).

2.0 THE IMPORTANCE OF STUDYING CRITICAL FACTORS OF TQM

There is a general consensus that we need more empirical and theoretical debate about TQM. We generally do not know, for example, what and how the key elements influence the TQM implementation process and how these elements should be addressed and managed in an organisation (Zink, 1995). We may need further empirical testing. For example, TQM is mainly designed from the developed world, and it is not clear if it is applicable in most developing countries.

Thiagrajan and Zairi (1998) argue that to study critical quality factors for effective TQM implementation, a descriptive approach is more appropriate than a normative one. The descriptive approach helps to ascertain and describe the detailed variation in a situation from an individual, organisational, industry, or any other perspective (Sekaran, 2003). This also involves the selection of the most suitable organisations meeting a set of quality factors critical to successful quality initiatives in their organisations. This approach involves three different levels of inquiry to address the "what and how" elements of TQM implementation and the issues involved prior to implementation.

3.0 RESEARCH OBJECTIVES

The various studies covered in this paper are based on a common methodology developed by Thiagarajan (1996). Thiagarajan (1996) used the triangulation methodology and used three different levels of analysis: 'what', 'why' and 'how' questions. The first level is concerned with the structure of the implementation process, which highlights what questions. The second level involves the understanding of TQM implementation regarding the process, i.e. 'how' questions. Finally, in the last level, there is an attempt to understand the issue of implementation, which are 'why' questions.

Each study in specific geographical context has follows the following structure:

Level 1: Identifying the critical quality factors (the 'what' element)

Level 2: Understanding the process of implementation (the 'how' element)

Level 3: Understanding the issues involved prior to implementation (the 'why' element)

3.1 Level 1: Identification of critical quality factors (the 'what' element)

By selecting a group of organisations, this level of inquiry intends to identify the structure of the implementation process in an attempt to search for a set of key quality factors of effective TQM. The use of a quantitative questionnaire survey is suggested for this level of inquiry, as both generalisability and data representativeness are expected from the analysis, and the reliability and validity of results are allowed to be measured. Consequently, a large sample is needed to represent a wide range of organisations. The suggestions from these organisations are used to make a representative and credible description of the key quality factors for effective TQM in the Kuwaiti context. The results are generally analysed using statistical techniques.

3.2 Level 2: Understanding the implementation process (the 'how' element)

Responding to the first level of analysis, this level is more concerned with the implementation of CQFs. In other words, it examines how Kuwaiti organisations effectively address and implement the CQFs identified in the previous stage. Through interviews, we collect all differences in opinions as to how best to address and implement the critical quality factors of TQM, as already noted in the literature review, and how it works in reality.

In this level of inquiry, qualitative research methods are useful. Interviews are used to describe how Kuwaiti organisations experience the process of implementation (Sekaran, 2003). Hence, a smaller case study approach using semi-structured interviews to collect data is used.

3.3 Level 3: Understanding issues involved prior to implementation

After completing the first two levels, we will precede to the last level. This level is more about 'why' – why TQM succeeds in some organisations, but

181

not in others. The use of a qualitative approach is again recommended, especially the case study approach. This may be of tremendous importance of investigating 'why' in the process. We should highlight the significance of case study because research and theory are in their early formative stage and that the experiences of the respondents are important, and the context of action is critical (Thiagarajan, 1996). We allow interviewees to define, to suggest or to argue what is important regarding the success of the quality management process in their organisation.

4.0 COMPARISON OF CRITICAL FACTORS – AN ANALYSIS OF 4 TQM STUDIES IN MALAYSIA, PALESTINE, SAUDI ARABIA AND KUWAIT

In this section, a comparison of four studies of Malaysia, Thiagaran (1996), Palestine, Baidoun (2000), Saudi Arabia, Omaim (2002) and Kuwait, Al-Nofal (2002a&b), will take place.

Table I shows the different size of companies in terms of the number of employees. In respect to business category, different researches have different emphasis. In Malaysia, the majority, more than 70%, are manufacturers, service comes second, and producer, government and consultancy are lower than 2.5%, respectively. In Palestine, service and industrial sector share 57% and 43%, respectively. In the Saudi Arabia research, 45% is from manufacturing; 31% from service, 20% from producer, and the rest, 4%, from construction. In Kuwait, the diversity of business is more evident. 41.5% are from manufacturing, 20.3% from service, 15.2% from producer, and the rest is from government and bank.

	Malaysia Thiagaragan, (1996)	Palestine Baidoun, (2000)	Saudi Arabia Omaim, (2002)	Kuwait (2003)
Size (number of employees)	54.5% (fewer than 500) 31.2% (500-999) 14.3% (>1000)		54% (fewer than 500) 14% (500-999) 32% (more than 1000)	16.5% (fewer than 100) 24.1% (100-199) 11.4% (200-299) 11.4% (300-399) 8.9% (400-499) 7.6% (500-599) 10.1% (600-699) 1.3% (900 and more)
Business category	70.4% (manufacturer) 22.2% (service) 2.5% (producer) 2.5% (government) 1.2% (consultancy)	57% (service) 43% (industrial)	45% (manufacturer) 20% (producer) 4% (construction) 31% (service)	15.2% (producer) 41.5% (manufacturer) 20.3% (Service) 2.5% (Bank) 5.1% (government) 5.1% (other)
Principal ownership	55.6% (Malaysian) 12.3% (American) 11.1% (European) 11.1% (Japanese) 8.6% (Other)		73% (Saudi organisation) 27% (joint venture)	10.1% (public sector) 81.0% (private) 8.9% (joint venture)

Table I: Comparison of Orgnaisational Classifications

4.1 Comparison of Critical, Important and Minor Quality Factors

There are three types of quality factors in TQM research. They are: critical, important, and minor quality factors. Hackett and Spurgeon (1998) and Bohan (1998) have both discussed the significance of the TQM in detail. The differences between critical, important and minor important quality factors are of great importance, which will be discussed later.

Regarding the CQFs, there are 22 in Malaysia, 19 in Palestine, 21 in Saudi Arabia, and 19 in our research in Kuwait. The difference is obvious. The higher quantity of critical factors may tell us something important, but the focus should not simply be put on the quantity. We should also take which critical factors have been taken into account. For example, in Malaysia, Q1,

Q2, Q3, Q4, Q6, Q7, Q8, Q9, Q11, Q12, Q14, Q15, Q16, Q17, Q18, Q19, Q20, Q21, Q22 are all critical factors. This is in contrast to our research in Kuwait, where only Q1, Q2, Q7, Q12, Q30, Q4, Q5, Q6, Q9, Q15, Q16, Q18, Q19, Q23, Q25, Q27, Q28, Q31 are included.

	Malaysia (1996)	Palestine (2000)	Saudi Arabia (2002)	Kuwait (2003)
Critical	Q1,Q2,Q3,Q4, Q6,Q7,Q8,Q9, Q11,Q12,Q14, Q15,Q16,Q17, Q18,Q19,Q20, Q22,Q23,Q20, Q21,Q22	Q1,Q2,Q3,Q4, Q6,Q7,Q8,Q9, Q12,Q15,Q16, Q19,Q20,Q21, Q25,Q27,Q28, Q30,Q31	Q1,Q2,Q3,Q4, Q5,Q6,Q7,Q8, Q9,Q12,Q15,Q16, Q19,Q20,Q21,Q23, Q24,Q25,Q27,Q30, Q31	Q1,Q2,Q7,Q12, Q30,Q3,Q4,Q5, Q6,Q9,Q15,Q16, Q18,Q19,Q23, Q25,Q27,Q28,Q31
	(n=22)	(n=19)	(n=21)	(n=19)

Table II: Comparison of 'what' and 'how' of actual implementation process

In respect to Table II, the number of important factors is different in different countries. In Malaysia, there are 8 important quality factors, while there are 1, 9, and 12 important factors in Palestine, Saudi Arabia and Kuwait respectively. In the Kuwaiti context, the number of important quality factors is the highest. Qualitatively, in the Kuwaiti study, Q8, Q10, Q11, Q13, Q14, Q17, Q20, Q21, Q22, Q24, Q26, Q29 were all found to be important factors. However, in Palestine, Q5, Q10, Q11, Q14, Q17, Q18, Q22, Q23, Q24, Q26, Q29 emerged as important. In Saudi Arabia, the situation is slightly different. Only 9 factors were empirically tested as important (Q10, Q11, Q14, Q17, Q18, Q22, Q26, Q28, Q29).

In so far as minor factors are concerned, The Kuwaiti study highlighted that there are no minor factors. The Malaysian context was similar. Only in Palestine and Saudi Arabia revealed the presence of minor factors. We should not over-emphasise this finding. The significance is not as big as we expect. This may be due to many factors: statistical error, wrong filing, mistakes in calculation, and interviewees' different responses. However, interestingly, both Palestine and Saudi Arabia have shown the same minor quality factor-that is, Q13. The reason for this is not very clear, but this factor is about employees' union support of the organisation's quality initiatives. Tsang and Antony (2001) have suggested an interesting point: the successful multinational corporation is one in which operating personnel and executives alike encounter appreciation and encouragement for what they are and what they can become.

4.2 Comparison of Identified Critical Quality Factors (CQFs)

It is a very interesting task to compare the CQFs between countries because it may show us the different organisational practice and emphasis in different cultures and countries. Havaleschka (1999) and Mann (2000) do both agree with this point. CQFs. We have also demonstrated the different number of CQFs in the 4 countries analysed. There are 22 in Malaysia, 19 in Palestine, 21 in Saudi Arabia and 19 in Kuwait. Malaysia has the most CQFs, while Kuwait and Palestine have the fewest. Saudi Arabia is in the middle. Harris and Ogbonna (2001) argue that none of these TQM enablers can guarantee better results.

Regarding the common factors, there are 13 CQFs in common: Q1, Q2, Q3, Q4, Q6, Q7, Q9, Q15, Q16, Q19, Q25, Q30, Q31. These common factors may tell us that these factors are cross-country and carry similar weight of significance in TQM implementation. Among the common factors identified, the first two are about the role of senior executives – Q1 is about their active responsibility for evaluation, and Q2, their commitment to quality and customer satisfaction is highlighted. Vision and goal are the core idea in Q3, Q4 and Q9. Q6 is about effective top-down and bottom-up communication. These results have been summarised in Table III.

	Malaysia (1996)	Palestine (2000)	Saudi Arabia (2002)	Kuwait (2003)
Important	Q5,Q10,Q13, Q21,Q24,Q26, Q27,Q28,Q29 (n=9)	Q5,Q10,Q11, Q14,Q17,Q18, Q22,Q23,Q24, Q26,Q29 (n=11)	Q10,Q11,Q14,Q17, Q18,Q22,Q26,Q28, Q29 (n=9)	Q8,Q10,Q11,Q1 3, Q14,Q17,Q20,Q 21, Q22,Q24,Q26,Q 29 (n=12)

	Malaysia (1996)	Palestine (2000)	Saudi Arabia (2002)	Kuwait (2003)
Minor		Q13 (n=1)	Q13 (n=1)	

	Malaysia (1996)	Palestine (2000)	Saudi (2002)	Kuwait (2003)	Common Factors
1	Q1	Q1	Q1	Q1	Q1
2	Q2	Q2	Q2	Q2	Q2
3	Q3	Q3	Q3	Q3	Q3
4	Q4	Q4	Q4	Q4	Q4
5	Q6	Q6	Q5	Q5	Q6
6	Q7	Q7	Q6	Q6	Q7
7	Q8	Q8	Q7	Q7	Q9
8	Q9	Q9	Q8	Q9	Q15
9	Q11	Q12	Q9	Q12	Q16
10	Q12	Q15	Q10	Q15	Q19
11	Q14	Q16	Q15	Q16	Q25
12	Q15	Q19	Q16	Q18	Q30
13	Q16	Q20	Q19	Q19	Q31
14	Q17	Q21	Q20	Q23	
15	Q18	Q25	Q21	Q25	
16	Q19	Q27	Q23	Q27	
17	Q20	Q28	Q24	Q28	
18	Q22	Q30	Q25	Q30	
19	Q23	Q31	Q27	Q31	
20	Q25		Q30		
21	Q30		Q31		
22	Q31				

Table III: Comparison of identified critical quality factors

Q15 and Q16 are both concerned with the training for employees, with different emphasis. The former is to improve interactive skills, such as communication skills, effective meeting skills, empowerment and leadership skills, and the latter is concerned with problem identification and solving skills. This point is also highlighted in the Antonacopoulou (2000) research on the concept of 'learning organisation'.

The next two points are system reviewer and analysis and cost of quality process to track network, waste, rejects and for continuous improvement. The last two points are more concerned with customers' satisfaction and comprehensive identification of customer needs. They are both customer-related and they are all common to these four researches in different countries. As Gunasekaran et al. (2001) have already mentioned: "Organisations are challenged to create demand for their products and services through outstanding customer support".

The most interesting finding from the comparison is that there is no factor, which can only be found in Kuwait. This is very different from the Malaysia, Palestine and Saudi Arabia studies. They all found some factors, which are only specific to their geographical contexts. The reason we may suggest is that there are already 3 similar researches, which have been conducted, and it is getting more difficult to find any special, exclusive factor in Kuwait.

4.3 Comparison of Unidentified Critical Factors

Apart from the identified factors, we need to discuss the unidentified factors, because they may give us an idea of how different cultural practices may affect the different performance of TQM in different countries.

Table IV suggests that Kuwait has two unidentified factors, which cannot be found in the other three researches. These two factors are Q8 and Q20. The first one is: 'the entire organisation understands that each individual and each process has internal customers and suppliers', and the second is: 'Problem-solving and continuous improvement processes, based on facts and systematic analysis'. They are particularly interesting in the Kuwaiti context, and only Kuwait has these unidentified factors. This may be explained by Kuwaiti culture, in the sense that not the entire organisation understands that each individual and each process has internal customers and suppliers (Denison, 1996; Reichers and Schneider, 1990; Zeitz et al, 1997). At the same time, we can also argue that problem-solving and continuous improvement processes are not commonly based on facts and systematic analysis.

We also see there are several common unidentified factors between these four countries. They are: Q13, Q26, and Q29. Q13 covers: employees' union support of the organisation's quality initiatives. Q26 suggests: zero defects as the quality performance standard. Q29 reflects: long-term relationship and working partnership with key suppliers.

	Malaysia (1996)	Palestine (2000)	Saudi Arabia (2002)	Kuwait (2003)	Common Factors
1	Q5	Q5	Q11	Q8	Q13
2	Q10	Q10	Q12	Q10	Q26
3	Q13	Q11	Q13	Q11	Q29
4	Q21	Q13	Q14	Q13	
5	Q24	Q14	Q17	Q14	
6	Q26	Q17	Q18	Q17	
7	Q27	Q18	Q22	Q20	
8	Q28	Q22	Q26	Q21	
9	Q29	Q23	Q28	Q24	
10		Q24	Q29	Q26	
11		Q26		Q29	
12		Q29			

Table IV: Comparison of Unidentified Critical Factors

It is difficult to explain why these three factors are both common to unidentified factors. This may be a pure coincidence or they are not important to all these four countries. One of the strongest explanations is culture. Malaysia, Palestine, Saudi Arabia and Kuwait are both Muslim countries. They believe in the same god, and share similar cultural and religious backgrounds. The cultural similarities may explain why these three factors are found common in these countries. Indeed, one might argue that the essence of TQM is culture change and that TQM practices are merely tools for cultural transformation (Flood, 1993; Zeitz et al., 1997). The answer to this puzzle depends on what is meant by organisational culture. In our view, culture consists of the beliefs, values, and underlying assumptions supporting behavioural patterns and artefacts (cf. Ott, 1989; Schein, 1992; Zeitz et al., 1997).

Regarding the number of unidentified factors, Palestine has 12, which are the top among these four countries. The research in Kuwait ranks second with 11 unidentified factors. Saudi Arabia has 10. Regarding the fewest numbers of unidentified critical factors, Malaysia has only 9.

An organisation's success or failure then depends on the relevance of these beliefs to the current opportunities and limitations confronting the organisation (Bass and Avolio, 1993; Dellana and Hauser, 1999). The variations cannot simply be explained by the face values. The plausible explanation may be the inclusiveness of TQM in each country. In Malaysia, only 9 unidentified factors are found. This may be because Malaysia has the highest absorption power, which keeps the unidentified critical factors the lowest. Reichers and Schneider (1990) and Zeitz et al. (1997) argues that this aversion to such general dimensions stems from the anthropological roots of culture studies, which prefer idiographic (emic) methodologies to nomothetic (etic), point on which Denison (1996) and Zeitz et al. (1997) elaborate.

SUMMARY

This paper discussed four different studies about TQM implementation in different places, Malaysia, Palestine, Saudi Arabia and Kuwait. Regarding the organisation breakdown, different studies have different size, business categories and principal ownerships. There are 31 critical factors in total, as identified by the original study conducted by Thiagarajan (1996) in Malaysia. Similar factors were identified in various geographical contexts and others made a distinctive difference between the various studies.

It is proposed that cultural factors may play a role in determining why and how some of the critical factors are identified. The process of selecting how TQM should be implemented will partly explain the success of its implementation. Leadership in these four studies has demonstrated a rather different picture. For example, in Malaysia, leaders help to build energy, but in Palestine, leadership suggests a clear belief in the benefits of TQM. In Saudi Arabia, the development of steering committees may help, but in Kuwait, the appointment of a TQM support manager may be more effective. Regarding internal stakeholders, these four studies have shown rather interesting patterns. In Malaysia, key employees are suggested to be informed but in Palestine and Saudi Arabia, training employees for interactive skills is more important. In Kuwait, the scenario is that there should be a need to allay middle management anxiety. There is no dispute about the importance of customer-driven process, but the emphasis may be different. In Malaysia, the concept of internal customer-supplier relationship is highlighted, while in Palestine, they suggest to identify the customers' needs first. In Saudi Arabia, a performance measurement system is more obvious, while in Kuwait, there is encouragement to deploy resources around major processes. Finally, regarding continuous improvement, Malaysia is more encouraging in introducing tools and techniques as a self-assessment tool to complement the framework. In Palestine, teamwork is promoted, and measuring customer satisfaction is recommended. In Saudi Arabia, problem-solving decisions are highlighted, and in Kuwait, continuous improvement is emphasised.

References

Oakland J. S. [2000]. "Total quality management – Text with cases", 2nd Edition, Butterworth-Heinemann

Thiagaran T. and Zairi M. [1997]. "A review of total quality management in practice: understanding the fundamentals through examples of best practice applications Part 1", The TQM Magazine, vol. 9 no. 4, pp. 270-286.

Cravens D. Piercy N. and Prentice A. [2000]. "Developing market-driven product strategies", Journal of Product and Brand Management, vol. 9 no. 6, pp.369-388

Zink K. J. [1995]. 'Total quality management and people management", In Kanji, G. K. (ed.) Total Quality Management. Proceedings, First world congress, London: Chapman & Hill

Thiagaran, T. and Zairi, M. (1998) An Empirical Analysis of critical factors of TQM: A proposed tool for self-assessment and benchmarking purposes'. Benchmarking for Quality Management and Technology. Vol.5, No.4, pp.291-303.

Sekaran, V. (2003) Research methods for business: A skill building. 4th ed. Wiley

Thiagaragan, T. (1996) An empirical study of total quality management (TQM) in Malaysia: A proposed framework of generic application'. Ph.D thesis. University of Bradford

Baidoun, S. (2003) 'An empirical study of critical factors of TQM in Palestinian organisations', Logistics Information Management. Vol.16, No.2, pp.156-171

Al-Nofal, A. and Zairi, M. (2002a) 'Sustainable excellence through quality transformations: an analytical review of winners of quality awards and conceptual framework of research construct'. Proceedings. 7th International Conference on ISO 9000 and TQM. Place: city campus, RMIT University, Melbourne, 2-4 April.

Al-Nofal, A. and Zairi, M. (2002b) 'Best practices and sustainable TQM implementation'. Proceedings. 7th World Congress for Total Quality Management: Business Excellence: Make it happen, Verona, Italy. 25-27 June.

Omaim, N. (2002) 'An empirical investigation of total quality management implementation in the Kingdom of Saudi Arabia'. Ph.D thesis. University of Bradford

Hackett, M. and Spurgeon, P. (1998) 'Developing our leaders in the future'. Health Manpower Management, Vol. 24, No.5, pp.170-177

Bohan, G. (1998) 'Whatever Happened to TQM? Or, how a good strategy got a bad reputation'. National Productivity Review, Vol.17, No.4, pp.13-16

Tsang, J. and Anthony, J. (2001) 'Total quality management in UK service organisations: some key findings from a survey'. Managing Service Quality, Vol.11, No.2, pp.132 -141.

Havaleschka, F. (1999) 'Personality and leadership: a benchmark study of success and failure'. Leadership and Organisation Development Journal, Vol.20, No.3, pp.114-132.

Harris, L. and Ogbanna, E. (2001) 'Leadership style and market orientation: an empirical study'. European Journal of Marketing, Vol. 35, No. 5, pp.744-764.

Mann, R. S. (1992) The development of a framework to assist in the implementation of TQM. Ph.D thesis: University of Liverpool.

Antonacopoulou, E. P. (2000) 'Reconnecting education, development and training through learning: a holographic perspective' Education + Training, Vol.42, No.4/5, pp.255-264.

Gunasekaran, A., Patel, C. and Tirtiroglu, E. (2001), 'Performance measures and metrics in a supply chain environment'. International Journal of Operations & Production Management, Vol.21, No.1/2, pp.71-87.

Denison, D. R. (1996) 'What is the difference between organisational culture and organisational climate? A native's point of view on a decade of paradigm wars'. Academy of Management Review, Vol. 21, No.3, pp.619-654.

Reichers, A. E. and Schneider, B. (1990) 'Climate and culture: An evolution of constructs'. In Schneider, B. (ed.) Organisational climate and culture (pp.5-39). San Francisco: Jossey-Bass.

Zietz, G, Johannesson, R and Ritchie, J. E. Jr. (1997) 'An employee survey measuring total quality management practices and culture: Development and validation'. Group & Organisation Management. Vol.22, No.4, pp.414-444.

Flood, R. L. (1993) Beyond TQM. Chichester, UK: Wiley.

Schein, E. H. (1992) Organisational culture and leadership. San Francisco: Jossey-Bass.

Ott, J. S. (1989) The organisational culture perspective. Chicago: Dorsey.

Bass, B. M., and Avolio, B. J. (1993). Transformational Leadership and Organisational Culture. Place: Pennsylvania, Publisher public admistration quarterly, Vol.17, No.1, pp.112-121.

Dellana, A. and Hauser, R. D. (1999) 'Toward defining the quality culture'. Engineering Management Journal, Vol.11, No.11, pp.11-15

> *Intrinsic is the belief that quality does not happen by accident, it must be Planned!*
>
> **- Joseph Juran**

Total Quality Management

Compiled and Edited by
Professor Mohamed Zairi
SABIC Chair for Best Practice Management
Head of the European Centre for TQM

Dr. Yasar Jarrar
Business Process Management
European Centre for TQM

In association with
Dr. John Peters
MCB University Press

First Published in

© MCB University Press and
the European Centre for
Total Quality Management

Creating a culture of total quality management

Culture in its simplest form can be described as It the way things are done, in particular organisational context". Most writers agree that culture is composed of values, expectations, behaviour, attitudes and norms. No two organisations are the same, nor are their respective cultures similar.

Culture has been described in many ways, with many distinct attributes and by many different writers. Whitehill (1991), for instance, describes culture as follows:

> We are immersed in a sea. It is warm, comfortable, supporting and protecting. Most of us float comfortably in the water; some bob about catching glimpses of different lands from time to time; a few emerge from the water entirely. The sea is our culture.

As far as the link between TQM and culture is concerned, there is a total inter-dependency between the two. TQM can help shape an organisational culture; existing culture, on the other hand, can facilitate the way TQM can be effectively implemented. Which comes first is of course the key question (the "chicken and egg" scenario). Most people believe that having the right culture in place is a pre-requisite for introducing TQM. This may not necessarily be true; culture can be a "soft" outcome from pausing on the "hard" necessities of TQM. In fact most TQM gurus acknowledge the importance of developing the right culture for benefiting from TQM:

- Crosby, for instance, as early as 1979 has reported that for a quality improvement strategy to succeed, it has to be supported by a culture change;

- Crosby did further stress the importance of focusing on values to what he refers to as the "tolerance level" of management, which brings about the right performance responses from workers (Crosby, 1967,1979).

- Feigenbaum, on the other hand, believes that the evolution of organisational quality values depends very much on the quality policy of the organisation (Feigenbaum, 1961).

- Other gurus, like Juran for instance, have argued that, in addition to values and policy, having the right structure will enhance team work, project management, employee involvement and their effective participation in improvement initiatives (Juran, 1951).

Why should culture matter in the context of modern competitiveness?

- Having the right culture can affect responses to world markets by affecting the overall organisational performance.

- The formulation and effective deployment of corporate strategy depends very much on whether enough focus is given to the inherent corporate culture.

- Organisational structure is a shaper of culture and can affect positively or negatively aspects of communication, interaction, effectiveness in synergising through the way roles and responsibilities are defined.

- Having the right culture can help an organisation move from being product-oriented to being customer-oriented.

- Culture if positively nudged can act as a precursor to change and continuous improvement.

On the other hand, culture could be an invisible barrier to change. Creating a culture which is TQ based does therefore mean that:

- the prerequisites are related more to senior management commitment to change than to having the right climate in the first place.

- culture of TQM needs to be shaped rather than grabbed by the "horns". Culture is a "soft" outcome; it depends on the right values to be inculcated, the right policy, the right structure, the right systems, the right people and the right skills.

An effective TQ-based culture will very much depend on effort, energy, belief and sustainable vision and dedication. Culture cannot be changed or developed rapidly, nor can it be totally transferable. Some people refer to a process called "acculturation".

Essentially, it has to be recognised that a TQ-based culture is synonymous with the following:

- culture comes from the brain rather than the genes;
- culture is a continuous process and tends to evolve throughout the lifetime of individuals;
- culture can be shared and can be communicated and reflected in groups.

Professor Mohamed Zairi
SABIC Professor of Best Practice Management
University of Bradford

References

Crosby, P.B. (1967), *Cutting the Cost of Quality: The Defect Prevention Workbook for Managers,* Industrial Education Institute, USA

Crosby, P.B. (1979), *Quality Is Free,* McGraw-Hill Book Company, New York, USA.

Feigenbaum, A.V. (1961), *Total Quality Control,* McGraw-Hill, London, UK.

Juran,J.M. (1951), *Quality Control Handbook,* McGraw-Hill, USA.

Whitehill, A.M. (1991*), Japanese Management - Traditions and Transition,* Routledge, London, UK.

Sustaining TQM: A synthesis of literature and proposed research framework

Abstract

Mohd Ashari Idris and Mohamed Zairi

ECTQM, University of Bradford School of Management, UK

As the new millennium progresses, TQM is expected to mature into a sustainability phase to support a universal business strategy. Its critical success factors will vary, in order to accommodate changes in the environment where the firms operate. Despite the fact that TQM initiatives have been recognised by many organisations as capable of transforming the quality culture and producing competitiveness, new initiatives or their improved versions are being suggested to retain TQM vigour and its sustainability. This has called for a continuous discourse and the development of a framework for sustaining TQM, which is the object of this paper.

The paper first traces the development of the concept of sustainability, leading to the conception of sustainable TQM. A framework of proposed research is presented drawing from literature on quality orientation, performance measurement, change management, and related organisational theories. Strategies for effectively sustaining TQM implementation are highlighted. A set of theoretical enablers and inhibitors for sustaining TQM are discussed, and a research model is proposed. From the model, various scenarios are constructed, and research propositions are deduced. Finally, a methodology for an empirical stage of research is offered.

Correspondence

M. A. Idris, PhD
ECTQM, University of Bradford School of Management
Emm Lane, BD9 4JL, Bradford, West Yorkshire, UK.
Tel: 01274-234312 and fax: 01274 -234311,
email: ashariaz @yahoo.co.uk

1. Introduction

Every twenty years in four decades, quality management has entered a new era (Feigenbaum, 1956), each of them more advanced and more strategic (Garvin, 1988; Dahlgaard, 1999), thus until this millennium TQM had survived the test of time as a corporate philosophy. However, will it sustain as a dominant logic of business corporate strategy in the future? This question, among the academics and practitioners, remains not fully answered by the past literature. Although there has been anecdotal and empirical evidence that supports TQM as a universal business strategy; the intensity of effective implementation of its success factors brings operational excellence, but the changing business orientation poses a challenge to TQM as a sustainable strategy for competitiveness.

A limited research had assessed at what levels of quality conditions that quality-performance relationship exists (Ismail and Hashmi, 1999). Despite Dale's (1996) positioning approach implied a longitudinal benchmark, but longitudinal research on conditions of TQM sustainability and its impact on long-term performance remain in paucity.

This paper tries to bridge the literature gap in quality orientation, and hence shed some light on the conditions for TQM sustainability in view of the changing critical factors over time as the new global business landscape is being created. The framework here is synthesised from the review of TQM theory, evolutions, and empirical studies in different economies. It then proposes research constructs and hypotheses for an empirical stage of study.

2. Literature review

Quality management as a managerial discourse (Witcher, 1994) is a moving paradigm (Aune, 1998; Dervitsiosis, 2000). Its evolutionary phases are discussed by many authors (Garvin, 1988; Kanji and Asher, 1993; Dale, 1994; Zairi, 1996; Dahlgaard, 1999) in reflecting continuous change in its philosophical ideas from functional-focus, such as inspection, to external-emphasis, such as market-based orientation (Gale, 1994; Gummesson, 1998; Idris, 2000). Building on these literatures, each era of quality management has its corresponding features reflecting the level of adoption by the industry in different economies. In illustrating the above transformational process, the ISO 9000:1987 for example, has been conceived to be equivalent to the early Japanese total quality control (TQC) (Akao, 1991; Ishikawa, 1985), forming a subset of company-wide quality control (Sullivan, 1986). Under the state of constant change, quality practices emanating from ISO 9000 aptly serve only as guidelines describing a minimal quality system (O'Connor, 1995), although the new ISO 9001:2000 has included customer satisfaction assurance over and above product quality assurance (Conti, 1999). Indeed, when more intense quality programmes are initiated and build-up of total quality approaching a maturity possibility for TQM success increases (Ahire, 1996; Zairi, 1996). This might improve the corresponding operational and corporate performance as a result of greater accumulation of enablers for progress.

According to Sullivan (1986), the build-up of total quality occurs in stages. This is partly because of limited roles played by the gatekeepers, and gradual acceptance by the organisational members (Zbaracki, 1998) after TQM being brought into a company. Therefore in each era, industry, or even within an organisation, the levels of adoption of quality management varies (Hackman and Wagemen, 1995; Haris 1995; Dale, 1996) depending on need and awareness of benefits of TQM. Some are driven by internal and external "push factors" such as competition and legislation.

On deduction, one could separate the emphasis of adoption by; hard and soft elements (Oakland and Porter, 1994), behavioural and technical (Myers and Ashkenas, 1993; Zbaracki, 1998; Baidoun, 2001), philosophical and operational (Deming, 1994, 1982), effectiveness and competitiveness (Zairi and Leonard, 1994; Zairi 1996), normative and rational (Giroux, 1998), operational excellence and strategic positioning (Porter, 1996), inside-out and outside-in views (Day, 1994; Webster, 1994; Gummesson, 1998), and internal-focus and customer-focus (Shiba et al., 1993; Day, 1994). These emphases have their corresponding industry conditions (Ansof, 1979; Webster 1988; Treacy and Wiersema, 1993; Mohr-Jackson, 1998; Idris, 2000), and to excel, firms should steer their emphasis to cope with the environmental forces. The coping process is the effort to reduce uncertainty in the operations and marketing, thus firms need to learn continuously about internal and external variables that have a strategic link to success. For example, Senge (1995) suggested that a TQM firm could be transformed into a learning organisation when all the 'old' and new seven tools of quality are pervasively used to drive change and embed the learning culture.

Some also suggested a higher order approach for TQM theory building (Idris, 2000). His approach, emphasising the learning-control dimension (Sitkin et al., 1994) and a content-process approach (Reed et al., 1996) legitimises the quality orientation as a continuum of adoption of quality principles and practices to create sustainable competitiveness. Each phase of orientation is best characterised by fundamental ideas or principles, core values or intervening principles (Svensson and Klefsjo, 2000), operating principles, and programmes and tools. For simplicity, this continuum can be reduced to converge into principle-practice categories (Dean and Bowen, 1994; Deming, 1994; Spencer, 1994; Hackman and Wageman, 1995; Hill and Wilkinson, 1995, Boaden, 1997), so as the practices truly reflect the extended principles of quality. When this linkage exists, firms can only gauge to measure real effectiveness, such as by applying scoring by self-assessment models.

Because of the diversity and compelling perspectives of quality management, achieving a consensual definition is difficult (Boaden, 1997), and making principle-practice categories hazy and not fully understood (Dean and Bowen, 1994; Grant et al., 1994; Witcher, 1994). As a consequence, many paradoxes emerge in its implementation (Thompson, 1998), which when solved and matched with the moving industry landscape can create organisational effectiveness (March, 1991; Sitkin et al., 1994; Reed et al., 1996). These underlie the calls for more empirical research to clarify how the TQM evolutionary path is related to critical success conditions (CSC) within an economic sector, industry, and era. In other words, CSC are relevant quality strategies for effectiveness and competitiveness, which are related but have a sequential event and are firm-specific. With more empirical proofs, an approach to sustainable quality strategy could be established. More needed is the longitudinal approach, because a snapshot design alone would fail to capture success conditions holistically.

2.1 Quality practices and competitiveness

Research has shown that there is strong positive correlation between quality practices and performance (Oakland et al., 1994; Flynn et al., 1995; Ahire, 1996; Hendricks and Singal, 1997; Idris, 2000) justifying that poor performance might result from practices at the lower orientation continuum (Dale, 1996; Ismail and Hashmi, 1999). It was argued that at a lower level, a company is more susceptible to poor performance and failure than at a much higher level of quality practices (Ismail and Hashmi, 1999). Also, matured TQM companies gain greater benefits from their quality programmes implementation (Ahire, 1996; Agus and Abdullah, 2000). Research has shown that a comprehensive rather than a piece-meal approach brings greater success (Flynn et al., 1995; Ahire 1996), particularly when the major concerns are directed at the contents elements which are tailored for specific sustainable performance factors within a firm (Reed et al., 1996; Idris, 2000).

Researchers have derived CSF (Flynn et al., 1995; Ahire et al., 1996; Black and Porter, 1996; Idris, 2000) spreading from manufacturing (Ahire, 1996, Ahire et al., 1996; Saraph et al., 1989; Agus and Abdullah, 2000), small and medium scale industries (Yusof and Aspinwall, 1999), higher education (Kanji et al., 1999), health care (Kunst and Lemmink, 2000), developing countries (Thiagarajan et al., 2001; Baidoun, 2001), non-Anglo-American (Chan et al., 2000). Collectively, these factors include all practices related to management commitment, education and training, feedback measurement, total employee involvement, empowerment, team-work, technological factors, customer satisfaction measurement, benchmarking, quality information and analysis, strategic quality planning, and supplier management. These main elements which represent the quality management models were further broken-down into their categories of quality initiatives, which can be self-assessed, such as in the MBQNA and European Excellence Models. On this basis, critical factors could be established by reviewing cases of quality award winners (McDonald et al., 2001).

Organisations could be classified according to the level of quality management practices (Dale, 1996). The varied intensity and diversity of practices made phases of transformational continuum (Bounds et al., 1994: Dale, 1998). It has been suggested that practices at a higher level on the continuum increase chances for greater competitiveness (MacDonald, 1993; Nadkarni, 1995; Ahire, 1996; Miyake et al., 1996), thus ascertaining TQM as an endless destiny to excellence. Agus and Abdullah (2000) confirmed that experienced TQM companies outperformed the short-term adopters. Award-winners in the USA outperform the control sample in operating income-based measures (Hendricks and Singal, 1997). Moreover, MBNQA winners realised performance benefits after only 5-10 years of its implementation (Nadkarni, 1995). High-performing hospitals in the USA exhibited significantly higher quality orientation than did the low-performing ones (Rapert and Babakus, 1996). All these suggest that more advanced quality practices have greater impact on organisational effectiveness, and hence improve managerial commitment to further strive for effective implementation. In other words, success breeds success.

Another stream of research has identified the level of orientation in terms of core quality management practices and supporting practices, and their impact on performance (Flynn et al., 1995; Idris, 2000). These researches were driven by the urge to drive competitive advantage through quality, hence the intensity of implementation of critical elements, and the comprehensiveness of the elements implemented determine failure or success in TQM. The third explanatory variable, the interaction between the critical elements, determines the level of synergy created that reinforced one another to provide support for creating value for the customer. The fourth contributory factor is the alignment of critical factors with the firm's corporate goal, which tend to overlap with each other or be subsumed by the appropriate critical elements, when quality orientation is already embedded as a core philosophy of the business.

2.2 Conception of Sustainable Excellence

To agree on success factors for each TQM paradigm, features of that paradigm need to be understood. When companies 'jump the paradigm curve' to higher quality orbit, a different set of characteristics becomes dominant. To generate conditions for sustainability, comprehensive literature review provided success factors, failure factors, change strategies, enablers and inhibitors, and their corresponding sets of organisational culture and climate, which become necessary for transformation to occur and be sustained. Having reviewed relevant literature, conceptual and empirical writings, a model of sustainable TQM-linking proposed constructs is presented. A methodology for the empirical stage is then proposed for advanced research.

For this, and foremost, the quality orientation is operationalised as a firm's quality initiatives at both strategic and operational levels, embraced as a corporate philosophy to affect its long-term performance. Sustainable TQM is therefore synonymous with continuous practices that create internal effectiveness and external competitiveness (Zairi, 1996). After all, good strategy is concerned with the structural evolution of the industry, as well as with the firm's own unique position within that industry (Porter, 1999).

Learning from strategic management literature, sustainable TQM exists for specific environmental conditions, firm-specifics, and will erode if not continuously renewed. From a cultural viewpoint, quality initiatives stay in vigour when they are embedded into the fabric of the day-to-day operations. Literature also suggests that sustainability is the product of efficiency and effectiveness in TQM implementation. This means that implementing the right critical factors efficiently is compulsory. In other words, sustainability is a cross-product between comprehensiveness of critical factors, because TQM is a systemic methodology, and intensity of implementation of critical elements (Ahire, 1996), because being efficient and effective are conditions for achieving operational excellence or best practice (Porter, 1999). Critical factors fall into a multi-tier model with the highest emphasis on leadership roles (Thiagarajan et al., 2001), consistent with the concept of transformational leadership as stressed by Deming (1993).

The issue of sustainability takes the centre stage of academic discussion at the beginning of the 21st century in disciplines such as sustainable development (Larson et al., 2000; Reinhardt, 2000), and quality orientation (Miles et al., 1995; Mohr-Jackson, 1998; Idris, 2000). Although the concept of sustainability in terms of quality initiatives is relatively of recent interest, its root had been long advocated by writers such as Deming (1982), through his "constancy of purpose" and "stability of society". However, much advanced debate progressed in the sustainable development discipline covering the various frameworks on how human needs could be satisfied without harming nature (Larson et al., 2000). In the context of sustainability, for example, the incorporation of environmentally aware stakeholders into the quality system has extended the ISO 9000 system to ISO9000: 2000 and ISO 14000.

The sustainable development framework, in a way, extends the standard TQM model to include the principles of sustainability (Larson et al., 2000), which brings associated consequences in terms of role of customers, suppliers, regulatory bodies and the publics in the concept of TQM. This captures stakeholders' interest in quality initiatives. Thousands of organisations, which includes Xerox, and AT&T in the USA and Electrolux in Europe have pioneered some of these frameworks. There has been a lack of reported cases in other parts of the world, though the ISO 14000 has been adopted in many countries. For example, in 1998, ISO 14000 was formalised in Malaysia, and EMAS programmes were adopted around the same period.

2.3 Conception of TQM sustainability

Within sustainable development, sustainability is defined as development that meets the needs of the present without compromising the ability of future generations to meet their own needs (Larson et al., 2000). Within the TQM lexicon, there has been no agreed meaning of sustainable TQM. Conceptually, TQM creates transitional states of excellence that deliver effective performance and, in turn, sustainable competitiveness. This implies that sustainable TQM precedes sustainable competitiveness.

The parallel term, business excellence, emphasises the aspect of competitiveness enhancement (Savolainen, 1997; 2000), although the use of excellence to replace quality in EFQA was heavily criticised by Dale et al. (2001), fearing the shift might affirm TQM as a fad. In terms of matrices, achieving 750 points or higher in EFQM assessment indicates business excellence (Dahlgaard et al., 1998). In a subsequent article, Dahlgaard et al., (1999) proposed a '4P' definition of business excellence related to people, partnership, process and product, which they claim has gained a wider acceptance and to closely consistent with the European model of Excellence.

TQM sustainability could be viewed from effectiveness of TQM implementation that is based on prescriptive critical factors, and effectiveness of critical factors that generate sustainable excellence. In addition to a pioneering work by Idris (2000), the work of Kunst and Lemmink (2000), in comparing between high and low hospital performance, concluded that there are different explanatory variables for progress in TQM implementation and for business performance.

Sustainable performance is a multi-dimensional concept, incorporating a balanced measurement of items of direct influence on competitive advantage, and thus the concept is contingent on sustainable environmental factors. It is an approach to measuring output performance against employed strategy from a long-term horizon. This two-stage (effectiveness-competitiveness) relationship suggests two types of critical factors exist, but at consecutive levels or perhaps integrative as shown in Figure 1. This two-stage analysis represents a TQM content-process approach to delineating critical factors for sustainable performance (Flynn et al., 1995; Reed et al., 1996; Idris, 2000).

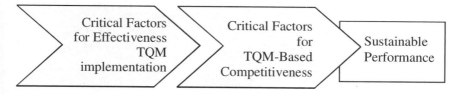

Figure 1: Critical Factors for TQM Implementation and Competitiveness

In this paper, we adopt the concept of TQM life-path (TQMLP) in order to investigate the conditions for TQM sustainability. The evolutionary path of quality management began in the early 1990s (Feigenbaum, 1956), incorporating primarily changes in managerial style (Deming, 1993) which can be symbolised by Introduction, Growth, Maturity, and Sustainability stage (IGMS). Adopting the field-force technique delineates the comprehensive enablers and inhibitors for each stage of TQM life-path.

The introduction stage can be equated to the inspection and quality control phase. The growth begins with adsorption of SPC and employee involvement to transform early stage quality management to TQC. This is later followed by wider applications of the concept of quality in service and thus brings the service quality era into TQM. The maturity stage is characterised by application of three levels of quality tools, including initial benchmarking and reengineering, making the concept of process management a common language in most organisations. This era was rampant in the early 1990s. In late 1990s, TQM began to absorb newer concepts, such as learning organisation and market orientation. As a result, today's TQM or modern quality management is an integrated improvement framework for sustainable performance. The integrated TQM benefits from the synergies of multiple improvement approaches and cost effectiveness in their concurrent implementation. The synergy mapping of TQM implementation is proposed in Figure 2.

Reliance /Comprehensiveness of Critical Factors

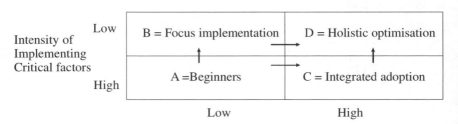

Figure 2: Synergy mapping of TQM strategy

Different strategies are usable to move from one stage to the next. Functional excellence could be achieved when a firm intensively improved any element of its critical success factors, such as design or delivery as appropriate. In order to move into a state of sustainable excellence, a firm might use multiple approaches to quality management, including reengineering and organisational learning. This is possible because history has shown that quality management has accommodated continuously to circumstances, and hence adopted new methods and tools (Dahlgaard, 1999).

The intensity of a TQM success factor should be assessed in terms of its immediate consequences, such as learning rate, innovation of new product or process, best practice goals achieved, and sustained continuous improvement culture in general. On the other hand, the comprehensiveness scale includes nature and degree of synergy achieved, integration of quality principles, and matching of critical factors with the strategic objectives of the firm. Figure 4 illustrates strategic choice of improvement approaches under the TQM umbrella using Ansof's (1979) product market matrix concept.

Scope of market definition / market orientation

	Current	New
Current	Continuous Improvement	Market-Oriented Best Practice
New	Technological-Oriented Innovation Best Practice	Radical Reengineering and Path-breaking approaches

Scope of Product / Technology

Figure 3: Strategic implementation of improvement approaches

2.4 TQM success and failure

Many authors (e.g. Harari, 1997; Gurnani, 1999) have discussed the success and failure of TQM implementation and proposed what constitute criteria for effective TQM. Critical success factors are those elements based on quality principles that should be present either as a tool, programmes or cultural, and infrastructures that influence the implementation of quality initiatives at the workplace (Zairi and Leonard, 1994). From these ad hoc definitions, organisational effectiveness it is thought, could be achieved by matching process performance with strategic goals - selecting critical processes that add value to business excellence (Dervitsiotis, 1999). Assessment of total performance therefore must rely on critical success factors.

Research has shown that reasons for TQM failure are numerous. Among them are lack of relevant measures for, or understated, cost of quality (Lakshmi and Roa 1996), poor initial planning, higher employee turnover, cultural difference between the management team (Gurnani, 1999), top management personality and preferences, resistance to change, and TQM environment (Krumwiede and Lavelle, 2000). These factors vary from company to company, and there has been no focused study done on the criticality of failure factors. However, generally they could be grouped as poor implementation rather than flaws in TQM contents (Zairi, 1996; Thiagarajan et al., 2001). Based on the 'important factor' lists, as well as relevant literature, a scenario for a quality paradigm could be constructed.

The each era's paradigms comprise factors such as change strategy, evolution of soft and hard elements, and critical success factors, emerging performance improvement strategies that influence adoption of TQM, such as re-engineering, benchmarking, high performance organisation, and trends in measurement.

2.5 Strategies for Sustainable TQM

The rise and fall of strategic movements such as strategic planning (Webster, 1988), BCG's experience-curve-effect, incremental improvement, downsizing and restructuring (Merrifield and Mitchell, 2000), and perhaps reengineering and 'Traditional TQM' sum up that those contemporary emphases, once sufficient to yield short-term competitiveness, are now no longer capable to shield that advantage from competitive pressure in the e-knowledge world. Firms need a holistic review and continuous innovation of strategy to match a their resources to the requirements of the future-oriented marketplace (Hamel and Prahalad, 1994), which involves making a tough choice about what you will do and what you will not (Porter, 1999).

In terms of TQM sustainability, making TQM a fabric of how a business is run is paramount to continuous success. Despite research having shown positive linkage between TQM and bottom line (Oakland et al., 1994), each individual organisation must understand how quality processes are linked to performance measures or accountability of their organisation. This includes understanding of financial-based performance and customer-based performance measure.

Holistic TQM implementation means achieving balance between conformance to customer satisfaction and internal process improvement, without losing flexibility and creativity in business improvement. Leverage quality initiatives and knowledge to create organisational agility, could enable firms to customise their mass customising strategies (Zairi, 2001). It is imperative that firms keep close to customers and partners with customers to track customers' value shifts (Woodruff, 1997; Day, 1998). This customer intimacy allows quick response to customer needs in a differentiated and co-ordinated way - differentiates customers in terms of the product they prefer, and the way they wish to acquire and experience the products.

Organisation at the paradigm edge should create an internal learning web to unite a dispersed workforce, promote unity of mental model by defining quality right, to quickly remove negative quality gaps, and create positive quality to stimulate customers (Zairi and Leonard, 1994; Kondo 2001). In the words of Porter (1999), "Companies must build advantages rather than just eliminate disadvantages."

Firm should optimise knowledge management (see Wayland and Cole, 1997) and capatalise on new research findings (Marrifield and Mitchel, 2000) or linking innovation as an outcome of quality initiatives (Nowak, 1997). For example, IP Malaysia utilises innovation to drive corporate growth, industry growth, and generate percentage of income stream from new products, and plans "phased-innovation". The company also uses global benchmarking study to set up path-breaking innovation (Idris, 2000).

There has been a continuous emphasis placed on creating superior skills and retaining employees (Hall, 1992; Pfeffer, 1994; Lawler, 2000) and optimising employee learning by sharing internal quality information and external customer information. Lawler (2000) suggested firms shifting a managerial culture to managing by incentives, to foster 'excellence employees' by tying incentives to employee contribution towards value creation. Luthans and Sommer (2000) urge that firms utilise high performance work practices (HPWP) to increase competitiveness by reducing employee turnover and increasing organisational effectiveness.

An organisation in search of sustainability should synergise efforts for internal quality initiatives and market-based initiatives (Idris, 2000). Initial research pointed to the emphasis on optimising TQM contents: reliability, processes, design, and market advantage, while simultaneously striving to be overall market-oriented. Over-relying on a specific component of market-oriented strategy, such as customer-oriented or competitor-oriented alone, could prove disastrous (Narver and Slater, 1990; Slater and Narver, 1993), because great strategies are based on lasting value propositions not transient value shifts (Porter, 1999). However, a specific quality-performance link is company-specific, therefore it is imperative that firms align their corporate goals with quality strategies to speeding up business growth. Subsequently, they should converge to synergism the conditions for growth into visible links of strategy-performance routes to sustainability.

2.6 Measuring TQM sustainability

One way of measuring performance is by meshing short-term and long-term financial and customer-based measures into an index of sustainable performance (Idris, 2000). The balanced scorecard approach permitted this where indicators could be tailored to match the proceeding strategies adopted by a firm (Kaplan and Norton, 1996). As a generic model, we propose the following measures to gauge sustainability of performance outcomes, which can be linked to individual critical factors of TQM implementation.

Financial measures:

- Relative profitability
- Relative sales growth
- Relative return on assets
- Relative market share

Customer measures

- Relative customer retention
- Relative corporate image
- Relative new products' success rate

212

A performance measure measures the effectiveness of a specific quality improvement initiative. Comprehensive indicators should provide holistic assessment of the strength, continuity, and sustainability of the total quality. The "Business Balanced Scorecard Approach" which is an overall method of tracking performance focuses on both the qualitative and quantitative measures which are the main ethos of performance measurement.

2.7 Enabling Conditions and Inhibitors to Sustainability

Enablers and inhibitors influence progress. Enablers are positive forces that impede the speed of positive progress, whereas inhibitors are negative forces that hamper the adoption of the concept, hence causing the delay of positive progress which could also result in diminishing effort on the initiatives. Enablers and inhibitors here refer to organisational antecedents such as climate, management support, and leadership style. Inhibitors are negative forces but not limited to the negatives of enablers, and these include TQM failure factors, as discussed in earlier part of this paper.

Sustainability of TQM is also about getting rid of inhibitors. Many of these inhibitors work the opposite way to the success factors. Inhibitors must be overcome or completely removed in order to facilitate the adoption of the concept, and to ensure quality initiatives can be successfully implemented. The major factors include lack of motivation for knowledge-sharing, lack of management support in quality programmes, under-estimate of the time-frame it requires for TQM to bear fruits, lack of total involvement in quality initiatives, and a host of factors related to structure, and organisational system.

2.8 Proposed model of TQM Sustainability

Any organisation could be placed on continuum of sustainability as implied by sustainability model shown in Figure 5, which links the goals, drives, and strategies and performance of TQM initiatives.

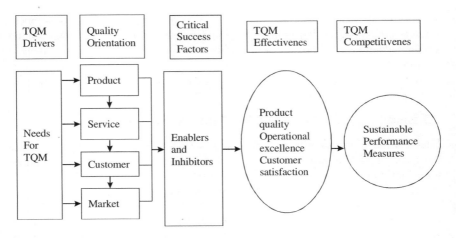

Figure 5: Model of Sustainable TQM and Performance

2.8.1 Description of model

The model is based on the following assumptions:

- TQM is an integrative and holistic approach for analysing the current status of continuous improvement within an organisation.

- TQM is not a "quick fix", and thus has to be approached from a long-term perspective.

- To begin the journey using this quality process to create competitive advantage requires a well-defined strategy to allow the transition as depicted by the model.

2.8.2 Stages of Orientation

In coping with the changing marketplace, a firm implementing TQM develops sustainable conditions to reap the benefits and retain its competitive position. For example, the Japanese have long using a low-cost strategy through utilising the experience-curve effect, hoping the volume of its global business provides sufficient return. This strategy is no longer sufficient in the knowledge-based economy, when speed and being ahead in information is the key to competitiveness (Marrifield and Mitchel, 2000).

The concept of orientation implied in this model therefore reflects the degree and nature of the Organisation's adaptation to a specific environmental context in which the firm operates (Miles et al., 1995). As the adaptation is time-dependent, the road to TQM requires gradual paradigm shift or jumping the 'paradigm curve' that takes into account the four significant transitional periods: "Production, Service, Customer and Market Orientations".

3. Scenario Development for each era

The objective of constructing a priori scenario of each TQM life-path is to help in clustering organisations into groups with differing emphasis. This construction is anecdotal in nature, and is based on selected reviews of secondary cases of various stages of companies implementing TQM. In this paper, the scenarios are meant to be non-exhaustive as this could vary to a great extent, therefore future research should build further on this approach.

Scenario 1: Blitz factors

Organisations at this stage tend to manifest inward-lookingness, where emphasis is on internal efficiency, product focus, low-cost producer mentality, and using control-oriented TQM goals, thus the ideology of TQM founders centres around traditional continuous improvement. Though companies might claim to have practised TQM, a business as usual attitude prevails and a high chance of TQM failure is expected.

Scenario 2: Certification fever

The organisation at this stage begins to adopt ISO 9000, thus TQM is synonymous with quality assurance. They are inward-looking, and most TQM initiatives are targeted at operational excellence in terms of internal efficiency measures. Documentation begins to take shape, and continuous improvement is nascent. Many of them perhaps have five years or less experience in TQM or ISO 9000. Managers might still think TQM is a fad. They might view customers as current users or suppliers.

Scenario 3: Piece meal drips

Early adopters of TQM tend to practise various initiatives and some might encounter resistance to change. The rise and fall of TQM happens at this stage, the successful implementation of particular initiatives prepares them for the next change. They achieve partial success. Some abandon it all together. During this stage, organisational emphasis might change from technical quality to rhetoric (Zbaracki, 1998).

Scenario 4: Transformed stage

The advanced TQM companies tend to benefit more from TQM implementation. Various initiatives are implemented, but getting more focus, where quality strategies are integrated to business goals and corporate strategy. They achieve success from effective TQM implementation and might look for implementing a self-assessment model to improve performance continuously. Here, firms have a high concern for customer and market knowledge. At this stage, firms display high market orientation and a good history of innovation, success on new products, high reputation, and brand equity. Many of them are exemplars of best practice and market leadership.

4. Proposed empirical study

An empirical study to verify the model could be done by questionnaire survey of TQM companies within a market economy. A pilot stage research is recommended to obtain the scope of understanding of the concept of sustainability within an industry. Studying secondary cases of quality management implementation over many years could generate the longitudinal data set. This will include the winners of MBNQA, EFQA, and the Deming Prize. If time permitted, primary data collection for targeted companies could be carried out as an exploratory stage. Next, the survey is to confirm the critical success factors for each era. The instrument should be is designed to discover the paradigm shifts necessary for each the transformational path.

4.1 Research Propositions

Having establish the research model and methodology the following hypotheses are proposed for empirical fieldwork:

1. TQM implementation is an evolutionary rather than a revolutionary process

2. TQM implementation process is constituted of soft and hard elements

3. TQM implementation requires a series of transformational changes

4. TQM process has to be integrated to business management

5. TQM implementation is measured through inside-out and outside-in measures

5. Conclusion

The paper reviewed TQM critical success factor related to the environmental context of the industrial eras. Having defined TQM sustainability, and traced the quality paradigms along TQM life-path, conditions for sustainability are discussed. The paper also highlights some initial strategies for sustainability, drawing primarily on past empirical and conceptual writing. A proposed sustainable model is presented, linking TQM implementation and competitiveness. Hypotheses and research constructs are generated to help further work in solving the growing concern for TQM sustainability.

Reference

1. Agus, A. and Abdullah, M. (2000), Total quality management practices in manufacturing companies in Malaysia: An exploratory analysis. *Total Quality Management*, Vol.11, No.8, pp.1141-1051.

2. Ahire, S. L. and Dreyfus, P. (2000), The impact of design management and process management on quality: An empirical investigation. *Journal of Operations Management,* Vol.18, No.5, pp.549-575.

3. Ahire, S. L., Golhar, D. Y. and Waller, M. A. (1996), Development and validation of TQM implementation constructs. *Decision Sciences*, Vol. 27, No.1, pp. 23-56.

4. Ahire, S.L. (1996), TQM age versus quality: An empirical investigation. *Production and Inventory Management Journal,* Vol.37, No.1, pp.18-24.

5. Akao, Y. (1991), *Hoshin Kanri: Policy Deployment for Successful TQM.* Portland: Productivity Press.

6. Ansoff, H. I. (1979), *Strategic Management.* London: Macmillan

7. Aune, A. (1998), Quality and quality management at a crossroads. *Total Quality Management,* Vol.9, No. 4/5, pp.6-12.

8. Baidoun, S. (2001), *An Empirical Investigation of Total Quality Management in Palestine: A proposed Generic Framework of Implementation.* PhD Thesis, University of Bradford School of Management, UK.

9. Black, S.A. and Porter, L.J. (1996), Identification of critical factors of TQM. *Decision Science*, Vol. 27, pp. 1-21.

10. Boaden, R. J. (1997), What is total quality management...and does it matter? *Total Quality Management*, Vol.8, No.4, pp.153-171.

11. Bounds, G. et al. (1994) *Beyond Total Quality Management: Toward the emerging paradigm,* New York: McGraw-Hill.

12. Broman, G., Holmberg, J. and Robert, K. (2000), Simplicity Without Reduction: Thinking Upstream Towards the Sustainable Society. *Interfaces,* Vol.30, No.3, pp.13-25.

13. Chan, A.M.Y., Chu, F.W.W. and Yuen, C.K (2000), A successful TQM Project in China. *International Journal of Commerce and Management,* Vol.10, No.2, pp.75-90.

14. Conti, T. (1999), Vision 2000: positioning the new ISO 9000 standards with respect to total quality management models, *Total Quality Management*, Vol. 10, No. 4-5, pp. S454-s464.

15. Dahlgaard, J.J. and Dahlgaard, S.M.P (1999), Integrating business excellence and innovation management: developing a culture for innovation, creativity and learning. *Total Quality Management*, Vol. 10, No.4/5, pp. S465-S472.

16. Dahlgaard, J.J., Norgaard, A. and Jakobsen, S. (1998), Profile for success. *European Quality*, Vol.5, No. 1, pp.30-33

17. Dahlgaard, S.M.P. (1999), The evolution patterns of quality management: some reflections on the quality movement. *Total Quality Management*, Vol.10, No.4/5, pp.S473-S480.

18. Dale, B. G. (1996), Benchmarking on total quality management adoption: a positioning model. *Benchmarking for Quality Management and Technology,* Vol.3, No.1, pp. 28-37.

19. Dale, B., Boaden, R., Mark, W. and Ruth, M. (1998), The use of quality management techniques and tools: An examination of some key issues. *International Journal of Technology Management,* Vol.16, No.4-6, pp.305-326.

20. Dale, B. Zairi, M., Wiele, A. and Williams, A.R.T. (2000), Quality is dead in Europe - long life excellence: true or false? *Measuring Business Excellence*, Vol. 4,No.3, pp.4-10.

21. Dale, B. (1994), *Managing Quality*. UK: Prentice-Hall International (UK).

22. Day, G. (1994a), The Capabilities of Market-Driven Organisations. *Journal of Marketing,* Vol.58, No.4, pp.37-52.

23. Dean, J. and Bowen, D. (1994), Management Theory and total quality: Improving research and practice through theory development. *Academy of Management Review*, Vol.19, No.3, pp.392-419.

24. Deming, E. (1982), *Quality, productivity and competitive position*. Cambridge, MA: MIT Center for Advanced Engineering Study.

25. Deming, E. (1993), *The New Economics: for industry, government, and Education*. Cambridge: M I T.

26. Deming, E. (1996), *Out of Crisis*. Cambridge, MA: MIT center for Advanced

27. Dervitsiosis, K.N. (2000), Benchmarking and business paradigm shifts. *Total Quality Management*, Vol.11, No.4-6, pp.s641-s646.

28. Dervitsiotis, K.N. (1999), How to attain and sustain excellence with performance-based process management, *Total Quality Management,* Vol.10, No.3, pp.309-317.

29. Feigenbaum, A.V. (1956, 1983), *Total Quality Control*. New York: McGraw Hill.

30. Flynn, B.B., Schroeder, R.G. and Sakakibara, S. (1995a), The impact of quality management practices on performance and competitive advantage. *Decision Sciences,* Vol.26, No.5, pp.659-692.

31. Gale, B. T. (1994), *Managing Customer Value*. New York: Free Press.

32. Garvin, D. A. (1988), Managing Quality: The strategic and competitive edge. New York: Free Press.

33. Giroux, H. and Landry, S. (1998), Schools of thought in and against total quality.*Journal of Managerial Issues*, Vol.10, No.2, pp.183-203.

34. Grant, R. M., Shani, R. and Krishnan, R. (1994), TQM challenge to management theory and practice. *Sloan Management Review,* Vol.35, No.2, pp.25-35.

35. Gummesson, E. (1998), Implementation requires a paradigm. *Academy of Marketing Science Journal*, Vol.26, No. 3, pp.242-249.

36. Gurnani, H. (1999), Pitfalls in total quality management implementation: The case of a Hong Kong company. *Total Quality Management*, Vol.10, No.2, pp.209-228.

37. Hackman, J. R. and Wageman, R. (1995), Total quality management: empirical, conceptual and practical issues. *Administrative Science Quarterly*, Vol. 40, No. 2, pp. 309-342.

38. Hall, R. (1992), The strategic analysis of intangible resources. *Strategic Management Journal*, Vol.13, No. 2, pp. 135-144.

39. Hamel, G., and Prahalad, C.K. (1994), *Competing for the future: breakthrough strategies for seizing control of your industry and creating the markets of tomorrow.* Boston, MA: Harvard Business School Press.

40. Harari, O. (1993), Ten reasons why TQM doesn't work. *Management Review*, Vol. 82, No.1, pp.33-38.

41. Haris, C.R. (1995), The evolution of quality management: An overview of the TQM literature. *Canadian Journal of Administrative Science*, Vol. 12, No.2, pp.95-104.

42. Hendricks, K. B. and Singhal, V. R. (1997), Does Implementing an Effective TQM Program Actually Improve Operating Performance? Empirical Evidence from Firms That Have Won Quality Awards. *Management Science*, Vol.43, No.9, pp.1258-1274.

43. Hill, S and Wilkinson, A. (1995), In search of TQM. *Employee Relations*, Vol.17, No. 3, pp.8-25.

44. Idris, M.A. (2000), *TQM and Market Orientation*, PhD Thesis. University of Bradford School of Management, UK.

45. Ishikawa, K. and Lu, D.J. (1985), *What Is Total Quality Control?* Englewood Cliffs, NJ: Prentice-Hall.

46. Ismail, M.Y. and Hashmi, M.S.J. (1999), The state of quality management in the Irish manufacturing industry, *Total Quality Management*, Vol.10, No.6, pp.853-862.

47. Kanji, G.K, and Tambi, A.M.A. (1999), Total quality management in UK higher education institutions, *Total Quality Management*, Vol.10, No.1, pp.129-153.

48. Kanji, G.K. and Asher, M. (1993), *Total Quality Management Process: A Systematic Approach.* London: Journal Oxford Ltd.

49. Kaplan, R. S. and Norton, D. P. (1996), *The Balanced Scorecard: Translating Strategy into Action.* Boston, Massachusetts: Harvard Business School Press.

50. Krumwiede, D. and Lavelle, J. (2000), The effect of top-manager personality on a total quality management environment. *Engineering Management Journal*, Vol.12, No.2, pp.9-14.

51. Kunst, P. and Lemmink, J. (2000), Quality management and business performance in hospitals: a search for success parameters. *Total Quality Management*, Vol.11, No.8, pp.1123-1133.

52. Larson, A.L., Teisberg, E.O. and Johnson, R.R. (2000), Sustainable Business: Opportunity and Value Creation. *Interfaces,* Vol.30, No.3, pp.01-12.

53. Lawler, III, E. (2000), *Rewarding Excellence.* San Francisco: Jossey-Bass.

54. Luthans, K. and Sommer, S. (2000), Helping RECs to compete: The comprehensive application of high performance work practices. *Management Quarterly*, Vol.41, No.2, pp.7-19.

55. MacDonald, M. (1993), Strategic marketing planning: A state of the art review. *Marketing Intelligence & Planning*, Vol. 10, No. 4, pp.4-22.

56. March, J.G. (1991), Exploration and exploitation in organisational learning. *Organisation Science*, Vol.2, No.1, pp. 71-87.

57. Maslennikova, I. and Foley, D. (2000), Xerox's Approach to Sustainability, *Interfaces,* Vol. 30, No.3, pp.226-233.

58. McDonald, I, Zairi, M. and Idris, M.A. (2001b), *Sustaining and Transferring Excellence: A framework of best practice of TQM transformation based on winners of Baldridge and European Quality Awards.* Research Paper Series. ECTQM, University of Bradford School of Management, UK.

59. McDonald, I., Zairi, M. and Idris, M.A. (2001a), *In Search of sustainable excellence: A contemporary perspective of total quality management.* Research Paper Series. ECTQM, University of Bradford School of Management, UK.

60. Merrifield, D. and Mitchell, G. (2000), Changing nature of competitive advantage. *Research Technology Management*, Vol.43, No.1, pp.41-45.

61. Miles, M. P., Russel, G. R. and Arnold, D. R. (1995), The quality orientation: An emerging business philosophy? *Review of Business*, Vol. 17, No.1, pp.7-18.

62. Miyake, D., Enkawa, T. and Fleury, A. (1995), Improving manufacturing system performance by complementary application of JIT, TQC, and TPM paradigms, *Total Quality Management*, Vol.6, pp.345-363.

63. Mohr-Jackson, I. (1998), Conceptualising total quality orientation. *European Journal of Marketing,* Vol. 32, No. 1 / 2, pp.13-22.

64. Myers, K. and Ashkena, R. (1993), Results-driven quality......now. *Management Review*, Vol.82, No.3, pp.40-44.

65. Nadkarni, R.A. (1995), A not-so-secret recipe for successful TQM, *Quality Progress*, Vol.28, pp.91-96.

66. Narver, J.C. and Slater, S. F. (1990), The Effect of a Market Orientation on Business Profitability. *Journal of Marketing*, Vol.54, No.4, pp.20-35.

67. Oakland, J.S. and Porter, L. (1994), *Cases in Total Quality Management.* Oxford: Butterworth-Heinemann.

68. Oakland, J.S., Zairi, M. and Letza, S. (1994) TQM and bottom-line results. *Quality World,* 20, pp. 600-604.

69. O'Connor, P. (1995), Achieving world class quality and reliability: science or art? *Quality World,* Vol.21, pp.712-715.

70. Pfeffer, J. (1994), *Competitive advantage through people.* Cambridge, MA: Harvard Business School Press.

71. Porter, M. (1999), Creating Advantage. *Executive Excellence*, November, pp.13-14.

72. Prahalad, C. K. and Hamel, G. (1990), The Core Competence of the Corporation. *Harvard Business Review,* Vol. 68, No.3, pp.79-91.

73. Rapert, M. I. and Babakus, E. (1996), Linking quality and performance. *Marketing Health Services*, Vol.16, No.3, pp.39-43.

74. Reed, R. L., David, J. and Montgomery, J. C., (1996), Beyond process: TQM content, and firm performance. *Academy of Management Review*, Vol.21, No.1, pp.173-203.

75. Reinhardt, F. (2000), Sustainability and the Firm. *Interfaces,* Vol.30, No.3, pp.26-41.

76. Saraph, J. V., Benson, G. and Schroeder, R.G. (1989), An instrument for measuring the critical factors of quality management. *Decision Science*, Vol. 20, No. 4, pp. 810-29.

77. Savolainen, T. (1997), *Development of quality-oriented management ideology: a longitudinal case study on the permeation of quality ideology in two family-owned manufacturing companies.* Jyvaskyld Studies in Computer Science, Economics and Statistics, No. 37, Dissertation, University of Jyvaskyld.

78. Savolainen, T. (2000), Leadership strategies for gaining business excellence through total quality management: A Finnish case study. *Total Quality Management*, Vol.11, No.2, pp.211-226.

79. Senge, P. (1995), The message of quality management. *Executive Excellence*, Vol.12, No.7, pp.5-7.

80. Shiba, S., Graham, A. and Walden, D. (1993), *A New American TQM*. Portland, OR: Productivity Press.

81. Sitkin, S.B, Sutcliffe, K.M. and Schroeder, R.G. (1994), Distinguishing control from learning in total quality management: A contingency perspective. *Academy of Management Review*, Vol. 19, No. 3, pp. 537-564.

82. Slater, S.F and Narver, J.C. (1993), Product-market strategy and performance: An analysis of Miles and Snow strategy types. *European Journal of Marketing,* Vol.27, No. 10, pp. 33-52.

83. Spencer, B. A. (1994), Models of Organisation and total quality management: A comparison and critical evaluation. *Academy of Management Review,* Vol.19, No.3, pp.446-471.

84. Sullivan, L. P. (1986), The seven stages of company-wide quality control, *Quality Progress*, pp.77-83.

85. Svensson, M. and Klefsjo, B. (2000), Experiences from creating a quality culture

for continuous improvements in the Swedish school sector by using self-assessments. *Total Quality Management*, Vol.11, No.4-6, pp.S800-S807.

86. Thiagarajan, T., Zairi, M. and Dale, B.G. (2001), A proposed model of TQM implementation based on an empirical study of Malaysian industry. *International Journal of Quality and Reliability Management*. Vol.18, No.3, pp.289-306.

87. Thompson, K.R. (1998), Confronting the paradoxes in total quality management. Organisational Dynamics, Vol.26, No.3, pp.62-74.

88. Treacy, M. and Wiersema, F. (1993), Customer intimacy and other value disciplines. *Harvard Business Review*, Vol.71, No.1, pp.84-93.

89. Wayland, R. E. and Cole, P. M. (1997), *Customer connections: Strategies for growth*. Boston, Massachusetts: Harvard Business School Press.

90. Webster, F. E., Jr. (1988), Rediscovering the Marketing Concept. *Business Horizons*, Vol.31, No.3, pp.29-39.

91. Webster, F. E., Jr. (1994), *Market Driven Management*. NY: John Wiley and Sons.

92. Witcher, B. (1994), *Clarifying total quality management*. Working Paper. Durham University Business School.

93. Woodruff, R.E. (1997), Customer value: The next source for competitive advantage. *Academy of Marketing Science Journal*, Vol.25, No. 2, pp.139-154.

94. Yusof, S.M. and Aspinwall, E. (1999), Critical success factors for total quality management implementation in small and medium enterprises. *Total Quality Management*, Vol. 10, No.4/5, pp. S803-s209.

95. Zairi, M. (2001). *From Cradle to Maturity, Annual Presentation*. Institute of Management, University of Huddersfield, UK.

96. Zairi, M. and Leonard, P. (1994), *Practical Benchmarking - Practical Guide to Benchmarking*. London: Chapman & Hall.

97. Zairi, M. (1996), *Benchmarking for Best Practice*. Oxford: Butterworth-Heinemann.

98. Zbaracki, M. (1998), The rhetoric and reality of total quality management. *Administrative Science Quarterly*, Vol. 43, No.3, pp.602-636.

[Authors' note]

Mohd Ashari Idris, PhD., is a senior lecturer in the Department of Marketing, National University of Malaysia since 1995, and is currently an Associate Researcher at ECTQM, University of Bradford School of Management, UK. He obtained an MBA from Cardiff University, Wales UK in 1986. Prior to his academic positions he had 18 years' industrial employment as a Senior Manager in multinational companies in Malaysia. His research interests include market-based quality orientation, TQM, best practice strategic marketing, and integrated management. Email: ashariaz@yahoo.co.uk

Professor Mohamed Zairi, PhD., holds the SABIC Chair of Best Practice Management, and Head of ECTQM, University of Bradford School of Management, UK. Email: M.Zairi@bradford.ac.uk

" I've got to repay a debt. I'm a member of the human race .... society needs a lot of improvement. "

- **Joseph Juran**
  on his motivation

Evolution & Development of the TQM concept

The Quality Improvement Continuum: An Integrative Approach

Professor Mohamed Zairi & John Whymark, 2005

1. Continuous Improvement: What is it?

This wide ranging philosophy has several meanings and can be applied in different contexts. It is very often referred to as the approach adopted to improve the management of key activities and tasks and thereby enhancing productivity and performance. Others describe it as a "philosophy" of continuous learning, creativity and innovation. There are perhaps three fundamental points to bear in mind when referring to Continuous Improvement:

• As stated, this approach is a continuous one and as such the gains and improvements achieved are relative ones and not absolute measures;

• Continuous Improvement does not depend on specialists but rather is a corporate approach which very much relies on wider involvement of employees at all levels;

• Continuous Improvement impacts on behavioural aspects and is geared towards changing people's mindsets and cultural settings.

However, we wish to define it, the philosophy of Continuous Improvement or Kaizen as it is known in Japan, has to be linked to the organisational System and its key constituents.

• Policy
• Process
• People
• Performance

The Concept of Business Process Management

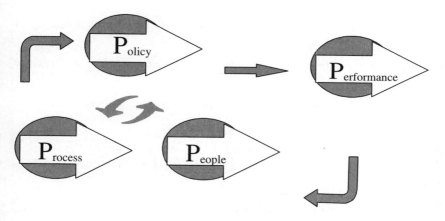

An Effective Process

Figure 1.1 The Concept of Business Process Management

As figure 1.1 illustrates, the organisational system and its dynamic functioning depends on the inter-play between enabling factors in order to achieve optimum performance. Continuous Improvement is the "envelope" which ensures that each of the four P's described can be optimised and that the integration and synergy levels built are capable of enhancing overall corporate performance.

A sustainable philosophy of continuous improvement cannot be achieved through a "bolting-on" approach to hierarchical structures and functional settings. As Figure 1.2 illustrates, and based on the Japanese experience, Continuous Improvement depends on:

- Being driven from a top-down perspective with good vision and strategic direction;

- Use C.I. as a means for achieving corporate goals and key objectives;

- Bring about the most appropriate transformational and necessary changes in order to achieve the desired gain;
- Build in enabling systems and processes;
- Educate all employees on problem-solving tools and the meaning of Continuous Improvement;
- Link Continuous Improvement to employee development and performance assessment;
- Locate a bottom-up performance perspective to change behaviour.

It is therefore important to recognise that at the heart of Continuous Improvement is the word organisational system and the key processes which make it function.

2. Understanding Organisations as Systems

The work on understanding organisations as systems is not new and indeed writers such as Ashby [1], Beer [2]; Cluckland [3] are well known in this field. A definition of a system found in Povey [4] describes the latter as:

	Top Management	Middle Management & Staff		Supervisors	Workers		
Determined to introduce kaizen as a strategy	TQC	Deploy and implement kaizen goals as directed by top management through policy deployment and cross functional management	TQC Detail Design of the Communication system	Use kaizen in functional roles	TQC	Engage in the kaizen through the suggestion scheme and small group activity	No individual Bonus Detail Design of the Communication system Behavioural Approach TQC Suggestion scheme
Provide support and allocate resources	Security / Flexibility Job Rotation	Use kaizen in functional capabilities	TQC	Formulate plans for kaizen and provide guidance to workers	Unions Detail design of the Communication system Ratio Supervisor: Worker	Practice discipline in the workshop	TQC Job Rotation Behavioural Approach
Policy for kaizen and cross functional goals	Cross Functional / Matrix Design TQC	Establish, maintain and upgrade standards	No individual Bonus Behavioural Approach	Improve communication with workers and sustain high morale	Unions Detail Design of the Communication system	Engage in continuous self development to become better problem solvers	Ambiguity of Roles Security / Flexibility Behavioural Approach
Realise kaizen goals through policy deployment and audits	Detail Design of Communication system TQC	Make employees kaizen conscious through intensive training programmes	TQC Union Experience Behavioural; Approach	Support small group activities (TQC) and the individual suggestion scheme	No individual bonus Behavioural Approach TQC	Enhance skills and job performance expertise with cross education	Security / Flexibility Unions Around Company Behavioural Approach Job Rotation
Build Systems procedures and structures conducive to kaizen	Detail Design of Communication system Behavioural Approach TQC	Help employees develop skills and tools for problem solving	Ambiguity of Roles Union Experience Behavioural Approach TQC	Introduce discipline in the workshop	TQC Behavioural Approach		
	Provide kaizen			suggestions	TQC Suggestion Scheme		

Figure 1.2 The Hierarchy of Kaizen

233

"A set of interactive components that transform inputs and has outputs, and is distinguished from its external environment by a boundary".

Povey [4] suggests the following list of key characteristics found to be common amongst all types of systems:

- A system has inputs

- A system does something (there are outputs)

- Additional or removal of a component changes the system

- Inclusion of a component effects the component

- A system has emerged properties (The whole is greater than the sum of the parts)

- A system has a boundary

- A system has an environment (outside the boundary) that effects it.

- Someone owns the system

The organisational system is improved through the management of processes and sub-processes as depicted by Figure 1.3.

An Effective Process

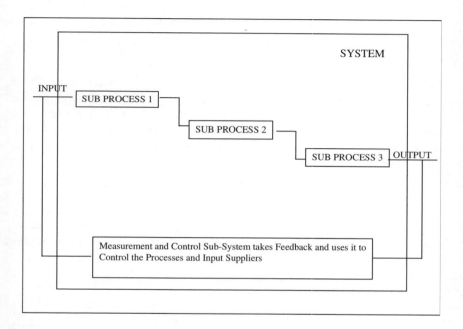

Figure 1.3 An Effective Process

A key contribution made in the understanding of organisations as system is by Dr Edward Deming.

3. Deming's Contribution to Systems Thinking

Dr Edward Deming is perhaps the key father of Continuous Improvement and organisations to function as systems. His philosophy which will be explained in later sections is very simple:

- Treat workers as partners rather than adversaries;

- Encourage them to use their minds as well as their hands'

- Concentrate on quality production rather than quantity.

Deming has had such an important and significant impact on modern management thinking that following his death on December 20th 1993, The Times newspaper wrote the following tribute about him:

"If there was ever a prophet without honour in his town, country, it was Edward Deming" Times, Friday, 24th December.

Deming views a business organisation being structured as a system whose sole purpose is to delight the customer. According to Deming, delighting the customer will not come just from a clear understanding of their needs, but rather through continually improving both its processes and its product. The whole purpose is therefore to optimise the entire system and not some of its components.

A system according to Deming [5] is:

"A network of functions or activities (sub-processes, stages) within an organisation that work together for the aim of the organisation. In fact systems are only one part of Dr Deming's Four Core Values of Profound Knowledge (Figure 1.4).

The Core Calues of Demings Theory of Profound Knowledge	The Four Cornerstones	The Fourteen Points
		1 Establish constancy of purpose
		2 Adopt the new philosophy
		3 Cease dependence on mass inspection
1 Appreciation for a system	The purpose of a business is:	4 End the practice of awarding business on price tag alone
2 Some knowledge of the theory of variation	1. to stay in business and to create jobs	5 Constantly improve every system
3 A theory of knowledge	2 to expand the market	6 Institute training
4 Some knowledge of psychology	3 to continually grow	7 Institute leadership
	4 to grow intelligently	8 Drive out fear
		9 Break down barriers between staff areas
		10 Abandon slogans
		11 Eliminate numerical quotas
		12 Remove barriers to pride of workmanship
		13 Promote education and self improvement
		14 Take action to accomplish the transformat'

Figure 1.4 The Core Values: The Cornerstones and the 14 points

Deming goes on to say [6]:

".......................A system must possess an aim, and this aim is a value-

236

judgement. Without an aim, there is no system. if you wish, you may call it a process - no matter".

He then says:

"ô.....................Management of a system is action based on prediction. Rational prediction requires systematic learning and comparison of predictions of short-term and long-term results from possible alternative courses of action.".

Deming is reported to have suggested the following flow diagram of an organisation as a System [7]. As Figure 1.5 depicts, Deming has stated in The New Economics [7] that:

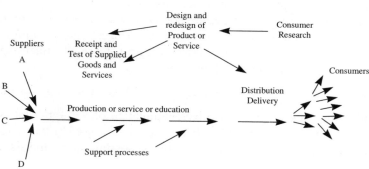

Figure 1.5 The Organisation Viewed as a System

"The flow diagram.......was the spark that in 1950 and onward turned Japan around. It displayed to top management and to engineers a system of production. The Japanese had knowledge, great knowledge, but it was in bits and pieces, uncoordinated. This flow diagram, directed their knowledge and efforts into a system of production, geared to the market - namely, prediction of needs of customers."

Essentially, and according to Deming's thinking, the systems view of an organisation means that:

237

(i) The organisation has horizontal focus on the customer and the flow of communication and activity is for problem-solving and value adding;

(ii) The linkages between various activities are based on corporate goals and synergy levels;

(iii) Work process design is not to keep the individual employees a "busy" but rather to fulfil organisational objectives both in the short and long term.

Underlining Dr Deming's thinking is that all endeavours need to focus on process and process optimisation.

Process: In relation to processes, Deming [8] states that:

"A diagram of any process will divide work into stages. These stages as a whole form a process. The stages are not individual entities, each running at maximum profit —work comes into any stage changes state, and moves on to the next stage. Any stage has a customer, the next stage. The final stage will send product or service to the ultimate customer."

He also states that: ".....Every activity, every job is a part of a process".

Optimisation   Of a system involves elimination of wasteful, undesirable variation. Inability to distinguish between variations caused by the system and that due to the people who work if this prevents optimisation. Indeed, it may well make things worse [5].

Deming stresses on optimisation of processes and systems in all of his talks. Together with Dr Walter Stewart, they have tried to convey the message that:

• Understanding of variation due to common and special causes

• Improvement of processes are at the heart of Continuous Improvement activity.

Unfortunately in many cases senior managers tend to view variation from a "judgmental perspective" and performance is viewed in absolute terms either as good or bad.

Deming argues that this approach does nothing to improve processes and is a way for looking for scapegoats and an approach to assign blame.

The use of statistical control tools and particularly SPC and control charts is a way for stabilising and optimising processes and removing the focus from individuals and rather to focus on process and system improvement.

4. The Deming Problem Solving Cycle:

The Deming Cycle was first originated by its founder, Walter Stewart. It was the Japanese who renamed it as Deming's Cycle back in 1950.The Cycle used to be referred to as P-D-C-A cycle (Plan-Do-Check-Act) and in 19909, Dr Deming renamed it as P-D-S-A (Plan-Do-Study-Act) because:

Deming argues that learning and innovation takes place at that stage and before acting, people need to analyse and understand the problem, gather data and look at possible solutions and alternatives, before suggesting how possibly problems could be improved.

As Figure 1.6 illustrates, the whole ethos of the Deming cycle is on innovation and improvement driven by change.

The PDSA Cycle

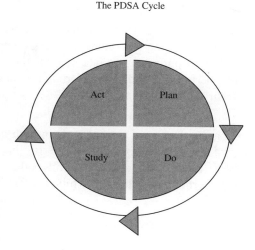

Figure 1.6 The PDSA Cycle

The Deming philosophy, supported by other gurus is based on the use of statistical tools and techniques, focusing on the process, involving and recognising people and their contributions. These aspects are the key ingredients for effective leadership.

To a question on how much influence did Dr Stewart's thinking influence him, Dr Deming replied [9]:

"Continually ....He provided the means to joy in learning; how to say it; how to think it; how to rank ideas; how to change emphasis. He led me to realise the importance of intrinsic motivation. Give the individual a chance, the way it was years ago. Everything we have has come from positions of economic security, where everybody is free to be responsible to himself. We must learn to think and grow; we must engage in a never-ending cycle of learning".

At the heart of the never-ending cycle of learning comes a set of rules for managers to subscribe to. These are derived from Tribus [10] and are detailed in Table 1.1. below.

A Checklist of Things that Managers need to Learn

Although in most cases the knowledge and usage of elementary statistical tools is more than adequate, non-the-less, there are many other tools that can be used for a wide variety of purposes. In fact many authors argue that the difference between high performing and low performing organisations is very often due to the extent of reliance on tools and techniques of quality management.

In a recent study comparing the use of quality tools in high quality and low quality organisations [11], the authors concluded for instance that the elementary SPC tools are used by all concerned, whilst other tools tended to be used more in high performing organisations (Figure 1.7).

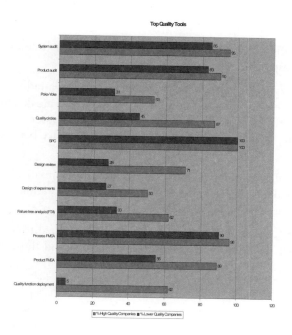

Figure 1.7 Intensive use of QA Tools in the Development Process

Table 1.1 A Checklist of things that Managers need to Learn

Every manager should be competent in elementary statistics:

1 Process Flow-Charting

2 Fishbone Diagrams

3 Run Charts

4 Histograms

5 Pareto Diagrams

6 Scatter Diagrams

7 Control Charts

8 Elementary Design of Experiments

Every manager should learn how to:

1 Recognise, define, describe, diagnose and improve the systems for which he or she is responsible

2 Diagnose the variability of a system and decide which variations are due to special causes and thus requires special action and which are due to common causes and will therefore require a change in the systems design and operation. The manager must be able to tell the difference between signals and noise

3 Lead teams of people from different educational levels in problem identification, data gathering, data analysis and the generation of proposals for solution, implementation and test

4 Diagnose the behaviour of humans and distinguish those difficulties which are due to the variations in human abilities (15%) and those which are caused by the system (85%) (Juran's rule)

The authors concerned concluded that:

"The outstanding quality that helps companies achieve top rates of growth and return is a management leadership task. it entails setting, communicating, and operationalising ambitions, objectives, redesigning business along the core processes, integrating customers and suppliers, and above all mobilising the workforce. It is not easy to do these things well, but some sophisticated quality tools can help. Managers ignore or abuse them at their peril".

5. Alternative Continuous Improvement Philosophies

There are similar continuous improvement philosophies to Deming's based on the teachings of Juran, Crosby, Ishikawa, Feingenbaum, Taguchi, Ouchi and Conway. A brief review of each approach is described in this section:

A. Juran's Philosophy and Contribution

Juran's philosophy of quality was originally developed during his work with Western Electric in the United States in the 1920s and in the 1940s he worked with Deming. Certain similarities, and equally importantly, differences, were established between the two theorists. Juran, like Deming, taught principles of quality management to the Japanese in the 1950s. His work was fundamental to their post-war reorganisation. Juran's approach has had considerable influence throughout the world. His overall approach was designated as "managerial breakthrough" (cited in Flood, 1993).

Juran echoed Deming's conclusion that US businesses faced a major crisis in quality due to the increase in poor quality products and services and the loss of sales to foreign competition. Both concluded that the solution to this crisis depended on developing new thinking concerning quality that would include all levels of the management hierarchy. Upper management in particular required training and experience in managing to achieve higher quality (Evans and Lindsay, 2001; Flood, 1993).

Unlike Deming, Juran specified a detailed procedure for quality improvement through his **Quality Trilogy** (Table 5.1) (Flood, 1993; Evans and Lindsay, 2001).

5.1: Illustrates Juran's Basic Quality Trilogy of Improvement Processes

Quality Planning	1) Identify the customers, both internal and external. 2) Determine customer needs. 3) Develop product features that respond to customer needs. 4) Establish quality goals that can meet the needs of customers. 5) Develop a process that can produce the needed product features. 6) Prove process capability - show that the process can meet the quality goals under operating conditions.
Quality Control	1) Choose control subjects – what to control. 2) Choose units of measurement. 3) Establish measurements. 4) Establish standards of performance. 5) Measure actual performance.

	6) Interpret the difference (actual vs. standard).
	7) Take action on the difference.
Quality	1) Prove the need for improvement.
Improvement	2) Identify specific projects for improvement.
	3) Organise a guide for the projects.
	4) Organise a diagnosis for the discovery of causes of problems.
	5) Diagnose to find these causes.
	6) Provide remedies.
	7) Prove that the remedies are effective under operating conditions.
	8) Provide for control to hold the gains.

Source: Juran, J.M. ('The Quality Trilogy' *Quality Progress*, Vol. 19, No. 8, Aug. 1986, pp. 19-24)

Quality trilogy consists of three basic managerial processes through which the management of an organisation can achieve quality (Juran, 1988).

1. *Quality control* emphasises the prevention of quality problems and the correction of defects to create a product that is free from deficiencies.

2. *Quality improvement* is based on looking for opportunities to improve quality before problems arise.

3. *Quality planning* provides the operating forces with the means of producing products that meet consumer needs.

'Fitness for use' is Juran's definition of quality. He uses this in the context of a user-based view, which signifies that quality lies with the actual use of a product or service. Juran applied two different meanings to quality – *features*, and *freedom from deficiencies*. Effective management of these quality types is achieved by using the Quality Trilogy (Juran, 1986). This emphasises the connection between quality planning, quality control, and quality improvement. Only the customer can determine the quality of the product or service using Juran's definition. James (1996) argues that '... consequently, manufacturers do not like to use it, but prefer a more controlled conformance to specifications'.

Therefore, fitness for use is a utility value concept, which varies from one customer to another. According to Juran (1974), this concept is based on five quality characteristics: -

1) technological (e.g. strength);

2) psychological (e.g. beauty);

3) time-oriented (e.g. reliability);

4) contractual (e.g. guarantees);

5) ethical (e.g. sales staff courtesy).

Juran emphasised a structured approach to planning for product quality. Within Juran's system, the quality of a manufactured product is defined primarily by technological and time-oriented characteristics, whereas a service product may involve all the characteristics indicated above. Further, he determined that fitness for use could be broken down into four elements:

1) quality of design,

2) quality control,

3) availability, and

4) field service.

Quality of design concentrates on quality of market research, product concept, and quality of specification; *Quality of conformance* includes technology, manpower, and management; *Availability* focuses on reliability, maintainability, and logistical support; *Field service* quality comprises promptness, competence and integrity (James, 1996).

Quality improvement was always Juran's focus, he determined that the goal was to increase performance to levels never achieved previously. To do this he indicated that companies must achieve a series of breakthroughs in attitude, organisation, knowledge, cultural patterns and results. Consequently, he developed six phases of problem solving (Figure 2.2) for quality improvement which include:

245

1) Identify the project;

2) Establish the project;

3) Diagnose the cause;

4) Remedy the cause;

5) Hold the gains;

6) Replicate and nominate (James, 1996).

	Steps	**Activities**
1.	Identify the Project	· Nominate projects · Evaluate projects · Select a project · Ask: 'Is it quality improvement' · Prepare a mission statement
2.	Establish the Project	· Select a team · Verify the mission · Analyse symptoms
3.	Diagnose the Cause	· Confirm/modify mission · Formulate theories · Test theories · Identify root cause(s) · Identify alternatives
4.	Remedy the Cause	· Design remedy · Design controls · Design for culture

		· Prove effectiveness
		· Implement
		· Design effective controls
5.	Hold the Gains	· Foolproof the remedy
		· Audit the controls
		· Replicate the results
6.	Replicate and Nominate	· Nominate the new project

Source: James (1996, Table 3.2, p. 65)

Figure 5.2: Juran's Six Steps to Problem Solving

In these phases, twenty-three activities are carried out. The first three phases and activities involved are described as the journey from 'symptom to remedy' and the remaining three phases and the activities are considered as the journey from remedy to further opportunity. According to Juran, the process is cyclic in nature and reflects the continuous spiral of quality development in an organisation.

Unlike Deming, Juran did not propose making a major cultural change to the organisation, but rather sought to improve quality by working within the system. Juran's programmes were designed to fit into an organisation's current business planning with a minimal risk of rejection. He argues that employees at different levels of an organisation speak in their own 'language' while Deming believes that statistics should be the common language (Flood, 1993; Evans and Lindsay, 2001).

Juran's approach recommends ten steps to quality improvement as follows:

1. Build awareness of the need and opportunity for improvement.

2. Set goals for improvement.

3. Organise to reach the goals (establish a quality council, identify problems, select projects, and appoint teams, designate facilitators)

4. Provide training.

5. Carry out projects to solve problems.

6. Report progress.

7. Give recognition.

8. Communicate results.

9. Measure all processes and improvements.

10. Maintain momentum by making annual improvement part of the regular systems and processes of the company (Juran, 1992).

B. Crosby's Philosophy and Contribution

Crosby worked as Corporate Vice President for Quality at International Telephone and Telegraph (ITT) for 14 years after working his way up from line inspector. Crosby's had a straightforward attitude to quality management. He states that top management in an organisation should adopt a quality management style, not because it is the right thing to do, but because it is good for the bottom line (Hunt, 1993; Crosby, 1979; 1984). This approach substantiates Juran's insight into management motivation for TQM.

Crosby states that quality is free and that "*unquality things*" cost money when organisations are not doing the '*right things right*' (Crosby, 1979; 1984). Crosby argues that quality does not cost money. "What costs money is not doing the job right the first time". He sets out four pillars of quality in terms of making quality certain:

1. Management participation and attitude

2. Professional quality management

3. Original programme

4. Recognition

In Crosby's approach, the focus is on altering the attitudes and behaviours of the workforce. He attributes quality problems to a lack of standards and attention to detail among employees (Harris, 1995). Crosby's quality slogan is 'conformance to the requirements and quality is free'. Crosby (1979) developed 'five absolutes of quality', these are:

1. Conformance to requirements. Once the requirements have been determined, the production process will exhibit quality if the product or service resulting from that process conforms to those requirements.

2. There is no such thing as a quality problem.

3. There is no such thing as the economics of quality – it is always cheaper to do the job right the first time.

4. The only performance measurement is the cost of quality.

5. The only performance standard is zero defects.

In the opinion of Crosby, the underlying philosophy behind these absolutes is a 'conformance mentality'. It breaks down if the design of the product or service is incorrect or does not match the actual customer requirements effectively. Crosby argues that since management deals predominantly in the language of money, putting the cost of non-conformance in cash terms makes sense. This concept clearly illustrates the effect of non-conformance and focuses attention on prevention issues. It is Crosby's basic thesis that *quality is free*.

Crosby (1979) believes that the first step for an organisation to move toward a quality management profile is to determine its current level of management maturity. A management maturity grid is developed based on the concept that there are five stages in quality management maturity:

1. Uncertainty exists – when management does not recognise quality as a positive management tool.

2. Awakening exists- when management starts to recognise that quality management can help but will not commit resources to it.

3. Enlightenment begins when management learns about quality management and becomes supportive.

4. Wisdom evolves when management participates personally in quality activities.

5. Certainty is established when quality management is a vital part of organisational management.

Crosby developed a fourteen-point plan for quality improvement. These points were meant to deal predominantly with implementation issues, they are as follows:

1. Management commitment: Determining where management stands on quality, developing a quality policy and management visibly becoming serious about quality.

2. The quality improvement team.

3. Quality measurement for each activity throughout the company.

4. The cost of quality: Crosby suggested that cost of quality is a 'catalyst that brings the quality improvement team to full awareness of what is happening'.

5. Quality awareness: According to Crosby this means providing the sort of support necessary to raise the level of concern and interest in quality amongst all staff in order for them to understand, acknowledge, and support the reason for the quality programme.

6. Corrective action: Crosby suggested that there is a need to develop systematic methods to solve problems previously exposed.

7. Zero Defects (ZD) planning: Crosby's main points of ZD planning are:

a. Explaining the concept and programme to all supervisors

b. Determining what material is required

c. Determining the method and process of delivery of the ZD programme

d. Identifying the error-cause-removal programme and making plans for its execution

8. Supervisor training: Crosby suggested this is necessary in order to ensure that supervisors are able to carry out the tasks and responsibilities of the quality improvement programme.

9. ZD day: Hold a ZD day to establish the new attitude.

10. Employee goal setting should take place.

11. Error causes removal.

12. Recognition.

13. Quality Councils.

14. Do it over again: Emphasising that quality in about continuous improvement. (Crosby, 1997)

In the opinion of Crosby, the above-mentioned points should be used as a guide to help in the rapid development of a programme. He also identified four absolutes of quality management:

1. Quality is conformance to requirements.

2. The system of quality is prevention.

3. The measurement of quality is the price of non-conformance.

4. The performance standard must be zero defects.

C. Feigenbaum

Feigenbaum's career in quality started more than 40 years ago as President and Chief Executive Officer of General Systems Co. He is widely regarded as one of the world's best quality control thinkers and practitioners. Feigenbaum (1991) coined the term Total Quality Control, which he defines as:

"An effective system for integrating the quality development, quality maintenance, and quality improvement efforts of the various groups in an organisation so as to enable marketing, engineering, production, and service at the most economical levels, which allows for full customer satisfaction".

Feigenbaum's work also emphasised employee involvement, teamwork, and long-term commitment to planning for continuous improvement. He made a major contribution by studying quality cost and indicated that quality and cost are a sum not a difference; they are partners not adversaries. Feigenbaum identified 10 benchmarks necessary for total quality competitive success:

1. Quality is a company-wide process.

2. Quality is what the customer says it is.

3. Quality and cost are a sum, not a difference.

4. Quality requires both individual and team work

5. Quality is a way of managing.

6. Quality and innovation are mutually dependent.

7. Quality is an ethic.

8. Quality requires continuous improvement.

9. Quality is the most cost-effective, least capital-intensive route to productivity.

10. Quality is implemented within a total system connected with customers and suppliers. (Stevens, Tim, 1994)

D. Ishikawa

Ishikawa was probably not known for his contributions to quality management through statistical quality control. His development of the Ishikawa Diagram (fishbone) and the employment of the seven tools of quality provided the capacity to use problem-solving techniques throughout an organisation. In Ishikawa's own words these seven tools were described as 'indispensable for quality control' (Bank, 1992), and include:

1. Pareto analysis,

2. Fishbone diagrams,

3. Stratification,

4. Cheek sheets,

5. Histograms,

6. Scatter diagrams,

7. Control charts.

With these tools, Ishikawa argues, managers and staff could tackle and solve the quality-problems facing them. According to James (1998), Ishikawa was more people-oriented than statistically oriented. He believed that everyone in the company is to be involved in quality development, not just the management who drove it, and he remarked that, in many Western organisations, grass-root workers were, and still are, denied the opportunity to make a contribution to quality. From the experience of Japan, he argues that the Japanese insistence on teamwork, and all staff being 'equal' on the basis of contributions to quality, illustrates the major gap existing between Japanese and Western management quality practices.

Ishikawa advocated Total Quality Control (TQC) in Japan prior to World War II. As a Professor at the University of Tokyo, he was one of the creators and early champions of quality circles, and founder of the Union of Japanese Scientists and Engineers (JUSE).

Ishikawa's philosophy for quality management is **Company-Wide Quality**, which involves both vertical and horizontal co-operation. Vertical co-operation occurs between managers, supervisors and the workers, whilst horizontal co-operation means looking beyond the internal organisation, caring about end customers through customer service and the quality that suppliers offer.

According to Ishikawa, TQC embraces 5 strategic goals:

1. Quality must be sought before profits.

2. The infinite human potential occurs when inspection is no longer necessary.

3. A long-term consumer orientation must be fostered within and outside the organisation.

4. Facts and statistical data must be used to communicate throughout the organisation, and measurement must be used as motivation.

5. A company-wide TQC/M system should be developed with the focus of all employees on quality implications of every decision and action (Brocka, 1992).

Key elements of Ishikawa's quality philosophy are as follows:

1. Quality begins and ends with education.

2. The first step in quality is to know the requirements of customers.

3. The ideal state of quality control occurs when inspection is no longer necessary.

4. Remove the root cause, not the symptoms.

5. Quality control is the responsibility of all workers and all divisions.

6. Do not confuse the means with the objectives.

7. Put quality first and set your sights on long-term profits.

8. Markets are the entrance and exit of quality.

9. Top management must not show anger when facts are presented by subordinates.

10. Ninety-five percent of problems in a company can be solved with simple tools for analysis and problem solving.

11. Data without dispersion information (i.e. variability) is false data (Evans and Lindsay, 2001).

E. Conway

Bill Conway is referred to as the "Deming disciple" (Zairi, 1991). In Conway's approach, quality management equates with management of all stages of development, manufacturing, purchasing, and distribution. Conway (1991) emphasises consideration of economic viability, improvement in activities to reduce material waste and time wastage.

Problems of failure in quality management often point to management's lack of conviction and commitment. In Conway's system, TQM combines consistency, pervasive application of a statistical approach and tools with a new way of management thinking. His system incorporates six guidelines or quality improvement tools (Table 2.2):

Table 5.2: Conway's List of Quality Improvement Tools

1 Human relation skills: Management responsibility to create working climate built on trust, mutual respect and common goals.

2 Statistical surveys: Use the power of surveys to identify areas for improvement and to be better informed about various development.

3. Simple statistical techniques: Use simple charts, diagrams to highlight problems, analyse them and propose various solutions.

4 Statistical Process Control: Minimise variations within various processes using control charts.

5. Imagineering: Problem solving techniques using problem visualisation with the view of identifying ways for waste elimination.

6. Industrial engineering: The use of various techniques to redesign work, methods, and plant layout for the purpose of achieving great improvements.

Source: Zairi (1991, p. 26)

F. Taguchi

Taguchi was awarded the Deming prize in 1960 in recognition of his techniques involving industrial optimisation. From 1978-1982 Taguchi acted as director of the Japanese Academy of Quality. Taguchi notably developed methods for on-line and off-line quality control. These methods comprise the basis of Taguchi's total quality control assurance approach. For his contribution to Japanese industrial standards, Taguchi received MITI's Purple Ribbon Award from the Emperor of Japan.

Taguchi's employment of statistics primarily focuses on their use by designers and engineers "to optimise the settings so that products are robust" (Zairi, 1991). In the early stages of product development, these approaches act as trouble-shooting/problem solving tools. Control variables, dealt with by SPC, and noise variables, are identified through Taguchi's methods. If left unaccounted these factors may affect product manufacture and performance.

Taguchi defined quality from a social perspective: "The loss imparted by the product to the society from the time the product is shipped" (Zairi, 1991).

Loss may include customer complaints, damage to company's reputation, market lead loss, and added warranty expense. Taguchi's argument concerning the loss function is that loss is not initiated until the product is out of specification. More critically, loss is initiated when deviation from target value exists. The QLF concept allows management awareness of deviation at the early stages of product development. Cost estimates are also provided. Taguchi's guidelines for quality improvement are indicated in Table 5.3:

Table 5.3: Taguchi's Quality Imperatives

1   Quality losses result from product failure after sale; product 'robustness' is more a function of product design than on-line control, however, stringent, the manufacturing processes.

2   Robust products deliver a strong 'signal' regardless of external 'noise' and with a minimum of internal 'noise'.

3   Any strengthening of a design, that is, any market increase in the signal-to-noise ratios of component parts, will simultaneously improve the robustness of the product as a whole.

4   To set targets of maximum signal-to-noise ratios develop a system of trials that allows you to analyse change in overall system performance.

5   To build robust products, set ideal target values for components and then minimise the average of the square of deviations for combined components averaged over the various customer-user conditions.

6   Before products go on to manufacturing, tolerances are set.

7   Virtually nothing is gained in shipping a product that just barely satisfies the organisation standard over a product that just fails. Get on target; don't just try to stay 'in specification'.

8   Work relentlessly to achieve designs that can be produced consistently.

9   A concerted effort to reduce product failure in the field will simultaneously reduce the number of defectives in the factory.

10 .Strive to reduce variances in the components of the product and variances will be reduced in the production system as a whole.

Source: Zairi (1991, p. 30)

256

G. Shingo

Shingo pioneered the area of Zero Quality Control (ZQC). He established that ZQC does not significantly raise production costs in any important way. Shingo has consistently promulgated his concepts that both statistical quality control and typical inspection processes should be totally eliminated. His basic idea is that control must occur at the problem's source, not after the problem emerges. Incorporation of inspection is used in the process where the problem is identified. At that point the problem is eliminated. Statistical Quality Control (SQC) focuses on effects, not the cause, of process imperfection and abnormalities. SQC concentrates on errors related to operators. Human error is completely eliminated with checklists for each operation. This checklist process is termed *Poka-Yoke,* this is similar to automation or *Vikhoda* in which operators stop automatically when operations are complete or mistakes occur. Shingo's guidelines are indicated in Table 5.4:

5.4: The implementation of Poka Yoke

1. Control upstream, close to the source of problem by, for example, incorporating devices to warn on defects in materials or abnormalities within the process.

2. Establish control mechanisms to deal with different problems to enable operators to know which problem to cure and how to cure it with minimal disruption to the operating system.

3. Take a step-by-step approach by taking small strides, simplifying control systems and having economic viability in mind. Efficiency, technological sophistication, available skills, work methods have all got to be carefully studied for effective usage of Poka Yoke.

4. Do not delay improvements by overanalysing: Although many manufacturers' main objective is to achieve closeness between design manufacturability, many Poka Yoke can be implemented as soon as the problems have been identified with no cost to the companies concerned. Poka Yoke encourages interdepartmental co-operation and is a main vehicle for continuous improvement because it encourages continuous problem-solving activity.

Source: Zairi (1991, p. 31)

H. Ouchi

Ouchi's famous contribution to management is '**Theory Z**'. Ouchi has examined overall Japanese management philosophy in terms of its effect on business in the United States. He concluded that Japanese success was built on a commitment to quality and a participative management style. US business is burdened with great inefficiencies - acute specialisation is the problem. Ouchi's plan for improvement is simply implementation of his analysis of the Japanese system (Zairi, 1991). The basis of Theory Z is outlined below (Table 5.5):

5.5: Ouchi's 13 Steps in Theory Z

1 Understand the *Type Z organisation* and your role.

2 Audit your company's philosophy.

3 Define the desired management philosophy and involve the company leader.

4 Implement the philosophy by creating both structures and incentives.

5 Develop interpersonal skills.

6 Test yourself on the system.

7 Involve the union.

8 Stabilise employment. Avoid layoffs and share the misfortune.

9 Decide on a system for slow evaluation and promotion.

10 Broaden career path development.

11 Prepare for implementation at the lowest level.

12 Seek out areas of implement participation.

13 Permits the development of relationships (for example, promote good communication).

Source: Zairi (1991, p. 32)

6. Making Business Process Improvement Happen: What Does it Take?

Perhaps in order to answer this difficult question, one needs to look at the experience of the Japanese and why did they manage to build world class competitiveness using the KAIZEN Management Philosophy? the three fundamental aspects which KAIZEN preaches include:

- CUSTOMER FOCUS through waste elimination

- EMPLOYEE INVOLVEMENT in problem solving

- PROCESS-ORIENTATION using Just In Time Techniques.

There is no "magic wand" or "Japanese miracle" as some would like to believe, except shear hard work, good discipline, unrelentless efforts to create customer satisfaction, teamwork, management by fact and more importantly, respect for people.

The following list summarises the Japanese management philosophy extremely well [12] and answers the previous question on how to crate a culture of Continuous Improvement, very eloquently:

- Leadership from the top

- Thirst for knowledge and new technology

- What we all have now is wonderful - but let us, together, find something different and better.

- Things are not black or white, but grey

- Logic alone is not enough: human nature must be considered

- Never hard decisions, but more of a choice-generation process

- Excessive energy is not burned up in overly egocentric behaviour

- Less emphasis on the cult of the individual

- We are in this for the long haul - time itself is not the issue

259

- Continuing self-development and self-fulfilment

- No overt confrontation, but long deliberation for consensus and harmony - and then rapid, effective implementation; and

- Co-operation between all groups.

7. The Essentiality of an Integrated Approach in Business Process Improvement

To support the arguments presented in the previous section, it becomes necessary to examine the issues that can "make or break" as far as creating a sustainable culture of continuous improvement.

The key issue of continuous improvement is one of mindset rather than structural and technological changes and enhancements. The various resolutions which took place in recent years and based on the latter options have all been marred with problems. Perhaps at the top of that list is the Re-Engineering and Radical Change process revolution.

As Hatten and Rosenthal (1999) conclude:

" Some companies unrealistically saw re-engineering as an almost magical silver bullet capable of solving all their problems in one fell swoop. Most simply failed to appreciate that achieving process-based cost, quality and efficiency gains ultimately depends on continuous effort - i.e. they failed to appreciate that re-engineering, like cost control, is essentially a social process".

The real shift in paradigm that will lead to a process-based culture driven by an ethos of continuous improvement, is one which has to be based on changes in management behaviour. A slight shift in the latter will induce a radical change in behaviour at the lower levels and so on. Process improvement comes through conviction and belief in the need for tackling problems and innovating for the customer. It does not however come through the super-imposition of technological and structural change on people with opposing views and beliefs.

Steering continuous improvement has to come from clearly defined vision/

260

mission and key objectives , their effective deployment and through the regularity of reviews and actions.

Without an organic process at the strategic level, a culture of continuous improvement and continuous learning cannot be developed. It will create what might be referred to as " a misfiring principle" a hit and miss approach.

Witcher and Butterworth (1999) in relation to the use of Hoshin Kanri, argue that "TQM provides the means and discipline for self management at any level of management, not just for the management of an operational process in daily work....daily pressures must be managed in such a way as to ensure that they are under control".

Hatten and Rosenthal (1999) on the other hand refer to "organisational slack" thrown away with waste. A practice attributed to the lack of taking a strategic perspective of short sightedness, short termistic and without any commitment to process improvement and continuous learning".

The arguments for an Integrated Approach is a legitimate one and self justifiable under the circumstances described in the previous paragraphs.

Whatever organisations do in the future, it has got to be clearly defined at the strategic level;, well articulated and effectively communicated.

Operational performance in all of its facets will continue to be the most critical aspect of evaluating organisational behaviour. It is however futile to review performance in isolation from strategic imperatives and key business objectives. An integration of strategic thinking with organisational performance is thus very critical.

Continuous improvement is not the outcome of various "bursts" of activity and will not be sustainable if it remains project-focused rather than process based.

The key outcome from Continuous Improvement has to be clear value to the customer through optimising process performance (i.e. ensuring there is no slack) and eliminating waste.

The key challenge for instigating a culture of continuous improvement and continuous learning is a "social" one, people-related rather than a technical one. An evolutionary approach based on paradigm shifts in thinking, believing and doing is a real pre-requisite.

An Integrative Approach is therefore not a question of choice but rather a necessary evil. Performance and Business results have in themselves got to present an integrated picture that is stakeholder orientated. They also have to be based on process-orientation, derived from continuous improvement activity, using resources available to the full (slack elimination) and more importantly they have to be driven by the social fabric of the organisation i.e. people who work through belief and conviction.

Lastly, an integrated approach has to be based on vision, strong leadership and clear strategic thinking.

References

[1] Ashby, W.R. (1965), Introduction to Cybernetics, Chapman & Hall, London, 1965.

[2] Beer, S. (1981), Brains of the firm, John Wiley, Chichester, 1981.

[3] Cluckland, P. (1981), Systems Thinking, Systems Practice, John Wiley, Chichester, 1981.

[4] Povey, B. F. (1997), Business Process Improvement, Master of Philosophy Thesis, University of Brighton.

[5] A System of Profound Knowledge, British Deming Association, London, 1992.

[6] A Perspective on Dr. Deming's Theory of Profound Knowledge, British Deming Association, London, 1992.

[7] Treite, M.D. (1995), The Deming Philosophy, New Ways to Think About the World, British Deming Association, London, 1995.

[8] Deming, W.E. (1986), Out of the Crisis, Cambridge University Press, USA.

[9] Profound Knowledge, British Deming Association, London, 1992.

[10] Tribus, M. (1993), The Germ Theory of Management, British Deming Appreciation, London, 1993.

[11] Romel, Gunter et. al. (1996), Quality Pays, MacMillan Press Ltd., London, UK.

[12] The Japanese and Business Transformation, British Deming Association, London,1995.

[13] Hatten,K.J: Rosenthal.S.R. (1999), "Managing the Process-Centred Enterprise". Long Range Planning, vol32:no 3 pp293-310

[14] Witcher, B; Butterworth, r. (1999). "Hoshin Kanri: How Xerox Manages", Long Range Planning, vol 32; no.3 pp323-332

"

Big organizations don't move on a broad front. They are more likely to move in single file. Some managers are more responsive than others. You need to use the responsive ones as pilots to stimulate the rest of the organization. "

- Joseph Juran
during a satellite seminar
"J.M. Juran on Quality,"
held on October 10, 1996

TQM Application

Leadership in TQM Implementation

Some Case Examples

Mohamed Zairi

First Published in

The TQM Magazine,
Vol. 6 No. 6, 1994, pp. 9-16
© MCB University Press, 0954-478X

Introduction

The leadership issue is frequently mentioned as being at the heart of many problems, not just those associated with the implementation of total quality management, but also in guiding organizations with sound strategies for the sustainability of superior competitive performance and long term prosperity.

This article makes some general points about leadership from the literature and discusses them in the context of seven organizational case studies and research on Baldrige Award applicants in the USA (A University of Chicago research project).

Strong leadership can perhaps be more associated with "soft issues" such as providing vision, direction and particularly with the ability of sharing, generating commitment, involving others and creating levels of synergy, consensus, congruence and enlightenment. Strong leadership has to be measured in situational and transformational terms. It is about reacting to adverse situations with wisdom, courage and object but also is about vision, risk taking and seeking success and advancement. Style, therefore, is dynamic and changes according to circumstances:

> The kind of leadership needed in times of crisis or great peril is very different from what is needed in times of stability, peace and prosperity[1].

Leaders can perhaps be compared to theatre directors, without whose contribution the play won't happen. Organizational processes are only the arena, and interpersonal processes represent the actors. Leaders need to identify what the priorities and agendas are for each actor, and have to bring the various people together so that the act is complete [2].

Leaders should not focus on themselves but rather be concerned with developing the vision and defining the mission for their organizations [3]. Leadership represents the general consensus and the level of readiness and focus there is to achieve the mission. This was compared by Stayer[4] with "a flock of geese on the wing". He argues:

> I didn't want an organizational chart with traditional lines and boxes, but a "V" of individuals who knew the common goal, took turns leading, and adjusted

their structure to the task at hand. Geese fly in a wedge, for instance, but land in waves. Most important, each individual bird is responsible for its own performance.

Leadership and Management: What Is the Difference?

Kotter[5]argues that leadership and management are different but complementary processes which are both required to steer organizations towards successful competitiveness. He comments:

> Leadership is different from management, but not for reasons most people think. Leadership isn't mystical or mysterious. It has nothing to do with having "charisma" or other exotic personality traits. It is not the province of a chosen few. Nor is leadership necessarily better than management or a replacement of it. Rather, leadership and management are two distinctive and complementary systems of action.

The distinction between leadership and management is perhaps in the fact that the former focuses more on setting the vision and relying on softer skills such as inter-personal skills to communicate the vision and generate commitment and enthusiasm to make it happen. To distinguish between the two, it may be useful to refer to the following definitions:

> Leadership means vision, cheerleading, enthusiasm, love, trust, verve, passion, obsession, consistency, the use of symbols, paying attention as illustrated by one's calendar, out-and-out drama (and the management thereof), creating heroes at all levels, coaching, effectively wondering around, and numerous other things [6]

On the other hand, effective management has been compared to "wagon masters of the Westward movement in the last century"[7]:

> A wagon master had two jobs. He had to keep the wagons moving toward their destination day after day despite all obstacles. He also had to maintain harmony and a spirit of teamwork among the members of his party and to resolve daily problems before they become divisive. A wagon master's worth was measured by his ability to reach the destination safely and to keep spirits high along the way. He had to do both in order to do either.

Leadership in the Context of TQM

Total quality management (TQM) requires a special type of leadership. In the 1990s productivity is defined in terms of human performance through creativity, problem-solving, teamwork, value adding contributions and a dedication and commitment to continuous improvement. Any effective style of leadership in this context will therefore have to have great impact on behaviour modification and changing people's attitudes.

It is no longer valid nor is it sufficient to rely on structural change or sound investment strategies on capital equipment and pioneering technologies. In the 1990s the challenge lies with leaders' ability to transform in a radical way cultures, attitudes, methods of working and so on. Performance of leaders in a modern context does not just hinge around one or two specific tasks. A recent study of 900 leaders has identified four areas where leaders focus their energies[8]:

- attention through vision;

- meaning through communication;

- trust through positioning; and

- the development of self-through positive self-regard.

Perhaps in the context of TQM what is expected of leaders is more of the doing, being more in touch, more aware and being much more concerned with developing *means* rather than being just concerned with *ends*. Leaders in the context of TQM are more focused on corporate performance rather than just their own. Leadership in the context of TQM is not about power, authority and control, it is more about empowerment, recognition, coaching and developing others.

Nowadays leadership is considered as a *must* for survival. It comes from the level of inspiration, commitment generated and corporate determination to perform. The power of modern leadership is in achieving congruence and getting wider ownership of the ultimate task of satisfying customers and building strong competitiveness. Warren Bennis, an author on leadership, is reported to have commented that:

Whips and chains are no longer an alternative. Leaders must learn to change the nature of power and how it is employed[9]:

The challenge for leaders in the context of introducing change and modem management philosophies such as TQM is best described in the following quotes [9]:

As the power of position continues to erode, corporate leaders are going to resemble not so much captains of ships as candidates running for office. They will face two fundamental tasks: first, to develop and articulate exactly what the company is trying to accomplish, and second, to create an environment in which employees can figure out what needs to be done and then do it well.

Executives who rose in traditional systems often have trouble with both. The quantitative skills that got them to the heights don't help them communicate. And if their intelligence, energy, ambition, and self-confidence are perceived as arrogance, it cuts them off from information, which makes the challenge of empowering the work force even more vexing.

Establishing Best Practice in Leadership

Results of an American Study

This study was conducted by Easton[10] as part of a research grant from the Graduate School of Business, University of Chicago. The work assessed 22 organizations representing a mixture of large and small companies and operating in both manufacturing and service sectors. The sample analysed represented organizations which submitted applications for the Malcolm Baldrige National Quality Award (MBNQA). Although the assessment of each individual company was considered to be subjective (using the MBNQA assessment criteria), the author has had vast experience as an examiner for the MBNQA for a number of years.

The assessment conducted during the study focused on the seven criteria covered by the MBNQA which include:

- leadership;
- information and analysis;

- strategic quality planning;
- human resource development and management;
- management of process quality;
- quality and operational results; and
- customer focus and satisfaction.

For the purpose of this discussion and in the context of this article only the first category will be considered. The major findings from the Easton study [10] have been grouped in terms of *strengths* and *areas for improvement*.

Key Strengths Identified

- Senior management commitment to quality is unwavering and they spend a substantial amount of their time reminding people of the importance of customers and improving quality. In addition, they put in a lot of effort in educating people, speaking in public, face to face contacts with customers, employees and so on.

- Senior management have developed a vision, a set of values to develop a quality culture in their organizations reflected by an obsession with the customer, continuous improvement, teamwork, problem-solving, respect for people, focusing on the process and so on.

- The vision achieving goal congruence in the form of customer understanding and focus and appreciating the importance of internal customers as well.

- Managing quality through a proper structure such as having a quality council, steering groups, and being active in managing quality improvement teams, the development of suggestion schemes and reward and recognition systems.

Areas for Improvement

- Senior managers' primary focus is on short- term strategic goals which tend to be financial in nature and their lack of appreciation of quality measures and improvement measures.

272

- Senior managers do not take a process-based approach in their decision making and their poor utilization of hard facts and information.

- Senior managers have very limited and poor understanding of TQM and its potential. Except from signing declarations, they devote very little time to making it work within their organizations and have little or no knowledge in defining roles for their subordinates for managing quality.

- Senior managers take a "results-oriented approach" rather than a "process-based approach". They set targets in isolation from the process and expect people to perform and deliver the expected results.

- Poor utilization of data relating to customers, suppliers and employees. As such they have very poor understanding of causes of problems and what causes variability in their organizations.

- Although a structure for quality might be present, senior managers tend to treat quality as a separate activity from the essentials of running a business and therefore can be given a low priority in comparison with activities which can lead to tangible results in the short term.

- Senior management take an "internal focus" rather than streamlining all their operations to meet external customer needs. This notion of "we know best" what the customer wants, means that quality improvements and measurement from the perspective of the end customer do not really take place.

Case Studies: Winners of Prestigious Awards

This section covers various case studies of companies that have won prestigious awards such as the MBNQA and the European Quality Award. In particular the various cases will highlight how leadership is defined, what kind of activities and initiatives are sponsored by senior managers and the level of activity they are involved in. In other words, the purpose of this analysis is really to determine the role of senior managers in TQM implementation.

Zytec Corporation

Zytec Corporation was an MBNQA winner in 1991. It designs and manufactures electronic power supplies, and also repairs them in addition to CRT monitors. It has a large industrial customer base both in the US and overseas and is considered as one of the largest multiple output switching power supply producers in the US. The company was formed in 1984 and has used quality principles since its inception.

Leadership at Zytec:

- Zytec's mission is based on three key words: *quality, service, value:*

  Zytec is a company that competes on value, it provides technical excellence in its products and believes in the importance of execution.

  We believe in a simple form and a lean staff, the importance of people as individuals, and the development of productive employees through training and capital investment.

  We focus on what we know best, thereby making a fair profit on current operations to meet our obligations and perpetuate our continued growth.

- To implement the above vision, Zytec's top management team relied on Deming's 14 points for the management of quality.

- Senior management created a structure for the management of quality, "The Deming Steering Committee", and acted as advisers to various Deming Implementation Teams whose task is to carry out major improvements to key processes.

- The senior management team developed and communicated the quality statement.

- The senior management team developed an approach for goal development, deployment and review based on best practice. This is referred to as the management by planning (MBP) process; it relies on employee involvement and feedback and drives Zytec towards achieving its short, medium and long- term goals.

- The MBP process is considered to be the best tool for communicating the quality mission, goals and objectives throughout the company.

- Senior managers are very active in promoting awareness of quality through training, seminars and open sharing of Zytec's key learnings. They are also active in talking to customers and suppliers and in major benchmarking initiatives.

Wallace Co. Inc.

This company was founded in 1942 and is family owned. It is a major industrial distributor to the US chemical market but also deals with overseas orders. The major market includes refining, chemical and petrochemical industries. It deals with maintenance and repair operations and engineering and construction projects.

Wallace became committed to quality because it has developed strong partnerships with its major customers who have very high standards of quality and who demand adherence to stringent levels of quality in every sense. Wallace won the MBNQA in 1990.

Leadership at Wallace:

- Wallace has established the quality Management Steering Committee (QMSC) which is represented by the senior management team.

- There is whole structure for managing quality which involves every manager and every employee. This structure is based on teamwork and includes, for example, quality improvement process teams, inter- departmental teams and so on.

- All senior managers have received training on TQM and its working.

- Communication on quality takes place through various vehicles such as visits, meetings, newsletters, posters and exhibitions. The major vehicle for communicating the quality message is, however, the mission statement.

- The mission statement is supported by 16 quality strategic objectives (QSOs). These are meant to drive the entire quality process.

Ritz-Carlton Hotel Company

This is a management company which develops and operates luxury hotels. It employs around 12,000 people and has subsidiary products including restaurants and banquets. Quality was introduced in the Ritz in order to set "gold standards" through having distinctive facilities and provide highly personalized services and deliver the best quality food and beverages. The Ritz-Carlton Hotel Company won the MBNQA in 1992.

Leadership at the Ritz-Carlton:

- The senior management team doubles up as the senior quality committee. They personally devise their quality strategy for the whole company.

- Senior management is actively involved in quality assurance and optimizing quality standards.

- The President and CEO communicate the quality vision throughout the organization.

- Quality at the Ritz-Carlton is implemented through the "gold standards" which include:

  - *The credo:* a guide for employees, highlighting that personalized customer satisfaction is the number one priority and also defining the critical characteristics of every product and service.

  - *The three steps of service:* defining activities and decisions related to customer interface.

  - *The Ritz-Carlton basics:* problem-solving process.

  - *A motto:* this is to emphasize commitment to serve customers in a warm and genuine manner.

Cadillac Motor Car Company

Cadillac was founded in 1902 and is a division of General Motors (GM). It competes in the luxury end of the car market and manufactures various models of vehicles. Although quality was always an important aspect of managing operations within Cadillac, the real breakthrough came in the mid-1980s through the introduction of simultaneous engineering (SE), parallel-oriented, process-based approach and a culture of work relying on teamwork and problem solving for continuous improvement. Cadillac won the MBNQA in 1990.

Leadership at Cadillac:

- Senior managers are responsible for developing and communicating the vision, values and ways for achieving intended business results.

- Senior managers have been instrumental in the change of work culture to a team-based one and the emphasis on the customer.

- In addition to the overall responsibility of implementing the business planning process (mission ===> strategic objectives ===> business objectives ===> goals ===> action plans) the top management team initiated the development of the mission:

  The mission of the Cadillac Motor Car Company is to engineer, produce and market the world's finest automobiles, known for uncompromised levels of distinctiveness, comfort, convenience and refined performance. Through its people, who are its strength, Cadillac will continuously improve the quality of its products and services to meet or exceed customer expectations and succeed as a profitable business.

- Senior managers review the annual business planning cycle and help set targets for the following years. These targets are then communicated throughout the organization and various group levels are empowered to develop their own specific goals to support the overall corporate targets.

Texas Instruments Defense Systems and Electronics Group (TI-DSEG)

This company is a manufacturer of precision-guided weapons and other advanced defence technology. It is a subsidiary of Texas Instruments Inc. Ninety-five per cent of its annual sales revenue comes from precision-guided weapons, airborne radar systems, infra-red vision equipment, electro-optic systems and electronic warfare systems. TI-DSEG is highly committed to TQM and believes that its quality goals and business goals are one and the same. The commitment to achieve the highest of quality standards can be demonstrated by TI's determination to achieve six-Sigma quality standards (a defect rate of 3.4 per million) by 1995 and to reduce new product development time by 25 per cent each year. TI-DSEG won the MBNQA in 1992.

Leadership at TI-DSEG:

- Senior management communicate the company's quality values and are very active in promoting and supporting TQM implementation, through attending meetings, talking to employees, answering written letters, using management by walk around (MBWA).

- TI evaluates the quality commitment of all its managers through their annual performance reviews.

- TI has a proper structure of deploying quality based on teamwork, quality improvement teams and other team structures.

- TI is very active in promoting quality externally and is a member of research groups on quality issues, benchmarking associations, and is actively helping the transfer of knowledge within the business community it is part of.

National Roads and Motorists Association (NRMA)

This Australian association was founded in 1920 and offers services to all its members on a national basis in the motoring field. It is one of the largest motoring organizations in the world with over two million members and is Australia's largest general insurer. NRMA was the winner of the Australian Quality Award (AQA) in 1992.

Quality within NRMA has evolved over the years. Its commitment to establishing a culture of never ending improvement is expressed in the mission statement:

To provide road service and a range of quality services for members, at the lowest possible cost consistent with sound financial management.

To promote the interests of motorists in good roads, safety and consumer protection.

Leadership at NRMA:

- The organizational structure supports the implementation of TQM.

- Each senior manager has direct line responsibility for continuous improvement in a specific area. The role encompasses many activities including innovation, problem-solving, monitoring progress, empowering teams to perform, reward and recognize efforts.

- The CEO is instrumental in the communication of company vision and creating a climate aware of the need continuously to improve quality.

- The deployment of quality takes place through the translation of corporate targets into individual unit plans, goals, reviews and action plan development at various levels.

Rank Xerox Limited

Rank Xerox Ltd is part of Rank Xerox Corporation. It is one of Europe's leading high technology companies. Its customer base represents commercial, industrial and public sector-based organizations. They deliver anything from small office copiers, workstations, laser printers, electronic printing systems and colour copiers. The company is represented by 19 operating units.

The implementation of quality at Rank Xerox Ltd started in 1984, gradually moving away from focusing on the product and service, to an obsession with improving processes and delivering value added to the customer base. Now quality drives the business of Rank Xerox and the culture is one of true quality based on thousands of teams working in different areas and using various tools for carrying out the necessary improvements. Rank Xerox Ltd were the first winners of the European Quality Award (EQA) in 1992.

Leadership at Rank Xerox Ltd:

- The senior management team is central to TQM implementation. It developed Rank Xerox's quality policy:

  Rank Xerox is a quality company. Quality is the basic business principle for Rank Xerox.

  Quality means providing our external and internal customers with innovative products and services that fully satisfy their requirements.

  Quality improvement is the job of every employee.

- The quality strategy by which the above quality policy is implemented has evolved from being a *goal* to a *strategy* and now into a *process* relevant to all levels within the organization. This is referred to as *leadership through quality.*

- Senior managers lead all training initiatives and on a continuous basis assess the requirements of all employees for continuously improving quality.

- Senior managers are expected to lead by example by using tools and techniques of TQM and taking a process perspective to solve various problems.

- The communication of the quality message tales place through the formal deployment process *(policy deployment process).* The deployment of goals and the generation of commitment takes place through weekly, monthly, quarterly and yearly meetings.

- Rank Xerox uses a quality improvement process and a six-step problem solving process to promote a culture of quality. Review of the culture development takes place through appraisal of individual performances, review of quality progress by looking at results and self-assessment.

- Senior managers reward quality achievements and recognize quality efforts. Recognition is delivered to individuals and groups of people, at departmental, national and international levels.

- Senior managers ensure that quality implementation is adequately resourced through networks, senior appointments and funding.

- Senior managers actively encourage the involvement of customers and suppliers in the quality effort.

- Senior managers promote quality outside Rank Xerox within professional associations, local community, attendance at conferences and seminars, and by writing books and articles.

Key Ingredients for Effective Quality Leadership

The discussion in this article, whether from the review of the literature or the case studies, indicates that leadership requirements for the 1990s are to a large extent different from those in the past. There are areas in which traditionally leaders tended not to be involved in but are now required to do so; in addition and in terms of style, leaders in the context of TQM for instance are expected to have more of a "hands on" role and have, in addition to their brilliance at financial skills and strategic skills, to be good communicators and efficient at inter-personal contacts.

Based on the analysis of the case studies and Easton's[10] review, the following are perhaps areas where leaders need to focus the core of their activities; they could be the pre-determinants of their effectiveness and could be used as a measure of their performance.

Setting the Vision and the Strategic Choice

Leaders in any organization will be expected to develop the vision of their organization reflecting aspirations for the short term, medium term and long term. A healthy mix will ensure that performance delivers in different ways and at different periods of time.

Communicating the Vision, Generating Corporate Commitment

Leaders can only be considered to be effective once they have shared their vision with all employees. Many efforts which result in excellent blueprints fail because they remain as "theory" and do not get shared and communicated effectively. The communication of the vision has to be based on a sound framework which reaches everyone in the organization and which encourages discussion, feedback and involvement. This is very critical since TQM's workings are more or less from a bottom-up approach and unless there is corporate ownership, no performance will ensue.

Developing a Process-based Culture

Part of a leader's role in a modern business context is to change the culture of the organization. One of the essential requirements of TQM is to focus more on the process and less on the individual. It is to organize work so that there is an inter-connectedness between the various roles and appreciation of everyone's efforts since what is delivered to the end customer is a team-based effort. Processes represent the capability of the organization to meet customer

281

requirements both in the short term and the long term. The capability to deliver is not dependent on any specific function and has to rely on all the various contributions. Traditional structural approaches do not support the process-based view. Leaders in the context of TQM, will, therefore, have to have a team-based structure which cuts across all the functions and boundaries and which will appreciate all the various contributions.

Recognition of People as Assets

One of the premises of TQM is that people are the most important asset for achieving high standards of competitive performance. This recognition has to be supported by:

- investment in training and employee development;
- involvement, participation in decision making;
- setting goals and targets;
- participation in team projects;
- creativity and innovation encouragement; and
- reward and recognition.

Performance Management

Leaders in a modern business context have to realize that performance is not solely measured in terms of financial *results* (short term) but efforts have to be measured in terms of strengthening the *processes,* building capability for future demands and ensuring that there is a high level of consistency and confidence in satisfying customer requirements time and time again (long term).

Performance reviews therefore have to take place at various levels and at different intervals in time. This will reflect wider ownership and will indicate that the notion of control is focused on the process rather than the individual.

Developing Partnerships

It is widely recognized that modern competitiveness has to rely on building strong partnership with customers and suppliers. Effective leadership will be based on creating a climate of *win-win* through, perhaps, working with fewer suppliers but on a strategic approach which will help deliver benefits for each party. Issues of capability, resources, commitment to continuous improvement, and technical know-how will be taken into consideration when trying to choose partners. Similarly, leaders can be very instrumental in generating customer commitment for agreeing on long-term working relationships. Regular visits, joint projects, additional services, joint exploitation of technological know-how and so on are opportunities which could be effectively exploited for developing partnerships.

External Ambassadors

Leaders have a very important role in promoting their organizations, through PR, seminars, conferences, professional associations, local academic institutions and within the wider community. Networking is absolutely essential in modern competitiveness. Through networking, benchmarking activities can take place, to compare practices, methods and performance, to learn new ways and inject them back in organizations concerned and more importantly networking ensures continuity, perseverance and avoids complacency.

Leaders have a role to play within the community by ensuring that there is social responsibility, a caring attitude and a development of the community concerned through the creation of jobs and prosperity.

Developing Leadership in the Organization

Effective leadership in a modern business context is taking time and effort to develop others and being humble, kind and generous with comments, advice, information, tips and so on. The following Chinese proverb expresses this last point clearly:

Of the best leader, when he is gone, they will say: we did it ourselves.

References

1. Dimma, W.A., "On Leadership", Business Quarterly, Winter 1989, pp. 17-20.

2 Zairi, M., Total Quality Management for Engineers, Woodhead Publishing Ltd, Cambridge, 1991.

3. Drucker, P.F., Managing the Non-profit Organization, Butterworth-Heinemann Ltd, Oxford, UK, 1990.

4. Stayer, R., "How I Learned to Let My Workers Lead", Harvard Business Review, November- December, 1990, pp. 66-83.

5. Kotter, J.P., "What Leaders Really Do", Harvard Business Review, May-June 1990, pp. 103-11.

6. Peters, T. and Austin, N., "MBWA (Managing by Walking Around)", California Management Review, Vol. 28 No. 1, Fall 1985, pp. 9-34.

7. Ninomya, J.S., "Wagon Masters and Lesser Managers", Harvard Business Review, March- April 1988, pp.84-90.

8. Bennis, W. and Nanus, B., Leaders: The Strategies for Taking Charge, Harper & Row, New York, NY, 1985.

9. Huey, J., "The New Post-heroic Leadership", Fortune, February 1994, pp. 18-22.

10. Easton, G.S., "The 1993 State of US Total Quality Management: A Baldrige Examiners' Perspective", California Management Review, Spring 1993, pp. 32-54.

**Mohamed Zairi is Unilever Lecturer in TQM,
Bradford University Management Centre, Bradford, UK.**

Total partnership for primary health care provision: a proposed model: part I

A.K. Aggarwal Meltham Road Surgery, Huddersfield, UK
Mohamed Zairi European Centre for TQM, Bradford University Management Centre, Bradford, UK

Presents the first of a two part paper, based on a study which examined the dynamics of primary health care provision. The study examined 49 general practices in the Kirklees area, UK, through a detailed questionnaire mode. The response was 67 per cent covering the views of 106 doctors. To capture further input for the study, an indepth seminar with nine doctors from a range of practices was conducted. Examines internal factors for managing general practices and the levels of competence in addressing financial, strategic, quality issues and whether general practices get involved in any external activities for new learning and benchmarking. Comprehensively covers common areas of concern and areas where expertise may be inadequate or lacking.

First Published in

International Journal of Health Care Quality Assurance
10/7 [1997] 277–284
© MCB University Press [ISSN 0952-6862]

Introduction

The National Health Service (NHS) was created on 5 July 1948 as a result of the passing of the National Health Service Act in 1946. In England and Wales the legislation laid a duty on the Minister of Health:

> To Promote the establishment of a comprehensive health service designed to secure improvement on the physical and mental health of the people and the prevention, diagnosis and treatment of illness and for that purpose to provide or secure the effective provision of resources.

It intended to make health services available universally and equitably with reference to clinically defined need, rather than ability to pay or other considerations.

There were five founding principles:

1 Universality: the service was available to all regardless of income, age, sex, employment, area of residence or insurance qualification.

2 Comprehensiveness: the service provided the full range of services covering physical and mental health – the prevention, diagnosis and treatment of all conditions.

3 Free at point of use: all services were initially provided free at the point of use to patients.

4 Accessibility: the service was intended to be readily available at the time of need.

5 Equity: the services were provided on the basis of need with priority for treatment being determined by need only and not by any other consideration.

Finance for the NHS was raised through general taxation and National Insurance. However, the cost of providing an equitable health service has caused increasing concern for governments. In 1948 expenditure on the NHS represented 3.9 per cent of Britain's Gross National Product (GNP) and in 1984 has risen to 6.2 per cent of GNP. In monetary terms, since 1984, total expenditure on the NHS has gone up from £16 billion to nearly £35 billion in 1992/93. Even accounting for inflation this represents a substantial increase in real terms.

The many changes in demography and society in the UK partly explain the increase in expenditure but the changes themselves had a profound impact on the running of the health service.

Some of the more important changes include:

- An increase in life expectancy from 60 years for males in 1948 to 72 years in 1994.

- The growth in the number of elderly people in the population.

- Continuing inequalities between social and ethnic groups and between geographical areas.

- Increased levels of real income for most people alongside the emergence of an underclass.

- The persistence of high levels of unemployment.

- Changes in the family, including an increase in divorce rates and in single parent families.

- The emergence of new patterns of work centring on an increase in self-employment, part-time work and job sharing.

In view of these changes and the escalating cost of running the health service, other principles have become important. They include[1-4].

1 Cost containment. The service should live within a budget set by the government to reflect the level of resources that can be afforded.

2 Efficiency. The resources that are made available should be used efficiently.

3 Responsiveness. The service should be responsive to the demands of patients and service users.

4 Choice. The service should offer users a choice whenever this is possible.

The net result of all this has been the restructuring of the NHS on several occasions, in 1974, 1982, 1985, 1991 and 1996.

From 1948-1974, the management structure of the NHS was highly centralized with most of the managerial control at the regional or national level. General practitioners were responsible to Family Practitioner Committees who, in turn, were responsible to the Ministry of Health via local Executive Councils. Figure 1 illustrates the NHS structure between 1948 and 1974.

The NHS in the 1990s

The NHS reforms of April 1991 involved:

- The separation of purchaser and provider roles.

- The creation of self-governing NHS Trusts.

- The transformation of District Health Authorities into purchasers of services.

- The introduction of GP fundholding (GPFH).

- The use of contracts or service agreements to link the purchasers and providers[5].

This process of change has gradually developed. In 1995 over 90 per cent of all hospitals had achieved Trust status. On the purchasing side by April 1994 there were 2,000 general practices which had become fundholders and covered 8,800 general practitioners and 36 per cent of the population. With more joining the scheme in 1995, it estimated that 50 per cent of the population would be registered with GPFHs. Research by Glennerster et al.[6] has demonstrated that general practitioner fundholding has led to a number of changes in service provision including employing a wider range of staff in the practice, negotiating shorter waiting times for hospital services and obtaining better value for money for drugs expenditure. The role of District Health Authorities as purchasers took off after a slow start. Many of them had to merge to form viable purchasing organizations and to consolidate managerial skills. Furthermore District Health Authorities and Family Health Services Authorities (FHSAs) engaged in joint working of various kinds. These initially loose arrangements have been cemented by new legislation and in April 1996 they merged to create Commissioning Authorities with a responsibility for primary care, purchase of secondary health care and for developing health plans and examining resource allocation. Also in 1996 Regional Health Authorities were abolished with the creation of regional offices to implement the strategy of a streamlined NHS Management Executive.

Figure 1 illustrates the structure of the NHS as at 1993 and Figure 2 the structure as from April 1996.

The need for a partnership approach in primary health care provision

As the NHS is a national service, parliament has had a centralizing influence on how the NHS budget is spent. In the 1980s it exerted increasing control over the affairs of NHS authorities who were held to account for the use of resources and their performance in delivering national policies and priorities. As costs rose and efficiency became the driving force, reforms were introduced involving a move away from a centralized administrative structure to a more pluralistic set of arrangements in which competition as well as management plays a part in determining how services develop. Providers of care, mainly NHS Trusts, will have to be more responsive to the needs of patients and the public if they are to attract contracts from purchasers. However, there are uncertainties. First, in a competitive internal market there are bound to be winners and losers and public pressure may force the Government to intervene on matters of hospital closures and service nationalization. Hence the market may not be allowed to operate without intervention. Second, the success of the reforms is likely to depend on the response of doctors and other professionals who have a significant influence over the direction in which services develop. Both GPs and hospital doctors value their clinical freedom and this limits the extent to which managers can influence the allocation of resources. Third, the ability and expertise of managers to manage the change process will influence success. Clinicians have traditionally been resistant to change and this poses new challenges for NHS managers. Methods to overcome this are already in use including the resource management initiative and appointing doctors to managerial posts. Their effect is yet to be determined. In primary health care, FHSAs appointed Medical Advisors and set up Primary Health Care Development Teams but yet doctors' decisions on which patients to treat and how to continue to have a major bearing on the provision of services and there is no guarantee that the priorities espoused either nationally or locally will be carried into action.

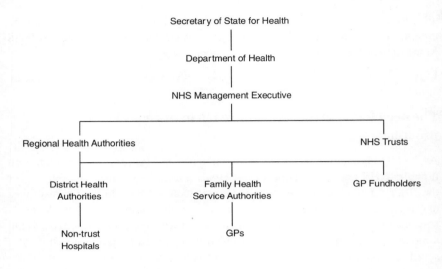

Figure 1 The NHS 1993

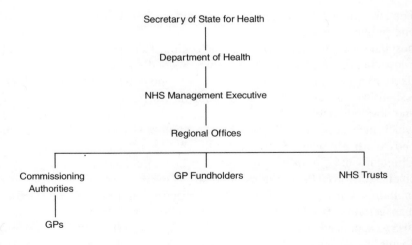

Figure 2 The NHS, 1996

Objectives of the study

The aims and objectives of this study are as follows:

1 To assess the effectiveness of the general practitioner/employed staff interface and working relationship.

2 To assess the effectiveness of the general practitioner/attached staff interface and working relationship.

3 To assess the effectiveness of internal management personnel and systems in a range of medical practices.

4 To assess the perceptions and effectiveness of the FHSA (Commissioning Authority)/ GP interface.

5 To assess the effectiveness of two key FHSA tools in improving standards in primary health care, i.e.

• The Independent Medical Advisers.

• The Medical Audit Advisory Groups (MAAGs).

6 To assess general practitioners' perceptions of future opportunities and threats which could affect their ability to provide a quality service.

7 To determine some of the critical factors both internal and external which would improve the quality of primary health care.

8 To determine, as far as possible, the present morale and motivation among general practitioners and possible reasons for dissatisfaction, if applicable.

Methodological approach used

The main part of the study entailed a questionnaire sent to 49 practices in the West Yorkshire area selected at random but with consideration to include practices of all sizes. There were five fundholding practices as the proportion of practices in the Kirklees area. The breakdown of the practices by size is as follows:

291

- One doctor: four.
- Two doctors: ten.
- Three doctors: ten.
- Four doctors: twelve.
- Five doctors: five.
- Six plus doctors: three.

The total number of general practitioners covered by the study is 157. The questionnaire was posted to the lead partner in the practice with a stamped addressed envelope for replies. They were asked to present a view of the practice as a whole.

The second and lesser part of the study involved a conference of eight senior partners from nine practices in the Kirklees area. The practices were chosen to reflect size and status with four fundholding practices represented. The aim of this meeting was to determine GPs' values and external management needs to improve the quality of primary health care provision.

Thirty-three out of 49 questionnaires were returned. This is a percentage response of 67 per cent. The number of doctors represented by the responses was 106 (67.5 per cent response). See Figure 3.

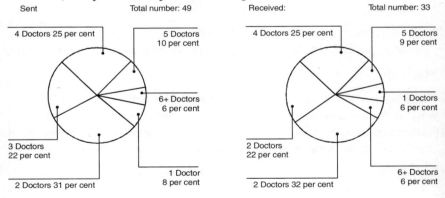

Figure 3 Questionnaire response by practice size

An analysis of internal management in general medical practices

Practice nurses and staff

In modern day general practice, practice nurses are considered an essential part of the primary health care team (PHCT) and it reflects quality of service provision. Six per cent of the practices have no practice nurse. If one considers that the optimum level is 0.5 WTE per one WTE general practitioner, then only 24 per cent of practices meet this standard.

It has been well accepted and is reflected by previous arrangements in terms of FHSA reimbursements for staff wages that the standard for practice staff numbers, including nursing staff, is 2 per WTE GP.

Hence, a reasonable standard for administrative practice staff is 1.5 WTE/GP. This study shows that 55 per cent of the practices fall below this threshold with 6 per cent employing a very low level of staff.

For a quality service, practices need to meet with the other members of the PHCT and this study shows that 33 per cent of the practices do not meet with the PHCT and, of those who do, only 36 per cent meet on a weekly basis.

The study shows that only 6 per cent of practices do not meet with their employed staff but of those who do, 26 per cent meet less than monthly.

Quality of management

Figure 4 shows the response to six questions indicating the internal quality in doctor/ employed staff relationships. This process is vital in service delivery. The proportion of respondents indicating that the internal customer/ supplier chain is effective only some of the time is significant.

When asked the question about the facilitating and inhibiting factors in practices that influenced a good working relationship with employed staff, the most common themes were:

Facilitating factors:

- a team building course;

- a staff room;
- staff social events;
- a Staff appraisal system;
- written office protocols;
- a culture of respect for each other.

Inhibiting factors:

- poor building design;
- lack of staff numbers;
- poor staff motivation;
- poor communication;
- lack of practice management skills;
- poor staff attitudes.

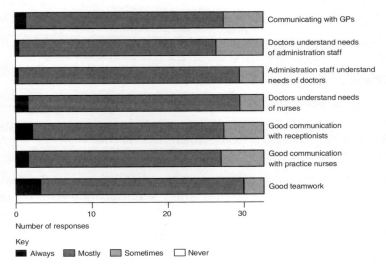

Figure 4 Quality in managing employed staff

Figure 5 illustrates the response to questions to determine the quality of working relationships between GPs and attached staff (district nurses, health visitors, midwives, etc.). It shows that a third of the practices feel that communication is good only sometimes. Also that the understanding of needs of each other is another area of concern with 42-54 per cent of the practices responding that this is good only some of the time.

The relationship between GPs and attached staff within a PHCT setting is very important in the provision of a quality and a comprehensive level of health care and this issue, therefore, needs to be addressed.

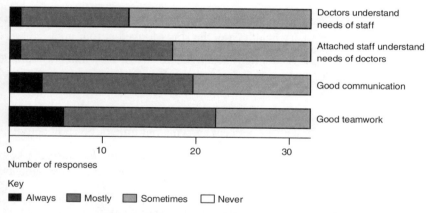

Figure 5 Quality in managing attached staff

Quality of internal practice management

Of respondents, 12 per cent, do not have a practice manager and, of those who do, only 6 per cent meet weekly. Remarkably 4 per cent of the practices never meet their practice managers! In terms of quality of communication, the study seems to show that, while this is good, practice managers communicate better with doctors than vice versa. Of the respondents, 35 per cent rated this to three or below, which does indicate that there is scope for improvement in a significant number of medical practices.

295

Information tools

In assessing the use of support tools to deliver a quality service, the study shows that, while 91 per cent of respondents had a computer system, only 88 per cent were able to use it to its potential. While the majority of practices collect information on hospital referrals, consultation rates and study prescribing data, only 18 per cent of them compare this information with other practices. Furthermore, the study shows that these are in the main GP fundholding practices.

Quality tools

In order to obtain an assessment of the application of some internal tools to facilitate quality in primary health care, the study looked at four areas:

1 Use of tools to assess practice effectiveness. Most respondents replied positively but 18 per cent of them carry out little or no assessment in this area.

2 Use of audit to evaluate and improve performance. Again, most respondents use this quality tool, with 12 per cent carrying out little or no audit activity.

3 Use of patient satisfaction scores/studies. This tool for measuring a key outcome in health care is vital. However, 66 per cent of these respondents carry out little or no such studies.

4 An enthusiastic and motivated team. Of the respondents, 91 per cent scored 1-3, indicating that the majority of responding practices have a motivated team – commitment and motivation are important requirements in delivering quality (see Figure 6).

External benchmarking activities

This part of the study was designed to evaluate the use and importance of comparison and benchmarking to drive up quality. Five areas were covered and the results are represented in Figure 7.

1 Visiting other practices. Of the practices, 63 per cent felt that this was not important to them. This could be considered as an opportunity being missed,

as one way of learning about best practice is through visiting other medical practices.

2   Comparing prescribing patterns. Of the responding practices, 82 per cent, did not feel this to be an important activity. This is most surprising as this study has also shown that 88 per cent of practices regularly scrutinize their prescribing data. The effectiveness of this would be greatly enhanced if there was comparison with colleagues from other practices.

3   Comparing hospital referral patterns. Of the respondents, 75 per cent do not feel this to be a useful tool. This may be because of the complexities in interpretation of this information but nevertheless gives an opportunity for self-audit, reflection and possible further evaluation of advancement.

4   Clinical meetings with colleagues. Only 12 per cent of the respondents felt this to be unimportant. This is a useful tool for benchmarking and learning best practice in clinical areas.

5   Meetings with FHSA for practice development. Of the respondents, 27 per cent felt that this was not important. Of the others, many made comments that, while they felt these were important, the FHSAs were disinterested and unhelpful.

It has to be said that, of practices strongly in favour of comparing data with other practices and using the FHSA for development, most of them were fundholding practices. It can be argued that they have an incentive for doing so but this opportunity needs to be extended to most practices.

Effectiveness of key areas of practice management

Six areas were examined (see Figure 8):

1   Business planning.

2   Setting clinical and administrative objectives and goals.

3   An internal Patient's Charter.

4   An internal complaints procedure.

5. Mechanisms to determine patient satisfaction.

6   A staff appraisal scheme.

Of all responding practices, most are effective in setting clinical and administrative objectives and have set up internal complaints procedures. However, over half have not taken up the issues of an internal charter for patients or mechanisms to determine patient satisfaction. As far as business planning and staff appraisal systems are concerned, there appears to be a dichotomy with approximately half the respondents finding these areas to be effective and others not. This may be due to a lack of managerial expertise. However, this same study has indicated that 97 per cent of the respondents with a practice manager consider them to be of a reasonable standard. It may be that these systems are viewed with suspicion and of being of little value.

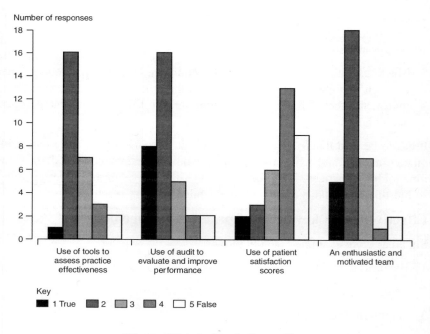

Figure 6 Internal tools for quality

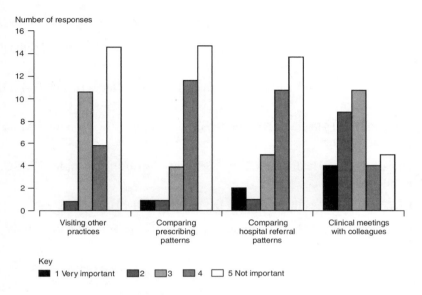

Figure 7 Activities for benchmarking

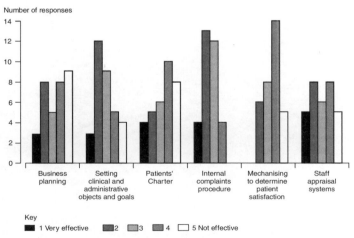

Figure 8 Effectiveness of key areas

References

1 Roberts, J., "Kenneth Clarke: hatchet man or remoulder?", British Medical Journal, Vol. 301, 1990, pp. 1386-6.

2 Department of Health and Social Security, Promoting Better Health, HMSO, London, 1987.

3 Department of Health and Social Security , Working for Patients, HMSO, London, 1989.

4 Department of Health and Social Security, Caring for People, HMSO, London, 1989.

5 Department of Health, Managing the New NHS, DoH, London, 1983.

6 Glennerster, H. et al., A Foothold for Fundholding, Kings Fund Institute, London, 1992.

Total partnership for primary health care provision: a proposed model: part II

A.K. Aggarwal Meltham Road Surgery, Huddersfield, UK
Mohamed Zairi European Centre for TQM, Bradford University Management Centre, Bradford, UK

This is the second part in a paper which studied the dynamics of primary health care provision. This paper examines external factors related to the management of General Practices. The study revealed that there are major problems at GP/FHSA interfaces involving poor communications, needs evaluation and understanding, and the lack of teamwork. The paper argues that attempts by FHSAs in terms of initiatives are so far failing and have not effectively been able to build strong partnerships between the parties concerned. The paper concludes by proposing a Model of Total Partnership for effective primary health care provision. The model suggests that structures need to be modified in a horizontal way, focusing on patients and building a collaborative way between FHSAs and GPs in a seamless fashion. The model is based on Total Quality Management (TQM) principles and is represented by the building of a customer-supplier chain, the spirit of continuous improvement and synergy through teamwork with the ultimate goal of Total Patient Satisfaction.

First Published in

International Journal of Health Care Quality Assurance
11/1 [1998] 7–13
© MCB University Press [ISSN 0952-6862]

An analysis of external management factors of general medical practices

As perceptions are indicative of the quality of relationships between any two bodies, it was felt important to assess GPs' perceptions of their FHSA. Results are illustrated in Figure 1. They clearly show that the majority of responding practices felt that:

- The FHSAs have too much authority.
- There is poor understanding between GPs and FHSA managers in terms of each other's roles and functions.
- There is poor communication between GPs and FHSAs.
- There is poor teamwork between GPs and FHSAs for the delivery of health care.

Effectiveness of the FHSA

This part of the study was designed to assess the effectiveness of the FHSA in six key areas. Figure 2 illustrates the results. They indicate that FHSAs rated well in terms of their skills in financial administration and in assistance to GPs with staff training. However, they rated less well on facilitating General Practice development. The main areas of deficiency were felt to be in terms of the FHSA's understanding of health needs and of problems in General Practice at the grassroots level.

This indicates that whilst FHSAs are good at the "harder" elements of management, e.g., finances, they are less good at the "softer" issues of developing understanding, rapport and communication with the suppliers of primary health care, the General Practitioners.

Effectiveness of MAAGs

Medical Audit Advisory Groups (MAAGs) were set up five years ago to stimulate the ethos of medical audit. These groups are part of the FHSA and funded by them. As their main objective was to improve the quality of health care provision, or at least to facilitate it, it seemed to be important to assess its effectiveness. The results are presented in Figure 3. The findings were that half the respondents felt that MAAGs have not achieved their main objective. From April 1996, MAAGs may take on different roles and will be allowed to develop, as individual FHSAs see it appropriate.

Effectiveness of the Medical Adviser to the FHSA

FHSAs have appointed Independent Medical Advisers with part of their brief being to improve prescribing and health promotion in medical practices. It was felt that they could stimulate practice development through analysis and providing feedback to practices on their annual reports.

Hence it was felt appropriate, as part of this study, to investigate the effectiveness of the Independent Medical Adviser. The results are illustrated in Figure 4. They show that they have hitherto not succeeded in any of the areas assessed, i.e.:

- Improving medical service provision.

- Improving prescribing.

- Improving health promotion.

- Assisting in practice development.

- Improving communication at the GP/FHSA interface.

It has to be said, however, that whilst Independent Medical Advisers have not been shown to be effective in the above areas, most respondents felt that they have not been a hindrance in providing medical services.

Practice needs for improving the quality of health care provision

All respondents in this study were asked to list the top six clinical factors which would enable them to raise standards of health care. The ten most commonly stated factors are as follows:

1 An increase in attached staff/practice nurses;

2 More time for patients/smaller list sizes.

3 Removal of the 24 hour responsibility.

4   Personal educational training and opportunities for self-advancement.

5   Reduced FHSA interference/bureaucracy.

6   Patient education programmes.

7   Improved communication/teamwork with the Primary Health Care Team (PHCT).

8   Efficiency in use of computers.

9   Motivation and enthusiasm of GP partners.

10 Setting regular goals and objectives.

The study then went on to determine the possible areas of assistance for GPs which would enable them to improve their quality of health care provision. Ten areas were assessed for a Yes/No response and, as represented in Figures 5 and 6, the majority of respondents require help in all the ten areas vis: (in order of strength of positive response).

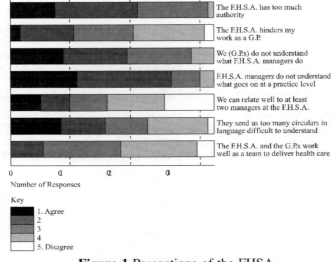

Figure 1 Perceptions of the FHSA

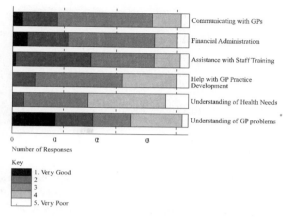

Figure 2 Effectiveness of the FHSA

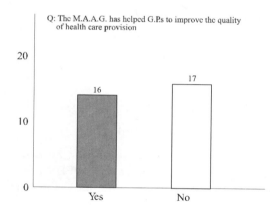

Figure 3 Effectiveness of medical audit advisory groups (MAAGs)

1 Learning about good ideas/best practice.

2 Improved staff training.

3 Continuing education for nurses.

4   Improving systems in the practice.

5   Continuing education for doctors.

6. Help with practice management skills.

7   Partnerships with secondary health care providers.

8   Comparing practice data with other practices.

9   Help with business planning.

10 Training in quality issues.

In an open question, respondents were asked to list key activities that they would like the FHSA to help them with to improve the quality of health care. In addition to the ten areas shown in Figures 5 and 6, other areas highlighted include:

- reduction in paperwork;

- improving communication;

- increased level of staff;

- better use of computers;

- practice development techniques; and

- bringing all practices to the gold standard.

Many respondents stated that a co-operative relationship with FHSAs with facilitation rather than policing and perhaps a named FHSA manager for each practice for personal contact could lead to better provision of primary health care.

Perceptions of the future

The threats

It has recently been widely reported in various literatures that one of the key reasons for GP stress is the threats they face. This part of the study has attempted to determine the possible areas of threats of stress to GPs. As shown in Figure 7, the majority of respondents feel that the FHSA will increase its control over GPs and that their future as an independent contractor is under threat. Furthermore, they feel that the administrative workload in General Medical Practice has distracted them from good clinical practice. Most worrying of all is the majority view and a probable consequence of the above factors that most GPs feel that they are unlikely to be able to raise the quality of health care provision.

The opportunities

Figure 8 illustrates that GPs are seeking opportunities and the majority view is for a collaborative partnership and more effective communication with FHSAs. There is hope that the new commissioning authorities will improve relations with GPs but there is a feeling of negativity in terms of the likely absence of a clear vision for General Practice. Above all, GPs are looking forward to opting out of a 24 hour commitment.

Reasons for dissatisfaction (low morale)

Almost 75 per cent of the respondents felt dissatisfied with the General Practice existing set up which can only have an adverse effect on their ability to deliver a quality service. The top three reasons stated in order of frequency of response were:

1   loss of recognition;

2   loss of status/esteem; and

3   loss of opportunities for self-advancement.

Other reasons stated were:

• increased patient demand/expectation;

• loss of ability to innovate;

• poor relations with the FHSA; and

• low importance of GP opinion.

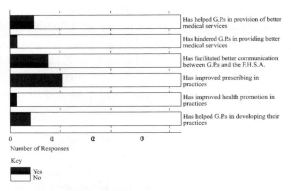

Figure 4 Effectiveness of the medical advisor to the FHSA

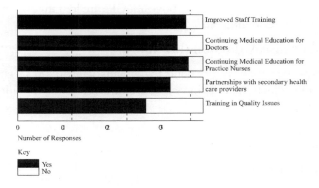

Figure 5 Areas of assistance

Towards a partnership model of primary care provision

The issues

The General Medical Services Committee of the British Medical Association in its publication General Practice: A British Success (1993) expressed the belief that:

> Primary Health Care of a high standard should be available to everyone in the United Kingdom.

308

Following this publication, the Department of General Practice at the University of Manchester carried out three large studies comprising the quality of service provision in five health districts (Wilkin et al., 1984; Wilkin and Metcalfe, 1984). Large variations in every measured parameter were found. The following year, Fountain (1985) concluded that: "Good quality practice needs good quality management". Donald Irvine (1990) in his book Managing for Quality in General Practice states that: "Producing high quality patient care will be best achieved by encouraging every practice to have the internal capacity to manage for quality."

Obstacles to quality: the GP dimension

GPs are in a unique position in the structure of the health service in terms of their autonomy as suppliers of primary health and yet there is managerial control from FHSAs and the NHS Management Executive.

On the whole, General Practices have not taken advantage of implementing the principles of TQM in their organisations. Laffel (1990) has suggested three possible reasons:

1   Doctors are trained to act primarily as advocates for patients.

2   Doctors are trained to assume responsibility for all aspects of the encounter between a patient and the health care system.

3   Doctors value their time in looking after patients rather than improvement projects.

Zairi (1993) found a similar set of reasons to be a barrier for implementing TQM in medical practice. There is evidence of this in this study which is best illustrated by first considering a model for delivering quality health care. Figure 9 links clinical core values which are at the heart of every GP and TQM values to drive internal GP processes.

Evidence from this study indicates that this model is not working in practice. The evidence is as follows:

•   Teamwork – It is shown that there are considerable problems in teamwork with employed and especially attached staff.

- Patient focus – This study shows that most respondents do not make any attempt to determine patient satisfaction.

- Process improvement – It is shown that a significant proportion of the respondents do not use measurement tools, e.g. audit to assess and improve performance. Support tools, e.g. computers, are used to theirmaximum potential in only 12 per cent of the respondents. Also, there is little benchmarking activity and this must impede performance improvement.

- Management of health care – This study shows that the majority of respondents have difficulty in this area, especially in terms of planning, human resource management and focus on improvement of care, e.g. Patients' Charter.

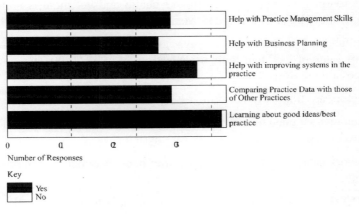

Figure 6 Areas of assistance

310

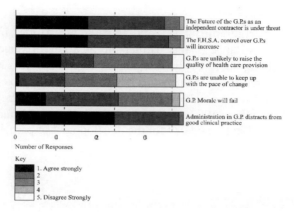

Figure 7 The future threats facing general practitioners

The reasons for this apparent failure are determined from the assessment of practice needs. Whilst GP morale is low and the era of consumerism has led to increased patient demands, the key reason for GPs failing to work to quality models is because of poor internal capability in terms of management skills, human resource management, benchmarking and quality assurance. As indicated in early discussions, the vast majority of respondents would like the FHSA to provide assistance in all these and other areas. Myerson (1992) in his study of 20 urban GPs found that their perceptions were very similar to those identified in this study.

The proposed model

It is quite clear from this study that the way forward for quality in primary health care is through a partnership between FHSAs and GPs, which hitherto does not exist. This view is echoed by another independent study by Zairi (1993).

Figure 10 illustrates the addition of a partnership between GPs and FHSAs to Figure 9, as another major driver for quality health provision and completes the proposed model. It is suggested that the partnership is based on the principles of TQM and linked by a "customer supplier" relationship.

311

The key elements

The GP-FHSA Partnership. The Total Partnership Model in Figure 10 emphasises the importance of this partnership as a key driver of quality. A recent conference organised by the Institute for Health Services Management entitled "From Hierarchies to Partnerships" (NHS Management Executive News, 1992) has reported on the value of partnerships within the health service. Metcalfe (1992) and Wall (1992) both write about the lost opportunities through present management styles and call for the development of partnerships based on trust.

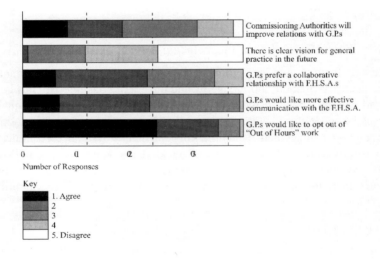

Figure 8 The future opportunities for general practitioners

312

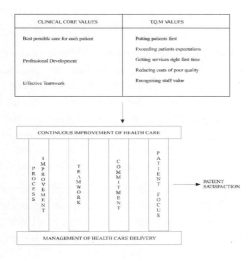

Figure 9 Driving for quality: the internal GP model

The key critical success factors of this partnership based on developing quality in General Practice are:

- Teamwork. This study has demonstrated that there is hitherto poor understanding and teamwork between GPs and FHSAs. Furthermore most GPs would like a collaborative partnership with FHSAs. Cameron (1990), Morley et al. (1990), Sloane (1994) and Wilson (1990), have all emphasised the importance of teamwork between GPs and FHSAs. May (1995) states that the new commissioning authorities in 1996 must move towards a primary care led NHS.

- Communication. This study has clearly demonstrated that there is a major obstacle in communication between FHSAs and GPs and also that GPs are looking for an improvement in this area. Effective communication is a key component of teamwork and through information sharing forms a bridge in a partnership. FHSAs need to set up strategies to improve on personal

313

communication and not rely on written memos which GPs find difficult to understand.

- Leadership. Fleishman (1973) and Hersey (1988) defined leadership as using communication processes to influence the activities of a group towards the attainment of a goal, leader behaviour is how a manager acts towards members of the system. The goal in primary health care needs to be delivery of quality primary health care and patient satisfaction. FHSAs need to use a high consideration leadership style with GPs for collaboration rather than policing. Furthermore, they need to consider and understand the reasons for low morale in GPs and attempt to remedy the situation.

- Strategy/vision. Most GPs in this study felt that there was not a clear vision for General Practice. FHSAs need to share strategies and a vision with GPs which is realistic and achievable. Hunter (1990) has advocated that FHSAs must develop a corporate direction and vision for the future to enable them to fulfil their role and this has to be in collaboration with primary health care providers.

- Resource allocation. FHSAs need to locate resources according to assessment and prioritisation of needs. This can only be done in partnership with GPs. This study shows that a large number of practices are understaffed and the reasons and effect of this need to be further explored.

- Process management and development. This key element in the GP/FHSA partnership is to optimise internal GP capability. This study has shown that GPs lack skills in human resource management, information technology, benchmarking, business planning and assessment of quality outcomes. It has also been demonstrated that GPs, because of their lack of management skills, perhaps feel that administration in their practices distracts them from good clinical practice. They are looking to the FHSAs to assist them in all the above areas and in providing training for doctors, nurses and staff, including training in quality issues.

Jenny Griffiths (NAHAT Briefing, 1991), General Manager and Oxfordshire

FHSA states in the publication FHSAs – Today's and Tomorrow's Priorities: FHSAs can do much through direct funding, training and support to ensure

314

that practices take opportunities open to them to build a team based approach and commitment amongst attached and employed staff.

Butland (1993) has argued that FHSAs should support General Practitioners in defining, adopting and developing quality standards. Essex FHSA has adopted the "Goals for 1995" quality standards scheme whereby it is supporting GPs to develop quality standards in six main categories – business planning, organisation and administration, procedures, staff development, premises and audit.

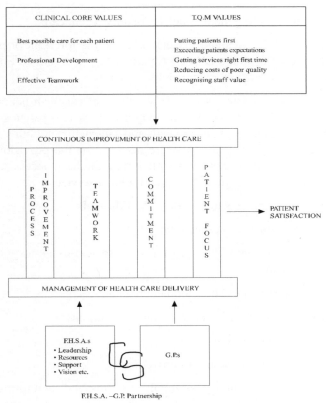

Figure 10 Driving for quality: the total partnership model

315

Benchmarking, as discussed earlier, is a very useful tool in process and quality management. FHSAs need to link in with GPs to use this tool. Dorset Health Commission, Southampton and S.W. Hampshire Health Commission are already using it as an information tool for GPs (Linden, 1995). This can then lead to Best Practice Initiatives whereby FHSAs take the facilitative role in disseminating Best Practice throughout the GP network. Such an initiative has just been started in East Yorkshire by a fundholding practice (Holdridge, 1995). In summary, an effective GP/FHSA partnership is a vital component of the Total Partnership Model, providing much needed management support for GPs and the PHCT and enabling them to deliver quality health care.

GPs and the PHCT. GPs and the PHCT are at the forefront of primary care and with support from the GP/FHSA partnership as described earlier need to develop the following key components of quality:

1 Patient focus – There needs to be a culture of excellent patient care with mechanisms to elicit and respond to information from patients. This would involve assessments of health needs and satisfaction at both a primary and secondary level. In addition, there needs to be the provision of quality service information to patients so that they can have access and choice to a comprehensive range of health and related services.

2 Teamwork – This has to be established through:

- Excellent internal communication.

- Staff empowerment through mutual role understanding and valuing individual team roles.

- Appraisal and personal development planning.

- Clarity of team objectives and member commitment.

- Task orientation to excellence.

- Support for innovation and improvement.

3 Process improvement – This involves setting and monitoring standards, outcomes and adverse events. It also encompasses developing a culture of

quality through audit – both clinical and organisational and ensuring "seamless" care with development and monitoring of collaborative plans. An example of this in practice is the introduction of jointly agreed disease management protocols between Huddersfield GPs and the Huddersfield NHS Trust.

- Management and organisation of total quality – This would entail internal leadership, a service vision, effective business planning, and a philosophy and practice of continuous improvement and one of getting services right first time.

Implementation of the Total Partnership Model

As described earlier, the Total Partnership Model for quality in primary health care has two forces or drivers – the GP/FHSA partnership and the GP/PHCT all working together with the same vision, direction and culture, and embraced by TQM core values.

Implementation of the model will require the following three "Cs" on the part of both FHSAs and GPs.

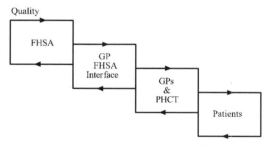

Figure 11 Dynamic steps of quality

1 Capability – Huntington (1993) in assessing the roles of the new Commissioning Authorities notes that they need to "contain members and managers experienced in primary care". Implementation of this model will require training in quality issues for both FHSA managers and GPs and their practice managers. Zairi (1993) in his study recommended that FHSA facilitator training was a priority in order to assist practices. This study has

317

shown the ineffectiveness of FHSA Medical Advisers and to some extent of the Medical Audit Advisory Groups – MAAGs in improving quality in primary health. Hence, the roles of both these "initiatives" need re-evaluation. Jolleys (1994) and Wood (1991) have both suggested that the role of the FHSA Medical Advisers needs to evolve and expand.

2   Commitment – Zairi (1993) suggested that the FHSA should be involved with all practice TQM initiatives. Jenny Griffiths, the General Manager of Oxfordshire FHSA states (1991):

FHSAs should take a lead in demonstrating the new emphasis on quality. Implementing a quality model requires firm commitment from both the FHSA and the PHCT. This commitment will lead to appropriate resource allocation for the purpose and fulfilment of training needs.

3   Culture –– "Quality is a journey without destination and is everyone's responsibility – its successful implementation requires participation and the involvement of all staff" (Zaire, 1993).

In summary, successful implementation of the Total Partnership Model will lead to the Dynamic Steps of Quality as illustrated in Figure 11, with the patient as the main benefactor.

References

Butland, G. (1993), "Commissioning for quality", British Medical .Journal, Vol. 306 No. 6871, January, pp. 251-2.

Cameron, J. (1990), "Best friends and all things to all people", Health Service Journal, Vol. 100 No. 5219, p. 1385.

Fleishman, E. (1973), Twenty Years of Consideration and Structure, Current Developments in the Study of Leadership, Southern Illinois University Press, Carbondale, IL.

Fountain, S. (1985), "Practice management – common problems", Journal of the Royal College of General Practitioners, Vol. 35, pp. 155-8.

General Medical Services Committee (1993), General Practice: A British Success, British Medical Association, London.

Griffiths, J. (1991), FHSAs – Today's and Tomorrow's Priorities, January, p. 31.

Hersey, P. and Blachard, K. (1988), Management of Organisational Behaviour: Utilising Human Resources, Prentice Hall, Englewood Cliffs NJ.

Holdridge, K. (1995), "Networking best practice on the Internet", VFM Update Primary Focus, Issue 1, July, p. 20.

Hunter, D. (1990), "Vision is the key", Health Service Journal, Vol. 100, No. 5223, October, p. 1559.

Huntington, J. (1993), "From FPC to FHSA to Health Commission", British Medical Journal, Vol. 206 No. 6869, January, pp. 33-6.

Irvine, D. (1990), Managing for Quality in General Practice, Kings Fund Centre, London.

Jolleys, J. (1994), "Directors forum", Health Director, No. 12, September, p. 10.

Laffel, G. (1990), "Implementing quality management in health care: the challenge ahead", Quality Progress, April, pp. 29-32.

Linden, M. (1995), "How will league tables affect GPs", General Practitioner, August, p. 39.

May, A. and Robinson, R. (1995), "Mapping the course", Health Service Journal, Vol. 1055 No. 5438, February, pp.22-24.

Metcalfe, D. (1992), "The chains of education, experience and culture", British Medical Journal, Vol. 305 No. 6884, July, pp. 33-4.

Morley, V., Dammers, J. and Pharoah, C. (1990), "Building a GP platform", Health Service Journal, Vol. 100, No. 5215, August, pp. 1246-7.

Myerson, S. (1992), "The new contract and relationships in general practice", Journal Management in Medicine, Vol. 6 No. 1, pp. 19-26.

NAHAT Briefing (1991), FHSAs – Today's and Tomorrow's Priorities, April.

NHS Management Executive News (1992), "From hierarchies to partnerships", No. 53, January, p. 8.

Sloane, R. (1994), "Open for business", Health Service Journal, Vol. 104, No.5432, December, p. 36.

Wall, A. and Webb, N. (1992), "The fax about your job", Health Service Journal, Vol. 102 No. 5309, July, p. 21.

Wilkin, D. and Metcalfe, D. (1984), "List size and patient contract in general practice", British Medical Journal, Vol. 289, pp. 1501-5.

Wilkin, D., Metcalfe, D. and Hallman, L. (1994), "Area variations in the process of care in urban general medical practice", British Medical Journal, Vol. 289, pp. 229-32.

Wilson, K. (1990), "At the top of the bill", Health Service Journal, Vol. 100 No.5224, October, pp. 1608-9.

Wood, J. and Bligh, J. (1991), "New directions", Health Service Journal, Vol. 101 No. 2572, October, p. 28.

Zairi, M. (1993), TQM in Primary Care: An Evaluation, European Centre for TQM, Bradford University, UK.

Quality function deployment : A main pillar for successful total quality management and product development

Mohamed Zairi
University of Bradford Management Centre, Bradford, UK and
Mohamed A. Youssef
Norfolk State University, Virginia, USA

First Published in

International Journal of Quality & Reliability Management,
Vol. 12 No. 6, 1995, pp. 9-23,
© MCB University Press, 0265-671X

Introduction

Recent trends in advanced manufacturing technologies (AMTs) and managerial philosophies have caused a major shift in quality definition. Manton[1] explained this shift. He argues that "...The concept of 'conformance to specification' within permitted tolerance is replaced by the philosophy of continual improvement in the achievement of target values for critical parameters that represent the customer requirement". We take this viewpoint one step further and argue that quality is no longer "conformance to specifications" or "fitness for use" because these definitions look at quality from a narrow perspective.

Quality function Deployment (QFD) is a technique which was born in Japanas a strategy for assuring that quality is built into new products. QFD was first used in 1972 by Kobe Shipyard of Mitsubishi Heavy Industries Ltd and wasthen referred to as the quality tables. While the use of QFD in Japan has increased over the years, its extension to the West was, however, very slow. The first examples of using QFD in the USA did not emerge until 1986 when companies such as Ford and Rank Xerox first introduced it. Subsequently other companies started to introduce it, for example: AT&T Bell Labs, Digital Equipment, Procter & Gamble and Hewlett-Packard. In the UK the uptake of QFD is very recent and there are only a few scattered cases of companies trying to experiment with it.

QFD has also been applied in non-manufacturing environments such as construction companies, hotels and airlines. Although in the main it has been linked to new product development (NPD), QFD can be used for reviewing existing products, services and processes.

QFD is an ideal opportunity to move away from "we know best what the customer wants" to a new culture of "let's hear the voice of the customer". In a sense it enables the organization to become very much proactive to quality problems rather than being reactive to them by waiting for customer complaints. QFD does also enable organizations to compare their product quality standards to those of their competitors thus helping them establish how a competitive edge can be established. QFD has three major objectives (to identify who the customer is, what the customer wants and how to fulfil the customer's wants).

322

The Japanese give a strong importance to the word deployment. eployment in Japan means extending involvement or broadening of various activities. QFD in Japan is considered as the best tool which spreads awareness on the need to focus on customer requirements and encourages company-wide responsibility and commitment towards achieving quality standards which would be consistent with customer expectations and the companies' own aspirations.The article is segmented into two main parts. In the first part, we discuss the theory and foundations of QFD and its relationship to some continuous improvement programmes. In the second part, we report the results of an empirical analysis of seven case studies.

Theory and foundations

In this part of the article we discuss some of the attempts to define QFD, show how QFD works, present some of the QFD benefits, and explain its relationship with other continuous improvement programmes such as total quality management (TQM), statistical process control (SPC), concurrent engineering (CE), and benchmarking. We also shed some light on the problems a company might face in an attempt to implement a QFD programme.

QFD defined
The power of QFD is in its effectiveness in re-examining customer defined hows in order to establish the true customer whats[2]. There have been many attempts to define QFD. Some of the definitions that have been widely reported in literature are listed below:

Lynch and Cross
QFD is a *system* for designing a product or a service based on customer wants, involving all members of the supplying organization. As such, it is a conceptual map for interfactional planning and communication [3].

Hauser and Clausing
A set of *planning and communication routines,* Quality Function Deployment focuses and coordinates skills within an organization, first to design, then to manufacture and market goods that customers want to purchase and will continue to purchase. The foundation of the [QFD] is the belief that products should be designed to reflect customers' desires

and tastes – so marketing people, design engineers, manufacturing staff must work closely together from the time a product is conceived [4].

Garvin

QFD may be defined as elaborate charts to translate perceptions of quality into product characteristics and product characteristics into fabrication and assembly requirements. In this way "the voice of the customer" is deployed throughout the company [5].

Bossert

QFD is a process that provides structure to the development cycle where the primary focus is the customer requirements [6].

Maddux et al.

Quality Function Deployment can be defined as a system for designing a product or service based on customer demands and involving all members of the organization [7].

Fortuna

A systematic means of ensuring that customer or marketplace demands (requirements, needs, wants) are accurately translated into relevant technical requirements and actions throughout each stage of product development[8].

Adams and Gavoor

A detailed planning and design process support technique applicable to any design process whether for services or products aimed at translating "the voice of the customer" into company specifications at every stage of the product introduction process [9].

Whether QFD is viewed as a process, a method, a system, or even a philosophy, it ensures that customer requirements are integrated into new products as early as the design stage. It is therefore necessary to survey customers and discuss these needs. In many of the Japanese companies which implemented QFD, customers are brought in and participate in the design of the product with teams of design and manufacturing engineers.

QFD benefits

Quality function deployment (QFD) can lead to a wide variety of benefits[10], it can help:

- define product specifications meeting the customer's requirements, while paying attention to the competitors;

- ensure consistency between the customer's requirements, and the measurable characteristics of the product;

- inform and convince all those responsible for various stages of the process of the relationship between the quality of the output of each phase and the quality of the finished product;

- ensure consistency between the planning and the production process;

- get things moving more quickly because planning takes place at an earlier stage and mistaken interpretations of priorities and objectives are minimized.

Adao[11] conducted a survey on QFD spread in Japanese industry. The survey concluded that the following benefits were reported by companies using QFD in their business processes. QFD enables organizations to achieve the following:

- Translate customer requirements into meaningful (technical) requirements at each stage of the development and production processes.

- Offer a structured method to tap into all the knowledge on NPD in any organization and facilitates its management and control.

- Brings people together from various disciplines and facilitates the formation of teams capable of meeting customer requirements.

Other benefits reported by Japanese manufacturers using QFD include :

- reductions in number of engineering changes (up to 50 per cent);

- squeezing of design cycle time (up to 50 per cent); and

- increased customer satisfaction and reductions in warranty claims (up to 50 per cent).

It seems that the bottom line of QFD is higher quality, lower cost, shorter timing, and a substantial marketing advantage.

QFD and continuous improvement programmes
There is a strong relationship between QFD and many of the continuous improvement programmes. In this part of the article we examine the relationship between QFD, SPC, SE, TQM, and benchmarking.

The Japanese who have pioneered QFD strongly believe that QFD can only be effective if it is strongly linked to a wide and encompassing quality programme. This is because QFD starts with the objective and works backward by establishing the customer-supplier chain which is capable of delivering to the end customer. It really maps the whole innovation process and ensures that there is a wide involvement and corporate ownership of innovating activity.

Kogure and Akao[12], writing on QFD and company-wide quality control (CWQC) in Japan, concluded that:

...QFD activities should not be confined to the process flow between upstream and downstream, but must be systematized to involve different levels of management, such as top executives, managers and engineering staff. Used in that way, it can help management apply CWQC as a truly effective corporate strategy.

Statistical process control. QFD is more concerned with design aspects and tends to work backward by starting with the end objective and then determining means by which the objective is achieved. SPC on the other hand is more "downstream" and is concerned with process improvement, the prevention of defects and the reduction of variability. QFD does not seek to replace SPC and the two techniques are very much compatible with each other.

QFD completes the picture by joining the voice of the customer with the voice of the process (determined by SPC). In addition to the prevention of product defects and process variability, both downstream activities, QFD makes right first time and zero defect both tangible goals since it aims at optimizing design for manufacturability and reflecting true customer requirements.

Simultaneous engineering and QFD. Simultaneous engineering, also known by other names such as concurrent engineering (CE), design for manufacturability (DFM), parallel engineering (PE), has been defined in various ways. The following are some of the definitions reported in literature:

Simultaneous Engineering attempts to optimize the design of the product and manufacturing process to achieve reduced lead times and improved quality and cost by the integration of design and manufacturing activities and by maximizing parallelism in work practices[13].

Simultaneous Engineering is not just project management by Task Force under another name. Vital elements include:

- Multi-disciplinary Task Force;

- Product defined in customer's terms, then translated into engineering terms in considerable detail;

- Design for Manufacture and Assembly (DFMA);

- Simultaneous development of the product, the manufacturing equipment and processes, quality control and marketing[14].

Simultaneous Engineering is also known as Concurrent Engineering or process-driven design. The performance of product design and process design is parallel. Considerable interaction between product and process design to assure the product is designed to be easily manufactured[15].

Youssef [16] defines DFM as:

A design philosophy that promotes collective and integrated efforts of a number of teams involved in planning, organizing, directing, and controlling all activities related to products and processes from idea generation to a finished product or a service such that:

- available design, manufacturing, and information technologies are efficiently utilized;

- team work is emphasized;

- redundancies and non-value added activities are eliminated; and

- customer requirements and quality are built in the design.

327

QFD is a great opportunity for making simultaneous engineering work. Its main principle is bringing people together representing different functions to agree on key parameters of the product, process and manufacturing methods.

Simultaneous engineering is a concept which was difficult to apply in the past because it tended to be initiated by certain groups of people without widening the involvement and without any serious attempt to change the culture of "business as usual". Basically, QFD helps establish the customer-supplier chain by getting rid of the "throw it over the wall" approach.

Simultaneous engineering takes over from QFD to ensure that the voice of the customer is used for the design of the *production* process. Its purpose is to improve the quality of process design and also to increase design efficiency.

The management of core processes based on QFD and simultaneous engineering practices is the best way of delivering innovation of high quality, at the right time, to the right customer and in the right quantities in a consistent manner. Managing core processes in this format is also the best way to instigate the "never ending improvement" philosophy as the above practices are constantly subjected to review and updating.

TQM. QFD is an essential pillar for achieving TQM. The TQM literature indicates that building the quality into the product starts with asking what does the customer need. QFD is a useful tool in answering this question. In addition, the "hows" of the QFD or the "voice of the company" are important for explaining how the company meets or exceeds the customer needs. It is our belief that QFD is a prerequisite for a successful TQM programme.

Benchmarking. QFD as a benchmarking technique gives information on customers' perceptions of suppliers' ability to fulfil their requirements in comparison with the competition. Competitive and tactical benchmarking techniques can be included in "house of quality" for this purpose.

How does QFD work?

QFD has three fundamental objectives. These are:

(1) to identify the customer;

(2) to identify what the customer wants;

(3) how to fulfil customer's wants.

A QFD matrix, or the house of quality tables is used to provide information on customer requirements ("whats"), design requirements ("hows"), priorities of the customer requirements, priorities of the design requirements, correlation between the hows, and correlations between the hows and whats. These six elements of the house of quality are depicted in Figure 1.

What are the benefits of QFD?

QFD instigates discipline throughout the various activities of the business delivery system. First of all it ensures that the starting point is listing customer requirements then translating the latter into physical and measurable outputs, then it examines the parts required, the process capability and the production capability.

Besides its power as a benchmarking tool, QFD offers a wide variety of benefits including the following:

• It takes the customer as a starting point.

• It cuts down on cycle time since it encourages designing right first time by closely sticking to customers' true requirements.

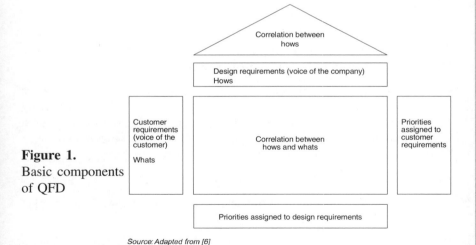

Figure 1.
Basic components
of QFD

Source: Adapted from [6]

329

- It is a tool for never-ending improvement. If offers the ability to prioritize customers' own preferences and following a ranking procedure, suppliers may not necessarily have to focus on customers' top priorities if these are strong enough on other aspects which they may be weak at.

- It is a team building process. QFD forms teams by encouraging input not just from marketing, development, manufacturing and distribution. It combines efforts which link in the emotional needs of customers to those which have to convert them into physical outputs which are produced and delivered to the satisfaction of the end customer.

- QFD helps create a strong database of customer understanding and internal effectiveness and external competitiveness.

- QFD provides firms with the opportunity to reduce costs and waste by using experiential learning and constantly working on reducing cycle time for product to market.

- QFD is a tool of innovation since it currently encourages people to rate their capabilities against those of competitors and others. It assesses the ability of the process to deliver the customer right first time and every time.

General problems with QFD implementation

There are however various reported problems with the use of QFD. Ernst & Young[2] identified the following problems associated with QFD implementation:

- Engineers think that QFD is a "false science", too focused on the mechanics of scoring. QFD however is an effective tool of capturing and displaying data and serves as a communication vehicle for generating structured discussions among team members, in order to meet customer requirements (the expertise is in the hands of the team members and not the tool!).

- It takes a long time to develop a QFD chart fully.

- Team members get caught in the details of the exercise while the market window closes on them[17].

Hewlett-Packard identified the following problems during the implementation of QFD[18]:

(1) Project scheduling (time to market) ruling as the dominant consideration.

(2) Inadequate management commitment to persevere.

(3) Looking for high return on investment with the first application of QFD.

(4) Lack of adequate facilitation:

- not timely;

- not continued long enough;

- not skillful enough in facilitation *per se;*

- not trained well enough in QFD.

(5) Taking on too large a product (especially if a first QFD project).

(6) Getting into too much detail (QFD tables become unmanageably large).

Empirical analysis of seven case studies
The methodology used

An interview proforma was designed to encapsulate various pieces of information which covered pre and post-implementational aspects of QFD. In one case the interview proforma was used in the form of a questionnaire which was mailed to the company concerned. The flexibility in its design permitted all the required information to be obtained from a distance. The questionnaire is depicted in the Appendix.

The companies involved

Company A is a "materials-science" company, with a $1.25billion annual turnover. Specializes in polymeric products such as:

- heat shrinkable tubing;

- moulded parts;

- wire and cable products;

- interconnection d evices;

- gels, adhesives; and

- self-limiting heaters.

331

Main markets include commercial and defence electronics, industrial produce and telecommunications. Company A employs over 10,000 people and operates in more than 40 different countries.

Company B is an international company with a turnover of £230million, employing 2,100 people. It specializes in electronic imaging equipment, colour scanners, article planners and creative design systems for the printing industry. It has sales offices in Europe, Canada and Australia and uses distributors elsewhere.

Company C is one of the largest health and beauty product manufacturers in the UK, with 10 per cent of the market. It employs approximately 1,400 people of which 700 are directly employed in manufacturing or production activities. Twenty-four per cent of the output is for export.

The customers are mainly the retail and wholesale trade. An increasing proportion of sales goes to major multiples such as Boots, Superdrug, Tesco, Asda, Safeway and Sainsbury. The company sells over 30 branded products.

Company D is part of a worldwide private company of 14,000 employees with corporate headquarters in the USA. It specializes in high-technology manufacture of textiles, chemicals and packaging. Company D employed 107 employees and specializes in woven textiles which form part of the construction of car and cycle tyres.

Company E is part of a large multinational organization which provides advanced technology systems, components and services to the world's aerospace, automotive and other selected markets. Company E comprises two related business units. One is the market leader in project management, planning and control software and technical service products. The other is a projects and systems engineering contracts business, covering business and manufacturing systems engineering design, engineering software and information technology services. Company E employs 410 people and has an annual turnover of £23million.

Company F is a large car manufacturing organization with 35,000 employees and a turnover of £4billion. It produces luxury cars.

Company G specializes in the manufacture of printed circuit boards. It employs 649 people.

Company H specializes in the manufacture of consumer goods such as indoor and outdoor power tools. It employs 1,500 people.

Key findings

- The above companies seem to have introduced QFD for similar reasons which, in the main, tended to be related to systemizing and organizing the process of developing new products. The urgent need to attempt to use QFD is often prompted by the need to speed up the innovation process, to reduce the number of changes at the design stages and to become much more competitive.

- Since these companies were at different stages of the learning curve with QFD, a wide variety of benefits were reported. On the whole, the key benefits seem to be related to the following areas.

- There is an enhancement of companies' ability to understand customer requirements and therefore incorporate the "voice of customers" in the new product development process.

- The less tangible and often "not expressed" customer attributes are made more visible with the use of QFD.

- The introduction of a new culture of new product development based on team work and an external assessment of customer needs before carrying out the need translation process.

- Decision making is based much more on facts and data rather than opinions.

- A climate of "sharing" and "co-operating" rather than a "throw it over the wall" type of approach, since the ultimate goal is delivering to the customer rather than internal competition.

- More positive innovation with speed, quality and cost effectiveness. In these companies, the problems encountered in the implementation and use of QFD include:

- Most people who attempted to use the technique came to the realization that it is very complex and requires a lot of detail.

- Many attempts fail because not enough time is given to the teams concerned to learn the technique and pilot it on simple projects to start with.

- Not enough facilitation and support is given to the teams in terms of "team building" and also in terms of resources and ideas/inspiration.

- Overambitious programmes and very high expectations from senior management.

- QFD tends to work better if there is a strong total quality programme in place and other tools and techniques to support it. Some organizations just attempted to bolt it on without having visible TQ commitments.

Conclusions

This pioneering technique which has only recently been taken seriously in the West is a very powerful tool for instigating a discipline which starts with the "voice of the customer" and a thorough knowledge and understanding of their true requirements. It encourages companies to be externally focused and to do more for the customer and aspire for higher standards of achievement and competitiveness.

In cases where it has been applied successfully, many benefits were reported both of a tangible nature and in shaping up a new culture of new product development. There are however certain prerequisites for QFD to lead to successful outcomes. These may include:

- QFD is not an exercise for building charts, the end result is to satisfy customer requirements using existing resources and optimizing process capability.

- QFD is heavily dependent on the contribution of key people, senior management commitment, since the technique is upstream and has strategic implications and the use of a facilitator to help the teams concerned progress positively with the use of the technique.

- QFD is resource dependent in terms of people, time, financial resources, among others. The choice of projects therefore has to be carefully planned where resource implications have been carefully examined.

- Finally, QFD is a culture change agent and has to be gradually integrated as part of a bigger umbrella of change, ideally a total quality management programme which drives for efficiency, effectiveness and continuous measurement for superior competitiveness.

References

1. Manton, S.M., "Engineering for quality", *IMechE*, Vol. 202 No. 32, 1988.

2. Selecman, W.H., "Quality improvement starts at the beginning with QFD", *Transactions from the Second Symposium on Quality Function Deployment,* 18-19 June 1990, MI.

3. Lynch, R.L. and Cross, K.F., *Measure Up: Yardsticks for Continuous Improvement,* Basil Blackwell, Cambridge, MA, 1991.

4. Hauser, J.R. and Clausing, D., "The house of quality", *Harvard Business Review,* May-June 1988, pp. 63-73.

5. Garvin, D.A., *Managing Quality,* Free Press, New York, NY, 1988.

6. Bossert, J.L., *Quality Function Deployment – A Practitioner's Approach,* ASQC Quality Press, Milwaukee, WI, 1991.

7. Maddux, G.A., Amos, R.W. and Wyskid, A.R., "Organizations can apply quality function deployment as strategic planning tool", *Industrial Engineering,* September 1991, pp. 33-7.

8. Fortuna, R.M., "Beyond quality: taking SPC upstream", *Quality Progress,* ASQC, Milwaukee, June 1988, pp. 23-8.

9. Adams, R.M. and Gavoor, M.D., *Quality Function Deployment: Its Promise and Reality,* Rockwell International, Automobile Operations, Troy, MI, 1990.

10. Zucchelli, F., "Total quality and QFD", *1st European Conference on Quality Function Deployment,* Milan, 25-6 March 1992, Galgano & Associati.

11. GOAL/QPC Research Committee 1989 Research Report, "Quality function deployment – a process for continuous improvement", *Transactions from the Second Symposium on Quality Function Deployment,* 18-19 June 1989, GOAL/QPC Research Committee, MI.

12. Kogure, M. and Akao, Y., "Quality function deployment and CWQC in Japan", *Quality Progress,* October 1983, pp. 25-9.

13. Broughton, T., "Simultaneous engineering in aero gas turbine design and manufacture", *Proceedings of the 1st International Conference on Simultaneous Engineering,* Status Meeting, December 1990, p. 6.

14. Hardley, J. and Mortimer, J., *Simultaneous Engineering: The Management Guide,* Industrial Newsletter Ltd in association with the Department of Industry, 1990.

15. Tompkins, J.A., *Winning Manufacturing – The How to Book of Successful Manufacturing,* Industrial Engineering and Management Press, Norcross, GA, 1989.

16. Youssef, M.A., "Design for manufacturability and time-to-market: theoretical foundations", *International Journal of Operations & Production Management,* Vol. 14 No. 12, 1994, pp. 6-21.

17. Burrows, P., "In search of the perfect product", *Electronic Business,* June 1991, pp. 70-4.

18. Daetz, D., "QFD – a method for guaranteeing communication of the customer voice through the whole product development cycle", *IEEE Conference on Communications,* Boston, Vol. 3, IEEE Press, Piscataway, NJ, June 1989, pp. 1329-33.

Further reading

Youssef, M.A., "Design for manufacturability and time-to-market: empirical findings", *International Journal of Operations & Production Management,* Vol. 15 No. 1, 1995, pp. 6-23.

Appendix. QFD questionnaire
1 – Background information

Organization name: _____

_____

_____

_____

Person(s) contacted: _____
Number of employees: _____
Annual turnover: _____
Industry sector: _____
Main products/services: _____

Site visited: _____
Location: _____

_____

_____

Ask host company whether it is possible to obtain an information pack on background of the organization itself plus some useful information relating to their TQM programme, i.e.:

- copy of mission statement;

- quality policy;

- implementation strategy;

- some of the results up to date.

2 – Level of understanding and awareness
- How is QFD defined in your organization?

- What was the general level of understanding on its meaning and the major appreciation of its benefits before you decided to introduce it?

- How did you evaluate its potential benefits?

    – Did you visit other companies who are users of QFD?

    – Did you send people on courses to learn about it?

    – Did you use consultants to help you appreciate its applicability and potential benefits to your business?

3 – Reasons for introducing QFD
- Why did you decide to introduce it in the first place?

- Who was responsible for its introduction?

4 – Extent of utilization of QFD
Can you give an indication on the level of utilization of QFD in relation to the following:

	%
Product development	_____
Product improvement	_____
Process development	_____

Product/process improvement _____

Still experimenting and learning how to use it _____

5 – Benefits

Some of the following are benefits reported by companies who had experience in using QFD.

Please state which ones are applicable to your organization.

Great reduction in no changes in design of product/service _____

Great reduction in NPD cycle time _____

Great reduction in total cycle time _____

Reductions in costs and waste _____

Reductions in warranty claims _____

Increases in customer satisfaction _____

Increases in effective team building for problem-solving activity

_____

Increases in number of innovations _____

Better understanding and tighter control over business processes

_____

Increases in competitive standards _____

Closer relationships with customers and suppliers _____

Better intelligence on customer preferences _____

Please specify other benefits which you have achieved from using QFD:

6 – Major problems

Some of the following are problems which users of QFD faced during its implementation. Which of the following is applicable to your own organization?

It is complex _____

Difficult to apply in all business contexts   _____

It is resisted by some employees   _____

It is not compatible with existing infrastructure   _____

It requires a change in culture   _____

Conflicting objectives among team members   _____

Does not lead to speedy results   _____

Difficulties in getting customers and suppliers to participate _____

Double pressure in having to deal with *customers* and *consumers (users)*

    _____

No other techniques in place to support it   _____

7– Link between QFD and TQM

- Do you consider your organization to be a TQM business?

- How long have you been using TQM principles?

- How effective do you think your organization is at the following?

	Efficient	Inefficient	Not applicable
Use of BS 5750/ISO 9000	_____	_____	_____
Use of teams	_____	_____	_____
Use of tools and techniques	_____	_____	_____
Performance measurement	_____	_____	_____

- What are your future TQM plans?

- Do you consider QFD to be an integral part of your TQM programme?

- What particular aspects of your TQM programme have helped in the introduction of QFD?

8 – Other tools and techniques

In addition to QFD, which of the following tools do you use for your product development/process improvement purposes?

Statistical process control   _____

Data analysis   _____

Design of experiments   _____

Taguchi methods   _____

Failure mode effect analysis   _____

Nominal group technique   _____

Time charting and analysis   _____

Cost of quality   _____

Force field analysis   _____

Value engineering and analysis   _____

Benchmarking   _____

Any others please specify:

9 – QFD implementation

- What process did you follow to introduce QFD?
- Who was the internal sponsor?
- Did you pilot it on a specific project first?
- How radical was the QFD approach in comparison with the traditional project management approach?
- How much training did you give to the teams involved?
- How did you select the team members?
- Could you give us an indication on the costs involved in setting up QFD?
- How long have you been using it now and how long did it take you to introduce it?

- At what stage did you decide to involve your customers and suppliers?
- What project management skills did the teams have prior to QFD?
- Who led the first activity and why?
- Where did you choose to pilot it and why?
- Could you take us through an example of a QFD project?
- Is it possible to have some information related to the example you described and which we can use in our report? (for example flow charts, matrices, houses…)

10 – Recommendations
- Based on company's experience in using QFD, what advice would you give to an organization considering the use of QFD as an additional technique for meeting customer requirements right first time?
- Could you recommend a 5-7 points action plan?
- Which do you consider are the *most critical factors* for successful implementation of QFD?
- What are the most tangible benefits companies should expect to achieve?
- What are the major pitfalls you would like to warn them against?

Best practice QFD application: an internal/external benchmarking approach based on Ford Motors' experience

David Ginn and Mohamed Zairi

School of Management, University of Bradford, Bradford, UK

Abstract

Purpose – This paper is based on a benchmarking exercise involving some 164 QFD practitioners within Ford Motor Company and 27 selected external QFD companies. The predominant response "cell" was from Vehicle Centre 1, Power-Train Systems Engineering, although there was both a US and non-power-train response content. The benchmarking focused on four parts: (1) criteria of success; (2) learning experience; (3) teamwork; and (4) future of QFD.

Design/methodology/approach - Quality function Deployment (QFD) is a bridge between the customer and the product (process/service) evelopment community. The QFD technique translates customer

First Published in

International Journal of Quality & Reliability Management
Vol. 22 No. 1, 2005, pp. 38-58,
© Emerald Group Publishing Limited
0265-671X DOI 10.1108/02656710510572986

requirements obtained from market research into product measurables using matrix diagrams and product development teamwork. Ideally this process continues throughout the product development cycle, from design to production, using a series of QFD phases, prioritising and trading off the key measurables at each step. The ideal result should be both perceived and actual improvements to quality, functional performance and reduced cost on key attributes to prompt higher customer satisfaction. Use of QFD is therefore seen as both a strategic and a tactical tool within a competitive market. The problem facing many QFD practitioners, including Ford Motor Company, is that the cost, complexity and commitment required to deliver effective QFD-driven targets in a timely manner either exceed available resources or represent a cultural anathema.

Findings – Following a discussion of the major findings from the Ford survey on usage pattern, the results were then benchmarked with a 1991 QFD usage survey conducted by MIT with 100 US companies.

Research limitations/implications – The concept of QFD was developed in the mid-1960s in Japan, with many Japanese companies now automatically incorporating QFD as an integral part of company-wide quality practice. In contrast, many Western companies, having used QFD only since the mid-1980s, either have already abandoned QFD in frustration or are in the process of radically rethinking its practice within their own changing quality improvement environments.

Originality/value – Senior and middle management support, including the release of resources, remains a critical component of successful QFD implementation. There is also a need to integrate a more flexible and timely QFD process within the requirements of the established product development process. All this depends on well-trained, cross-functional and multi-disciplined teams with unified goals and focus.

Keywords Quality function deployment, House of quality, Customer satisfaction, Team working, Performance management, Quality

Paper type Research paper

1. Some working definitions and descriptions of quality function deployment

In the Ford Quality Function Deployment Executive Briefing (Ford Motor Company, 1987) it was stated that there was no single definition for quality function deployment, but the following definition was proposed as a starting point:

A system for translating customer requirements into appropriate company requirements at each stage (of the product development cycle) from research and product development to engineering and manufacturing to marketing/sales and distribution.

Despite there being revisions to this definition within Ford Motor Company, the essence of the definition remains the same, although more recent QFD definitions within Ford Motor Company have added breadth by including key words such as "quality", "value", "target setting process", "planning tool", "customer driven product development process", "customer focused engineering" and "customer satisfaction". A selection of excerpts over time includes:

"A planning tool for translating customer needs and expectations into appropriate company requirements" and "Customer Driven Product Development" (Ford Motor Company, 1989); and

"A planning tool that identifies the significant few items on which to focus time, product improvement efforts and other resources" (Ford Motor Company, 1992).

Other descriptions and definitions of QFD, include amongst others, the following. Kathawala and Motwani (1994) simply state: "QFD can reduce the risk of misinterpreting customer requirements". Kathawala and Motwani (1994) urther quote from the work of Maddux et al. (1991), that "QFD's objectives are to: identify the customer, determine what the customer wants, and provide a way to meet the customer's desires". Asaka and Ozeki (1988) place great emphasis on the word "planning" in their descriptions of QFD, as do Sullivan (1988), McElroy (1989), and Ford Motor Company (1983). Asaka and Ozeki (1988), however, prefer to shorten the term "quality function deployment" to just "quality deployment", and state that quality deployment (or QFD) "defines the functions of planning, development, design and manufacturing of a product to satisfy the quality requirements of customers". This shortening of QFD to just "quality deployment" is consistent with Akao (1990). Quality deployment refers to the charts, tables and descriptive matrices used to design in the quality (or "goodness") required by the customer in the product. Akao (1990) has two definitions for QFD, one narrow, and one broad:

(1) narrow QFD definition: "The business or task functions responsible for quality (design, manufacturing, production)"; and

(2) broad QFD definition: "A combination of these business or task functions responsible for quality (design, manufacturing, production etc.) and the quality deployment charts".

Akao (1988) adds that "function deployment is often a later step in QFD where the basic functions of the product or service are identified by experienced people at the production company". Akao (1990) likens function deployment to the "voice of the engineer" who has the task of identifying the "must be" attributes of the product, where Akao (1990) gives the example of "must be" as an unspoken customer requirement, an attribute that must be there, otherwise it is a source of dissatisfaction to the customer (such as a bed and a bathroom in a hotel, which the customer must have). However, Akao (1990) asserts that to have these "must be" attributes, or functions, does not guarantee customer satisfaction: it only ensures no strong dissatisfaction. Akao (1990) summarises this argument by stating that when a customer's spoken quality demand opposes these "must be" attributes or functions, then the producer of the product or service must balance the spoken demands with practical functional requirements of the product or service. Akao (1990) ties in the purpose of the quality charts or quality tables (which have already been referred to as "houses of quality" or "QFD matrices" by the previously referenced authors) as a "means to" and not "an end in themselves", that is to say they are there to provide insight into the nature of the product or service and what is necessary to improve it with relation to the spoken quality demands of the customer.

Slinger (1992) neatly proposes that "Quality Function Deployment is a design tool which is a powerful support to "encouraging" engineering design teams to take a structured, thorough approach to product design". Slinger (1992) and Metherell (1991) further describe a four-stage (phase) QFD process as part of an integrated engineering process, which they illustrate as linked into simultaneous engineering using teamwork, training and planning. Metherell (1991) adds to the setting of QFD and simultaneous engineering in context with integrated engineering by emphasising the focus for team effort. Metherell (1991) also intimates that QFD as part of this integrated engineering process is consistent with the highest "opportunity for change" at the concept levels, and offers traceability throughout the product cycle.

Consistent with the previous two authors, Hauser and Clausing (1988) propose a definition of QFD through reference to its classic house of quality matrix, which reads: "the house of quality is a kind of conceptual map that provides the means for interfunctional planning and communications". They further suggest that people with different problems and responsibilities can thrash out design priorities by referring to patterns of evidence from the house of quality. This interpretation adds to argument for QFD being more than just a planning tool scenario, but also a tool for interdisciplinary communications within any company. Hauser and Clausing's (1988) definition proposes that QFD is both a planning and communications tool that helps focus and coordinate skills within an organisation from design to manufacture into a product customers want and will continue to buy.

Sullivan (1988) corroborates this view that QFD is a both a planning tool and an aid to communication, and observes that several US companies (notably Ford) show case studies being very successful in applying the QFD matrix charts, which in turn has helped integrate the various diverse activities within that company. Sullivan develops this argument, however, by suggesting that QFD can be used as the "hardware" through which "policy management", which he refers to as the "software", can be integrated. The difference with policy management to "objective management", the more typical style of management, is that the latter is based on measuring performance by results, while the former focuses on developing the means of achieving results through methods, systems, or resources. Sullivan (1988) suggests that the foundation of policy management is "business planning". Business planning in turn is based on employee ownership or entrepreneurship to set goals through a comprehensive planning process across the whole organization, by reducing the void between departments. The results from this level of detail then become the results of the policy means and a measure of policy management success. In summary, Sullivan (1988) proposes that "soft technologies" such as policy management are important to achieve the business plan, and that this must be integrated through congruent objectives with the use of "hard technologies" such as QFD, Taguchi methods and SPC to deploy product requirements. All these elements combined deliver the key goal of meeting customer expectations. This argument for QFD is an integral part of business planning and is corroborated by Barlow (1995), who refers to "policy deployment" in the same context. Greenall (1995) describes policy deployment as process-focused, rather than management by objectives.

The idea of using QFD within an organization as an aid to business planning becomes clear when placed in the context of its numerous and varied benefits, which will now be discussed. Zairi (1993) summaries four key benefits as being:

(1) higher quality;

(2) lower cost;

(3) shorter timing; and

(4) marketing advantage.

Akao's (1990) survey of QFD benefits within Japanese industry quotes five key process benefits:

(1) decreased start-up problems;

(2) competitive analysis becomes possible;

(3) control points clarified;

(4) effective communications between divisions; and

(5) design intent carried through to manufacturing.

Aoki et al. (1990) relate the benefits of QFD as being in conjunction with "quality charts, related procedures of new product development and quality assurance activities", and summarises these into two broad benefits that lead to:

(1) the development of new products that both meet customers' demands and wins their trust as well as being developed in a timely manner to lead the market; and

(2) the improvement of interdepartmental communication on product development by identifying problems from early pre-design stage to ensure development and process time reductions.

It would appear, however, that QFD is only one of many techniques available to companies wishing to improve product development times. Reinertsen (1991) reviews how companies can overcome 15 common barriers to timing product-development cycles, and refers to QFD and CE (concurrent engineering) as valuable in trimming development cycles down, but from the 15 common barriers, QFD is only completely successful in just two areas while CE is successful in only five areas. These are:

- "hitting moving targets" (QFD);

- "lack of concurrency" (CE);

- "moving locus of control" (CE);

- "phased development systems" (CE); and

- "focus on communication" (QFD/CE).

The Reinertsen (1991) list of remaining barriers (which are largely self-explanatory) that QFD specifically does not adequately address include:

- taking giant steps;

- ignoring market clocks;

- overloading capacity;

- ignoring queue time;

- burn rate management;

- lack of concurrency;

- inattention to architecture;

- moving locus of control;

- phased development systems;

- inappropriate testing strategies;

- failure to quantify the problem;

- make/buy decisions; and

- when efforts pay off.

Reinertsen (1991) does, however, acknowledge the crucial role of communications in developing products rapidly.

Finally, a description of QFD is given by Reynolds (1992), who proposes that the planning process of quality function deployment is the major development in the quality sector of business. Reynolds (1992) describes QFD as a tool that uses "a sophisticated subjective analysis to design an "optimal" product with maximum customer satisfaction assured". This definition places emphasis on the subjective approach QFD offers, and that optimisation of the product is the route to maximum customer satisfaction. Miguel (2003), on the other hand, further emphasizes the importance of establishing a customer-centric approach, using the magic of QFD.

2. The background, method and intention of the QFD practitioner survey

The purpose of the benchmarking survey on QFD usage patterns was to check the importance of having consistently well trained and well maintained cross-functional teams with multi-disciplinary skills supported by senior management, all of which are factors highlighted in previous studies.

The research was based on a questionnaire which was sent out to 283 internal Ford employees, including core team, support team and ex-team members worldwide, as well as some 80 external QFD practitioners, representing some 27 companies. The areas of the study covered include aspects related to QFD project management, QFD training and experience, QFD teamwork, and finally the future of QFD.

Part of the analysis is to benchmark the internal QFD practices within Ford with external QFD practices where applicable. Like the internal responses, the external responses include a cross-section of experience and application expertise that ranges from the complete beginner to long-established team members who are at the forefront of QFD development within their respective companies.

3. Response profile for the QFD practitioners survey

From within Ford Motor Company responses were polled from current core and support team member distribution lists to active QFD efforts within the company worldwide. These distribution lists were based on the authors' own e-mail QFD distribution lists and were customised into three key lists of "core", "support" and "ex-QFD" team members. These three lists, although given "pigeon-holed" titles of core, support and ex-team members, in reality represented a more complex distribution of interest. The areas represented within Ford, although extensive and comprehensive in many cases, still had a strong Power-Train Systems Engineering bias. Details of QFD usage questionnaires sent, returned and lost are given in Table I.

From the external responses, as already noted some 27 companies or QFD user groups were represented. The companies which agreed to participate in the questionnaire included:

- ASI QFD User Group;

- Jaguar Car Company;

- Martin Smith & Partners;

- University of Derby;

- Sporting Body Mind;

- British Sugar;

- MIL Research;
- Lever Brothers Ltd;
- Unilever plc;
- ICL;
- Cabot Leiden TC;
- ITI (UK) Ltd;
- Birds Eye Walls Ltd;
- Abbey National;
- Van den Bergh Foods;
- Elida Gibbs;
- TSB plc;
- Mars plc;
- IBM International;
- The CIM Institute;
- Lucas Engineering;
- MDI (UK) Ltd;

Questionnaire groups	Number sent out	Number returned	Number lost
Internal			
Core team members (VCI-Europe)	94	64	
Support team members (VCI-Europe)	88	36	+2

352

Ex-team members (VCI-Europe)	45	18	
Core team members (VC2-5 – USA)	56	9	
Internal totals	283	127 (45)	+2
External totals	80	37 (46)	+11
Combined totals	363	164 (45)	+13

Note: Numbers in parentheses are percentages

Table I. QFD usage questionnaires sent, returned and lost in post

- Ward Dutton Partnership;
- Edwards High Vacuum International;
- Four Square Drinks; and
- University of Bradford Management Centre.

4. Analysis of the QFD questionnaire findings

The key findings will be discussed from the five main parts, which include:

(1) respondent details;

(2) criteria for effective QFD application;

(3) the learning experience;

(4) the QFD team; and

(5) the future of QFD.

A comparison within the 1991 QFD implementation survey conducted by Pandey and Clausing (1991) at MIT, with some 79 companies in the USA with 203 responses, will take place at the end of this paper. The results from the internal and external responses have not been separated for two reasons. The first reason is that the original draft of results did not show a great difference across the complete response range between the internal and external responses. The second reason was that with the constraint of time, it was considered more important to get the fullest content analysed question by question. The focus on a detailed question-by-question breakdown of results broadly showed a greater contrast of results than would have been seen by focusing on splitting the two key response groups of internal and external.

The following five sections mirror Parts A to D of the questionnaire, as well as the initial "Respondent details" that all respondents completed before talking all or part of the questionnaire: Section 1 – Respondent details; Section 2 – Part A: Criteria for effective application; Section 3 – Part B: Learning experience; Section 4 – Part C: The QFD team; and Section 5 – Part D: The future of QFD.

The first level of detail is the respondent details, which all 164 respondents completed. From this profile of the respondents was set. The total of 127 internal (Ford Motor Company) respondents compared to just 37 external respondents must be put into context of a 45 and a 46 per cent response level to the total number of questionnaires sent out to internal and external respondents, respectively.

Partly due to the bias of the source of the internal distribution lists, and partly due to the historic bias for QFD application within Ford Motor Company, the power-train versus non-power-train respondent level internally is 3 to 1 (94 to 33 absolute counts). The respondent levels externally are the opposite, with non power-train responses outnumbering power-train responses five to one. Overall, however, power-train respondents outnumber non-power-train respondents by almost two to one.

By far the most overwhelming fact in the personal respondent profile is the 92 per cent versus 8 percent male to female overall response levels. This ratio is higher internally within Ford than externally (96 to 4 per cent and 77 to 23 per cent, respectively).

All respondents were asked to identify where in their respective company's product development cycle they saw their job function role. This question framed the terms as "upstream versus downstream ratios" (such as 80/20, upstream/downstream). With this came the finding that three-quarters (75 per cent) of the respondents saw themselves spread evenly within the 70/30 to 100/0 upstream/downstream band of the product development cycle, with barely upwards of 3 per cent in the remaining mid- to downstream area of the product development cycle. There was one "population" of 12 per cent in the 50/50 band.

The split between management role and general safety role (GSR) internally within Ford Motor Company was largely even, 54 to 46 per cent respectively. However, externally it was very much management-role biased (81 to 19 per cent, respectively). Overall this places the bias towards management role at 59 per cent to 41 per cent GSR.

The penultimate aspect of the respondent details was the years that respondents had spent in the (their) company. The response profile looked at the bands as follows: 0-1 + , 2-5 + and then in five-year bands, from 6-10+ finishing at 36-40. Although this produced a broad spread for both internal and external respondents, there was a combined peak within the 2-5 þ band of 24 per cent that flattened off to 17 and 18 per cent (6-10 + and 11-15 +), and tailed off to 12 per cent and below from 16-20 + years.

The overall results for the current interests in QFD practice produced a fairly even spread of interest across all the five areas, with option d, "A potential new QFD Team member" receiving the least (10 per cent), but the main option was option e, "An interested party to QFD efforts", with 37 per cent response levels (although this was with the highest multiple count of 23, or 14 per cent). The second and third options were very close, with 30 and 26 per cent for option a, "QFD Core Team member/leader" and option c, "Past QFD Team member", respectively.

5. Criteria for effective QFD application
In this section, a series of questions were asked to establish both the "forced" and "unforced" responses to criteria critical to the successful implementation of QFD. The questions and responses covered a range of criteria across both

the technical (hard) and human (soft) aspects considered important when
progressing a QFD project.

5.1 Issues critical to the success of QFD

Overall, all six criteria proposed in the questionnaire received good response
levels, with "Training" (87 per cent) the highest, followed by "Team selection"
(81 per cent) and "Senior management role" (79 per cent). The key to the
question asked how critical each of the criteria were to the success of QFD,
with "3" being the most critical and "1" the least. The results broadly showed
that all six of the criteria were heavily weighted towards the "2" and "3"
ratings, indicating that respondents considered all the criteria had a moderate
to critical influence on the success of QFD. However, three criteria in particular
had all four key response cells ratings between 60 and 90 per cent in the "3"
critical to QFD success. These were "Training", "Team selection" and "Project
targets and deliverables". "Senior management role" came a close fourth in
importance. Overall, it can be said that two criteria held consistently high
responses levels and ratings, being criteria 1 and 2 of "Training" and "Team
selection", respectively.

The second part of this process was to identify the most important issues
supporting the criteria of success. The top seven keywords for "Training and
team selection" can be seen in Table II.

From the results, it can be seen there is an even spread of the top four issues
for "Training", while for "Team selection" it is more specifically cross-
functional technical expertise that is most important.

5.2 QFD project type experience and usefulness in support of task activity

This question simply aimed at understanding the profile of experience in QFD
projects. In summary of the four project types given, i.e. "(a) New product
development", "(b) Current product improvement", "(c) New process
development" and "(d) Current process improvement", there was clearly an
emphasis on "New product development" in particular, followed by "Current
product development". The ratings show that QFD was seen as largely critical
(36 per cent) followed by moderate (29 per cent) to the success of "New
product development", while for "Current product development" it was seen
largely as moderate (27 per cent) to success.

5.3 Key benefits experienced as a direct result of using QFD

A total of 76 per cent of the respondents identified 16 areas of benefits (with response levels of 3 per cent and above) plus a group of others/miscellaneous as a direct result of using QFD. The top seven benefits out of the total of 16 are summarised below as keywords with their response level percentages shown in Table III. As can be seen in Table III, "Understanding the customer" received nearly a 50 per cent response level, with "Teamwork" a strong second.

5.4 Key problems experienced as a direct result of using QFD

Respondents were also asked to identify all the key problems experienced as a direct result of using QFD. This prompted a 71 per cent response level, just slightly lower then the benefits response level of 76 per cent. However, unlike the benefits which descended in order fairly evenly from a response of 47 per cent to 31 per cent to 26 per

Top seven keywords for "Training and team selection"	Percentage
"Train together in team"	27
"More adequate training"	22
"Team/technical skills (required, i.e. EQUIP)"	21
"Timing of training (i.e. just in time)"	21
"Team selection (cross-functional)"	41
"Technical expertise"	40
"Commitment"	28

Table II. Training

Benefit	Response level (per cent)
"Understanding the customer"	47
"Teamwork and team focus"	31
"Supports quality improvement"	26
"Prioritisation of (customer) wants and resources (to support QFD)"	22
"Assists engineering and product knowledge"	21
"Structured, systematic and data-driven approach"	18
"Corporate knowledge and documentation"	18

Table III. Top seven benefits from direct QFD application

cent down to 18 per cent for eights, the problems identified with an equivalent 18 per cent response level (or above), number only four, almost half the number of the benefits. The difference this time is that the top problem of "Slow/time consuming/lengthy process", with a response level of 45 per cent, similar to the top benefit, is double the count for the second problem response of only 23 per cent. One of the notable differences, however, is the total number of problems (with counts of 3 per cent and above) reaches a total of 27, compared to a total of only 16 benefits. This finding illustrates a general frustration with the QFD process that perhaps outweighs its benefits. The top eight problems are shown in Table IV.

5.5 Effectiveness of QFD to support technical and human criteria of success

Overall this question received a high response level for both "Technical criteria of success" and "Human criteria of success" (87 and 85 per cent, respectively). Both headings had four criteria given with an opportunity for respondents to identify any other criteria of success within both headings. The aim was to establish the effectiveness of QFD to support these criteria. All criteria under both headings received around 130-140 responses each. However, the ratings of 1, 2 and 3 (for QFD being marginal, moderate or critical to criteria of success) varied. The "Technical criteria of success" that QFD was considered of greatest benefit was "Quality improvement", which corroborates the findings of key QFD benefits, where "Supports quality improvement" was third most important (26 per cent). The other three technical criteria of "Innovation", "Cost reduction" and "Speed of delivery" all displayed a reasonable to strong response in the rating "1" (marginal) to "2" (moderate), with a range of 28-44 per cent. All the "Human criteria of success" had high response levels for both ratings "2" (moderate) and "3" (critical) of between 41 and 49 per cent and 35 and 41 per cent, respectively. This strongly suggests that perhaps the key measure of QFD benefits are less tangible "human" aspects.

6. Learning experience

The overall combined responses levels for Part B, the "Learning experience" was very good, with the lowest at 75 per cent ("Format of QFD believed to hold the greatest benefit to the company") to 93 and 94 per cent ("Initial contact with QFD" and "QFD software skills"). Most were around 85-90 per cent. Part B covers some 13 questions covering initial contact and learning experiences of QFD through to post-training experience and observations, as well as QFD software application knowledge. The last two questions include experience of other supporting quality tools and processes used in place of or in conjunction with QFD.

Problem	Response level (per cent)
"Slow/time-consuming/lengthy process"	45
"Inability of team to stay together"	23
"Poor understanding/poor image of QFD"	22
"Lack of funding/high cost of surveys"	20
"Bureaucratic/too complex/too much detail"	16
"Inappropriate/poor training of QFD"	16
"Poor understanding of the customer"	15
"Lacks focus/poor direction"	15

Table IV. Top eight problems from direct application of QFD

6.1 Initial contact with QFD

"In a QFD team" was by far the most important initial contact for 43 per cent of the respondents, in particular internally within Ford Motor Company. The second most important form of initial contact with QFD was through "Training" (28 per cent), closely followed by "Colleagues" (21 per cent). These second two formats, however, equally represented the most important initial contact to QFD externally (40 per cent and 35 per cent of all external responses). "Literature" represented only a very small proportion of initial contacts (11 per cent), with "Other" contacts even less (4 per cent).

6.2 Poor image of QFD

After "Training", QFD appears to be equally as likely to be spread by word of mouth by "Colleagues". Any current poor images of QFD within Motor Ford Company may get an even poorer image, especially if the "colleagues" in question are untrained or poorly informed in the first place. Certainly from the perspective of a large company like Ford, where effective communications will be tested to the limits of efficiency, quality tools such as QFD, which are simple in principle but difficult in effective application, are susceptible to distortion or misuse, which does nothing for its long-term credibility.

6.3 Formal training experiences (B.2)

The results from the "Formal training" experience question provided a three-level response for each of the four response cells. This meant many respondents with formal training experience will have given a multi-response answer. That is to say an internal (or external) respondent may have experienced training from ASI Quality Systems (American Suppliers Institute), as well as with internal formal training modules in QFD, such as Ford EQUIP or Quick QFD.

6.4 Format of QFD thought to offer the greatest benefit to the company

These results suggests that there is an opportunity to develop and offer a QFD process that is not constrained by an specific number of phases, formats or rigid rules, while still retaining the option to deliver customer-generated targets down through the PDC. Such an opportunity has been tackled with limited success by the Ease of Start QFD.

The key conclusion here is that most QFD practitioners, although keen to retain the option of deploying QFD through as many phases as possible — depending on resources, timing, and task required – do not want too many constraints before either starting a QFD or whilst conducting a QFD. This supports the need to teach a flexible QFD approach, and has an impact on how teams are trained. A summary of the four QFD formats in order of preference is shown in Table V.

Rank	Percentage	Format
1	77	Customised (flexible to task)
2	17	Single phase (phase 0 or phase 1 only)
3	12	Four-phase (traditional ASI taught)
4	9	Multiphase (four-phase plus sub-system phases 1A and 1B)

Table V. Order of importance for QFD format considered most beneficial

6.5 Initial impressions of QFD before training or current experience

The respondents were asked to give three keywords that expressed their initial impressions of QFD "before" training or current experience. The top five initial impressions before training are:

(1) "Unknown/unheard of/unaware";

(2) "Time consuming/lengthy/slow";

(3) "Vague/sceptical/suspicion";

(4) "Gimmick/fashionable/management jargon"; and

(5) "Logical/structured/systematic".

The top six impressions after training are:

(1) "Worthwhile/helpful/useful";

(2) "Valuable/powerful/important";

(3) "Time consuming/lengthy/slow";

(4) "Logical/structured/systematic";

(5) "Laborious/demanding/work"; and

(6) "Complex/difficult/complicated".

6.6. The issue of "customer" understanding

The first observation is that after training/current experience, "Worthwhile/ helpful/useful" remains as the consistent top (positive) keyword group/ impression. This result, coupled with the drop from second place at 34 per cent before training/experience to sixth place with 10 per cent for "Complex/ difficult/complicated", and the fact that there are an equal number of positive impressions in the top six places in the "after" training experience section, strongly supports the benefits that training provides to QFD by way of a positive impression. This argument for training to support not only better understanding of the QFD process but to act as a vehicle for improving the image of QFD is an important lesson to learn. Of all the positive impressions within the original list of 22, a total of 11, virtually all except two, of the positive keyword group/impressions either show an increase in response levels or appear for the first time. Of the two that do not, "Simple" remains the same (3 per cent) and "Customer focused/driven product" disappears completely. It does seem strange that this key positive impression using the key word "customer" appears so low before and not at all after.

6.7 Teamwork issues

One surprising finding was that the positive keyword group of "Team building/ teamwork/empowerment" showed such a low response count both before and after (2 and 6 per cent, respectively) training and/or current experience. The low response may be explained by the fact that respondents perceive teamwork as a derivative of QFD rather than an active ingredient or prerequisite.

6.8 Negative and positive impressions and a possible measure for success

It is of critical importance to review the few negative keyword groups/ impressions that remain after training and current experience (see Table VI). These negative impressions will result in an ongoing poor image of QFD for those who do not actively

Negative keyword groups/impressions	Before (per cent)	After (per cent)
"Time-consuming/lengthy/slow"	21	25 (down)
"Laborious/demanding/work"	1	14 (up)
"Complex/difficult/complicated"	34	10 (down)
"Misunderstood/misused/ underdeveloped"	N/A	9 (new)
"Inefficient/ineffective/indecisive"	7	7 (same)
"Frustrating/disappointed/results not accepted"	N/A	6 (new)
"Lack of expertise/specialists/ facilitators"	N/A	3 (new)
"Team too big/untrained/ lost momentum"	N/A	3 (new)
"Inflexible/cumbersome"	5	2 (up)
"Waste of time/not much help/ not applicable"	N/A	2 (new)
"Not supported by senior management"	N/A	1 (new)
"Bureaucratic (prescriptive/ mechanistic)"	5	1 (down)
"Vague/sceptical/suspicion"	15	N/A (lost)
"Gimmick/fashionable/ management jargon"	13	N/A (lost)
"Optimistic/theoretical/academic"	3	N/A (lost)
"Expensive/costly"	3	N/A (lost)
"Does not fit into Ford culture"	3	N/A (lost)
"Advanced and research only/ selective"	2	N/A (lost)

Table VI. Eighteen negative impressions of QFD before and after training

participate in QFD. It is negative impressions that will most likely be remembered rather than the benefits, which as described already, tend to be less tangible or visible to those not involved with QFD, or embarking on a QFD for the first time.

6.9 Key elements still missing from training

All of the top four elements still missing from respondents' understanding of the QFD process are linked very closely to each other. A statement summarising the findings would read: "Respondents require 'more training' on how, when and with what to 'apply QFD', including a greater 'understanding of customer wants' and the opportunity to 'practice QFD within a Team'" (see Table VII). This finding emphasises the importance to respondents of four key elements of training of QFD, integration of QFD with other tools, the customer and practical application.

6.10 QFD software application skills and expertise

This section of the questionnaire response had a high response level. However, the total number of respondents who had used or had training on QFD software applications was very small, with only 33 (21 per cent) out of 154 responses. By default most practitioners using QFD software used the current Ford QFDNET (48 per cent) or the old Ford QFDplus (36 per cent), with the rest (including mostly external respondents) using ASI AFD Designer (36 per cent). The other QFD software packages used

Rank	Element	Percentage
1	"Complete/general/more training on QFD"	17
2	"Global coordination/alignment/integration of QFD"	14
3	"Reach/getting/understanding customer wants"	10
4	"Work/involve/practise/do it/train with a team"	10

Table VII. Top four key elements still missing from QFD training

included examples from the companies participating, including ITI QFD Capture, Lucas Teamset, and IBM Strategic Pointer 2000.

When asked to identify the key improvements to the QFD software package respondents currently used, there was consistency across the response cells and packages used. The three most important improvements are shown in Table VIII.

6.11 Other quality tools and processes used in conjunction with QFD

Of the "top" nine tools and processes, there was some variation to the response levels between "used" and "essential" with each tool or process considered. All the tools or processes drew between 17 and 50 per cent for either the "used" or "essential" category. A list of the top nine quality tools and processes in order of being "essential" to QFD success support are shown in Table IX.

7. The QFD team

The respondents who answered Part C, "The QFD team", answered either from their current teamwork experience or from the perspective of their past QFD teamwork experience. The teamwork "experience" covered a broad baseline from active core team members or support team members to occasional participants, such as from the perspective of facilitators, trainers or consultants. The overall response level to this section in Part C was 70 per cent of the total respondents.

7.1 QFD team's objectives, goals and aims (C.1)

The respondents were asked to identify whether or not their QFD team's objectives, goals and aims were clearly defined and understood by:

- their management;

- by the team itself; and

- by the team's next "internal" customer.

Rank	Improvement	Percentage
1	"Easier/better printing/plotting capability"	30
2	"Transferability into standard applications" (e.g. Word, Excel, FMEAplus)	27
3	"Improved layout/display of graphics"	24

Table VIII. Top three improvements required for QFD software

Rank	Quality tool or process	"Essential" response (per cent)	"Used" response (per cent)
1	Experimentation	47	40
2	Systems engineering	43	25
3	Taguchi (robustness)	39	34
4	FMEA		35
5	Quality engineering	32	18
6	Systems design specifications	27	20
7	Process management	25	23
8	Concurrent engineering	24	17
9	TOPS 8D	21	43

Table IX. Top nine quality tools/processes essential to QFD success

Overall, only option b, "By the team" showed a strong 75 per cent "yes" response, followed by option a, "their management" at 47 per cent, and lastly by option c, "by the team's next internal customer". This finding first raises the issue as to the viability of gaining adequate management support in the first place, a constant criticism throughout the questionnaire. Second, it raises a concern that communication, particularly downstream from the QFD team, is lacking, which will seriously affect the chance of the QFD team effectively deploying its targets.

7.2 The cross-functionality of the team

Overall respondents were happy that their teams were suitably cross-functional to meet the QFD objectives set. This response level was a yes to no ratio of two to one (60 to 30 per cent). This result so clearly illustrates the awareness respondents have of the need for cross-functional teamwork when conducting QFD projects.

7.3 QFD team members' roles and tasks

To the question "Are the QFD team members' roles and tasks sufficiently identified to meet the team's objectives?", the split becomes skewed when looking at internal and external responses. The external response is four to one "yes", while the internal response is almost two to one "no". This shows a weakness in the internal (Ford Motor Company) QFD team structures. Despite there being people skills and teambuilding exercises internally within the EQUIP training process (before full "globalisation" of the Ford Engineering Techniques Programme) within Ford Motor Company, it was either too late, never completed, or there was little to put it into practice.

7.4 The level of QFD process knowledge within the QFD team

This question was intended to determine the current level of understanding of the process knowledge within respondents' QFD teams. Not surprisingly, judging by the responses already received in Part A and Part B, only 28 per cent of the respondents considered their teams to be comprised of teams with most of the members up to speed with QFD process knowledge. The biggest response of 35 per cent focused on "Only a few of the team area up to speed with QFD (process knowledge)". The findings from this simply reinforce previous findings that training in the QFD process is still incomplete for most people actively involved within QFD teams.

7.5 The regular QFD team meeting schedule

This question was simply intended to identify where geographically QFD team meetings were typically being held. There were three options:

(1) on-site at place of work;

(2) 50/50 on-site at/off-site from place of work; and

(3) off-site from place of work.

Although the order by response levels was off site (45 per cent), on-site (30 per cent) and 50/50 on-site/off-site (18 per cent), the split was 80 per cent on-site for external respondents, while internal respondents confirmed off-site as a preference by 48 per cent (almost half), with the other two options split with about 25 per cent each.

7.6 The eight criteria of success for QFD team meetings
Respondents were asked to review eight criteria of success for their QFD team meetings, and rate one of three options for each criterion. The three options were:

(1) "criterion is never met";

(2) "criterion is only partly met", and

(3) "criterion is successfully met".

In common with most of Part C, the responses show an overall bias to option 2, which identifies the criteria of success being only partly met. This is the case for seven of the eight criteria and displays a response level range of between 42 and 60 per cent. The only criterion that shows option 3 as top (with a response level of 43 per cent), indicating that the criterion is successfully met, is "Tasks are clearly defined and assigned". This is marginal, however, as option 2, "criterion is only partly met" still drew a 38 per cent response level. The criteria of success that display the most predominant bias towards option 2 and the three strongest response levels for option 3 of "criterion is only partly met" and "criterion is successfully met", respectively, are shown in Table X.

8. The future of QFD
8.1 The future challenges of QFD implementation within the company
There were a total of 16 keyword groups identified, with the top six drawing between 10 and 19 per cent response levels. The response levels to the keyword

groups showed differences between the internal and external respondents to the point where although 16 keyword groups still remained for internal respondents, with the same top six, only ten keyword groups were identified by external respondents, with only three drawing response levels above 10 per cent (see Table XI).

Overall, apart from the third external response above, all of the top six are consistent for both internal and external responses. All of the above seven challenges are consistent throughout the questionnaire. These seven combined can be summarised into four key categories of challenges in relative order of importance, are shown in Table XII.

	Criterion of success	"Criterion is only partly met" (per cent)
1	"Tasks are completed on time"	60
2	"Agenda are completed in time allocated"	57
3	"Optimum meeting frequency for progress"	51
4	"Optimum meeting attendance for progress"	51
5	"QFD process checks are regularly scheduled"	50
6	"Optimum meeting length for tasks/agenda"	42
7	"Schedule/agenda posted well in advance"	42

		"Criterion is successfully met" (per cent)
7	"Tasks are clearly defined and assigned"	43
7	"Schedule/agenda is posted well in advance"	40
6	"Optimum meeting length for tasks/agenda"	34

Table X. Eight criteria of QFD team meeting success

		Response levels (per cent)
Top six internal keyword groups		
1	"Resources identified and applied"	22
2	"Integration of/standardisation of QFD practice"	19
3	"Senior management buy-in/support/champions"	15
4	"Time management/faster/flexible QFD"	13
5	"Prioritisation/discipline/goals/aims/objectives"	13
6	"Better understanding of QFD/effective training"	10

Table XI. Future of internal and external challenges for QFD use

Top three external keyword groups		
1	"Better understanding of QFD/effective training"	30
2	"Senior management buy-in/support/champions"	18
3	"Link product success with use of QFD"	12

Table XII. Four key challenges to the future of QFD use

	Challenges to future of QFD	Relative response level (per cent)
1	Management support for QFD process and resources	35
2	A more flexible, speedier standard process	25
3	More effective training/communicate success stories	19
4	Discipline and prioritisation of goals /aims/objectives	11

8.2 Best chance for QFD being adopted by most people within the company
Broadly, the top five "best chances" of QFD being adopted by most people within the company followed a consistent descent in order for all the four key response cells, with only the fifth "chance" keyword group being heavily weighted by the external response, which would have made it the second most important external best "chance" (see Table XIII).

8.3 QFD becoming a company standard to meet high customer satisfaction
Respondents were simply asked if they thought QFD would become the company standard for meeting high customer satisfaction. Although, there was no intention to just obtain a "yes/no" answer, this was how most respondents replied. The response levels were consistent with the sample sizes across the four key response cells, with a cautious overall answer given, with only 39 per cent saying "yes", 33 per cent saying "maybe/only if" and 23 per cent saying "no".

	Best chance for QFD adoption by most people	Response level (per cent)
1	"Benefits need to be seen/success stories"	33
2	"More training/information on QFD process"	20
3	"Integrate/institutionalise QFD with PD process"	15
4	"Simplify/rationalise/speed up QFD process"	13
5	"Driven by senior management/champions/ sponsors"	13

Table XIII. Five best chances for QFD adoption by most people

8.4 QFD use bringing strategic benefits to the company

To this question the response in D.4 was "yes" with a 70 per cent response level, followed by "maybe/only if" at 13 per cent and "no" at 9 per cent. This finding contrasts dramatically with the many negative or highly critical findings within the questionnaire. This finding perhaps more clearly demonstrates how the image of QFD, although poor in practice, does have a good or positive image in theory.

8.5 Advances most liked to see within QFD

The overall top five "advances" are shown in Table XIV.

8.6 Other statements on the topic of QFD and a preliminary conclusion

Two key responses arose from this last question from a total of seven:

(1) "Senior and middle management vision is required" (17 per cent); and

(2) "Keep pushing/promoting QFD (through training)" (9 per cent).

Although the overall response levels are low, these two responses reflect two of the broad themes discovered in the questionnaire findings, which are critical to the future success of QFD use within both internal and external environments. The first is that support for all areas of resources, from time given to the process to allow it to run, headcount allocation to teams and funding of market research through to benchmarking, are all critical to QFD. This support for resources can only be sanctioned by senior and middle management. Without it the QFD process may exist within a company by name, but not by action.

9. Benchmark comparison between the Ford results and the 1991 QFD usage survey results

To assist the conclusion and validation of the Ford benchmarking survey on QFD practice, a comparison was made with a similar QFD implementation survey run by Pandey and Clausing (1991) in the summer of 1991. The MIT QFD Implementation Survey had a similar large response level of 203 (compared with 164) and a broad response profile, with some 79 companies from the consumer goods to aerospace industries represented. Although the response range of the current survey was smaller with only 27 companies represented, there was still a broad range of responsibilities represented within the internal Ford responses. Within the internal Ford response profile, approximately ten organisations from Power-Train to Programme Office were represented. Even within Power-Train itself, there were many disciplines represented. A key focus of both surveys included establishing the extent of use of QFD within the companies and factors of the perceived success of QFD.

	Advances most liked to see in QFD	Response level (per cent)
1	"Streamlined/speedier/more flexible process"	25
2	"Improved QFD/market research techniques /links"	11
3	"Improve communication of QFD results"	10
4	"Link QFD with other quality tools/processes"	9
5	"More practical/product/programme application"	7

Table XIV. Top five advances most liked to see in QFD

Both the 1991 survey results and the Ford survey results showed that the majority of companies used QFD mainly in the pre-production phase. In the 1991 survey, 63 per cent of QFDs were at the advanced, planning or design end of the product cycle, which compares to 78 per cent within the Ford survey. This also needs to be balanced with "East versus West" cultural usage of QFD, and in fact reinforces the fact that the West uses QFD mainly as up-front planning tool rather than a downstream deployment tool with regard to product development. Although the findings of the 1991 survey showed that most companies had only applied ten or fewer QFD projects, this question was not directly asked in the study. However, this correlates well with the literature search findings. Certainly within Ford Europe, and particularly within the organisation of Power-Train only 10-14 QFD projects had even been attempted. Of these, less than ten had been successfully completed.

Of the top factors related to successful implementation in the 1991 survey, there were a number of differences with the forced ranking of the top criteria for successful implementation within Part A of the Ford survey. In Part A of the Ford survey, both "senior management role" and "team selection" were in the top three key criteria of success, which was comparable with the 1991 results. Also in common with the Ford survey, the 1991 survey reported that 40 per cent of respondents did not feel QFD was "catching on" and that their team was "incomplete". This matches very closely the Ford survey results on teamwork in Part C. Also when considering all four parts of the Ford survey, there are many parallels with the top five factors for successful implementation in the 1991 survey.

The Ford survey also produced a response that reinforces the top two factors of success in the 1991 survey, i.e. that "Senior and middle management vision is required".

A comparison of the 1991 top five factors related to successful implementation and the Ford top five future "challenges" of QFD implementation is given in Table XV.

The main limitations of this research study are related to the fact that a standardized QFD methodology was not used. This is further exacerbated by the fact that we are often dealing with dynamic customer needs, which require dynamic usage of QFD. The need to standardize the QFD methodology is acknowledged by Akao (2003) who argues that:

QFD will also be positioned as an effective tool for quality assurance systems in the information age. For these goals, QFD methodology needs to be standardized.

In conclusion, it can be stated that senior and middle management support, including the release of resources, remains a critical component of successful QFD implementation. There is also a need to integrate a more flexible and timely QFD process within the requirements of the established product development process. All

1991 top five factors	Ford top five challenges
Top management support	Resources identified and applied
Middle management support	Integration/standardisation of QFD with PD
Completeness of multi-functional teams	Senior management buy-in-support/teams champions
Integration of QFD into PD process	Time management/faster/flexible QFD
Flexibility in adapting QFD	Prioritisation/discipline/goals/aims/methodology objectives

Table XV. 1991 versus Ford QFD survey top five factors of success

this depends on well-trained, cross-functional and multi-disciplined teams with unified goals and focus.

References

Akao, Y. (Ed.) (1990), Quality Function Deployment: Integrating Customer Requirements into Product Design (originally published as Hinshitutenkai katsuyo no jissai, Japan Standards Association, Tokyo), Productivity Press, Cambridge, MA.

Aoki, H., Kawasaki, Y. and Taniguchi, T. (1990), "Using quality deployment charts: subsystems, parts deployment, quality assurance charts", in Akao, Y. (Ed.), Quality Function Deployment: Integrating Customer Requirements into Product Design (originally published as Hinshitutenkai katsuyo no jissai, Japan Standards Association, Tokyo), Productivity Press, Cambridge, MA, pp. 83-111.

Asaka, T. and Ozeki, K. (1988), Handbook of Quality Tools: The Japanese Approach (originally published as Genbacho no tameno QC Hikkei, Japanese Standards Association, Tokyo), Productivity Press, Cambridge, MA.

Barlow, K. (1995), "Policy deployment in action at Kawneer", ASI Quality Systems 6th European Symposium for Taguchi Methods & QFD, Kenilworth, May 16-18.

Ford Motor Company (1983), Module 7, Customer Focused Engineering, Level 1, QFD Manual, Engineering Quality Improvement Programme, EQUIP Centre, Ford Motor Company, Boreham Airfield.

Ford Motor Company (1987), Quality Function Deployment, Executive Briefing, QFD00250, ASI Press, Dearborn, MI.

Ford Motor Company (1989), QFD Awareness Seminar, Quality Education and Training Centre, Ford Motor Company, Dearborn, MI.

Ford Motor Company (1992), QFD Reference Manual: Car Product Development, Technical Training and Educational Planning, Ford Motor Company, Dearborn, MI.

Greenall, R. (1995), "Policy deployment", ASI Quality Systems 6th European Symposium for Taguchi Methods & QFD, May 16-18, Kenilworth.

Hauser, J.R. and Clausing, D. (1988), "The house of quality", Harvard Business Review, pp. 63-73.

Kathawala, Y. and Motwani, J. (1994), "Implementing quality function deployment: a systems approach", The TQM Magazine, Vol. 6 No. 6, pp. 31-7.

McElroy, J. (1989), "QFD: building the house of quality", Automotive Industries, January, pp. 30-2.

Maddux, G.A., Amos, R.W. and Wyskidcy, A.R. (1991), "Organisations can apply quality function deployment as a strategic planning tool", Industrial Engineering, Vol. 23, September, pp. 33-7.

Metherell, S.M. (1991), "Quality function deployment, less firefighting and more forward planning", IFS Conference Proceedings.

Miguel, P.A.C. (2003), "The state-of-the-art of the Brazilian QFD applications at the top 500 companies", International Journal of Quality & Reliability Management, Vol. 20 No. 1, pp. 74-89.

Pandey, A. and Clausing, D.P. (1991), "QFD implementation survey report", working paper, Laboratory for Manufacturing and Productivity, MIT, Cambridge, MA.

Reinertsen, D. (1991), "Outrunning the pack in faster product development", Electronic Design, January, pp. 111-24.

Reynolds, M. (1992), "Quality assertive companies to benefit from recovery", Elatometrics, February, p. 19.

Slinger, M. (1992), To Practise QFD with Success Requires a New Approach to Product Design, Kontinuert Forbedring, Copenhagen.

Sullivan, L.P. (1988), "Policy management through quality function deployment", Quality Progress, May, pp. 18-20.

Zairi, M. (1993), Quality Function Deployment: A Modern Competitive Tool, TQM Practitioner Series, European Foundation for Quality Management/ Technical Communications (Publishing), Eindhoven.

*What we've learned from Baldridge Award
winners is that:*

1. the CEO personally took charge

*2. they provided a lot of training at senior
levels and throughout the organization*

*3. they used accelerated continuous
improvement*

*4. they opened up the business plan to
include quality goals*

*5. they set up measures to assess progress
toward those goals*

*6. they made provision for participation
by the workforce, and*

*7. they provided a great deal of
recognition*

- Joseph Juran
during a satellite seminar
"J.M. Juran on Quality,"
held on October 10, 1996

Beyond TQM Implementation: The New Paradigm of TQM Sustainability

D Professor Mohamed Zairi
Head of The European Centre for TQM
School of Management
University of Bradford UK.
m.zairi@bradford.ac.uk

Abstract

The concept of sustainable development has been touted as a new planning agenda (Beatley and Manning, 1998). As such, it becomes a fundamental concept, which should be an important aspect of all further policy developments (Loffler, 1998). Sustainable development is based on a perceived need to address environmental deterioration and to maintain the vital functions of natural systems for the well being of present and future generations. Sustainability is defined as 'the ability of an organisation to adapt to change in the business environment to capture contemporary best practice methods and to achieve and maintain superior competitive performance' (Zairi, 2001). This concept implies that sustainability is a mean for an organisation to maintain its competitiveness. Quinn (2000) has a similar idea on sustainability. He describes it as the development that meets the present without compromising the ability of future generations to meet their own needs. Gladwin et al. (1995) on the other hand, defines it as "development, which meets the needs of the present, without compromising the ability of future organisations to meet their own needs".

Total Quality Management (TQM) represents an integrative approach for the pursuit of customer satisfaction (Chin, et al. 2001). However, facing intense pressure of global competition, organizations need to consider incorporating the idea of sustainability in TQM in order to sustain their competitive advantage and performance improvement. In addition, the interest of organisational survival, growth and prosperity has therefore got to be concerned not just with the present but also the future. The concept of sustainability does however remain unclear and it is therefore worth exploring further how it can be applied.

It is the purpose of this paper to highlight some of the key issues of sustainable TQM, to trace transformational evolutions that bring different orientations over time. The paper will then describe how various critical factors can create a sustainable competitive advantage, when working in harmony. Finally, a wide range of best practices will be illustrated to support a proposed model for TQM sustainability.

Key words: Sustainability, competitive advantage, TQM transformation, orientation, performance measurement, Balanced Scorecard, paradigm.

Introduction

Total quality management (TQM) represents an integrative approach to pursue customer satisfaction (Chin, et al. 2001). However, facing intense pressure of global competition, organizations need to consider incorporating the idea of sustainability in TQM in order to sustain their competitive advantage and performance improvement. In addition, the focus of maintaining competitiveness does not simply emphasize present time, but also in future. However, the concept of sustainability remains unclear and how it applies in TQM is worth further exploration. It is the purpose of this research to highlight some of the key issues of sustainable TQM, to trace the transformation of different orientations over time, for example, from product orientation in the 1950s and 1960s to market orientation in the 1990s and 2000s. Then we shall discuss the different factors of creating competitive advantages. Finally, the measurement of sustainability, in particular the rising trend in strategic performance measurement by the business balance scorecard measures, is highlighted.

Notion of Sustainability

What is sustainability?

The concept of sustainable development has been touted as a new planning agenda (Beatley and Manning, 1998). As such, it becomes a fundamental concept, which should be an important aspect of all further policy developments (Loffler, 1998). Sustainable development is based on a perceived need to address environmental deterioration and to maintain the vital functions of natural systems for the well being of present and future generations. Zairi (2001), the pioneer who applies the concept of sustainability in TQM, defines sustainability as 'the ability of an organisation to adapt to change in the business environment to capture contemporary best practice methods and to achieve and maintain superior competitive performance'. This concept implies that sustainability is a mean for an organisation to maintain its competitiveness. Quinn (2000) has similar idea on sustainability: 'development that meets the present without compromising the ability of future generations to meet their own need'. Gladwin et al. (1995) defines it as "development, which meets the needs of the present, without compromising the ability of future organisations to meet their own needs".

Garvare and Isaksson (2001) define sustainable development as 'the process to reach a steady state where both humanity and nature thrive' (p12). To succeed with this, a global management process for sustainable development is needed and management processes are needed on the personal, organizational and societal levels. The reasons for pursuing sustainability are: morality, intergenerational equity, survival, and organizational benefits and risks.

Sustainable performance

Sustainability is crucial to company performance. The organisational goal describes where the organisation is headed based upon the business environment and consistent with the corporate vision. Mission statements are used by individual sub-business units (e.g., distribute centres, manufacturing sites, specific operations or modules, etc.) to articulate how they contribute to the business unit's vision. A mission statement defines the purpose of a business unit. Value statements are time-independent principles that articulate how individuals in the organization are expected to behave as they pursue the vision and mission. Value statements can especially make an impact when the value represent changes in behaviour required for the organization to achieve its vision and deliver its mission. Measuring Performance through assessment of the organisation's vision and mission statements is the foundation of a sustainable effective performance measurement system (Hacker and Brotherton, 1998).

Garvare and Isaksson (2001) suggest that many different concepts can be applied as measurements and indicators of sustainable development. They propose four categories of indicators divided as: 1. Driving forces; 2. State; 3. Reactive response; and 4. Active response. They argue that excellence for sustainable development can be built on the triangle 'person-organization-society'. One way of doing this is to redefine stakeholder priorities.

In other words, TQM effectiveness and organisational performance can be measured by using self-assessment framework of quality management, such as the European Quality Award (EFQM), Deming Prize (Japan), and the Malcolm Baldrige National Quality Award (Kunst and Lemmink.2000). Quality awards have also been established at the national and region framework for analysing different factors, such as processes, leadership, and personnel management and business results, which play a role in the functioning of organisations. The criteria cover a wide range of subjects that are all relevant to quality performance in organisations (Dessler and Farrow, 1990). Awards are indeed strongly based on the foundations of TQM (Bemowski and Sullivan, 1992;Stauss, al levels (Harjono and Hes, 1993). Kunst and Lemmink (2000) believe that quality awards could be applied to both profit and non-profit sector. Sustainability of TQM in an organisation is determined by the successful implementation of CSFs as proposed by the award criteria.

The Path to Sustainability: the Various TQM Transformational Stages

During the transformational eras, the focus of quality gradually moved from product control to process improvement, thus shifting the profession from inspection to prevention. The view of quality as an added cost gradually changed to cost-reduction and improved productivity. Two major changes of the post-war period were a better understanding of the role of management in quality improvement, and the understanding that quality applied everywhere, not just to the production line. Juran must be given credit for initiating the first of these changes, whilst Deming, who earlier promoted statistical quality control, added his voice to Juran's call for management involvement (Burrill and Ledolter, 1999). Juran cautioned top management to be quality-minded, because in the absence of sincere manifestation of interest at the top, little will happen below. On a cursory review of the world of quality today, one recognises that other quality gurus have built various parts of a richly detailed quality model, on the original foundation of Shewhart. In some instances, these parts seem to interlock, at times there is an element of overlap, and in other cases, the quality gurus approach similar concepts from extremely different vantage points. Figure 1 illustrates the changes that have taken place in the quality movement since the 1970s to the current era, and in the process, it highlights some of the critical success factors in the respective eras.

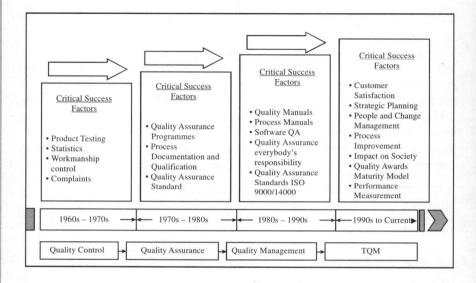

Figure 1: Evolution from Quality Control to Total Quality Management

The second major change in the direction of the quality effort emerged during the 1960s, when the focus shifted from the factory floor to the entire production process. Feigenbaum (1961), who proposed extending the quality effort to all functional areas, expounded this view. He then dubbed it total quality control (TQC), which was an attempt to integrate the quality development, quality maintenance and quality improvement efforts within all areas of the organisation, in order to achieve the most economical levels of production and service, and for complete customer satisfaction. This concept broadened the horizon of the quality movement to the entire production process at that time, which included marketing, engineering, purchasing and manufacturing.

The 1970s were difficult times for the United States and, by extension, the western world. Dogged by political problems, a faltering economy and a severe recession, which followed the huge oil price hikes early in the decade after the rise of OPEC, quality thus received very little attention as an issue of the day. In the interim, Japan's eroding of the American markets went unnoticed for

384

years, and it was not until the US car industry, which represents a large part of its GNP, came under siege and captured much attention, as the United States which had won the war with Japan was in serious danger of losing the peace.

The dawn of the 1980s brought the promise of salvation to dispel the worries of the late 1970s as the United States discovered quality circles and Phillip Crosby (Burrill and Ledolter, 1999). In the light of the recession and increasing Japanese competition, interest in quality circles, but it was Crosby (1979) who had a more dramatic impact on the United States as he expounded the absolutes of quality in his book 'Quality is Free'.

A major quality event of the 1980s was the establishment in 1987 of the Malcolm Baldrige National Quality Award. Suffice to add nevertheless, by the 1990s, a small number of American organisations had raised their quality to world-class levels and those successful Baldrige Award winners displayed characteristics that can be described as a total quality management (TQM) approach to quality.

The large and growing importance of world trade is a phenomenon of this current era. To deal confidently with any supplier, a customer needs to be assured that quality products will be supplied, and such assurance becomes even more salient in this era of trade liberalisation or globalisation. The growing acceptance of ISO 9000, an internationally acknowledged quality management standard, is the main quality story of the 1990s. The ISO 9000 series, which will be also discussed later, are generic standards for quality management and quality assurance that apply to all types of companies (large and small) in all sectors of the economy.

Classification of the various eras

Each quality era built on the previous one, and during the first three eras, quality was viewed as a problem to be solved, with the focus being on the internal operations of the organisation. In the 1980s, however, quality was seen for the first time as a competitive opportunity or a strategic weapon that could be used against competitors. Thus, in the fourth quality era, the focus was on the customer, and organisations became more proactive in anticipating and responding to both customer and market needs (Kaye and Anderson, 1999).

A similar view was earlier advanced by Zairi and Leonard (1994), who suggested that quality by definition referred to certain standards and the procedures by which those standards were achieved, maintained and improved upon, until gradually quality became to be more associated with what the customer wanted. In this regard, they cited two examples, to wit: quality is driven by the market place, by the competition and especially by the customer; also, quality is a key attribute that customers use to evaluate products or services.

The continued commitment and involvement of top management is crucial to ensuring the full integration of quality into business strategy and plans, also its adequate deployment throughout the organisation. Kaye and Anderson (1999) also submit the view that the strategic quality management approach is however, still inadequate to meet today's rapidly changing business environment, which is characterised by uncertainty and unpredictability.

In order to meet these challenges, Kaye and Dyason (1995) identified a fifth quality era: competitive continuous improvement. Here, it is suggested that the primary concern is forming organisational flexibility, responsive and capable of adapting quickly to needed changes in strategy as a result of feedback from customers and from benchmarking against competitors. The implementation of a sound strategy of continuous improvement is therefore essential, if an organisation is to cope and benefit from changes within the environment in which it operates.

For the past decade or more, there seem to have been a proliferation of TQM implementation frameworks in the literature, and Jamal (1998) provides a useful synthesis of this literature based on the work of several academics. His approach seeks to suggest that:

- TQM is strategically linked to business goals.
- Customer understanding and satisfaction are vital.
- Employee participation and understanding at all levels are required.
- Management commitment and consistency of purpose are compulsory.
- The organisation is perceived as a series of processes that incorporate customer and supplier relationships.

386

Economic and business pressures that drive an increased focus on continuous benchmarking, global competitive benchmarking, adapting new best practice, and innovating to become world-class stimulated the growth of the TQM framework. A world-class organisation is one that has the production and /or service capability that is competitive in the dynamic global economy.

The Rationale for a TQM Sustainability Model

Increasingly, organizations in the USA and Europe accept that TQM is a way of managing activities to gain efficiency, effectiveness and competitive advantage thereby ensuring longer-term success in meeting the needs of their customers, employees, financial and other stakeholders and the community at large. The implementation of TQM programs can achieve significant benefits such as increased efficiency, reduced costs and greater satisfaction that all lead to better business results.

Regardless of business sector, size, structure or maturity, to be successful organizations need to establish an appropriate management system. The MBNQA Model and the EFQM Excellence Model are practical tools that can help organizations do this by measuring where they are on the path to excellence, helping them to understand the gaps and stimulating solutions.

It must be recognised that there are many approaches to achieving sustainable excellence, but within a non-prescriptive framework there are some fundamental concepts, which underpin both models. Excellence however, is dependent upon balancing and satisfying the needs of all relevant stakeholders. Hence, to achieve business excellence, organisations must demonstrate that they excel across various performance areas, each of which is covered by agreed measurement criteria.

This business scorecard approach does not prescribe which performance areas should be used or how they should be measured. However, from the study of the literature it is clear that organisations need to adopt a TQM process and the critical success factors if they are to achieve business excellence. While these two business excellence models are non-prescriptive frameworks, the issue of measurement is at the heart of everything that is done. It is a behavioural issue and not one of design or control.

Measurement gives strength, continuity and sustainable performance. As excellent organisations develop and improve, and regularly upgrade their strategic 'scorecard', overtime this will translate into effective leadership at all levels that practices management by fact, and inculcates a continuous improvement culture that enhances people performance that produces customer delight and good business results.

Best Practice Applications for Sustainable TQM

As Table 1 illustrates, the various critical factors thought to be impinging mostly on TQM sustainability in relation to each of 20 organisations examined (Appendix 1), were identified and grouped under the broad criteria of the MBNQA and EQA Models. The list of critical factors identified are totally compatible with those identified and empirically tested by various researchers referred to in earlier sections.

Leadership & Top management commitment	Strategic planning & policies	Information Analysis	Customer resources
-Leading in markets, in customer service, in employee development & Care, in speed of operation, and business Results	-Develop strategic is aside on customer requirement -Strategic management processes	-Competitive Comparisons Benchmarking -Customer scorecard -Management of data information	-Direct customer contact, -Customer relationship management -Complaint management process -Consultative sales approach
-Training, teamwork, -Communication, Reward recognition -Company-wide meetings, open door policy	-Strategic quality planning -Competitive comparison & Networking	-Employee & Customer satisfaction -Develop goals & implement plans	-Scoring customer expectation, customer surveys -Empower customer-contact personnel To resolve complaints immediately

-Corporate vision, goal Mission & non-negotiables -Building products Operations	-Key data & Information, Measurement of organisational Performance	-5key quality indicators: safety, Internal/ external Customer Satisfaction, six sigma quality business Performance	-Future requirements Expectations -Customer satisfaction measurement, Evaluation Improvement
-Employees receive Regular communication on quality improvement -Operate a top-down, Bottom up approach	-4 standard measures: Quality, time Liness, cycle time & Efficiency	-Measures linked To key business drivers -All employees benchmark	-Building relationship -Attention to sales, Service teams -Multi-layered data gathering
-Public responsibility -Driving the continuous improvement process -Lead by example Involvement -Exemplify the highest ethical & quality values	-Team-mate training & recognition, Customer satisfaction, Supplier relation Cost of quality	-Performance reported formally, quarterly - Self-reported, non-threatening information	-Customer complaints -Future customer Requirement -Customer input on outstanding competitor information pursued
-Set direction & priorities, quality first, Followed by schedule, Then cost. -Organise plan align & Perform to plan	-Competitive benchmarking, -Empowerment, Community awareness	Strategic development process: analysis of external environment, Comparative position internal resource	-Concentration on fewer, larger client-partners -The surprise delight System -Dual measures of client satisfaction
-Focus on customers & driving quality improvement -Listening to staff, & Recognition of Individuals & earns -Customer & suppliers are identically important	-Developed Strategic plan & Define long-term Improvement goals for each business priority -The development Process is adopted, linking up the mission, Vision values	-Competitive comparisons Benchmarking data -Quality & performance data	-Focus on exceeding expectations as the measure of client satisfaction -Complete service standards by client & project

Partnership & resources	People management	Process management
-Human resource Planning & evolution -High performance Work systems -Training job-related Skills, TQ leadership Training.	-People, capability are Sustained developed by Identifying, classifying & Matching skills to roles, & Work-based learning	-Management of supplier performance -Support service -Scoring, customer satisfaction process: Evaluation improvement
-Education, financial, aid, employee empowerment	-People agree targets Continuously, review performance, develop team skills promote Continuous learning	-Dazing & Introduction of Product services -Product service production delivery
-Employee recognition Programs -Continuous improvement Philosophy of fully Empowered associates	-Improvement, of effective dialogue to share information	-Reduce, waste & increase efficacy -Use, benchmark information
-Training effectiveness -Leadership skills	-People are involved, Empowered recognised	-Product service production delivery
-A well-defined selection process -Extensive, ongoing Communications	-Stress teamwork as a learning process -Tests are used to select the best fit	-Transportation, improving Supply management, costs -Team problem solving
-Total team participation -Highlight, the use Of technology	-Employee satisfaction surveys -Effective top-down Bottom-up communication	-New advertising item development -Management of process Quality
-Supplies, materials, Buildings & equipment	-Promoting involvement & Empowerment	-Quality management and benchmarking
-Evaluation of investment Decisions use of cost of Quality measure	-Agreeing target Improving performance By aligning objectives with corporate goals	-Process, thinking environment -Supplier performance Evaluated against key requirements
-Information resource -Financial resource	-Organisation development -Human resource target	-Process are improved using innovation Creativity
-Two strategic financial goals: to maximise long term shareholder value -to manage risks -to minimize financial losses	-Aligning, terms Of employment with policy strategy	-Process ownership, Standards of operation

Table 1: Critical factors of TQM in the sample of organisations studied

Proposed Framework for Sustainable Development

Having reviewed the literature it has become quite clear that organizations are unable to survive without constantly meeting the changing needs, wants and requirements of their customers and withstanding the pressures of their competitors. Competitive pressures have forced organizations to think of delighting customers rather than simply satisfying them. This process has been institutionalised by the creation of the MBNQA that is mirrored by the establishment of the EFQM, which has similar attributes.

It can also be gleaned from the literature review that the leadership system of the MBNQA/EQA winners, demands, models and assures continuous improvement in all business processes, and promotes an environment for innovation in products and services through the use of a strategic business plan, business environment, operating plan and regular key indicator reports The literature also confirms that TQM is not a "quick-fix"- "off-the-shelf" solution to competitiveness for any organization. It must be a totally integrated, continuous, professional system based on the commitment of employees and top management, working together with customers so that the needs of all are met.

Discussion and Implications of Model

This TQM Maturity and Sustainable Performance Model (Figure 2.0) proposes the creation of an organizational system that fosters cooperation, learning and innovation in order to facilitate the implementation of process management practices. This in turns leads to continuous improvement of processes, products and services, and to employee fulfilment, both of which are critical to stakeholder satisfaction and ultimately to the survival of the organization.

Implicit in this proposition is the crucial role that organizational leadership has to play in order to ensure the success of quality management. It is the responsibility of leaders to create and communicate a vision that moves the organization toward continuous improvement, also to be supportive, in order to enable the creation and sustenance of an organizational system that is receptive to process management practices.

• Driver – (Need for TQM)

The "Driver" can be interpreted as the TQM approach to quality that exemplifies characteristics that an organization needs to display, to successfully compete in the market place. As a business imperative, it must re-establish itself to be quicker to market, customer-focused, innovative, flexible and better able to cope with rapid change. A summary of the key drivers that were identified in the literature include – work process improvement, positive work experience, customer focus and satisfaction, supplier relationships and performance, support services and competitive advantage.

- Stages of Evolution - (Paradigm Shift Required –Orientation)

The stages of evolution encountered during the review of the literature, are in support of the proposed TQM model, it bears repeating that several pundits have advanced different definitions and concepts of quality. However, the reality of present day globalisation is that markets have expanded in size, and the volume of activity in both manufacturing and service sectors has outgrown the capacity to manage by personal direction. With the emergence and growth of technology, products and processes have become increasingly complex when one considers the totality of environmental forces.

The concept of orientation implied in this model therefore reflects the degree and nature of the organization's adaptation to a specific situation or environment in which it has to operate. It is thus suggested that the road to TQM requires a paradigm shift that takes into account the four significant transitional periods found in the literature:

"Production, Service, Customer and Market Orientations".

- Sustainable Performance – (Paradigm Shift required – Measures)

TQM looks at quality as a long-term business strategy, which strives to provide products and/or services to fully satisfy both the internal and external customers by meeting their explicit and implicit expectations. At the core, is the issue of measurement, which is the source of strength, continuity and sustainable performance?

The "Business Balanced Scorecard Approach" which is an overall method of tracking performance, forms an integral part of the proposed model. This concept helps to focus on both the qualitative and quantitative measures, which are the main ethos of performance measurement.

- Learning and Innovation

Incremental improvement is grounded in the literature on learning curves [Cochran, 1968; Dutton et al, 1984; Yelle, 1979]. These authors have proposed

392

that extended production experience provides the employee with an opportunity for learning that may lead to a predictable decrease in the manufacturing cost per unit over time. Innovation is also integral to the concept of continuous improvement and to the proposition that visionary leadership enables the simultaneous creation of a cooperative and learning organization [Deming, 1986]. According to Deming, organizational learning generates and encompasses two types of knowledge – the process task knowledge akin to the "science of the process", complete with the understanding of technology, human and task requirements as explicated with precise operational definitions that guide activity and the measurement of quality.

• Culture of Continuous Improvement

The culture of continuous improvement in the context of the proposed model, means better and better quality, less and less variation which results from process management practices that bring forth incremental improvements and innovations in products, services and processes. The organization must be capable of adapting to changing opportunities and the requirements of all key stakeholders. Fact-based decisions must be made from the analysis of data collected from sources including – key customers, supplier and stakeholder interaction. These sources can only contribute to an effective communication system that will enable the organization to become more flexible and responsive to changing needs, and to continuously improve business practices.

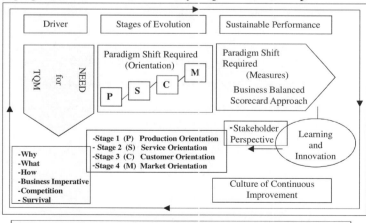

Figure 2 : TQM Maturity and Sustainable Performance Model (TQM-MSPM)

393

APPENDIX 1

The Malcolm Baldrige National Quality Award

YEAR	COMPANY
1990	Cadillac
1991	ZYTEC
1992	AT&T
1993	Ames Rubber Corporation
1994	GTE DirectoriesWainbridge Industries, Inc.
1995	Armstrong Building Products Operation
1996	Trident Precision Manufacturing IncCRI Custom Research IncDANA Commerical Credit
1998	Boeing Airlift and Tanker Programs
1999	STMicroelectronics
2000	DANA corporationKarlee company

The winners of the MBNQA (Source: NIST 2000)

The European Quality Award for Excellence

1992	Rank Xerox Ltd
1994	Design to Distribution Limited
1995	Royal MailTexas Instruments Europe
1996	Ulster Carpet Mills Limited*Mortgage Express Holdings Limited*
1997	Elida Faberge*British Telecommunication
1998	NETAS
1999	Sollac

Winners of EQA (source: www. Efqm.org/award)

• Denotes British Quality Award

394

Bibliography

Beatley, T., & Manning, K (1998). The ecology of place: planning for environment, economy and community. Washington DC: Island press.

Burrill, C. W. and Ledolter, J (1999). Achieving quality through continual improvement, John Wiley & Sons, Inc.

Chin, K. S., Pun, K. F., and Hua H.M. (2001), "consolidation of china's quality transformation efforts: a review" International Journal of Quality & Reliability Management, Vol. 18, No. 8., pp. 836-853.

Cochran, E. (1968) Planning production using the improvement curve. San Francisco: Chandler.

Crosby, P. (1979) Quality is free: The art of making quality certain. New York: McGraw-Hill.

Deming, W. E. (1986). Out of Crisis, Cambridge: MIT, Center for Advanced Engineering Study.

Dessler, G. and Farrow, D. (1990), "Implementing a successful quality Improvement programme in a service company: winning the Deming prize" International Journal of Service Industry Management; Vol. 1, No. 2.

Dulton, J., Thomas, A. and Butler J. (1984). The history of progress functions as a managerial technology. Business History Review. Vol 58, Summer, pp. 204-233.

Feigenbaum, A. V. (1961) Total Quality Control, Second Edition, New York: McGraw-Hill.

Garvare, R and Isaksson, R (2001) 'Sustainable development: extending the scope of business excellence models' Measuring business excellence. Vol. 5., no 3. Pp 11-15

Gladwin, Th.N., Kennely, J. J. BC Shelomith, T-Krause, T. (1995) Shifting paradigms for sustainable development: implications for management theory and research, Academy of management review, 20, pp. 874-907.

Hacker, M. E., and Brotherton, P.l A., (1998) Designing and installing effective performance measurement systems. IIE Solutions; Aug., Vol. 30 Issue 8, pp. 18-23

Kaye, M. and Dyason, M. D (1995). The Fifth Era. TQM Magazine, Vol. 7, No. 1., pp. 33-37

Kunst, P., and Lemmink, J., (2000) Quality management and performance in hospitals: A search for success parameters. Total Quality Management; Dec., Vol. 11, Issue 8, pp 1123-1133.

Loffler, P (1998) Sustainable development in Europe; a cause for regional environment, 8, pp. 133-120.

Quinn, B., (2000) Sustaining New Jersey's Industrial Future. Pollution Engineering; Dec., Vol. 32, Issue 13, pp. 25-27

Strauss, B. (1993), 'Service Problem Deployment: Transformation of Problem Information into Problem Prevention Activities', International Journal of Service Industry Management, Vol. 4, No. 2

Yelle, J., (1979) The learning curve: Historical review and comprehensive survey. Decision Sciences, Vol. 10, No. 2, pp 302-308.

Zairi, M. and Leonard P. (1994). Practical Benchmarking: The complete guide. London: Chapman and Hall.

Zairi, M. with Liburd, I.M. (2001), "TQM Sustainability - A Roadmap for Creating Competitive Advantage", Integrated Management, Proceedings of the 6th International Conference on ISO 9000 and TQM, Paisley, Ayr, Scotland, 17th - 19th April, Scotland, pp. 452 - 461, Published by Hong Kong Baptist University Press (ISBN 962-86107-2-4)

ACHIEVING SUSTAINABLE PERFORMANCE THROUGH TQM AND MARKET ORIENTATION

A proposed Framework for Empirical Investigations

by

Dr. M. Idris-Ashari and

Professor Mohamed Zairi

European Centre for TQM, University of Bradford, July 2005

ACHIEVING SUSTAINABLE PERFORMANCE THROUGH TQM AND MARKET ORIENTATION

Dr. Idris Ashari, Associate of The European Centre for TQM

Professor Mohamed Zairi, Juran Chair in TQM, European Centre for TQM.
University of Bradford. UK

m.zairi@bradford.ac.uk

Abstract

TQM and market orientation as strategic initiatives have been associated to improved organisational effectiveness and financial performance. However, each orientation is often discussed as a separate discipline in the literature. This paper integrates these orientations into a conceptual model of coherence business practises. It highlights the critical components of the model in relation to firms' efforts to sustain high performance through delivering superior customer value for the end customers - the basis for sustainable performance. An empirical investigation is proposed to operationalise this market-based quality orientation.

Key Words: Sustainable performance, market orientation, Customer Value Chain, TQM, Performance, Competitiveness

TQM and Market Orientation Routes to Sustainable Performance: A framework for an empirical investigation

Background literature on TQM, market orientation and performance

In coping with the environmental challenges and to sustain performance, firms practice a different relative emphasis on business orientation during the last three decades. The traditional business orientations evolve from production to sales, to marketing to entrepreneurial (Kotler, 1977; Webster, 1988). A different form of orientations is dominant in different industrial eras thus classifying relative emphasis between internal focus and customer focus behaviour of the firm (Ansoff, 1979; Webster, 1988, 1994; Treacy and Wiersema, 1993). Quality orientation evolves from conformance quality to customer satisfaction to competitive market perceived quality and value to customer value management (Gale, 1994, Garvin, 1988). The earlier two stages are internally focused while the latter forms are more externally oriented.

The recent decades have observed the rising of TQM and market orientation approaches to strategic movement. Whereas market orientation off shoots from marketing concept and is rooted in resource-based theory to competitive advantage (e.g. Webster, 1994; Kohli and Jaworski, 1990). TQM discipline originated in statistical theory, but first developed within manufacturing and operations management before its adoption into services, health care, publics, education and not for profit organisations (e.g. Haris, 1995; Hackman and Wageman, 1995).

Recent descriptive literatures pointed to the convergence of the these two business orientations into an integrated management discipline and practices based on a common objective that is to achieve customer satisfaction through quality (e.g. Webster 1988, 1994; Day 1994; Kotler 1977; Gummesson, 1994, 1998; Mohr-Jackson, 1998). Many other authors implied this integration in their writing. For example, Spencer (1994), and Dean and Bowen (1994) found substantial overlapping between TQM and management theory. As Grant et al. (1994) propose that TQM orientation is a superior model to classical management theory but incompatible hence challenges the traditional economic and behavioural theory of the firm.

399

Mohr-Jackson (1998) states that total quality orientation and market orientation are complementary philosophies with potential benefits for improving business results. Such congruence benefits marketing function from taking greater responsibilities in quality management. He echoed O'Neil and LaFiet (1992) to suggest that the adoption of TQM is critical for successful application of the marketing concept within a firm. Additionally, TQM provides vehicle for increasing communication and co-operation between marketing and other functions, including operations and production.

Gummesson (1992) proposes a quality-focused orientation as an organisational response to environmental dynamics, which integrate and may supersede production and marketing orientation. Production orientation argues Gummesson (1998) is consistent with internally driven quality management while marketing orientation is closely tied to external quality management. Strategic success is the trade-off between those two. Moreover, he argues that quality management has fortified the relationship between operations management and marketing management and has united production orientation with marketing orientation. All these trends hint the potential viability of a 'market-based quality orientation' as advocated in this research.

From strategic viewpoint, both quality and market orientations represent the demand-side strategy, where obsession with customer satisfaction through quality as the source of competitive advantage and predecessor to business performance (e.g. Webster, 1994; Wayland and Cole, 1996). Deming (1982) calls for transformation of management style based on company-wide quality orientation would lead to future competitive advantage and survival for the organisation. In discussing the paradigm for implementing marketing, Gummesson (1998) stresses that quality management can be approached externally from the market, or internally from the organisation. He asserts that the former is market driven quality management extended from "fitness for use" in Juran's (1992) terms, whereas the latter is driven by technology, organisational structure, systems, and internal goals and values.

Since the literature pointed to the existence of multiple orientations, it appears that firm might employ several orientations simultaneously. However, as Kotler (1977) suggested firms normally adopt only one of the many mutually exclusive orientations as their core philosophy. Moreover, since orientation as part of the corporate culture (Desphande et al.,1993; Webster, 1994), resource-consuming to implement, and lapse in producing results, therefore, implementing them require investment in resources and commitment by top managers and employees. As such, firms nurturing a specific orientation require appropriate strategic focus in their value chain activities. This, demands a balanced approach in implementing strategic contents (effectiveness factors) and processes (efficiency factors) of the chosen orientation (Hofer and Schendel, 1978; Reed et al.,1996), which suit the firm's goals (Sitkin et al., 1994).

A firm's orientation as a business strategy could be studied from "process-content" perspective. In particular to quality orientation, Reed et al. (1996) pointed out the process elements and content elements of TQM, in the context of firm strategy, and identify four strategic TQM contents as market advantage, design optimisation, process optimisation and product reliability. The first two contents are associated with the consequences of being external or customer-focused, while internal or operation-focused leads to firms strive to optimise operational processes and product reliability. They see the contents as the substantive elements that actually cause the changes in performance outcome. The strategic contents are therefore the core activities of the business orientation, which influence performance either singly or in synergy with other supporting practices. Those elements by themselves are necessary for superior performance but might not be sufficient to hold a sustainable outcome. TQM and market orientation supporting practices form the infrastructure that supports the value creation for the external customer.

Firm Internal- External Orientation

As earlier noted, Internal-external focused as one of the dimensions of business orientation reflects the relative emphasis of the firm's activities during the duration of a particular strategy implementation. Quality advocates such as Shiba et al., (1993) also referred to the concept of 'company-focused' and 'customer-focused' in terms of process aspects of TQM. Explicitly, the external orientation is reflective of customer-focused TQM behaviour, which concerns with the front end of the business that is the transaction of company's products and services with the buyer customers. It is concerned about the relationships with the external customers as sources of revenue to the firm.

Among others, external orientation aims to optimise design processes, gaining market advantage, and enhance firms' market value by exploiting those advantages to increase the revenue (e.g. Reed et al., 1996). It thus represents a proactive response to market dynamics and management of environmental opportunities to create and sustain its "outside-in capabilities" or "market-based orientation" that is guided by the customers and other market forces (Day, 1994).

This behavioural emphasis consequently leads a firm to be either oriented more towards the customers or its internal operations. Therefore, the firms that adopt TQM can either be operation-focused or market-focused (customer oriented) as their primary emphasis. Since TQM fundamental advocates customer satisfaction, it is self evident that TQM firms display some degree of customer focus. However, their intensity of customer focus varies depending on the TQM goals and the kinds of TQM programmes implemented. It is expected that the degree of customer focus in TQM companies is lower than of market-oriented firms that embrace TQM.

Customer focus is a primary pillar of market orientation that is the behavioural characteristic of market-driven organisation (e.g. Narver and Slater, 1990; Kohli and Jaworski, 1990; Day, 1994). TQM firms and market-oriented firms though embrace the customer focus as their central philosophy, but might have applied different operating principles and tools thus achieved different degree of customer focus. Since TQM philosophy and market orientation themes converge, and for simplicity of our discussion, internal operations emphasis for TQM companies is equivalent to low concerned to external customers in market-driven organisations. In another word operation focused firms tend to be less customer orientated, which could mean that internal efficiency does not necessarily suited to meeting customers' critical requirements - one of conditions for winning and retaining customers.

Furthermore, some of the important and unique market-based behaviours might be obscured in firms that only practice TQM. For example, continuous improvement typically focuses on operational processes and procedures are targeted at satisfying existing customer needs better. Whereas, external market focus stimulates new ideas and responsiveness to market dynamics hence targeted at anticipated needs (Day, 1994; Jaworski and Kohli, 1993; Sinkula et al., 1997, Slater and Narver, 1994, 1995), thus more proactive to future needs of the customers. Based on these arguments, firm's orientation is a trade-off between a customer focused and internal-external emphasis. Customer focused is a subset of external emphasis, which could also means competitor focused or technology-led. Therefore, external emphasis does not necessarily mean customer focus. Figure 1.1 below illustrates the firms' orientation in terms of operations and customer emphasis.

Figure 1.1 Firm relative emphasis on customer and operations.

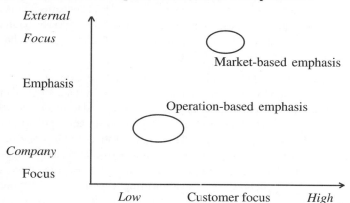

In stressing a different emphasis, firm may have followed a set of operating principles. Because firm operates in contextual environment and under varied uncertainty levels, the same precepts or philosophical orientations could mean different things among the firms. Its actual operating principles are context-specific and determined to a large extent by what the firms want to achieve and how to go about achieving it. Some authors argue for example, firm pursues TQM effort for enhancing operational control: improving existing activities, for learning and exploration or a balanced combination of these goals (Sitkin et al., 1994; Reed et al., 1996).

Conversely, different goals require different operating principles, which yield a particular emphasis in the firm's business orientation. A growing research in market orientation (e.g. Desphande et al., 1993; Jaworski and Kohli, 1993; Narver and Slater, 1990; Pelham and Wilson, 1995; Slater and Narver, 1994), showed that firms are market oriented to a different extent, which suggests that emphasis on different elements of market orientation will yield a particular form of firm's orientations.

Control-oriented and learning-oriented goals of TQM.

Besides the 'internal-external' perspective earlier discussed, the learning-control dimension is another perspective to describe the goals pursues by a firm adopting TQM. This perspective provides an avenue to disentangle the complex elements of

TQM and hence facilitates the theory building (Sitkin et al., 1994). According to this view firm focuses on internal operations more than its external concerns is consistent with control-oriented goal of TQM, whereas heavier external emphasis on markets and customers is more related to learning, exploration and adapting to the changing environment.

Control-oriented is an expanded closed system view to include suppliers, employees, and customers, yet remain focus on internal operations (Sitkin et al., 1994). Control-oriented goal means the firm emphasises internal efficiency and its related objectives, as the firm attempts to control and reduce both production and marketing costs. However, for simplicity it is generalised to an input-output definition of efficiency (Sitkin et al., 1994). Moreover, firm has greater control over costs than it does over activities undertaken in the marketplace (Dickson, 1992). By the same token, downsizing, restructuring, delayering or reengineering, which involve 'remodelling the organisation' to increase productivity, operational efficiency and reduced costs reflect firm's control-oriented goals.

Efficiency objective is a deliberate attempt to achieve operational excellence; that is doing 'right first time and every time' and excels in doing the individual activities along the process of value delivery. The strategy of zero defects and zero defection are also consistent with this emphasis. Control-oriented goals aim to optimise the firm's operational performance, which in TQM terms can be indicated by its operational process optimisation, product reliability, and cost effectiveness (Reed et al., 1996).

The control-oriented goals implies that TQM focuses on improvement activities on processes for current products to satisfy today's customers (Dervitsiotis, 1998) in the existing served markets. This strategy of searching for operational excellence is effective, when no trade-offs required between lower costs and unique position in the marketplace (porter, 1996). According to porter simultaneous improvement of cost and differentiation is possible only when the firm's best practises are far behind the productivity frontier or when the frontier shifts quickly outward.

On the contrary, learning-oriented goal is based on open system view, stressing challenges to those system boundaries from the outside, and keeping boundaries as permeable as possible to facilitate second order learning (Sitkin at al., 1994). For example, controlled-oriented goal may view customer satisfaction encircles the present served market, while the learning-oriented goal concerns more with the new customer segments, and with developing products with features beyond what the expressed needs of existing users. Because learning focus is related to experimentation, it encourages exploration of new market or technology to create a new marketspace through industry foresight (Hamel and Prahalad, 1994). Hence, learning-oriented goals promote firm's exploration efforts, beyond its existing served market, and thus stimulate new products development, technology diffusion, and process innovation.

Learning-control goals, like internal-external dimensions are not mutually exclusive options for a firm to pursue. Such dimensional perspectives however, challenge the standardised TQM packages, which rely on a rigid set of operating parameters and universal approach to quality orientation. By analysing the quality orientation in this manner, it could help to explain the possible reasons for some TQM failures, partly attributed by the 'mismatch' of TQM goals with practices, which in the past has tarnished the great potential benefits from its effective implementation.

The quality orientation adopted in this thesis is clearly synthesised from the goal perspectives and firm's internal-external dimensions. As illustrated by Figure 1.2, it is the resultant of learning emphasis and a firm's focus, and is depicted in relation to stages of quality evolution and market orientation practices. The proposed model provides a framework for analysis of TQM orientation in terms of its internal emphasis and its external dimension.

Dale (1996) based on his extensive practical work on TQM proposed five clusters of organisations on a quality orientation continuum. Each cluster displays a unique set of operating characteristics with potential 'hybrid' boundaries between clusters as an organisation progresses to a more advanced stage of quality practices. His positioning model of TQM adoption suggests organisations benchmark against advanced practices, hence begin a series of continuous improvement along the TQM journey.

By assessing the degree of firms' adoption of TQM, based on critical lists of operating principles, it is possible to cluster organisations on the basis of similar practices. Subsequently, each cluster can be correlated to their market orientation practices and their corresponding performance measures.

Figure 1.2 Quality orientation continuum

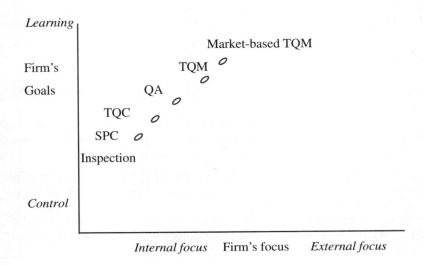

Effect of TQM practices on market orientation

Quality performance under TQM perspective directly affects customer perceived quality outcome, such as of Garvin's (1988) eight dimensions of quality. For example, product features, reliability, operations flexibility, singly and in combination enable strategies of product variety, reputation, and customisation. Additionally, these factors form the basis for product differentiation; offering product with distinctive features by design, engineering variables or communication variables (Webster, 1994, p. 104). Product differentiation in combination with market knowledge, in turn made possible the variety-based positioning, need-based positioning, and access-based positioning, which constitute three sources of strategic positioning (Porter, 1996). In conclusion, quality performance will enable firms to exploit advantageously market opportunities.

406

Earlier, market advantage is identified as a strategic content of TQM (Reed et al., 1996) and also as one of the objectives of market driven companies. Gaining market advantage is the objective of market orientation that is the result of responding to changing customer needs earlier or better than competitors (Day, 1994). According to Reed et al., (1996) a market advantage means a firm is generating supernormal profits by getting more customers, keeping them longer, or charging higher price for the products that are valued by the customers. Other than differentiation (pricing) and customer relationships, market advantage can be exploited through intangible strategic assets like reputation, patents, trademarks, brand equity, knowledge and learning orientation. Achieving market advantage is also possible by leveraging technological innovation, mass customisation, globalisation, and competitive orientation strategies such as benchmarking, positioning and competitive objective setting.

Some of the strategic assets are purely the result of 'creative phase' in the firm value added chain, but generally they are supported by the performance of 'productive phase'. Branding, for example, is a most powerful form of differentiation that can create lasting market advantage because of its not imitable characteristic. Brand equity, the newer concept than brand image and brand loyalty, is putting value to the brand and nurturing this value through investment in advertising and communication (Webster, 1994). Brand equity is therefore a measure of market advantage created by the brand. Customer patronage of a brand however, is sustainable only when operation performance and product reliability eventually meet the expectation of the brand, Similarly, patents, trademarks, reputation all are dependent on the effectiveness of operational excellence to produce consistency of quality performance in the marketplace.

Deployment of strategic assets to create market advantage can possibly be achieved when firm has a high degree of market orientation. The reasons being those with extensive customer database and greater customer knowledge are able to leverage those knowledge as well as technology to connect with customers (Wayland and Cole, 1997), thus can stay close to customers and ahead than competitors (Day, 1990, 1994). Additionally, knowledge-rich firms are better able to exploit targeting, positioning, customising, and adjust marketing strategies to the market requirements. This also means that market oriented firms can offer superior solutions and experience on matters that customer value most highly e.g. "always the low price" at Wal-Mart and "mass customising" at Dell Computers (Day, 1998).

Market advantage in terms of customer oriented strategies mean that firms can improve customer retention rate thus lead to substantial improvement in profits (Buchanan, 1990; Reicheld and Sasser, 1990). Additionally, as Gronrooss (1990) noted that marketing or transaction costs for every customer can be reduced within long-term relationship, in particular it could lead to facilitation of relationship customisation. Long-term customer relationships would likely easier to create structural bonding such as joint investment in value delivery system (Berry and Parasuraman, 1991), which create difficult-to-imitate competitive advantage hence are likely sustainable. Customer-oriented firms should convert customer satisfaction to customer retention and loyalty (Day, 1998) and creating customer partnership realising that all those are important drivers to profitability. It can be postulated that TQM companies that establish customer relationships are likely to retain customers and achieve higher profitability.

Positional advantage is created in the market place when firm perform the value delivery activities differently from competitors, or perform different activities from competitors. This is the meaning of strategy (Porter, 1980; 1996). In either case, it is also means strategic positioning or differentiation strategy-deliberately choosing a different set of activities to deliver a unique mix of value. Specifically, Porter (1980) identified low-cost advantage and differentiation as the sources of competitive advantage, which businesses may emphasises either or both (Hall, 1980). According to these sources of advantage, differentiation or market niche is also interpreted to be additional product benefits and can take many forms including brand image, product image, product features, customer service, dealer network, and technology (Porter, 1996).

Despite of its many sources, differentiation is most often characterised by superior quality of the products (Phillips et al., 1983). The unique product offering permits higher prices thus allow excess return to the firm. However, a firm actual profitability is determined by its relative cost and differentiation (price) advantage over and above its relative potential profit attributed to the industry or segment 'attractiveness' factors (Hamel and Prahalad, 1994, p. 301). These differentiation effects are essentially external and concerned with an attempt to shift a business's demand curve upward (Narver and Slater, 1990). These arguments clarify the simplified statement that market advantage leads to increased revenue and sustainable performance (e.g. Reed et al., 1996).

On the contrary, a low cost advantage is essentially the effect of operational excellence that can be shared between provider and customer buyer as lower acquisition and use costs. Total customer cost is the bundle of costs customer expects to incur in evaluating, obtaining, and using the product or service (Kotler, 1997, p.38). Total customer value is the difference between total customer costs and the total benefits gained from purchase and product use. The cost saving may be derived from economies of scale, volume, or cost reductions in value delivery processes such as R&D, production, service, sales-force, and advertising (Narver and Slater, 1990). For example, IKEA co-produces furniture with customers and share the cost saving thus increasing value for both parties (Gummesson, 1998).

Firms pursuing cost leadership strategy could accept cheaper components, use standardised processes, and advancing market share in order to reduce unit costs (Phillips et al., (1983). Some TQM practices such as process improvement, changeover flexibility, variety flexibility and efficient design, zero defect and the like, allow some cost containment be achieved. Simply stated, TQM efforts help to make cost leadership strategy possible. At the same time TQM efforts also help firms to support market advantage created by their marketing activities.

Prior to TQM era, firms view cost leadership and high quality are mutually exclusive, otherwise their profitability stuck in the middle. Within TQM perspective, market performance may be related more to the intensity of commitment to quality strategy rather than to the polarity of differentiation or low cost. Current thinking and industrial experience shows that product quality and cost leadership are compatible strategies. Phillips et al., (1983) for example, empirically conclude that quality and cost control interact to generate above average ROI. Although mutually supportive capabilities, these two emphases operationally compete for management time and employee attention, therefore, those firms not attaining leading edge in both areas should focus on variety and cost in sequence (Hamel and Prahalad, 1994, p. 178).

In their study, Narver and Slater (1990) found a higher correlation between the three market orientation components and differentiation strategy (.45) than between those components and low cost strategy (.27), which they claim has provided supports for concurrent validity of the market orientation constructs used in the study. This implies that conceptually differentiation strategy being an external emphasis is more compatible to an SBU with a strong market orientation than a low cost strategy, which is not likely external emphasis. Since TQM efforts could affect differentiation and positioning therefore, TQM and market orientation is related through this relationship. Furthermore, as earlier argued firms' market advantage could be supported by activities that constitutes both quality and market orientation practices.

While conceptually, the two approaches are compatible, simultaneous implementation of a comprehensive system as separable initiatives are less favourable in light of commitment, resources and time required for effective implementation. Given the right resources and organisational culture, TQM and market orientation can promise a powerful contribution in enhancing firm performance. This effect would be empirically tested in this thesis.

Integrating TQM and market orientation elements.

Miles, Russell and Arnold (1995) propose that the firms attempt to leverage strategic quality to create customer value should integrate quality orientation precepts comprising customer focus, continuous improvement, and system perspectives. Mohr-Jackson's (1998) field-based view of total quality constitutes four pillars: organisation-wide commitment, continuous improvement, customer perceived quality, and customer satisfaction. His finding supports the notion of customer-perceived quality that includes all products and service attributes that meet customer requirements better than competition. This supprts the assertion that customers judge quality relative to competition and is consistent with earlier literatures (e.g. Buzzel and Gale's (1987) on perceived quality; Garvin's (1988) user-based definition of quality; Marketing Science Institute's (1991) market driven quality; Zeithaml et al's. (1990) service quality).

Such integration suggest that quality orientation to be a commitment to maximise firm's long-term value and stakeholder satisfaction by constantly reducing the product related cost to society. A further integration between quality and market orientation requires a complete delineation of the principles and elements of each approach to find their common themes and peculiar practices.

When discussing TQM and market orientation relationships it is important to differentiate between practices (elements) and performance. Practices, being inputs to achieve performance outcome influence the latter directly and singly or through interaction with other input variables. TQM and market orientation elements generated in chapter two and three respectively are collection of practices available for managers to steer their firms toward certain types of performance.

Despite authors implied the convergence of TQM and market orientation (e.g. Webster, 1994; Day, 1994; Gummesson, 1994, 1998; Reed et al., 1996; Mohr-Jackson, 1998) but there has been no explicit and precise listing of those practices that comprise the combined orientation. Perhaps the extensive overlapping between those practices (e.g. Webster, 1994; Spencer, 1994; Grant et al., 1994; Dean and Bowen, 1994) makes precise integration difficult. Descriptive literatures suggest that quality and market orientation practices may be mutually supportive, which means, TQM improves product quality and firm's performance but TQM efforts could also improve market orientation performance. The converse may also be true.

This research begins to empirically articulate the relationship between TQM and market orientation, in terms of both elements (practices) and performance. Since TQM fundamentals, like market orientation concept, generate an array of peripheral principles, this research took the approach of dividing the TQM and market orientation elements into unique TQM practices, unique market orientation practices, and common practices. This method is consistent with approach taken by Flynn et al. (1995), who studied TQM and JIT relationships, although their basis for classifying unique and common practices are different.

Consistent with system approach and contingency view points each common practice in isolation or combined supports the effectiveness of the firm's orientation. Common elements, which formed the foundation for integrating TQM and market orientations, become the organisational infrastructure that influences the attainment of firm's core practices. Those conceptually different and similar elements based on related literatures are shown in table 1.1. Customer value is the unifying purpose for both orientations. These elements are assembled into an integrated conceptual model called market-based quality (MBQ) orientation as shown in figure 1.3.

Table 1.1: Unique and common elements of MBQ orientation

Unique TQM Elements	Common Elements	Unique Market Orientation Elements
1.Supplier management	1.Customer orientation	1. Technological orientation
2. Usage of quality/SPC tools	2 Management commitment	2. Marketing-mix modification
3. Operations optimisation	3. Interfunctional coordination	3. Competitor orientation
4.Employee involvement	4. Knowledge and learning	4. Customer relationships
5. Product / Service reliability	5. Design optimisation	5. Innovation orientation
6. Continuous improvement	6. Market advantage	6. Strategic positioning
7.Quality training	7 Measurement	7. Branding
8. Empowerment	8. Customer satisfaction	8. International marketing
9. Teamwork		9. Marketing research
10. Benchmarking		

Market Focus Initiatives

Customer focus has been traditionally construed as being equivalents to the marketing concept (echoes Levitt, 1969: and subsequent writers (Webster, 1994; Kohli and Jaworski, 1990; Narver and Slater, 1990). Recent literatures have indicated that customer orientation is also a pillar of TQM thus enlarging the concept into a much broader dimension. The view that customer orientation with obsession with quality and customer satisfaction advocated by Deming in 1950's implied that customer orientation is the pillar of TQM. Also, Kotler's total quality marketing concept (1997.) links quality and market orientation through customer orientation. These arguments and others place customer orientation as one of the common factors in the conceptual model to be studied. Customer orientation, under the new marketing concept and TQM thinking means that:

1. Firm is able to create value for customers because it understand their value chain (Porter, 1985),

2. Firm is committed to the generation of market intelligence and organisation-wide response to it (Jaworski and Kohli, 1993; Kohli and Jaworski, 1990; Narver and Slater, 1990).

3. Firm position itself to the target market based on the capabilities and competence to provide superior value, stay close to customer, and ahead of competition (Day, 1990: 357).

4. Firm constantly innovates or continuously improves its business process to enhance customer value and amaze customer (Deming, 1986, Hamel and Prahalad, 1993).

7. Firm Manages customer portfolio, competitive market including technology to improve customer relationships (Webster, 1994; Wayland and Cole, 1997).

The degree of customer orientation reflects the relative emphasis the firm places between the customer (and other market orientation factors) and the internal efficiency or 'company focus' in implementing TQM (refer figure 1.1). In other words a firm pursuing TQM can strive to be either customer focus or operation focus or emphasise both. Literatures accepted that TQM is a business culture and resource consuming to implement thus firm only pay attention to a particular emphasis during different phases of its implementation. If it is suggested to be mutually exclusive like differentiation and low-cost duality of Porter's (1980), TQM orientation thus assumed along unidimensional scale between customer and operation focus (see Figure 1.2). Consequently, it is argued that TQM firm with external orientation emphasis and exhibits high customer focus is market oriented.

Since TQM also emphasises both quality of conformance (producing product to customer specification) and quality of performance (serving customers by improving product quality) (Deming, 1986; Juran, 1992), customer needs become a key input to TQM. Quality inputs derived from effective environmental scanning, competitor analysis, technological forecasting, and customer feedback among others are subsumed under intelligence generation. The customer and competitor information: intelligence generation and dissemination are the processes of market orientation (Kohli and Jaworski, 1990) but involve interdepartmental role, though suggested could be championed by marketing personnel (Webster, 1998; 1994). These market-based activities aim at meeting "quality of performance": customer perceived quality in the marketplace leading to market advantage, whereas ensuring the "quality of conformance to design" is the job of the internal operation. However, both require interfunctional co-ordination.

413

High market orientation, particularly of customer orientation will directly affect 'quality of design' since market-oriented TQM companies will be able to improve all practices associated to quality of design. Optimisation of design processes is the result of team participation especially by marketing and operations personnel. Moreover, communication, networks and involvement with suppliers and customers have been shown to facilitate innovation.

Since TQM emphasises the use of cross-functional team approach towards solving quality problems, this practice and teamwork that it creates will enhance interfunctional coordination. This in turn improves internal information flow, though not necessarily reduces departmental conflicts, but help to keep members focus on important issues. It is postulated that TQM companies achieve greater interfunctional co-ordination through cross-functional activities and greater flow of quality and customer information, which result in improved response to market. This, conceptually clarify linkages between quality orientation and market-based behaviour in terms of improved organisational co-ordination.

Furthermore, quality award models such as MBNQA, Deming prize, and EFQM award consider customer's requirements, expectation and satisfaction as criteria for effective quality programmes, which are consistent with contents of marketing concept: customer primacy and long-term satisfaction. Conceptually, TQM and market orientations are two parallel concepts, mutually supportive and rely on common elements such as customer orientation, competitive orientation, innovation, and interfunctional co-ordination. However, only selective deployment of both orientations simultaneously can lead to firms exhibit the highest form of customer orientation.

Market oriented (Customer-focused) TQM companies

Customer-focused TQM companies are firms that exhibit high market orientation practices, place customer related objectives in their quality orientation practices, promote learning about market to develop market-based (outside-in) capabilities such as customer connection, customer relationships, customer retention, customer visits, etc. They practice a host of TQM programmes as well as market oriented behaviours that leverage activities during the 'creative phase' (see figure 1.4) to enhance market advantage as the primary source of revenue and competitiveness.

These companies fulfil the customer demands on customer oriented measures such as high quality, low cost, short lead time, and flexibility, all of which are external measures of successful operations, though they are measurable inside the firm (Schonberger, 1986, p.205). These measures, unlike the traditional internal oriented measures such as cost variance, internal due dates, efficiency, and utilisation, which customer don't really care about, characterise world-class practice. By definition, market oriented measures are closer to measuring firm's competitive advantage. A comprehensive measurement system in market oriented companies that embrace TQM should cover total perspective from design quality to conformance quality and performance quality.

Market-oriented TQM firms use market intelligence to anticipate customer's changing needs and expectation thus become close to customer and deliver superior value earlier than rivals. Being market oriented means gaining and sustaining competitive advantage through customer focus behaviour (e.g. Narver and Slater, 1990; Day, 1994). As they actively collect information about customers and competitors thus would have extensive customer database. Good use of customer database would create knowledge about customers and enable firms to meet the customers' requirements better and earlier than the rival firms. Subsequently, firms with exceptional knowledge of portfolio of customers would be able to focus on developing and on keeping profitable customers. It is also able to employ and leverage technology effectively to connect with customers better (wayland and Cole, 1997). As a result of these activities, firms that are customer oriented would enjoy a growth advantage over their peers.

Additionally, Customer-focused TQM company gains competitive advantage by providing customer satisfaction through quality (Deming, 1982). Product quality precedes customer value as the former is internally determined but the latter is measured in the marketplace after the customers experience with the products and realise its' "value-in-use". The 'Market–based quality orientation' must deploy both product quality and customer value emphases in order to not only create competitive advantage but to translate those advantages into sustainable performance.

Under this approach, firm emphasis covers both quality of 'conformance to design' and quality of 'performance'. Balancing these internal-external concerns creates improved value to external customers. Continuously Improved customer value is the unifying mission for market-based quality oriented companies. By implication, customer-focused TQM companies should strive for revenue growth through optimum market advantage and achieve cost leadership through operational excellence. They benefit from both strategies by practising all the common TQM and market orientation practices as well as unique practices as necessary. In doing so, the contents of TQM and market orientation as generated in the literature review are meshed into the conceptual model, on which to be empirically studied.

TQM companies constantly evaluate its processes in order to improve the value delivery processes. Within TQM literature, process management and continuous improvement are central to quality improvement. Alternatively, improvement could be derived through benchmarking-an outward view of constant improvement by 'copying and improved from the best' so as to continuously achieve best practice. To nurture superior ability to deliver customer value, market-driven firms must compare their value delivery processes with "best-in-class" competitors (Day, 1998). Improvement for market driven companies encompasses product innovation, continuous process improvement and "benchmark improvement".

Benchmarking or similar competitor-centred activities such as technological forecasting, setting competitor-centred objectives are contingent to the goals of the orientation itself. For example, a firm operating under stable market demand and facing little technological turbulence, might want to pursue continuous improvement, which could be cheaper and less risky to implement as opposed to more costly competitive benchmarking. In this competitive market, customer-focused TQM companies are likely to adopt competitor-centred initiatives such as strategic benchmarking in order to acquire best practice in delivering customer value.

In competing for customer value delivery, organisations must become highly information driven in managing the operations side and equally information driven in the marketing side (Woodruff, 1997). According to his value framework, achieving overall customer satisfaction is related to customer value dimensions derived from three equivalent satisfaction levels; i.e. goal-based (customer motive) satisfaction, consequence-based (usage) satisfaction, and attribute-based (product attributes) satisfaction. In this context, he suggested that by marrying the skills in managing quality of internal processes and product with customer value orientation firms would enhance customer value delivery practices as sources of competitive advantage.

416

This dual emphasis requires effective deployment of TQM tools as well as customer value tools such as QFD, benchmarking, customer satisfaction measurement and customer value-oriented marketing information system (CVOMIS) (Woodruff, 1997). Customer-focused TQM companies are likely to exhibit effective use quality tools, internal quality information and external customer knowledge. As noted earlier, these are possible through improved communication, cross-functional team activities and interfunctional co-ordination. As a result, market oriented TQM companies would be better able to satisfy customer needs earlier than rivals, achieve better market growth hence better performance than the internally focused TQM companies.

Figure 1.3: MBQ Orientation: Conceptual Integrated Model

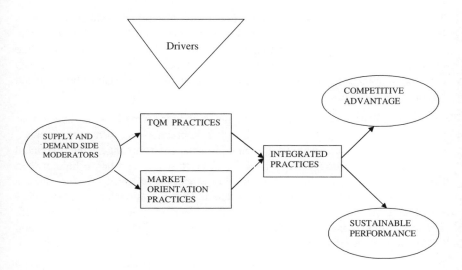

Description of the conceptual Model

This model combines the elements of both quality orientation and market orientation into an integrated approach. Market-based quality (MBQ) orientation is defined as business philosophy that guides managers to choose the way of doing business. It is a business culture-organisational culture, climate, and style that are oriented toward satisfying profitable customers. "The culture, climate and style pertain to the interrelationships which exist within a firm's micro-environment", while the orientation pertains to how firms interact with all environment (Miles et al., 1995). Explicitly, the actual orientation defines how firm relates to its external, internal and the contextual competitive environment. As firm faces unique situations within their internal and external environment, the actual orientation represents selecting the contents and processes from the model that compatible to the firm resources and skills in an attempt to develop a sustainable advantage.

This model assumes that the philosophy held by organisational members influences both the strategic and tactical decisions in all business activities and is consistent with Foxal (1984) that organisational orientation influence the actions and "the attitudes and behaviour of all members of the company". This implied that MBQ orientation should be pervasively deployed throughout the organisation and led by top management.

The model incorporates all critical elements derived from market-based behaviour and quality-focused characteristics. However, in practice each firm may display a set of operating principles that suit their contextual environment especially related to their control-learning oriented goals. In order to study the relationship between firm's actual orientation (measured on set of practices) and firm's performance, a causal model (see figure 1.4) is constructed. These relationships between core elements in the model and performance form the main hypotheses in this research. The causal model extracts the "content elements" from the conceptual model and the list of practices in table 1.1.

Research model (figure 1.5) shows the contents and processes of the MBQ orientation. The contents are the core practices (elements) that truly create competitive advantage, which have been identified from the literature as operational optimisation (process efficiency), products / service reliability, design optimisation and market advantage. These core elements are by no mean exhaustive but are thought as sufficient to embrace the peripheral concepts delineated from market orientation and TQM fundamentals. The causal model separates the process elements from the contents though they may be equally important in securing the sustainable advantage.

These contents elements are derived directly from Deming three stage definition of quality; i.e. quality of design and redesign; quality of conformance; and quality of performance [Gitlow et al., (1987, p. 8)] and Juran's four elements definition; quality of design, quality of conformance; availability; and field service (Juran and Gryana, 1988). Juran is more explicit than Deming to state quality of performance in terms of availability and field service, which can be translated into product reliability consistent with SERVQUAL model by Zeithaml et al., (1990).

Reliability, a primary element of TQM is a multi-construct concept encompassing product usable age, ease and speed of maintainability, parts replacement availability, promptness of correction, delivery as promise, on-time service, and integrity of service in correcting problems. Reliability is at the core of product offering supported by services as 'augmented product' making a bundle of benefits to the customer. High reliability is not only a core determinant of product performance but also perquisite to customer satisfaction.

Market advantage in this context is the result of leveraging the product reliability and customer satisfaction relative to the competition in the industry. In another word market advantage is the consequence of product/service reliability and customer satisfaction. The latter two concepts are the purpose of all quality strategies. Therefore quality of performance is measured in the marketplace and can be enhanced externally, for example through customer education and after sale service. Similarly, relationship-marketing strategies are primarily concerned with enhancing and translating the outcome of quality of performance to create market advantage.

Quality of conformance in operations management or engineering term means meeting standards in production process (Crosby, 1979) and associated with process control. Operational optimisation is largely affected by optimum design. Design and operational optimisation in turn result in high reliability products/ service being delivered to customer. This value-added chain is continuously improved through various TQM efforts and market oriented behaviour thus making firms achieve both operational excellence and unique market position to sustain their performance.

Figure 1.4 MBQ Orientation: Content - process model

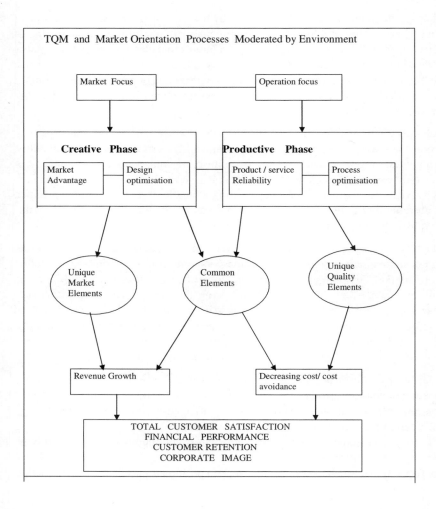

Figure 1.5 MBQ Orientation: Research Model

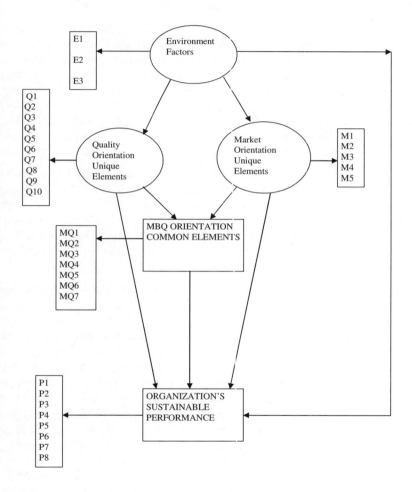

MBQ elements and sustainable performance

Firm that implement TQM can derive competitive advantage in the market place as well as from the operational processes. In the market place, created positional advantage can produce increased market share and increase revenue. Dean and Bowen (1994) argue about the relationship between TQM and competitive advantage by linking improved quality with high prices and increased market share. Internally, improved design can lead directly to efficient process, which can reduce defective production. This argument is also consistent with Deming's quality chain that improved quality lead to reduced cost, which in turn increase market share and profit (Deming, 1982).

Effective and efficient design would yield directly both improved product reliability and market reputation (Reed et al., 1996). Improved reliability is a resulted after the customers use the product or experience the service, hence has its time lapse before its effect can be recognised. However, once reputation on reliability has been built, repeat purchase is more likely. Reputation, rooted in product reliability is therefore a source of competitive advantage, which is more sustainable because it is harder for competitor to imitate (e.g. Kay, 1993).

Design optimisation, process optimisation and product or service reliability by themselves are sources of quality advantage. Design process is a combination of managerial responsibilities and customer analysis which include identification of core customer benefits, benefits positioning, and development of physical products, strategy, and service policy to fulfil the key benefits. Design optimisation includes activities that allow firms to use cost-effective input in product design and develop better product faster than competitors thus reduce new product cycle time to meet time-based competition. Optimisation in design would improve defect in production through design for produceability and by using fewer components. It would also enable firms to increase process optimisation through efforts such as plant modernisation, facilities expansion, and re-layout, redesign and reengineering. Design optimisation is often driven by internal processes as opposed to product reliability which is more stimulated by market response, such as customer complaint (Garvin, 1988). In essence, design optimisation, process optimisation and product reliability are prerequisites to lowering product costs and achieving operational excellence. Also as has been discussed in earlier section design optimisation is antecedent to an array of strategic assets, which in turn can contribute to market

422

advantage leading to sustainable competitive advantage.

Design optimisation and sustainable performance

Design quality is the process and activities that ensure providers fully meet customer requirements. This means designing include identifying customer need, developing what satisfies the need, checking the conformance to the need, and ensuring that the need is satisfied (Oakland, 1993, p. 45). These entail to carefully manage the entire design process by using effective design management framework such as concurrent engineering or total design.

Cost reduction in TQM context can be associated to design optimisation, often subsumed under the concept of concurrent engineering (Schmidt and Finnigan, 1992). Concurrent engineering enables participation of multi-division personnel early in the design process. This is a highly critical process because as much as 80% of the product cost is committed at the design stage (Pye Andy, 1998).

Simultaneous or concurrent engineering includes techniques like the Taguchi design method, design for manufacturability, design for assembly, and quality function deployment (Reed et al., 1996). QFD is concerns with selection of critical customer expectation into design features to create product with market advantage and cost effective to produce. By various claims QFD has reduced design time by 40% and design costs by 60% while maintaining or enhancing the quality of the design (Hauser and Clausing, 1988). In tandem, all synergistic effect of efficient design-robust and manufacturability, reliable product with less defective production can lead to reduced costs and sustaining advantage.

Computer aided design (CAD) is one of the enabling technologies for concurrent engineering. Through this, consistent design data provides an ideal mean of co-ordination and bridging information across divisions and disciplines. Related to CAD, electronic data management (EDM) can make a major contribution to concurrent engineering. The ability to produce, access and revise critical documents quickly can lead to competitive advantage through reduced new product development life cycle, increased product complexity, and reduced time to market.

TQM and market orientation cultures promote flat structure, speedier corporate communication, and team approach to decision making. All the above, particularly cross-functional teams can simplify design process. It also facilitates modular approach to design, which enables firms to combine and utilise existing standardised components to create new models or services more effectively and drastically reduce product development costs (Lau, 1996). According to Lau modular design results in firm's flexibility to meet changing market demand faster. The entire process is seen as making value delivery processes into modules of dynamic network of skills and capabilities, which allow integration of resources to customise product or services.

Design determines what elements of tangible and intangible features should be included in the product or service. This decision in turn determines the key financial factors in an operation: revenue, cost, and capital employed, which all affect profitability. For example, redesign that applies substitution with lower cost materials lead to reduced total cost. Redesign for produceability (or ease of operations in service) leads to increased labour productivity and increases capacity of existing facility.

The above arguments support the notion that TQM companies, either customer focus or operation focus, tends to benefit from optimum design and product or service reliability therefore can translate into higher degree of customer focus and market orientation. Flynn et al., (1995) propose that optimise design create direct impact on quality performance through its effects on product reliability, product features, and serviceability. The indirect effects of design on quality performance take root through its impact on produceability, which in turn affect operation flow management. It is hypothesised that TQM companies produce reliable products and employ optimum design will achieve lower cost and hence better performance. Consequently, the market oriented TQM companies, which employ optimum design and produce reliable products are more likely to maintain sustainable performance.

Process optimisation and performance.

Process optimisation refers to various organisational capabilities and practices to control and achieve efficient operations in the value delivery processes. It aims to lower product costs while ensure quality of conformance to design. Constant improvement in process may lead to best practices, which can be reflected through high plants and facilities utilisation; labour efficiency; reduced scrap, waste and rework; increased product and service reliability; and reduced relative operating costs. This emphasis is consistent with cost leadership advantage, although not all process optimisation emphasis leads to lowest cost in the industry.

Internally focused revenue growth can be derived from either cost saving in operation or reduction in capital employed, which mean in either case managing effectively existing resources. In another word firm's TQM contents are tailored to improve productivity that is by getting more output from the same resources or getting the same outcome from fewer resources. Through TQM efforts productivity is achieved without specifically resulting in reduced headcount, unlike downsizing, rightsizing, delayering, or reengineering, which almost always do (e.g. Hamel and Prahalad, 1994).

Cost avoidance through holding capital expansion, cutting promotion, deferred physical investment or making employees redundant (through downsizing, restructuring or reengineering) are common practices in times of economic malaise, but cost reduction by continuous process improvement can be a continual pursuit irrespective of economic conditions. Lower cost can be the result as well as the cause to increased productivity. In the context of operation, increased productivity is parallel to process optimisation, which can be derived from improved design, improved reliability or conformance to specifications. Flynn et al., (1995) suggest that effective process management improve quality performance through reduction of process variance and defective production. They noted that process flow management practices include reliance on preventive maintenance (echoed Garvin, 1993), foolproofing or poka-yoki, flexible and effective scheduling, and teamwork between managers and operatives in quickly solving operations problems. Therefore, TQM companies that improve process optimisation will be able to control operational costs and achieve sustainable performance.

Product and service reliability and performance

Quality leadership is based on thrust to become a leader in industry through achieving high standards in the product performance, reliability and features, at competitive cost. High reliability creates product or service reputation, which is also a component of company reputation and source of market advantage. By leveraging this reputation as strategic asset firm can charge premium price in the market. High product and service reliability has been shown to be associated with fewer complaints, lower warranty costs, reduced service costs after sale, higher customer satisfaction and perceived market quality. Perceived product performance relative to competitor's products can create differential advantage and reputation, which are likely to sustain firm's performance.

425

Reliability is affected by design, quality control in operation, control of suppliers and maintenance. These activities must be co-ordinated with appropriate resources suitable to the requirements of the product. Product requirements for reliability may involve varied degrees of customer and supplier involvement and must be determined by market assessment, warranty cost considerations and the customers. Since reliability affects availability, repairs, spare units, support technician, customer defection recovery efforts, etc, the improvement in delivered customer value can be achieved by improving total aspects of reliability.

Operation-focused firm and sustainable performance

This category of companies is concerned with operational excellence: effective operation and efficient process to achieve lower costs. They search for improved operational results and best practices as the sources for competitiveness. They operate in opposite direction to the customer-focused TQM companies. This strategy is not necessarily ineffective, especially in stable market environment and less dynamic technological change.

Garvin (1988, p. 90) has depicted the relationship between improved quality and lowering cost. Gummesson (1994) links quality to both productivity and profitably. The Crosby's (1979) slogan 'Quality is free' suggests that substantial saving can be achieved by doing job right first time that avoid rework and prevent dissatisfied customers. This means a cheaper product or service cost at the end, while firm enhances its image among customers. As a consequent it encourages repeat purchase, attracting new customers resulting from word of mouth recommendation, and increasing revenue.

Crosby (1979) suggests that cost of quality arising from producing 'non-quality' as much as 35 %, which 95% of it is accounted by failure and appraisal cost. Because TQM emphasises cost effectiveness through continuous improvement and process management, there is a massive potential reduction in overall cost, even by allocating prevention cost such as TQM planning and implementation cost above 5% level. As has been earlier pointed out in chapter two one of the assumptions of TQM principles is that the benefits from TQM implementation by far outweigh the costs of not implementing TQM.

TQM literature clearly indicated that efficient production through prevention of defect along the production stages lead to cost saving and lower cost of production

(Crosby, 1979, 1984; Deming, 1982, 1986), and the earlier the defect is detected, the less expensive it is to correct (Garvin, 1988). The quality gurus address many aspects of management issues in improving efficiency and control of the firm operation. Unlike customer orientation construct, operation focus has never been fully defined or measured although wide acceptance of the concept exist in the classical scientific management and current management theory that deal with the internal control of the firm and the governance of its activities (Reed et al., 1996).

Operation focus firms aim to excel through quality leadership via product performance, reliability and features and cost effectiveness. Therefore their emphases are more likely associated with operational excellence indicated by process efficiency and product and service reliability. TQM programmes such as process management, statistical control, continuous improvement, employee involvement, supplier management and inspections are all related to operational effectiveness, which can lead to lower cost.

Continuous improvement and performance

Cost advantage is one of the routes to competitive advantage (Day and Wensley, 1988; Porter, 1985). For operation focus firm, a cost-based advantage may be seen as corresponding to market advantage in the customer oriented firm (Reed, et. al., 1996). Operation focus TQM companies are construed as relying on continuous improvement tool for improving design improvement, reliability improvement and process optimisation.

Continuous improvement in the context of people oriented efforts is seen as kaizen-incremental reduction in effort and time to conduct operation (Schmidt and Finnigan, 1992). Others see Continuous improvement as a broader concept which includes innovation in process resultant from the application of new technologies and research and development effort, while it resembles the economic concept of experience-curve effects (Reed et al., 1996). These arguments are consistent with Gilmore (1990), who projected that with continuous improvement, long-run average cost curves getting below the previous one as the firm adopted new methodologies in technology, manufacturing methods, or materials. Lowest cost producer strategy for Market-oriented firm is thus consistent with operation focused strategy for TQM company. In other words TQM firms pursuing continuous improvement in operation will achieve lower production cost, which in turn lead to improved market share and market performance.

Continuous improvement philosophy captures the desire to enhance the reliability and control of performance (doing it right first time and every time), and to enhance learning and experimentation (continuous learning) in order to develop new skills and capabilities. In practice, most quality programmes focus on enhancing the organisational performance through continuous improvement by systematically reduces or eliminates sources of customer dissatisfaction. Extensive data collection, analysis, and feedback systems that help to identify problems and direct the employees' attention to those problems achieve this (Day, 1990). Continuous improvement is the lowest step in improvement activity as opposed to benchmarking and reengineering, which are more complex to implement.

Employee involvement, Empowerment and Teamwork.

TQM advocates employee involvement in decision making to solve workplace problems. This in normally achieved via project teams, QCC, suggestion system, or self-managed team and the like. For example, the QCC teams choose routine problems where members have ability to overcome them. Generally, the identified problems are routine and low in uncertainty (i.e. problems are analysable), therefore dramatic result in efficiency are some time achieved.

Similarly, the suggestion system also confines employees to suggest improvement within which employees themselves or their sections' members can implement the improvement. The problems of interdepartmental in nature, often concerned with creation of customer value would be left unsolved. It can be proposed that organisation with TQM programmes that involve employees in enhancing control-oriented goals will not improve customer value delivery. These companies also fail to realise the full benefits of employee participation when the firm operates in a highly uncertain environment.

Empowerment is a 'state of mind' that exist in employees when companies implement practices that distribute power, information, knowledge, and rewards throughout the organisation. This 'high-involvement-high-performance' approach is guided by non-bureaucratic and participation-oriented philosophy (Bowen and Lawler, 1995). They argued that empowerment creates superior performance capabilities, which are organisationally embedded thus become a source of sustainable competitive advantage. Others also suggest that successful organisations empower their employees (e.g. Kotter and Haskett, 1992; Milliken, 19996; Scotto, 1996).

Teamwork is collaboration between managers and non-managers, between functions and between customers and suppliers. The non-managerial employees contribute to the organisation when they are empowered and prepared. Functional teamwork follows the notion of system optimisation, whereas the customer-supplier collaboration is based on the perceived benefits of partnerships (Dean and Bowen, 1994). Deming's (1993) system thinking even suggests teamwork among competitors, where competition should be directed to expand the market thus meets the customers' needs not yet served. To Deming, competition between people, teams, department, divisions are actually destructive.

Dean and Bowen (1994) echoed Ciampa (1992) regard teamwork practices include identifying the needs of all groups and organisation involved in decision making, searching for mutually benefited solutions, sharing responsibility and credit. These practices are promoted by forming teams and team building techniques such as role clarification and group feedback. Superior performing companies value cross-functional teams and people working together in teams (e.g. Beck and Yeager (1996); Kern, 1997; Milliken, 1996).

The complete elements of MBQ orientation are listed under table 1.2 as research constructs. Primarily, consisting of TQM elements therefore their meanings are consistent with the current definitions discussed in many related literatures. The main relationships among the elements and firm's performance have been formulated into the research hypotheses to facilitate the empirical work.

Proposed Research Constructs

Table 1.2 Research Constructs

Code	Research constructs as represented by figure 1.5
Q1	Operation focused-process optimisation
Q2	Operation focused-product and service reliability
Q3	Continuous improvement
Q4	Supplier management
Q5	Usage of quality tools
Q6	Employee involvement
Q7	Quality information and planning
Q8	Quality training
Q9	Benchmarking
Q10	Empowerment
M1	Competitor orientation
M2	Technological orientation
M3	Innovation orientation
M4	Customer relationship (final customers)
M5	Channel relationship (agents and distributors)
M6-N	Strategic positioning & segmentation -(not tested)
M7-N	Marketing mix modifications (e.g. mass customisation)
M8-N	Branding
M9-N	International marketing (e.g. globalisation)
M10-N	Marketing research
MQ1	Customer orientation
MQ2	Market advantage
MQ3	Design optimisation
MQ4	Interfunctional co-ordination
MQ5	Top management commitment
MQ6	Teamwork
MQ7	Customer satisfaction (internal and external)
MQ8	Knowledge and learning (not tested)
MQ9	Measurement (not tested)
P1	Sales growth
P2	Return on assets
P3	Customer retention
P4	Success in new products or services
P5	Corporate image or company reputation
P6	Sales over revenue ratio (profitability)
P7	Customer satisfaction
P8	Relative market share
E1	Market turbulence
E2	Competitive intensity
E3	Technological turbulence

Proposed research hypotheses are:

General hypotheses:

P1: Firms with customer-focused TQM practices (IV) tend to display high degree of market orientation (DV).

P2: Firms with operation-focused TQM practices (IV) tend to display low degree of market orientation (DV).

P3: Firms with customer focused TQM practices tend to display higher degree of market orientation than firms with operation focused TQM practices.

P4: Firms with low market orientation (IV) that use TQM but operation focused (MV) will achieve medium to low sustainable performance (DV).

MBQ orientation contents and performance:

P5: Firms with a high degree of market orientation (MV) that use TQM to generate market advantage (IV) will realise benefits of growth in revenues and achieve high sustainable performance (DV).

P6: Firms with a high degree of market orientation (MV) that use TQM to improve design optimisation (IV) will realise benefits of reduction in costs and achieve high sustainable performance (DV).

P7: Firms with a high degree of market orientation (MV) that use TQM to improve process optimisation (IV) will realise benefits of reduction in costs and achieve high sustainable performance (DV).

P8: Firms with high degree of market orientation (MV) that use TQM to improve product reliability (IV) or (pursuing continuous improvement) will realise benefits of growth in revenues and achieve high sustainable performance (DV).

P9: Firms with low market orientation (MV) that use TQM to improve process optimisation (IV) will realise benefits of reduction in costs and achieve medium sustainable performance (DV).

P10: Firms with low degree of market orientation (MV) that use TQM to improve product reliability (IV) will realise benefits of growth in revenues and achieve medium sustainable performance (DV).

431

MBQ orientation processes and sustainable performance

P 11: The higher the interfunctional co-ordination (IV) the greater the TQM effectiveness (DV) . (TQM effectiveness is positively related to interfunctional co-ordination).

and the higher the interfunctional co-ordination (IV), the higher the market orientation (DV) (Degree of market orientation is positively related to interfunctional co-ordination).

P12: TQM companies that apply customer-oriented tools (IV) such as QFD, competitive benchmarking tend to be able to satisfy customer needs better than competitors hence are more market-oriented and achieve better growth and sustainable performance (DV).

P13: TQM companies that established customer relationships (IV) programmes has higher retained customers and achieved market growth and sustainable performance (DV).

P14: Organisational climate determines the top management decision making style which control structure, system, corporate culture, and values, moderate the TQM and market orientation effectiveness and hence sustainable performance relationship. The better the organisational climate (IV) the higher the sustainable performance (DV)

P15: The higher the innovation orientation (IV) the higher the TQM effectiveness and market orientation thus the higher the sustainable performance (DV).

P16: Customer focused TQM and sustainable performance relationship is stronger in the high environmental uncertainty.

P17: Operation focused TQM and sustainable performance relationship is stronger in the low environmental uncertainty.

Conclusion

This article has constructed the research model from the conceptual framework integrating the elements of quality and market orientation. The resultant causal model, which can be empirically tested in the research fieldwork, is called market-based quality orientation approach to managing business. The MBQ model is the extended TQM model with integration of market orientation elements thus making it the integrated approach to business strategy. It is a business philosophy based on quality management principles that is guided by market factors thus seeks to deliver sustainable competitive advantage hence sustained performance. The model amalgamates both orientations and has a powerful link to improved performance.

BIBLIOGRAPHY

Ansoff, H. I. (1979), *Strategic management,* London: Macmillan

Beck, J.D.W. and Yeager, N.M. (1996), How to prevent teams from falling, *Quality Progress*, March.

Berry, Leonard L. and Parasuraman, A. (1991), *Marketing Services: Competing Through Quality,* New York: The Free Press.

Bowen, David E. and Lawler, Edward E III, (1995), Empowering service employees, *Sloan Management Review*, vol. 36, no. 4, pp. 73-

Buchanan, R.W.J. (1990), '*Customer Retention: the key link between customer satisfaction and profitability',* Unpublished paper, Bain & co.

Buzzel, R.D. and Gale, B.T. (1987), *The PIMS Principles: Linking Strategy to Performance*, New York: Free Press, p.79-82.

Ciampa D. (1992), *Total Quality: A user's guide for implementation,* Reading, MA: Addison-Wesley.

Crosby, P.B. (1979) *Quality is free,* London: Penguin Books Ltd.

Dale, Barrie G. (1996), Benchmarking on total quality management adoption: a positioning model, *Benchmarking for Quality Management and Technology,* vol.3, no.1.

Day, G.S. and Wensley. R. (1988), Assessing advantage: A framework for diagnosing competitive superiority. *Journal of Marketing,* 52 (2), 1-20.

Day, George S. (1990), *Market Driven Strategy: Process for Creating Value.* New York: The Free Press

Day, George S. (1994), "The Capabilities of Market-Driven Organizations," *Journal of Marketing,* 58 (October), 37-52.

Day, George S (1998), What Does it Mean to be Market-Driven?, *Business strategy Review*, vol.9 (1), pp1-14.

Dean, J.W. and Bowen, D. E. (1994), Management Theory and total quality: Improving research and practice through theory development. *Academy of Management Review*, 19: 392-419.

Deming, W.E. (1982), *Quality, productivity and competitive position*, Cambridge, MA: MIT center for Advanced Engineering Study.

Deming, W.E. (1986), *Out of the crisis*, Cambridge, MA: MIT center for Advanced Engineering Study.

Deming, W.E. (1993), *The New Economics: for industry, government, and Education*, Cambridge: M I T.

Dervitsiotis, Kostas A., (1998), The challenge of managing organizational change: Exploring the relationship of re-engineering, developing learning organizations and total quality management, *Total Quality Management*, vol.9, no.1, pp.109-122.

Desphande, Rohit, John U. Farley and Frederick E. Webster, Jr. (1993), "Corporate Culture, Customer Orientation, and Innovativeness in Japanese Firms: A Quadrad Analysis," *Journal of Marketing,* 57 (January), 23-37.

Dickson, Peter R. (1992), "Toward a General Theory of Competitive Rationality," *Journal of Marketing*, 56 (January), 69-83.

Flynn, B.B., Schroeder, R.G. and Sakakibara, S. (1995a), The impact of quality management practices on performance and competitive advantage, *Decision Sciences,* Vol.26, no.5, pp. 659-

Foxall, G. (1984), *"Corporate Innovation: Marketing and Strategy"*, New York: St. Martin's Press.

Garvin, David A. (1988), *Managing Quality: The strategic and competitive edge.* New York: Free Press.

Garvin, David A. (1993), "Building a Learning Organization." *Harvard Business Review*, vol.7, no. 4, pp. 78-91.

Gilmore, H. L. (1990), Continuous incremental improvement: An operations strategy for higher quality, lower costs, and global competitiveness. *Advanced Management Journal,* 55(1): 21-5.

Gitlow, Howard S. and Gitlow, Shelly J. (1987), *The Deming Guide to Quality and Competitive Position*, Prentice Hall Inc. New Jersey, USA.

Grant, R. M., Shani, R., and Krishnan, R. (1994), TQM challenge to management theory and practice. *Sloan Management Review,* 35 (2): 25-35.

Gronroos, C. (1990a), "The Marketing Strategy Continuum: Towards a Marketing Concept for the 1990,"*Management Decision*, 29, No.1, p.9.

Gummesson, E. (1994), "Broadening and Specifying Relationship Marketing", *Asia-Australia Marketing Journal*, 2, No1, pp.31-43.

Gummesson, E. (1998), Implementation requires a paradigm, *Academy of Marketing Science Journal,* vol.26, no.3, pp.242-249.

Hackman, J.Richard and Wageman, Ruth (1995),Total Quality Management: Empirical, Conceptual, and practical Issues, *Administrative Science Quaterly.*

Hall, W. K. (1980), "Survival Strategies in a Hostile Environment," *Harvard Business Review,* 58 (5), 75-85.

Hamel, G., and Prahalad, C.K. (1994), *Competing for the future: Breakthrough strategies for seizing control of your industry and creating the markets of tomorrow.* Boston, MA: Harvard Business School Press.

Haris, C.R. (1995), The evolution of quality management: An overview of the TQM literature, *Canadian Journal of Administrative Science*, vol. 12, no.2, pp.95-

Hauser, J. F. and Clausing D. (1988), The house of quality, *Harvard Business Review,* vol. 66 (3) : 63-73.

Hofer, C. W. and Schendel, D. (1978), Strategy Formulation: Analytical concepts. St. Paul, MN: west.

Jaworski, Bernard J. and Ajay, K. Kohli (1993), "Market Orientation: Antecedents and Consequences." *Journal of Marketing*, 57 (July): 53-70.

Juran, J.M. (1992), *Juran on quality by design: The new steps for planning into goods and services.* New York: Free Press.

Juran, J.M. and Gryna, F.M., eds. (1988), *Juran's Quality Control Handbook*, fourth edition, McGraw-Hill, New York.

Kay, John A. (1993*), Foundations of Corporate Success: How business strategies add value,* New York: Oxford University Press.

Kern, A. (1997), No team is an island, Quality Progress, May.

Kohli, A.K., Jaworski, B.J., And Kumar, A. (1993), MARKOR: A measure of market orientation, *journal of Marketing Research*, 30: 467-477.

Kohli, Ajay K. and Bernard J. Jaworski (1990), "Market Orientation: The Construct, Research Propositions, and Managerial Implications," *Journal of Marketing*, 54 (April), 1-18.

Kotler, P. (1997), *Marketing Management: Analysis, Planning, Implementation, and Control, 9th. Ed. Prentice Hall International.*

Kotler, Phillip (1977), "From Sales Obsession to Marketing Effectiveness," *Harvard Business Review*, 55 (November-December) 67-75.

Kotter, J. R. and Heskett, J. L. (1992), *Corporate Culture and Performance*, New York: Free Press.

Lau, R.S.M., (1996), Strategic flexibility: A new reality for world-class manufacturing, *S.A.M. Advanced Management Journal*, vol.61.,n.2, pp.11-

Levitt, Theodore (1969), *The Marketing Mode*, New York: McGraw-Hill.

Miles, Morgan P.; Russel, Gregory R. and Arnold, Danny R. (1995), The quality orientation: An emerging business philosophy? *Review of Business*, vol. 7, no.1, pp. 7-

Milliken, W. F. (1996), The Eastman way, *Quality Progress*, October.

Mohr-Jackson, Iris (1998), Conceptualizing total quality orientation, *European Journal of Marketing*, vol. 32, no. 1 / 2.

Narver John C. and Stanley F. Slater (1990), "The Effect of a Market Orientation on Business Profitability," *Journal of Marketing*, 54 (October), 20-35.

Oakland John S. (1989, 1993), *Total Quality Management*, Heinemann Professional Publishing Ltd, Oxford, UK.

Phillips, L., D. Chang, and R. Buzzell (1983), "Product Quality, Cost Position and Business Performance: A Test of Some Key Hypotheses", *Journal of Marketing*, vol.47, Spring, pp. 26-43.

Porter, M. E. (1985), *Competitive Advantage: Creating and Sustaining Superior Performance*, New York: Free Press.

Porter, M.E. (1980), *Competitive strategy: Techniques for analysing industries and competitors.* New York: Free Press

Porter, M.E. (1996), What is strategy, *Harvard Business Review,* Vol. 74, issue 6., pp. 61-

Pye, Andy (1998), Making European Industry World Class; The role of document management, *Document World,* vol. 3, no. 1, pp. 52.

Reed, R, L., David J. and Montgomery, Josept C., (1996), Beyond process: TQM content, and firm performance, *The Academy of Management Review*, Vol. 21, no. 1:173.

Reichheld, F. F. and Sasser, W. E. (1990), 'Zero deflections: quality comes to services', *Harvard Business Review*, September-October, pp. 105-111.

Review 71 (July-August) 78-91.

Schmidt, W. H., & Finnigan, J. P. (1992), *The race without a finish line.* San Francisco: Jossey Bass.

Schonberger, Richard J. (1986), *World class manufacturing*, The Free Press, New York: Macmillan Inc.

Scotto, M. J. (1996), Seven ways to make money from ISO 9000, *Quality Progress,* June.

Shiba, S., Graham, A. and Walden, D. (1993), *A new American TQM,.* Portland, OR: productivity Press.

Sinkula, J.M., Baker, W. E. and Noordewier, (1997), "A framework for market-based organizational learning: Linking values, knowledge, and behaviour." *Academy of Marketing Science Journal,* Vol. 25 (Fall): 305-

Sitkin, S. B., Sutcliffe, K. M., and Schroeder, R.G. (1994), Distinguishing control from learning in total quality management: A contingency perspective, *Academy of Management Review*, 19: 537-564.

Slater, S.F. and Narver, J.C. (1994), Does competitive environment moderate market orientation-performance relationship? *Journal of Marketing*, 58:46-55.

Spencer, B. A. (1994), Models of organization and total quality management: A comparison and critical evaluation, *Academy of Management Review,* 19: 446-471.

Wayland, Robert E. and Cole, Paul M. (1997), *Customer connections: Strategies for growth*, Harvard Business School Press.

Webster, Frederick E., Jr. (1988), "Rediscovering the Marketing Concept," *Business Horizons,* 31 (May-June), 29-39.

Webster, Frederick E., Jr. (1994), *Market Driven Management*, John Wiley and Sons.

Woodruff, R. E. (1997), Customer value: The next source for competitive advantage, *Academy of Marketing Science Journal*, vol. 25, no. 2, pp. 139-

Zeithmal, V., Parasuraman A. and Berry, Leonard C. (1990), *Delivering quality service: balancing customer perceptions and expectations,* New York: The Free Press, A division of Macmillan, Inc.

" ...every successful quality revolution has included the participation of upper management. We know of no exceptions. "

- Joseph Juran

A proposed model of TQM implementation based on an empirical study of Malaysian industry

T. Thiagaragan and M. Zairi
University of Bradford, Bradford, UK, and
B.G. Dale
UMIST, Manchester, UK

Keywords TQM, Model, Malaysia, Implementation

Abstract This paper is based on an empirical study of TQM implementation in the Malaysian industrial context. The main focus of the study was to identify quality factors for effective TQM implementation, which are critical for TQM to flourish in Malaysian industries, and to understand the dynamics of TQM implementation in a Malaysian context. The paper presents the outcomes from this research in the form of an implementation framework, constructed through the use of practical guidelines, the key steps of which have been validated and supported empirically.

First Published in

International Journal of Quality & Reliability Management,
Vol. 18 No. 3, 2001, pp. 289-306.
© MCB University Press, 0265-671X

Introduction

According to Crosby (1989) quality, as a key attribute that customers use to evaluate products and services, has emerged as a vital point of management focus in many parts of the world. Many corporate enterprises have found that the key to competitive success lies in emphasising product and service quality as a strategic issue when doing business (see Kano, 1993; Belohav, 1993; Pulat, 1994). The following quote by John Young, former president and CEO of Hewlett-Packard, puts into perspective the critical importance of quality to the success of corporate business:

> In today's competitive environment, ignoring the quality issue is tantamount to corporate suicide (Shetty, 1987).

The emergence of quality as a top priority in many corporate entities is primarily due to the globalisation of world trade and the competitive pressure brought about by the escalating demands of consumers, who want better products and services. According to Feigenbaum, quoted in Townsend and Gebhardt (1992) quality was given priority equal to price in 80-90 percent of all buying decisions by consumers in 1988 The figure was only 30-40 percent a decade earlier and since that time, quality has become an important consideration for executive thinking. Crosby (1989) also talks about the increased awareness of senior executives, who have begun recognising that quality is a key strategic issue and an important focus for all levels of the organisation. In particular, senior management have started to take charge of quality as part of their primary responsibilities. This all-encompassing management philosophy, termed total quality management (TQM) has generated a tremendous amount of interest and has emerged in the forefront as a major management movement, influencing many sectors of the economy in countries around the world. Kanji (1990) aptly called this development the "second industrial revolution'.

Implementing TQM involves defining and deploying several key elements or factors (these are termed quality factors for the purpose of the study described in the paper). They include both the so-called "soft" aspects of management such as leadership, employee empowerment and culture (e.g. Wilkinson, 1992) and the "hard" aspects such as systems and improvement tools and techniques (e.g. Oakland, 1993). However, it is claimed by writers such as Burr (1993) and Black (1993) that the set of quality factors or essentials of TQM implementation cited in the available literature are not formulated on the basis of systematic empirical research. Each author tends to emphasise a selection of quality factors based on their judgement and experience in working with different organisations.

The gap in the literature is hardly surprising given that research and theory in TQM implementation are still at a very early stage in the West (e.g. Dale et al, 2000; Sitkin et al, 1994). To date, there are only a handful of empirical studies reported in the literature that have attempted to identify what constitute the levers of TQM that can be manipulated to implement TQM effectively (Baker and Starbird, 1992; Black, 1993; Garvin, 1983; Mann, 1992; Martinez et al, 1998; Motwani et al, 1994; Ramirez and Loney, 1993; Saraph et al., 1989; Sinclair, 1994). The majority of these studies have been undertaken in developed economies.

Description of the problem area and research opportunity

Lack of empirical research

Dean and Bowen (1994) claim that TQM as a ubiquitous organisational phenomenon has been given little research attention. As mentioned above, the bulk of the TQM literature is based on personal experiences and anecdotal evidence (Baker and Starbird, 1992), with very little emphasis on empirical testing (Sitkin et al, 1994). Given this lack of empirical work, Black (1993) argues that TQM risks losing credibility as a management philosophy for improving organisational effectiveness. There are three possible reasons for the lack of attention given to empirical investigation of TQM experiences. First, TQM is a relatively recent phenomenon outside Japan. Second, its origin lies mainly outside the academic world (Spencer, 1994). The third reason is highlighted by Dean and Bowen (1994):

> TQ researchers ... will be much more productive if there is a theoretical base upon which they can draw ... TQ because of its interdisciplinary nature means that it often transcends the boundaries of existing theories. Thus, it is unlikely that the existing theories will be sufficiently broad based to support research on TQ.

Lack of empirically sound TQ implementation models

A number of writers including Dale (1999) and Kanji (1990) argue that implementing TQM should be a top priority of all corporate leaders. While the literature is full of "everything you need to know about TQM implementation", most of the information is based on personal experiences and anecdotal evidence. It is also evident in the literature (e.g. Coulson-Thomas, 1992; Glover, 1993) that, while there is general consensus regarding the importance of issues related to leadership and employee involvement for effective TQM implementation there are many differences in opinion about the other relevant components and the appropriate emphasis among the various components (e.g. Smith, 1994; Creech, 1994). There is also much disagreement concerning the details of implementation even in the areas in which there is general consensus (Easton, 1993). As a consequence, organisations wanting to implement TQM are not only overwhelmed by the numerous precepts (e.g. Juran, 1993), principles (e.g. Deming, 1986), models (e.g. Oakland, 1993) and prescriptions (e.g. Crosby, 1979), but also are often left confused as to where to begin. This problem is described as "total quality paralysis" by authors such as Smith (1986).

Unsuccessful TQM implementation attempts are not uncommon; see Cole (1993) and Gilbert (1992) for examples. To quote Atkinson (1990), "the road to total quality is littered with failures". Mann (1992) and Sitkin et at (1994) argue that the lack of clear guidelines and implementation methods may have contributed to a number of failed implementation attempts. In a survey carried out by Yui (1995), 41 percent of the 138 respondents agreed that they did not understand what was required to introduce and implement TQM, even though they understood its concepts. According to Dean and Bowen (1994) leaders of organisations recognise that the available approaches to implementation are organisationally and politically naive and they question the lack of empirically sound models to assist in effective quality management.

The development of a model to explain effective TQM implementation by organising, synthesising and empirically validating the various key quality factors should help to serve the needs of practitioners. Such a model is the focus of this paper.

Lack of empirical research outside the developed economies Hurd (1992) outlines how the growing importance of quality has spread to many enterprises outside the developed world, especially nations in the South East Asian region. It is appropriate, therefore, that studies in TQM implementation be conducted for the benefit of managers in these countries, where the need is confounded by a lack of information relating to TQM. In addition, given the acknowledged limitations of the findings of some of the earlier studies in their applicability across national boundaries (e.g. Dawson, 1994), the outcome of such systematic studies will create a new critical mass of TQM thinking under different cultural environments.

Malaysia as a focus of research

In Malaysia, the 1990s witnessed the intensification of interest in quality management activities in literally every sector of its economy. A study by Lasserre and Probert (1994) showed that quality sophistication and expectations in Malaysia are better than in other growing economies of Asia; indeed, in some quality dimensions, Malaysia is grouped with Japan. Malaysia has also taken on itself the challenge of attaining the status of an industrialised nation by the year 2020. Malaysia therefore provides an interesting and, more importantly, a practical arena for empirical study of effective TQM implementation in a developing economy.

In summary, the importance of TQM in practice, the lack of theory and research and the need to develop knowledge specifically for the benefit of organisations outside the developed economies, indicates that expanding the existing knowledge of TQM implementation is a valid topic for research.

Purpose of the study

The main purpose of the study described in the paper was to construct a TQM implementation framework that can be used as a guide in the selection and/or formulation of an effective TQM implementation approach in Malaysian organisations. The form of framework will be used to present the "what" and "how" of TQM implementation and is intended to provide non-prescriptive guidelines.

Constructing such a framework can best be approached by studying

445

organisations that have implemented TQM. The aim is to identify the so-called critical quality factors of TQM implementation and understand how they are addressed. This is the approach which has been adopted for this study and central to this are the following core requirements:

- understanding how the current knowledge of TQM implementation is developed;

- investigation of TQM implementation experiences in Malaysian organisations;

- identification of the key quality factors for effective TQM implementation in Malaysian organisations;

- analysis of how the key quality factors are deployed.

In constructing the TQM implementation framework, consideration is given to its practical value. Such an objective is best achieved by presenting the central component of the framework in the form of implementation guidelines (see Mann, 1992), with the critical quality factors superposed as a "checklist". Information from the TQM literature suggests that in developing guidelines for effective implementation, there is a need to:

- List the key quality levers that have to be manipulated to implement TQM. These are termed as key organisational requirements (KORs).

- Describe the organisational activities needed to deploy and implement the KORs.

- Present the guidelines in a recognisable structure.

- While the framework was constructed using inputs "closer to the phenomenon" to offer Malaysian management support for decision making for TQM implementation, it is not intended to be prescriptive. The quality management literature is clear that models and frameworks cannot take the responsibility from the management as to "how to go about implementing TQM" (e.g. see Deming, 1986).

The general purpose of this study was to construct a TQM implementation framework that can be used as guide in the selection and/or formulation of an effective TQM implementation approach in a Malaysian organisation. Constructing a TQ implementation framework as a research topic can best be approached by studying organisations that have implemented TQM. The aim therefore was to identify the so-called critical quality factors of TQM implementation and to understand how they were addressed. This was the approach adopted for this study and central to the approach were the following core requirements:

* an understanding of the current knowledge of TQM implementation was developed;

* investigations of TQM implementation experiences in Malaysian-based TQM organisations were carried out;

* an analysis was conducted to identify the key quality factors for effective TQM implementation in Malaysian-based organisations;

* an analysis was carried out to identify how key quality factors were deployed.

Specifically, there were three objectives in this study which were synthesised primarily from the core requirements. These are detailed below.

The first objective was to identify quality factors that are critical to effective TQM implementation based on current knowledge of implementation in the West. The effort required an in-depth review of the available literature, interviews with best companies in the UK, and a survey using experts as respondents.

The second objective was to identify the quality factors that are critical for TQM to flourish in Malaysian organisations. The enquiry involves Malaysian-based TQM organisations agreeing on a set of quality factors based on their implementation experiences.

The third objective was to understand the dynamics of TQM implementation in a Malaysian environment. The investigation involved in-depth case studies of selected organisations.

Development of the framework

The elements of the central component of the framework are now described.

Key organisational requirements (KORs)

KORs are the actual quality levers that management need to deploy and manipulate to implement critical quality factors; they can be considered as the foundation blocks. A key organisational requirement is described in the form of verb plus an object(s). The critical quality factors and foundation elements offer a practical step-wise framework of "most critical first" and "least critical last" in addressing the KORs. A three-stage approach is proposed and three categories of KORs adopted:

(1) Stage zero KORs. These are the KORs needed during the pre-TQM introduction stage. Foundation factors and tier I critical quality factors define stage zero (SO) KORs.

(2) Stage one KORs. These are KORs needed during the early stages of TQM implementation. Tiers I and II critical quality factors define stage one (SI) KORs.

(3) Stage two KORs. Stage two (S2) KORs are employed after stage zero and stage one KORs have been met. The KORs are defined primarily by tiers II and III critical quality factors.

Organisational activities (Oas)

Oas describe what is involved and/or what must be done to implement the key organisational requirements. The primary aim of Oas is to describe the tactics and techniques employed in deploying and implementing the KORs and where appropriate the structure of individual KOAs.

Structure

In presenting the critical quality factors and KORs, it was felt that a provision of a recognisable structure will facilitate a user friendly framework. The identification of a constellation or underlying constructs to represent variables offers the means of achieving such a structure. Information from the TQM literature also suggests that there is a need to attempt to explain the constructs of TQM implementation. Those writing on TQM find it all but impossible to discuss and explain TQM models without using words relating to constructs to define the important aspects of TQM (e.g. Cullen, 1991; Creech, 1994; Clemmer, 1990; Leonard and Sasser, 1982; Kilmann, 1985; Kanji, 1990; Kano, 1993, Oakland, 1993). The constructs which are given a range of terms (e.g. conditions, quality, levers, tracks for change, general governing principles and pillars) are generally presented as "areas" at which an organisation planning to implement TQM should aim to excel.

The concept of constructs has also been used by researchers to group variables into a number of underlying factors (e.g. Black, 1993; Saraph et at, 1989; Mann, 1992). Black (1993) used statistical procedures of factor analysis to explore and identify ten factors. Mann (1992), on the other hand, used a judgmental process grounded in the literature to group variables into five underlying factors and accorded them recognisable labels.

Given the nature of the task at hand, the latter approach is appropriate and has been adopted in this study. In identifying the underlying constructs to group the critical quality factors and associated KORs a conscious effort was made to: ensure that the constructs reflect the key findings of the three levels of investigations; maximise clustering of items of similar criticality; maximise clustering of items that are actionable together and limit the number of groups. In this way the constructs will have empirical validity and practical value within the implementation framework. Four separate but interrelated and mutually supportive categories can be identified - institute leadership; maximise internal stakeholders' involvement; manage by customer-driven processes; and adopt continuous improvement. They have each been accorded a recognisable label from a descriptive perspective which describes the interrelationship between the items within the categories (see Rummel, 1970). As the categories are "distilled" from the critical quality factors they put into perspective the broad critical areas that an organisation planning to implement TQM should aim to create.

Figure 1 conveys the interrelationship of the critical categories and also portrays the soft-hard aspects of essentials of TQM implementation. Figure 2 shows the proposed structure of the TQM implementation framework.

449

Guidelines for TQM implementation

The guidelines are now presented from a senior management perspective.

A Critical category I: institute leadership

Leadership and corporate quality strategy means a united senior management
team which is committed to customer satisfaction and communicating the
"vision" in such a way as to mobilise all employees towards its attainment.

Figure 1. Getting to organisational excellence: critical categories

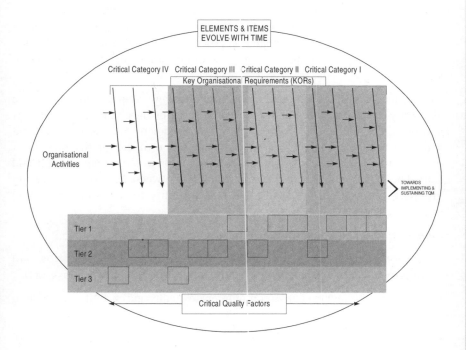

Figure 2. Elements of the TQM implementation framework

Critical prerequisites to developing the necessary commitment are a clear belief in the tangible business and operating benefits of TQM and the recognition that the traditional management system is no longer an option in a competitive business environment. An early responsibility of management is the development of a corporate quality policy incorporating a statement of mission/vision, quality goals and guiding principles. Effective communication of mission ensures all employees understand and are committed to the organisation's direction. The deployment and implementation of goals at all levels ensure congruence of individual efforts and corporate expectations.

Given the considerable time and ability required during the early stages, a steering group for quality, chaired by the chief executive, is usually set up to design and manage the implementation process. A TQM support manager may be appointed, depending on the size of the organisation, and co-opted into the steering group to assist in the early tasks.

As the quality process gets under way, the steering group continues to serve as the key custodian of the quality process by creating the enabling mechanisms and resources. Below the steering group, management establishes additional activities to take ownership of the implementation of the quality process at divisional and site levels; such sub-groups comprise local management and staff. The TQM manager provides the vital links between the corporate steering group and the sub-groups, and takes responsibility for the implementation support functions.

Implementation guidelines. Critical quality factor checklist:

- Senior executives assume active responsibility for evaluation and improvement of management system, and leading the quality drive (Tl).

- Visibility of senior executive commitment to quality and customer satisfaction (Tl).

- Comprehensive policy development and effective deployment of goals (Tl).

- Clear, consistent communication of mission statement and objectives defining quality values, expectations and focus (Tl).

- Elements of quality management structure in place to manage the organisation's quality journey (T3).

SO build energy. Develop a clear belief in the tangible business and operating benefits of TQM to generate the energy to start and sustain the transformation. This involves investing time and effort to understand the content of TQM and would usually require study of TQM literature and conducting benchmarking visits to superior performing organisations.

(S0) Develop consensus among the top team. Ensure that there is consensusamong the senior management on what should be done to implement and sustain TQM. It requires understanding the challenge and opportunities, and the change process.

(S1) Set up a quality council. Set up a quality steering committee/council to provide strategic direction to TQM and plan for its implementation. Develop a TQM implementation plan by active consensus. Ensure senior managers serve on the council, with the chief executive as the chairperson and co-opt the TQM support manager.

(SI) Appoint a corporate TQM support manager. Appoint a TQM support manager to advise and assist the quality council in the planning and implementation of TQM; the post may be on a full- or part-time basis.

(SI) Develop and implement policy and strategy based on total quality. Develop a policy based on the concept of TQM that includes mission statement, corporate values, expectations and focus. Take into consideration the needs of all organisational stakeholders (i.e. customers, suppliers, employees, shareholders, legislators and society), competitive position {vis-a-vis competitors), and process capability in developing the policy. Where appropriate, involve employees in the development process. Benchmark policy development and deployment processes.

Incorporate conditions critical to the success of the organisation achieving its policy and identify critical success factors (CSFs) and define key performance indicators (KPIs) for each CSF. Set targets for KPIs and measures to track gaps in target performance and review performance at agreed intervals.

Effective policy deployment and implementation will help to ensure organisational goal alignment and congruence with set goals and targets at process and individual levels. The necessary resources and training need to be provided for a successful implementation.

(SI) Communicate the statement of mission. Communicate the statement of mission and objectives defining quality values, expectations and focus organisation-wide. Ensure senior managers accept responsibility for and commitment to the mission before communicating it to employees. Gather all employees together to communicate and explain the mission; where this is not possible, use a cascade approach. Use a wide variety of modes to communicate the statement of mission, with emphasis on face-to-face meetings rather than artefacts and encourage discussion and feedback by allowing time for questions and answers.

(S1) Ensure visibility. Ensure visibility of senior management's commitment to quality and customer satisfaction. This may require devoting a substantial portion of time to quality-related matters. For example, actively communicating the organisation's vision, values, and focus, attendin quality courses, teaching the courses to others, attending training courses with staff, regular meetings with staff, giving informal and formal recognition and celebrating successes, visiting customers, regularly reviewing of quality issues in management meetings, and using quality tools and techniques in daily work.

(S2) Set up local steering committees. Set up steering committees at divisional and site levels to take responsibility for overseeing and managing the quality processes at the local level. Each committee is represented by local key personnel, and chaired by the manager. Effective liaison and links with the corporate quality council is vital.

B. Critical category II: maximise internal stakeholders' involvement

Internal stakeholders are middle management and non-management employees. Maximising internal stakeholders' support and involvement involves mobilising the entire workforce to attain the quality goals of the organisation through buy-in, skills training and recognition.

Those writing on TQM (e.g. Manz and Sims, 1993; Clemmer, 1990; Creech, 1994; Oakland, 1993; Kanji, 1995; Zairi, 1991; Blackburn and Rosen, 1993) are unanimous that maximising employees' support and involvement in quality initiatives is the most basic requirement for making TQM work in an organisation. It is through the combined efforts of middle managers and employees, led by senior managers, that the offerings to customers can be continuously met and improved.

Once there is employee buy-in to adopting TQM and an understanding of the corporate mission and quality goals, employees need to develop the necessary skills and abilities to carry out the quality mandate. In addition to learning the fundamentals of TQM, early training should support values and expectations as defined by the quality policy, and developing continuous improvement and problem-solving skills. Employees also need the appropriate teamworking skills. Aligning rewards and recognition is an important ingredient for maximising employees' involvement in TQM and associated quality initiatives.

Implementation guidelines. Critical quality factors checklist:

- The entire workforce understands and is committed to the vision, values, and quality goals of the organisation (Tl).

- Supervisors, unit heads and divisional managers assume active roles as facilitators of continuous improvement, coaches of new methods, and mentors and leaders of empowered employees (Tl).

- Training for employees in problem identification and solving skills, quality improvement skills and other technical skills (Tl).

- System for recognition and appreciation of quality efforts and success of individuals and teams (Tl).

- Training for employees to improve interactive skills (T2).

  (SO) Soft-sell TQM. Disseminate information about TQM and its operating and business benefits, before it is formally launched. This may involve incorporating relevant TQM news and articles in the in-house bulletin and sending key personnel to TQM conferences, seminars and visits to other companies who have made the adoption.

  (SI) Foster employee buy-in to TQM. Communicate the need to set up an integrated management system based on TQM.

  (SI) Orientate the perspective of everyone towards corporate objectives. Communicate on an organisation-wide basis the statement of mission and corporate objectives defining quality values, expectations and focus. Ensure the entire workforce understands and is committed to the mission.

(SI) Allay middle managers' anxiety. Recognise and allay the anxiety and concern of middle managers as the organisation develops a TQM ethic. Mentoring and guidance can assist with this, as can direct interaction with senior managers during the initial phase of the implementation. Organise visits to organisations with good TQM experience to provide the opportunity for middle managers to meet peer groups.

(SI) Nurture middle managers to assume new roles. Recognise that in a TQM approach middle managers require new knowledge, skills and abilities. Provide training so that they can assume roles as facilitators of continuous improvement, coaches of new methods and leaders of em-powered employees. Align rewards and recognition to reinforce the behaviours for their new roles.

(SI) Provide the necessary training in scientific continuous improvement skills. Provide training in continuous improvement, problem identifica-tion and problem-solving techniques; e.g. training in the seven basic QC tools. Introduce teamwork and decision-making based on facts and systematic analysis as one of the guiding values of continuous improvement (see critical category IV).

(SI) Set up a reward system and recognition programmes. Align the re-ward system and recognition (monetary and non-monetary) programmes to maximising employee support and involvement. Em-ployees need to be consulted regarding what form of recognition is a motivator for them; an ad hoc committee may be set up to make rec-ommendations. Visit best-in-class organisations to study best prac-tice. Also strive for balance between recognising individual and team performance based on the organisation's quality goals.

(SI) Set up effective top-down and bottom-up communication. Review the internal communication strategies in maximising employee support and involvement. This may involve using feedback from employee sur-veys and/or other measures. An ad hoc committee may be set up to review and make recommendations for improvement. Identify oppor-tunities for improvement by visiting best in class organisations.

(S1) Keep employees informed. Keep employees regularly informed of business performance and development, and factors such as individual and team successes, using a variety of modes of communication. Where possible, emphasis should be on face-to-face meetings rather than artefacts; however, organisations with fragmented businesses may need to rely on effective use of the latter.

(S2) Institute training in interactive skills. Provide training in interactive skills such as leadership, training and effective communication.

C. Critical category III: manage by customer-driven processes

Managing by customer-driven processes for value means the organisation conducting its business and implementing its quality goals primarily by deploying its employees and other resources along processes, rather than the organisation structure. Central to this approach is the concept of internal customer supplier relationship. A focus on processes and internal customer supplier relationship and their management has been widely documented by authors (e.g. Kanji, 1995; Snee, 1993; Oakland, 1993; Zairi, 1994; Creech, 1994).

For organisations that are managed on a functional (departmental) basis, a critical early task is to promote internal customer supplier attitude. This involves employees/functions relating the things they are doing to delivering values for the customer and identifying the requirements of their immediate customers.

Implementation guidelines. Critical quality factor checklist:

- The entire organisation understands that each individual and process has internal customers and suppliers (Tl).

- Comprehensive identification of customers and their needs (internal and external), and the alignment of processes to satisfy these needs (T2).

- Systematic review and analysis of key process measures that have a direct or indirect impact on value addition to customer satisfaction (T3).

    (SI) Promote the concept of internal customer supplier relationship. Promote the concept of customer supplier relationship as a discipline to identify, control and improve activities that add value to customer satisfaction.

457

Ensure everyone, including senior management, understands the concept of process management and internal customer supplier chain.

> (S2) Identify external and internal customer requirements. Identify external customer requirements; initially this may involve marketing and sales personnel providing inputs. The use of other formal techniques such as customer surveys and focus groups may be introduced at a later stage to collect data.

Order everyone within the organisation to seek out his or her customer requirements.

> (S2) Carry out process mapping. Conduct training in process mapping. This may involve just the senior managers and middle managers who will take on the responsibility of process champions. Carry out process mapping of major processes that together impact on the organisation's ability to achieve customer requirements. Involve employees responsible for performing the processes in the exercise. Document the processes. Include information of process owners, internal customers and suppliers, their requirements, critical and non-critical activities and measures and targets.

> (S2) Deploy resources around the major processes. Deploy resources, including manpower, for the effective and efficient execution of the major processes.

Assign a process champion (this may be a senior manager) to be responsible for the execution of each business process. Involve employees responsible for performing the process. Break down individual business process into sub processes and identify new sets of process ownership. Set up process improvement teams wherever inter process dependencies are identified.

Recognise and reward individual contributions to the process team.

Improve communication across functional units involved in performing the critical processes, for example, by setting up of new modes of communication, improved management of meetings and the use of information technology.

(S3) Develop a performance measurement system. Develop a performance measurement system to track process performance and for continuous improvement of processes (see critical category IV).

Establish measures and targets to be used as evidence of the success of attaining customer values attached to business and sub processes and benchmark standards. Ensure the measures and targets are mutually agreed by supplier and customer. These need to reflect the needs and wants of the customers, process capability and benchmark standards. Devise procedures for data collection and measure performance against target performance. Develop plans for handling non-conformance, including establishing target time scales for resolving non-conformance. Incorporate mechanisms for continuously improving business processes. Establish a standardised corrective action method to maximise the sharing of experience.

D. Critical category IV: adopt continuous improvement

Adoption of continuous improvement means that every activity and process aligned to the customer is continuously undergoing improvement. Continuous improvement of customer-driven activities and processes is a basic philosophy that underlies continuous customer satisfaction (McNair and Liebfried, 1992).

There are a number of early initiatives, some fundamental, that should be pursued to support continuous improvement. These include: every improvement step taken is based on facts (Kanji, 1995; Johnston and Daniel, 1991), teamwork to promote a bottom-up thrust for improvement (Hoeveymeyer, 1993; Heath, 1989), and deliver a synergistic enhancement of quality efforts (Bank, 1992).

At a later stage, tools and techniques such as benchmarking, self-assessment against a quality/excellence model and cost of quality should be introduced to initiate and guide continuous improvement efforts.

Implementation guidelines. Critical quality factor checklist:

- Problem-solving and continuous improvement processes based on facts and systematic approach (T2).

- A team approach to problem solving and continuous improvement (T2).

- The use of customer surveys and feedback process, and tracking of other key measures to assess customer satisfaction (T2).

- The use of self-assessment tools and other mechanisms to track and improve performance gaps in the implementation and effectiveness of systems, processes and practices. (T3).

- Competitive benchmarking against primary competitors (T3).

- Cost of quality to track rework, waste, rejects and to facilitate continuous improvement (T3).

- Informal benchmarking and other forms of information sharing with organisations in different sectors and industries to identify best practices for improvements and opportunities (T3).

  (SI) Instil discipline that continuous improvement and problem-solving decisions are based on facts and systematic analysis. Ensure that decision making based on facts and systematic analysis is one of the organisation's guiding values.

Provide employees with training and assistance to help them to use appropriate facts in their decision making. This may include training in the use of specific analysis tools such as the seven basic QC tools, and the seven management and planning tools. Make available a pool of experts to assist individuals and teams to use the tools and make systematic analysis to arrive at decisions. This may be set up as a part of the quality management structure.

Encourage ideas for improvement (e.g. in suggestion schemes) that are substantiated with data.

  (SI) Encourage team effort. Encourage the formation of a broad scope of improvement team types. Make teamwork one of the organisation's guiding values and align rewards and recognition to reinforce teamwork.

  (S1) Measure customer satisfaction. Establish metrics to track customer satisfaction and to identify improvement opportunities. This may in-

460

clude methods such as customer surveys to solicit information and internal data such as delivery times.

(S2) Introduce tools and techniques. Introduce tools and techniques to identify improvement opportunities. This should include benchmarking, self-assessment and quality costing. Develop a pool of personnel trained in the various tools and techniques.

Conclusions

The construction of the TQM implementation framework is primarily based on findings representing the experiences of TQM organisations, the vast majority which are two to three years into the implementation. It has been shown that the core elements (i.e. the critical quality factors) used to construct the framework are generalisable; however, the framework is presented more as a guide for organisations contemplating a TQM initiative. It is envisaged that the framework should provide useful advice in the critical first two to three years of TQM implementation as a practical and systematic tool for assessing, measuring and evaluating the progress made.

The framework is applicable to organisations in a wide range of industries, since it provides practical guidance for the development of a TQM implementation plan to suit, for example, individual business situations and available resources.

Although the "key concepts" of the framework represent most, if not all, of the current philosophical understandings which underpin TQM, it is recommended that organisations complement the guidelines by continually seeking out and studying best implementation practices to understand how others are achieving success in implementing and sustaining TQM. Even the developers of well-established TQM frameworks such as the Baldrige award recognise the evolution of implementation approaches (see for example, Neves and Nakhai, 1995).

The framework has been constructed based on questionnaire findings from 81 organisations and 16 case studies analysis. Therefore it only represents a snapshot of the industry at a point in time, but it presents more of a picture, albeit far from complete, than what is available in the literature.

The proposed framework does, however, make a significant contribution for the following reasons:

- First, from a theoretical standpoint, the development of empirical research in TQM has lagged far behind the fast growing acceptance of TQM as a management philosophy for improving organisational effectiveness. The problem is even more acute outside the developed world where knowledge or TQM is almost non-existent. The research described in this paper has attempted to bridge the gap between existing theories and knowledge and approaches required for increased effectiveness of TQM implementation a developing economy like Malaysia.

- Second, from an application standpoint, the framework is aimed at increasing the degree of effectiveness in implementation by assisting Malaysian managers to develop a step-wise implementation roadmap.

References

Atkinson, P.E. (1990), Creating Culture Change: The Key to Successful Total Quality Management, IFS Publications, Kempston.

Baker, G. and Starbird, S.A. (1992), "Managing quality in California food processing firms", Agribusiness, Vol. 8 No. 2, pp. 155-64.

Bank, J. (1992), The Essence of Total Quality Management, Prentice-Hall, London.

Belohav, J.A. (1993), "Quality, strategy and competitiveness", California Management Review, Vol. 35 No. 3, pp. 55-67.

Black, S.A. (1993), "Measuring the critical factors of total quality management", unpublished PhD thesis, University of Bradford, Bradford.

Blackburn, R. and Rosen, B. (1993), "Total quality and human resources management: lessons learned from Baldrige award-winning companies", Academy of Management Executive, Vol. 7 No. 3, pp. 49-66.

Burr, J.T. (1993), "A new name for a not so new concept", Quality Progress, Vol. 26 No. 3, pp. 87-8.

Clemmer, J. (1990), Firing on All Cylinders, Judy Piatkus (Publishers), London

Cole, R.E. (1993), "Introduction", California Management Review, Vol. 35 No. 3, pp. 7-11.

Coulson-Thomas, C.J. (1992), "Quality: where do we go from here?", International Journal of Quality & Reliability Management, Vol. 9 No. 1, pp. 38-55.

Creech, B. (1994), The Five Pillars of TQM, Penguin Group, New York, NY.

Crosby, P. (1979), Quality Is Free: The Art of Making Quality Certain, Penguin Books, New York, NY.

Crosby, P. (1989), Let's Talk Quality: 96 Questions that You Always Wanted to Ask Phil Crosby, McGraw-Hill, New York, NY.

Cullen, J.M. (1991), "Organising for TQM", in Oakland, J.S. (Ed.), Proceedings of the 4th International Conference on Total Quality Management, IFS Ltd, Stratford-upon-Avon.

Dale, B.G. (Ed.), (1999), Managing Quality, 3rd ed., Blackwell Publishers, Oxford.

Dale, B.G., Zairi, M., Williams, A.R.T. and van der Wiele A. (2000), "Total quality management: an exploratory study of contribution", Total Quality Management (under review).

Dawson, P. (1994), "Quality management: beyond the Japanese model", International Journal of

Quality and Reliability Management, Vol. 11 No. 7, pp. 51-9. Dean, J.W. and Bowen, D.E. (1994), "Management theory and total quality: improving research

and practice through theory development", Academy of Management Review, Vol. 19 No. 3, pp. 392-418.

Deming, W.E. (1986), Out of the Crisis, Cambridge University Press, Cambridge.

Easton, G.S. (1993), "The 1993 state of US total quality management: a Baldrige examiner's perspective", California Management Review, Vol. 35 No. 3, pp. 32-54.

Garvin, D. (1983), "Quality on line", Harvard'Business Review, Vol. 61 No. 5, pp. 65-72.

Gilbert, J.D. (1992), "TQM flops: a chance to learn from the mistakes of others", National Productivity Review, Autumn, pp. 491-9.

Glover, J. (1993), "Achieving the organisational change necessary for successful TQM", Internationaljournal of Quality and Reliability Management, Vol. 10 No. 6, pp. 47-64.

Heath, P.M. (1989), "The path to quality achievement through teamwork plus commitment", Internationaljournal of Quality and Reliability Management, Vol. 1 No. 2, pp. 51-9.

Hoeveymeyer, V.A. (1993), "How effective is your team?", Training and Development, Vol. 47 No. 9, pp. 67-71.

Hurd, W.L. Jr (1992), "Quality in the Asia Pacific", International Journal of Quality and Reliability Management, Vol. 9 No. 3, pp. 14-20.

Johnston, C.G. and Daniel, M.J. (1991), Customer Satisfaction through Quality. An International Perspective, The Conference Board of Canada, Ottawa, Ontario.

Juran, J.M. (1993), "Made in USA: a renaissance in quality", Harvard Business Review, Vol. 71 No. 4, pp. 42-50.

Kanji, G.K. (1990), "Total quality management: the second industrial revolution", Total Quality Management, Vol. 1 No. 1, pp. 3-11.

Kanji, G.K. (1995), "Quality and statistical concepts", in Kanji, G.K. (Ed.), Total Quality Management: Proceedings of the First World Congress, Chapman and Hall, London.

Kano, N. (1993), "A perspective on quality activities in American firms", California Management Review, Vol. 35 No. 3, pp. 12-31.

Kilmann, R.H. (1985), Beyond the Quick Fix, Jossey-Bass, San Francisco, CA.

Lasserre, P. and Probert, J. (1994), "Competing on the Pacific Rim: high risks and high returns", Long Range Planning, Vol. 27 No. 2, pp. 3-11.

Leonard, F.S. and Sasser, W.E. (1982), "The case of the quality crusader", Harvard Business Review,Vol.66No.3,pp.l2-20.

Mann, R.S. (1992), "The development of a framework to assist in the implementation of TQM", unpublished PhD thesis, University of Liverpool, Liverpool.

Manz, C.C. and Sims, H.P. (1993), Business without Bosses, John Wiley, New York, NY.

Martinez, A., Rodriguez, A.G. and Dale, B.G. (1998), "Total quality management and company characteristics: an examination", Quality Management Journal, Vol. 5 No. 4, pp. 59-71.

McNair, C.J. and Leibfried, K. (1992), Benchmarking: A Tool for Continuous Improvement, Harper Business, New York, NY.

Motwani, J.G., Mohamoud, E. and Rice, G. (1994), "Quality practices of Indian organisations: an empirical analysis", International Journal of Quality and Reliability Management, Vol. 11 No. 1, pp. 38-52.

Neves, J.S. and Nakhai, B. (1995), "The evolution of the Baldrige award", Quality Progress, June, pp. 65-70.

Oakland, J.S. (1993), Total Quality Management, Buttevworth-Ueinemann, Oxford.

Pulat, B.M. (1994), "Total quality management: a framework for application in manufacturing", The TQM Magazine, Vol. 6 No. 4, pp. 44-9.

Ramirez, C. and Loney, T. (1993), "Baldrige award winners identify the essential activities of a successful quality process", Quality Digest, January, pp. 38-40.

Rummel, R.J. (1970), Applied Factor Analysis, NW University Press, Evanston, IL.

Saraph, J.V., Benson, P.G. and Schroeder, R.G. (1989), "An instrument for measuring the critical factors of quality management", Decision Sciences, Vol. 20 No. 4, pp. 810-29.

Shetty, Y.K. (1987), "Product quality and competitive strategy", Business Horizon, May-June, pp. 46-52.

Sinclair, D.A.C. (1994), "Total quality based performance measurement: an empirical study of best practice", unpublished PhD thesis, University of Bradford, Bradford.

Sitkin, S.B., Sutcliffe, K.M. and Schroeder, R.G. (1994), "Distinguishing control from learning in total quality management: a contingency perspective", Academy of Management Review, Vol. 19 No. 3, pp. 536-64.

Smith, S. (1986), How to Take Part in the Quality Revolution: A Management Guide, PA Management Consultants, London.

Smith, S. (1994), The Quality Revolution, Management Books 2000, Didcot.

"Creating robust work processes", Quality Progress, Vol. 26 No. 2, pp. 37-41.

Spencer, B.A. (1994), "Models of organisation and TQM", in Oakland, J.S. (Ed.), Proceedings of the

4th International Conference on Total Quality Management, IFS Ltd, Stratford-upon-Avon.

Townsend, P.L. and Gebhardt, J.E. (1992), Quality in Action, John Wiley and Sons, New York, NY.

Wilkinson, A. (1992), "The other side of quality: 'soft' issues and the human resource dimension", Total Quality Management, Vol. 4 No. 1, pp. 323-9.

Yui, H. (1995), "Key issues in introducing and promoting TQM", in Kanji, G.K. (Ed.), Total Quality Management: Proceedings of the First World Congress, Chapman and Hall, London.

Zairi, M. (1991), Total Quality Management for Engineers, Aditya Books Pvt, New Delhi.

Zairi, M. (1994), Measuring Performance for Business Results, Chapman and Hall, London.

Impact

An evaluation of TQM in primary care: in search of best practice

Mohamed Zairi and Ajit Matthew

Assesses the effectiveness of a TQM initiative in general practice

First Published in

International Journal of Health Care Quality Assurance,
Vol. 8 No. 6, 1995, pp. 4-13
© MCB University Press Limited, 0952-6862

Introduction

Recently, within the Yorkshire and Humberside region, there have been initiatives to focus on total quality management (TQM) in primary care. The research proposal consisted of research into how TQM could be incorporated into general practice and implementation of this research into a pilot project. The experience from these projects formed the basis of the initiatives to introduce TQM into primary care. The overall aim was to provide a comprehensive package of materials for GPs and managers in order to facilitate the development, establishment and monitoring of quality through all practice activities for the benefit of patient care. The process will enable effective change in all areas of the practice.

It is hoped that this project will be expanded nationwide but prior to this, the NHS Management Executive commissioned an independent evaluation of the project. The evaluation findings had a strong bearing on the strategic direction on this project. The evaluation looks at the TQM initiative from an expert's view and also from the view of the beneficiaries of the seminars through structured interviews with general practitioners.

The methodological approach used was designed to:

- assess the effectiveness of the model used in the launch of TQ in primary care which is to be tested against other models of TQM implementation;

- measure the impact of the model used in general practices that benefited from the knowledge and expertise available; and

- produce guidelines and recommendations in order to strengthen the workings of the model used.

Established TQM implementation models

Total quality management has widely been regarded as essential by progressive organizations. TQM is regarded as a fitness for purpose in terms of product or service to customer requirements. To take this further, one must regard one's role as customer or supplier where appropriate and ensure that the customer, whether internal or external is satisfied.

470

Total quality management is seen as a management-led approach in which top management commitment is essential. The emphasis is on quality in all aspects and functions of the organization's operation, not just the provision of a service to the patient. To achieve this, employee awareness and motivation are essential.

All are responsible for ensuring quality in terms of satisfying the patient in what they do. The approach is one of prevention of errors and faults rather than detection and correction. Major cultural changes are required.

Data acquisition is seen as essential to: facilitation and measurement of the process of change including attitudes; clarification of internal customer relationships; and ascertaining costs of quality.

TQM implementation techniques

There are various techniques for the implementation of TQM, which leads to discord as a divergence in thinking occurs. The techniques most quoted are:

- the systems approach – BS 5750/ISO 9000;

- the tools approach – statistical process control, benchmarking; and

- the teamwork approach.

Each of these techniques has appropriate uses. The systems approach is ideal in organizations which produce a standard product and use standard processes, skills and systems. The teamwork approach works well in a paternalistic environment where information, jobs and responsibilities are shared. The tools approach is used in an environment which uses high technology and has a high skills profile environment where large batch manufacturing is predominant.

The discord concerns which techniques should be used to dominate the others. Crosby advocates that quality is free and that systems organization is the only way forward. Juran believes that there is an optimum point of quality and advocates process capability, teamwork and training rather than the systems approach. Although discord still exists, it is possible to merge certain aspects of the various techniques to form an appropriate implementation model.

TQM in primary care

The applicability of TQM in a service or health care setting

In order to establish a high standard of service quality, it is important first to define customer requirements and to define what behaviour is required by the customer and appropriate for the particular situation. Unfulfilled expectations form a large proportion of customer dissatisfaction. Service levels set by an organization must define and relate to individual customer requirements.

Applying this principle to health care organizations, TQM has to take the patient as the starting point. The process of delivery to the patient is very much dependent on staff attributes and an organization commitment for enabling and empowering individuals to fulfil patient expectations.

> In the competitive environment of the 1990s, especially as that environment focuses on health care, hospitals must operate under multiple constraints. Limited resources of capital, market and manpower force us to do better with what we already have or less. The cutting edge of competition increasingly centres eon quality; quality as defined by a myriad of regulators and professional accrediting bodies, quality as defined by the customer who is the physician and the employer, quality as defined by the patient, the family and the employee[1].

TQM has gained prominence in the health care industry for various reasons. First, health care expenditure has experienced a rapid growth. In the USA, health care accounted for 12 per cent of its GNP in 1991 and is expected to reach 20 per cent by the year 2000. There is evidence that high-quality health care can cost less than poor-quality health care. Second, the advent of The Patients' Charter and fundholding means that patients and GPs can be more involved in the selection of their doctors and contracted secondary services respectively. Finally, there is the possible increase in the cost of real practice litigation due to the rise in patients' expectations and awareness.

Comparison with established TQM implementation models

Most current quality implementation approaches are based on the established models of Crosby, Juran, Deming, etc. This section compares the primary care TQM initiatives with them in the following areas:

- definition of quality;
- degree of senior management responsibility;
- performance standard/motivation;
- general approach;
- structure;
- statistical process control;
- improvement basis;
- teamwork;
- costs of quality;
- purchasing and goods received; and
- vendor rating.

The comparison model used is adapted from Oakland[2].

Definition of quality

- Crosby. Conformance to requirements.
- Deming. A predictable degree of uniformity and dependability at low cost and suited to the market.
- Juran. Fitness for use.
- Oakland. Identify and meet the requirements of customers whether external or internal.
- Primary care. A service that is designed to: meet present and future customer requirements in respect of use, quality and satisfaction; and address problems that are likely to be encountered in the use of a service and resolve them prior to delivery.

Degree of senior management responsibility

- Crosby. Responsible for quality.
- Deming. Responsible for 94 per cent of quality problems.
- Juran. Less than 20 per cent of quality problems are due to workers.
- Oakland. Responsible for quality.
- Primary care. Responsible for quality.

Performance standard/motivation

- Crosby. Zero defects.
- Deming. Quality has many scales, hence use of statistics to measure performance in all areas, emphasis on monitoring variation.
- Juran. Avoids campaigns to do 100 per cent perfect work, set achievable goals.
- Oakland. Measure, control and ensure conformance to customer requirements and agreed standards.
- Primary care. No defined standards of quality stated – i.e. variation, agreed standards, etc.

General approach

- Crosby. Prevention, not inspection.
- Deming. Reduce variability by continuous improvement.
- Juran. General management approach to quality – especially human elements.
- Oakland. Total satisfaction of all customers.
- Primary care. Management approach to human aspects – practice culture, staff approach, etc.

Structure

- Crosby. Fourteen steps to quality improvement.

- Deming. Fourteen points for management.

- Juran. Ten steps to quality improvement.

- Oakland. Thirteen steps to total quality management.

- Primary care. Absence of any structured implementation approach.

Statistical process control

- Crosby. Rejects statistically acceptable levels of quality.

- Deming. Advocates statistical methods of quality.

- Juran. Recommends statistical process control (SPC) but discourages total dependence as it would lead to a tools-driven approach.

- Oakland. An important tool to measure and control conformance to customer requirements continuously and to correct defective measures quickly.

- Primary care. Not addressed at all.

Improvement basis

- Crosby. An essential process not a mere programme.

- Deming. Reduction of variation.

- Juran. Project-by-project team approach to set goals.

- Oakland. Culture based – teamwork to instigate, encourage and implement continuous improvement throughout.

- Primary care. This topic is addressed but not the means or basis of improvement.

Teamwork

- Crosby. Formation of quality improvement teams and quality councils.

- Deming. Employee participation in decision making, removal of interdepartmental barriers.

- Juran. Team and quality circle approach.

- Oakland. Team and quality circle approach.

- Primary care. Team approach, emphasis on quality circles involving staff from specific areas or cross-functional teams where appropriate.

Costs of quality

- Crosby. Cost of non-conformance – quality is free.

- Deming. Continuous improvement to reduce quality costs.

- Juran. Quality is not free, there is an optimum.

- Oakland. Continuous improvement to reduce quality costs.

- Primary care. Not addressed.

Purchasing and goods received

- Crosby. State requirements, treat supplier as extension of the business. Faults can be attributed to purchasers also.

- Deming. Use statistical evidence and control charts to assess purchased goods.

- Juran. Problems are too complex, conduct formal surveys.

- Oakland. Customer focus and total supplier involvement to ensure good teamwork and proper definition of requirements.

- Primary care. In the model, the suppliers are defined for example, secondary care providers, computer system suppliers; however the need for clearly stating requirement does not seem to be stressed.

476

Vendor rating

- Crosby. Important but quality audits have no impact on them.

- Deming. Critical of most systems.

- Juran. Advocates this but aids supplier in achieving improvements.

- Oakland. Advocates this and specifically promotes good teamwork with supplier to achieve improvements.

- Primary care. Not addressed. However, as a result of geographical constraints in some areas, this may not always be appropriate.

Conclusion

The primary care initiative concentrates on interpersonnel relations. It deals with specific issues such as communication, teamwork and patient satisfaction. The research found that most practices interviewed gained the most in this area from attending the initiatives. The need for commitment from higher levels is quite rightly stressed.

What is strongly evident is the lack of any structured implementation approach. The "ends" have been defined but not the "means". As quality itself is a process of continuous improvement, a credible means of composing and measuring one's progress is important. This is where tools such as SPC should be used to help provide a basis for improvement. The cost of quality (internal, external, prevention, appraisal) has been totally ignored.

The need to incorporate providers has not been fully addressed. Their presence is acknowledged but not the need for total involvement to ensure total patient care. Aspects such as mutually agreeable standards of secondary care and partnership strategies with secondary care providers have not been addressed. It is true that this may not be totally achievable at present because of geographical and funding constraints but this should be addressed – by both parties. Total quality is dependent on partnerships both within and outside an organization.

The evaluation had three objectives:

The evaluation methodology

(1) To assess the effectiveness of the primary care model from the point of view of its suitability to general practice and also its impact on negative quality and positive quality.

(2) To compare the primary care approach with other alternatives in order to determine its applicability in different practices and whether it is replicable from practice to practice.

(3) The production of guidelines and recommendations based on the state-of-the-art knowledge and TQM best practice in health care to ensure that the primary care model will remain effective and lead to results in both the long and short term through the ultimate measurement of the effect on patient care.

The methodology consisted of the following three factors:

(1) *Effectiveness of the primary care model.* This stage benchmarked the primary care approach against other quality implementation models. The objective was to assess whether the necessary prerequisites to ensure quality and its implementation had been reviewed.

(2) *Relevance of TQM to primary care.* This stage was carried out by conducting a series of interviews with selected practices who attended the relevant TQM in primary care seminars. A data capturing tool was designed in the form of a questionnaire. This is further described later in this article.

(3) *Guidelines and recommendations to strengthen the workings of the model.* The findings from (1) and (2) will form the basis of this section. The analysis of the data gained from the interviews together with research into health care trends will enable suitable recommendations to be made.

The questionnaire was designed to address the following:

478

- impact of TQM in general practice;

- benefits from TQM and the attendance of pertinent seminars;

- attitudes to quality;

- organization prerequisites for quality (quality circles, commitment, systems, partnerships);

- aspects of measurement, benchmarking and quality costing;

- interlinks with suppliers (secondary care providers);

- communications within and outside the practice;

- issues that affect the quality of patient care (NHS reforms, audits, Patients' Charter); and

- future quality needs.

The questionnaire was divided into two parts – Part A and Part B. The information from Part A was gained from interviewing the doctors and their practice managers. The interviews lasted for about 30-45 minutes. As it would be difficult to interview doctors for a longer time period, they were asked to fill in Part B of the questionnaire in their own time. This also enabled them to reflect on various issues. Most of the questions in Part B were rating scales. This enabled us to quantify measurements and observe trends.

Sample population

All the practices interviewed were situated in the Yorkshire and Humberside region. The total sample number was 156. Of these, the attendance of 16 practices to the seminars was considered too recent to be representative, hence the realistic sample population was 140. Thirty practices participated in the survey. The criteria to be noted were as follows:

- a total of 37 per cent of the interviewees were fundholding practices;

- of the interviewees, 33 per cent were situated in inner cities or deprived areas; and

- of these practices, 50 per cent had attended both seminars (Seminar 1: an introduction to TQM in general practice; Seminar 2: total quality management within the practice).

Analysis of the survey

The interviews addressed specific aspects of practice administration and patient care. The conclusions and findings from the interviews are discussed under the various classified aspects.

Background issues

- The high degree of teamwork that is apparent will help to facilitate the introduction and the continued implementation of TQM within the practice. The fact that secondary care personnel who work within the practice are incorporated in all relevant matters reflects this.

- Quality is dependent on staff satisfaction; the low staff turnover rates in most practices means that this is feasible.

- The degree of proactivity of a practice is dependent on the consistency of the patient population profile.

- Fundholding was perceived to be a strength as it could offer a higher quality of secondary care.

- The quality of communication in multi-site practices is sometimes poor.

- Continual training and team-building exercises were seen as a strategy to improve staff effectiveness continuously. This attitude will enable TQM to be promoted actively within the practice.

- Accessibility for appointments is related directly to the magnitude of the patient population and the quality of patient responsibility. Those which were able to limit their patient population were able to offer a high standard of accessibility. Those practices in densely populated areas with a poor level of patient responsibility reported poor accessibility. This was because of the high number of patients who walked in without any appointments, and was further compounded by those who did not attend their appointments.

Awareness and expectations about TQM

- Quite a large proportion (37 per cent) of the interviewees had a strong awareness about TQM prior to the seminars. They saw the need to introduce TQM as an essential means to improve patient care and staff satisfaction.

- Only 6 per cent of the respondents attended the seminars in order to gain PGA accreditation. It is quite heartening to note that the majority of the practices did not attend the seminars for this reason. This shows that the impetus to improve the quality of patient care exists.

- Interaction with other practices was regarded as a vehicle to exchange ideas and techniques to improve continuously and thus further promote TQM.

Information technology

- This aspect was not addressed in the primary care model and the relevant seminars. This is essential for TQM as it has a role for recording and presenting data required for setting and measuring levels of quality.

- The survey addressed three particular dimensions of the quality of data – accuracy of data, ease of recording, ease of analysis. The majority of the respondents rated accuracy of data from average to good. Ease of recording was rated from mediocre to average. Ease of analysis was rated between average and good. This implies that there is a strong need to improve the ease of recording data. It is possible that accuracy of data depends on the ease of recording it in order to avoid mistakes.

- In most cases, no mechanism, it seems, exists to form a partnership with suppliers. This is essential so that the supplier is able to understand the needs of a customer. The majority of the respondents (86 per cent) did not rate their supplier as good.

- Pressure groups have been formed to force suppliers to improve and incorporate suggestions. This suggests the lack of partnership between supplier and customer.

- Instead of pressure groups, it would be more effective for a representative group comprising various practices to form a partnership with a supplier. This group should agree to optimum parameters and specifications. By concentrating on this group, the supplier can concentrate his efforts on a common strategy and not be distracted by variations. Ways of standardizing information in order to benchmark and compare information outside practices would be highly desirable.

Organizational and administration systems

- The primary care model has not addressed the importance of having a formal written administrative system. This is essential to ensure the consistency of process or procedure.

- The majority of practices (67 per cent) had formal administrative systems in place. A further 16 per cent had a formal system for prescriptions only. In order to form a framework to implement TQM further, formal systems are a necessity. It is imperative that more practices formalize all procedures.

- Although a significant majority of practices review their procedures on a continual basis, very few practices incorporate any relevant quality standards or performance measurements within their administrative system. This raises the question about how a procedure is reviewed and compared objectively .

Staff

- A high degree of cross-functionality exists among staff. This is conducive to TQM implementation.

- Team effectiveness between practice partners and staff was rated poorer compared to the team effectiveness between the manager and staff. This could hamper TQM implementation as all initiatives for change start from the top.

- Many practices are actually improving and sustaining team effectiveness through continual training.

- Of the practices interviewed, 74 per cent have seen major improvements in staff effectiveness as a result of various TQM initiatives. Of these, 27 per cent have attributed this to the seminars.

- Quality circles were a regular feature of 70 per cent of the sample practice population.

- The frequency of cross-functional meetings is low – as mentioned earlier, this could be a result of poor availability. Nevertheless, this could lead to distortion in communication and possible discord because of a lack of opportunity to reach a consensus.

Secondary care providers

- From the practices surveyed, only the fundholding practices were able to set levels of quality in secondary care provision.

- These levels of quality related to lead times for appointments and waiting times at various stages, lead times for discharge letters, issues about communication – accessibility, information, protocols and the level of seniority in referral.

- The various dimensions of quality levels in secondary care that the practices were asked to measure were not rated too highly.

- Since secondary care has not been rated as totally satisfactory whether fundholding or not, this poses a threat to the quality of care provided by the practice (especially to non-fundholders).

- Non-fundholders had to accept what was provided by the secondary care providers. This hampered their efforts to provide the patient with care of the highest quality.

- Fundholders have developed a strategy to form partnerships with secondary care providers. This has been done either by forming regional practice groups or several practices appointing a contracts manager to liaise with the providers on their behalf. Non-fundholders have attempted to meet secondary care providers to form better partnerships and improve standards but to no avail. This leads to further evidence of a two-tier system for the provision of secondary care.

- Improved communication and information from secondary care providers was regarded as an essential need. There was plenty of room for improvement in various aspects.

Benchmarking

- Of the practices interviewed, 60 per cent do not formally benchmark their performance at all. The remaining practices that did used Family Health Services Authority (FHSA) information about clinical targets.

- With the exception of two practices, no attempt had been made to benchmark performance in areas outside the FHSA information. This includes the comparison of the practice's own performance over a particular period with that over a similar period.

- It is difficult to compare practices like for like as they differ in terms of practice size and population characteristics. However, it could be possible to measure various aspects. An attempt should be made to develop measurements which take account of these variables. While the practices may not have the resources to develop this, opportunities are available for the higher authorities to conduct research into this aspect.

- The lack of any formal benchmarking mechanism is a serious omission when implementing a TQM system.

Performance measurement

- Performance measures were limited to a few common areas. These areas were as follows: meeting FHSA clinical targets, formal staff appraisal and waiting times.

- No one had attempted to use numerical measures to set standards of patient satisfaction.

- The omission of any procedure or mechanism to measure performance formally in every area is a serious impediment to implementing a TQM mechanism. The questions that would be raised are: without measurements, how does one improve or set targets to improve? How does one improve oneself without any measurable targets? How does one know that one is improving oneself? Measurements are central to providing a framework to ensure continuous improvement.

- It is possible that practices could be willing to consider aspects of performance measurement and benchmarking. The positive attitude to medical audits proves this.

Quality costing

- Quality costing has not been given much emphasis by the TQM initiative. Only one practice was aware of the meaning of this term.

- The internal costs of quality have been the only quality cost that has been addressed. This cost dimension has been addressed in terms of wastage of material and manpower. The other quality costs have not been addressed at all.

- External quality costs have not been addressed but these costs could possibly be recorded in terms of medical audit results.

- Again, the poor emphasis with regard to the cost of quality leads to the question of whether the presence of any framework or basis exists to drive the mechanism for continuous improvement.

Patient communication

- Of the practices interviewed, 50 per cent use, or are about to use, newsletters to communicate general issues and preventive medicine.

- In order to ensure that patients had realistic expectations about the service available, one practice specifically explained to new patients the practice's capabilities and the responsibilities that would be expected from the patient. This procedure facilitates mutual awareness of the standards to be set by both parties and also ensures that all patients are informed.

Patient feedback

- Patient satisfaction was monitored on a subjective basis only (i.e. gauging patient attitudes, etc.). None of the practices measured patient satisfaction based on any scoring system addressing various dimensions.

- Of the respondents, 50 per cent used questionnaire surveys.

- Only two practices of those surveyed used patient participation meetings. Another practice discussed various issues with patients at random while they were waiting. As a supplement to questionnaire surveys, this method of feedback would provide a good response. This is because it offers the opportunity for spontaneity of response and avoids the distortions that written opinions might convey.

Future quality strategy

- It is very encouraging to find that 93 per cent of the practices consider that quality is essential in planning their future strategy.

- The practices that did not consider quality as a strategic issue were situated in deprived areas.

- It is very difficult to incorporate quality into future strategic planning if the quality of patient responsibility is poor.

Medical audits

- The majority of the practices (63 per cent) had a positive opinion about medical audits. They regarded audits as a vehicle to identify opportunities to improve constantly the quality of patient care and identify strategic direction.

- Improvements which would lead to a higher standard of quality of patient care would be more effective if individual practices were allowed to plan their audit strategy.

- Reservations exist about audits in their present form. Audits are imposed on practices, which result in auditing of areas where there may not be specific weaknesses or relevance. This is a waste of resources; the losses incurred are even higher for the practice as they have to bear the cost of the audits, and also the opportunity costs of the wasted resources. This results in an extremely high cost of quality appraisal.

The Patients' Charter

- *The Patients'* Charter has had no positive effect on the quality of patient care in the majority of the practices interviewed (77 per cent). It did help increase patient expectations and awareness. Non-fundholding practices found that aspects of *The Patients'* Charter pertaining to secondary care made a useful negotiating tool.

- There is a greater onus on the GP. Although the GP profile has been increased, the resources have not been provided to help maintain this profile.

- The charter ignores any need for the patient to observe certain responsibilities. This coupled with increased (and sometimes unrealistic) expectations leads to practices wasting resources in resolving unnecessary and unfounded complaints usually as a result of poor accessibility to the detriment of the quality of patient care.

- The complaints mechanism means that the practice does not have the initial opportunity to resolve complaints. This leads to a slower response in improving care or resolving matters. Ideally, the complaints should be referred directly to the practice and the FHSA should be notified of this. The FHSA should monitor what action has been taken to resolve the matter and intercede or arbitrate when necessary.

NHS reforms

- Positive effects on the quality of patient care were reported by 40 per cent of the respondents. It is noted that all these effects have been to do with secondary care and fundholding.

- An overwhelming majority of the respondents (93 per cent) felt that the NHS reforms threatened the quality of patient care. The threatening factors centred mainly on the resources spent on the everincreasing paperwork and bureaucracy, constantly having to adapt to an inconsistent strategy (the moving goal post syndrome) and the two-tier system because of fundholding.

FHSA partnerships

- Practice-FHSA relationships were regarded as generally good by all respondents though a lot was needed to improve partnerships. This needed to be done in various ways: better stability of FHSA staff positions; improving communications, assuming a supportive role as opposed to that of a policing one and the provision of more resources.

- In any organization, commitment to quality must come from the top authority. This is essential to ensure that there is a commitment to direct resources to ensure the success of a quality strategy. In a primary care practice, it would be expected that the commitment to quality comes from the practice partners. However, they may not always be the ones who are able to direct the resources. The lack of available resources could lead to flagging commitment. It is essential that the FHSA, which controlls the resources, is committed to TQM within primary care and enables resources to be available to ensure this.

Benefits from the TQM initiative

- Individuals gained much from interaction with people outside their practices and future initiatives should consider this aspect when planning future strategies.

- Most of the other benefits from the TQM initiative have been centred around communication and quality circles. It has also caused some practices to reflect on their present environment and the concept of quality.

Quality aspects not addressed by the TQM initiative

- Not much attention had been given to the aspect of TQM implementation. This led to some practices feeling that the quality standards discussed in the seminars were too far-fetched or unrealistic. It must be stressed that one has to work to attain achievable targets and then review future targets in a similar way. If not, it can cause one's enthusiasm to flag.

- The importance of partnerships with external organizations was not addressed. The benefits, whether subjective or objective, need to discussed. Strategies to form partnerships need to be looked into.

- The importance of measuring and the use of quality measurement tools such as SPC was not addressed. The importance and description of a quality system needs to be addressed.

Problems encountered when implementing TQM

- The biggest problem encountered by most practices was time as a resource. They felt that more staff time was needed to be released to address quality issues more thoroughly. The constraints as a result of the contracts hampered this. This in turn did not allow some practice partners to commit resources for the introduction of a quality management system.

- Aspects of implementation were not addressed; there is a need to explain what common implementation problems could occur and how these are overcome.

Applicability of the primary care model

- Quite a few of the practices that were situated in deprived areas found it difficult to provide a high standard of quality of care because of the poor quality of patient education and responsibility.

- Non-fundholding practices, especially those with less than three partners, would not be able to commit sufficient time and resources to address quality issues.

- Non-fundholding practices are not able to offer a high standard of total patient care because unlike fundholding practices, they do not possess the leverage to demand a quality secondary care service.

Conclusions and recommendations

This section lists recommendations and conclusions for the future strategy of the TQM initiatives in primary care and various issues to be addressed.

Role of FHSA

- The FHSA should be involved with all practice TQM initiatives from the start. They should be represented on the quality steering committee. As a customer, they will be able to incorporate their needs into the quality process; as a supplier, they will be aware of the resources which are required by the practice in terms of manhours and finance required for training and addressing quality issues.

- The FHSA are in an ideal position to introduce facilitators required to impart a quality culture. They will be able to identify practice needs and provide them.

- FHSA facilitator training is advocated as a priority in order to assist practices.

- The FHSA should focus on a more supportive role rather than a policing one.

- As a consequence of this, the FHSA would not be the ideal body to handle initial patient complaints. Complaints should be addressed to the practice concerned to reduce response time and avoid factual distortion. The most effective way of tackling the problems is for the practice to resolve them from within. The FHSA should be notified of the complaint and follow up the outcome after a certain period. It need only intervene if the problem cannot be resolved between both parties.

Applicability of TQM

- At present, TQM could be applicable to most fundholding practices because they are in a position to control and release resources for addressing quality issues and are able to control the quality of secondary care.

- The non-fundholding practices that could implement TQM to an extent are those which have a finite patient list size and those that have a patient population who are responsible and have realistic expectations.

- An attempt should be made to research the quality needs of different types of practices (in terms of size, location, fundholding status, etc.) in order to address specific problems which impede TQM implementation, if the project is to be propagated further.

Patient education and responsibility

- Quality of patient care depends directly on the quality of patient education and responsibility.

- Practices should attempt to ensure patient responsibility by explaining to patients about their responsibilities and the practice's capabilities. The ideal way is to explain to new patients about the responsibilities required from them and make observance of these responsibilities as a condition for enrolling. This could also be applied to present patients.

- Knowledge of the practice capabilities and responsibilities required would facilitate realistic patient expectations.

- Patient participation forums will help reinforce these responsibilities and enable the practice to get an idea of actual patient expectations. Performance measurement

- The primary care model has overlooked the aspect of measuring and using data to drive the impetus for continuous improvement.

- There are no standard measures which can be applied from practice to practice. One can borrow and adapt measurements as a starting point. Measurements are best developed by the owner and/or customer of a particular process.

Benchmarking

- It is very difficult to benchmark practices as a whole. However, it is possible to benchmark different aspects of practice activity with adjustments for various parameters (size of practice, patient population characteristics, etc.).

- More efforts should be made to benchmark practice performance. This will permit identification weaknesses and make the practice more competitive.

Quality costing

- Quality costing must be given more emphasis. Reducing the costs of quality is an opportunity to improve productivity further.

Audits

- Audits were regarded as a positive measure to improve the quality of patient care.

- Audit strategies are best left to the practices as they themselves are aware of the clinical areas where audits are required. The necessary authorities need only be aware of the strategies and outcomes of the audits.

- If practices are asked to carry out audits from an external body, these audits should be relevant and should address a specific weakness within the practice.

Quality training

- There is a need for more project-based training on quality. This enables one to view TQM in the context of the practice.

- Training in supplier partnership development is seriously lacking. This aspect had not been addressed in the primary care model and it also was not apparent in the relevant literature on health care in the UK. Provision of secondary care

- As mentioned above, developing partnerships with the suppliers has not been addressed.

- Non-fundholding practices cannot offer a total quality patient care because of the low priority given to them by the secondary care providers.

- There is a lack of interest by secondary care providers in developing a partnership with the non-fundholding practices as they are captive customers.

Quality system

- The need for a quality system needs to be emphasized.

- Administrative systems do exist in the majority of practices. These could easily be adapted to incorporate the issue of quality and performance measures. More emphasis needs to be given on process ownership.

- The process owners must participate in the design and continuous improvement of the quality system.

- A mechanism for performance feedback must be incorporated.

Quality implementation

- Commitment for quality needs to come not only from the practice partners but from the FHSA who provide the resources.

- A well-defined implementation strategy must be formulated and adhered to.

- It is important to gain the commitment for TQM from all the staff. This can only be done through investment in training and the provision of resources, more empowerment, a fair system of reward and recognition and an open environment.

Changing the culture of primary health care provision

- Quality is a journey without a destination. It addresses long-term issues and the sustainability and consistency of offering quality care. Results and benefits, therefore, have to be quantified in relative rather than absolute terms.

- Quality and its management should reflect the management of practice hierarchy. Quality, therefore, has to be managed and controlled from the top and not left as an act of faith.

- Quality is everyone's responsibility. Its successful implementation requires participation and the involvement of all staff.

- Quality strategies have to start with the patient first through a focus on the process of health care delivery.

References

1. Gordon, D.R. and Cannon, S.C., "Building quality into the structure, process and outcomes of health care", 1989 Conference Proceedings of the QQ and PHS Quest for Quality and Productivity in Health Services, Washington, DC, 1989, pp. 35-8.

2. Oakland, J.S., Total Quality Management. The Move to Improving Performance, 2nd ed., Butterworth Heinemann, Oxford and Boston, MA, 1993.

Mohamed Zairi is Unilever Lecturer in TQM and Ajit Matthew is a Research Assistant both at Bradford University Management Centre, Bradford, UK.

Total Quality Education for Superior Performance

Mohamed Zairi

The author

Mohamed Zairi is Unilever Lecturer in TQM, Bradford University Management Centre, Bradford.

Abstract

Total quality management continues to spread in industry and commerce on a global basis. Despite the various levels of scepticism and doubt expressed on its potential to lead to competitive benefits, TQM continues to reshape organizations at all levels. When one looks at providers of education and training, there is little evidence to suggest that there is a high degree of enthusiasm and positive response to the challenges that industry has to face. Analyses how education is responding to TQM implementation and highlights the various obstacles. Discusses the critical aspects of TQM implementation in education and the areas which need to be addressed for a complete and radical transformation of education and training provision capable of meeting modern business requirements. Finally, suggests a way forward for developing an integrated approach to total quality education (TQE) which will assist providers of education and training to become more competitive.

First Published in

Training for Quality
Volume 3 · Number 1 · 1995 · pp. 29–35
© MCB University Press · ISSN 0968-4875

Gauging the mood for quality in education

As TQM continues to change the face of organizations and reshape the nature of competitiveness in industry and commerce, educational institutions continue to retrench themselves and stand further apart from the realities of business life. The quality revolution proved to be a formidable challenge and its implementation quite hard and painful. This is particularly true since TQM does not lead to instant results and requires an integrated and customerdriven approach. Although organizations that have seriously embarked on TQM initiatives are reporting great benefits all the time, it is comments from the cynics and stories of failures which make the headlines. Similar reactions take place in academic institutions, where success enjoyed by industry through quality principles is totally ignored, and failures, problems and obstacles are widely publicized and clearly highlighted. This indicates the level of cynicism and degree of rejection of TQM as a modern approach to competitiveness.

Most of the cynicism linked to TQM is due to the lack of understanding of its workings and the lack of appreciation that, as a philosophy of modern management, TQM requires:

- a long-term focus;
- an outward, customerbased approach;
- the measurement of value rather than of activity;
- non-financial performance measurement.

Various studies talk about failure of TQM without necessarily attempting to qualify what is meant by failure[1,2]. There is also a school of thought which argues very strongly that there is nothing wrong with traditional methods of management[3]: financial management is the only way to secure effective business results[4] and TQM (referred to as an activity-centered approach) has a flawed logic which confuses ends with means and processes with outcomes[5]. Those sceptical of TQM[5] argue that:

Any payoffs from the infusion of activities will be meagre at best. And there is in fact an alternative: results-driven improvement processes that focus on achieving specific, measurable operational improvements within a few months. This means increased yields, reduced delivery time, increased inventory turns, improved customer satisfaction, reduced product development time. With resultsdriven improvements, a company introduces only those innovations in management methods and business processes that can help achieve specific goals.

The type of cynicism covered in the previous section is matched by a similar level of questioning and rejection from academic professionals. Typical comments made by people in academia include[6]:

- "We have no real control over the quality of the 'material' entering the schools";

- "We have no control over outside influences which will continue to thwart educational efforts to achieve a quality product";

- "Business has little disagreement over how best and how often to evaluate a product – educators cannot decide on how best or how often to evaluate or exactly what needs to be evaluated, when it comes to student performance";

- "Unlike businesses, whose products yield resources which can be channelled back into the organization for research in product improvement, educators have limited available resources and little control over how much money will be allocated in the future".

These are some of the many misconceptions and unacceptable arguments presented by cynical academics who perceive TQM as a practice not really applicable to the field of education. Most of the arguments presented need to be challenged.

Understanding who the customer is

The concept of "the customer" is still alien to many academics. Many will not really perceive the student as a customer and this is demonstrated by how they teach, what they teach and how performance is assessed. In addition, and when it comes to industry, many academics will not address urgent needs from industry; the research undertaken is not really applicable nor is it useful to practitioners. This therefore demonstrates a somewhat arrogant attitude, one of "we know best", "a throw and catch" approach of take it or leave it.

The meaning of academic freedom

Academic freedom is something always talked about; but what does it really mean? Academics operate in a free environment and their performance and contributions are judged in an entirely different manner from that of industrialists. Academic freedom is freedom for creating, designing, delivering, researching and disseminating knowledge, concepts, information and practical solutions. However, it is all the deliverables covered which often raise questions. The intellectual freedom is one of doing the right things for the customer(s) and ensuring that they get done in an effective manner. In many cases however, academic freedom is taken to mean: "I know best – what I recommend is what should be applied" or, worse still, contributions from academics are so ineffective that nobody benefits in the end.

Who measures performance

Performance evaluation and measurement is another area of controversy. In teaching, for instance, performance is measured from the lecturer's perspective. Students' performance is seen as their own responsibility. While one would agree that quality assurance and "technical" measurement have to be conducted by the provider (i.e. the lecturer), students who are the recipients of the service (acquiring knowledge/information) are the ones who should measure the quality of the output. If one considers the student to be a customer then, similarly to the industrial context, the customer is the ultimate judge of quality, and that has to apply in the academic context.

What is an effective and competitive academic outcome?

In industry one can talk about technical success versus commercial success. Many organizations are good at inventing new technologies and producing prototypes which are then shelved until a commercial opportunity does arise. This is currently a concern to many organizations which would like to see a speedier return to their investment on R&D. Technical success is quantified only in terms of costs until it becomes commercially exploited to generate benefits.

A similar analogy does apply in academia. Many research programmes carried out by academics produce theories and concepts which are not applicable in industry and are of little benefit to practitioners. Many courses taught do not reflect business realities and fail to equip students with the skills required by employers. Competitive outcomes from academic work therefore have to be measured in terms of usefulness, commercial exploitation and degrees of applicability in various contexts. That is the real challenge for academic institutions where academic freedom can be exploited more positively to meet current and future demands of customer(s) and various stakeholders.

Through gauging the mood of quality in education one can conclude that there is a rejection of TQM as a new way of working and there is a difficulty to accept that academic delivery systems have to start with the customer(s). TQM in education means complete reengineering and radical culture change. This is very painful and demands hard work, discipline, and a new mindset. The need for culture change is recognized by many writers. Sink[7] for example argues that:

We, in higher education, are uncomfortable using terms like "customers", "value added", "processes", and "systems" because we feel they are applicable only for business and industry. Or, perhaps, is it really because we resist the very concepts themselves and hide behind the excuse of language.

The growth of TQM in education

There is a growing interest in applying TQM in education for a wide variety of reasons including: pressures from industry; government schemes allocating moneys which encourage research and teaching in the field of quality; increasing competition between various academic institutions; and a reduction in the pool of money for research and teaching, thus meaning that only reputable institutions will have a likely chance of gaining access to various moneys.

Various surveys were conducted to assess the TQM spread in education:

(1) A US study[8] reports that over 1,200 US colleges and universities have included courses or modules on quality in their curricula.

(2) An ASQC survey[9] had responses from 139 universities and 46 community colleges which reported great benefits from the use of TQM including:

- increased employee empowerment;
- customer satisfaction;
- teamwork;
- culture change.

Other findings from this survey were that:

- most institutions are at the early stages of TQM; implementation
- over 50 per cent have quality councils, officers or centres to co-ordinate their TQM efforts;
- process improvement activity is mainly concentrated in administrative functions, followed by teaching methods;
- TQrelated courses are to be found mainly in schools of management followed by other disciplines such as engineering;
- about 28 per cent of respondents offer degree, masters and doctoral programmes in quality-related fields.

In addition, various doctoral programmes have attempted to scrutinize the levels of awareness, understanding and application of TQM concepts:

(1) One study[10] assessed the spread of quality in non-academic processes of a large university, using the Malcolm Baldrige national quality award criteria: 29 departments were surveyed to find that the majority were interested in quality improvement, particularly in the area of human resource utilization.

(2) Another study[11] looked at the applicability of Deming's 14 points to education in Tennessee: a survey instrument was sent to a sample of 139 superintendents with an 81 per cent response rate; 51 per cent of the respondents were found to be using some form of TQM programme.

(3) The purpose of a third study[12] was to measure the effectiveness of TQM implementation in the two year colleges of Texas: faculty members (n = 113) and administrators (n = 148) completed a mailed questionnaire with the purpose of measuring the applicability of Deming's 14 points. The specific points considered included:

- the adoption of a new philosophy;

- implementation of training on the job;

- implementation of effective leadership;

- elimination of fear in the workplace.

The findings indicate that there is little application of the TQM concept. They also indicate that there is a major disagreement between administrators and faculty members, with the former being much more positive about the implementation of TQM.

In Europe the pace of introduction of TQM in education is much slower, and there are very few documented cases of TQM implementation. However, there is a lot of research underway to assess the level of spread and application of TQM in academic institutions. One of the reasons, it is thought, that TQM implementation in academic institutions in Europe is slow, is the industry's lack of commitment to invest in education and training on quality-related topics. A survey on business needs[13] came to the conclusion that European organizations do not invest sufficient money in TQM education and training, unlike Japan, where quality improvement is fundamentally dependent on employee knowledge and degree of competence.

This brief review indicates that the momentum is building up for educational institutions; those that will rise to the challenge will undoubtedly benefit and those that do not will perhaps have to face the painful consequences of: huge drops in student recruitment levels; lack of adequate moneys for conducting meaningful research; inability to attract and retain high-calibre staff; and poor standing in the immediate communities.

The size of the challenge for TQM implementation in educational establishments

It is perhaps right to start at the top management level and challenge the leadership of educational institutions. In most cases, leaders of academic institutions are professors who gained seniority levels through personal achievements and who demonstrated good administrative skills. They have a good approach to cost management, human resource management and planning and organization. Many of those individuals are no longer in touch with the real world and therefore are unable to assess the challenges facing the organizations they lead.

When it comes to TQM, for instance, this is the biggest obstacle to leaders who do not see anything wrong with the "old" and who would rather ask: "what is wrong with industry?" As Sink[7] argues:

> ...there is not enough leadership in higher education to create a vision of what the system[TQM] could look like ... responsibility for implementing TQM in higher education lies with presidents, provosts and deans. They are the ones who must lead positive change and create a vision of what the higher education system must be in the context of the larger system.

The first challenge for educational institutions, therefore, is the establishment of leadership styles which can bring about real change capable of meeting the challenges of the modern business world. What is required are change masters and not masters of complacency. Masters of change are described as:

Those people and organizations adept at the art of anticipating the need for, and of leading, productive change[14].

Leadership for TQM in education is also about entrepreneurship in education, defined as:

Someone who intends to change long established practices to enable the future of the institution to be changed at least partly by the institution itself and not simply by external factors[15].

502

The key attributes for an educational entrepreneur include:

- vision;
- ability to allocate resources to ensure quality provision;
- ability to delegate;
- ability to organize;
- ability to reduce individual and team stress;
- ability to think long term;
- accepts responsibility of leadership;
- ability to motivate at all levels;
- ability to select a good team;
- ability to develop a good team.

Doing the right things right all the time

The second biggest challenge perhaps is for educational institutions to re-examine everything they do and ensure that the right–things from the perspective of the customer are being–done and, through building a culture of continuous improvement, get all the things done right all the time, with effectiveness and consistency. At the present time, however, most institutions use quality assurance as a means to comply with standards set by accreditating bodies and government regulatory organizations.

Compliance with standards does, however, breed mediocrity[16], and the auditing exercises are considered as no more than a once in-a-while exercise, a burden, something that needs to be done quickly. Quality assurance, however, as defined by international standards such as ISO 9000, is much broader and more encompassing and starts with the customer first. The challenge for academia therefore is to redefine the meaning of quality assurance (QA) and to establish a culture of continuous improvement for building consistency (through measurement of the valueadded to customers) as opposed to compliance with bureaucracy (through the measurement of activity).

The student as customer

The student is not only the "raw material" but also the "primary customer". Without students there is no education and, in an environment where students can afford to choose, only providers who are focused on customers and their needs will attract the best recruits and in large quantities, thus enabling them to achieve superior competitive standards.

A commitment to students as the "primary customers" must be demonstrated through all activities and the building of a value-added chain, including academic and support functions. The customer is the starting point of all activities. In industry, for instance, prior to designing new products or services, many organizations started to use a technique called quality function deployment (QFD) for establishing customer wants and developing a translation process of the wants through focusing on the right activities and developing strength in all of then via a continuous improvement process. QFD has been used in education to assess student (customer) satisfaction with courses delivered[17]. The technique was used to appraise the whole process of delivering courses and included:

- an evaluation of the effectiveness of the courses in achieving their declared aims;

- an evaluation of the degrees of integration between subjects;

- an assessment of the original aims of the course to determine the philosophy in designing a revised course.

The seven tools of TQM can also be used to achieve customer satisfaction. A five-phase process of improvement to courses delivered has been successfully adopted[18]. The five stages are based on Deming's plan-do-check-act. They include:

(1) identify (gaps, variations) from students' feedback;

(2) analyse (instructional process);

(3) plan (through QFD, introduce actions to improve quality);

(4) implement (actions);

(5) evaluate (by customer satisfaction surveys).

Tools and techniques of TQM are very powerful in building a culture focused on customers and customer satisfaction. QFD and the seven simple tools, as demonstrated by the above examples, can lead to effective outcomes. A focus on the customer, however, has to be sustainable and will not require merely changes in existing procedures: it is very much behavioural. This is the only way forward for being an effective and competitive provider of educational needs. As stated[16]:

Identifying students as the primary customers and striving to meet their needs is an ethically correct strategy. Recognizing other important customers, such as employers, reflects the reality that postsecondary-education organizations are constantly engaged in complex efforts to satisfy many parties. But it is vital that educational institutions recognize that conflicts in the needs and expectations of different customers should be resolved in favor of the student.

The concept of partnership

Education providers have started to come to the realization that competitiveness in education is heavily dependent on the ability to build links with industry and to be continuously selected as the preferred supplier of education and training needs. IBM has demonstrated a serious commitment to assist education providers in building cultures of quality based on a partnership approach. The former chairman[19] was reported to have said:

Education isn't just a social concern, it's a major economic issue. If our students can't compete today, how will our companies compete tomorrow?

IBM's own commitment to the development of TQM in education was demonstrated in October 1991 when the company launched an initiative entitled: "An IBM total quality management (TQM) competition for colleges and universities in the USA"[20]. The scheme was to offer eight awards in the amount of $1,000,000 in cash and $3,000,000 in IBM equipment. The beneficiaries would enter into partnership with IBM in the following manner:

- loaned IBM executives;
- IBM speakers;
- faculty and student internships at IBM;
- classes on IBM's approach to market-driven quality;
- co-operation on research;
- participation in a network of TQM companies, colleges, and universities to share information, research or "best practice".

IBM received 204 applications to choose from and only nine institutions were chosen for the awards.

The chairman and CEO of Rank Xerox, Paul Allaire, talking about partnerships between industry and academia[21], argues that the new breed of graduates required for industry:

- are customer oriented;
- are systems thinkers;
- understand work as a process;
- are committed to improvement;
- make decisions based on fact;
- are active learners;
- have practical knowledge of and can apply quality tools;
- are team oriented.

Allaire strongly believes that graduates will suffer if universities do not respond to the challenges set by industry and follow the change process. He argues[21]:

Those universities that ignore the quality movement are failing their customers ... their students are going to come into a business world that is very strange to them. They won't understand today's basic concepts of management, or tomorrow's, for that matter.

To appreciate the need for developing a partnership approach to "TQM for competitiveness", even the US government has put down guidelines for education providers to respond to the TQM challenge. The US Department of Labor produced a document entitled Learning a living: a blueprint for high performance, referred to as the SCANS report (Secretary's Commission for Achieving Necessary Skills) (cited in [22]).

Some of the key parameters laid down in the report include the following expectations of graduates joining industry:

(1) competences in managing resources, including:

- managing information;
- monitoring their own performance;
- improving systems;
- selecting and applying technology;

(2) interpersonal competences:

- ability to work in teams;
- customer service;

(3) basic arithmetic and communication skills:

- reasoning and problem solving
- personal qualities for responsible self-management.

Total quality education (TQE) for effective competitiveness

The way forward, as far as education providers are concerned, is to respond to the challenges facing industry by providing employers with graduates competent in all modern aspects of performance and by developing the skills and knowledge of graduates who will manage to secure employment and perform effectively. A proposed approach, illustrated in the list below, can lead to a radical transformation, and a complete re-engineering, of educational institutions to change from an internal focus (a reactive mode, through piecemeal change with little effectiveness) to an external focus (continuous breakthroughs to enhance competitiveness):

Key elements for TQE

(1) Leadership in education for excellence:

- vision for future competitiveness;
- a partnership approach;
- goals, communication and congruence;
- support infrastructure;
- corporate commitment and management;
- process-focus;
- performance management.

(2) Process-driven delivery systems:

- building a value chain;
- focus on core processes;
- building strong support base;
- quality assurance and audit;
- cross-functional culture;
- breakthroughs through innovation;
- a culture of continuous improvement;
- best practice for benchmarking;
- emphasis on measurement.

(3) Winning formula for success:

- total quality education delivery through partnerships;

- totally re-engineered processes for optimum capability;
- continuous improvement through continuous learning;
- time-to-market approach to delivery;
- measuring for competitiveness rather than effectiveness;
- competing on innovation breakthroughs;
- a commitment to customer satisfaction.

Leadership in education for excellence

This is perhaps a prerequisite to bring about the necessary changes required for achieving the desired transformation.

Process-driven delivery systems

Competitiveness can come only through the building of strong capability and the ability of "offering" in a consistent manner but also with innovation, major breakthroughs, state of the art thinking and the use of best practice provision elements.

Winning formula for success

The ability to build a value chain through the creation of a total education delivery process, based on external focus, a commitment to customer satisfaction, re-engineered processes to optimize capability and the provision of breakthroughs and major innovations in a speedy manner.

Total quality education (TQE) is about creating opportunities for continuous learning through continuous improvement. Productivity measurement in the context of education institutions is the measurement of learning. Learning comes from newness and innovation. TQE has to carry education institutions towards their vision of being "preferred suppliers for learning".

Competitiveness in education is based on the amount of new learning and inspiration provided. That is the main distinguishing feature, and perhaps the only one, as the following statement explains:

I don't divide the world into the weak and the strong, or the successes and the failures, those who make it or those who don't. I divide the world into learners and nonlearners. There are people who learn, who are open to what happens around them, who listen, who hear the lessons. When they do something stupid, they don't do it again. And when they do something that works a little bit, they do it even better and harder the next time. The question to ask is not whether you are a success or a failure, but whether you are a learner or a nonlearner[23].

References

1   Taylor, P., "Faith in the religion of quality is starting to waver", Financial Times (management section), 21 October 1992.

2   Taylor, P., "Why customers must come first", Financial Times(Management section), 26 October 1992.

3   Zairi, M., Measuring Performance for Business Results, Chapman & Hall, London, 1994.

4   Schaffer, R.H., "Demand better results – and get them", Harvard Business Review, March-April 1991, pp. 14-29.

5   Schaffer, R.H. and Thomson, H.A., "Successful change programs begin with results", Harvard Business Review, January-February 1992, pp. 80-9.

6   Weller, L.D and Hartley, S.A., "Why are educators stonewalling TQM?", The TQM Magazine, Vol. 6 No. 3, 1994, pp 23-8.

7   Sink, D.S., "Quality priorities of higher education", Quality & Productivity Management, Vol. 1 No. 2, 1993, pp. 5-6.

8   Golomski, W.A.J., "TQM in education", EOQ '93 World Quality Congress Proceedings, Helsinki, 1993.

9   Horine, J.E., Hailey, W.A. and Rubach, L., "Shaping America's future", Quality Progress,October 1993, pp. 41-5.

10 Fritz, S.M., "A quality assessment using the Baldrige criteria: non-academic service units in a large university", PhD thesis, University of Nebraska, Lincoln, NE, 1993.

11 Wilcox, R., "A study of the W. Edwards Deming total quality management concept as it applies to education in Tennessee", EdD thesis, East Tennessee State University, TN, 1992.

12 Partin, J.C., "A measurement of total quality management in the two-year college districts of Texas", EdD thesis, East Texas State University, TX, 1992.

13 Dale, B. and Van Der Wiele, T., "TQM UMIST and ERASMUS", TQM, April, 1992, pp. 77-80.

14 Kanter, R.M., The Change Masters, Simon and Schuster, New York, NY, 1983.

15 Boyett, I. and Finlay, D., "The emergence of the educational entrepreneur", Long Range Planning, Vol. 26 No. 3, 1993, pp. 114-22.

16 Hittman, J.A., "TQM and CQI in postsecondary education", Quality Progress, October 1993, pp. 71-7.

17 Smith, J.A., Baker, K. and Higgins, S., "The assessment of customer satisfaction in higher education – a quality function deployment approach", EOQ '93 World Quality Congress Proceedings, Helsinki, Finland, 1993.

18 Zaciewski, R., "Improving the instructional process", Quality Process, April 1994, pp. 75-80.

19 Schargel, F.P., "Total Quality in Education", Quality Progress, October 1993, pp. 67-70

20 Beaumariage, K.D., "IBM grant proposal overview", Quality & Productivity Management, Vol. 10 No. 2, 1993, p. 40.

21 Rubach, L. and Stratton, B., "Teaming up to improve US education", Quality Progress, February 1994, pp. 65-8.

22 Chappeli, R.T., "Can TQM in public education survive without co-production?", Quality Progress, July 1994, pp. 41-4.

23 Hyatt, C. and Gottleib, L., When Smart People Fail, Penguin, Harmondsworth, 1993.

" " Only 1-2% of companies are role models for quality. Less than 20% of companies are adequate in terms of quality. " "

- Joseph Juran
during a satellite seminar
"J.M. Juran on Quality,"
held on October 10, 1996

The Critical Factors Requested to Implement Pharmaceutical Care in Saudi Arabia hospitals: A Qualitative study

Waleed Al-Shaqha,[1] PharmD., Ph.D. and Mohammed Zairi[2]
1-Visting Scholar, School of Pharmacy, UNC at Chapel Hill
2-Professor of TQM Management Centre, University of Bradford.

Abstract

A revolution is underway in health care delivery system that is deriving fundamental, sweeping change. While much of the cost savings in health care have come from eliminating waste and inefficiency, further savings in health care will come from better patient care, better health outcomes, prevention and better management of disease conditions. Pharmacy as a major component in the health care system is also under reprofessionalisation. Pharmaceutical care requires pharmacists to change their practice from product oriented to patient oriented care. In this article the implication of the transformation of hospital pharmacy departments from the traditional pharmacy practice approach to patient care approach, they embark on the mission of pharmaceutical care is reviewed. It explores the role adopted by clinical pharmacists in hospitals providing pharmaceutical care in the Kingdom of Saudi Arabia hospital contexts. The successful implementation of clinical pharmacy services is a critical factor for implementing a comprehensive pharmaceutical care management approach. The successful implementation of pharmaceutical care management approach in the KSA hospital context through an empirical research of critical pharmaceutical care factors is the focus of this thesis. Reviews of the literature review on pharmaceutical care management verified the need for research in this area. The research design, involving a qualitative methodology and field work in the KSA hospital context, included:

1. The identification of key pharmaceutical care commonly cited in the literature, and endorsed by practitioners and experts as important for the effective implementation of pharmaceutical care,

2. Determining how these so-called critical pharmaceutical care management factors are addressed and implemented via the use of semi-structured interviews, and

3. Understanding the pre-implementation process using in-depth case studies.

The findings of the study indicated that critical prerequisites to establishing pharmaceutical care are administration and pharmacist commitment to the pharmaceutical care concept.

In addition, the findings of the study emphasis that developing a strategic plan, including clear mission, goals, organisational structure, and technical and human resources, is a prerequisite for pharmaceutical care implementation.

Introduction

The principles of practice of pharmaceutical care demonstrate the knowledge required of a pharmacist and the level to which the pharmacist must participate with other healthcare professionals in order to provide the best care. The use of these principles would foster consistency in the provision of pharmaceutical care in all hospitals. It would support the continuity of care within practice settings. Further, these principles of practice of pharmaceutical care would establish consistency in documentation, so that patient-specific and medication-related information could be shared from pharmacist to pharmacist and among health professionals.

Although Saudi Arabia has been mentioned in the ACCP1 directory one of three countries applied clinical pharmacy outside the USA, still the pharmacy services do not meet pharmacist's expectations. Overall, hospital pharmacy in Saudi Arabia is in a transitional phase. The last two decades of the 20th century have witnessed a reasonable progress of pharmacy practice with the rapid expansion of healthcare institutions.

The research design, involving a qualitative methodology and field work in the KSA hospital context, included:

1. The identification of key pharmaceutical care commonly cited in the literature, and endorsed by practitioners and experts as important for the effective implementation of pharmaceutical care,

2. Determining how these so-called critical pharmaceutical care management factors are addressed and implemented via the use of semi-structured interviews, and

3. Understanding the pre-implementation process using in-depth case studies

However, these critical factors could be extended to be a standard or main element to implement pharmaceutical care in any global hospitals. In addition, this article shows the barriers that could be considered as obstacles to implement pharmaceutical care from the sight of decision-maker and practitioner pharmacists in many lead hospitals in KSA.

Research Method

The research method of the study consisted of three general steps: conducting an interdisciplinary literature search; conducting ethnographic interviews with pharmacy managers, clinical pharmacy services directors, clinical pharmacists in Saudi hospitals; and analysing the data in order to clarify the theme and develop a pharmaceutical care model.

Interdisciplinary literature review

For this study, the literature review focused on pharmaceutical care management. By completing the literature search, this provided a better understanding of the nature of the pharmaceutical care concept and clinical pharmacy services and the identification and clarification of the important role of the pharmacist in the healthcare system. The research also heightened an awareness of new concepts in pharmacy, i.e. patient-focused care, re-engineering, TQM and critical pathway, and possible relationships between them.

Case Study Semi-Structured Interviews and Participant Observation

Participant observation and the semi-structured interview are probably the two most common types of data collection in a qualitative research. However, the interviews and the observation are also essential sources of case study information. The aim of the semi-structured interviews is to understand the nature of the pharmaceutical care management and the process of clinical pharmacy service implementation, by investigating how the critical factors of the pharmaceutical care concept identified in the literature survey are addressed and implemented. The case studies are the primary method used to probe the how, what, and why questions in this study.

There are a variety of approaches to conducting an interview, ranging from a totally unstructured interview in which the content is completely controlled by the subject, to interviews in which the content is similar to a questionnaire, with the possible responses to questions carefully designed by the researcher. Another type of interview is called the semi-structured interview. This lies roughly half-way between the two types of interview described above. Although the encounter between interviewer and respondents is structured and the major aspects of the study are explained, respondents are given considerable liberty in expressing their definition of a situation that is presented to them.

The semi-structured interview was chosen for the collection of data during this research since:

1. Open questions encourage pharmacists to describe their pharmacy department activities in their hospitals and to formulate their own views about the pharmaceutical care concept. A number of pharmacists had not carefully considered the pharmacist's role in the healthcare team prior to the interview, and extra time was required for thought-provoking questions in these cases. This formulation of concepts was necessary before interviewees could communicate their thoughts.

2. Open questions helped to ensure content validity of data gathered during data collection.

3. The use of a set of predetermined questions facilitated categorisation of responses and comparison between cases. However, the semi-structured schedule allowed the researcher flexibility of probing when appropriate.

Thus, semi-structured interviews were appropriate for the collection of data which would meet the objectives of this research.

Design of Interview Schedule

The design of the initial schedule was based on the literature review, discussions with colleagues and the experience of preliminary, pre-pilot and pilot interviews. The questions were ordered so that there would be a natural flow from one question to another and from one topic to another. Each new section or topic was introduced to enable the interviewee to focus thought on the new topic. The semi-structured interview schedule was designed to define the interviewee's views on the value of the currently provided and potential clinical pharmacy services, the reasons for current service development, and possible barriers and facilitators to currently provided and future services. In addition, general questions about the pharmaceutical care concept were designed to explore the pharmacist's understanding of this concept, and the current levels of involvement of pharmacists and their staff in specific pharmaceutical care activities. The interview schedule was divided into two main parts, as follows:

1. Part (I) Open-ended questions about establishing and changing practices for pharmaceutical care.

This part can be divided into six sections, which included questions on the following:

A. Hospital characteristics and utilisation

B. Pharmacy department activities in hospitals

C. Clinical pharmacy services in hospitals and how useful and valuable these services are in the overall provision of good patient care

D. Functional and structural prerequisites for clinical pharmacy services

E. Pharmaceutical care concept

F. Integration of pharmaceutical services.

Pilot Interviews

Interviews were conducted with 8 hospital pharmacists at the 5 hospitals, who volunteered to take part, as a pilot of the interview schedule

These pilot interviews with the 8 pharmacists highlighted the need to reduce the length of the interview schedule and to increase the specificity of questions. During the pilot study, a few minor alterations were made to the wording of questions and the instructions of the interviewer were clarified. The mean time taken to conduct the pilot interview, including interruption time, was 90-120 minutes. Despite the length of time needed to complete the interviews, a decision was made to proceed to the main study without omitting any of the interview schedule, due to the quality of data obtained and the positive feedback from interviewees about participation in the study.

Selection of Sites and Respondents.

The sites selected for benchmarking are not a random sample. Based on grounded theory, the sampling has to be directed and deliberate, with conscious choices made about whom and what to sample in order to obtain the necessary data [3]. As the purpose of this research is to develop guidance based on the best practice model for pharmaceutical care management, the sampling strategy has to meet the nature of functional benchmarking which compares specific functions with the best in the class. The literature review helped to clarify the construct of pharmaceutical care management. The qualitative portion of the study was conducted within five hospitals in KSA to explore the extent to which clinical pharmacy and the pharmaceutical care concept have been implemented.

The nature of the interviews and observation methods required the interviewer to spend some time at each site (hospital). This requirement, plus time and resource constraints, limited the number of sites to the five hospitals. Selection of a representative sample of all Saudi hospitals was desirable, but the use of random or stratified sampling was impractical, given the limited size of the sample. Instead, judgmental sampling or purposeful sampling [5] was used to select a theoretically representative sample based on prior knowledge of factors that were thought to be important in the development of hospital clinical pharmacy. This knowledge was obtained from the preliminary research, numerous informal contacts, from information gleaned on pharmacy practice in the Saudi Arabia literature review, and personal communication. Purposeful sampling was used to identify informants for this phase of the study. As a result, hospitals were categorised and selected using the criteria:

1. Teaching status

2. Reputation of clinical pharmacy service

3. Total number of clinical pharmacy services provided.

Additional factors were considered in hospital selection. Hospitals that provided a broad perspective of clinical pharmacy services and that allowed the interviewer easy access to all areas and persons of interest there[6] were selected.

This enabled suitable hospitals to be selected for this research which would involve in-depth case study to probe the how, what and why questions. Those emerging as highest adopters of the pharmaceutical care concept, and additionally a small number of medium and low-adopters, were chosen. A contact person, usually the pharmacy director or clinical pharmacy supervisor or co-ordinator, was selected at each site who would help in choosing interviewees and organising the visit. Interviewees were chosen in advance from specific groups that would inform the study[6]:

1. Those managing the pharmacy department (pharmacy department director)

2. Those managing the clinical pharmacy service (clinical pharmacy service supervisor)

3. Those providing the clinical pharmacy service (clinical pharmacist)

The majority of interviewees were selected in consultation with the contact person at the hospital. The consultation process included discussion of a potential interviewee's responsibilities and duration of service at the hospital. All interviewees had worked at the hospital for at least a year; most had been at the site for several years. Clinical pharmacists who were viewed by their managers as having a relatively high proportion of positive patient care experience were encouraged to participate in the research.

Arranging and Conducting Interviews

Hospital participants were recruited through the use of an announcement memo, which was sent from the Security Forces Hospital (SFH, the researcher's sponsor) administrator to the directors of five selected hospitals in Saudi Arabia. Three or 5 pharmacists were recruited from each hospital's major clinical pharmacy service, including the pharmacy director. In the memo to hospital directors, they were urged to discuss the study with their pharmacy department staff members. The pharmacy director at each hospital was contacted by telephone and agreement for the visit to take place was obtained. This was confirmed in a letter that introduced the researcher, explained the purpose of the research very generally, named the sponsors, guaranteed confidentiality and anonymity, and requested help in the selection of interviewees. Follow-up telephone calls were made to those individuals contacted in order to gain agreement to participate in the survey, and to arrange suitable times and dates for the interview. In fact, every hospital contacted agreed to participate in the survey. All individuals were informed of the approximate time necessary for the interviews; it was explained that it would take about 90-120 minutes. Individuals were also given further details on the nature of the survey to ensure that interviewees understood what was being required of them. All meetings took place in a private setting at the respondent's office and during office hours. Interviews were carried out usually at the interviewees' place of work in a quiet place, where the process was unlikely to be interrupted or overheard. In all of the cases, the respondent was ready for the interview and had made arrangements to make the period of the interview free of interruptions or distractions caused by official duties. Formal group interviews were carried out in similar conditions with groups of 3-5 interviewees. Informal group and individual conversational interview opportunities were taken also. The respondent would then be asked to present his/her views regarding the issue(s) to be explored.

All interviews were conducted by a single researcher thereby eliminating the potential effects of interviewer differences on results[7]. There is evidence that recording responses by note-taking during interviews results in selective recording, and any substantial systemic error is incorporated into the data[6]. The only way of reducing errors in recording of data is by obtaining a verbatim report of the interview, e.g. by tape-recording the responses. Therefore a Sony Professional Walkman and microphone were used to record responses during this phase of data collection where possible.

In addition to the 17 formal interviews, the researcher had many informal discussions with many people on the same topic at various pharmacy seminars, meetings, and in other situations. Informal discussion is another way of capturing opportunities to enhance theoretic sensitivity[8]. To improve validity and reliability, up to five interviews were conducted in each hospital. The 8 pilot interviews have been added to the entire study due to the valuable information that has been extracted from them. Additionally, where available, documentation was gathered to support the interview; typically, this would

521

include mission statements, objectives statements, policy and procedures, organisation structure/charts, pharmacy practice standards, and training materials.

Data Analysis and Interpretation

Case analysis method was used in combination with a constant comparative method in the analysis of the data from the case studies. This involves analysing the data from each individual case to explore the full richness of the data obtained. The case analysis involves producing descriptive summaries of each case based on the data obtained and presenting the cases in a uniform structure. The structure chosen for presenting the cases was largely to follow the design of the interview schedule. At the end of each descriptive case study, conclusions were then made about each case, based on the information provided. The constant comparative analysis lies at the heart of the grounded theory approach and is the principal method of data analysis used to generate categories and properties from the interview data of the five sites.

The fundamental aim for case analysis is to deepen understanding and explanation. Another reason is to enhance generalisation[9]. The recorded data were transcribed. Field notes derived from observation were converted into write-ups. The transcriptions and the field notes were coded and categorised, seeking internal convergence and external divergence among the categories[10].

Coding and Categorising

With the large amount of descriptive information obtained from the case studies, it was necessary to code and categorise the data. The approach used was that suggested by Easterby-Smith et al. (1991)[11]. Coding involves the derivation of codes for qualitative information based on grouping data together under suitable headings. The first step in coding involved transcribing all tape-recordings of the interviews, and defining codes for the responses from each respondent under each unstructured question. It is necessary to read and re-read the data transcription to enable concepts to emerge. Responses are then grouped on a "fram sheet" and similar responses are put together. Any responses not conforming to an existing code are then given a new code, until all responses have been tabulated.

The second phase in grouping qualitative data involves categorising responses. Categorising is a classification of concepts. This involves grouping cases into different categories, based on the responses to one or more questions. Categorisation allows interpretation of case study data, which may be difficult to achieve if cases are presented randomly (Strauss and Corbin, 1990)[8]. Case study analysis commenced with the preparation of descriptive reports following a uniform structure along the lines of the interview proforma or schedule.

Research Findings and Discussion

The research presented in this article represents an exploratory study of pharmaceutical care critical factors to implement pharmaceutical care in KSA hospitals. The finding of the study will now be discussed and presented. In order to create best practice models of clinical roles for hospital pharmacists, the measurement of "what" is not enough for the purpose of understanding the process that creates best practice. Detailed explanations of "how" and "why" are therefore needed. To achieve these goals, the case studies approach using a certain number of hospitals in Saudi Arabia was adopted. In addition, secondary analysis of case studies in both USA and UK hospitals was used. The history of each hospital was studied in depth with particular emphasis on critical factors and processes supporting the implementation of the pharmaceutical care concept, and determining the extent to which the hospital pharmacy department was involved in patient–focused care models and patient care plans. This was followed by in-depth interviews with individual pharmacy managers and clinical pharmacy directors, and participant observation study in KSA hospitals. The interviews were semi-structured and informal. Interviewees' opinions on a variety of topics, including clinical pharmacy services, the pharmaceutical care concept, and pharmacists' contributions to patient care were explored using a range of open and probing questions. The in depth-interviews were combined with direct observation. Direct observation is a useful data collection technique in pharmacy practice research as it allows detailed information to be collected without disrupting the pharmacists' normal work patterns. It emerged that there was variation in implementing the concept of pharmaceutical care management between the five hospitals in KSA. Given the considerable time and ability required for planning and implementing a pharmaceutical care management approach, hospitals involved in this study usually tended to have some sort of support infrastructure that facilitates and manages their processes. The study indicated that the variations observed in the approach to provision of pharmaceutical care management in the KSA hospitals involved in this study are not random. Out of the five hospitals, KFSH&RC and KFNGH have found to have the required success factors to implement the pharmaceutical care management approach. These two hospitals appear to have generally succeeded in putting their approach on the right track. Several critical success factors that help set the foundation of the pharmaceutical care management within the case study hospitals were identified. These, aptly termed "foundation critical success factors of pharmaceutical care management" are described below:

Foundation critical success factors of pharmaceutical care management

This section discusses the outcomes of the interview analysis, assessing issues that affect the provision of pharmaceutical care management in the Saudi Arabian hospitals involved in this study. The last two decades of the twentieth century have witnessed a reasonable progress of pharmaceutical services provided in the country, which has come in conjunction with the rapid expansion of healthcare services, including building several new hospitals and other healthcare institutions. Overall, hospital pharmacy in Saudi Arabia is in a transitional phase. Availability of resources and dedicated pharmacists have overcome many difficulties and produced progress, in some cases impressive, in a relatively short period of time. Interviewees' opinions on a variety of topics, including pharmacists' contributions to patient care were explored using a range of open and probing questions. The purpose of this section is to isolate factors found to critical for the effective provision of pharmaceutical care management. A second aim is to highlight the major barriers for the implementation of pharmaceutical care in Saudi hospitals.

The Critical Factors Requested to Implement Pharmaceutical Care

524

1. Pharmaceutical Care Definition Understanding

All of the pharmacists interviewed in the five hospitals had some knowledge of the term "pharmaceutical care". Definitions ranged in complexity, indicating the varying extents of understanding of the concept. Some pharmacists considered pharmaceutical care to be basically patient-oriented, whilst others provided definitions of pharmaceutical care which included monitoring the outcomes of therapy, and undertaking increased responsibility for patient outcomes.

"It is looking at the whole patient in general or taking the patient as a whole, not just focusing on one medication in one area" Pharmaceutical Care Supervisor.

"It is the concept that the pharmacist acts on behalf of the patient's interest before medical staff or nursing staff or everybody else, so the pharmacist becomes really an active healthcare provider" (Clinical Pharmacist)

"The Pharmaceutical care concept means complete patient care, where pharmacists act on behalf of patient's interest and take the responsibility to achieve definite outcomes and improve patient's quality of life" (Pharmacy Director)

Only three pharmacists considered the pharmaceutical care concept to be a product service function which focuses on the medication itself as a product:

"It is really the advice on drug-drug interaction drug formulary, and the way to produce pharmaceutical care that meet the needs of a patient" (Assistant Pharmacy Director).

Different authors have defined and addressed the pharmaceutical care concept in different ways. The definition of the concept presented by pharmacists were interviewed is similar to the existing definitions proposed in the literature review. Pharmaceutical care was first defined by Mikeal et al.[12], in 1975 as:

"the care that a given patient requires and receives which assures safe and rational drug usage".

Brodie[13] et al. (1980) also emphasised that pharmaceutical care includes the determination of the drug needs for a given individual and the provision not only the required drugs but also the services necessary (before, during, and after treatment) to ensure optimally safe and effective therapy. Hepler[14] (1988) defined pharmaceutical care as:

"a conventional relationship between a patient and a pharmacist in which the pharmacists performs drug use control functions governed by the awareness of and commitment to the patient's interest".

In 1989, Hepler and Strand[15] defined the pharmaceutical care concept as:

"the responsible provision of drug therapy for the purpose of achieving definite outcomes that improve a patient's quality of life".

According to Strand[16] (1997) pharmaceutical care is a practice in which the practitioner takes responsibility for a patient's drug related needs and is held accountable for this commitment.

A review of the definition revealed in fact that there is a consistency between the definition of pharmaceutical care from the interviewees involved in this study and definition of several authors in the literature. The implication is that pharmacists in those hospitals are eager to move towards the patient care more than being product-oriented, and this also supports that pharmacy practice is in a global transitional stage. Many interviewees emphasised new terms used for the first time by pharmacists in KSA hospitals, such as "patient outcomes, responsibility, focusing on the patient as a whole". It can be argued that all these items give evidence that pharmacists in KSA seem to be looking for a new role and through it improve patient care and enhance the therapy outcome.

2. Availability of Patient-Oriented Services

Patient-oriented pharmacy practice in Saudi hospitals has made considerable progress over the last decade or so. Clinical pharmacists are now practising alongside physicians, nurses and other healthcare professionals in some Saudi public hospitals other than those operated by the Ministry of Health. Recently, the pharmacy profession in Saudi Arabia has begun to shift its emphasis from technical product-oriented issues to patient-oriented informational and cognitive services. Provision of a cognitive service begins with the recognition of a possible patient drug therapy problem and is followed by intervention to verify that the problem is clinically relevant and to determine an appropriate solution. The results from this study show that the intervention may include changes in drug therapy and patient counselling. Although claims were made in all the five hospitals that patient counselling was available, in reality it was observed that most of such services were brief and available only to outpatients, and only one hospital from the five in question provided counselling for its discharged patients, while in other hospitals, clinical pharmacists might provide counselling for selected groups of outpatients and discharge patients. Such a service was provided by pharmacists at some hospitals when patients were nearing discharge, usually for those who were felt to be in greatest need, such as the elderly. However, most of these hospitals depended on nurses to provide routine patient counselling prior to discharge.

The concept of "clinical pharmacy" and the term "clinical pharmacist" were first discussed by Pratt and colleagues[17] (1968). They defined the clinical pharmacist as one who, in addition to academic preparation for the practice of pharmacy, has been intimately involved with patient services and is able to serve as an active member of the medical team. Ideally the clinical pharmacist will work side-by-side with the physician in rendering bedside services to patients. Many authors have pointed out the benefits of pharmacists attending the rounds with the medical team.

"The goal of department is to direct our resources to areas where patient care needs are most critical. Patient-focused care forces us to adopt radically new perspectives. One of the fundamentals of our pharmacy department objective is that the patient and the pharmacist have a direct relationship" Pharmacy department director.

"We identify clinical pharmacy activities through literature review and the experience of other hospitals in Saudi Arabia and in the USA. We establish the goal of our clinical programme to relocate the pharmacist from the basement to the patient care area to provide the patient in our hospital with the most effective, safest and cost-efficient therapies" (Clinical pharmacy co-ordinator).

There have been several studies published, evaluating the effectiveness of implementation of patient-oriented pharmacy services [18] [19]. All the studies had similar findings that pharmacists can be effective on ward rounds being used by physicians as a source of drug information, as well as making unsolicited suggestions, resulting in improved patient care and increased quality of care[20,21]. This implies that there have been significant changes in opinion in recent years over demarcation lines in the pharmacy departments of KSA hospitals regarding the role of pharmacists in patient care process. The interview results give support that pharmacists should be patient-oriented rather than products oriented should move from a reactive to a proactive. Furthermore, this finding supports the evidence in the literature that pharmacists should move from waiting for a prescription to initiating the prescription and, from providing all services from the central department of pharmacy to providing some services from the patient care areas. It emerged that the many of the pharmacy departments in hospitals involved in this study are still in transition. Some of them are in the midst of changing from providing reactive services to delivering proactive services in keeping with the changing needs of their hospitals.

3. Attitudes towards pharmaceutical care and role of pharmacist

All the pharmacists interviewed regarded pharmaceutical care as the future model for comprehensive patient-care and believed that the pharmacist has a major role to play in the provision of this patient-oriented service in Saudi Arabia

"Saudi Arabia is the best country to practice pharmaceutical care. Pharmaceutical care needs only the knowledgeable pharmacist who has a commitment to be a pharmaceutical care provider. Pharmaceutical care means that the pharmacist has knowledge and a readiness to share this knowledge with the other (patients). Pharmaceutical care is a paradigm shift in the pharmacist thinking. The pharmacists should change the way they think and be patient-oriented" (MOH, Ministry Consultant).

"Pharmacists are capable of making a worth while contribution to the patient care process and participation in the healthcare team" (**Clinical Pharmacist**).

However, whilst agreeing with the concept in theory, most pharmacists have an intention to extend their role to practice pharmaceutical care. All the pharmacists interviewed believed that they were involved in pharmaceutical care provision, but in each case, this role focused on medication distribution, patient education, drug information provision, and participation in multidisciplinary committees such as the Pharmacy and Therapeutic committee. The number of pharmacists interviewed indicated that their long- term goal is to provide pharmaceutical care as a complete package across the hospital medication process in order to increase the effectiveness and quality of patient care.

"Our aim is to expand the role of the pharmacists to encompass new tasks and duties traditionally fulfilled by the medical and nursing staff. In addition, typical clinical pharmacist functions were performed in greater depth and on a routine rather than an irregular basis, and this allowed time for the pharmacist to become fully integrated into medical teams" (Pharmacy Department Director).

Only 10 pharmacists interviewed claimed that they were involved in patient monitoring including monitoring the physiology outcomes of therapy, such as normalizing blood glucose or cholesterol level. A few pharmacists indicated that they advised patients on their disease state. Within the sample, it therefore appeared, that pharmaceutical care provision, particularly in relation to therapeutic outcomes monitoring and patient education on their disease state was implemented in these hospitals only to a limited extent. During the observation of activities carried out by pharmacists who provided more in-depth definition of pharmaceutical care in their hospitals, it was found they did not implement comprehensive pharmaceutical care activities to as high a degree as they had claimed.

It is clear from the results obtained from the interviews' survey that most of the pharmacists involved in this study have an interest to become pharmaceutical care providers, but most of them do not have the necessary tools to meet the requirements of pharmaceutical care.

Pharmaceutical care is an outcome-oriented concept that has been proposed as a model for pharmacy practice in resolving the issue of preventable drug-related problems[15]. The question remaining for them is whether pharmacists possess the skills and knowledge to accomplish these goals. Hepler[24] (1990) believes that pharmaceutical care is pharmacy's future as healthcare evolves and pharmacy matures. The concept of pharmaceutical care evolved from clinical pharmacy. Rendering pharmaceutical care is now considered the mission of pharmacy practice by most national pharmacy practice organisations[25]. The concept of pharmaceutical care as espoused by Hepler and Strand[15] (1990) requires pharmacists to have a covenantal relationship with patients concerning the appropriateness of their drug therapy. It also requires pharmacists to share responsibilities and be held jointly accountable for patient care outcomes with other healthcare professionals. Most pharmacy practitioners currently provide only some elements of pharmaceutical care that is primarily directed at making sure that patients receive, take, and understanding their drug therapy, drug distribution, and patient counselling responsibilities[26]. Pharmaceutical care is a process which pharmacists, in cooperation with patients and physicians, design, implement and monitor the drug therapy of patients. It requires operative procedures and an attitude of responsibility to the client for achieving a purpose. The pharmacists must examine what their resources are and what additional resources are needed[24]. The results obtained from the pharmacists involved in this study are very consistent with the literature review presented earlier. The study's findings validate the anecdotal evidence and intuition of academic views presented in the literature, for example by Hepler and Strand[15] (1990), Hepler and Grainger-Rousseau[27] (1995), Starnd[16] (1997). This implies that although most pharmacist interviewed have a commitment to provide pharmaceutical care theoretically, many of them have not read, digested, or comprehended the original paper (Hepler and Strand, 1990)[15] describing pharmaceutical care.

Some of the interviewees made statements such as:

"I have been providing pharmaceutical care for 15 years because I counsel every patient"; "I have been providing pharmaceutical care for 10 years because I attend rounds on every patient and review every drug regimen".

It is obvious many of pharmacists interviewed have trouble taking in this thing called pharmaceutical care. On this issue, Winslade[28] et al. (1996) describe how the faculty of pharmacy at the University of Toronto developed a pharmaceutical care process. The first premise is that pharmacists must accept responsibility for all a patient's drug-related problems, real and potential, and provide a plan to achieve an optimal outcome. Many of the pharmacists interviewed claim that they do this. However, accepting responsibility does not mean that pharmacists do so only during the times the patient is in their presence. Who provides pharmaceutical care and prevents drug-related problems at weekends or during holidays when they are not there? Most of the pharmacists, if not all, said that no body does. This indicates that a minority of pharmacists in those hospitals actually provide pharmaceutical care as it is defined. If they do not do so by taking ultimate responsibility for all aspects of drug therapy, their role in the future will be bleak.

Pharmacists who were interviewed were asked to comment on factors believed to influence the provision of pharmaceutical care in hospitals. From the interview data, it became clear that important changes are required in a number of aspects of pharmacy practice in Saudi Arabia if pharmacists are to provide high quality pharmaceutical care. The data collected supported previous literature, as well as personal experience, that a number of important factors which influence pharmaceutical care provision both positively or a negatively should be taken into consideration. These are:

1. Mission of pharmaceutical care.

2. Organisational structure.

3. Quality and number of pharmacists.

4. Technology and automation support.

5. Pharmaceutical care practice standards.

6. Healthcare professionals' communication.

Information from the pharmaceutical care literature does also suggest that there is a need to explain the constructs of the implementation of the pharmaceutical care management approach. See for example Hepler and Strand[15] (1990); Hatoum[29] et al.; (1992); Hepler[30], (1993); Mcallister[31], (1995); Cotter[32] et al., (1996); Winslade[28] et al., (1996); Odedina[33] et al., (1996). Smith and

Benderev[34] (1991) provided a theoretical basis for expecting a relationship between the development of a management system and pharmaceutical care implementation. He argued that explicit detailing of practice functions is a prerequisite to the development of management systems for the implement of pharmaceutical care.

The results from analysis related to each factor will be discussed below.

1. Mission of Pharmaceutical Care

All of the pharmacists interviewed agreed that departments of pharmacy in their hospitals have to have a clear mission statement and definite goals in order to implement pharmaceutical care. A successful pharmaceutical care practice in these hospitals requires a practice management system that facilitates the work that must be done to implement pharmaceutical care.

"The pharmacy department should determine its mission and also it should be translated into the provision of pharmaceutical care" (Pharmacy Director).

"We update our mission to focus on providing patient-care and outcome-driven drug therapy. The most important decisions we make are those related to the pharmaceutical care implementation in our hospital" (Pharmacy Director).

The pharmacists interviewed indicated that pharmacy departments have to develop annual goals in order to achieve their mission. They reported that stated goals serve to guide and track accomplishment, assign responsibility, and provide clear direction. Of the 15 pharmacists interviewed, 7 indicated that specifically written, documented goals and objectives are developed for the department. The majority of interviewees indicated that the goals and objectives include scope and purpose of service offerings, and department character, quality and reputation.

"Clear goals provide a framework on which to design the pharmaceutical care practice approach. When gaols are clearly set, they are more likely to generate support to the major work of the practice" (Assistant Director of Pharmacy for CQI).

All five cases reported having a clear mission statement and goal that place great emphasis on providing pharmaceutical care to all patients. This finding supports the view that critical prerequisites for developing the necessary commitment are a clear belief in the tangible professional and operating benefits of pharmaceutical care, and the recognition that the traditional pharmacy practice is no longer an option in the competitive healthcare environment[24]. The initial step in organising pharmaceutical care practice is to articulate its mission of the practice. This statement for the fundamental reason of the practice's existence should reflect the practice's commitment to pharmaceutical care. A mission statement is a broad declaration of the basic, unique purpose and scope of operations that distinguishes this practice from others of its type[35]. In highlighting the importance of mission statements, Drucker[36] asserts that it defines that the organisation believes that only a clear definition of mission and purpose of the business makes possible clear and realistic business objectives. It is the foundation of priorities, strategies, plans and work assignments[36]. Furthermore, for the managers concerned, the mission statement can be a benchmark against which to evaluate success. For employees, a mission statement defines a common purpose, nurtures organisational loyalty, and fosters a sense of community[37]. The corporate mission and goals must be conveyed to every employee to be appropriately implemented. In this regard, the findings from all the cases indicate an early responsibility of pharmacy directors is developing a corporate policy and procedures incorporating a statement of mission, department's goals and guiding principles. However, these results supported the intuition that effective communication of mission ensures all employees understand, and are committed to the organisation's direction. Researchers over several decades have highlighted the importance of goals in enhancing organisational efficiency and effectiveness[38]. In this regard, Janning[39] et al., (1996) described implementing comprehensive pharmaceutical services at an academic tertiary care hospital. They indicated that the change to pharmaceutical care requires a clear vision that incorporates pharmaceutical care with practice goals for members. As a result of the commitment to pharmaceutical care at their institution, the department's mission and vision statements were modified to embrace comprehensive pharmaceutical care as the top priority.

2. Organisational Structure

All pharmacists interviewed have stated that the department of pharmacy should establish its own organisational structure. Organisational structure was also found to determine the pharmaceutical care practice. Pharmacists interviewed indicated that their department has a plan to re-evaluate organisational structures to integrate management responsibility for both products and clinical services to maximise quality of service delivered. The majority of pharmacists interviewed indicated that the organisational structure is considered a very important factor to facilitate the pharmaceutical care implementation. They believed that departments that have well-established clinical services may find it to their benefit, from both a resource and quality of service standpoint, to eliminate the separation of the management of clinical pharmacy and product service. They argued that the elimination of this separation will allow for a further expansion of clinical service. All but one case indicated that the pharmacy director reports to the Associate Executive for Patient Service in their hospitals. This finding provides strong support that an appropriate structure can do much to recognise, empower, and encourage the growth of practitioners and practice leaders[40]. This finding validates the anecdotal evidence and intuition of many authors presented in the literature, for example Anderson[41] (1986); Gouveia[42] (1993); Santell[43] (1995); Giese[44] (1996); Chamberlain[45] (1998). Anderson[41] (1986) described changes in the organisational structure at M.D. Anderson Cancer Centre in 1986. Until early 1986, the pharmacy department was part of the hospital and clinics administrative structure. The pharmacy director reported to an associate administrator who in turn reported to the hospital administrator. Through presentations of the department's strategic plan to upper-level system administrators, including the chancellor and the board of regents, pharmacy's visibility increased substantially. The plan demonstrated that pharmacy's role had expanded from the traditional focus on drug distribution to include clinical, research, and academic elements. Based on this perception, the system administrator asked the pharmacy department to develop a plan for establishing pharmacy as a clinical division rather than a hospital and clinics' operational department. In this regard, Raiford[46] et al. (1991) reported that therapeutic drug monitoring and medication counselling were considered by hospital administrators to be important functions of the pharmacy department. Of the 500 administrators responding to the survey, 61% indicated that the pharmacy was grouped with clinical departments, although some had no grouping of clinical or support departments. Furthermore, in a telephone survey conducted by ASHP and Health Concept Inc. (Anon[47], 1991), 85% of senior executives viewed the pharmacy director as effective and very effective in management and communication, respectively; 62% viewed the pharmacy as a clinical service. A national survey was conducted in 1994 in the USA by Santell[43] (1995) which identified the departmental reporting structure and responsibilities of management. The type of executive to whom the pharmacy director reported varied significantly with the occupied-bed size, urban or rural location, and federal and non-federal ownership. As hospital size increased up to 399 beds, pharmacy directors were most likely to report to a hospital executive who primarily manages clinical departments as opposed to operational departments. Moreover, these findings also share some common theme with that of Gouveia[42] (1993); Giese[44] (1996); Woodward[48] (1996); and Chamberlain[45] (1998). They argue that integrated delivery systems are built by teams that make use of professionals from all disciplines in the healthcare organisations. They claimed that the key requirements for comprehensive pharmaceutical care services in integrated healthcare systems are: a shared vision for the pharmacy; establishing a leadership position for the pharmacy; absolute commitment to pharmaceutical care for all patients; and developing a customised portfolio of pharmaceutical services and programmes. So, the study's findings provide strong support that pharmacy departments should redraw the organisational charts, so that all pharmacists may contribute to pharmaceutical care (May[49], 1993).

3. Quality and Number of Pharmacists

Most pharmacists interviewed indicated that the number of qualified pharmacists is a very important factor for the implementation of the pharmaceutical care.

"When you have good and qualified pharmacists and clinical pharmacists, who are willing to be pharmaceutical care providers, then, pharmaceutical care might be implemented" (Clinical pharmacy co-ordinator).

All pharmacists interviewed believed that identifying and acquiring the right number of knowledgeable pharmacists with the necessary skills and motivating them to achieve high performance level is necessary for becoming a pharmaceutical care provider.

"In our pharmacy department, we need to have an adequate number of pharmacists with a high degree in their knowledge and clinical skills" (Pharmaceutical Care Supervisor).

Many authors question the ability of pharmacists to perform all the activities their new role requires. The lack of adequate training for pharmacists is one challenge, to there being more universal availability of these services. A survey of hospital pharmacists in Macon, Georgia, USA, showed that 50% cited lack of training as a barrier to implementing the new concept (Gannon[51], 1992). The study's findings support that one key to increasing the availability of patient-centred pharmacy is the training/retraining provided to them. The findings of this study are very consistent with the findings of Cotter[52] et al. (1996). Their paper focused on observed variations in the overall provision of clinical pharmacy service in UK NHS hospitals and the underlying reasons for such variations. They found that the number of clinical pharmacy services provided was influenced by the number of pharmacists employed. A critical mass of pharmacists was required in order to provide many services.

4. Technical and Automation Support

The data collected supported the view that automation of the traditional services provided by pharmacists such as drug distribution and dispensing should be delegated to pharmacy technicians or automation systems for such service to free pharmacists for quality pharmaceutical care activities.

"All the technical services provided by pharmacists can be easily delegated to the pharmacy technicians or the recent technology advances can be used. The recent technological advances have provided devices that automatically fill medication carts with unit doses and other time saving distributive systems. These automation systems will free up the pharmacist time to assume more responsibility for drug therapy monitoring and patient counselling" (Clinical Pharmacist)

"In my hospital's current economic position, it is not easy to obtain expensive new technology. But, I believe the new technological systems will help so much to free up the pharmacist for clinical tasks" (Pharmacy Director)

The study's findings are very consistent with the earlier findings that automation and technology will lighten the burden of distributive tasks on pharmacists, then enabling pharmacists to redirect their effort towards pharmaceutical care (Macallister[58], 1993; Maine and Penna[59], 1996). In this regard, Gouveia [42] (1993) emphasised that the pharmaceutical care model may exist until the pharmacy departments can develop drug distribution and information systems that require minimal intervention by pharmacists. He argues that automation of drug distribution and the development of a fully integrated clinical information system will give the pharmacy staff the time they need to fulfil their new roles. Ogden[60] et al., (1997) described the transformation of Veterans Affairs (VA) pharmaceutical services. They reported that the VA invested heavily in automation for both inpatient and outpatient dispensing to assist pharmacy staff in meeting dispensing and clinical responsibilities. Bayles[61] et al. (1997) described comprehensive pharmaceutical services in the Unites States Navy. They reported that Navy pharmacy continued to look to automation as one means of meeting many challenges. Navy hospitals have implemented automated prescription-filling equipment. They believed that increased automation of the distribution process will enable the Navy pharmacy staff to spend more time on direct patient care. Furthermore, they indicated that pharmacists will play a greater role in managing patient compliance and take more responsibility for outcomes. The finding of this study is very supportive of the evidence in the literature. All hospitals involved in this study reported that some of the pharmacy distribution processes were automated to reduce the technical tasks of the pharmacist. Although they indicated that automation of these services is costly in establishment, they believe it is worth it on long-term running. They indicated that a pharmacist who spent most of his/her time focussing on distribution tasks, after the automation some of distribution process is now able to spend more time on direct patient care.

5. Pharmaceutical Care Practice Standards

The data analysed do also support the idea advocated in the literature that each hospital should have its own pharmaceutical care practice standards which do not necessary need to resemble those of other hospitals. These standards should be based on clear job descriptions for the various pharmaceutical care tasks needed and should have clear procedures for these tasks.

"We also need clear departmental pharmaceutical care practice standards that establish pharmacists' responsibilities and functions. The practice standards should also state the knowledge and skills needed by pharmacists to meet their new responsibilities" (CQI Pharmacist)

The road of change to pharmaceutical care will not be without difficulties. Standards of practice are expected to be as dynamic as the new practice of pharmacy itself. A broad review of pharmacy literature reveals the absence of most steps of the basic process standard needed for the pharmacy practice (Hatoum[63] et al., 1992; Hutchinson and Schumock[63], 1994). There have been numerous calls for standards of pharmaceutical care practice in the literature. Hutchinson and Schumock[63] (1994) state that:

"Pharmaceutical care will fail if each pharmacy organisation or individual pharmacists are allowed to define pharmaceutical care for their own agenda".

In this regard, Hatoum[62] et al., (1992) argue that pharmacists have not agreed on what constitutes relevant standards for the practice of pharmacy, nor did they decide on meaningful measures to ensure adherence to these standards. According to Hatoum[62] et al. (1992), these steps are not only essential for the definition of pharmacy practice, but also for the assessment of the quality of pharmaceutical care provided. Janning[64] et al. (1996) described implementing comprehensive pharmaceutical services at an academic tertiary care hospital. They reported that the pharmacy department have developed a document identifying standards of pharmaceutical care to be met for all patients in the institution. ASHP [65] (1996) published guidelines on a standardised method for pharmaceutical care. The purpose of this document is to provide pharmacists with a standardised method for the provision of pharmaceutical care in component settings of organised healthcare systems. It has been noted that there is considerable variation in pharmacists' provision of pharmaceutical care in all practice settings. ASHP emphasises the use of this method would foster consistency in the provision of pharmaceutical care in all practice settings. Further, a standardised method would establish consistent documentation, so that patient-specific and medication-related information could be shared from pharmacist to pharmacist and among health professionals (ASHP[65], 1996). Findings from this present study are very consistent with the literature which stresses that pharmacists have to use a standardised process for patient care[66].

6. Pharmacist Authority and Responsibility

Data obtained from the various interviewees provided further piece of evidence concurring with what has already been established in the literature [15, 30]. It was established that pharmacists need well defined authority and responsibility which set the limits of their engagement in providing patient care.

"The hospital should define the boundaries of authority and responsibility for each profession practice in the hospital. For the pharmacy profession, the hospital should revise the pharmacist's responsibility and authority to reflect the hospital's support for the new role of the pharmacist as a pharmaceutical care provider" (Pharmacy Director)

Helper[30] (1993) indicates that after a clear statement of purpose has been identified and agreed upon, planners should be ready to identify the activities necessary to achieve that purpose and to decide the "who, when, and how" of performing those functions. According to Winslade[28] et al. (1996), the pharmaceutical care concept primarily represents a general statement of pharmacists' responsibilities for ensuring optimal therapeutic outcomes for individual patients. They argue that further elaboration of the concept is necessary to facilitate practitioners' understanding of the responsibilities relative to patient care providing. In this regard also, Campagna and Newlin[67] (1997) conducted a study with the purpose of examining factors that may determine why pharmacists perform at different levels of drug therapy decision-making, and suggest factors which could facilitate higher performance. They believe that law and regulation is considered as a key factor affecting many pharmacists' drug therapy decisions. They indicate that laws and regulations define the boundaries of authority and responsibility that society grants to the practice of a profession. So, the finding from this study provided further piece of evidence concurring with what has already been published in the literature.

In general, to maximise the pharmacist's effort to implement the pharmaceutical care concept, these factors should be complemented and established to improve the environment required to provide the pharmaceutical care activities.

Barriers to Pharmaceutical Care implementation in Five Saudi Hospitals

Data analysis from the interviewees conducted in this study indicated that a number of barriers hindering the quality of pharmaceutical care practice do exist. Ironically, these have been found in previous similar empirical studies (Penna[68], 1990; May[49], 1993; Louise and Robertson[69], 1993; Strand and Cipolle[70], 1993; Venkataraman[71] et al., 1997; Bell et al., 1998) to be major obstacles to pharmaceutical care provision in various acute settings. However, the barriers identified tend to fall into five major categories. These are:

1. Lack of time

2. Personnel

3. Lack of administration support

4. Acceptance of these services from other healthcare professionals;

5. Lack of documentation systems

Their importance varies greatly among the five sites. A barrier that has been overcome in one hospital may be a major problem at another. The results of the analysis related to each barrier is presented in the following sections.

1. Lack of Time

Out of 15 pharmacists interviewed in this study, 5 reported that lack of time deters them from providing pharmaceutical care to a very small extent. 3 reported that a lack of time prevents their pharmacists from providing patient-oriented-services at all.

"Pharmaceutical care activities consumed a long time. Much of this time can be utilised in predefined tasks including medication chart checking, drug information, pharmacokinetic dosing and monitoring, and so on, but with the pressure of time, We can not extend the pharmaceutical care activities to cover all our patients" (Clinical Pharmacists).

"Perhaps the most important challenge facing us in this hospital is the lack of time to practice pharmaceutical care. Often, there is not enough time to ensure that our pharmacists review the drug profiles of all patients for drug-related problems within 24 hours of admission" (Clinical Pharmacy Supervisor)

The findings of this study provide strong support that lack of time affects the provision of pharmaceutical care services. In this regard, Venkataraman[70] et al. (1997) conducted a study to assess the extent of pharmaceutical care services offered by community pharmacies in rural West Virginia, and to determine the influence of various facilitators and barriers on the provision of pharmaceutical care services. They reported that the pharmacists' attitude is favourable when adequate time is available for the performance of a pharmaceutical care service. In the acute care setting, May[49](1993) indicates that lack of time to provide pharmaceutical care is commonly cited by pharmacists. In this regard also, Cotter[72] et al. (1997); Bell[73] et al. (1998) reported that lack of time is cited as making routine pharmaceutical care provision difficult to implement. The majority of interviewees involved in this study too stress that lack of time to provide pharmaceutical care is considered a very important barrier to performing the new role of pharmacists.

So, the finding from this study has provided a further piece of evidence concurring with what has already been published in the literature, the direct observation of author in those five hospitals and his own experience as a clinical pharmacist in one of the hospitals involved in this study.

2. Lack of administration support

The analysis of qualitative data indicated that the lack of administration support was considered a major obstacle facing the pharmacists to extend their activities to be pharmaceutical care providers.

*"The major obstacle that we are facing in our hospital is the lack of
administration support to extend the pharmacist's role. The pressure from
administration forces us to spend more time to project and control drug budgets
and less time planning to extend the pharmacists-patient-oriented activities"*
(Pharmacy Director).

In this regard Penna[68] (1990) indicated that if management fails to recognise
the value of pharmaceutical care, no effective system will be created to
encourage practitioners to become professionally involved in the outcomes of
care. Louie and Robertson[69] (1993) argued that pharmacy managers lack
sufficient time to plan for pharmaceutical care and an evolving, patient-centred
practice. Furthermore, May [49] (1993) indicated that hospital administrators
represent a significant barrier. The pressure from the administration may force
the pharmacy managers to spend more time scrutinising the budget for the
next fiscal year and less time planning for pharmaceutical care. The
administrative barrier seems to be strengthened by a lack of statistically sound
studies that clearly demonstrated the value of pharmaceutical care. Cotter [72] et
al. (1997) believe that pharmacy managers have a key role to play in enhancing
pharmaceutical care because they could seek resources from others in the
hospital, allocate resources within the pharmacy and set pharmacy priorities.
They, could, therefore, influence factors such as the amount of time that
pharmacists spend on the ward participating in teams or providing care directly
to patients.

The implication of the finding from the interviews of study is that the pharmacy
department management does not support the activities of those pharmacists
committed to pharmaceutical care. Many of them noted that pharmacy
department in their hospital is one of the weakest departments in the hospital
because the top managers in the hospital administration do not pay any attention
to improve the pharmacy department in the hospitals.

3. Acceptance of pharmaceutical care by other healthcare professionals

Results from the interviews conducted indicated that a number of pharmacists,
particularly clinical pharmacists, reported that physicians and nurses may

perceive that pharmacists are attempting to encroach on their territories.

"Some physicians in my hospital can make problems because they may be unwilling to admit they might be wrong, or need help, and qualified pharmacists often threaten them" (Clinical Pharmacist)

"I feel that some physicians and nurses are reluctant to allow pharmacy to have a large involvement in the provision of clinical services and to expand our role into patient–oriented care" (Pharmacy Director).

"A minority of our physicians in this hospital wanted subservient pharmaceutical care activities. The majority were simply glad that pharmacists were not aggressively promoting the extension of their role" (Clinical Pharmacist)

"Many physicians and nurses did not know what pharmacists could do and the pharmacy department often made little effort to inform them of potential contribution" (Clinical Pharmacist)

There has been much published literature regarding the nature of the relationship between pharmacists and other healthcare professionals (Hepler and Strand[15], 1990; Penna[68], 1990, May[49], 1993; Hepler[74] 1996; Cotter [72] et al., 1997). Hepler and Strand (1990) stated that:

"Pharmaceutical care, as a co-operative activity, would not detract from the other actors in the drug-use process. It would in fact add to their effectiveness by improving the quality of patient care"

It is considered likely that there will be those who will attempt to keep pharmacists in their traditional role by misrepresenting the pharmaceutical care goals and aligning physicians and other healthcare professionals against it[68]. Penna[68], (1990) argues that some healthcare professionals fear that sharing responsibility means sharing the control through which they have maintained successful careers. Physicians have been cited as a potential barrier to the implementation of pharmaceutical care, since they may have traditionally viewed the responsibility for patient outcomes as primarily theirs[49]. Louie and Robertson[69] (1993) contend that many physicians do not accept a non-distributive, clinical role for pharmacists, and that physicians and other healthcare professionals are often unaware that pharmaceutical care could meet a unique need to complement them, without duplicating or threatening their role.

Finding from this study did not indicate, however, when it was better for
pharmaceutical care to be provided directly to patients or through team services.
It is obvious from the Cotter and MicKee[72] (1997) study that most pharmacy
activities tended to initiated and presented through physicians or nurses, then
to patients. This approach seems opposed to the Hepler and Strand[15] (1990)
approach for pharmaceutical care. The significant element of the pharmaceutical
care concept definition includes the element of the process through which
pharmacists cooperate with a **patient** and other professionals in designing,
implementing and monitoring a therapeutic plan. This study has similarly
established that physicians and other healthcare professionals in UK NHS
hospitals viewed the pharmacist's role in a medical team to be not more than
an advisory role. In reality, however, the pharmacist's role, according to the
Hepler and Stand [15] (1990) pharmaceutical care model, base to be responsible
directly to the patient for the purpose of achieving definite outcomes that
improve the patient's quality of life.

4. Lack of documentation system

The majority of pharmacists interviewed indicated that their pharmaceutical
care activities and intervention outcomes are rarely documented, because of
the lack of well-established documentation systems. They believe that greater
attention to the documentation of pharmaceutical services provided by
pharmacists is a prerequisite to ensuring pharmaceutical care in their hospitals.

*"The pharmaceutical care activities and professional functions of pharmacists
must be documented because the role pharmacists are now assuming is different
from what has occurred previously. Unfortunately, the absence of such a
documentation system is a very important obstacle to demonstrate the need for
pharmaceutical care"* (Pharmacy Director).

There has been much published literature regarding the beneficial impacts of
having well established documentation systems in the pharmacy department[15, 29].
Providing pharmaceutical care means documenting the pharmacist's activity[15].
Louie and Robertson [69] (1993) considered a lack of documenting mechanisms
of pharmaceutical care activities as a barrier in the healthcare environment,

and they note that documentation of pharmaceutical care is essential for recording clinical information and drug outcomes, and for assessing the therapeutic benefits and cost-effectiveness of the care. They report that many pharmacists enjoy providing direct patient care, but view documentation of the care as a bureaucratic hassle. Generally, documentation systems are needed to provide evidence that a pharmacist is performing up to expectations and that patients are seeing a significant improvement in outcomes.

Data obtained from this study provided further evidence concurring with what has already been established in the literature that many hospital pharmacy departments have no well documentation systems. Many pharmacy directors involved in this study indicated that one of many challenges that the pharmacy department facing is to measure the clinical pharmacist's performance and to document the interventions of the clinical pharmacist and the impact of these intervention on the patient and hospital outcomes.

Conclusion

In this article, the findings of the study were discussed in general. Although the interpretation of findings showed that the five hospitals in Saudi Arabia are classified as the best government hospitals, only two hospitals have so far implemented a portion of the pharmaceutical care concept, and the rest of the case studies have a plan to introduce this concept in their pharmacies. This article considered the critical factors influencing pharmaceutical care implementation approach and the barriers.

Two of the five hospitals involved in this study have adopted the pharmaceutical care approach as the department mission, and both hospitals articulate their mission to meet the pharmaceutical care requirements. In addition, they are the first two hospitals in KSA to have changed their pharmacy department name from Pharmacy Services Department to Pharmaceutical Care Department. They strive to make the pharmaceutical care idea real, and have used restructuring to tie pharmaceutical care to the actual service. They defined the short-term and long-term goals of the pharmacy department based on their new mission statement. Both hospitals redefined the responsibilities and accountability of all staff to meet their new role. In addition, both hospitals established their own principles and standards for pharmaceutical care practice. The rest of the three hospitals involved in this study were found to be in a transition phase. Although they have a plan to move towards the pharmaceutical care concept, they first have to solve some challenges they are facing. Overall, hospital pharmacy in Saudi Arabia is in a transition phase. Availability of resources and dedicated pharmacists have overcome many difficulties and produced progress in a relatively short period of time.

Attitudes towards Extending the Role of Pharmacists to be Clinical-Oriented

1. The findings of the study suggest the role of pharmacists should be changed from product-orientated to patient-oriented. The study has examined the attitude of pharmacists to change in their role and responsibilities in the hospital.

2. The findings indicated that the majority of pharmacists in both contexts feel the pharmacist's role should be activated and utilised to add value to patient care and reduce overall healthcare cost. Many pharmacists considered the adoption of this approach will save the pharmacy profession from obsolescence. They indicated that a move to patient-centered care with the pharmacist assuming responsibility and liability for the client's care is consistent with the highest calling of a profession.

References

1-ACCP Directory of Residency and Fellowship. American college of Clinical Pharmacy. 1998.

2- Hakim, C. (1994) Research design: Strategies and choices in the design of social research. Routledge Publications, London.

3- Eisenhardt, K. (1989) Building theories from case study. Acad Man Rev, 14:532-50.

4- Zairi, M. (1992) Competitive benchmarking: An executive guide. Technical Communications, Letchworth.

5- Miller, D. C. (1991) Handbook of research design and social measurement, Fifth Edition. Sage Publications Inc, London.

6- Oppenheim, A. N (1992) Questionnaire Design, Interviewing and Attitude Measurement. Second Rev. Edition. Pinter Publishers, London.

7- Moser, C. A. and Kalton, G. (1971) Survey methods in social investigations. Second Edition. Gower Publishing Company Limited, Aldershot.

8- Strauss, A. and Corbin, J. (1990) Basics of Qualitative Research: Grounded Theory Procedure and Techniques. Sage Publications, Newbury Park, CA; London.

9- Miles, M. B. and Hubermans, A. M. (1994) Qualitative data analysis. Sage Publications, London.

10- Guba, E. G (1978) Toward a methodology of naturalistic inquiry in educational evaluation. CSE Monograph Series, 8: ULCA Center for the Study of Evaluation, Los Angeles.

11- Easterby-Smith, M., Thorpe, R. and Lowe, A (1991) Management research. Sage, London.

12- Mikeal, R. L., Brown, T. P., Lazarus, H. L. and Vinson, M. C. (1975) Quality of pharmaceutical care in hospitals. Am J Hosp Pharm, 32:567-74.

13-Brodie, D. C., Parish, P. A. and Poston, L. W. (1980) Societal needs for drugs and drug-related services. AM J Pharm Ed, 44:275-8.

14- Hepler, C. D (1988). Unresolved issues in the future of pharmacy. Am J Hosp Pharm., 45:1071-81.

15- Hepler C. D. and Strand L. M. (1990) Opportunities and responsibilities in pharmaceutical care. Am J Hosp Pharm, 47:533-43

16- Strand, L. (1997) Pharmaceutical care: The Minnesota model. Pharm J, 258:899-904.

17- Pratt, S., Beck, A. and Sperandio, G (1968) Experience in a new clinical pharmacy training program. Am J Hosp Pharm, 25:559-63.

18- Eadon, H., Batty, R. and Beech, E. (1996) Implementation of patient-oriented pharmacy service. Int J Pharm Pract, 4:214-20.

19- Ketley, D., Qualie, J. and Godfrey, B. (1998) The near patient clinical pharmacists:1- From design to pilot. Pharm J, 261:247-49.

20- Cavell, G, Bunn, R. and Hodges, M. (1987) Consultants' view on the developing of the role of the hospital pharmacist. Pharm J, 239:100-2.

21- Fletcher, P. and Barber, N. (1995) The pharmacist's contribution to clinicals ward rounds: analysis by the stages in the drug use process. Int J Pharm Pract, 3:241-4.

22- Haigh, G. and Kiser, L. (1991) Effect of pharmacists' participation on a medical team on costs, charges and length of stay. Am J Hosp Pharm, 48:1457-62.

23- Milliken, B. and Rea, Y. (1997) A clinical pharmacist's contribution to discharge planning and patient counselling. Pharm J, 258:777-8.

24- Hepler, C. (1990) The future of pharmacy: Pharmaceutical care. American Pharmacy, NS30:23-9.

25- Schwartz, M. (1990) Envisioning pharmacy's future: A further commentary on strategic planning. AM J Pharm Edu, 54:167-74.

26- Miller, W. (1997) ACCP strategic planning conference: Issues and trends in clinical pharmacy practice. Pharmacotherapy, 17:1063-7.

27- Hepler, C. and Grainger-Rousseau, T. (1995) Pharmaceutical care versus traditional drug treatment: Is there a difference? Drugs, 49:1-10.

28- Winslade, N., Strand, L., Pugsley, J. and Perrier, D. (1996) Practice functions necessary for the delivery of pharmaceutical care. Pharmacotherapy, 16:889-98.

29- Hatoum H. T., Witte, K. W. and Hutchinson R. A. (1992) Patient care contributions of clinical pharmacists in four ambulatory care clinics. Hosp Pharm, 27:203-9.

30- Hepler, C. (1993) Issues in implementing pharmaceutical care. Am J Hosp Pharm, 50:1635-41.

31- McAllister, J. III (1995) Collaborating with re-engineering consultants: Maintaining resources for the future. Am J Health Syst Pharm, 52: 276-80.

32- Cotter, S., Barber, N. and Chalmers, C. (1996) Factors influencing the provision of clinical pharmacy services in United Kingdom National Health Services hospitals. Inter J Tech Assess Health Care, 12:475-86.

33- Odedina, F., Segal, R., Hepler, C., Lipowski, E. and Kimberlin, C. (1996) Changing pharmacists' practice pattern. J Soc Admin Pharm, 13:74-88.

34- Smith W. E. and Benderev, K. (1991) Levels of pharmaceutical care: a theoretical model. Am J Hosp Pharm, 48:540-6.

35- Pearce, J. and Robinson, R. (1988) Strategic Management. Irwin, Illinois.

36-Drucker, P. (1973) Management: Tasks, responsibilities, and practices. Harper&Row, New York.

37- Nach, L. (1988) Mission statements-Mirrors and Windows. Harvard Business Rev, March-April:155-6.

38- Lee, T., Locke, E. and Latham, G. (1989) Goal setting theory and job performance. In: Pevin, L. (ed). Goal concepts in personality and social psychology. Lawrence Erlbaum, Hillsdale, New Jersey. 291-326.

39- Janning, S., Stevenson, J. and Smolarex, R. (1996) Implementing comprehensive pharmaceutical services at an academic tertiary care hospital. Am J Health-Syst Pharm. 53:542-47.

40- Lazarus, H. and Duncan, W. (1994) Restricting pharmacy department for survival. Am J Hosp Pharm, 51:2827-31.

41- Anderson, R. (1986) Strategic planning for clinical services: The University of Texas M.D. Anderson Hospital and Tumor Institute. Am J Hosp Pharm, 43:2169-73.

42- Gouveia, W. (1993a) Caring for the patient: The implications of assuming responsibilities for patient outcomes. Am J Hosp Pharm, 50:1596-601.

43- Santell, J. P. (1995) ASHP national survey of hospital-based pharmaceutical services-1994. Am J Hosp Pharm, 52:1179-98.

44- Giese, R. (1995) Contribution of pharmacy management to systems' success Scott & Abbott Northwestern Hospital. Am J Hosp Pharm, 53:S18-S22.

45- Chamberlain, M. (1998) The vertically integrated pharmacy department. Am J Hosp Pharm, 55:669-75.

46- Raiford, E., Clark, T., and Andeson, R. (1991) Hospital administrators' perceptions of pharmacy directors. Am J Hosp Pharm, 48:1948-51.

47- Anon. (1991) Hospital executive give pharmacy director high marks. Am J Hosp Pharm, 48:1846-7.

48- Woodward, B. (1996) Contribution of pharmacy management to systems' success Scott & White hospital, clinics & health plan. Am J Hosp Pharm, 53:S13-S18.

47- Chamberlain, M. (1998) The vertically integrated pharmacy department. Am J Hosp Pharm, 55:669-75.

49- May, J. (1993) Barriers to implement pharmaceutical care in the acute care setting. Am J Hosp Pharm, 50:1608-11.

50- Kusserow, R. P. (1990) The clinical role of community pharmacist. Office of the Inspector General, January:1-21.

51- Gannon, K. (1992) Pharmaceutical care, challenge or threat? Hosp Pharm Rep, 6:1-8.

52- Cotter, S., Barber, N. and Chalmers, C. (1996) Factors influencing the provision of clinical pharmacy services in United Kingdom National Health Services hospitals. Inter J Tech Assess Health Care, 12:475-86.

53- Ajzan, I. (1988) Attitudes, personality, and behaviour. Open University Press, Milton Keynes, England.

54- Kiriking, D. A. (1986) Drug utilisation review: A component of drug quality assurance. In: Final Report of APHA Pharmacy Commission on Third Party Programs.American Pharmaceutical Association.Washington, D. C.: 81-91.

55-Lee, M. Fjortoft, N. Gender differences in attitudes and practice patterns of pharmacists. American Journal of Pharmaceutical Education. 57(4): p 313-319. 1993.

56-Fjortoft, NF. Lee, MW. Developing and testing a model of professional commitment. American Journal of Pharmaceutical Education. 58(4): p 370-378. 1994.

57- Odedina, F., Segal, R., Hepler, C., Lipowski, E. and Kimberlin, C. (1996) Changing pharmacists' practice pattern. J Soc Admin Pharm, 13:74-88.

58- McAllister, J. III (1993) Opportunities and imperatives for pharmaceutical care. Am J Hosp Pharm, 50:1621-30.

59- Maine, L. and Penna, R. (1996) Pharmaceutical care—an overview. In: Knowlton, C. and Penna, R. (eds). Pharmaceutical Care. Chapman & Hall, New York:133-153,.

60- Ogden, J., Muniz, A., Patterson, A., Ramirez, D. and Kizer, K. (1997) Pharmaceutical services in the Department of Veterans Affairs. Am J Health-Syst Pharm, 54:761-5.

61- Bayles, B., Hall, G., Hostettler, C., Gibson, J. and Worker, D. (1997) Pharmaceutical services in the United States Navy. Am J Health-Syst Pharm, 54:778-82.

62- Hatoum H. T., Witte, K. W. and Hutchinson R. A. (1992) Patient care contributions of clinical pharmacists in four ambulatory care clinics. Hosp Pharm, 27:203-9.

63- Hutchinson, R. and Schumock, G. (1994) Need to develop a legal and ethical base for pharmaceutical care. Ann Pharmacother, 28:954-56.

64- Janning, S., Stevenson, J. and Smolarex, R. (1996) Implementing comprehensive pharmaceutical services at an academic tertiary care hospital. Am J Health-Syst Pharm. 53:542-47.

65-ASHP (1996) ASHP guidelines on a standardized method for pharmaceutical care. Am J Health-Syst Pharm, 53:1713-6.

66- Filibeck, D., Petroroff, B., Sinsnowski, L. and Teahan, J. (1999) Developing managed care plan. Am J Health-Syst Pharm, 56:1348-9.

67- Campagna, K. and Newlin, M. (1997) Key factors influencing pharmacists' drug therapy decisions. Am J Health-Syst Pharm, 54:1307-13.

68- Penna, R. (1990) Pharmaceutical Care: Pharmacy's mission for the 1990s. Am J Hosp Pharm. 47: 543-49.

69- Louise, N. and Robertson, N. (1993) Barriers to pharmaceutical care in the managed care setting. Am J Hosp Pharm, 50:1614-17.

70- Strand, L. M., Cipolle, R. and Morley, P.C. (1990a) Drug-related problems: Their structure and function. DICP, 24:1093-97.

71- Venkataraman, K., Madhavan, S., and Bone, P. (1997) Barriers and facilitators to pharmaceutical care in rural community practice. J Soc Admin Pharm, 14:208-19.

72- Cotter, S. and McKee, M. (1997) A survey of pharmaceutical care provision in NHS hospitals. Pharm J, 259:262-68.

73- Bell, H., McElnay, L., Hughes, C. and Woods, A. (1998) A qualitative investigation of the attitudes and opinions of community pharmacists to pharmaceutical care. J Soc Admin Pharm, 15:284-95.

74- Hepler, C. D. (1996) Pharmaceutical care. Pharm World Sci, 18: 223-25.

Quality has to be learnt before it gets practised: Teaching Principles of Excellence Using the European Quality Award Model

By Prof. Mohamed Zairi
Head of the European Centre for
TQM University of Bradford UK
March 2005

Abstract

As the Business Community moves into the 21st Century through pioneering
with the Quality Concept, the academic debate on the merits / de-merits of
TQM as a sound management approach will continue to rage on.

The paper argues the case for TQM in the education provision context. It
highlights the importance of TQM to providers of academic courses, particularly
in a Higher Education environment. The paper pinpoints the importance of
focusing on core processes, customer orientation and the emphasis on
continuous improvement, measurement and TQM-based competitiveness.

In order to support the various arguments presented, the paper discusses an
approach adopted at Bradford Management Centre (UK) to teach TQM at
postgraduate MBA level, using the European Quality Award Model as the
framework for the course design and delivery. The paper then concludes by
presenting some key arguments on the importance of 'linkages' for a total
approach to delivering academic excellence. An evaluation of the 'Bradford
Pilot' is also included, together with useful comments from some of the
participants in the MBA programme.

1. The TQ Imperative in Higher Education

The upsurge of TQM introduction in Higher Education and in particular Business Schools, has been quite significant over the past few years. Froiland (1993) argues that the spread of TQM can be found in courses, classroom methods and administrative processes. Similarly, Bruce & Tseng (1993) through a survey of 117 U.S. Business Schools, have looked at the impact of TQM on organisational changes, faculty development and curricular changes. Although the benefits reported have been modest, it is however generally agreed that TQM is perceived to be a 'necessary evil' in this day and age (Ardaiolo, 1994; Clayton, 1993). Bhattacharya et al (1998), in outlining the initiation of a TQM program in an academic department and the research centre of a business school, have concluded that the whole process brought with it a keener awareness of the goals of the school and its constituent departments. One of the key outcomes they reported was particularly a stronger focus on the needs of customers/constituents of the departments and pilot projects when applying TQM concepts to selected key activities.

Although other writers have been more cautious with their views on the usefulness and level of impact TQM brings with it when applied in the context of Higher Education, and in particular Business Schools, non-the-less, there seems to be a consensus reached on the appropriateness, applicability and usefulness of TQM in the aforementioned context. Koch & Fisher (1998) argue that TQM encourages colleges and universities to collect data that enables them to measure their progress in key areas and this, against themselves and against others. Michael et al (1997) referred to TQM as 'the saving grace' for the future of Higher education institutions.

2. TQM In Business Schools: What Are The Benefits?

The changes in teaching and learning have been accelerated by the advent of new technology, low cost publications, electronic media and the computer. They all have had a significant impact on the provision of education in Business Schools to date. The drive for achieving superior quality standards and delivering excellence is well noted and highlighted by various researchers (Sallis, 1993; Cowles, 1993). Others have also noted that quality improvement has

become important to give Business Schools better control over their destiny
(Tang & Zairi, 1998; Sallis, 1993). Williams (1993) argues that TQM has
becomes part of the education vocabulary through the provision of business
studies degrees.

Motwani and Kumar (1997) reported that some of the tangible benefits often
observed are improved communication, higher employee morale, increased
productivity, improved process efficiency, reduction in defects and costs.
Peters (1999) on the other hand, suggests that TQM can give business schools
the opportunity to enter new markets and to jockey for position against
competitor providers. Melan (1998) highlights the importance of leadership
and 'constancy of purpose'. He points out that leadership and change facilitation
are additional contingencies influencing the outcome of introducing TQM.

Kanji & Tambi (1999) suggest that TQM can be evaluated in institutions of
higher learning such as Business Schools, and that there is compatibility between
the academic and business ethos; with similar arguments Reavill (1998)
introduces the notion that the quality assessment process has contributed and
will continue to contribute to the improvement in the provision of education in
Business Schools. Greensted (2000) puts a view, based on the UK experience,
that existing quality assessment processes are often unable to lead to a
significant impact since they rarely provide opportunities for benchmarking
Business Schools against Best In Class practices. He suggests that a migration
from concentrating on subject specific quality assurance or an accreditation
of specific programmes (from professional membership to a total accreditation
approach), is the most logical way forward. Models such as the Malcolm
Baldrige National Quality Award (MBNQA) and the European Quality Award
(EQA), will permit such a progression, since these two approaches are capable
of providing a total examination.

3. The European Quality Award Model as a Model for Teaching Quality

The European Quality Award (EQA) Model similarly to the Malcolm Baldrige
Award, despite several criticisms for some shortcomings (Garvin, 1992; Crosby
et al, 1991), are representing a significant step in offering a more holistic and

widely accepted TQM framework.

The EQA Model is based on the premise that Excellence is business dependent on 8 fundamental concepts. These include:

- Customer Focus

- Leadership and Constancy of Purpose

- Management by Processes and Facts

- People Development and Involvement

- Continuous Learning, Improvement and Innovation

- Partnership Development

- Public Responsibility

- Results Orientation

The EQA Model is thought to have predictive ability on Business Performance. As stated by Sir Peter Bonfield, CEO, British Telecom (1999):

"A Business is not just about measuring profit and loss. You can't keep score just using profit and loss, which is essentially a measure of yearly outcomes, the result of decisions taken several years ago. You need something which says 'if you do that then you will have long term success'…and the Model allows you to do that."

(EFQM, 1999)

The 8 Fundamentals of Excellence are therefore an extremely useful start for developing teaching courses related to the notion of quality excellence. It seems that the EQA Model offers academics with 2 sets of opportunities:

- Re-aligning the processes of academic delivery and related support functions so that the emphasis is on quality improvement and customer satisfaction;

- Preaching what is practised by teaching the concepts that really add value in terms of modern learning and in terms of developing the right competencies which are compatible with business needs.

In 1999, a revised version of the European Quality Award Model was launched to re-emphasise the point that Excellence comes from being results-orientated, customer focussed and through harnessing organisational capability to the full.

Figure 1 illustrates the Revised Version of the Excellence Model, which is deemed to be more dynamic, simple, holistically orientated and generic. The arrows in the framework capture the dynamic aspects, in which innovation and learning improve the enablers, leading in turn to improved results. The improved model is also more attuned to modern business requirements. Concepts such as innovation and the learning organisation are much more evidently stressed. The revised model also places emphasis on such as the management of partnerships and knowledge, and strengthens the focus upon customer and staff satisfaction.

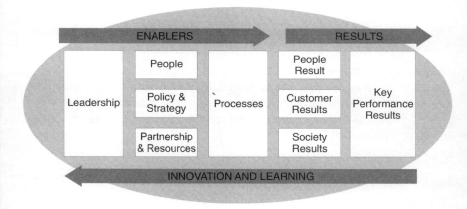

Figure 1.0 The Enhanced Excellence Model

In sum the model is premised on the notion that excellent results with respect to Performance, Customers, People and Society are achieved through Partnerships and Resources, and Processes.

The boxes, shown in Figure 1, represent the criteria against which to assess an organisation's progress towards excellence. Each of the nine criteria has a definition, and is broken down into sub-criteria that help develop the meaning of that criterion. The criteria are defined in table 1.0 below.

Table 1.0: The Excellence Models' Criteria for Assessment

Criterion 1: Leadership

How leaders develop and facilitate the achievement of the mission and vision, develop values required for long term success and implement these via appropriate actions and behaviours, and are personally involved in ensuring that the organisation's management system is developed and implemented.

Sub-criteria:

Leadership covers the following four sub-criteria that should be addressed.

1a. Leaders develop the mission, vision and values and are role models of a culture of Excellence

1b. Leaders are personally involved in ensuring the organisation's management system is developed, implemented and continuously improved

1c. Leaders are involved with customers, partners and representatives of society

1d. Leaders motivate, support and recognise the organisation's people

Criterion 2: Policy and Strategy

How the organisation implements its mission and vision via a clear stakeholder focused strategy, supported by relevant policies, plans, objectives, targets and processes.

Sub-criteria:

Policy and Strategy cover the following five sub-criteria that should be addressed.

2a. Policy and Strategy are based on the present and future needs and expectations of stakeholders

2b. Policy and Strategy are based on information from performance measurement, research, learning and creativity related activities

2c. Policy and Strategy are developed, reviewed and updated

2d. Policy and Strategy are deployed through a framework of key processes

2e. Policy and Strategy are communicated and implemented

Criterion 3: People

How the organisation manages, develops and releases the knowledge and full potential of its people at an individual, team-based and organisation-wide level, and plans these activities in order to support its policy and strategy and the effective operation of its processes

Sub-criteria:

People cover the following five sub-criteria that should be addressed.

3a. People resources are planned, managed and improved

3b People's knowledge and competencies are identified, developed and sustained

3c People are involved and empowered

3d People and the organisation have a dialogue

3e People are rewarded, recognised and cared for

Criterion 4: Partnerships and Resources

How the organisation plans and manages its external partnerships and internal resources in order to support its policy and strategy and the effective operation of its processes.

Sub-criteria:

Partnerships and Resources cover the following five sub-criteria that should be addressed.

4a. External partnerships are managed

4b. Finances are managed

4c. Buildings, equipment and materials are managed

4d. Technology is managed

4e. Information and knowledge are managed

Criterion 5: Processes

How the organisation designs, manages and improves its processes in order to support its policy and strategy and fully satisfy, and generate increasing value for its customers and other stakeholders.

Sub-criteria:

Processes cover the following five sub-criteria that should be addressed.

5a. Processes are systematically designed and managed

5b. Processes are improved, as needed, using innovation in order to fully satisfy and generate increasing value for customers and other stakeholders

5c Products and Services are designed and developed based on customer needs and expectations

5d Products and Services are produced, delivered and serviced

5e Customer relationships are managed and enhanced

Criterion 6:Customer Results

What the organisation is achieving in relation to its external customers.

Sub-criteria:

Customer Results cover the following two sub- criteria that should be addressed.

6a. Perception Measures

6b. Performance Indicators

Criterion 7: People Results

What the organisation is achieving in relation to its people.

Sub-criteria:

People Results cover the following two sub- criteria that should be addressed.

7a. Perception Measures

7b. Performance Indicators

Criterion 8: Society Results

What the organisation is achieving in relation to local, national and international society as appropriate.

Sub-criteria:

Society Results cover the following two sub- criteria that should be addressed.

8a Perception Measures

8b. Performance Indicators

Criterion 9: Key Performance Results

What the organisation is achieving in relation to its planned performance.

Sub-criteria:

Key Performance Results cover the following two sub-criteria that should be addressed. Depending on the purpose and objectives of the organisation some of the measures contained in the guidance for Key Performance Outcomes may be applicable to Key Performance Indicators and vice versa.

9a Key Performance Outcomes

9b Key Performance Indicators

Amongst some of the key areas where improvement has taken place include the explicit incorporation of the importance of supply chain management and partnerships, as a key driver for the former. The second improvement relates to innovation and learning. A third feature of improvement is in the development of RADAR logic (see Figure 2), which helps operationalise the model for self-assessment. RADAR provides the central logic, at the heart of the model, determining the search for performance improvements. The fundamental building blocks of the concept underpinning corporate excellence are Results, Approach, Deployment, Assessment and Review

The RADAR logic consists of four elements:

Results	-	Determining results required.
Approach	-	Planned and developed approaches that deliver effective results.
Deployment	-	The systematic implementation of approaches.
Assessment of Review	-	The analysis, monitoring, learning and prioritisation of Improvement plans.

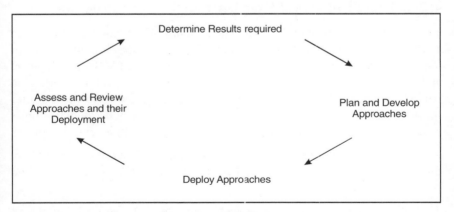

Figure 2. Radar Logic

According to RADAR logic an organisation needs to:

Determine the Results the organisation is aiming for as part of its policy and strategy making process. These results should cover the full range of performance metric (financial, operational, and the perceptions of its stakeholders). Next it should plan and develop an integrated set of sound Approaches to deliver the required results, now as well as into the future. The company should then attempt to reap the benefit from the fruits of its labour by Deploying the selected approaches in a systematic way to ensure full and proper implementation. Finally the organisation should assess and Review the approaches adopted by monitoring and analysing the results achieved. Based on this it should identify, prioritise, plan and implement improvements where needed and subsequently embed the learning into the organisation.

The Excellence Model provides a framework that can assist businesses to gauge themselves against the 8 fundamentals of excellence (discussed previously), from the point of view of answering the question: *" Where are we now?"* and *"Where should we be in the future?"* These 8 fundamentals of excellence are applicable to the academic context, as was the case of The Bradford MBA Programme.

4. Teaching Principles of Excellence on the MBA Program

The review of the Bradford Management Centre MBA conducted between 1995 and 1996 highlighted a number of problems with the curriculum. One of the main criticisms to emerge out of the literature review of MBA development and discussions with members of the department is the lack of integration between courses. As businesses are increasingly moving towards flatter organisational structures and cross-functional management it would be remiss of the Management Centre not to reflect these changes in its curriculum.

The intention is to introduce a cross-functional management "core" throughout the whole programme, which will reflect these trends in industrial and commercial developments.

The rationale for an Integrative Management Course based on Principles of Excellence.

The underlying intent of introducing a cross - functional management "core" into the programme is the need for managers to understand the challenges of working in a cross - functional way and think beyond functional disciplines in developing innovative and creative solutions to management problems. The cross-functional management stream, as envisaged, is multi-faceted.

The main elements to be included reflect:

- the skills required to operate in a cross functional organisation

- critical elements of "good practice" with which modern organisations are currently grappling

The Integrative Management compulsory core course therefore plays a vital role in the cross-functional core: principally it is concerned with outlining the importance of interfaces between business functions and the value of viewing organisations as holistic entities where actions in one area impact on decisions in another.

The aims of the course

The aim of the course is to extend student knowledge and understanding beyond business functions into the realm of inter - disciplinary management. Many organisations are now recognising that competitive advantage can be best derived from managing the interfaces between disciplines. This course focuses on why this should be the case and how firms can manage processes rather than functions.

It could be possible to argue that by simply adding a subject labelled "Integrative Management" this course perpetuates the compartmentalisation of business disciplines. However, its positioning within the structure of the programme (a course which ties themes together and build links between previously studied functional disciplines) should avoid this being the case.

What makes attending this course essential?

" Nothing in the world of business is static: processes, products, cash, service to customers, should be changing for the better all the time. The pressures for change in this modern world will never stop and there is never a perfect business - simply one which is temporarily better than- its competitors"

Source: Sir John Harvey - Jones "All Together Now" Mandarin 1995.

Managers face accelerating levels of change in their working environment as business strives for superior performance through increased competitiveness and improved efficiency. This intensity of change and commitment is universal across both the private and public sectors as organisations seek to maximise the benefits to be gained from their finite resources.

Since the early 1990s a growing number of organisations have emerged who are committed to the principles of total quality management. This is hardy surprising given the international research and in particular the Bradford Studies of 1996 and 1991 which clearly indicated that organisations committed to total quality management sustain significantly improved bottom line results compared to their peers in the same industry sectors. What underpins their success is the integrative rather than disparate approach adopted to business management. Vertical cross-functional structures have replaced the traditional horizontal and functional structures and with it a completely different managerial approach.

What has not been available, until now, is the knowledge and learning which managers can gain from a close look at the integrative management practices and behaviours which underpin superior performance.

Many traditional management practices have been challenged by these organisations and superseded by new practices which address the requirements of today's market. This course will expose delegates to these modern approaches to business management and in particular the critical success factors, which have emerged from these successful organisations.

How has this course been researched?

Research was focused on the management practices and behaviours of leading organisations who were committed to total quality management. Typically these were organisations who were recipients of the various prestigious quality awards such as the Malcolm Baldrige National Quality Award (USA), the European Quality Award, the British Quality and the Deming Prize (Japan). All the organisations examined have a clear and consistent purpose together with a flair for innovation and continuous improvement that produce exceptional results.

What has emerged from the research are new management practices that have challenged the traditional practices and produced outstanding results. Furthermore, now that quality has reached a higher level of maturity in many organisations critical success factors for total quality management are beginning to emerge.

This course offers a unique opportunity to gain insights into these management practices, critical success factors and understanding of the methodology, which underpins the application of best practice management.

Who will benefit from this course?

The course will specifically benefit senior and middle managers wishing to update and enhance their managerial skills through a practical course based on the experience of leading organisations across different industry sectors.

It is envisaged that many of the best practice approaches will spark the imagination of delegates and with adaptation where appropriate, enable implementation back at their work place.

What will be the key learning from this course?

The course is designed to expose delegates to the latest management tools and techniques, which address such current issues as:

- How can managers balance the need for customer focus with the requirements of all the stakeholders?

- How can world class practices be developed which lead to competitive advantage?

- Is the role of manager a thing of the past in an empowered environment?

- How can staff who perform a support role understand the need for customer focus?

- How can managers work smarter by measuring and managing the right things and not wasting time on trivialities?

- How can quality move from talk to full integration within the business?

- How can managers build a learning organisation where staff is committed to life long learning?

- Should an organisation have a social conscious?

- How can teamwork and people management be so important today with increased technology and automation?

- Is the quality system an administrative nightmare or managerial asset?

The core elements of the syllabus are drawn from the European Quality Award framework now familiar to many world-wide organisations. The course will comprise the following elements:

- Overview and perspective of integrative management

- The role of leadership in the modern business context

- Formulation and integration of policy and strategy into the business

- Managing people resources in the work place

- Deployment of resources to optimise effectiveness

- Managing business processes

- Determining the level of customer satisfaction

- Measuring people satisfaction within the organisation

- Establishing corporate responsibility to Society

- Measuring business performance

- World class performance

Some of these elements will inevitably cut across areas of business management studied further in the elective stage of the programme. Such overlap is not considered problematic, indeed it will enable students to better understand the context of areas of management studied later in the programme.

In terms of knowledge, students should be able, by the end of the course to:

- understand how functions are linked together in an organisation by way of critical processes
- identify frameworks for summarising business processes

The main skills and competencies being sought relate to:

- an ability to identify linkages between functions in an organisation
- an ability to be proactive in suggesting appropriate business solutions to process-based problems
- an ability to synthesis and interpret complex information
- an ability to co-operate and work in teams.

How is the course taught?

The course runs as an intensive week long module and comprises a wide range of teaching methodologies including:

- Formal lectures / seminars
- Group discussion and workshops
- Video presentations

The rationale for the intensive teaching mode is that the course is not knowledge intensive: it focuses on applying existing knowledge and extending understanding through exploration of key issues.

The course comprises 80 hours of learning and is made up as follows:

- 20 hours session preparation and reading
- 40 hours teaching and group interaction
- 20 hours preparation time for project

What is the structure of the course?

Block 1 - The role of leadership in the modern business context

- Organisational vision, values and mission
- Management training and commitment
- Role model behaviour
- Developing a continuous improvement environment
- Involving customer and suppliers
- External promotion of quality culture

Block 2 - Formulation and integration of policy and strategy into the business

- Planning process
- Data sources and feedback loops
- Determining business priorities
- Benchmarking and competitive analysis
- Policy deployment process
- Review and updating process

Block 3 - Managing people resources in the work place

- People selection, assessment and development.
- Investors in People
- Core skill requirements.
- Development, training and career maps
- Role of teamwork and target setting
- Communication process

Block 4 - Deployment of resources to optimise effectiveness

- Financial strategy formulation, budget preparation and review process

- Investment decision making models
- Supply chain management
- Technology application
- Creativity
- Cost of quality using different models

Block 5 - Managing business processes

- Identification of critical processes
- Development of performance measures
- Management of processes
- Role of quality systems and standards
- Process management using measurement tools and techniques
- Review and improvement of processes
- Innovation

Block 6 - Determining the level of customer satisfaction.

- Critical attributes of customer satisfaction.
- Direct measures of customer satisfaction
- Indirect measures of customer satisfaction
- Collecting satisfaction data through surveys, mystery shoppers, competitor analysis
- Complaint handling and root cause analysis
- Deployment of customer satisfaction data systems

Block 7 - Measuring people satisfaction within the organisation

- People satisfaction attributes
- Health, safety and security

- Data collection methods.
- Deployment of data systems
- Reward and recognition systems

Block 8 - Establishing corporate responsibility to Society
- Preserving global resources
- Impact and involvement on local communities
- Developing environmental responsibility awareness within the business
- Support for education and training
- Establishing effective measures for environmental awareness.

Block 9 - Measuring business performance
- Challenging the traditional approach to performance measurement
- Determining operational effectiveness
- Asset management
- Competitive analysis
- Measuring innovation

Block 10 - World class performance
- Dispelling the myth of world class performance
- Identifying who are world class players
- Implications of world class on your business
- Taking the course learning back into the workplace
- Questions and answers

How is the course assessed?

The course is assessed by way of an individual project (100%). An examination would be inappropriate in a course of this nature given it is not primarily knowledge based. •

For full - time students this is based on case study material from which students are expected to extrapolate information about business functions to build a picture of business processes.

For part - time students, the project is company - based, students being required to build a picture of business processes within their own organisation.

The aim of the assessment is to ensure that students understand how different business functions interact within an organisation and can make prescriptions about how these cross - function processes can be effectively managed.

6. Programme Evaluation and Students' Feed back:

Surveying various cohorts of both full time and part-time students who have attended the course carried out the evaluation of the programme. Since this was a new innovation, it was deemed to be necessary to gauge students' feed back on a variety of aspects. Table 2 illustrates the outcomes of the survey:

Evaluation Criteria	Student Cohort (both Full & Part Time)					Mean
	1	**2**	**3**	**4**	**5**	
Relevance of Course content	5	5	4	5	4	**4.6**
Presentation Quality	5	5	5	5	4	**4.8**
Appropriateness of teaching/learning mode	4	4	4	4	3	**3.8**
Understanding of subject	4	5	4	4	4	**4.2**
Value of Assessment	4	3	4	4	3	**3.6**
Appropriateness of Skills Development	5	5	5	4	4	**4.6**
Overall Impression	5	5	5	5	4	**4.8**
Level of Prior Knowledge (%)	30	30	30	40	15	

Table 2: Teaching TQM by using the European Excellence Model

The various groups of students who have participated in this program have found the course of high relevance, with high learning outcomes and very appropriate for the development of skills and expertise. Although they all had relatively low experience with TQM in the past, their understanding of the subject has significantly increased (4.2 out of 5). The students would have liked to space out the course over a longer period of time so that the learning outcomes from the teaching mode used can be better enhanced, through regular discussions and mini-projects on each of the teaching blocks. Furthermore, suggestions were made on the usefulness of introducing the key elements of the course during the foundation induction week (at the beginning of the academic year), in order to enable an accelerated and advanced approach when the course is scheduled to run. Overall however, the students have had a very good impression of the course (4.8 out of 5), with many comments saying that this is the best course they have ever attended.

7. Conclusion: Excellence in Business is dependent on linkages

The premise of the course was to demonstrate that MBA courses should demonstrate the levels of synergy between them without any sub-optimisation and certainly with no reference to 'prima donna' effects. It seemed that the EQA Model would provide the ideal opportunity for doing so. As far as the various linkages are concerned, students were taught that the various principles of Excellence, as defined by the EQA Model, would converge in one focal point (i.e. the overall corporate performance. Individual aspects of excellence which implicitly explain how functional business topics are taught was shown from the point of view of WHAT type of contribution they make and WHERE are the likely areas they link with and thereby influence.

The usefulness of the Bradford Program concurs with findings from similar experiments. For instance the experience of using the MBNQA in the U.S., reported by Karathanos (1997) and Bernard (1999) who looked at the usefulness of TQM in Business Studies, at Rochester Institute of Technology. Bernard concluded that a TQM approach can increase students' learning in a class, help students support one another in a co-operative learning environment, and foster feelings towards the instructor.

Professor Mohamed Zairi

Professor Zairi is the Juran Chair in Total Quality Management based at the University of Bradford in the UK. Professor Zairi holds a BSc. (Hons) in Polymer Sciences and Technology, a MSc. in Safety & Health and a PhD in Management of Advance Manufacturing Technology.

Professor Zairi has written over 300 papers and 20 books covering different aspects of management, 4 of them in the area of Benchmarking specifically. He is recognised as a leading authority in the fields of Benchmarking and Performance Measurement. Professor Zairi lectures world-wide and has acted as adviser to many large organisations and various government bodies in different countries such as the Middle East, Malaysia and Europe.

Professor Zairi is the Head of the European Centre for Total Quality Management. He oversees a large portfolio of research projects in the TQM and related fields, and leads various sponsored projects on TQM. He is the company-Editor of the TQM Magazine and the founder editor of Business Process Management Journal and benchmarking: An International Journal.

References

Crosby, Philip B.; Reimann, C. (1991), 'Criticism and support for the Baldrige Award', Quality Progress, March pp.21-21

EFQM (1999), Eight Essentials of Excellence – The Fundamental Concepts and their Benefits, European Foundation for Quality Management, Brussels, Belgium

Garvin, D.A. (1992), 'Does the Baldrige Award Really Work?', Harvard Business Review, Vol.70, No.1, pp.126-147

Karathanos, D. (1997), 'Using the Baldrige Criteria to teach an MBA level TQM Course', Quality Management Journal, Vol.6, Issue 1, pp.19-28

Froiland, Paul. (1993), "Total Quality Management is being introduced into courses and classroom methods in business schools and in higher education overall", Training, Vol.30, No7, pp. 52-56, July 1993

Melan, E.H. (1998), "Implementing TQM: A contingency approach to intervention and change", International Journal of Quality Science, Vol. 3, Issue 2, pp. 1 – 16

Reavill, L.R.P. (1998), "Quality Assessment, Total Quality Management and The Stakeholder in the UK Higher Education System", Managing Service Quality, Vol. 8, Issue 1, pp. 1 – 9

Kanji, G.K. & Tambi, M.A. (1999), "Total Quality Management in UK Higher Education Institutions", Total Quality Management, Vol. 10, No 1, pp. 129 – 153

Peters, J. (1999), "Educational Accreditation Through ISO 9000", Quality Assurance in Education, Vol. 7, Issue 2, pp. 1 – 6

Motwani, J. & Kumar, A. (1997), "The need for implementing total quality management in education", International Journal of Educational Management, Vol. 11, Issue 3, pp. 1 – 6

Bhattacharya, T.; AlDiab-Zoubi, T.; Sukar, A. (1998), "Application of total quality management concepts to a business school", International Journal of Technology Management, Vol. 16, Issue 4-6, pp. 520 – 531

Koch, J.V. & Fisher, J.L. (1998), "Higher Education and Total Quality Management", Total Quality Management, Vol. 9, No 8, pp. 659 – 668

Michael, R.K.; Sower, V.E.; Motwani, J. (1997), "A comprehensive model for implementing total quality management in higher education", Benchmarking for Quality management & Technology, Vol. 4; Issue 2, pp. 1 – 12

Barnard, J. (1999), "Using Total Quality Principles in Business Courses: The Effect on Student Evaluations", Business Communication Quarterly, Vol. 62, No 2, June 1999, pp. 61 – 73

Tseng, D.P; Stern, B. (1993), "U.S. Business School's Reaction to the Total Quality Management Movement", Journal of Education for Business, Vol. 69, No 1, pp. 44 – 48

Ardaiolo, F.P. (1994), "Using Total Quality Management (TQM) to Enhance Weekend Student Life", Journal of the Freshman Year experience, Vol. 6, No 1, pp. 53 – 68

Clayton, M. (1993), "Towards Total Quality Management in Higher Education at Aston University – A Case Study", Higher Education, Vol. 25, No 3, pp. 363 – 371

Tang, K.H. & Zairi, M. (1998), "Benchmarking quality implementation in a service context: A comparative analysis of financial services and institutions of higher education – Part II", Total Quality Management, Vol. 9, No 6, pp. 407 – 420

Sallis, E. (1993), Total Quality management in Education, Kogan Page Ltd, London, UK.

Williams, G. (1993), "Total Quality Management in Higher Education: Panacea or Placebo?", Higher Education, Vol. 25, No 3, pp. 229 – 237

Cowles, D. and Gilbreath, G. (1993), "Total Quality Management at Virginia Commonwealth University: An urban struggle with the realities of TQM", Higher Education, Vol. 25, No 3, pp. 281 – 302

Greensted, C. (2000), "Measure for Measure or A Pound of Flesh? (A comparison of quality assurance schemes)", The International Journal of management Education, Vol. 1, No. 1, November 2000, pp. 3 – 10

An Empirical Investigation on HR-TQM Relationship in Education:

The Case of Malaysian Universities

by

Noor Azman Ali, ECTQM, Bradford University,
n.a.ali1@bradford.ac.uk
Mohamed Zairi, ECTQM, Bradford University,
m.zairi@bradford.ac.uk

Abstract

The aim of this paper is to provide evidence on the reliability and validity tests of human resource (HR) related critical success factors (CSFs) in TQM implementation. This involves identifying and defining the HR-related CSFs from an exhaustive source of literature reviews on quality initiatives. In higher education (HE) contexts, TQM programmes emphasise very much on management commitment, effective HR management and quality working attitudes towards achieving customer satisfaction. Therefore, the 'soft' or HR aspects in the literature review stand as the fundamental issue for organisational management in quality planning and creating a quality working climate to ensure successful expected performance. Using SPSS, ten HR-related CSFs that have high arithmetic mean scores and reliability coefficients, were further validated using exploratory factor analysis method. The HR-related CSFs were re-examined and revised into nine factors, and are recommended to be included in similar research in other service contexts than simply HE.

Keywords: TQM, Human Resource Management, Critical Success Factors, Service Quality, Reliability, Higher Education

1.0 INTRODUCTION

TQM is not just an organisational management programme or management-initiative package, but a complete change in an organisation's culture and the way people behave at work. TQM definitions, philosophy, approaches and models have been discussed in many organisational contexts by many quality gurus from various perspectives. Oakland (1989) defined TQM relevant to HRM perspective as:

> "An approach to improving the effectiveness and flexibility of business as a whole. It is essentially a way of organising and involving the whole organisation; every department, every activity, every single person at every level. For an organisation to be truly effective, each part of it must work properly together, recognising that every person and every activity affects and in turn is affected by others."

This definition focuses on functional integration and employee involvement, but says nothing on the customer. However, it recognises the importance of organisational co-ordination for quality, which can be enhanced, for example, by conducting departmental purpose analysis - tasks negotiated between organisational members, thus smoothing workflow and inter-departmental co-ordination.

Generally, a study on TQM implementation can be focused on either 'hardware' (especially the tools and techniques) or the 'software' (mainly the human resource aspects) (Wilkinson, 1992). This study is mainly concerned with the soft or people issues, and usually the more qualitative aspects of a TQM programme, consisting of HRM policies and activities to generate commitment to quality and the dissemination of management vision and ideology that may reinforce the maxims of quality working environment, cultural change, continuous improvement and customer orientation.

The phrase critical success factors (CSFs) itself indicates the importance of the concept to ensure the success of any particular process or project. From the perspective of decision management, Ferguson and Dickinson (1982) define CSFs as those internal and external factors that must be identified and reckoned with, as they are capable to support or threaten the achievement of a company's objectives. In other words, they should be seen as opportunities or threats in the organisation's strategic planning process. Therefore, CSFs are the key areas that need to be carefully identified where 'things must go right' for a programme or business to succeed.

2.0 HR-RELATED CSFs IN QUALITY INITIATIVES

The following discussions will define ten HR-related CSFs that were used in previous research on quality initiatives, and mostly in service organisations contexts.

2.1 Visionary leadership

The 2003 Education Criteria of the Malcolm Baldridge National Quality Awards (MBNQA) define visionary leadership as:

> " The organisation's senior leaders who should set directions and create a student-focused, learning-oriented climate, clear and visible values and high expectations, which should balance the needs of all stakeholders."

(NIST, 2003)

Top managers carry the primary responsibility for commitment to quality and support efforts necessary to achieve the organisational goals, and as the architects of change initiatives who provide a sense of direction for the workers and organisation, particularly in successful TQM implementation (Crosby, 1979; Garvin, 1983). In TQM implementation, leaders are responsible for developing and communicating the company vision, and then building organization-wide commitment in the people in order to achieve the specified goals.

2.2 Customer- focus orientation

Like other industries, customers in HE institutions are the main element for quality initiatives. It is essential to identify them, along with establishing the processes to determine each of their needs to be satisfied (Spanbauer, 1995; Owlia and Aspinwall, 1996). Gap 5 in the SERVQUAL model (Parasuraman et al., 1990) indicates that it could be a major service deficiency if the organisation fails to identify and provide the right specification for customer needs. Therefore, customer-focused organisations involved in quality initiatives should believe that business operations would improve by satisfying customers' needs and requirements. The customers' degree of satisfaction will be the main indicator to determine the level of quality performance.

2.3 Effective communication

Effective communication ensures employees' clear understanding about the TQM programme, and is also useful to overcome barriers to changes leading towards the quality improvement. In TQM, communication should happen at all level, through all aspects of operations (Dale and Cooper, 1993). Furthermore, in the HE context, Lewis and Smith (1994) suggest that effective communication will break down barriers between departments and programmes, and between faculties, administration, staff, and students. Sherr et al. (1992) argue that the working culture of most colleges and universities would have to be transformed through effective communication in training and education, and that top management alone can develop the total quality mindset in people throughout the organization. Therefore, in the HE environment, quality communication is indicated within the function to adapt quality programmes to the internal and external customers, and to promote a network of cooperation between staff and students.

2.4 Congruent objectives

Deming (1986) suggests that congruent objectives in quality management will drive out the fear of uncertainty in people, and is the best way to create a quality environment. According to Juran (1974) and Oakland (1993), to keep quality objectives aligned with the employees' efforts, results should be communicated to every member and be made a basis for continuous improvement. Meanwhile, Gaps 2 and 3 in the SERVQUAL model by Parasuraman et al. (1988) explain clearly the effect of a lack of congruent objectives between management on the service provided by employees, in terms of service perception. Nonetheless, the common objectives in TQM are to increase productivity, maximise resource utilisation (or total cost and capacity management), and at the same time, be sure of customer satisfaction.

2.5 Staff selection and deployment

Employee selection is a HRM decision process that is made on the basis of an assessment on the suitability of a group of potential individuals who might fill job vacancies (Redman and Wilkinson, 2001; Canziani, 1996; Rees and Doran, 2001) and suggests that, from a TQM perspective, selection processes are designed to identify individuals who possess quality-related competencies. However, according to Ahmed and Schroeder (2002), selection criteria may involve the 'hard' or tangible aspects, such as technical and academic qualifications, and also the 'soft' aspects or behavioural skills. Staffing or staff deployment through the 'rightsizing' and 'ability-job-fit' technique in quality management essentially involves analysing a unit's or department's personnel needs based on its long-term quality objectives, and the overall company needs, and finding the combination of permanent and temporary employees with the best skills and competencies to meet those needs (Rhinehart, 2000).

2.6 Competent staff

Woodruffe (1993) defined competencies as " the set of behavior patterns that the incumbent needs to bring to the position in order to perform its tasks and functions with competence". Deming (1985) suggests that TQM requires specific technical knowledge and the ability to maximise the impact from each of the methods applied, which would determine the quality of performance. Meanwhile, the Carter et al. (2000) findings suggest there is a need for management staff to have the skills and commitment in key strategic decisions, and there is a need for employees to be involved in more tactical decisions. These are both important in the success of TQM. In order for the employees to perform an excellent job as expected, they need to have the knowledge, skills and capabilities relevant to the tasks specified which are critical to provide quality services.

2.7 Teamwork spirit

Teamwork in the TQM perspective is seen as " everyone in an organisation is personally managing and continuously improving their own process, and working together in teams to improve their service to the customers". Hackman and Wageman (1995) and Behara and Gundersen (2001) find that TQM practices emphasize teamwork and cross-functional relationships that provide many opportunities for social interaction and social reinforcement. These show that the spirit of team working is one of the main features of TQM culture. The Black and Porter (1996) study identifies teamwork structures to represent efforts made to develop organizational structures in support of quality improvement initiatives. The study also explicitly ties teamwork to the importance of integrated management at all levels of service and organization in the overall quality performance. Therefore, a quality working culture of teamwork spirit is an important condition for successful TQM implementation.

2.8 Rewards and motivation

A reward policy in HRM which involves a selection of a range of rewards being designed and administered (such as being linked to a performance assessment exercise) is crucial, with the ultimate aim of motivating employees to contribute effectively to a set of organisational mission. Hackman and Wageman (1995) claim that among the evidence they reviewed for the discriminant validity of TQM was the fact that TQM explicitly eschews a number of popular motivational devices, including work redesign (e.g. job enrichment), goal setting (e.g. management by objectives), and performance-contingent rewards (e.g. pay for performance). Therefore, the studies suggest that organisations must develop formal systems to encourage, track, and reward employee involvement to maintain a high level of employee motivation towards excellent performance.

2.9 Training and education

Deming (1982) explains that what an organisation needs in TQM implementation is not just good people, but people who are continually improving with training and education. Dale and Cooper (1993) and Oakland (1995) claim that training is one of the most important factors for continuous improvement. Saraph et al. (1989) suggested that TQM requires technical and attitudinal knowledge, and specific training for employee understanding is necessary. Ramirez and Looney (1993) and Thiagarajan (1996) categorised quality education as the first tier factor, which specifies one of the roles of top management in implementing an excellent quality programme, in a validity survey, ranking the importance of CSFs in TQM implementation. Moreover, HR development and management examine the key elements of how the HE institutions develop and realise the full potential of their workforce in pursuing the quality and excellent performance objectives.

2.10 Innovation and creativity

The MBNQA defines innovation in the 2003 Education Criteria Version (NIST, 2003) as" ... making meaningful change to improve programmes, services, and processes, and creates new value for students and stakeholders. It involves the adoption of ideas, processes, technology, or product that is new or new to its proposition." In the service quality context, Ziethaml, Parasuraman and Berry (1990) suggest that service design is a form of architecture involved in process, interaction and the evaluation of outputs to ensure customer satisfaction. However, the creative idea is to design high quality into service systems after considering and responding to customers' expectations. In the HE context, the design of teaching systems, the course materials and content delivery to the students are the important interactions in the overall quality product/service design.

585

3.0 HR-RELATED CSFs IN TQM RESEARCH FRAMEWORK

Based on the above discussions, it is hypothesized that Visionary leadership, Customer- focus orientation, Congruent objectives, Effective communication, Staff selection and deployment, Competent staff, Teamwork spirit, Training and education, Rewards and motivation, and Innovative product/service design are the HR-related CSFs in TQM implementation for HE. Figure A illustrates how the hypothesized relationships are seen to be the valid composition for the CSFs' elements in quality initiatives for the HE context. The conceptual model suggests that those critical factors identified, as they have been used in previous research, as HR-related for the management of the higher institutions to put special attention as to ensure successful quality initiatives. However, this research would only give a quantified measurement of each factor on the reliability of the claim in the higher education context. The causal equation this paper considers is that successful quality initiative (Y) is affected by ten HR-TQM critical factors. That is,

$$Y = f(X_1, X_2, X_3, X_4, X_5, X_6, X_7, X_8, X_9, X_{10})$$

The equation suggests that the ten HR-TQM critical factors are the determinants for successful TQM implementation. However, this research is not keen to analyse the coefficients of each factor, which are more relevant in the regression projection research objective.

The reliability of a measure or research element is established by testing both consistency and stability (Sekaran, 2003). Consistency indicates how well the items measuring a concept hang together as a set of research constructs. Stability indicates the ability of a measure to remain the same over time, despite uncontrollable testing conditions and low vulnerability to changes in the situation. Consistency of measures that are free from random error means reproducibility of the same answer, and are therefore reliable. The larger the measurement error, the lower the reliability of the measure. Reliability in the test is shown by a high correlation between measures, which means the homogeneity of items underlying the construct (Bryman, 2001).

Figure A: CSFs in TQM Implementation for HE Context

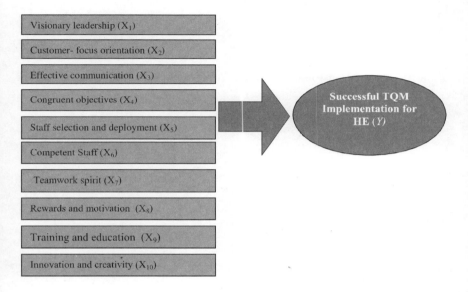

The internal consistency was measured using Cronbach's alpha reliability coefficient. Cronbach's alpha is a common reliability coefficient that indicates how well the items in a set are positively correlated to one another (Sekaran, 2003). It is computed in terms of the average intercorrelations among the items in measuring the concept. The closer alpha is to 1, the higher the internal consistency reliability.

4.0 FINDINGS AND DISCUSSION

Using the SPSS reliability analysis program, an internal consistency analysis was performed separately for the items of each critical factor. Table A shows the values of alpha (i.e. reliability coefficient) computed for each factor. Generally, an alpha of 0.60 or higher will be considered adequate in exploratory research (Black and Porter, 1996; Hair et al., 1999).

The alpha values range from 0.6381 to 0.8981, thus providing strong evidence that the scales developed are judged to be 'acceptable' in term of reliability. The high alpha coefficients indicate that since inter-item correlations are high, there is evidence that the variables are measuring the same underlying construct of factors specified. The low variance of mean given by the output supports the research evidence that the items used have minimum variability of scores.

Table A: Internal Consistency Reliability Analysis for HR-TQM Critical Factors

HR-TQM CSFs	Cronbach's α value	Standardised item α	Variance of mean
	0.8981	0.8977	0.0025
	0.7562	0.7563	0.0261
	0.8302	0.8323	0.0210
	0.6454	0.6652	0.0850
	0.6393	0.6381	0.0460
	0.7026	0.7090	0.0358
	0.7234	0.7318	0.0928
	0.8639	0.8655	0.0097
	0.7835	0.7797	0.0465
	0.7606	0.7665	0.0062

The analysis can improve the measurement construct by either removing low coefficient variable/s, or combining several variables into a particular construct, and of course with justifiable reason. The original 4 items for the critical factor Staff selection and 5 items for Staff competency were combined, and the alpha value increased from 0.6381 and 0.7090, respectively, to 0.7485. The new alpha coefficient can be used with justification that staff selection and competent staff are perceived as common in broader perspective (Rees and Doran, 2001). The factors were reviewed using exploratory factor analysis outputs, and were combined and renamed Staff selection and competencies.

5.0 CONCLUSION

The theoretical discussions and empirical analysis from the data collected justify ten HR-TQM critical factors, which are relevant to quality initiatives in the HE context. They are visionary leadership, customer focus, effective communication, congruent objectives, staff selection and deployment, competent staff, teamwork spirit, training and education, rewards and motivation, and innovation and creativity. The survey suggests that HR-TQM factors given as independent constructs are significant as determinants of successful quality initiatives in Malaysian HE context. The reliability internal consistency test suggests that all of those factors are acceptably reliable to be used in a similar research context. The improved internal consistency of Cronbach's alpha suggests that if research would take a relatively high reliability coefficient (that is above 0.70) the critical HR-TQM factors that can be revised. It is suggested to revise the variables with justifiable theoretical grounds, supported with further statistical analysis, and with renaming when necessary. The findings signify the degree of criticality, and nine variables were included as HR-related CSFs. The reliability of variables and construct validity of HR-related CSFs in a quality initiative measured the concept and phenomena that were appropriate to be applied in related research.

References

Ahmed, S. and Schroeder, R.G. [2002] The importance of recruitment and selection process for sustainability of total quality management. International Journal of Quality and Reliability Management, vol.19, no.5, pp. 540-550.

Behara, R.S. and Gunderson, D.E. [2001] Analysis of quality management practices in services. International Journal of Quality and Reliabiltiy Management, vol.18, no.6, pp. 584 -604.

Black, S.A. and Porter, L.J. [1996] Identification of the critical factors of TQM. Decision Science, vol.27, no.1, pp. 1-21.

Bryman, A. [2001] Social Research Methods. Oxford University Press: N.York.

Carter, J.R., Smeltzer, L.R. and Narasinham, R. [2000] Human resource management within purchasing management: Its relationship to total quality management success. Journal of Supply Chain Management, vol.36, no.2, pp.52 -62.

Crosby, P. [1986] Quality is Free . McGraw Hill: New York.

Deming, W.E. [1986] Out of Crisis. MIT Press; Cambridge

Ferguson, C.R. and Dickinson, K. [1982] Critical success factors for directors in the eighties. Business Horizon, vol.25, no.3, pp. 14-19.

Field, A.[2000] Discovering statistics using SPSS for Windows. Sage: London

Garvin, D.A. [1983] Quality on the line. Harvard Business Review, vol.61, no.5, pp. 65-75.

Hackman, J. and Wageman, R. [1995] Total quality management: Empirical, conceptual and practical issues. Administrative Science Quarterly. vol.40, no.42, pp. 309-342.

Hair, J.F., Anderson, R.E., Tatham, R.L. and Black, W.C. [1995] Multivariate data analysis (4th edition). Prentice-Hall: New Jersey.

Juran, J. M. [1981] Product quality: A prescription for the west (Part I). Management Review,vol.70, no.6, pp. 8-14.

Juran, J.M. [1974] The Quality Control Handbook, 3rd Edition. McGraw Hill: New York

NIST [2003] MBNQA Criteria 2003, Malcolm Baldridge Award 2003 Education Criteria for Performance Excellence, National Institute of Standards and Technology, www.quality.nist.gov/

Oakland, J.S. [1993] Total Quality Management. Heinemann: Oxford.

Parasuraman, A., Zeithaml, V. and Berry, L. [1988] SERVQUAL: a multiple-item scale for measuring consumer perception of service quality. Journal of Retailing. vol.64, no.1, pp. 12-40.

Redman, T. and Wilkinson, A.[2001] Contemporary human resource management: Text and cases. London: Prentice-Hall.

Rees, C.J. and Doran, E. [2001] Employee selection in total quality management context: taking a hard look at a soft issue. Total Quality Management, vol.12, no.7/8, pp. 855-860.

Rhinehart, E. [2000] Quality management is a journey, not just a destination. Managed Healthcare. vol.10, no.5, pp. 52-54.

Saraph, J.V., Schroeder, R.G. and Benson, P.G. [1989] An instrument for measuring the critical factors of quality management. Decision Sciences, vol.20, no. 4, pp. 810-829.

Sekaran, U. [2003] Research Methods for Business: A Skill Building Approach. 4th Edition, John Wiley: New York.

Thiagarajan, T., Zairi, M. and Dale. B. G [1996] A proposed model of TQM implementation based on an empirical study of Malaysian Industry. International Journal of Quality and Reliability Management. vol.18, no.3, pp. 289-306.

Wilkinson. A. [1992] The other side of quality: 'soft' issues and the human resource dimensions. Total Quality Management. vol. 3, no.3, pp. 323-329.

Woodcruffe, C. [1993] What is meant by a competency? Leadership and Organisational Development Journal, vol.14, no.3, pp. 29-36.

Author's Background

Dr Noor Azman Ali is a Research Associate at the European Centre for TQM, Bradford University, working as a part of the post-doctoral programme at the School of Management. Since 1998, he has been a Lecturer at the University Putra Malaysia, and in 1987-1998, he served as a Finance Officer at the same university in Malaysia. His wide range of educational background covers Doctor of philosophy (Bradford University), Master of Business Administration (Wolverhampton University), Bachelor in Business Administration (Ohio University, Athens), Diploma in Research Methods (Bradford University) and Diploma in Business Studies (Universiti Teknologi MARA). Dr Noor Azman is actively involved in various research areas, particularly in the applied TQM scope including; TQM in education, HRM-TQM relationships in quality initiatives, Organisational behaviour in quality programmes, ISO9000 implementation in higher education contexts, Customer satisfaction survey in universities, Integrated Performance Management and Performance measurement in service quality. The author can be contacted at: ECTQM, Bradford University, Bradford, BD9 4JL United Kingdom, or email at n.a.ali1@bradford.ac.uk. Telephone contact numbers are: 00-44-1274 234317 (o) and 00-44- 7900 677283 (m).

Professor Zairi is the Juran Professor of Total Quality Management based at the European Centre for TQM, University of Bradford in the UK. Professor Zairi holds a BSc.(Hon.) in Polymer Sciences and Technology; and MSc. in Safety & Health and PhD. in Management of Advanced Manufacturing Technology. He has written over 300 papers and 10 books covering different aspects of management, 4 of them in the area of benchmarking specifically. He is recognised as a leading authority in the fields of Benchmarking, Best Practice Management and Performance Measurement. Professor Zairi lectures world-wide and has acted as adviser to many large organisations and various government bodies in different countries such as the Middle East, Europe and Malaysia. He can be contacted at: ECTQM, Bradford University, Bradford, BD9 4JL United Kingdom, or email at m.zairi@bradford.ac.uk. Telephone contact numbers is: 00-44-1274 234311.

Does
TQM Impact on
Bottom-line Results?

by

M. Zairi, S.R. Letza and J.S. Oakland

Introduction

In discussions of business behaviour, very often one hears expressions such as "TQM is a journey not a destination". These are meant to highlight that the business quest for progress and advancement is never ending. This can create, however, a dichotomous situation in so far as managing business organizations is concerned. Many managers, while not denying the need for continuous improvements, are presented with a difficult situation. They are expected to show consistent results in the marketplace in the short term while having to reconcile the short-term gains with the long-term opportunities for improvement.

Nearly all the published literature on TQM and the models of implementation consider the need for management commitment. Management commitment, however, while very instrumental in the whole process of introducing TQM, may not be enough to generate success in the market place. Many failures in TQM implementation have been attributed to factors such as:

- the executive promotional ladder;

- executive bonuses and the resultant interest in short-term results;

- shareholder pressures.

There are, however, wider and more complex factors which make the need for commitment more encompassing and more widely spread. There is a need, for example, for internal commitment of all employees and a willingness to combat waste, reduce costs and carry out

consistent improvements. There is also required the commitment of shareholders and financial institutions, in taking a long-term interest in business performance. This is crucial if performance sustainability is to be the objective. Finally, commitment of governments in preparing the right climate for business, right incentives and adequate protection is also crucial for results to be consistently achieved.

The issues in relation to TQM, therefore, are twofold. There are needs for:

(1) short-term benefits in enhancing profit levels and initiating growth; and

(2) long-term benefits through ensuring sustainability and consistency in achieving repeated superior performance standards;

In order that TQM can be conducive to (1) and (2), its implementation has to be carried out in a very systematic way, without any wavering in commitment levels, without any hesitation and deferral in the decision-making process.

The following questions need to be observed for TQM to start leading to pay-offs:

- Does the organization understand its purpose?
- Is there a vision/mission and some clear goals?
- Has the vision and the TQM plan been communicated effectively?
- Have all the goals been deployed effectively?
- Have employees been trained, educated and motivated (empowered) to carry out the improvement efforts?
- Is the organization externally focused?
- Does it understand its customer requirements?
- Is it confident in understanding and appreciating what takes place in the market place?
- Are appropriate tools, techniques, teams and systems in place?
- Do improvement efforts get measured?

Increasingly, comments such as: "TQM failed to help businesses perform in the marketplace" appear in the literature, but what about the question: did businesses fail to introduce TQM effectively and as such failed to perform in the marketplace? Many examples of poor business performance could be traced back to poor implementation of TQM. In many instances TQM implementation has lacked strategic focus and has been introduced as a bolt-on to unchanged business culture. The link between TQM and business performance may be established only if the previous questions have been answered honestly.

The Malcolm Baldrige National Quality Award (MBNQA) came under severe criticism recently. The fate of some of the Baldrige winners led them to face business difficulties which were reflected in bottom-line results. In addition, the organizers of the MBNQA may have conveyed the message to the business community and the public at large that, by winning the award, there is guaranteed business success. In particular, MBNQA came under attack in three main areas:

First, winning the award requires such high resource commitment and high levels of expenditure that it can be considered a "purchased item". Reference was particularly made to Rank Xerox which was reported to have spent in excess of $800,000, and to the finalists, Corning, which devoted approximately 14,000 man hours preparing the application.

The alternative argument is, of course, that both companies were investing in a five-year quality improvement programme and decided to use the MBNQA as the driving force. In a sense, they were using the award criteria as an audit and self-assessment framework. This is why Garvin[1], who interjected to defend the MBNQA, suggested:

The best way to understand the Baldrige criteria is as an audit framework, an encompassing set of categories that tells companies where, and in what ways, they must demonstrate proficiency – but not how to proceed. The categories are in no sense a "to do" list, and it is simply incorrect to suggest that the criteria specify particular programs or techniques.

There is no Baldrige system to be bought off the shelf.

Second, the MBNQA fails to lead to superior quality standards. Reference was made to Cadillac, which won the award in 1990. Cadillac failed to rank at the top among other automobile producers in terms of quality and reliability of its products. The director of the MBNQA, Curt Reimann[2], defended by arguing that:

We've taken a lot of flak on Cadillac...I think they really ought to see the improvements that are being made in these companies and see how much they have dug in with quality systems, getting workers empowered and trained and educated...My belief is that you could walk out of Cadillac with a very long list of very impressive things to do.

Third, winning the MBNQA does not lead to improvements in business results. Critics once again picked on the performance of some previous winners such as Cadillac, Federal Express and Motorolla in which market shares have dropped and which suffered decreases in general profitability levels. The argument presented to defend the MBNQA was that its purpose is really to strengthen business long-term survival rather than to enhance profit improvement, as Garvin[1] explains:

The Baldrige Award and short-term business results are like oil and water: they don't mix and were never intended to.

He also argued that the MBNQA was intended as a strong predictor for long-term survival and this is really how Wall Street and the public at large should look at it. It is very easy to locate companies with good bottom-line results but not so easy to locate those with a good quality improvement approach.

There is, however, a major shortcoming of the MBNQA in its approach. By placing less emphasis on results, it almost suggests that quality should be taken on board as an act of faith. By giving attention to leadership and management of processes, companies may devote too much effort in putting the structural and methodological aspects in place but fail to capture the benefits. Without measuring the impact of TQM, efforts may be doomed to failure. Indeed, it has been reported by one major consultancy that some organizations are expressing serious concern about not seeing "daylight" with their TQ initiatives[3]. The pursuit of a vision without any clear results, has been explained nicely by a Japanese professor, Shoji Shiba[3], who said that:

"When you consider something 'ideal', you lose the opportunity to improve it."

The US General Accounts Office (GAO) Study

A report published by the GAO in 1990 represented the first attempt ever to link TQM practice and bottom-line results. The study focused on the top 20 scorers of the MBNQA in the period 1988-1989. Using a combination of questionnaire and interview method, the companies concerned were asked to provide information on various performance measures, including:

- employee related indicators;

- operating indicators;

- customer satisfaction indicators;

- business performance indicators.

Consistently the respondents saw improvements in all the suggested indicators (Table I). A list of factors was identified, which were thought to be critical in leading to improvements in business performance:

- a customer focused approach to quality;

- strong leadership;

- employee empowerment;
- corporate culture;
- use of hard facts;

Type of indicator	Number of companies	Score (Favourable)	(Unfavourable)	No change
Employee-related indicators				
Employee satisfaction	9	8	1	0
Attendance	11	8	0	3
Turnover	11	7	3	1
Safety/Health	14	11	3	0
Suggestions	7	5	2	0
Operating indicators				
Reliability	12	12	0	0
Timeliness of delivery	9	8	1	0
Order-processing time	6	6	0	0
Errors or defects	8	7	0	1
Product lead time	7	6	0	1
Inventory turnover	9	6	1	2
Cost of quality	5	5	0	0
Cost savings	9	9	0	0
Customer satisfaction indicators				
Overall customer satisfaction	14	12	0	2
Customer complaints	6	5	1	0
Customer retention	10	4	2	4
Financial performance indicators				
Market share	11	9	2	0
Sales per employee	12	12	0	0
Return on assets	9	7	2	0
Return on sales	8	6	2	0
Source: GAO (1991)[4]				

Table I.

TQM-based Performance Achievement of Top 20 Companies (Highest Scorers in Malcolm Baldrige Criteria)

- developing strong partnerships with suppliers.

598

The GAO study, even with its various shortcomings, is a major initiative in trying to establish cause-effect relationships between TQM practice and bottom-line results. There are, of course, issues which could be raised about the study.

For instance:

- Sample of companies examined. It could be argued that these are all "blue-chip companies" and, therefore, would have been expected to perform well, regardless of TQM.

- The list of indicators used is not exhaustive. For example, they do not reflect investment programmes, market changes and conditions and other factors which may have caused improvements in bottom-line results.

- The information is supplied in a subjective manner by the companies concerned. There is no real proof to support or dismiss the claims made.

- The size of the companies examined. Although 20 companies were examined, only nine companies tended to answer consistently all the questions.

The US GAO study, in spite of its shortcomings, prompted the Bradford researchers to examine the link between TQM and bottom-line results, using a different approach.

The Bradford Study

The Bradford Study was conducted in order to establish whether similar patterns of behaviour were emerging within European companies which are pioneering TQM and trying to enhance their competitiveness.

Unlike the Japanese and US situations, where TQM has tended to be more widely publicized, it is not easy in Europe to identify companies which have truly adopted TQM. Choosing companies for the study was, therefore, a much more difficult process.

An additional difficulty was the quality of information to be used for analysis. It is difficult to obtain internal information on how companies measure performance and results in the context of TQM. This is because TQM performance-based measurement is not a very advanced practice in Europe and companies find difficulty in establishing the extent of TQM in enhancing competitiveness, in terms of specific performance measures. The authors believe that to enable this to happen, there will need to be a focus on patterns and trends over a long period of time.

Taking the argument presented by Garvin and others, the authors believe that TQM is more likely to lead to long-term impact rather than short-term gains. As such, it was the intention not to look for absolutes in terms of achievements but rather to obtain a picture of positiveness and improvements in financial performance, over a reasonable time period.

It was considered inappropriate to use information collected directly from companies for the following reasons:

- a wide diversity of internal measurement methods are employed by companies and consequently comparison would be, at the very least, difficult;

- access to sensitive information would be prohibitive. This was experienced by the GAO study in which only 45 per cent of the companies approached provided information.

Methodology

For the reasons suggested above, the Bradford study focused on externally reported information which is more readily available, and more importantly, which is subject to external standards as specified in company law and the accounting profession's statement of standard accounting practice. The information is also subject to independent scrutiny by professionally qualified auditors. Externally reported information was, therefore, considered a reliable source of information from which patterns of behaviour and performance could be examined.

One of the questions which had to be established was the time frame over which it was reasonable to expect TQM to deliver benefits. Using the experience of the researchers and information from the multitude of case studies in the literature of companies which have implemented TQM, it was decided that, if TQM had been introduced with a clear mission, tangible goals, a sound plan and real action, then it is reasonable to expect benefits within a period of five years.

The sample of companies was carefully selected for the study, based on direct knowledge and understanding of specific TQM approaches adopted by each individual company. In all, 29 companies were selected. The analysis focused on their performance over a five-year span.

The mean for each company was calculated over the five years for each performance indicator. The performance under each indicator for each company was compared to the appropriate industry median. The median rather than the mean was used to avoid distortion of the results from very large or very small companies.

The sample of the 29 companies does not represent any specific industry sector. The companies chosen are of different size and reflect different resource availability and different standing in the marketplace.

How Was TQM Defined?

An all-encompassing definition of TQM was chosen for the purpose of this study. Since the different companies were at different stages of TQM implementation and, since they were likely to have adopted different routes and approaches, it was felt necessary to place emphasis on the positive drive for quality improvement in satisfying the end customer. The chosen definition was:

A positive attempt by the organizations concerned to improve structural, infrastructural, attitudinal, behavioural and methodological ways of delivering to the end customer, with emphasis on: consistency, improvements in quality, competitive enhancements all with the aim of satisfying or delighting the end customer.

In all the TQM initiatives carried out by the selected companies the following critical factors were visible:

(1) Leadership elements:

- mission/vision statement,
- quality policy,
- direction,
- goals,
- communication processes,
- measurement,
- quality decisions,
- strategic planning and deployment, and
- customer/market focus.

(2) Hard elements:

- tools and techniques,
- measurement,
- systems,
- procedures,
- specifications, and
- standards.

(3) Soft elements:

- problem-solving approach,
- team work,
- innovation/creativity,
- continuous improvement philosophy,
- empowerment,
- incentives, and
- process-based approach.

Findings

The findings indicated that a high proportion of the companies examined exhibited above industry average performance:

- For profit per employee 79 per cent of the companies showed positive quanta in comparison with industry median.
- Average remuneration in 93 per cent of the companies studied is higher than their industry median.
- Total assets per employee is positively exhibited in 79 per cent of the companies.
- A total of 76 per cent of the companies are showing positive returns on total assets.
- Turnover per employee in 79 per cent of the companies is higher than the corresponding industry median.

602

- A total of 76 per cent of the companies studied showed healthier profit margins than industry median.

- A total of 72 per cent of the companies examined showed an above industry median fixed asset trend.

- Number of employees trend is not conclusive but 17 of the 29 companies studied have, over the five years studied, increased rather than shed employees.

The eight indicators chosen for carrying out the comparisons reflect business performance both in the short term and the long term. They include "softer" or people related measures, such as employee trends and remuneration. In combination, the eight performance indicators show a consistently positive pattern of performance between the selected companies and industry medians.

The authors believe that these patterns suggest that there is a positive association between the introduction of TQM and tangible benefits. The companies studied were selected on the basis of existing knowledge of their TQM initiatives and not their standing in the marketplace.

Although it is not possible to prove direct causation, since other factors may be present, the consistency of the results does point towards a

strong association. This European-based study, together with the US GAO study and other studies in Japan, provides strong evidence that total quality management does have a direct impact on financial results, provided its implementation is well directed and planned and provided there is strong commitment in sustaining continuous improvements which focus on benefits for the end customer.

The results of this study by no means suggest that TQM leads directly to improvements in bottom-line results. TQM merely offers companies the opportunity to carry out improvements and focuses on getting closer to customers. It is only a license to practice. Companies must still have the right strategies in place, the right products and services, the right commitment, and the right investment strategies in order to be successful.

Further Research

There are opportunities for further research and the following themes are the subject of current research under way at Bradford Management Centre:

- subsequent trends in performance of the 29 companies concerned, in order to establish increases or decreases in performance since TQM introduction;

- examination of companies which are known not to subscribe to TQM philosophy, in order to assess patterns of performance, using the eight indicators;

- examination of newly emerging companies to see whether they take TQM on board and what kind of performance levels they exhibit.

Finally, the crucial question: How can TQM impact on bottom-line results?

In order to answer this question, the authors refer to the following comments from John Hudiburg[5], previous chairman and CEO of Florida Power & Light, the first overseas company ever to win the Japanese Deming Prize. He strongly believes that, by focusing on the customer, any organization can achieve healthy business results. In relation to the Japanese, he explains:

The Japanese study the customer. Then they study the customer again. Their entire process, internal as well as external, is directed towards the customer. By serving the customer they believe they will gain market share and corporate health. It is taken as a given that, if they are better than anyone else at serving the customer, they will have strong sales and thereby make greater profits. Their ideology says first comes customer satisfaction, then sales, then profits.

References

1. Garvin, D.A., "How the Baldrige Award Really Works", Harvard Business Review, November-December, 1991, pp. 80-93.

2. Lopez, C.E., "The Malcolm Baldrige National Quality Award: It's Really Not Whether You Win or Lose", The Quality Observer, November 1991, pp. 1, 5, 13-14, 20, 23.

3. Dickson, M., "Bouquets and Barbed Ire", Business Times, 3 February 1992, p. 10.

4. General Accounts Office Study, USA, 1991.

5. Hudiburg, J.J., Winning with Quality – The FPL Story, Quality Resources, a division of the Kraus Organization Limited, New York, NY, 1991.

Further Reading

Clark, F. , Money, A. and Tynan, C., Total Quality Management: Senior Managers' Views, Henley Management College, 1991.

Goulder, J., "Stop Paying Lip-service and Start Measuring", Business Marketing Digest, Vol. 16 No. 2, Q2, 1991, pp. 39-46.

Howard, D., "A Limited Understanding", Total Quality Management, April 1991, pp. 91-4.

M. Zairi, S.R. Letza and J.S. Oakland are at the University of Bradford Management Centre, Emm Lane, Bradford BD9 4JL, UK. Tel: 0274 733466; Fax: 0274 546866.

> " *Technology confers wonderful benefits on society, but it also makes society dependent on the continuing performance and good behavior of technological goods and services. This is 'life behind the quality dikes' - a form of securing benefits but living dangerously. Like the Dutch who have reclaimed much land from the sea, we secure benefits from technology but we need good dikes - good quality - to protect us against the numerous service interruptions and occasional disasters.* "

- Joseph Juran
on a Seminar titled
"An Abbreviated History of
Managing for Quality in the U.S.A."

Wider Issues

Perspectives
Social Responsibility
and impact on
society

Mohamed Zairi

First Published in

The TQM Magazine
Volume 12 . Number 3 . 2000 . pp. 172±173
© MCB University Press . ISSN 0954-478X

The author

Mohamed Zairi is SABIC Chair in best practice management, Management Centre, University of Bradford, UK.

Keywords

Social responsibility, Corporate image, Environment

Abstract

Discusses an area which is growing in terms of significance and proven to impact on business performance, reputation and corporate image. Discusses social responsibility from the point of view of environmental issues and ethical considerations. Useful examples of models for the effective management of environmental issues are provided, together with examples of best practice. Finally, proposes a framework for auditing this very pertinent area of business excellence.

Electronic access

The research register for this journal is available at
http://www.mcbup.com/research_registers/quality.asp

The current issue and full text archive of this journal is available at
http://www.emerald-library.com

Business and organisations have a privilege denied to ordinary mortals - they don't have to die. This makes them especially responsible (Charles Hardy).

Focusing on community issues

One would have thought that, at a time of global recession and great mergers, the business community would be more concerned with financial, rather than social, issues. In fact, what is emerging very strongly is a determination and commitment to address both environmental and societal concerns.

Elkington (1999), argues that:

Environmental reporting is now well established, as of course is financial reporting. But further challenges lie ahead for companies looking to evaluate social indicators in such areas as community, employee and supplier relationships. The pressure for accountability, together with the significant expense of producing the data, will develop powerful pressures towards the integration of financial, social and environmental accounting and reporting . . . Companies - and their stakeholders - will have no option but to address this merging "triple bottom line". They will have to work harder to assess what really matters to them and which indicators will be seen by key stakeholders (including financial analysts) in assessing the triple bottom line performance of companies and sectors alike.

It is widely argued that the business ethos generally speaking has started to subscribe to the principle "show me" rather than just "trust me". Corporate social accountability and reporting is therefore seen as a key driver for engaging the wider community as an important stakeholder in business activity.

There are conferences and global events organised to promote this new principle. For instance, the World Business Council for Sustainable Development (WBCSD), the Institute for Social and Ethical Accountability (ISEA), among many organisations, have staged conferences to debate the theme of social accountability and social responsibility. For instance, ISEA organised an important conference in January 1999 to address the following key areas:

- the concepts and principles behind organisational social reporting, accountability and sustainability and the business drivers for change;

- how the social reporting system is linked with existing financial, environmental and risk-reputation systems;

- the range of issues that can be included in a social statement and how organisations can embark on the process of social reporting;

- techniques and methods to establish social reporting as a powerful audited system for improved market performance; and .

- the value of developing effective stakeholder dialogue to inform measurement and reporting strategies.

Focusing on community issues is not, however, a new concept. Many gurus in the TQM field have, for instance, stressed the importance of "stakeholders". Dr Edward Deming, as far back as 1946, had argued that statistical quality techniques ought not to be limited to economic applications. Deming argued on the significance from social contributions that would emerge, through the application of quality tools and techniques (Jacques, 1999).

Deming's views were further stressed by Juran (1994), who has often urged quality institutions such as The American Society for Quality to expand its mandate by placing more emphasis on rendering service to society.

Definition and meaning of corporate social reporting

A useful report on social reporting by Elkington et al. (1998) describes in a useful way, the various meanings of corporate social reporting:

- In short, this concept covers social, ethical accounting, auditing and reporting.

- A little bit more than just philanthropy. The report argues that companies like BP and United Utilities, measure, evaluate and benchmark their social activities. Furthermore, they tend to view the community's perception of them as a critical factor for their business success.

- Ethics versus social concerns. The inter-dependency between the two is undisputed. Organisations have, first of all, got to operate with a high code of ethics so that everything else can follow on from this.

How to create optimum societal value-added

The key drivers for adding optimum value to society and the communities in which specific business organisations operate is through having strong commitment to corporate and social governance, having an open dialogue with external stakeholders and having the determination to achieve environmental sustainability.

Nelson (1998) proposes an approach based on three elements for building societal value added. Table I illustrates how this can be carried out in practice.

Nelson (1998) argues that companies that have started to make real headway in the area of societal value-added tend to share four characteristics:

(1) they rely on value-based transformational leadership (i.e. sponsor-headed by the CEO and reflected in the company's vision/mission and value statements);

(2) cross-boundary learning (a commitment to learning, innovation and through networks and global partnerships);

(3) stakeholder linkages (mutual benefits through various modes of relationships); and

(4) performance levers (use of a wide range of financial and non-financial performance measures, supported by auditing, verification, reporting and recognition systems).

Standards of social accountability and reporting

There are various principles and standards that the global business community has started to adhere to on a voluntary basis.

The CERES Principle

A ten point code of conduct on companies' environmental performance and accountability. Any organisation that pledges to endorse the CERES Principles will agree to monitor and improve its behaviour in the areas outlined in Table II.

Table I Creating societal value-added: a proposed approach

Approach	Example of area of application
1. Efficient and ethical pursuit of core business activities	Making environmentally and socially responsible decisions
	Investing in the responsible sourcing production, distribution by taking into account access to the poor.
	Creating local jobs
	Paying taxes and royalties
	Implementing social human resource policies
	Adopting international accepted business standards
	Supporting technology co-operation
2. Social investment and philanthropy	Offering training programs to the community at large
	Running employee volunteering schemes for social or cause-related initiatives
	Business education projects
	Community health projects
	Sponsoring community development trusts
	Resource mobilisation and civic improvement
3. Contribution to the policy debate	Tackling obstacles to private sector policy debate development and responsible foreign investment
	Contribution to social and environmental policies and frameworks in areas such as education, training, local economic development, employment and environmental management.
	Supporting progress for good governance, including anti-corruption initiatives and human rights standards

Other principles and standards

* principles for global responsibility (benchmarks for measuring business performance);

* the CAUX round table (principles for business);

* the business charter for sustainable development (principles for environmental management); and

* social responsibility initiative by the Foundation for Ethics and Meaning.

One of the organisations that is recognised as a leading example for its commitment to corporate responsibility is Levi Strauss & Co.

Operating in over 60 countries, with a turnover in excess of $7 billion, Levi Strauss stresses values and social standards.

According to its chairman and CEO, Robert Haas:

A company's values - what it stands for, what it believes in - are critical to its competitive success. Indeed, values drive the business.

Levi Strauss's mission statement is:

To sustain responsible commercial success as a global marketing company of branded apparel. We must balance goals of superior profitability and return on investment, leadership market positions and superior product and services. We will conduct our business ethically and demonstrate leadership in satisfying our responsibilities to our communities and to society. Our work environment will be safe and productive and characterised by fair treatment, teamwork, open communications, personal accountability and opportunities for growth and development.

Levi Strauss was given several recognitions and awards for its commitments to global socially responsible practices.

Best practice examples in social responsibility and accountability

Royal Mail and its focus on the community

As one of the largest employers in the UK, Royal Mail has made significant commitment to enhance its performance in community issues, to encourage and support employees in various community activities and to ensure that the whole corporate organisation acts as a good and responsible corporate citizen. Royal Mail North East, for instance, has two key aims in its community policy:

(1) to support and encourage employees in their chosen community services; and

(2) to demonstrate to the community that as a business, Royal Mail North East is committed to improving its environment and the opportunities available for the diversity of people that live in it.

Table II The CERES Principles

1. **Sustainable use of natural resources**	We will make sustainable use of renewable natural resources, such as water, soils and forests. We will conserve non renewable natural resources through efficient use and careful planning
2. **Protection of the biosphere**	We will reduce and make continual progress toward eliminating the release of any substance that may cause environmental damage to the air, water or the earth or its inhabitants. We will safeguard all habitats affected by our operations and will protect open spaces and wilderness, while preserving biodiversity

616

3. Reduction and disposal of wastes	We will reduce and where possible eliminate waste through source reduction and recycling. All waste will be handled and disposed of through safe and responsible methods
4. Energy conservation	We will conserve energy and improve efficiency of our internal operations and of the goods and services we sell. We will make every effort to use environmentally safe and sustainable energy sources
5. Risk reduction	We will strive to minimise the environmental, health and safety risks to our employees and the communities in which we operate through safe technologies, facilities and operating procedures and by being prepared for emergencies
6. Safe products and services	We will reduce and where possible eliminate the use, manufacture or sale of products and services that cause environmental damage or health or safety hazards. We will inform our customers of the environmental impacts of our products or services and try to correct unsafe use
7. Environmental restoration	We will promptly and responsibly correct conditions we have caused that endanger health, safety or the environment. To the extent where this is feasible, we will redress injuries we have caused to the environment and will restore the environment
8. Informing the public	We will inform in a timely manner everyone who may be affected by conditions caused by our company that might endanger health, safety or the environment. We will regularly seek advice and counsel through dialogue with persons in communities : our facilities. We will not take any action against employees for reporting dangerous incidents or conditions to management or appropriate authorities

9. Management commitment	We will implement these principles and sustain a process that ensures the board of directors and CEO are fully informed about pertinent environmental issues and are fully responsible for environmental policy. In selecting our board of directors, we will consider demonstrating environmental commitment as a factor
10. Audits and reports	We will conduct an annual self evaluation of our progress in implementing these principles. We will support the timely creation of generally accepted environmental audit procedures. We will annually complete a CERES report which will be made available to the public

Source: Adapted from Green Money Journal (1996)

The process of getting requested support for community-based activity is illustrated in Figure 1.

The request sheets for getting support is illustrated in Figure 2.

Lever Bros. Ltd

Lever lays down the following principles for employees to follow in order to effectively focus on societal value-added:

(1) We recognise that our employment policy, not least the commitment to training and personal development and our emphasise on safety, health and environment, has a positive impact on the world outside the working environment.

2) We improve the well-being of society at large both by the generation of employment in companies which service and supply us and in our marketing activities.

618

Figure 1 Support for community-based activity process

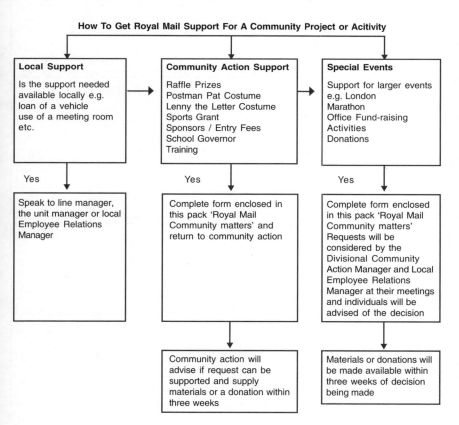

How To Get Royal Mail Support For A Community Project or Acitivity

Local Support	Community Action Support	Special Events
Is the support needed available locally e.g. loan of a vehicle use of a meeting room etc.	Raffle Prizes Postman Pat Costume Lenny the Letter Costume Sports Grant Sponsors / Entry Fees School Governor Training	Support for larger events e.g. London Marathon Office Fund-raising Activities Donations

Yes   Yes   Yes

Speak to line manager, the unit manager or local Employee Relations Manager	Complete form enclosed in this pack 'Royal Mail Community matters' and return to community action	Complete form enclosed in this pack 'Royal Mail Community matters' Requests will be considered by the Divisional Community Action Manager and Local Employee Relations Manager at their meetings and individuals will be advised of the decision
	Community action will advise if request can be supported and supply materials or a donation within three weeks	Materials or donations will be made available within three weeks of decision being made

Figure 2 Community action support request sheets

Community Action
Special Event Support

1. Please give details of the project or event you would like support for, including the date

2. What type of support would you like Royal Mail to provide?

3. If you are raising money please give an estimate of how much you hope to raise.

4. What Opportunities are there for publicity at the event?

5. Have you spoken to your Area Communications Manager or Courier about publicity for the event?

Yes   No   If you take photos of your event or activity please send them in. We would like to see them!

☐   ☐   Just put your name and address on the reverse so we can return them to you.

(3) We use a world class expertise base in human safety to ensure the consumer safety of our products.

(4) We take great care to minimise the environmental impact on all our operations from raw material procurement, product design, manufacture and distribution to use and disposal.

(5) Lever has a long and proud tradition of involvement with the community. This originated when William Hesketh Lever first established Port Sunlight village to improve the living conditions and well-being of his employees.

Some of the specific activities that Lever is involved in to add value to the community at large include:

(1) *Lever as a source of business/employment.* As Figure 3 illustrates, Lever has considerable expenditure in generating opportunities for industrial people and businesses in the communities where it has operations. Employment is generated in many areas including:

* raw and packaging material suppliers;

* packaging and process plan manufacturers;

* distribution and transport providers;

* market research and advertising agencies;

* design and artwork agencies;

* mechanical electrical and civil contracts; and

* service and support agencies.

(2) Environmental policies and activities:

- Lever is a founder member of ERRA (The European Recovery and Recycling Association); and

- Lever has recently become a committed signatory to the AISE code of good environmental practice with specific European targets to be achieved in the next five-year period.

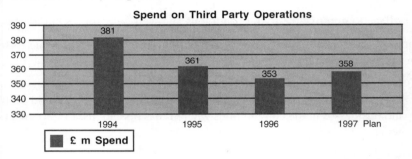

Figure 3 Lever's support for business and employment

(3) *Lever corporate citizenship.* There is involvement in various schemes, including:

- the Merseyside Industrial Consumer Awards (MICA) (offering solutions to business nominated problems);

- supply of training/support to the introduction of Investors in People schemes in local schools;

- European summer placement scheme which provides 10-12 week industrial placements for students from other countries in Europe; and

- factory tours specifically targeted at schools.

As far as community involvement programmes are concerned, this is founded on three principles:

622

- the company devotes the equivalent of at least 1 per cent of its pre-tax profit to community involvement in the form of donations, time and materials (Figure 4);
- Lever's involvement is targeted and focused on charitable work, supporting education, health and welfare; and
- Lever encourages direct contact between employees and the local community.

Auditing organisational commitment to environment and social responsibility

The framework shown in the Appendix, which is based on a distillation of best practices found to be inherent in world class organisations can be used as a useful tool for assessing organisational effectiveness vis-a -vis practices

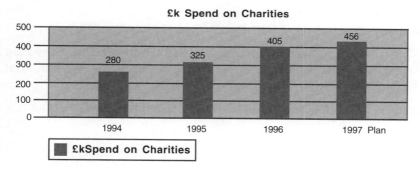

Figure 4 Lever's charitable contributions

related to environment and community-based, socially-oriented practices. The framework is also a useful tool for drawing together action plans for improvement and can provide significant assistance in steering organisations towards world class status as far as social responsibility and environmental practices are concerned.

References

Elkington, J. (1999), "The link between accountability and sustainability - theory put into practice", Conference on the Practice of Social Reporting for Business, ISEA, 19 January, Commonwealth Conference Centre, London.

Elkington, J., Van Dijak, F., Delbe, C. and Terry, V. (1998), *The Social Reporting Report,* Sustainability Publication, London.

Green Money Journal (1996), Fall, available at: http:// www.greenmoney.Com/ gmj/Fall96/htm

Jacques, M.L. (1999), "Applying quality concepts to community issues", *Quality Progress,* March, pp. 49-56.

Juran, J.M. (1994), "The upcoming century of quality", *Annual Quality Congress Proceedings*, ASQC Quality Press, Milwaukee, WI.

Nelson, J. (1998), "Leadership companies in the 21st century: creating shareholder value and societal value", *Visions of Ethical Business,* Financial Times Management, No. 1, October, pp. 21-6.

Appendix

Table AI

Best practice application from MBNQA winners	Degree of importance[a]	Degree of effectiveness[b]
1. The organisation's principal business activities include systems to analyse, anticipate and minimise public risk from hazards	1 2 3 4 5 ☐☐☐☐☐	1 2 3 4 5 6 7 8 9 10 ☐☐☐☐☐☐☐☐☐☐
2. Indicators for risk areas are identified and monitored	1 2 3 4 5 ☐☐☐☐☐	1 2 3 4 5 6 7 8 9 10 ☐☐☐☐☐☐☐☐☐☐
3. Continuous improvement strategies are used consistently, and progress is reviewed regularly	1 2 3 4 5 ☐☐☐☐☐	1 2 3 4 5 6 7 8 9 10 ☐☐☐☐☐☐☐☐☐☐
4. The organisation considers the impact that its operations, products and services might have on society and considers those impacts in planning	1 2 3 4 5 ☐☐☐☐☐	1 2 3 4 5 6 7 8 9 10 ☐☐☐☐☐☐☐☐☐☐
5. Employees at various levels in the organisation are encouraged to be involved in professional organisations, committees, task forces or other community activities	1 2 3 4 5 ☐☐☐☐☐	1 2 3 4 5 6 7 8 9 10 ☐☐☐☐☐☐☐☐☐☐
6. Employees participate in a variety of professional, quality and business improvement associations	1 2 3 4 5 ☐☐☐☐☐	1 2 3 4 5 6 7 8 9 10 ☐☐☐☐☐☐☐☐☐☐

Overall actual score (maximum = 60)

Notes:
[a] 1 = not very important,. 3 = relatively important,. 5 = very important
[b] 1 = not effective at all,. 5 = relatively effective,. 10 = extremely effective

Commentary

Practical guidance and useful insights into this key area of modern business.

The Learning Organisation: Results of a Benchmarking Study

Mohamed Zairi
University of Bradford Management Centre, Bradford, UK

The author
Mohamed Zairi is Chair of Best Practice Management at the University of Bradford Management Centre, Bradford, UK

Keywords
Benchmarking, Learning organizations, Model, Surveys

Abstract
This paper is based on a survey which benchmarked two large conglomerates in the area of "corporate learning". One of the problems with the theme of the learning organisation is clear understanding of its meaning, constituent elements, the way learning gets applied, is measured and can be kept sustainable. To ensure that learning is given an all-encompassing approach, a model proposed by Carr (1994) was adapted and used to survey Unilever plc and Allied Domecq. Consumer focus through effective branding is core to their business, which could be described as more creative than productive. In both cases, the harnessing of human potential and its development is crucial to their competitive success. The survey indicates that Unilever plc has got the edge over Allied Domecq in many areas. The paper discusses the type of learning organisation each case is and the degree of their effectiveness in each of the six areas scrutinised.

First Published in

The Learning Organization
Volume 6 · Number 2 · 1999 · pp. 76–81
© MCB University Press · ISSN 0969-6474

1. Securing tomorrow through learning

Most, if not all, CEOs talk about business imperatives for the future and building a better tomorrow for their organisations. This is perhaps at a time when they are placing more and more emphasis on short-term results and getting the financials right. Is there, therefore, a paradox? Do they mean what they say? What is their real vision?

Perhaps to answer all of the above questions one could refer to an inquiry conducted by the Royal Society for the Encouragement of Arts (RSA, 1995). The inquiry, made up of senior managers representing 25 top companies, concluded that in the UK there is:

- an overall gap in perfomance at a worldclass standard because UK companies suffer from complacency and ignorance of world standards;

- a national culture which is very adversarial;

- An overreliance on financial measures of performance and a short-term focus.

The RSA (1995) report concludes that in order to create tomorrow's organisation there has to be a radical shift through the creation of a more "inclusive" approach and taking a stakeholder perspective. In particular the report stresses the following:

- The need to define purpose, values and their effective communication at all levels.

- Using the purpose, values, etc., as a baseline for designing individually tailored formulas for success and a meaningful framework for performance measurement.

- Organisations need to recognise the importance of reciprocal relationships, and learning from all those who have a stake in the business in order to compete effectively.

- Building close partnerships with customers and suppliers.

The report stresses the importance of learning in order to create tomorrow's companies. For instance, by specifically referring to the role of leadership and focusing on people:

- *Business leadership* includes "defining, discussing, measuring and reporting on success in more inclusive ways" (QWL, 1995).

- *People* includes realising the creativity and learning potential of all people with whom the company has contact, not just employees: "Participating in exploring the future of work, on the basis that successful companies can only flourish in a successful society".

It is very apparent, therefore, that creating tomorrow's organisation requires a fundamental shift in attitudes towards people as the major asset and investing in the development of means of creativity, innovation and high business impact.

Jack Welsh, CEO and chairman of General Electric introduced the philosophy of "Change before you have to" to create a global organisation, which is fit for competing in the 1990s. Since he joined GE in 1981, this change master embarked on a programme which stretched GE to become a global competitor, lean and mean, with annual revenues of $60 billion. He believes that it is the role of leaders to create a climate which constantly reminds people that change is a continuous process. Some of Jack Welsh's famous words include: boundarylessness, speed, stretch.

According to Welsh, "Change should not be an event but rather a continuous process in the quest for success" (Salazar, 1995).

Visionary leaders are referred to in a variety of ways such as:

- change agents;

- transformational leaders;

- corporate revolutionaries;

- change masters.

2. Learning is synonymous with change management

The best way to describe learning is perhaps through the impact this can have on changing things, changing processes and changing organisations in their entirety. If effective change management is going to happen, organisations have to manage a variety of things through direct and indirect means of encouraging learning. Wood (1995) suggests a very useful list, which was observed in the effective management of change in various organisations such as Rank-Hovis for instance:

- Corporate change through a top-down, bottom-up and middle-out approach relies on changing people's mindsets (how they think) and the culture of work (how they behave). This is the only way for creating ownership and commitment of the strategic task and also on relying on people's creative contributions.

- There is a need to stress the importance of developing skills both at process management level and for the purpose of driving change and managing its implications. This can happen through various means and methods such as teamwork and dynamic visual interaction.

- Change can only happen through the development of robust processes and eliminating functional barriers in order to secure effective performance.

- A specific role for managers and supervisors is to become change facilitative leaders, and develop everyone around them through coaching, guiding, mentoring and the encouragement of continual personal learning experiences.

- Change has to be managed and cannot be left to occur in an *ad hoc* fashion. When change is induced it has to be closely related to strategic planning and the competitive arena outside. Change for the sake of change is worse than no change at all. Change has to be considered as a means with ends, the end being effective competitiveness:

- It is imperative for managers to link in employees' individual learning agendas to the business priorities and the core competencies required for the organisations concerned to achieve effectively their agenda in the marketplace. This link is so vital as it enables individuals to plan and manage their own learning tasks with the view of helping the accomplishment of the corporate goal and making a significant contribution.

As Wood (1995) argues:

> Above all the change process is about people, and about unleashing their innate human potential to be the best they can be. If this is not recognised as the most fundamental principal of all, bottom-up and middle-out change lose their energy and meet with major barriers to change, resulting in eventual breakdown of the change programme.

The following is a list of critical factors for creating effective change (Wood, 1995):

- Having a clear vision, leadership and communication and an effective decisionmaking process at all levels, driven by business imperatives.

- It is important to have overwhelming support for change, otherwise if there are pockets of resistance, these can hamper progress and advancement. One effective way of securing commitment and support is to encourage access to decision-making processes.

- Building trust through openness and selling change as an opportunity for better competitiveness rather as a threat to job security. It is important to link change to learning, empowerment and risk taking and sell it as an opportunity for individuals' strengths and expertise to be applied to new roles to deliver corporate goals and achieve the desired transformational state.

- Having a change management policy which is well communicated and supported by all.

- Focus and keeping the momentum going is crucial in continuing to empower people and get their full commitment

- Having champions, advocates and enthusiasts for change who are going to propagate the need and benefits at all levels within the organisation. This is to be done through coaching and mentoring for instance.

- Tracking and monitoring success is critical to ensure that change is effective and leading to the desired outcomes.

- Using external catalysts for help, assistance, support and inspiration.

3. Benchmarking learning

Since learning is an all-encompassing approach, an adaptation of a model proposed by Carr (1994) was used to assess corporate learning within Unilever plc and Allied Domecq plc. Both are operating in the fastmoving consumer sector and have more similarities than dissimilarities.

Unilever plc

Unilever's aims are to effectively meet the needs of the global consumer in its specific markets. Its strength is in branded and packaged consumer goods, in foods, detergents and personal products. Unilever has over 1,000 strong and successful brands being marketed worldwide.

Some of the strengths of Unilever are in the following areas:

- understanding the needs of customers and consumers;
- product innovation;
- investment in R&D;
- creative and effective marketing;
- expertise in manufacturing technology;
- people.

As far as people are concerned, and this is the area scrutinised in this paper, in a corporate document issued in 1992, the following statement was written:

> Unilever recognises that its employees are the lifeblood of the business; it is their skills and commiment which determine success.

Allied Domecq plc

Allied Domecq is a world leader in spirits and retailing. Spirits and wine account for 62 per cent of Allied Domecq's trading profit (1995 figures) and retailing for 26 per cent. It has additional areas which include brewing and food manufacturing. Similarly to Unilever, Allied Domecq has very strong brands such as Ballantine's, Beefeater, Kahlua, Courvoisier, Teacher's. In retailing, it has 13,800 retail outlets, comprising 4,100 pubs, 1,500 offlicences and 8,200 franchised stores with brands such as Victoria Wines, Big Steak Pubs and Mr Q's. There is a determination at Allied Domecq to drive through the strengths of its brands, such as in the case of Unilever. This is expressed by A.D's chairman, Michael Jackaman, in the 1995 company report, as follows:

> Our consumer brands are all-important to our future growth. We focus on them intently giving them consistent and imaginative support. The quality of our brands and the speed of our service are key determinants of success.

4. The survey instrument

The survey instrument was based on a questionnaire proposed by Carr (1994). The questionnaire was structured in six areas, covering the following:

(1) core qualities for creativity;
(2) key characteristics of a creative organisational system;
(3) measures of organisational flexibility;
(4) measuring diversity and conflict;
(5) developing creative organisational systems;
(6) developing effective and successful teams.

Ten functions were represented within Unilever plc and 12 from Allied Domecq. Responses were received from eight Unilever businesses and four from Allied Domecq. In all, 26 questionnaires were received out of a total of 100 sent (Table I).

The results are discussed in the following sections, under each of the six elements used and based on Carr's model (1994).

Table I Background to data collection

Elements of comparison	Unilever	Allied Domecq
Number of respondents	14	12
Number of functions represented	10	12
Number of businesses represented	8	4

5. The seven core qualities of a creative organisation

In this area, which covers core elements of being a learning organisation and operating a total quality management approach, Unilever, overall, has a better profile than Allied Domecq. The gap appears to be in three specific areas:

(1) Within Unilever, there is a better approach to people's contributions.

(2) Within Unilever, there is a better approach to problem-solving.

(3) There is a more ad hoc, trial and error approach within Allied Domecq than is the case within Unilever (Figure 1).

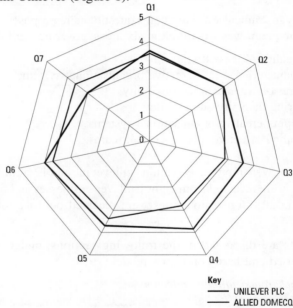

Key
——— UNILEVER PLC
——— ALLIED DOMECQ

Figure 1 The seven core qualities of a creative organisation

6. The basic characteristics of a creative organisational system

This area examines how both Unilever and Allied Domecq put learning into practice. Both organisations appear to be lacking in many areas and in particular:

- There is a big concern overall about the allocation of resources for problem solving.

- There is not a true culture of problem solving in both organisations and using problems for injecting in new learning.

- The evidence about pioneering approaches and innovativeness in relation to other organisations is not particularly strong (Figure 2).

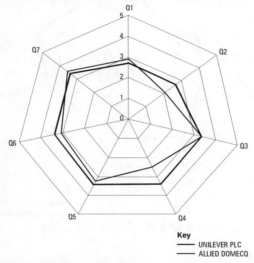

Figure 2 The basic characteristics of a creative organisational system

7. The ten attributes of a flexible organisation

This area attempts to map whether there is clear evidence of a positive culture of total involvement, a proactive approach to managing change and whether the notion of true empowerment is really visible. Both profiles once more do not appear to be of world-class status. In particular the following areas appear to be of concern:

- It appears that there is not a positive climate for creativity and an approach which enthusiastically gets people to experiment and learn.

635

- The notion of empowerment is not widely recognised and there is still concern over hierarchies and rigid structures (Figure 3).

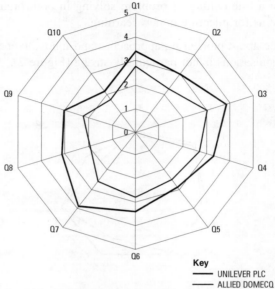

Figure 3 The ten attributes of a flexible organisation

8. Using diversity and conflict

There is a lot of concern about diversity and how conflict is considered. Both profiles once again do not appear to reflect best practices in the development of a corporate climate where goals and targets are effectively communicated and closely linked to individual development needs and where opportunities for promotion, and participation in the decision-making processes are not widely abundant. In particular, the following areas need to be highlighted:

- opportunity to apply for positions at all levels;
- individual goals and needs are not integrated effectively into the structure of organisations (Figure 4).

636

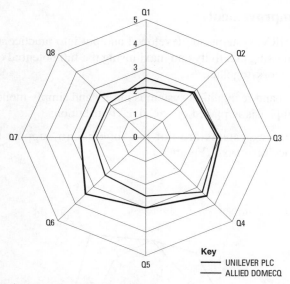

Figure 4 Using diversity and conflict

9. The eight rules for a creative HRM system

This is again one of the most critical areas for creating the learning organisation. It is very much about people's choice, selection and development, how they are motivated and rewarded and how levels of synergy are obtained by encouraging teamwork. Although Unilever appears to be much better than Allied Domecq in this respect, nonetheless, apart from one or two areas, there are many of concern.

Positives

- Effective training and its link to functions.
- The quality of people hired (creative potential).
- Tasks and projects are made to be the key motivator for people.
- People are hired for keeps and not just to fill in a short-term need.

637

Areas for improvement

- The way HRM systems are developed and put into practice are not really about harnessing creativity and maximising the full potential of people and how they work together.

- The reward and recognition system is purely and simply monetary and not enough emphasis is placed on creative contributions.

- The incentive systems are not put together to support the creative performance of people (Figure 5).

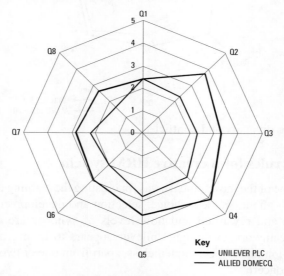

Figure 5 The eight rules for a creative HRM system

10. The nine characteristics of successful teams

This is the last area examined and specifically relates to aspects of teamwork, goal clarity, culture of supporting teams, whether values and guiding principles are shared and how the goal deployment process concentrates on the work of teams. Once again, Unilever appears to have a slightly better profile than Allied Domecq. The general indication is that this is not really an area of great concern, although there is not one single practice which highlights world-class status. Nonetheless, the effort deployed indicates above average practices. Perhaps, one or two areas which need to be highlighted and would require improvement, cover:

- Renewals for team performance. There is still a strong focus on individuals.

- There is clear recognition that individuals within the teamwork context do add value and efforts are recognised.

11. Conclusions

This brief benchmarking exercise indicates that Unilever has the edge over Allied Domecq and perhaps is more advanced in its effort to create a learning organisation. The efforts, however, do not indicate world-class status and there are many deficiencies which may need to be attended to.

When plotting the aggregated responses of all the respondents from each organisation for each of the six parameters examined, Unilever appears to be much stronger than Allied Domecq, as Figure 6 illustrates.

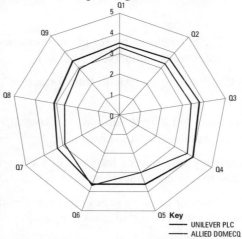

Figure 6 The nine characteristics of successful teams

639

Figure 7 illustrates the gaps in performance between Unilever and Allied Domecq under the six key elements of developing a learning organisation.

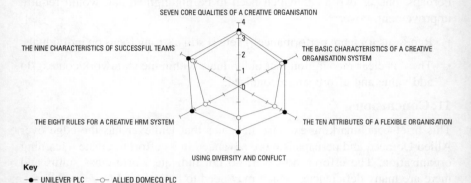

BENCHMARKING LEARNING IN FMCG
A COMPARISON BETWEEN UNILEVER AND ALLIED DOMECQ

SEVEN CORE QUALITIES OF A CREATIVE ORGANISATION

THE NINE CHARACTERISTICS OF SUCCESSFUL TEAMS

THE BASIC CHARACTERISTICS OF A CREATIVE ORGANISATION SYSTEM

THE EIGHT RULES FOR A CREATIVE HRM SYSTEM

THE TEN ATTRIBUTES OF A FLEXIBLE ORGANISATION

USING DIVERSITY AND CONFLICT

Key
UNILEVER PLC   ALLIED DOMECQ PLC

Figure 7 Six key elements of developing a learning organisation

References

Carr, C. (1994), "The competitive power of constant creativity", *AMACOM,* American Management Association, New York, NY.

Salazar, R. (1995), "Leading corporate transformation", *World Executive's Digest,* August, pp. 10-12.

"Tomorrow's company" (1995), *Quality of Working Life (QWL)* News and Abstracts, No. 124, Autumn, ACAS, London, p. 4

"Tomorrow's company: the role of business in a changing world" (1995), The Royal Society for the encouragement of Arts (RSA), July, London.

Wood, R. (1995), "New articipative series on people, work and change", *The Strategic Planning Society News,* November, pp. 4-5.

Training Evaluation: An Empirical Study in Kuwait

Ahmad Al-Athari

European Centre for TQM, University of Bradford, Bradford, UK

Mohamed Zairi

SABIC Chair in Best Practice Management, European Centre for TQM, University of Bradford, Bradford, UK

First Published in

Journal of European Industrial Training
26/5 [2002] 241-251
© MCB UP Limited [ISSN 0309-0590]
[DOI 10.1108/03090590210424911]

Keywords

Training, Evaluation, Model, Human resource development, Organisational development

Abstract

This paper is based on a study which examined the current training evaluation activity and challenges that face Kuwaiti organisations. The study sample was five UK organisations (recognised as best practice organisations in their T&D activities) and 77 Kuwaiti organisations (40 government and 37 private). Interviews and questionnaires were used. The study reveals that the majority of respondents, both in government and in private sectors, only evaluate their training programme occasionally. The most popular evaluation tools and technique used by government and private sectors were questionnaires. The most common model used by Kuwaiti organisations is the Kirkpatrick model, while the most common level of evaluation for both government and private sector is reaction type.

Introduction

The Manpower Services Commission (1981) in its Glossary of Training Terms defines evaluation as:

The assessment of a total value of the training system, training course or programme in social as well as financial terms. Evaluation differs from validation in that it attempts to measure the overall cost-benefit of the course or programme and not just the achievement of its laid-down objectives. The term is also used in the general judgmental sense of the continuous monitoring of a programme or of the training function as a whole (McDougall, 1990).

The Glossary of Training Terms also defines the validation of the training as:

- Internal validation. A series of tests and assessments designed to ascertain whether a training programme has achieved the behavioural objectives specified.

- External validation. A series of tests and assessments designed to ascertain whether the behavioural objectives of an internally valid training programme were realistically based on an accurate initial identification of training needs in relation to the criteria of effectiveness adopted by the organisation (Rae, 1986).

Evaluation has become a very important task for the organisation, and there are several very sound reasons for starting to put more effort into it. According to Kearns and Miller (1996, p. 9):

- It is about building credibility and a solid foundation for T&D decisions.

- Provides a basis for maximising return on investment.

- Helps to categorise training by the type of return you will get from your investment

- For those who get it right, it should lead to building up the training function, not depleting it.

- Automatically links T&D with strategic and operational business objectives.

- Ensures buy-in and commitment at all levels.
- Produces results that can act as a great reinforcer of learning and further motivate individuals to develop themselves.

The most forgotten stage in any training programme is the evaluation. Magdy (1999), in his research in the USA, found out that organisations spend $30 billion annually on training programmes and only 10 per cent of that expenditure goes to evaluation. Often, the value of conducting training evaluations is overshadowed by the necessity simply to gain participation's immediate post-course reactions, the results of which are sometimes mistakenly viewed as indicating whether or not the course was successful overall. In addition, budgetary and other constraints have caused many trainers and designers to employ standardised, commercially available, evaluation instruments. These have many disadvantages: generally, not focused, offer little assistance in assessing long-term effects, one size fits all (McClelland, 1994).

So to get the best benefit from the evaluation instrument it has to be designed to meet the goals and objectives of the programme. Designing training to meet goals or objectives is not a new concept. Nor is the concept of attempting to measure changes that have occurred as a result of the training and determining what benefits the organisation has received for its investment. However, to accomplish both tasks is a challenge. Add to that variables such as multiple functional as well as behavioural objectives, and decisions of what process or procedures to use become more complex.

Study objectives and methodology

The study in this paper is part of a larger research project aimed at identifying best practice of training and its impact on employees' and organisations' effectiveness and performance. The part being discussed in this paper had the main objective of identifying the training evaluation activities and challenges in Kuwaiti organisations.

To achieve this objective, the study identified what was present by the literature and published case studies as reward and appraisal best practice and training (Nadler, 1970; Hamblin, 1974; Laird, 1978; Robinson, 1985; Kenney and Reid,

1986; Kirkpatrick, 1986; Rae, 1986; Camp et al., 1986; McDougall, 1990; Hames, 1991; Oakland, 1993; McClelland, 1994; Kearns and Miller, 1996; Buren and Bassi, 1999; Newman, 1999; Magdy, 1999). These have been reproduced in a generic format and structured in questionnaires to assess the applicability and the viewpoint of experienced practitioners toward them.

The survey focused on targeting government and private (joint venture) organisations in Kuwait to see how many subscribed to the idea proposed, thus providing further proof of whether these ideas were the right approach to a successful human resource development in the future. The questionnaire was designed and piloted to assess: time required to complete the questionnaire, simplicity, clear language, clarity of instructions, comprehensiveness and item sequence. The pilot sample includes NatWest Bank, British Airways, IBM, Elida Faberge, ICL and University of Bradford. Once the final questionnaire version was available, the survey sample was selected. For the purpose of the study, the only criterion for sample selection was the size of the organisations and their financial statutes. The sources used to select the sample were Ministry of Planning and case studies analysis in the literature. The selected populations for this research are training department managers and HRD managers in all government and joint venture organisations. For the government sector, there are currently 48 authorities and, for the private sector, the investigator will study only the main shareholding companies (joint venture with the government, only 38 companies working in investment, insurance, industrial, real estate, transport, and services) (Ministry of Planning, 1998) and in addition the banking sector (eight banks) and hotels sector (14 hotels).

In order to identify the training evaluations activity and to compare government with private organisations in relation to these activities, a sample of 108 organisations was selected from the Kuwaiti organisations population. A total of 96 questionnaires were collected and 77 were processed and analysed. The sample represents both government and private sectors and is divided almost equally between government (40, representing 51.9 per cent) and private organisations (37, representing 48.9 per cent of the sample).

The majority of the sample, accounting for 23 organisations in both government and private sectors, work in the services sector, representing 29.9 per cent of the sample, followed by 14 organisations working in the manufacturing sector, which accounted for 18.2 per cent of the sample. Banking and finance sectors accounted for 13 organisations, representing 16.9 per cent, while hotels and catering organisations accounted for 11, representing 14.3 per cent of the sample. Transportation and storage, and construction sectors accounted for eight, each on 10.4 per cent.

Study finding

Initially, the study participants were presented with several statements to assess the perceived importance of training evaluation, evaluation models, evaluation tools and techniques, evaluation input and output, and challenges. Participants were requested to show how strongly they agreed with these statements on a five-point Likert scale.

Figure 1 Importance of evaluation

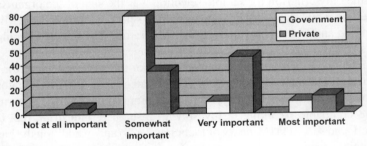

Importance of evaluation

In order to identify how Kuwaiti organisations view training evaluation, the respondents were asked about the level of importance of the evaluation process in their organisation. Their answers reveal that only eight government organisations out of 40, representing 20 per cent, believe that training evaluation is important, while 32 government organisations, representing 80 per cent, believe that it is somewhat important. On the other hand, 22 private organisations out of 37, representing 59.4 per cent, believe that training evaluation is very important, while 13, representing 35.1 per cent, believe that it is somewhat important. In addition, only two private organisations do not believe in its importance (Figure 1).

646

The above findings show that private organisations believe in the importance of training evaluation more than the government organisations. This could be attributed again to the nature of each sector. The private organisations believe that each dinar (Kuwaiti currency) they spend has to pay off, or give them returns, so training must pay off. This conclusion is consistent with ASTD (1997) research; they found out that organisations in the USA with higher annual sales were especially likely to say that they conducted evaluations, while services sector organisations were the least likely to evaluate their training. ASTD (1997) conducted a survey on the importance of evaluation to US organisations; 81 per cent attached some level of importance, while 84 per cent felt that it is important only for HRD.

Figure 2 Frequency of training evaluation

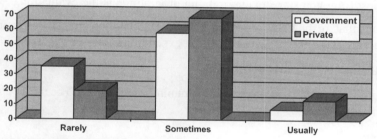

Frequency of training evaluation

In order to investigate the importance of training evaluation and to support the previous findings, the respondents were asked about the frequency of conducting evaluations for their training programme (Figure 2). Their answers show that the majority in both government and private sectors sometimes evaluate their training programme, while only 7.5 per cent of government and 13.5 per cent of private organisations usually evaluate their training programme. Furthermore, 35 per cent of government and 18.9 per cent of private sector organisations rarely evaluate their training programme.

One of the main difficulties faced by the training efforts in Kuwaiti organisations is that no specific body is in charge of evaluating the training programme. The responsibility for training evaluation is formally left to the training co-ordinator, who occasionally evaluates the programme just for reporting to the management and submitting it in the annual report. That is why most Kuwaiti organisations only occasionally evaluate their training programmes. So these organisations have to work on finding a specific body to be in charge of evaluation, either the training department or HR management department.

This result is also consistent with Al-Ali (1998). He stated:

We could see the lack of professional management thinking that could find a training programme which suits the work environment and employees' needs (Al-Ali, 1998, p. 165).

Magdy (1999, p. 21) stated that:

The most forgotten stage in any training programme is the evaluation.

He found that, in the USA, organisations spend $30 billion annually on training programms and only 10 per cent of that expenditure goes to evaluation.

Evaluation tools and techniques

Many instruments are used in evaluating training effectiveness. The most popular in the field include:

- tests;
- questionnaires;
- interviews;
- observations; and
- performance records.

In the training context, all known evaluation instruments can be used to collect necessary data. However, evaluation purpose and strategy will govern what evaluation instruments are most appropriate.

The evaluation tool and technique most used by the government and private sectors is the questionnaire (Table I), which is used by 70 per cent of government organisations and 81 per cent of the private sample. Observation and performance records are no less important for the private sector, as they had been used respectively by 81 per cent and 70 per cent. Furthermore, 62 per cent of the government organisations sample use performance records as evaluation tools. Test, interview, other management tool, attitude survey, and CAT, CAL were used by less than 54 per cent of the private and government samples.

Table I Evolution tools and techniques

Tool/technique	Small extent (%)	Considerable extent (%)	Great extent (%)	Total (%)
Questionnaire				
Government		30	70	100
Private	5	14	81	100
Interview				
Government	8	45	47	100
Private	27	41	32	100
Test				
Government	8	38	54	100
Private	30	22	48	100
Observation				
Government	15	45	35	100
Private	5	14	81	100
Attitude survey				
Government	40	43	17	100
Private	68	19	13	100
Performance record				
Government	3	35	62	100
Private	11	19	70	100
CAT, CAL				
Government	90	5	5	100
Private	86	14		100
Other management tools				
Government	88	5	7	100
Private	36	39	25	100

Al-Muraifea (1993) found in his study that the only method used to evaluate the training courses was direct observation in the classroom. Also, Al-Ali (1999) found that the most common evaluation tool used by Kuwaiti organisations is the questionnaire. Another finding by ASTD (1997) is consistent with the above; they found that 94 per cent out of 300 US organisations use the questionnaire. Furthermore, they found that 100 per cent of public sector organisations use the test to evaluate their training programme.

The above discussion has indicated that the entire samples in both sectors use the questionnaire (see Table I). This is widely used in training programmes, and it included trainees' evaluations of training, often assessed on a "smile sheet". Robinson and Robinson (1989) stated:

Almost all HRD professionals provide end-of-course questionnaires, which are completed by participants and given to the instructor. However, these reaction evaluations, too frequently, are poorly designed and yield minimally helpful information.

So, whatever was the evaluation instrument used by Kuwaiti organisations, it must be designed to meet the goal and objectives of the programme. Designing training to meet goals or objectives is not a new concept. Nor is the concept of attempting to measure changes that have occurred as a result of the training and determining what benefits the organisation has received for its investment. However, to accomplish both tasks is a challenge. Add to that variables such as multiple functional, as well as behavioural, objectives, and decisions of what process or procedures to use become more complex.

Evaluation models

The selection of an evaluation model is very important in relation to what the training activity sponsor organisation aims to get out of it. Is it to benchmark the organisation training activity, or to see how much organisations benefited from the training programme, what is the employees' reaction, how much did they learn, did they change their behaviour, and what is the result?

The respondents were asked about the type of evaluation model and methods they use for their evaluations. Their answers show that the entire sample in both government and private sectors use the Kirkpatrick model to evaluate their training programme to a different extent, while only 5 per cent of the private sector use the CIRO model. Furthermore, none of the sample in either sector uses Investor in People standard or benchmarking (Table II).

As the study shows, the entire sample uses the Kirkpatrick model to conduct training evaluation. This finding is consistent with ASTD (1997) research; they found that 67 per cent out of 300 US organisations reported that they use the Kirkpatrick model. Large organisations were much more likely to use the Kirkpatrick model than smaller organisations.

Evaluation of training outcomes

When the respondents were asked about the evaluation of training outcomes, especially with use of the Kirkpatrick model, their answers indicate that the most common evaluation for both government and private organisations is trainee reaction. For government organisations, 47 per cent of them evaluate learning, and 40 per cent evaluate result, and 35 per cent of them evaluate job behaviour. On the other hand, 48 per cent of private organisations evaluate result, 11 per cent evaluate job behaviour, and only 10 per cent evaluate learning (Table III).

Table II Evolution models

Model	Small extent (%)	Considerable extent (%)	Great extent (%)	Total (%)
Kirkpatrick				
Government	52	28	20	100
Private	46	43	11	100
CIRO				
Government	100	0	0	100
Private	95	5	0	100
Investor in People				
Government	100	0	0	100
Private	100	0	0	100
Benchmark				
Government	100	0	0	100
Private	100	0	0	100

Table III Evolution models

Model	Small extent (%)	Considerable extent (%)	Great extent (%)	Total (%)
Reaction				
Government	0	15	85	100
Private	3	24	73	100
Learning				
Government	0	53	47	100
Private	49	41	10	100
Job behavior				
Government	5	60	35	100
Private	35	54	11	100
Result				
Government	5	55	40	100
Private	22	30	48	100

This finding is consistent with ASTD (1997); they found that 67 per cent of the organisations included in the study used Kirkpatrick, 92 per cent of them evaluate reaction, 51 per cent evaluate learning, while 32 per cent evaluate job behaviour, and only 26 per cent evaluate result.

To evaluate the trainees' reaction to the training programme by asking them what they thought of it in order to determine their degree of satisfaction with the training without moving to the second step, their answer would sometimes be misleading. Their answer will sometimes be based on how much they like the instructor, or whether they had a good time or not. This means that, if it is a good programme but they felt unsatisfied or they did not like the instructor, they will kill the programme by their answer (see Table III). Saari et al. (1988) stated that organisations typically use only "happy sheets", and ignore whether training has had an impact on learning, behaviour and performance of the trainee on the job.

Evaluation has become a very important task for the organisation, and there are several very sound reasons for starting to put more effort into it, such as to build credibility for T&D decisions, to see the return on investment and to build up the training function. But, for Kuwaiti organisations, the problem is that nobody is interested in the findings of the evaluation process. The only target for such evaluation is the instructor. Al-Muraifea (1993) stated:

One of the defects in the structure of the Training Department in most Kuwaiti organisations is that there is nobody or division in charge of the results of such assessments, so ultimately nobody ensures the effectiveness of employee training in Kuwait. It is necessary to know whether objectives have been achieved or not.

Measuring training input

To continue with the evaluation section, and also to reach a conclusion about evaluation activity in Kuwait, the respondents were asked whether they measure their training input or not. Their answers indicate that almost the entire sample measures their training input, while only 2.5 per cent of the government sample do not perform any such measurement (Figure 3).

Input measurement

In order to identify the kind of training input measurement, the sample was provided with a list from which to choose. Their answers show that private sector organisations measure their total training expenditure, number of employees receiving training, and number of courses they offer to their employees. In addition, 97 per cent of them measure their payments to outsider training providers, 81 per cent measure their trainee travel expenses, and 68 per cent measure their training expenditure per employee. The most popular training input measurement for the government organisations is number of employees receiving training and number of courses which they offer to their employees. A total of 79 per cent of government organisations measure their total training time/days, and 72 per cent of them measure their cost of paying for training facilities and equipment.

As a conclusion, the entire private organisations sample chose measurement of the quantitative input, while the government organisations had chosen the qualitative input (Table IV). That also could be attributed to the nature of each sector and the responsibility for payment. Almost all government organisations' payment comes from the civil services authority (Dewan). So the lack of measuring the quantitative input by the government sample could be attributed to the monopoly of the civil services authority (Dewan) in the training activity and payment, while the private sector is responsible for its own payment. As indicated before, the private sector is always looking for payback on expenditure, and that is why this sector measures the quantitative input.

Figure 3 Measuring training input

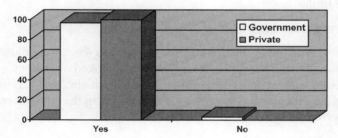

This finding is consistent with ASTD (1997); they found in their research that total expenditures on training and the number of employees receiving training were measured by nearly nine out of ten organisations that evaluated their training in the USA (88 per cent). Just over three-quarters (77 per cent) of these organisations kept track of the number of courses they offer.

Table IV Input measurement

Input	Yes (%)	No(%)	Total(%)
Total training expenditure			
Government	31	69	100
Private	100		100
Number of employees receiving training			
Government	97	3	100
Private	100		100
Payment to outside training providers			
Government	28	72	100
Private	97	3	100

Total training time/days			
Government	79	21	100
Private	51	49	100
Trainee travel expenses			
Government	31	69	100
Private	81	19	100
Course development expenditures			
Government	28	72	100
Private	51	49	100
Cost of facilities and equipment			
Government	72	28	100
Private	54	46	100
Training expenditure per employee			
Government	13	87	100
Private	68	32	100
Training expenditure as % of payroll			
Government	8	92	100
Private	30	70	100
Course development time			
Government	23	77	100
Private	30	70	100

Organisations with high volumes of annual sales tended to measure total training expenditures, training as a percentage of payroll, and tuition reimbursements, more than other organisations. Tracking training as a percentage of payroll and the cost of facilities and equipment was also more prevalent among large firms. Other comparisons by industry group indicated that none of the organisations in the service sector or in agriculture, mining and construction recorded their course development expenditures.

Measuring training output

The respondents were asked whether they measure their training output or not. Their answers indicate that the entire private organisations sample measures their training output, while only 40 per cent of the government sample do so (Figure 4).

Training output measurement

In order to identify the kind of training output measurement, the sample was provided with a list from which to choose. Their answers show that the entire sample of government which measure their training output measure their employees' job satisfaction and their productivity (Table V). In addition, 80 per cent of them measure their employees' absenteeism, and 69 per cent measure their customer satisfaction as an output for their training programmes. The private organisations also match the government organisations in measuring their employees' productivity and their job satisfaction, which are measured respectively by 97 per cent and 95 per cent of the private organisations sample; 92 per cent measure their customer satisfaction, 84 per cent measure their profitability, and 76 per cent measure their sales as training output.

Figure 4 Measuring training output

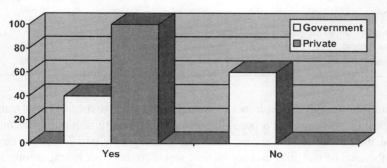

As a comparison between Kuwaiti organisations and US organisations concerning training output measurement (Table V), it appears from the ASTD (1997) research that customer satisfaction is the most commonly measured outcome, tracked by 69 per cent of organisations. Surprisingly, profit-making organisations were less likely to track this measure than non-profit organisations. Job satisfaction was a distant second at 38 per cent (63 per cent among health-care firms). Organisations in the finance, real estate and insurance sectors were more apt to measure return on expectations and sales as outcomes than other organisations.

Evaluation challenges

The evaluation process for assessing T&D effectiveness is not easy; it requires special techniques, financial resources and the availability of required information. However, there are some challenges which might minimise the evaluation process. The respondents were asked to determine the most important evaluation challenges that face them in conducting sound evaluation. More than 50 per cent in both sectors believe that finding evaluation methods that suit a variety of courses, cost of doing evaluations well, translating evaluation results into top management's language and determining specific actions to take based on evaluation results are the most important challenges they faced (Table VI). These are in addition to determining the impact of training on financial performance, time required to do evaluations well, identifying appropriate quantitative and qualitative measures, getting top management buy-in, finding qualified measurement and evaluation professionals, and getting trainees and managers to participate in evaluations.

Figure 5 Difficulty in obtaining information needed for evalution

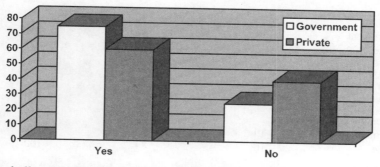

The challenges of translating evaluation results into top management language and determining specific actions to take based on evaluation results are consistent with the previous finding. This indicates that evaluation activity in Kuwaiti organisations is not well designed to meet their objectives, and also shows that no action is taken to improve training activity and training results based on the evaluation, because they cannot determine the kind of action they should take based on its results (see Table VII). This result also contrasts with Al-Ali (1998, p. 165); he stated that there is a big gap between the training

Table V output measurement

Output	Yes (%)	No(%)	Total(%)
Customer satisfaction			
Government	69	31	100
Private	92	8	100
Job satisfaction			
Government	100		100
Private	95	5	100
Productivity			
Government	100		100
Private	97	3	100
Return on expectations			
Government	19	81	100
Private	27	73	100
Sales			
Government	18	82	100
Private	76	24	100
Return on investment			
Government	25	75	100
Private	24	76	100
Cost/benefit ratio			
Government	19	81	100
Private	16	84	100
Profitability			
Government	18	82	100
Private	84	16	100
Absenteeism			
Government	80	20	100
Private	22	78	100

Table VI Evolution challenges

Challenges	Small extent (%)	Considerable extent (%)	Great extent (%)	Do not know (%)	Total (%)
Cost of doing evolutions well					
Government		23	70	7	100
Private		14	86		100
Determining the impact of training on financial performance					
Government	20	18	57	5	100
Private	5	41	54		100
Time required to do evaluations well					
Government	18	28	54		100
Private		14	86		100
Identifying appropriate quantitative measures					
Government	10	20	62	8	100
Private	11	30	37	22	100
Identifying appropriate qualitative measures					
Government	10	10	57	23	100
Private	11	30	37	22	100
Finding evaluation methods that suit a variety of courses					
Government		13	87		100
Private	3	22	75		100
Getting trainees and managers to participate in evaluations					
Government	33	18	49		100
Private	16	14	65	5	100
Getting top management buy-in					
Government	8	28	64		100
Private	24	16	60		100
Finding qualified measurement and evaluation professionals					
Government	10	35	65		100
Private	35	19	38	8	100
Translating evaluation results into top management's language					
Government		28	72		100
Private	3	24	70	3	100
Determining specific actions to take based on evaluation results					
Government		30	70		100
Private	8	11	78	3	100

department and employees in relation to the training need analysis and training evaluations. In addition, the smaller evaluation challenges that face private organisations are in identifying appropriate qualitative measures and finding qualified measurement and evaluation professionals, which represent respectively 37 per cent and 38 per cent of the private organisations sample, as Table VI shows.

Difficulty in obtaining information needed for evaluation

HRD professionals who must perform training evaluations rely on a variety of resources to do their work. However, not all the information they require to use these resources is widely available (Figure 5). To continue with the same section, the respondents were asked whether they faced any difficulty concerning obtaining information needed for evaluations. Their answers indicate that 75 per cent of government and 59.5 per cent of private organisations face difficulty in obtaining the information needed.

Table VII Kinds of information difficult to obtain

	Small extent (%)	Considerable extent (%)	Great extent (%)	Do not know (%)	Total (%)
Information on the latest advances in measurement and evaluation					
Government		27	73		100\
Private		23	77		100
Tools/methods for benchmarking training outcomes against other companies or organizations					
Government		27	73		100
Private	5	18	72	5	100
Information on what other companies or HRD executives or doing					
Government	17	17	66		100
Private	9	23	65	5	100
Information on measurement and evaluation tools themselves					
Government	33	10	57		100
Private	14	27	59		100
Information on how to conduct sound measurement and evaluation					
Government	7	50	43		100
Private	14	27	59		100

Information on the evaluation skills HRD professionals will need in the future

Government	17	20	63	100
Private	27	23	50	100

Information on all the measurement and evaluation resources available

Government	22	26	52	100
Private	2	32	63	100

Information about outside providers of measurement and evaluation assistance

Government	17	33	50	100
Private	23	18	59	100

Information difficult to obtain

More than 60 per cent of the entire sample for both government and private organisations faced some degree of difficulties in obtaining the following (Table VII):

- Information on the latest advances in measurement and evaluation.

- Information about tools/methods for benchmarking training outcomes against other companies or organisations.

- Information on what other companies or HRD executives are doing.

- Information on measurement and evaluation tools themselves.

- Information on how to conduct sound measurement and evaluation.

- Information on the evaluation skills HRD professionals will need in the future.

- Information on all the measurement and evaluation resources available.

- Information about outside providers of measurement and evaluation assistance.

This finding is also consistent with Al-Ali (1999, pp. 7-38), who stated:

The most important challenges facing the Kuwaiti organisations are difficulties in measuring performance improvement in certain jobs (services), difficulties in measuring the change in behaviour of individuals over a short period of time, and the absence of a follow-up process after T&D programmes. Other difficulties such as lack of knowledge about the evaluation process seem to exist in the government sector more than in the private sector.

For the purpose of comparison, respondents to the ASTD (1997) survey reported that information on the latest advances in evaluation and training was the most difficult to locate, followed closely by information about how to benchmark their training outcomes against other companies. Executives whose organisations used the Kirkpatrick model were also likely to perceive a lack of information on evaluation and measurement geared towards HRD executives.

Conclusion

A minority in the government sector and the majority in the private sector believe that training evaluation was the single most important for their training system success. However, the majority in both government and private sectors only occasionally evaluate their training programme. The most popular evaluation tools and technique used by government and private sectors were questionnaires, followed by observation and performance records. The most common model used by Kuwaiti organisations is the Kirkpatrick model, while the most common level of evaluation for both government and private sector is reaction.

Furthermore, almost the entire study sample measured their training input, which included measuring the total training expenditure, number of employees receiving training and number of courses they offer to their employees, payments to outside training providers, trainee travel expenses, training expenditure per employee, total training time/days and amount they pay for training facilities and equipment. On the other hand, all the private and a minority of government organisations measured their training output, which includes employees' job satisfaction, productivity, employees' absenteeism and customer satisfaction.

The most important evaluation challenges that deter Kuwaiti organisations from conducting sound evaluation were as follows: finding evaluation methods that suit a variety of courses, cost of doing evaluations well, translating evaluation results into top management's language and determining specific actions to take based on evaluation results. The study also revealed that the majority in both sectors face difficulty in obtaining the information needed for evaluations.

References

Al-Ali, A. (1999), "HRD training and development practices and related organisational factors in Kuwaiti organisations", PhD thesis, University of Bradford, Bradford.

Al-Ali, S. (1998), Scientific Research, Kuwait Library Co., Kuwait.

Al-Muraifea, K.M. (1993), "Employees' training programs of public authority for applied education and training", PhD thesis, University of Hull, Hull.

ASTD (1997), "Training industry trend", November, American Society for Training and Development, Alexandria, VA, available at: www.ASTD.com

Buren, E. and Bassi, J. (1999), Sharpening the Leading Edge, Report code 99ASTDIR, American Society for Training and Development, Alexandria, VA.

Camp, R., Blanchard, P. and Huszczo, E. (1986), Towards a More Organisational Effective Training Strategy and Practice, Areston Books, Englewood Cliffs, NJ.

Hamblin, A.C. (1974), The Evaluation and Control of Training, McGraw-Hill Book Company, Maidenhead and London.

Hames, R.D. (1991), "Dynamic learning: a quality approach to quality training", Total Quality Management, Vol. 2 No. 1, pp. 39-44.

Kearns, P. and Miller, T. (1996), Measuring the Impact of Training and Development on the Bottom Line, Technical Communication Publishing.

Kenney, J. and Reid, M. (1986), Training Interventions, Institute of Personnel Management, London.

Kirkpatrick, D. (1986), "Do training classes change attitudes?", Personnel, Vol. 63 No. 7, pp. 11-15.

Laird, D. (1978), Approaches to Training and Development, Addison-Wesley, London.

McClelland, S. (1994), "A model for designing objective-oriented training evaluations", Industrial and Commercial Training, Vol. 26 No. 1, pp. 3-9.

McDougall, N. (1990), "Management training evaluation for decision making", MSc dissertation, UMIST, Manchester.

Magdy, A. (1999), "Measuring and evaluating salesforce training effectiveness", PhD thesis, Old Dominion University, Norfolk, VA.

Manpower Services Commission (1981), Glossary of Training Terms, HMSO, London.

Ministry of Planning (1998), "Annual statistical abstract", Statistics and Information Sector, Kuwait Times, Edition 34, Kuwait.

Nadler, L. (1970), Developing Human Resources, Gulf, Houston, TX.

Newman, J. (1999), "An evaluation of a professional development technology training program as reported by selected school administration", PhD thesis, University of Sarasota, Sarasota, FL.

Oakland, J.S. (1993), Total Quality Management, 2nd ed., Butterworth-Heinemann, Oxford.

Rae, L. (1986), How to Measure Training Effectiveness, Gower Publishing, Aldershot.

Robinson, D. and Robinson, J. (1989), Training for Impact, Jossey-Bass Publishers, San Francisco, CA.

Robinson, K.R. (1985), A Handbook of Training Management, Kogan Page, London.

Saari, L., Jo, T., McLaughlin, S. and Zimmerle, D. (1988), "A survey of management training and education practices in US companies", Personnel Psychology, Vol. 41 No. 4, pp. 731-43.

Competition: What does it Mean?

Mohamed Zairi

First Published in

The TQM Magazine
Volume 8 · Number 1· 1996 · pp. 54–59
© MCB University Press · ISSN 0954-478X

Abstract

Examines a modern approach to competitiveness and describes current phenomena which have altered the principles which underlie competitive success. Discusses the meaning and implications of several key competitive principles including market-driven strategies, time-based competition, global competition, competition based on core competences and learning. Emphasizes the significant role of benchmarking and presents a model that positions benchmarking as a strategic tool for modern competitiveness.

Emphasis on front-end quality has changed the very definition of competition. I maintain that benchmarking is the key to competitive strategies that build on speed and customer focus.

A crucial question needs to be asked regularly by every organization competing in the modern business environment. Namely, what does it take to compete today?

Numerous competitive variables determine competitive success, and new factors are emerging and interacting all the time. Phrases such as "market-driven strategies", "customer-based competitiveness", and "time-to-market" express a sense of urgency and a business attitude where winning strategies are based on a mix of criteria which focus more on the market and the end customer, and less on internal operations, technologies, products and services.

Perhaps we in the West learned some lessons from the Japanese and their long-time grip on global supremacy. In trying to imitate their obsession with the customer, have we identified the trigger for their continued success? Turpin[1] explained a key difference between the Western and Japanese approaches to competitive success this way: "The most obvious source of potential conflict lies in the different ways of keeping score. Corporate objectives can vary considerably between Japanese and Western companies. While the Japanese partner is managing the business so as to increase market share and the ratio of new products, and the Western partner is looking for a high ROI, and maximizing the shareholders' return, troubles lie ahead. Japanese executives typically manage their businesses for long-term benefits, with little attention paid to the shareholder, while they consider, as one Japanese put it, that US firms have become the slaves of Wall Street".

In truth, being competitive in the 1990s requires an unprecedented set of extraordinary strengths. For one thing, the dynamics of the market are more turbulent where there is parity in terms of product/service technological capability and intense competition in the less tangible, "soft" aspects, such as customer service, quality, responsiveness. Market dynamics mean more unpredictability. Consider this metaphor:

As water has no constant form, there are in war no constant conditions[2].

For another thing, successful competitiveness often is the result of the ability to determine rational capability (through strengths and weaknesses) and a rigorous attack to fulfil customer needs that are well defined through closeness to the market (voice of the customer). Consider:

Invincibility depends on one self; the enemy's vulnerability on him... invincibility lies in the defenses; the possibility of victory in the attack[3].

Finally, winning comes through innovation, uniqueness (differentiation), teaching rather than following, a culture of continuous improvement and learning. Under these conditions, benchmarking can be a key catalyst for defining the necessary gap of success and superiority. Consider again:

Generally, in battle, use the normal force to engage; use the extraordinary to win[4].

Market-driven strategies: a first requirement

As alert companies come to grips with the need to be much more dynamic and responsive in the marketplace, developments such as downsizing, reorganizing, repositioning, forming strategic alliance with other firms, focusing on core competences (niche markets) and revamping the business portfolio are common recurrences. Having a marketdriven approach today means more than making incremental changes to existing cultures and old ways of managing. Being a market-driven organization nowadays means:

- reorganizing the business to focus entirely on the customer/market of operation;

- deploying resources and expertise only in core activities that reflect the strengths of the organization;

- defining strategies, making technological choices, and building delivery capability through an accurate and thorough understanding of who the customer is and what the requirements are;

- building a competitive advantage not only through an ability to deliver uniqueness and excellence in products and services but also, more importantly, through time compression – being first and good matters more than being last and best;

- establishing superior standards of performance by achieving customer satisfaction through continuous review, measurement and action on those value-added activities which are most important to the customer;

- driving business competitiveness through innovation. Understanding the value of customer-driven innovation is vital for business survival. The various activities of innovation should yield a strong line of products/services that focuses on:

  - replacing the old with the new;

  - improving the existing products/services;

  - developing new products/services for unfulfilled needs; and

  - pioneering new technologies to build supremacy.

Market-driven strategies require a commitment to changing existing business cultures by streamlining and focusing all activities on adding value which benefits the end customer. If value-adding activity can be equated with quality, market-driven strategies reflect a commitment to factors like innovation, responsiveness, quality and reliability. As the Siemens quality motto says: "Quality is when your customers come back and your products don't".

A market-driven organization will probably have undergone radical changes in its culture, perhaps akin to the three stages cited by Naumann and Shannon discussing customer-driven marketing[5]:

(1) *Bliss:* Establishing an internal system dealing with quality deficiencies and gaps in quality performance. This stage reflects a reactive culture focusing on negative quality aspects such as waste and customer complaints.

(2) *Awareness:* Becoming aware that customer satisfaction is critically important. In addition to dealing with deficiencies, organizations reflecting this culture use a more proactive approach to measure what is important to the customer through, for instance, customer satisfaction surveys.

(3) *Commitment:* Operating in a totally proactive way through a continuous effort to capture the voice of the customer and translating it internally through the conduct of activities which add value to customer satisfaction.

Moving from a "blissful" culture to one totally dedicated to customer satisfaction and delight requires effort and performance. Wishful thinking will not work. As Shapiro[6] put it: "…the term *market-oriented* represents a set of processes touching on all aspects of the company. It's a great deal more than the cliché "getting close to the customer".

Time-based competition

Expressions such as "time-to-market", "concurrent" or "simultaneous engineering", "parallel working", "integrated engineering", "forward engineering" describe an approach to competitiveness based on speed, quality, and being first in the marketplace. The expressions, however, also reflect changes in existing cultures of work where working hard is no longer desirable.

Time-based competition expresses the need to:

• deliver products and services to the end customer faster than competitors can;

• surprise competitors by continuously launching new products/services in the marketplace faster and in innovative ways that they would find difficult to imitate; and

• work in harmony with suppliers so that deliveries take place on time.

Effective time-based competitiveness means that cycle times must be tracked in all aspects of business operations, for example:

- *Right first-time design.* The translation of the physical/emotional needs of the customer into tangible prototypes which reflect production capability.

- *Make-to-market cycle time.* The planning, scheduling, production and delivery of products and services.

- *Innovation sequence.* Time required to receive feedback on customer satisfaction levels, assess future customer requirements, and translate the latter into new innovations.

Essentially time-based competition is the instigation of a culture where time-based performance measures are developed and continuously tracked in all activities and processes, in order to identify bottlenecks and remove them, and inject new learning in order to achieve faster methods of operation.

Time-based competition is not just an expression of hope. It is not about superimposing time-reduction targets on existing processes and methods of work. Achieving effective time-based strategies comes from a high level commitment to challenge existing methods and scrutinize all processes closely.

The advantages of time-based competition are numerous. Besides an improved ability to remove waste and optimize value-added activity by evaluating the whole delivery system, time-based competition gives an organization the ability to:

- innovate more quickly than competitors and offer new products and services with higher standards of quality and lower prices;

- discontinue existing lines that are poor performers by continuously developing better lines;

- leverage time savings for future innovations and new developments;

- harness various levels of synergy through teamwork and cross-functional involvement; and

- steadily speed up time cycles through sequential recycling and the injection of new learning.

Reports indicate that time-based competition consistently allows organizations to leapfrog their competitors and that "…the competition can get overwhelmed by this strategy as happened to Yamaha where Honda introduced 113 new motorcycle models in just 18 months in the early 1980s"[7].

Synchronicity[8] or incremental innovation is a practice at which most Japanese companies excel. Basically, it means developing an ability to present the customer with a continuous stream of new products and services and yet use time savings effectively by synchronizing all activities to improve existing methods and inject new learning.

This means that quality standards are raised constantly and a continuous improvement culture is in evidence all the time. True leaders never rest; the more they learn the more they realize how naïve they were. For example, in 1985, it took Motorola three years to develop the cellular phone. By 1991, they had reduced that time by 50 per cent and were committed to reducing development time to less than six months[9]. Similarly, 3M, considered by many as perhaps the best example of a leading innovator, has developed a time-conscious culture where new ideas and methods are continuously encouraged and supported, and where speed – the ability to make things happen very quickly – is emphasized constantly.

Being a global competitor

Operating in a global environment means more than building supremacy in transferring technologies, managing global supply sources and developing global distribution networks – though those challenges are substantial.

Creating a global company means operating in a world without walls. It means becoming a company without a country.

The challenge is to establish a global corporate culture, and that goes beyond changing management structures and strategies to include all the necessary means to understand the needs of customers globally and how competitors are trying to address similar issues. Being a global competitor requires the ability to:

• establish global efficiency and effectiveness through the transfer of technology, knowhow and effective deployment of resources, thus sharing best practices becomes a big leverage;

- proactively harness innovation activity globally in order to establish superiority and offer unique and differentiated products and services, worldwide;

- stay close to the market(s) and develop a flexible, structured approach which ensures responsiveness, i.e. being capable of delivering products/ services which meet the various needs of the customer, at a global level.

Having the abilities described above means that global organizations can retreat, advance, integrate, and split global operations according to the needs of their customers and in response to market changes and competitor threats. For example, as early as 1991, one report[10] described how Matsushita Electric Company developed a global strategy to counter competitive threats from Philips and to exploit the weaknesses in the latter company's approach. The key to their strategy was:

- making effective use of input from all subsidiaries for global management strategies;

- getting close to markets and focusing all development work on meeting market needs and requirements; and

- assessing all key activities (i.e. development, marketing, manufacturing) and ensuring smooth transfer of responsibility.

Another report[11] described how ABB allocates worldwide responsibility for decision making, in relation to key products, to centres with the greatest degree of competence. In another example, Unilever has developed a new structure which moved from local production to concentrated manufacturing. In 1973, it had 13 factories in 13 countries; by 1989, its manufacturing was concentrated in four factories in four countries.

Procter & Gamble too has reorganized to focus more on product groups that are managed across geographical boundaries. IBM has shifted its global headquarters for communication systems from New York to London, and has moved all its R&D activities for laptop and notebook PCs to Japan[11].

Global competitors challenge their existing corporate cultures and radically attack existing management systems and structures in order to streamline all processes and add value. This leverages information technology as a powerful means to communicate effectively and continuously. One example of the power of global communication is Hewlett-Packard's success in launching new products. Reports[10] indicate that 50 per cent of HP's sales volume comes from products launched in the past two to three years. HP does this by encouraging creativity through global R&D co-ordination and integration which allows HP to access its best ideas worldwide and to bring them to the most appropriate markets.

Global competition requires management executives capable of understanding global markets and managing various conflicts. It means developing global management skills through global career planning and transfer and by encouraging mobility and secondments. It means developing global centres of excellence through the exploitation of material resources, human resource strength and cultural strengths.

As Rhinesmith put it: "Developing a global corporate culture is, for most corporations, the last step in the globalization agenda. It is not just a matter of doing business internationally or even having subsidiaries abroad. Developing a global corporate culture involves forming the integrated values, mechanisms, and processes that allow a company to manage change successfully in a competitive global marketplace"[10].

Core competences: competing through learning

Core competences are all those skills and levels of know-how, knowledge and expertise that give organizations big advantages in the competitive arena and enable them to be highly competitive through either smooth or turbulent times. Core competences are the answer to the question: "What do we excel at?"

Generally speaking, core competences represent a blend of hard and soft skills which are difficult to copy or imitate, which provide access to a wide variety of markets, and which add value which benefits the end customer. All successful global companies tend to have specific core competences, e.g. Sony's skill in miniaturization, American Airlines' expertise in IT, and Corning's know-how in glass and ceramics[p. 12].

Deep understanding of their strengths and weaknesses – as well as how all processes function – enables organizations to harness their strengths (core competences) and develop effective strategies to protect them. It also makes it possible to improve those areas of weakness. In short, it enables organizations to compete effectively. However, core competences must be exploited fully. That means setting stretch objectives through a searching and ambitious vision. Otherwise, whatever effort is deployed is likely to achieve only small, incremental gains.

Core competences are established through doing things beyond the norm, through discontinuous innovation. Consequently, the current emphasis on innovation and creativity is hardly surprising. As Sterne[12] puts it: "Core competences are the muscles of the organization. They make it possible to accomplish much of the work that is carried out every day. But as any marathon runner knows, muscles are not enough to win a race. A high level of aspirations is also needed for remarkable achievement".

Competing through benchmarking: a proposed model

To be competitive in the future, organizations will depend on getting close to their markets and responding quickly to customer needs – on countering competitive threats and fully exploiting opportunities. The following model depicts a dynamic, benchmarking approach to competitiveness. Its two stages represent "push forces" – the ones that organizations can control least – and "pull forces" – the capability of response, i.e. those forces that can be controlled effectively.

Stage 1

This represents all the steps necessary for continuously scanning the business environment to identify the level of demand for products/services. In this stage, benchmarking is a powerful tool for understanding market conditions. As shown in Figure 1, forces which apply pressure and which represent the key parameters for establishing competitive criteria include:

- customer;
- global markets;

- shareholder;

- environment;

- technology; and

- time/speed.

Stage 2

This represents the type of responsiveness an organization exhibits when operating in the marketplace. In this stage, benchmarking provides a very powerful tool for helping build a strong capability for delivering goods and services, based on best practice and on quality outputs which are economically viable. Capability represents the various levels of energy, strengths and competences that an organization should be able to control and harness positively and effectively. The pull forces that comprise the "offering" (Figure 2) include:

- innovation and creativity;

- teamwork;

Figure 1 A model of establishing modern competitiveness – stage 1 the demand

Figure 2 A model of establishing modern competitiveness – the offering

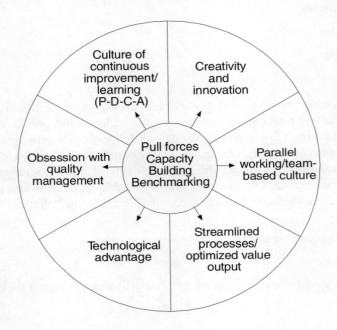

- streamlined processes;

- technology;

- measurement; and

- a culture of continuous improvement.

The model is analogous to a living cell. Cells live, grow and prosper according to their ability to protect themselves from adverse bodies and their ability to create a good climate and nourish themselves to become strong and healthy.

References

1 Turpin, D., "Strategic alliances with Japanese firms: myths and realities", Long Range Planning, Vol. 26 No. 4, 1993, pp. 11-15.

2 Tzu, S. The Art of War, Vol. 1 No. 29.

3 Tzu, S., The Art of War, Vol. 4 No. 1.

4 Tzu, S., The Art of War, Vol. 5 No. 5.

5 Naumann, E. and Shannon, P., "What is customer-driven marketing?", Business Horizons, November/December 1992, pp. 44-52. (References in Benjamin, C., "Honda and the art of competitive manoeuvre", Long Range Planning, Vol. 26 No. 4, 1993, pp. 22-31.)

6 Shapiro, B.P., "What the hell is 'market-oriented'?", Harvard Business Review, November/December 1988, pp. 119-25.

7 Spanner, G.E., Nuño, J.S. and Chandra, C., "Timebased strategies – theory and practice", Long Range Planning, Vol. 26 No. 4, 1993, pp. 90-101.

8 Starr, M.K., "Accelerating Innovation", Business Horizons, July/August 1992, pp. 45-51.

9. Kotler, P. and Stonich, P.J., "Turbo marketing through time compression", The Journal of Business Strategy, September/October 1991, pp. 4-29.

10 Rhinesmith, S.H., "Going global from the inside out", Training and Development, 1991, pp. 43-7.

11 Theuerkauf, I., "Reshaping the global organization", The McKinsey Quarterly, No. 3, 1991, pp. 102-19.

12 Sterne, D., "Core competencies: the key to corporate advantage", Multinational Business, No. 3, 1992, pp. 13-20.

Commentary

Quality improvement can be treated as a closed system, but in the end it's important to be able to understand the whole environment within which an organization works and the competitive dynamics of an industry. It won't help directly in quality improvement, but it puts actions back into the wider context where they need to be seen.

Defining organisational knowledge: A Best Practice Perspective

Yasar Jarrar[1], Giovanni Schiuma[2], and Mohamed Zairi[3]

1. **Dr. Yasar Jarrar**
   Visiting Research Fellow, European Center For TQM
   Bradford School of Management, Bradford, BD94JL, UK
   Yasar.Jarrar@cranfield.ac.uk

2. **Dr. Giovanni Schiuma**
   Assistant Professor, Laboratorio di Ingegneria Economico-
   Gestionale, Università degli Studi della Basilicata, Italy
   Giovanni.Schiuma@Cranfield.ac.uk

3. **Professor Mohamed Zairi**
   Director, European Center For TQM
   Bradford School of Management, Bradford, BD94JL, UK
   m.Zairi@bradford.ac.uk

Abstract

In today's digital economy, the emerging patterns are that intellectual capital will replace natural resources, commodities, finance, technology and production processes as the key factor influencing competitive advantage. However, knowledge management is still in its infancy. This paper aims to identify the critical success factors and best practices of knowledge codification for knowledge management through analysing the experiences of several organisations. The paper starts by defining what is meant by 'knowledge' and 'knowledge management', and follows on by presenting the knowledge processes which are at the basis of knowledge management practices. Moreover, and based on a systematic analysis of 6 case studies of leading organisations in knowledge management, the paper focuses on the practices these organisations deployed to define and understand organisational knowledge.

1. Introduction

The field of Knowledge Management (KM) is of growing interest in today's business and academic world. Today organisations are living in a world of expanding knowledge with more and more people being described as knowledge workers, and knowledge being widely accepted as the only true business asset. Global organisations have started using KM technologies to heighten their competitiveness in ways that were impossible a few years ago. Hewlett-Packard executive stated that "If HP knew what HP Knows, we would be three times as Profitable" (cited in Coates, 1999) With the importance of KM being realised, companies are viewing KM as a critical factor for their success (Lim, Ahmed and Zairi 1999). According to James Dalton, CAE, president, Strategic Counsel, in the USA, the "downsizing of the 1980s led corporate America to realise that they were haemorrhaging an asset that wasn't on their balance sheets. Today, however, many people deem knowledge-based assets to be the new organisational wealth. Acquisition and enhancement of these assets have become crucial management concerns" (Kirrane, 1999). Many authors and practitioners (Quinn, et al., 1996, Matinez, 1998, Numri, 1998, Albert and Bradly, 1997) argue that the emerging patterns are that intellectual capital will replace natural resources, commodities, finance, technology and production processes as the key factor influencing competitive advantage. This is because, with the exception of intellectual capital, everything else (IT, materials, end technical information) is available to everyone on more or less the same terms. So it does not come as a surprise to find many organisations have already embarked on some form of 'knowledge management system'.

2. Knowledge and Knowledge Management

There has been a great deal of debate in the literature about the meaning of the term "knowledge management". Most of the debate revolves around the differences between the term's 'information' and 'knowledge'. Even though in some instances they may have been used interchangeably, many have suggested that the two concepts are distinctly different (Gore and Gore, 1999). It is frequently suggested that information is a component part, but not the whole of knowledge. Knowledge itself is a much more all-encompassing term

681

which incorporates the concept of beliefs that are based on information (Machlup, 1983).

In order to successfully manage knowledge, it is prudent to clearly define it. The definition of knowledge adopted here is "information combined with experience, context, interpretation, and reflection. It is a high-value form of information that is ready to apply to decisions and actions" (Albert and Bradley, 1997).

Based on cognitive science theories, knowledge can be defined as an abstract concept that is consciously or unconsciously built by the interpretation of a set of information acquired through both experience and meditation on the experience itself, and that is able to give its owner a mental and/or physical ability (Polanyi, 1962; 1966; Kim, 1993; Kolb, 1984; Johnson-Laird, 1993). This definition highlights that knowledge has three characteristics: structural, process and functional, that are tightly interconnected. From a structural point of view, knowledge is formed by information. However, knowledge is not a simple aggregation of information: while information, defined as a structural set of data, is neutral, i.e. independent from the owner (individual or organisation), knowledge is a set of information associated to a meaning by an individual or organisational interpretation process (Huber, 1991; Weick, 1979). This aspect is the process characteristic of knowledge. The interpretation process concerns new or existing information by which both individuals and organisations develop new knowledge (Daft and Weick, 1984). Therefore, to deal with the concept of knowledge it is necessary to separate the simple information from information associated to a meaning (i.e., the knowledge). Finally, from a functional point of view, all the knowledge owned by individuals or organisations defines their skills and core competencies, respectively, and enable them to carry out some tasks. In fact, every skill always makes reference to a specific task defined as a goal that can be achieved in given conditions (Leplat, 1990).

Business knowledge generally is of two types; explicit knowledge (can be written down, transferred, and shared. It is definable and can be protected by the legal system) and Tacit knowledge (know-how, and is by nature difficult to describe. It can be demonstrated but rarely codified, and resides with its holder. It gets transferred through demonstration and on-the-job training). Within this context, knowledge management means the "strategies and processes of identifying, capturing, and leveraging knowledge to help the firm compete" (APQC, 1997). In general, knowledge management is the process of continually managing knowledge of all kinds to meet existing and emerging needs, to identify and exploit existing and acquired knowledge assets and to develop new opportunities. It is a systematic process of underpinning, observation, instrumentation, and optimisation of the firm's knowledge economies. Its overall purpose is to maximise the enterprise's knowledge related effectiveness and returns from its knowledge assets and to renew them constantly.

3. A framework for knowledge management processes

In Figure 1 the fundamental knowledge processes underpinning the knowledge management practices are depicted. It addresses the possible knowledge management practices that an organisation might implement to continuously maintain and develop its knowledge.

The framework is structured around the knowledge codification process. It is considered the most relevant process on which other knowledge processes are based. In fact the knowledge codification represents a cross-sectional process which affects all other knowledge processes. In accordance with the 'knowledge creating company' model, proposed by Nonaka and Takeuchi (1995), knowledge generation is deeply affected by the ability of an organisation to adopt knowledge codification. By knowledge codification a company stimulates the organisation knowledge creation mechanisms as well as allows the acquisition of public and private knowledge available outside the company context in form of formalised knowledge. Knowledge codification increases the effectiveness of knowledge transfer and sharing processes, allowing to overcome the constrains of the socialisation processes to exchange tacit knowledge. Moreover the knowledge codification is at the basis of both knowledge mapping and knowledge storing. In fact in order to map knowledge, it is necessary, at least, to classify it. While the knowledge storing is only possible if the knowledge is put in some information codes.

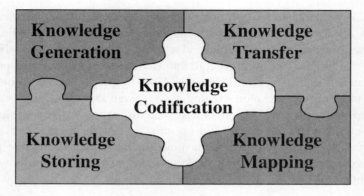

Figure 1. Relevant knowledge processes underpinning knowledge management practices

3.1 Knowledge Codification - From a semantic point of view, to codify knowledge means to put knowledge into a code. Within an organisation the knowledge codification process involves three main interrelated processes which are: knowledge externalisation, knowledge representation and knowledge organisation. Knowledge externalisation is the process by which tacit knowledge rooted in an individual's actions is transformed into explicit knowledge, i.e. knowledge that can be described and transferred by a verbal communication process. This transformation has a fundamental role since tacit knowledge is not describable by its owner and it can only be observed through the ability that it allows (Albino et al, 2001).

Knowledge representation is the process which gives explicit knowledge a graphic form and it is possible to use different information and communication code, such as natural language, figures, drawings, pictures, ideograms, flow charts, and so on. Until explicit knowledge is represented by an information and communication code, it is informal knowledge. For an organisation, the value of informal knowledge is increased when it is formalised or represented. In fact in this way the knowledge becomes the property of the organisation rather than of the individual. It can be stored, easily spread in the organisation and also sold. The representation of knowledge involves the description of the explicit knowledge by a specific information and communication code. The choice of code to be used is strictly related to the goal of the codification process and depends on the information and communication technologies that will be adopted to store and spread the codified knowledge.

Knowledge organisation is the process designed to categorize, structure and/ or contextualise the codified knowledge. Usually a lot of codified knowledge is recorded in organisations in different types of documents that are dispersed in diverse databases. The result is that their access and retrieval can be difficult. Through the organisation of knowledge the organisational codified knowledge is identified and structured according to specific rules. In this way the knowledge utilization value is increased. Knowledge organisation can also involve a contextualisation process. This is a process which aims to change the communication code of specific codified knowledge in order to make knowledge more transferable and absorbable in contexts different from the original one. In fact the information code used to represent knowledge could be strictly related to a specific context. This requires that the codified knowledge is understood and used properly only within the context in which the code is well understood.

3.2 Knowledge generation - includes a set of processes executed in order to increase the stock of corporate knowledge assets. There are two main sub-processes of knowledge generation - knowledge acquisition and knowledge creation.

Knowledge acquisition is the process of capturing and bringing knowledge from the external environment into the internal context of a company. The most direct way of acquiring knowledge assets from the external environment of the company is to buy it. Knowledge can be acquired by scanning the external environment and identifying and, for instance, capturing knowledge in the form of patents, practices and technologies. Alternative methods are either to acquire knowledge assets or to rent them, e.g. paying consultants to resolve specific problems, or to obtain them by building up relationships, e.g. setting up joint ventures or other forms of agreements (Neely et al., 2000).

Knowledge creation is the process of developing new knowledge assets within the company. Adopting a cognitive approach, it can be considered as the result of an information interpretation process performed by individuals within the organisation. Knowledge creation within a company is then strictly tied to individual learning processes and can be the result of either fortuitous individual activity or planned organisational policy. The most effective way of creating knowledge within an organisation is to motivate employees to be creative and learning-oriented and to dedicate specific resources to these processes. A common way of generating knowledge is to establish organisational units specifically for this purpose, such as a R&D departments.

3.3 Knowledge transfer - is the process of passing on knowledge between cognitive systems. When it takes place within a firm, among different units, groups or individuals, it overlaps with knowledge sharing. When it involves the inter-organisational dimension, it has common characteristics with many knowledge acquisition processes. The main difference between the two knowledge transfer processes is the disparity in their use. The former is intended to make individual or team knowledge organisational knowledge. The latter works towards creating a channel and context to enable the organisation to acquire knowledge which has been generated from outside. Both intra and inter-organisational knowledge transfers are based on a communication processes that involve both information and interpretation in order to allow the knowledge owned by the sender to be acquired and absorbed by the receiver. It is important to point out that the nature of the transferred knowledge should determine the method of communication. For instance, when the knowledge is tacit the communication is best performed by socialisation or facilitated by multimedia communication technology. The effectiveness and efficiency of knowledge transfer processes is affected by the absorptive capacity of the receiver, which is related to a shared knowledge background between sender and receiver. If they share a common technical and cultural experience the performance of the knowledge transfer process is improved by reducing the ambiguity of the information interpretation process.

3.4 Knowledge mapping - is the process of identifying knowledge assets within the organisation and of defining ways of accessing them. Often, much of the knowledge people require to solve problems already exists within an organisation, but it is not readily available when needed. All organisational knowledge has to be accessible, as this makes the process of creating new knowledge assets more efficient and effective. Knowledge mapping is usually supported by knowledge storing technologies that make knowledge either available on demand or enable employees to locate it and show how it can be acquired.

3.5 Knowledge storing - is the process of saving knowledge within the organisation. But knowledge needs to be available anytime and anywhere. Knowledge storing is at the heart of knowledge mapping and can take the form of either knowledge databases, in which codified knowledge is stored in appropriate information codes, or of yellow pages, which provide links to people with specific know-how. The former is based on the idea that knowledge can be codified and made available to be retrieved electronically. This is an approach followed by many consulting organisations companies such as Ernst & Young who have developed and adopted best practices databases to support the activities of consultants spread out around the world. The only information stored is that required for identifying the people and the places where knowledge resides. For example Hoffmann-LaRoche (Jarrar and Zairi, 2001), as a part of its overall Drug Approval Process knowledge map, included a Yellow Page catalogue of relevant experts, arranged according to know-how, questions and issues.

4. Learning from organisational experience

The practices presented in this paper are based on a wide literature survey, and in depth interviews and analysis of leading organisations. The literature review included a systemic analysis of 40 cases of KM applications in organisations that reported successful initiatives. These cases were analysed using the format shown in Figure 2. The organisations included Dow Chemical, Chevron, KPMG, BT, McDonald's, Oracle, Saatchi &Saatchi, 3COM, Nortel, Kodak, DHL International, IBM, Royal Mail, Skandia Life, Xerox, HP, Rolls Royce, Hughes Space, Boston Consulting Group, among others. The approach was to analyse the methodologies pursued, IT used, and results achieved in order to identify the success factors. This resulted in developing the framework structure and documenting various Best Practices (Jarrar and Zairi, 2001)(Jarrar, 2002).

To further understand the practice and techniques used, in-depth interview-based case studies where undertaken. The case study organisations that took part in this study include: British Telecom, British Airways, IBM, Unilever, Ernst & Young, and Yorkshire Water. These companies were based on several criteria including: experience with KM (reported success); blue chip; and willingness to share their experience. The cases were based on in-depth, semi-structured, interviews with organisational directors. In most organisations, two directors were present at each interview (usually MD and KM Director levels). The interview focus and structure was based on understanding the knowledge management methodologies pursued by the organisation, the processes implemented, Information Technology used, and the results achieved. Such a structure allowed the investigation of the perceived success factors (best practices) and challenge areas. The interview structure is shown in the framework below (Figure 2). The data collected from the interviews was mostly qualitative and various qualitative analysis techniques (including Coding and Critical Incident Techniques) were used, however, the detailed methodology of analysis is outside the scope of this paper.

The interview structure above was within a Best Practice Knowledge Management framework (Figure 3) which, as noted, was in-itself based on a comprehensive study of Best Practices (Jarrar, 2001). The objective of this study, was to understand in more depth the practices, processes, and techniques that underlay that generic framework of knowledge management. The study covered all four aspects of the framework, but the final part of this paper will focus on the area of 'Defining and Understanding Organisational Knowledge'.

Drivers for KM: *background of the initiative, and context highlights*		
	Success factors	Challenges
Culture	*Experiences in changing the culture and applying knowledge management*	
Processes	*The way KM was actually applied*	
IT	*The use of Information technology*	
Structure	*How it was changed to allow effective implementation and communication*	
Lessons learnt : *the main lessons (recommendations)*		
Results achieved : *the improvements (Or problems) achieved*		
Tools used : *the use of certain tools and techniques that have facilitated the effort*		

Figure 2: Case Study Interview Structure

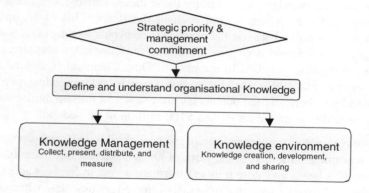

Figure 3: Knowledge Management Framework

5. Define and understand organisational knowledge

For a successful start to KM, an organisation should engage in a clear understanding of how, and where, knowledge resides, and is developed, in the company. Organisations like BT and Ernst & Young have pursued this step and gone as far as developing their own models for defining organisational knowledge. Other organisations can learn from these best practices (to avoid re-inventing the wheel) and start by clearly defining what knowledge means to them. This can be achieved by studying the definitions and mapping the organisational knowledge. An organisation must identify its knowledge assets as a first step to develop plans for acquiring, retaining, building, and leveraging those assets on a continuous basis. All organisations that valued knowledge saw it imperative to know how and where to access it, and successful attempts so far have started by classifying intellectual portfolio by producing an organisational 'knowledge map' (Bontis, 1996). Organisations like BT and Unilever, undertook knowledge mapping and produced guides to in–house experts (a 'yellow pages' directory that directs the user to the people in the firm who know about particular topics of interest). Ernst & Young charted the key business processes or areas covered by the knowledge management system, how knowledge flows among these areas, and the key knowledge requirements for each step within each of the flows. This clear, up-front definition for users of what to do and what not to do avoids wasting organisational resources on unfocused activities. Furthermore, knowledge mapping could result in immediate benefits. In the case of Dow Chemical (Caulkin, 1997) (Davenport et al., 1998), just by arranging such a 'knowledge map' and understanding where all their patents lay, they saved $4 million during the first year, expected to generate more than $100 million in the second.

The most common initiative was building some form of 'knowledge repositories' which was intended to take some form of knowledge that has been extracted from people's heads and store it in an information system for later access. For example, IBM have systems that store sales-oriented documents—white papers, presentations, marketing collateral, for access by their field sales forces in selling computers. Other knowledge repositories are less structured, consisting of the insights and observations of employees, sometimes called 'discussion databases' or 'lessons-learned' systems. Some repositories do not hold the knowledge itself, but point to those who have knowledge. IBM, for instance, has expert repositories for researchers in its Laboratories and Corporate Education groups.

The cases analyzed revealed the following main knowledge repositories:

1. External knowledge – by definition, the easiest to acquire, organise, and communicate. This includes knowledge about the market place, competitors, customer information, etc.

690

2. Internal knowledge -

2.1 Formal / Structured – this type of knowledge includes research reports, marketing material, processes and methods, etc. HP (Davenport et al, 1998) used artificial intelligence software to manage such knowledge. They created an 'electronic sales partner' which contained technical product information, sales and marketing information, customer account information, etc. Sales support area reported having phenomenal feedback from both submitters (of knowledge) and users.

2.2 Informal – the most important area, and most difficult to manage. It mainly deals with tacit knowledge. To transfer tacit knowledge from individuals into a repository, organisations usually use some sort of community based electronic discussion and 'lessons learnt' databases. For many companies the issue is not acquiring or retaining organisational knowledge, instead it is figuring out how to more effectively capture and share the knowledge that already exists within a department, division, or even employees' minds. Chevron, (Stivers and Joyce, 1997) for example, saved over $20 million a year by comparing information on the operation of gas compressors in fields from all over the world. A recent survey of consulting firms by Consultants News (Stivers and Joyce, 1997) showed that about 75% of firms surveyed, reported that they had a process in place for capturing best practices, sharing information from one project to another, and documenting innovative ways of solving client problems. The creation of such knowledge repositories is not just about collecting data. The knowledge collected must be directly related to a business process. Broad-based employee participation in determining what knowledge is essential, is critical in determining what types of information should be collected and shared. In Dow Chemical's (Petrash, 1996) experience, it was more difficult determining which in-house know-how added value and which did not. They tackled this by setting up teams and establishing a single criterion to determine value. Similarly, Hughes Space and Communications (Bontis, 1996) has editorial teams that analyse and store knowledge posted by individuals on its web site in order to be shared by all areas. Buckman Labs (Martinez, 1998) ensures its knowledge system contains validated knowledge through 'Content experts' who monitor the information that is placed on the network.

In case of creating transfer and access channels the case studies have highlighted the following best practices for designing an effective system for knowledge connectivity, access, and transfer:

- Minimise the number of transmissions of knowledge between individuals to achieve the least distortion.

- Provide 24 hour access to every employee from any location.

- Allow and encourage each person to contribute and make the system easy to use.

- Design a flexible system that is automatically updated as questions and answers are given.

- Design multiple channels for knowledge transfer, ranging from intranet to face-to-face. Each has its benefits and techniques and times to be used.

Finally, a practice that was common to all organisations studied was clear planning for KM. Before attempting to understand and capture organisational knowledge, there are a number of questions that the organisation should seek to answer. These are essential to clarify why the organisation is going down the path of KM and to justify the costs (which can be substantial) of the initiative(s). The main questions at this stage include:

(1) What is the objective of KM? Objectives could vary for leveraging implicit knowledge, retaining knowledge of employees as they exit the organisation, or more efficient access to knowledge repositories. While these objectives might fall under one strategy for KM, they require different tactics and tools.

(2) What is the scope of KM in relation to the types of knowledge that the organisation should embrace? Explicit and tacit knowledge require different approaches to acquire and manage.

(3) What technologies and techniques are to be employed? These can vary from document creation and management technologies to group working technologies. Each approach requires different approaches, skills, training, and investments.

5. Conclusions

In today's business context, knowledge represents a strategic resource for company competitiveness. Thus knowledge management is a key strategic lever for a continuous improvement of business performance. In fact all company's capabilities are based on a knowledge base which is specific to any company. Organisations need to develop KM capacity to be able to survive in a knowledge-based, global marketplace.

This paper provided a clear definition of Knowledge and Knowledge Management. This should provide managers with a conceptual interpretation of this intangible resource in order to guide them in implementing knowledge management practices. A framework presenting the most relevant knowledge processes is also introduced. It allows the understanding of what the knowledge processes underpinning the knowledge management practices are. The first step in successful KM is to understand what knowledge is currently available at one's own organisation. A systemic analysis of 6 leading organisations provided a discussion of best practices deployed in this area. This can be seen as a generic approach that can form a starting point for managers and researchers alike to start working with KM.

6. References

Albert, S.; and Bradley K. (1997) Managing Knowledge – Experts, agencies, and organisations. Cambridge: Cambridge University Press.

Albino, V., Garavelli, A., Schiuma G., (2001) "Measuring knowledge codification in learning organisation", Technovation Journal, Vol. 20.

APQC (1997) Identifying and transferring internal best practices. www.apqc.org

Bontis, N. (1996) There's a price on your head: Managing Intellectual Capital Strategically. Business Quarterly. Summer, 1996, pp. 41 – 47

Caotes F. (1999) –The inevitability of knowledge management- Research Technology Management – Vol. 42- Issue 4- PP. 6-7. USA.

Caulkin, S. (1997) The knowledge within. Management Today. August. pp. 28

Daft, R.L. and Weick, K.E. (1984) "Toward a model of organisations as interpretation systems", Academy of Management Review, 9: p. 284-295.

Davenport, T.; De Long, D.; and Beers, M. (1998) Successful Knowledge Management Projects. Sloan Management Review. Winter. pp. 43 – 57

Gore and Gore (1999) knowledge management the way forward – Total Quality Management – Vol. 10- Issue 4/5- PP. 554-560. UK.

Huber, G.P. (1991) "Organisational Learning: The Contributing Processes and the Literatures", in Organisation Science, 2(1), February: p. 88-115.

Jarrar, Y. (2002 - *forthcoming*) Knowledge Management - learning from organisational experience, Managerial Auditing Journal, Volume, 4.

Jarrar, Y. and Zairi, M. (2001) Knowledge Management - learning from organisational experience, Proceedings of the 6th International Conference on ISO9000 and TQM, Edited by Ho, S and Donnelly, M. Scotland, April 2001

Johnson-Laird, P. (1993) The Computer and the Mind. An Introduction to Cognitive Science, William Collins Sons & Co. Ltd., London.

Kirrane (1999) Getting wise to knowledge management – Association Management – Vol. 51- Issue 8- PP. 31-40. USA.

Kim, H. (1993) "The Link between Individual and Organisational Learning", Sloan Management Review, Fall: p. 37-50.

Kolb, D.A. (1984) Experimental Learning: Experience as the Source of Learning and Development, Englewood Cliffs, New Jersey, Prentice-Hall.

Leplat, J. (1990), "Skills and tacit skills: A psychological perspective" Applied Psychology: An International Review, 39(2): p. 143-154.

Lim, K.; Ahmed, P.; Zairi, M. (1999)- Management for quality through knowledge management- Total Quality Management journal- Vol. 10- Issue 4/5- PP.615-621. UK.

Machlup (1983) Semantic quirks in studies of information. In F. Machlup & U. Mansfield. The study of information – John Wiley – NY.

Martinez, M. (1998) The collective power. HRM Magazine. February. pp. 88 – 94

Neely A., Marr B., Schiuma G. (2000) "Assessing knowledge in the New Economy", 1th European Knowledge Management Conference, 28-30 Ottobre, Slovenia.

Numri, R. (1998) Knowledge Intensive Firms. Business Horizons. 41, 3. pp. 26 – 31

Nonaka I., Takeuchi H., (1995), The Knowledge-creating Company: How Japanese Companies Create the Dynamics of Innovation, Oxford University Press, New York.

Petrash, G. (1996) Dow's journey to a knowledge value management culture. European Management Journal. 14(4). pp. 365 – 373

Polanyi, M. (1962) Personal Knowledge - Towards a Post-Critical Philosophy, Routledge & Kegan Paul, London.

Polanyi, M. (1966) The Tacit Dimension, Garden City (N.Y.), Doubleday.

Quinn, P. (1992) Intelligent Enterprise: A knowledge and Service Based paradigm for Industry – The free Press- New York.

Stivers, B. and Joyce, T. (1997) Knowledge management focus in US and Canadian firms. Creativity and Innovation Management. 6(3). pp. 140 – 150

Weick, K. (1979) The Social Psychology of Organising, Addison-Wesley, Reading, Mass.

> *"Without a standard there is no logical basis for making a decision or taking action."*
>
> **- Joseph Juran**

Index